The International Criminal Court

The International Criminal Court

Legal, Policy, and Political Challenges

Edited by

Richard H. Steinberg

Foreword by

Karim A. A. Khan KC

BRILL | NIJHOFF

LEIDEN | BOSTON

Library of Congress Cataloging-in-Publication Data

Names: Steinberg, Richard H., 1960- editor. | Khan, Karim A. A., writer of foreword.
Title: The International Criminal Court : legal, policy, and political challenges / edited by Richard H. Steinberg ; foreword by Karim A. A. Khan KC.
Description: Leiden ; Boston : Brill Academic Publishers, Inc., 2025. | Includes bibliographical references and index.
Identifiers: LCCN 2025024542 | ISBN 9789004686748 (hardback) | ISBN 9789004686755 (pdf)
Subjects: LCSH: International Criminal Court. | International Criminal Court--Political aspects. | International criminal courts.
Classification: LCC KZ7312 .I5825 2025 | DDC 345/.01--DC23/eng/20250521
LC record available at https://lccn.loc.gov/2025024542

Typeface for the Latin, Greek, and Cyrillic scripts: "Brill". See and download: brill.com/brill-typeface.

ISBN 978-90-04-68674-8 (hardback)
ISBN 978-90-04-68675-5 (e-book)
DOI 10.1163/9789004686755

Contents

PART 2
Completion Strategies for Situations under Investigation

PART 3
The Emerging Use of Cyber Evidence and Open Source Material at the ICC

PART 7
Non-Western Law at the ICC: What Is Its Place?

PART 8
Decentralized Accountability: ICC Prosecutorial Engagement with State Courts and Regional Entities

Foreword

Since its inception, in 2009, the *International Criminal Court Online Forum* ("*ICC Forum*") has served as a virtual intellectual space, showcasing wide ranging expertise on important legal, policy and practical questions and challenges facing the International Criminal Court ("ICC"). Over the years, the Forum has exerted commendable efforts in raising awareness and cultivating a richer understanding of international criminal justice writ large, and issues relevant to the Office of the Prosecutor at the ICC, more specifically through high-level expert exchanges, lectures, and scholarly debate. The ICC Office of the Prosecutor has been a direct beneficiary of those efforts and their intellectual by-product. Indeed, the Office under three successive ICC Prosecutors has benefitted from the meaningful discussions and the bazaar of ideas that have been enabled and hosted by the ICC Forum. *The International Criminal Court: Legal, Policy, and Political Challenges* is a compilation of much of that intellectual output as penned by prominent scholars, jurists and practitioners.

The *ICC Forum* has historically been organized and operated by a dedicated team at the University of California, Los Angeles (UCLA) School of Law, under the guidance and editorial direction of Professor Richard H. Steinberg, with the support of the *Promise Institute for Human Rights*. On behalf of my Office, I extend our deep appreciation and gratitude for the pioneering work the *ICC Forum* has conducted under his able leadership, and for the support of the Forum.

To be sure, the *ICC Forum* has covered over 20 issues of interest to the Office, the most recent eight of which appear in the present volume. Topics which have been analysed since the publication of the 2nd volume, and included in the 3rd volume, are the decentralization of accountability question, the debate on superior or command responsibility, cyber/digital evidence, and the all too important question of how to wind down and close situations before the ICC in a principled reflective manner, and on the basis of a coherent strategy. Further questions addressed in this collection engage with a variety of topics such as non-Western legal traditions, cyber operations and warfare, the gravity threshold, resource constraints and prosecutorial discretion, and finally, coercive measures and pressures placed on the ICC.

Throughout the years, the *ICC Forum* has reached inquisitive minds far and wide with nearly one million unique visitors from all corners of the world on its website. This publication and the significant body of work that it represents builds on that contribution.

I congratulate Prof. Steinberg and his team for this latest volume. It serves as a notable depository of considered reflection on key issues in the discipline. As with previous volumes, it is recommended reading for those interested and, indeed, genuinely invested in the ever necessary field of international criminal justice and humanity's aspiration for a more just world.

I wish the ICC *Forum* continued success with its important work.

Karim A. A. Khan KC
Prosecutor of the International Criminal Court
The Hague, The Netherlands

Preface

The *International Criminal Court: Legal, Policy, and Political Challenges* is a collection of analyses and reform proposals written by leading commentators on eight contested issues. Each of the issues and analyses were posted on the *International Criminal Law Online Forum* ("*ICC Forum*"), a global online venue for debating issues of importance to the Office of the Prosecutor (OTP) of the International Criminal Court (ICC). The *ICC Forum* was established in 2009 at the University of California, Los Angeles (UCLA) School of Law, with the support of the ICC. Almost all issues posed on the *ICC Forum* were framed in collaboration with the Prosecutor in office at the time the issue was posted. In 2012, the Forum was named one of the world's top three justice innovations by *The Hague Institute for the Internationalisation of Law*. Since then, the *ICC Forum* has become the world's largest online community of scholars, jurists, lawyers, government officials, and others interested in international criminal law and the ICC. The *ICC Forum* can be read on the web at iccforum.com.

The issues addressed here were raised initially on the *ICC Forum* in the 2018 to 2023 period, but they deal with problems that will persist or re-emerge in different forms throughout the life of the Court. While the problems endure, the discussions contained in this book are best understood in the context in which they first emerged. Each debate in this book is presented as a separate Part, maintaining the same chronological order in which it originally appeared online.

Part 1, *Superior Responsibility after the Bemba Decision*, analyzes and critiques the Appeals Chamber decision that reversed Jean-Pierre Bemba Gombo's conviction on charges of war crimes and crimes against humanity. That decision has set a high bar for proving that an accused superior knew or should have known of criminal behavior by those under their authority, or that they failed to take all necessary and reasonable measures to curb that behavior. The decision came as a shock to many lawyers in the OTP, has been criticized by many commentators (including some in this volume), and its implications are likely to reverberate in future cases.

Part 2, *Completion Strategies for Situations under Investigation*, raises a set of questions facing Prosecutors as they attempt to wind down investigations. At the time the issue appeared on the *ICC Forum*, the OTP's capacity to continue addressing all of the situations that had been referred to it was, for the first time, under considerable strain. Some situations were in the preliminary examination phase; others in the investigation stage; and still others had become dormant, due partly to OTP's limited resources. In that context, and since many investigations were thought to have run their course, the OTP was faced for the first time with questions about whether, to what extent, and how to close investigations, issues that are certain to present themselves continuously in the future.

Part 3, *The Emerging Use of Cyber Evidence and Open Source Material at the ICC*, is one of two issues in this volume arising from new technologies that pose emerging challenges. While cyber evidence and open source material have offered the Court new sources of information for use in its work, relevant sources of law, such as the Rome Statute and the Rules of Procedure and Evidence, do not specifically address the use of such evidence. Digital evidence presents issues related to authentication; a risk of over-collection; algorithms or AI tools that skew searches; deep fakes; security issues; authentication and chain of custody issues; and other challenges, all of which are explored.

Parts 4, 5, 7, and 8 must be seen in the context of the Court's long term development and the serious *political* challenges it began to confront in 2012 and continues to address. Of course, at each stage of its development, the ICC has faced serious tests in its efforts to advance international justice. Following the Rome Statute's entry into force in 2002, the States Parties faced the monumental challenge of building an operational institution consistent with the terms of that document. And once operational, the Court had to develop ways to function effectively on such matters as evidence collection, effectuating arrests, establishing effective representation of victims and survivors located in remote places, and many other matters.

By 2012, when the second Prosecutor, Fatou Bensouda, assumed office, the Court had begun to face a serious political problem: all ICC investigations, arrest warrants, and trials were focused exclusively on situations in Africa, yet atrocity crimes were also being perpetrated elsewhere around the globe, creating an impression of bias. The first Prosecutor had concluded that many situations outside of Africa were not subject to the Court's jurisdiction or were inadmissible; at the same time, most of the Africa situations were required to be investigated, as they had been referred by states or the U.N. Security Council, which had been inconsistent by not referring other situations that were similarly grave. The Security Council had referred the situations in Libya and Sudan to the Prosecutor, but not Afghanistan, China (Xinjiang), Myanmar, Syria, or other situations. Many African states, and a majority of the African Union (AU), complained bitterly that the ICC was biased against Africa, with the AU Chair in 2013 asserting provocatively: "The ICC is hunting Africans." Several states threatened to withdraw from the

Rome Statute, and the AU and many African governments favored contravening various Rome Statute mandates and ignoring many ICC practices. Many scholars and government officials, particularly from the developing world, began asserting that the ICC was a European neo-colonial institution aimed at Africa.

By 2018, when the debates addressed in this volume began, Prosecutor Bensouda's tenure was already marked by efforts that seemed aimed at reducing African party state complaints about bias by way of using creative and expansive jurisdictional theories to pursue investigation of non-African nationals, such as behavior by some British forces in Iraq, and behavior by non-party state nationals, including Russian actions in Georgia and Ukraine, American actions in Afghanistan, and Israeli actions in the *Situation in the State of Palestine*. Meanwhile, except for the situation in Burundi, the Office of the Prosecutor had stopped addressing new atrocity crimes in Africa. In the period covered by this volume, the U.K. government objected to investigation of its actions in Iraq, and many non-party state governments had come to see the Court as acting illegitimately against them. These challenges merged to suggest the debates addressed in Parts 4, 5, 7, and 8 of this volume.

Part 4 addresses *U.S. Sanctions on the Court: Support, Opposition, and Off-Ramps*. In 2020, triggered by the Prosecutor's investigations of U.S. behavior in Afghanistan and of Israel's in the *Situation in the State of Palestine*, the first Trump Administration issued an Executive order sanctioning Prosecutor Bensouda and her deputy, and threatening criminal and civil penalties for any American who would provide material assistance to the Court. Part 4 features essays opposing the sanctions, some others supporting them, and still others suggesting political solutions that might improve relations between the U.S. and the ICC and resolve the standoff. Indeed, off-ramps suggested by two of the contributors to Part 4 seem to have been taken in 2021, when the U.S. government, by then under the Biden Presidency, lifted U.S. sanctions on the Court, and the third Prosecutor, Karim A.A. Khan, refocused the Afghanistan investigation on the Taliban. The events following the October 7, 2023, Hamas attack on Israel, and the Prosecutor's subsequent issuance of arrest warrants for the Israeli Prime Minister and Defense Minister, reignited U.S. government and Congressional dissatisfaction with the Court, which rekindled demands for sanctions on the ICC, suggesting that the type of problem covered in Part 4 may be an ongoing feature of the Court's political relations with some states.

Part 5, *The Gravity Threshold*, raises another set of issues not unrelated to tensions over the investigations of U.S. and British activities in the Middle

East: what should be the gravity threshold for ICC investigations? When the issue was posed, American and British leaders were arguing, among other claims, that the alleged crimes under investigation in Afghanistan and Iraq had affected so few victims and were of such a nature that they did not clear the gravity threshold appropriate for Court engagement. Of course, the gravity question also raises broader and enduring issues over how the Court should employ its limited resources. Should it address only the most grave situations, a larger number and scope of situations, or all situations that might be admissible and subject to its jurisdiction?

Part 6, *Cyber Operations and Cyberwarfare under the Rome Statute*, is the second debate in the volume concerning technological change: the extent to which the Rome Statute is positioned to adequately address cyber operations and cyber warfare, each central elements of the emerging phenomenon of hybrid warfare. Cyber warfare is often non-kinetic, stealthy, and conducted remotely, making it especially challenging to assign criminal liability to individuals.

Part 7, *Non-Western Law at the ICC: What Is Its Place?*, addresses a complaint, often raised by lawyers, scholars, and politicians from Africa and other developing countries, that the Court does not employ, understand, or lend enough deference to non-Western law, and that it inappropriately dismisses traditional modalities of justice and reconciliation when considering complementarity. Greater use or consideration of non-Western law within the ICC has the potential to dampen African leaders' complaints about the institution. Moreover, disagreements on this issue are sure to be a consistent theme in North-South relations at the Court.

Part 8, *Decentralized Accountability: ICC Prosecutorial Engagement with State Courts and Regional Entities*, considers how the Court might engage with state or regional entities, including those in Africa, to facilitate their application of justice to situations of alleged atrocity crimes. Proactive complementarity, and other Court support for the development or use of justice mechanisms in the country or region where alleged crimes occurred, could enable the substitution of local justice for justice carried out in The Hague, also dampening some African country perceptions of Court bias against them, while reducing demands on an overstretched Court.

Consistent with the *ICC Forum*'s longstanding practice, the issues in Parts 1 through 3 were framed in collaboration with the Office of the Prosecutor. However, when the issues in Parts 4 through 7 were posed, the U.S. government's Executive order imposing criminal and civil sanctions on Americans providing material assistance to the Court was in force. As a result, those issues were framed independently by *ICC Forum* staff rather than in formal collaboration with the Prosecutor. After President Biden lifted the sanctions, the ICC Forum resumed its collaboration with the Prosecutor, then Karim A.A. Khan, in framing the question for Part 8.

Richard H. Steinberg
Los Angeles, California
January 2025

Acknowledgements

This book is a collection of analyses by legal experts and social scientists on crucial issues that faced the International Criminal Court (ICC) from 2018 to 2023 and that are likely to persist or re-emerge in different forms throughout the life of the Court. Each of the issues and analyses has been posted on the web at ICCForum.com (ICC Forum), a global online venue for debating issues of importance to the Office of the Prosecutor (OTP) of the ICC. The ICC Forum was established in 2009 at the University of California, Los Angeles (UCLA) School of Law, with the support of the ICC OTP.

As founding Editor-in Chief of the ICC Forum, and Editor of this volume, I am indebted to each of the three successive ICC Prosecutors and their staff for their ongoing support of the ICC Forum. Luis Moreno Ocampo, the first ICC Prosecutor, brainstormed the idea of the ICC Forum with me, continuously communicated what would be most useful to the OTP, and organized his office to support the work of the ICC Forum. In addition, Moreno Ocampo was intrepid in his willingness and desire for the ICC Forum to tackle highly controversial issues so that his Office could garner as much insight as possible on important but divisive issues. Fatou Bensouda, the second Prosecutor, continued to facilitate collaboration with the ICC Forum, as did the third Prosecutor, Karim A.A. Khan.

Senior staff in the Office of the Prosecutor have also been indispensable. Shamila Batohi and Hans Bevers, each Senior Legal Advisors to the three successive Prosecutors, working with Associate Legal Advisors Yayoi Yamaguchi and Sarah Hishan, were crucial in coordinating the ICC Forum's work with the OTP, suggesting issues of interest and ways to frame questions so as to generate a dialogue that could be useful to the Office. While the final selection of issues and their framing have been the responsibility of the ICC Forum's editorial team, I am grateful for the OTP's partnership.

The ICC Forum was built and has been maintained by Christopher and Olga Werby of Pipsqueak Productions, LLC, from San Francisco, without whom this project would have been impossible. Their creativity, sensibilities about the subject of the site, understanding of the Internet and what it takes to create an online community, technical skill, capacity to fight endless hacker attacks, patience, and passion have driven the success of the project. Pipsqueak was there from the beginning, helping to crystalize the concept, then designing, building, updating, and refining it. Their work is responsible for the popularity of the ICC Forum and for the awards that it has received, including as one of the top three justice innovations in the world from The Hague Institute for the Internationalisation of Law in 2012, and the Gold Medal Laureate Award for World Good from Computerworld magazine.

Many others have been instrumental in making this book possible. Dozens of UCLA Law students have assisted with the ICC Forum, helping edit the contributions, including all of those contained in this volume, and assisting in communicating with contributors and the OTP. Research Assistants Kasper Jastrzebski, Alden Thiriot, and Austin Damiani, provided thoughtful and detailed assistance in preparation of the manuscript. Brill/Nijhoff's Bea Timmer patiently provided guidance in preparation of the volume.

Finally, this volume would not have been possible without generous support from the Promise Institute for Human Rights at UCLA, which has funded the ICC Forum since 2018. Successive Promise Institute Executive Directors, Kate Mackintosh and Hannah Garry, have each provided wise and judicious advice on the direction of the ICC Forum, and have exuded a passion for international justice that has helped inspire all those who work on the ICC Forum at UCLA.

Richard H. Steinberg
Los Angeles, California
January 2025

Abbreviations

ACA	Atrocity Crimes Advisory Group
ACJHR	African Court of Justice and Human Rights
ACLU	American Civil Liberties Union
AI	Artificial Intelligence
AP	Additional Protocol
API	Application Programming Interface
ASP	Assembly of States Parties
ASPA	American Servicemembers' Protection Act
AU	African Union
BBC	British Broadcasting Corporation
CAR	Central African Republic
CIA	Central Intelligence Agency
CIJA	Commission on International Justice & Accountability
COIN	Counterinsurgency
COVID	Coronavirus Disease
C3	Command, Control, Communications
DARPA	Defense Advanced Research Projects Agency
DDOS	Distributed Denial of Service
DDPD	Doha Document for Peace in Darfur
DDRRR	Disarmament, Demobilization, Repatriation, Reintegration and Resettlement
DRC	Democratic Republic of the Congo
EAC	Extraordinary African Chambers
ECCC	Extraordinary Chambers in the Courts of Cambodia
EO	Executive Order
EU	European Union
E-LAMP	Event Labeling Through Analytic Media Processing
FA	Forensic Architecture
FARC	Revolutionary Armed Forces of Columbia
FARC-EP	Revolutionary Armed Forces of Colombia – People's Army
FDLR	*Forces Démocratiques pour la Libération du Rwanda*
FIDH	International Federation for Human Rights
GA	General Assembly
GAOR	General Assembly Official Records
GC	Geneva Convention
GDPR	General Data Protection Regulation
GIFCT	Global Internet Forum to Counter Terrorism

GLAN	Global Legal Action Network
G7	Group of Seven
HRW	Human Rights Watch
ICC	International Criminal Court
ICJ	International Court of Justice
ICL	International Criminal Law
ICMP	International Commission on Missing Persons
ICPA	International Centre for the Prosecution of the Crime of Aggression against Ukraine
ICPCA	International Centre for the Prosecution of the Crime of Aggression
ICRC	The International Committee of the Red Cross
ICT	International Criminal Tribunal
ICT	Information and Communications Technologies
ICTY	International Criminal Tribunal for the former Yugoslavia
ICTR	International Criminal Tribunal for Rwanda
IER	Independent Expert Review
IEEPA	International Emergency Economic Powers Act
IHL	International Humanitarian Law
IHRL	International Human Rights Law
IIIM	International, Impartial and Independent Mechanism
IIMM	Independent Investigation Mechanism for Myanmar
IMTFE	International Military Tribunal for the Far East
IP	Internet Protocol
ISIL	Islamic State of Iraq and the Levant
ISIS	Islamic State of Iraq and Syria
JCCD	Jurisdiction, Complementarity and Cooperation Division
JEP	Special Jurisdiction for Peace
JIT	Joint Investigation Team
LRA	Lord's Resistance Army
MLC	Movement for the Liberation of Congo
MLF	Multilateral Force
MOD	Ministry of Defence
MOU	Memorandum of Understanding
NATO	North Atlantic Treaty Organization
NIAC	Non-International Armed Conflict
NGO	Non-governmental Organization
OAU	Organization of African Unity
OAS	Organization of American States
OCR	Optical Character Recognition
OLA	Office for Legal Affairs

OTP	Office of the Prosecutor
OPCON	Operational Control
OPCW	Organisation for the Prohibition of Chemical Weapons
OPR	Office of Professional Responsibility
OSCE	Organization for Security and Cooperation in Europe
PCC	Police Contributing Countries
PE	Preliminary Examination
PTC	Pre-Trial Chamber
QC	Queen's Counsel
RAW	Uncompressed and unprocessed image data
RPE	Rules of Procedure and Evidence
RSCSL	Residual Special Court of Sierra Leone
SAS	Special Air Services
SC	UN Security Council
SCADA	Supervisory Control and Data Acquisition
SCSL	Special Court for Sierra Leone
SEA	Sexual Exploitation and Abuse
SGBC	Sexual and Gender-Based Crimes
SGBV	Sexual and Gender-Based Violence
SIJ	Syrian Institute for Justice
SPSC	Special Panels for Serious Crimes
STA	Special Tribunal for the Crime of Aggression
STCOA	Special Tribunal for the Crime of Aggression
TCC	Troop Contributing Countries
TWAIL	Third World Approaches to International Law
UAE	United Arab Emirates
UC	University of California
UCLA	University of California, Los Angeles
UJ	Universal Jurisdiction
UK	United Kingdom
UN	United Nations
UNHCR	UN High Commission for Refugees
UNSC	United Nations Security Council
UNITAD	United Nations Investigative Team to Promote Accountability for Crimes Committed by Da'esh/ISIL in Iraq
UNTAET	United Nations Transitional Administration in East Timor
URL	Uniform Resource Locator
US	United States
USB	Universal Serial Bus
USC	United States Code

VFRAME	Visual Forensics and Metadata Extraction
VK	VKontakte
WMD	Weapons of Mass Destruction
YJIL	Yale Journal of International Law

Notes on Contributors

Raja Althaibani
is Senior Program Manager for the Middle East and North Africa at WITNESS.

Diane Marie Amann
is Regents' Professor of International Law, Emily & Ernest Woodruff Chair in International Law, and Faculty Co-Director of the Dean Rusk International Law Center at University of Georgia School of Law, Athens, Georgia.

Kai Ambos
is Professor of Law, Chair for Criminal Law, Criminal Procedure, Comparative Law, International Criminal Law, and Public International Law at Georg August Universität Göttingen, Göttingen, Germany, and Judge at Kosovo Specialist Chambers, The Hague, The Netherlands.

Jay D. Aronson
is Professor of Science, Technology, and Society in the History Department and founding Director of the Center for Human Rights Science at Carnegie Mellon University, Pittsburgh, Pennsylvania.

Mohamed Elewa Badar
is Professor of Comparative and International Criminal Law and Islamic Law at Northumbria Law School, University of Northumbria at Newcastle, Newcastle upon Tyne, England, Middle East and North Africa Regional Forum Liaison Officer at International Bar Association War Crimes Committee, and Legal Consultant for Al Hassan Defense Team at the International Criminal Court.

John B. Bellinger, III
is Adjunct Senior Fellow for International and National Security Law at the Council on Foreign Relations, and Co-Chair of Global Law and Public Policy and Partner at Arnold & Porter LLP, Washington, D.C.

Gary D. Brown
is Professor at the Eisenhower School, National Defense University, Washington, D.C.

Todd F. Buchwald
is Special Coordinator at U.S. Department of State Office of Global Criminal Justice, Washington, D.C., and Professorial Lecturer in Law at George Washington University Law School, Washington, D.C.

William W. Burke-White
is Professor of Law at Penn Carey Law School, University of Pennsylvania, Philadelphia, Pennsylvania, Non-Resident Senior Fellow at Brookings Institution Foreign Policy Program, and Senior Advisor to White & Case LLP.

Douglass Cassel
is Professor Emeritus of Law at Notre Dame Law School, Notre Dame, Indiana and Counsel at King & Spalding LLP, New York, New York.

James Cavallaro
is co-founder and Executive Director of University Network for Human Rights.

Róisín Á Costello
is Assistant Professor of EU and International Law at Trinity College, Dublin, Ireland.

Margaret M. deGuzman
is James E. Beasley Professor of Law and Co-Director of Institute for International Law and Public Policy at Temple Law School, Philadelphia, Pennsylvania, and Judge of the Residual Mechanism for International Criminal Tribunals.

Elizabeth Evenson
is Director of the Human Rights Watch International Justice Program, New York, New York.

Rebecca J. Hamilton
is Professor of Law at Washington College of Law, American University, Washington, D.C., an Executive Editor at Just Security, and a Member of the Council on Foreign Relations.

Ladislav Hamran
is President and National Member for Slovakia at Eurojust, The Hague, The Netherlands, and Prosecutor at the General Prosecution Office of Slovakia, Bratislava, Slovakia.

Oona A. Hathaway
is Gerard C. and Bernice Latrobe Smith Professor of International Law and Director of Center for Global Legal Challenges at Yale Law School, Professor of International Law and Area Studies at the MacMillan Center, and Professor of Political Science at Yale University, New Haven, Connecticut, and a Member of the Council on Foreign Relations.

Kevin Jon Heller
is Professor of International Law and Security at University of Copenhagen's Centre for Military Studies, Copenhagen, Denmark, Professor of Law at Australian National University, Canberra, Australia and Associate Professor of Public International Law at University of Amsterdam, Amsterdam, The Netherlands.

Devika Hovell
is Associate Professor of Law at LSE Law School, London School of Economics and Political Science, London, England.

Alexandra Huneeus
is Professor of Law and Director of Global Legal Studies Center at University of Wisconsin Law School, Madison, Wisconsin.

Miles Jackson
is Associate Professor of Law in the Faculty of Law and Sir David Lewis Fellow and Tutorial Fellow in Law at Jesus College, University of Oxford, Oxford, England.

Dia Kayyali
is Senior Case and Policy Officer at the Oversight Board and was previously Associate Director for Advocacy at Mnemonic and Program Manager at WITNESS.

Alexa Koenig
is Executive Director and Co-Founder of the Human Rights Investigations Lab at the Human Rights Center and Lecturer in Residence at University of California Berkeley Law School, Berkeley, California.

Máximo Langer
is David G. Price and Dallas P. Price Professor of Law, Director of the Transnational Program on Criminal Justice, and Faculty Director of Promise Institute for Human Rights at University of California Los Angeles School of Law, Los Angeles, California, and President of the American Society of Comparative Law.

Carrie McDougall
is Senior Lecturer in Law at Melbourne Law School, The University of Melbourne, Melbourne, Australia.

Luis Moreno-Ocampo
was the first Prosecutor of the International Criminal Court and is Senior Fellow at the Carr Center for Human Rights Policy at Harvard Kennedy School, Harvard University, Cambridge, Massachusetts.

Ray Murphy
is Professor at the Irish Centre for Human Rights, School of Law, National University of Ireland Galway, Galway, Ireland.

Michael A. Newton
is Professor of the Practice of Law and Political Science and Director of the International Legal Studies Program at Vanderbilt Law School, Nashville, Tennessee.

Yvonne Ng
is Archives Program Manager at WITNESS.

Ray Nickson
is Senior Lecturer in Criminology at Newcastle School of Law and Justice, University of Newcastle, Newcastle, Australia.

Bernard Ntahiraja
is Associate Professor of International Law at University of South-Eastern Norway, Drammen, Norway.

Melanie O'Brien
is Associate Professor of International Law at UWA Law School, University of Western Australia, Perth, Australia, and President of the International Association of Genocide Scholars.

Jamie O'Connell
is Lecturer in Residence at Stanford Law School, Stanford, California.

Enrique Piracés
is Director of the Center for Human Rights Science Technology Program at Carnegie Mellon University, Pittsburgh, Pennsylvania.

Fausto Pocar
is Professor Emeritus of International Law at the University of Milan, Milan, Italy, and Judge ad hoc of the International Court of Justice, The Hague, The Netherlands.

Nadia Carine Fornel Poutou
was President of the Association of Women Lawyers of Central African Republic.

Theresa Sophia Reinold
is Junior Professor of Global and Transnational Cooperation Research at the Institute of Political Science, Duisburg-Essen University, Duisburg, Germany.

Marco Roscini
is Professor of International Law at Westminster Law School, University of Westminster, London, England, and Swiss Chair of International Humanitarian Law at the Geneva Academy of International Humanitarian Law and Human Rights, Geneva, Switzerland.

Cedric Ryngaert
is Professor of Public International Law at Utrecht University, Utrecht, The Netherlands, Chair at the Dutch Advisory Committee on Public International Law, and Editor-in-Chief of Utrecht Law Review and Netherlands International Law Review.

Leila Nadya Sadat
is James Carr Professor of International Criminal Law at Washington University School of Law, St. Louis, Missouri, Special Adviser on Crimes Against Humanity to the International Criminal Court Prosecutor, and a Member of the Council on Foreign Relations.

David Scheffer
is Senior Fellow at the Council on Foreign Relations, Washington, D.C., Clinical Professor Emeritus and Director Emeritus of the Center for International Human Rights at Northwestern University Pritzker School of Law, Chicago, Illinois, and Professor of Practice at Arizona State University School of Politics and Global Studies, Washington, D.C.

Alison A. Smith
is Legal Counsel and Director of the International Criminal Justice Program at No Peace Without Justice, Brussels, Belgium.

Carsten Stahn
is Professor of International Criminal Law and Global Justice at the Leiden Law School, Leiden, The Netherlands, and Professor of Public International Law and International Criminal Justice at Queen's University Belfast School of Law, Belfast, Northern Ireland.

Richard H. Steinberg
is Jonathan D. Varat Professor of Law and Professor of Political Science at University of California Los Angeles, Los Angeles, California, a Member of the Council on Foreign Relations, and founding Editor-in-Chief of www.ICCforum.com.

Ivana Stradner
is Research Fellow at the Foundation for Defense of Democracies' Barish Center for Media Integrity, Washington, D.C. and Special Correspondent at Kyiv Post, Kyiv, Ukraine.

Beth Van Schaack
is Ambassador-at-Large for Global Criminal Justice at the U.S. Department of State, Washington, D.C.

Maartje Weerdesteijn
is Assistant Professor at the Department of Criminal Law and Criminology and Researcher at the Center for International Criminal Justice at Vrije Universiteit Amsterdam, Amsterdam, The Netherlands.

Alex Whiting
is Deputy Prosecutor at the Kosovo Specialist Prosecutor's Office, The Hague, The Netherlands, and Visiting Professor of Law from Practice at Harvard Law School, Cambridge, Massachusetts.

Lachezar Yanev
is Associate Professor of International Criminal Law at the Department of Criminal Law and Criminology, and Researcher at the Center for International Criminal Justice at Vrije Universiteit Amsterdam, Amsterdam, The Netherlands.

John Choon Yoo
is Emanuel S. Heller Professor of Law, Faculty Director of the Korea Law Center and Public Law & Policy Program at University of California Berkeley School of Law, Berkeley, California, and Visiting Fellow at the Hoover Institution, Stanford University, Stanford, California.

PART 1

Superior Responsibility after Bemba

Introduction to Part 1

The following question was featured on www.ICCForum.com from June 2019 through February 2020:

What does the *Bemba* Appeal Judgment say about superior responsibility under Article 28 of the Rome Statute?

On June 8, 2018, the Appeals Chamber of the International Criminal Court decided, by majority, to acquit Jean-Pierre Bemba Gombo from the charges of war crimes and crimes against humanity.

The Appeals Chamber's Judgment reversed Trial Chamber III's decision of March 21, 2016, that Mr. Bemba was criminally responsible pursuant to article 28(a) of the Rome Statute for the crimes against humanity of murder and rape and the war crimes of murder, rape and pillaging committed by the MLC troops in the Central African Republic (CAR) from on or about October 26, 2002 to March 15, 2003, as a person effectively acting as a military commander and with effective control over the Mouvement de libération du Congo (MLC) troops.

Having considered all submissions the Appeals Chamber found, by majority, that Trial Chamber III had erred on two important issues:

1. It had erroneously convicted Mr. Bemba for specific criminal acts that were outside the scope of the charges as confirmed; and
2. In its assessment of whether Mr. Bemba took all necessary and reasonable measures to prevent, repress or punish the commission by his subordinates of the other crimes within the scope of the case, the Trial Chamber made serious errors. More specifically, the Trial Chamber erred in its evaluation of Mr. Bemba's motivation and the measures that he could have taken in light of the limitations he faced in investigating and prosecuting crimes as a remote commander sending troops to a foreign country; in whether he made efforts to refer the allegations of crimes to the CAR's authorities; and in whether he intentionally limited the mandate of commissions and inquiries that he established. Furthermore, in the view of the Appeals Chamber majority, there was an apparent discrepancy between the limited number of crimes within the case's scope for which Mr. Bemba was held responsible and the Trial Chamber's assessment of which measures Mr. Bemba should have taken.

The Appeals Chamber concluded, by majority, that Mr. Bemba's conviction must be reversed, that Mr. Bemba cannot be held criminally liable under article 28(a) of the Rome Statute for the crimes within the scope of the case that

 | DOI:10.1163/9789004686755_002

were committed by MLC troops during the CAR operation, and that he must be acquitted thereof.

In this context, what does the Bemba Appeal Judgment say about superior responsibility under article 28(a) of the Rome Statute?

CHAPTER 1

Weakening Command Responsibility Doctrine? The Bemba Appeals Judgment

Dianne Amann

Few acts carry a weightier burden than the acceptance of authority over persons permitted to kill. The gravity of the commander's responsibility stems from practical as well as moral concerns, and is reflected in legal doctrine dating back centuries. But a 2018 judgment of the International Criminal Court Appeals Chamber appeared to lighten this burden, reversing, in *Bemba*, convictions of an accused it described as "Commander-in-Chief" of the "military branch" of a political party over which he also presided.[1] The ruling's construction of Article 28(a) of the ICC's Rome Statute erodes not only the foundations of command responsibility doctrine, but also societal aspirations, given voice in the *Statute's* preamble, "that the most serious crimes of concern to the international community as a whole must not go unpunished..."[2] Recognizing the likelihood the question again will confront some future ICC chamber, this essay argues for an interpretation that is grounded in the purposes of the command responsibility doctrine and of the Court itself.

> Men who take up arms against one another in public war do not cease on this account to be moral beings, responsible to one another and to God.

So wrote Professor Francis Lieber in his milestone *Instructions*, issued in 1863, during the United States' Civil War.[3] The statement pointed to the

1 Prosecutor v. Jean-Pierre Bemba Gombo, Case No. ICC-01/05-01/08 A, Judgment on the Appeal of Mr Jean-Pierre Bemba Gombo against Trial Chamber III's "Judgment Pursuant to Article 74 of the *Statute*," (June 8, 2018).

2 International Criminal Court, Rome Statute of the International Criminal Court, U.N. Doc. A/CONF.183/9 (July 17, 1998) [hereinafter Rome Statute].

3 War Dep't, General Orders No. 100, Instructions for the Government of Armies of the United States in the Field, art. 15 (Apr. 24, 1863), reprinted in D. Schindler and J. Toman (eds.), *The Laws of Armed Conflicts: A Collection of Conventions, Resolutions, and Other Documents*, (Dordrecht: Martinus Nijhoff Publishers, 1988), pp. 3–23.

 | DOI:10.1163/9789004686755_003

heavy individual burden that permission to kill imposes, particularly when that permission is conferred within a system professing to place high value on the life of every human and on the liberty and security of every person. By the time of Lieber's compilation, the moral onus already had found expression in the laws and customs of war, extensive even then and since amplified, through practice, codification, and commentary. Today, even as this body of law permits killings in combat, it also constrains them, by application of principles like necessity and by humanitarian injunctions against unnecessary suffering. At least since the post-World War II trials at Nuremberg and Tokyo, moreover, a person who acts outside these constraints risks individual punishment for violations of international criminal law.[4]

Leadership status does not relieve a person of this risk of punishment. Quite to the contrary. For in accepting authority over troops given permission to kill, a commander accepts the duty to be responsible for her troops' actions as well as her own. The moral dimension of command responsibility is apparent. Supervision of permitted killings, no less than the killings themselves, stands in tension with societal valorizations of human life; indeed, tension may be greater for the reason that the commander has power to control the behavior of many persons beyond herself. A dimension of military practicality also inheres in the doctrine of command responsibility. Both the effectiveness of military operations and the protection of one's own military forces depend on military discipline, and it is the commander's duty to instill and maintain discipline in all persons under her authority, through training, oversight, and, when warranted, reprimand. Indicative of this moral and practical significance are command responsibility's deep roots: many commentators date the doctrine to 1439, and some to a couple millennia before that.[5] Its many legal expressions range from a 1907 treaty according "rights…of war" only to persons in a unit that is *inter alia* "commanded by a person responsible for his subordinates" to the 2017 terms of

4 *See Principles of International Law Recognized in the Charter of the Nürnberg Tribunal and in the Judgment of the Tribunal*, ¶ 97, [1950] 2 Y.B. Int'l L. Comm'n 374. ("Any person who commits an act which constitutes a crime under international law is responsible therefor and liable to punishment."). For a definitive account of pre-World War II underpinnings for this principle, *see* William A. Schabas, *The Trial of the Kaiser*, (Oxford: Oxford University Press, 2018).

5 *E.g.*, Gary D. Solis, *The Law of Armed Conflict: International Humanitarian Law in War*, 2d ed., (New York, NY: Cambridge University Press, 2016), p. 418 (quoting 1439 edict first quoted in Leslie C. Green (ed.), *Essays on the Modern Law of War*, 2d ed., (Ardsley, NY: Transnational Publishers, 1999), p. 283); W. H. Parks, 'Command Responsibility for War Crimes' (1973) 62 *Mil. L. Rev.* 1, 3 (quoting Sun Tzu circa 500 AD).

reference for the Syria investigative mechanism.[6] As with other modes of international criminal liability, persons have endured trial, conviction, and punishment on charges of command responsibility ever since the post-World War II period.

It bears stressing that convictions have hinged upon the commander's own behavior; that is, on his own failure to act as military, moral, and legal considerations require him to do. An oft-quoted passage by Professor Yoram Dinstein encapsulates the point:

> It must be accentuated that command responsibility is all about dereliction of duty. The commander is held accountable for his own act (of omission), rather than incurring 'vicarious liability' for the acts (of commission) of the subordinates.[7]

It is not a matter of strict liability, for guilt may not lie simply because of command status. Conviction is based, rather, upon proof that a commander breached his duty by failing to act when he knew, or should have known, that subordinates were about to, or already had, committed violations of the laws of war. Allowing conviction upon proof of a *mens rea* lower than actual knowledge avoids what Professor Roger S. Clark called "an invitation to the commander to see and hear no evil," which would undermine "serious effort to make the command structure responsive to the humanitarian goals involved."[8]

Drafters at the 1998 Rome Diplomatic Conference embraced these views, so that Article 28(a) of the *ICC Statute* states:

> A military commander or person effectively acting as a military commander shall be criminally responsible for crimes within the jurisdic-

6 Hague Convention No. IV, Respecting the Laws and Customs of War on Land art. 1, Oct. 18, 1907, 36 Stat. 2277, T.S. 539. U.N. Secretary General, *Terms of Reference of the International, Impartial and Independent Mechanism to Assist in the Investigation and Prosecution of Persons Responsible for the Most Serious Crimes under International Law Committed in the Syrian Arab Republic since March 2011*, ¶ 6, U.N. Doc. A/71/755 (Jan. 19, 2017), https://digitallibrary.un.org/record/857709 (stating that the mechanism "focuses on evidence pertaining to *mens rea* and to specific modes of criminal liability, including under the principle of command or superior responsibility established under international criminal law.").

7 Yoram Dinstein, *The Conduct of Hostilities Under the Law of International Armed Conflict*, (Cambridge: Cambridge University Press, 2004), p. 238 (parentheticals in original).

8 R. S. Clark, 'Medina: An Essay on the Principles of Criminal Liability for Homicide' (1973) 5 *Rutgers-Camden L.J.* 59–79 at 78.

tion of the Court committed by forces under his or her effective command and control, or effective authority and control as the case may be, as a result of his or her failure to exercise control properly over such forces, where:

i. That military commander or person either knew or, owing to the circumstances at the time, should have known that the forces were committing or about to commit such crimes; and
ii. That military commander or person failed to take all necessary and reasonable measures within his or her power to prevent or repress their commission or to submit the matter to the competent authorities for investigation and prosecution.

This subpart (a) text, coupled with subpart (b)'s application of the doctrine to "other superiors," has led to description of Article 28 as expanding liability.[9]

That is not what happened in last year's appellate ruling in *Bemba*, however. The accused, a Congolese national, stood trial on two counts of murder and rape as crimes against humanity, plus three counts of murder, rape, and pillage as war crimes based on his liability as a commander for acts that his militia's troops had committed in the Central African Republic. In 2016, a Trial Chamber entered convictions on all counts and sentenced him to eighteen years' imprisonment. Two years later, the Appeals Chamber, by a vote of 3 to 2, applied a *de novo* standard of review and fully acquitted the accused.

Central to this result was the appellate majority's discussion of the element set forth in Article 28(a)(ii), concerning the commander's failure to "take all necessary and reasonable measures within his or her power to prevent or repress their commission..." The words "all" and "necessary" militate in favor of setting high expectations on what it is "reasonable" to expect of a commander. But the appellate majority placed the bar quite low. For example, Paragraph 191 stated:

> [T]he Trial Chamber's failure to fully appreciate the limitations that Mr Bemba would have faced in investigating and prosecuting crimes

9 *See* Solis, *The Law of Armed Conflict*, supra note 5, p. 437–38 (writing that Article 28(a)(ii) could be construed to enlarge potential liability, yet noting, via quotation of William Schabas, *An Introduction to the International Criminal Court*, (Cambridge: Cambridge University Press, 2001), p. 85, that "other superiors" liability under Article 28(b) requires a mens rea higher than that for military commanders).

> as a remote commander sending troops to a foreign country had an important impact on the overall assessment of the measures taken by Mr Bemba.

At odds with doctrine that holds willful blindness is no defense to a charge of command responsibility, the statement goes far to excuse a commander for absenting himself, figuratively and literally, from the field.

Paragraph 170, meanwhile, declared, without citation to authority:

> Commanders are allowed to make a cost/benefit analysis when deciding which measures to take, bearing in mind their overall responsibility to prevent and repress crimes committed by their subordinates.

The concept of "cost/benefit analysis" derives from economics, of course, and tends to prefer quantitative assessment. It thus seems ill-suited to evaluating the qualitative concerns about protection – force protection, as well as protection of civilians and persons *hors de combat* – that underlie command responsibility doctrine.

The apparent welcome of defense assertions of "costs" said to outweigh the "benefits" is curious for yet another reason. The Trial Chamber found a failure to satisfy the Article 28(a)(ii) duty of care after positing a list of measures that it ruled the accused could have taken to prevent or repress the crimes his subordinates committed. But the appellate majority rejected this line of reasoning on the ground that the accused had not been given notice that such possibilities would be taken into account. Rejection on this basis likely will astound a myriad of attorneys who have litigated complex criminal cases, and of judges who have presided over them. Removal of this method of legal reasoning provokes questions about what methods the majority would allow to the ICC's courts of first instance. As yet there are no answers. But one thing is known: the majority's construction treats an accused commander like an ordinary defendant, and in so doing disregards a duty of care that is justified by military practice as well as humanitarian concerns, and prescribed in law. Purporting to do so to ensure a fair trial, it ignores that there is no unfairness in holding a commander to the duty that he himself accepted when he assumed command. The doctrine of command responsibility, and not the responsible commander, has been made to step down.

This is no mere cavil. Given the *Statute's* directive to concentrate on the "most serious crimes," coupled with resource constraints and the sheer numbers of potential defendants, the actual committers of atrocities seldom will appear before the ICC. In the dock instead will be their commander, who led, acquiesced, or turned a blind eye to their criminality – or failed to punish them after crimes occurred. To tolerate such derelictions of duty is to condone indiscipline and so to increase the risks of the very harms that the doctrine of command responsibility is intended to dispel. In the court that was established to entrench a new era of accountability, the result may be that no one can be held to account.

CHAPTER 2

Bemba's Legacy: Motivations and Geographic Remoteness in Article 28 Liability

Miles Jackson

1 Introduction

Commanders are required to take all necessary and reasonable measures to prevent and punish the crimes of their subordinates. The decision of the Appeals Chamber in *Bemba* raises the issue of the relevance of a commander's (a) motivations and (b) geographical remoteness to an evaluation of their conduct. In this comment, I argue that the decision in *Bemba* did not introduce a new legal rule in respect of either motivations or remoteness, and discuss the potential relevance of both to a contextual assessment of the commander's conduct.

In its judgment of June 8, 2018, the Appeals Chamber of the International Criminal Court acquitted Jean-Pierre Bemba Gombo of charges of war crimes and crimes against humanity. Much has been said about the acquittal – of procedural questions concerning the relationship between trial and appeal, of its implications for politics in the Democratic Republic of the Congo, and of the exchange it prompted between the Office of the Prosecutor and Presidency. In this comment, I will focus on two issues relating to the applicable standards for determining whether a commander has discharged his duty to take all "necessary and reasonable measures" under Article 28 of the *ICC Statute*. These concern:

a) the role to be given to a commander's motivations in evaluating those measures; and
b) the relevance of a commander's remoteness from the scene of the crimes in evaluating those measures.

I argue that the *Bemba* Appeals Judgment does not introduce a new legal rule on either of these issues. However, I suggest that the Separate Opinion of Judges Van den Wyngaert and Judge Morrison shows a renewed emphasis on the culpable link between senior commanders and the specific crimes of their subordinates.

 | DOI:10.1163/9789004686755_004

2 A Commander's Motivations

A preliminary question regarding the role of a commander's motivations in assessing the adequacy of her measures is why we are discussing them at all? In the voluminous scholarship on command responsibility, the issue seems, at least on a cursory glance, to have garnered very little attention. Likewise, the issue does not seem to have been discussed at length in previous case law – whether after the Second World War, at the ICTY, at the ICTR, at the SCSL, at the ECCC, at the ICC, or in the domestic prosecution of international crimes. Why, then, is the issue of a commander's motivations now a question for discussion? It is a question for discussion because the Appeals Chamber in *Bemba*, seemingly mischaracterizing the judgment of the Trial Chamber, held that the latter had materially erred in the way that it treated Mr. Bemba's motivations in taking measures to prevent and punish the crimes of his subordinates.

More specifically, the Appeals Chamber held that the "Trial Chamber's preoccupation with Mr. Bemba's motivations appears to have colored its entire assessment of the measures that he took"; that "in effect the Trial Chamber appears to have treated the motives as determinative, in and of themselves, of the adequacy or otherwise of the measure"; and that "the Trial Chamber's error in considering Mr. Bemba's motivation had a material impact on the entirety of its findings on necessary and reasonable measures because it permeated the Trial Chamber's assessment of the measures that Mr. Bemba had taken."[1] Despite the forcefulness of these assertions, their characterization of the Trial Judgment is not correct. This has been argued at more length elsewhere.[2] This mischaracterization, though, is mostly a matter that goes to an evaluation of the acquittal itself. For future cases, the more interesting question is what the Appeals Judgment says on the issue of motivations as a matter of law.

In this respect, there appears not to be disagreement across the various opinions. In response to the Appeals Chamber's framing of the issues, during the appeal proceedings Mr. Bemba's counsel argued that a commander's motivations ought to play no role in a court's evaluation of their measures:

1 Prosecutor v. Jean-Pierre Bemba Gombo, Case No. ICC-01/05-01/08 A, Judgment on Appeal of Mr Jean-Pierre Bemba Gombo Against Trial Chamber III's "Judgment Pursuant to Article 74 of the Statute", ¶¶ 178, 191 (June 8, 2018) [hereinafter Bemba Appeals Chamber Judgment].

2 Miles Jackson, *Commanders' Motivations in Bemba*, EJIL TALK (June 15, 2018), https://www.ejiltalk.org/commanders-motivations-in-bemba/ (last visited June 21, 2023).

> The reason why a commander in the field decides to take measures to prevent and punish crimes is irrelevant to an assessment of the adequacy. Adequacy is assessed objectively; motivation is necessarily subjective.[3]

This claim of irrelevancy was rejected in the Majority Judgment in the following terms:

> …the Appeals Chamber rejects Mr. Bemba's submission that the motives of an accused commander are always irrelevant to the assessment of "necessary and reasonable measures" because a commander is required to act in good faith in adopting such measures and must show that he *genuinely* tried to prevent or repress the crimes in question or submit the matter to the competent authorities…[4]

This holding in the Majority Judgment was explicitly referred to and approved of in the Joint Dissenting Opinion of Judges Monageng and Hofmański.[5] The President's Separate Concurring Opinion only briefly touches on the issue, noting that:

> [A]cting to protect the image of his organization (if that were truly the case) needed not be seen in the particular circumstances of the case as forensically synonymous with non-genuineness of measure.[6]

Finally, the Separate Opinion of Judges Van den Wyngaert and Judge Morrison does not address the issue of motivations at all.

Thus, in short, where is the law on the relevance of a commander's motivation in an assessment of command responsibility? Two points seem clear.[7] First, adequacy is adequacy – an adequate measure or set of measures of prevention, investigation, or punishment remains adequate no matter

3 Prosecutor v Jean-Pierre Bemba Gombo, Case No. ICC-01/05-01/08-T-373-ENG, Appeals Hearing Transcript, 57–58 (Jan. 10, 2018).

4 *Bemba Appeals Chamber Judgment*, supra note 1, ¶ 176.

5 Prosecutor v. Jean-Pierre Bemba Gombo, Case No. ICC-01/05-01/08-3636-Anx1-Red, Dissenting Opinion of Judge Sanji Mmasenono Monageng and Judge Piotr Hofmański, ¶ 70 (AC, June 8, 2018) [hereinafter Bemba Appeals Chamber Dissent].

6 Prosecutor v. Jean-Pierre Bemba Gombo, Case No. ICC-01/05-01/08-3636-Anx3, Concurring Separate Opinion of Judge Eboe-Osuji, ¶ 16 (AC, June 14, 2018) [hereinafter Concurring Opinion of Eboe-Osuji].

7 Jackson, *supra* note 2.

the reason driving the commander's decision to take it. This follows from command responsibility's basic nature as an objective doctrine of responsibility. Second, a commander's motivations in taking a measure may be relevant, evidentially, to a determination of its genuineness, and, consequently, to its adequacy. Evidence that a commander was really seeking to set up a sham process may be relevant to a court's assessment of the adequacy of the measure.

3 Remoteness

A second substantive question concerns the potential relevance of a commander's geographical position in assessing the adequacy of their measures. As with the previous issue, a preliminary question here is likewise why this is a matter for discussion? As noted elsewhere,[8] it is up for discussion because in assessing the measures taken by Mr. Bemba the Majority Judgment appears, at least on first glance, to emphasize the fact that he – Mr. Bemba – was what the judgment calls a "remote commander." Specifically, the Majority Judgment held as follows:

- Nevertheless … the Trial Chamber paid insufficient attention to the fact that the MLC troops were operating in a foreign country with the attendant difficulties on Mr. Bemba's ability, as a remote commander, to take measures.
- In sum, the Appeals Chamber has identified the following serious errors in the Trial Chamber's assessment … (i) the Trial Chamber erred by failing to properly appreciate the limitations that Mr. Bemba would have faced in investigating and prosecuting crimes as a remote commander sending troops to a foreign country…
- The Appeals Chamber finds that the errors that it has identified have a material impact on the Trial Chamber's finding that Mr. Bemba failed to take all necessary and reasonable measures. […] Furthermore, the Trial Chamber's failure to fully appreciate the limitations that Mr. Bemba would have faced in investigating and prosecuting crimes as a remote commander sending troops to a foreign country had an important impact on the overall assessment of the measures taken by Mr. Bemba.
- Indeed, in faulting the results of measures taken by Mr. Bemba, the Trial Chamber failed to appreciate that, as a remote commander, Mr. Bemba

8 Miles Jackson, *Geographical Remoteness in Bemba*, EJIL TALK (July 30, 2018), https://www.ejiltalk.org/geographical-remoteness-in-bemba/ (last visited June 21, 2023).

> was not part of the investigations and was not responsible for the results generated. Had it done so, the Trial Chamber's assessment of the measures Mr. Bemba had taken would have been necessarily different.[9]

The repeated references to Mr. Bemba's status as a remote commander might otherwise have passed unnoticed but for other recent doctrinal developments in international criminal law. More specifically, in the course of the extensive doctrinal controversy prompted by the decision of the ICTY Appeals Chamber in *Perišić* concerning aiding and abetting, a similar discussion centered on the Appeals Chamber's reference to Mr. Perišić's remoteness from the scene of the crime.[10] Here, the Appeals Chamber of the ICTY introduced the additional element of "specific direction" in circumstances where "an accused aider and abettor is remote from relevant crimes"[11] and, as one potential factor relevant to determining a culpable link between the aider and principal, included "geographic distance."[12]

This is not the place to revisit either the overarching controversy around *Perišić* or the complex question of how to appropriately inculpate accomplices in situations of large-scale assistance. One thing seems clear, though. The relative geographical remoteness of accomplices does not provide a ground on which to draw principled distinctions amongst them. Historically, as a number of scholars have pointed out, the common law did distinguish between participants in crime on the basis of whether the party was at the scene of the crime. This has been long-abandoned. In Stewart's words, the position of those who assist at the scene of a crime and those who are geographically remote is "morally irrelevant."[13]

This relatively recent controversy perhaps explains an initial apprehension to the *Bemba* Appeals Chamber's repeated reference to Mr. Bemba's status as a remote commander. Is there, then, a new substantive distinction in the law of command responsibility relating to the geographical position of the commander?

In short, the answer is no. In the first place, it is not clear that the Majority Judgment itself was attempting to draw a substantive distinction between differently-placed commanders. Another reading of the Majority

9 Bemba Appeals Chamber Judgment, supra note 1, ¶¶ 171, 189, 191, 192.

10 Prosecutor v. Momčilo Perišić, Case No. IT-04-81-A, Judgement (Int'l Crim. Trib. for the Former Yugoslavia AC, Feb. 28, 2013).

11 *Id.* ¶ 39.

12 *Id.* ¶ 40.

13 James G. Stewart, *The ICTY Loses its Way on Complicity – Part 1*, OPINIO JURIS (Apr. 3, 2013), http://opiniojuris.org/2013/04/03/guest-post-the-icty-loses-its-way-on-complicity-part-1/ (last visited June 21, 2023).

Judgment is that the references to Mr. Bemba's remote position was simply part of its contextual assessment of what was necessary and reasonable. Second, and more importantly, both the President's Separate Concurring Opinion and the Joint Dissenting Opinion of Judges Monageng and Hofmański explicitly reject any substantive distinction on the basis of geography. To take the President first, he held:

> [Mr. Bemba] was a commander, and was at all material times remotely located in another country. While remoteness of location is not a controlling factor of innocence, it can complicate the question of guilt (as it does in this appeal) depending on the particular circumstances of a given case.
>
> […] I would not subscribe to any interpretation of the Majority Opinion as suggesting that the geographic remoteness of a commander is a factor all of its own, which would necessarily insulate him from criminal responsibility. Geographic remoteness is only a factor to be considered among other circumstances or peculiarities of a given case. It serves its greatest value in the assessment of what is reasonable as a measure to prevent or repress violations to submit them to competent authorities for investigation and prosecution.[14]

Turning to the Joint Dissenting Opinion, Judges Monageng and Hofmański held:

> We note that in a case concerning actors operating across international borders, the traditional criteria have been applied. The specificities of the particular case, such as the structure and functioning of the military groups involved, as well as the remoteness of the commander are part of the factual considerations that the Trial Chamber must assess in order to determine whether the accused had the material ability to prevent, repress or report the commission of crime.[15]

On this basis, it is clear that there is no substantive distinction between remote and non-remote commanders in the doctrine of command responsibility at the ICC. Rather than a substantive distinction, there is agreement

14 Concurring Opinion of Eboe-Osuji, *supra* note 6, ¶¶ 3, 258.

15 Bemba Appeals Chamber Dissent, *supra* note 5, ¶ 127.

here that the remoteness of the commander is a factual consideration in the specific case.

But is it possible to be more precise here? In addition to recognizing that geographical remoteness does not entail a substantive distinction among commanders, it is also crucial to understand that its potential relevance as part of the circumstances does not operate in a single direction. By that, I mean that it there is no implication at all along the lines that "the more remote the commander the less they are required to do." Geographical remoteness entails neither a legal distinction nor a factor that necessarily diminishes the obligations of a commander the further away she is.

To illustrate, as I wrote in a previous contribution:

> [C]onsider a commander in possession of credible information that her subordinates have committed war crimes. A remote geographical position may render the taking of certain measures: (i) more difficult or (ii) less difficult, or indeed (iii) may be irrelevant to the determination of whether a measure taken was required. Thus, for instance, taking the initial investigative steps to secure evidence may be rendered more difficult by remoteness; securing funding and political support for a proper inquiry may be less difficult where the commander is remote from the battlefield; and setting the terms of the investigative mandate of an inquiry, including which crimes it investigates, isn't straightforwardly informed by geographical position. Everything turns on the specific measure at issue and the specific circumstances at hand. It makes no sense to assert that limitations on capacity necessarily flow from a commander's remote position.[16]

4 A Wider Point

On this, I think, there is agreement. There is, though, something else that comes out of the Separate Opinion of Judges Van den Wyngaert and Morrison which is distinct from, but related to, the idea of geographical remoteness. The Joint Separate Opinion is at pains to emphasize that command responsibility is not what they call a "one-size-fits-all" offense.[17] By

16 Jackson, *supra* note 8.

17 *The Prosecutor v. Jean-Pierre Bemba Gombo*, Case No. ICC-01/05-01/08-3636-Anx2, Separate Opinion of Judge Christine Van den Wyngaert and Judge Howard Morrison, ¶ 33 (AC, June 8, 2018).

this they mean to emphasize that the position of the commander within the hierarchy *really* matters for how she is to discharge her obligations. At first glance, this might not seem worth noting at all – as a matter of principle I would be surprised if there were much disagreement at all as to the contextual nature of the doctrine of command responsibility and the critical importance of the commander's hierarchical position in determining precisely what it was appropriate to expect her to do.

However, it may be that, as a matter of emphasis, the Joint Separate Opinion suggests a stricter standard for the prosecution to prove the responsibility of senior commanders. To give three examples, the opinion proposes that "[i]n principle, higher-level commanders are thus entitled to rely on lower level commanders to keep their troops in check and to deal with deviant behavior"; that "[a]lthough article 28 of the *Statute* can very well be applied to senior commanders, it is not always the right tool to link them directly to the conduct of the physical perpetrators"; and that "in applying the test [(i) effective control, (ii) knowledge or should have known, and (iii) necessary and reasonable measures] the Court should abide by the principle that command responsibility is not strict liability and that we do not ask the impossible of the military commander."[18] Again, these statements in and of themselves do not seem controversial – it is a matter of emphasis that runs through the Joint Separate Opinion. In future prosecutions, it would make sense for the Prosecutor to take pains to focus on culpable omissions relating directly to the superior's place in the hierarchy of command.

5 Conclusion

The opinions in *Bemba* provide a rich set of disagreements on specific and fundamental issues in the law of command responsibility and the procedural law of the International Criminal Court. Though significant in the case itself, the two issues discussed here – a commander's motivations and geographical position – do not indicate a change in the law. Nonetheless, the decision in *Bemba* suggests closer scrutiny of evidence of the culpability of senior commanders in relation to the specific crimes of their subordinates.

18 *Id.* ¶¶ 33, 35, 36.

CHAPTER 3

Bemba's Balance: Aligning the Rome Statute with Military Realities

Michael Newton

1 Introduction

The *Bemba* Appeals Judgement preserved the normative power of Article 28 of the Rome Statute insofar as it reversed judicial presumptions that were strikingly at odds with centuries of military practice and established tenets of command responsibility. If left uncorrected, Trial Chamber findings would have disincentivized commanders from their non-delegable duty to prevent or ameliorate war crimes alleged against subordinate forces. Operational control is an essential element of command relationships in every national and multinational force, including NATO operations, United Nations peacekeeping missions, and multinational military coalitions created to enforce Security Council Chapter VII resolutions. Trial Chamber findings would nevertheless have eviscerated forms of operational control that provide strategic coherence and help ensure tactical level Unity of Command.

Judicial explication of the standards for assessing whether remote commanders exercise effective control over non-linear military campaigns waging non-international armed conflicts involving an array of non-state participants is wholly warranted. That aspect of *Bemba* is a welcome extension of the jurisprudence related to command responsibility.

However, the *Bemba* Trial Chamber's findings related to effective control relied upon evidence that he continued to receive reports from his forces after they deployed to another nation and fought in a composite command under the operational authority of foreign commanders in areas where the civilians spoke a different language.[1] No responsible commander should sever communications with forces deployed under the operational control of another command. Mr. Bemba's MLC staff continued to monitor operations from a distance and arranged for the exercise of punitive authority at his direction when supported by sufficient evidence from the field. The evidence of effec-

1 Prosecutor v. Jean-Pierre Bemba Gombo, Case No. ICC-01/05-01/08-3343, Judgment Pursuant to Article 74 of the Statute, ¶¶ 700–05 (TC III, Mar. 21, 2016).

 | DOI:10.1163/9789004686755_005

tive control was predicated in part on the Trial Chamber's findings that "rather than referring all matters" to foreign authorities "as would be consistent with a complete resubordination of the forces, Mr. Bemba continued to represent the MLC forces in the CAR in external matters, including, for example, in discussions with the U.N."[2]

By imputing a negative inference into Mr. Bemba's communications with deployed forces, the Trial Chamber would have created perverse incentives for commanders to abdicate their core duty to use every ounce of their moral and legal authority to repress violations of the law of armed conflict and redress any transgressions. Compounding that error, the Trial Chamber based criminal liability on an unprecedented finding that commanders have a legal obligation to withdraw their forces at some unspecified point upon receipt of reports of violations. The Appeals Chamber recognized the appropriate bounds of deference and held that the scope of "necessary and reasonable measures" is contextually determined rather than relying on rigid bright line standards. Trial Chamber rulings would predictably have discredited the Court in the eyes of military practitioners around the world. Responsible commanders seeking to enforce the law do not face a binary choice to abdicate all authority over forces deployed in an OPCON role or arbitrarily abandon the military mission through withdrawal or retreat.

The Rome Statute echoes centuries of military practice by stipulating that the gravamen of personal criminal liability imposed on military authorities (or civilian superiors) is the failure to prevent crimes committed by forces under his/her "effective control" when such crimes occur "*as a result* of his or her failure to exercise control properly over such forces."[3] The causation factor is an important aspect of this legal test. Although, the *Bemba* Appeals Judgment did not extend its analysis to address this aspect of Article 28 based on pragmatic restraint because it was unnecessary as the basis of decision, this chapter will conclude by briefly alluding to its implications for future cases. Article 28 requires that the *actus reus* of the offense is that the commander (or person effectively operating in that capacity) "failed to take all necessary and reasonable measures within his or her power to prevent or repress" violations committed by subordinate forces or "submit the matter to the competent authorities for investigation and prosecution." This phraseology consolidated the

2 *Id.* ¶ 702.

3 International Criminal Court, Rome Statute of the International Criminal Court, arts. 28(a) and (b), UN Doc. A/CONF.183/9 (July 17, 1998) [hereinafter Rome Statute] (emphasis added).

textual strands of Articles 86(2) and 87(1) of Additional Protocol I.[4] These legal predicates represent the essence of the *Bemba* Appeals Judgment analysis *vis-à-vis* Article 28.

Article 28 represents the culmination of a long developmental arc supported by centuries of pragmatic professional military practice. In lieu of extending the principles of command accountability into a non-traditional, non-linear battlefield in which the commanders utilized fluid mechanisms of control in the midst of rapidly evolving operations, the original OTP filings relied upon assertions of "co-perpetratorship" predicated on precedents interpreting the individual responsibility criteria of Article 25. Any organization united under the authority of a superior exists by definition with some shared or common purpose. The MLC under Mr. Bemba was no exception. That is the very essence of authority and command. The pretrial transformation of the *Bemba* case away from theories of co-perpetratorship towards Article 28 was salutary because command responsibility analysis provided the strongest basis of responsibility for the crimes alleged in the Central African Republic. That trend in charging should be sustained, and the *Bemba's* Appeals Judgment may well foreshadow similar characterization in the pending litigation related to the *Bashir* case.

2 The Nature of Command

To command is an active verb. A commander at any level of authority employs military force to achieve military objectives yet knowingly does so at the risk of personal criminal liability for the actions of subordinates. The - existence of superior responsibility as a form of vicarious liability rests upon the legal and moral necessity for controlling the lethal application of violence while simultaneously maximizing respect for the rights of non-combatants. In the words of the *Čelebići* bench, criminal responsibility of commanders and others in authority is:

> [P]redicated upon the power of the superior to control the acts of his subordinates. A duty is placed upon the superior to exercise this power so as to prevent and repress the crimes committed by his subordinates, and a failure by him to do so in a diligent manner is sanctioned by the

4 Protocol Additional to the Geneva Conventions of 12 August 1949, and Relating to the Protection of Victims of International Armed Conflicts (Protocol I), Arts. 86(2), 87(1), June 8, 1977, 1125 U.N.T.S. 3 [hereinafter Additional Protocol I].

> imposition of individual criminal responsibility in accordance with the doctrine.[5]

The notion that commanders on the battlefield are vested with the primary enforcement of the laws and customs of war represents the essence of the developed law of command responsibility. Article 28 distills this long line of authority into the mandate that the commander "exercise control properly" over subordinate forces.

At the same time, jurisprudence is quite clear that a perpetrator can never be convicted based upon a norm which an accused could not reasonably have been aware of at the time of the acts, and this norm must make it sufficiently clear what act or omission could engage his criminal responsibility.[6] This tenet operates in the shadow of the prosecutor's obligation to prove each element of each charged offense beyond a reasonable doubt. In the context of Article 28, the inarguable corollary is that military commanders or civilian superiors cannot be convicted based on strict liability incurred by virtue of their position.[7] The ICRC Commentary explaining Article 87 of Additional Protocol I makes plain in paragraph 3558 that as "regards commanders of higher levels than that of company commander, they will have corresponding obligations within the confines of the area of their competence."[8]

---

5 Prosecutor v. Zejnil Delalić, et al., Case No. IT-96-21-T, Judgement, ¶¶ 340, 377 (Int'l Crim. Trib. for the Former Yugoslavia TC, Nov. 16, 1998) [hereinafter Čelebići Trial Chamber Judgment] (The Čelebići case was the first litigation to involve superior responsibility since World War II and resulted in the acquittal of Zejnil Delalić who had been charged with eleven counts of grave breaches of the 1949 Geneva Conventions and violation of the laws and customs of war on the basis of his alleged command over the Čelebići prison-camp at the relevant time. The Trial Chamber found that Mr. Delalić did not have command and control over the Čelebići prison-camp and over the guards who worked there, such as to entail his criminal responsibility for their actions); see also Prosecutor v. Clément Kayishema and Obed Ruzindana, Case No. ICTR-95-1-T, Judgement, ¶ 202 (TC II, May 21, 1999).

6 Prosecutor v. Mitar Vasiljević, Case No. IT-98-32-T, Judgment, ¶ 193 (Int'l Crim. Trib. for the Former Yugoslavia TC II, Nov. 29, 2002).

7 Prosecutor v. Laurent Semanza, Case No. ICTR-97-20-T, Judgement and Sentence, ¶ 404 (TC III, May 15, 2003) ("Criminal liability based on superior responsibility will not attach on the basis of strict liability simply because an individual is in a chain of command with authority over a given geographic area. While the individual's position in the command hierarchy is considered a significant indicator that the superior knew or had reason to know about the actions of his subordinates, knowledge will not be presumed from the status alone").

8 International Committee of the Red Cross, Protocol Additional to the Geneva Conventions of 12 August 1949, and relating to the Protection of Victims of International Armed Conflicts (Protocol I), 8 June 1977: Commentary of 1987, art. 87 at ¶ 3558 (1987),

The *Bemba's* Appeals Judgement recognized that the Trial Chamber failed to support its reasoning with evidence sufficient to establish linkage between the actions of Mr. Bemba and the actual commission of crimes on the ground in the adjacent nation. The concurring opinion by Judges Van den Wyngaert and Morrison summarized this defect by noting that jurists must avoid:

> [The] mind-set that gives priority to the desire to hold responsible those in high leadership positions and to always ascribe to them the highest levels of moral and legal culpability. Although Article 28 of the *Statute* can very well be applied to senior commanders, it is not always the right tool to link them directly to the conduct of the physical perpetrators. Of course, it is the responsibility of every commander at every level of the chain of command to do what they can, within their own sphere of competence and authority, to avoid that crimes are committed. However, this is a shared responsibility, in which every commander has a specific role to play.

In other words, the evaluation of "necessary and reasonable measures" is context specific and unique to each commander's particularized circumstances and operational role.

3 The Importance of OPCON

Omission of any recognition or discussion of modern state practice whereby commanders around the world delegate operational control (OPCON) represents one of the most striking lacunae in the Trial Chamber analysis. The Trial Chamber asserted that the continuing flow of information from deployed MLC forces back to MLC staff and thence to Mr. Bemba provided him with ongoing authority over daily operations. In fact, commanders around the world delegate OPCON to subordinate commanders or allied officers on a daily basis; which in turn gives them authority to control the day-to-day flow of military planning and tactical operations. OPCON is particularly important when forces from a variety of nations are operating in close proximity and must deconflict friendly fires, designate zones of operation, and ensure tactical coordination.

---

https://ihl-databases.icrc.org/en/ihl-treaties/api-1977/article-87/commentary/1987 (last visited June 21, 2023).

U.S. doctrine (reflective of accepted practice in many nations, U.N. operations, and multilateral coalitions) is that OPCON delegated to another commander entails:

> [T]he authority to perform those functions of command over subordinate forces involving organizing and employing commands and forces, assigning tasks, designating objectives, and giving authoritative direction necessary to accomplish the mission. Operational control includes authoritative direction over all aspects of military operations and joint training necessary to accomplish missions assigned to the command.[9]

In that light, imputation of command responsibility flows from the very nature of the laws and customs of war. The entire conception of military structures is premised on some sort of operational hierarchy of authority, which explains why the principle of Unity of Command emerged as one of the universally recognized Principles of War.[10] In layman's terminology, too many cooks in the kitchen will lose every war.

In the context of the *Bemba* Appeals Judgment, the Trial Chamber's failure to discuss OPCON relationships meant that it essentially substituted its own subjective assessment regarding the actual extent of Mr. Bemba's authority as a remote commander to control tactical operations or the selection of military objectives. The repeated assertion by the Trial Chamber that MLC forces operated with a designated *modus operandi* to attack undefended civilian areas was actually undercut by the *viva voce* testimony of OTP witnesses. The Trial Chamber repeated that assertion without any discussion of the interface between a purported MLC policy (presumably promulgated or at a minimum supported by Mr. Bemba) and the actual control of operations on the ground exercised by Central African Republic commanders.

To be clear, delegation of OPCON in no way relieves senior commanders of their obligations to ensure compliance with the laws of war. However, it establishes important contextual framing for the implementation of command prerogatives, the flow of information, and analysis of actions that are "necessary and reasonable" on the part of each commander. Similarly, Mr. Bemba's

---

9 *See* JP 1-02, OPERATIONAL CONTROL IN DEPARTMENT OF DEFENSE DICTIONARY OF MILITARY AND ASSOCIATED TERMS, p. 253 (Nov. 8, 2010, as amended through Aug. 15, 2011), https://www.bits.de/NRANEU/others/jp-doctrine/jp1_02%288-11%29.pdf (last visited June 21, 2023).

10 John Whiteclay Chambers II and Fred Anderson (eds.), *The Oxford Companion to American Military History*, (New York: Oxford University Press, 1999), p. 557.

ability to conduct investigations was curtailed by both geographic and operational constraints that necessitated his reliance on intervening layers of command. In that light, his repeated petitions to U.N. officials and to leadership within the Central African Republic seem far more appropriate than the evidentiary weight accorded by the Trial Chamber.

In the real world, no responsible commander completely severs communication with forces deployed to another nation in an OPCON relationship to multinational commanders or wholly relinquishes command authority. Maintaining reporting channels to forces deployed overseas in an OPCON relationship is *prima facie* evidence of accepted state practice. The Trial Chamber adduced not a shred of evidence to support the assertion that the failure to surrender all authority over deployed military forces sustains criminal accountability. The ICTY *Perišić* Appeals Chamber observed that the "circumstantial nature of the relevant evidence" relied upon by judges means that "a finding of effective control is possible only if that is the sole reasonable inference from this evidence." The take away is plain. Finders of fact must be clear to document the evidentiary basis for findings of effective control, particularly in the absence of testimony that the perpetrator was engaged in tactical level planning for forces that would operate in the vicinity of civilian areas nor any basis in the record indicating an ability to even implement tactical Rules of Engagement.

Without clearly identifying its analogue, the Trial Chamber implicitly analogized Mr. Bemba to the Japanese Foreign Minister, Kōki Hirota, who was convicted by the IMTFE. The Tribunal noted that when Japanese forces in Nanking committed widespread atrocities, Hirota "was content to rely on assurances that he knew were not being implemented while hundreds of murders, violations of women, and other atrocities were being committed daily."[11] Of course, actual awareness of rampant criminality is an important distinguishing factor in the two cases. There is also a matter of contrasting scale in comparing the crimes in Nanking to the twenty instances documented by the Trial Chamber as the basis of Mr. Bemba's conviction. In contrast to other commanders who knowingly facilitated rampant criminality, the defense brief argued that Mr. Bemba:

> [Was] the commander that international law would have him be. He trained his army, he gave them a Code of Conduct, he actively pursued rumors of crimes, he punished those identified to him. The ICC should

11 United States, et al. v. Sadao Araki, et al., Judgment (Kōki Hirota), 49791 (Int'l Mil. Trib. for the Far East, Nov. 4, 1948).

> go out of its way in this its first command responsibility case to reinforce the principles of responsible command rather than to create a self-fulfilling construct of criminality.[12]

The *Bemba* Appeals Chamber made a contextual analysis of whether the steps actually taken were "necessary and reasonable" based on the information available to Mr. Bemba and his ability to actually exercise investigative authority on the ground. The response of the International Federation of Human Rights (FIDH) is illustrative of the context. Upon receipt of information from FIDH regarding allegations against MLF forces, Mr. Bemba phoned the President and then replied via letter on February 20, 2003. The letter informed FIDH of the investigative steps already taken and requested documentation of the instances uncovered by FIDH investigators. The reply from Sidiki Kaba on February 26, 2003 noted only that evidence in its possession had been formally referred to the ICC as early as February 13, 2003 followed by the snarky observation that "for the purposes of completion of the file, I am sure that the ICC will appreciate receiving all information contributing to the establishment of facts and responsibilities."

The *Bemba* Appeals Judgment does not provide credence to the two assertions by the Trial Chamber that became the load bearing pillars of its finding that the measures actually undertaken were not "necessary and reasonable" under the particularized circumstances of the case. In particular, the commander's subjective motivation for taking steps to respond to allegations of criminal conduct is not relevant to the determination whether the legal threshold of "necessary and reasonable" has been met. Adequacy of such measures is an objective standard evaluated based on each commander's relative knowledge, role, and operational authority. Motivation is entirely subjective. Judicial superimposition of a duty to withdraw military forces from ongoing operations as the granddaddy of all "necessary and reasonable measures" was similarly unsupported by even a hint of state practice or jurisprudential support.

Commanders on the battlefield who control their fighters are the most important modality for suppressing violations of the laws of war in real time either proactively by proper training or reactively through the imposition of appropriate investigations and discipline. Despite that moral and pragmatic imperative, Judge Eboe-Osuji summarized the gravamen of the Majority decision on Appeal by observing that:

---

12 Prosecutor v. Jean-Pierre Bemba Gombo, Case No. ICC-01/05-01/08, Public Redacted Version of Appellant's Document in Support of the Appeal, ¶ 549 (AC, Sep. 28, 2016).

> Since command criminal responsibility entails a degree of separation between the commander and the actual perpetration of the acts amounting to crimes, coupled with the mental disposition to commit the crimes, it is important that the finding of criminal responsibility must result from a clear analysis of the evidence in a manner that reveals beyond reasonable doubt that the commander's failings suggest his own connivance in the crimes or his condonation of them – in the manner of willful subscription or callous indifference – such as would convincingly approximate a mental disposition to commit the crimes that he failed to prevent or punish. I saw no such clear analysis in the Trial Judgment – nor, for that matter, that the revealed evidence would sustain it. In the absence of such clear analysis (especially when the charges are so grave as here), I do not accept it as correct that the Appeals Chamber should, through a methodized theory of 'appellate deference,' consign the fate of a convicted person to the undoubted good faith of the Trial Chamber whose verdict of conviction has been appealed. That would be to suffer an Orwellian catch that ill-serves any criminal justice system that purports a right of appeal against conviction. The benefit of ambiguity in a conviction judgment does not belong to the trial court that authored it. It belongs to the convicted person: by sheer operation of the requirement that guilt must be established beyond reasonable doubt.

4 Implications for the Future

The *Bemba* Appeals Judgement reveals three related implications for future command responsibility cases. Technical experts and jurists must avoid a victim-centric approach that clouds good faith assessment of the timely responses necessitated in the midst of conflict. For example, rather than working with MLC officials or U.N. investigative authorities or even local commanders to identify and isolate known perpetrators of what were grievous crimes, FIDH refused to coordinate. Responding to Mr. Bemba's conviction at trial, Ms. Bensouda stated that: "Justice for the victims has been our primary and sole objective in this case." Such worthy sentiments must coexist with the recognition of the commander's primary role in investigating and ameliorating violations during armed conflict. The goals of enforcing the law and ensuring good order and professional discipline need not be deemed incompatible. In any event, the needs and concerns of victims should not obviate the importance of careful analysis of the predicate elements of personal criminal culpability.

By extension, the modern law of armed conflict provides a sort of centripetal force that helps ensure cohesion to modern multinational coalitions. As the *Bemba* Appeal Judgment notes:

> The scope of the **duty to take "all necessary and reasonable measures" is intrinsically connected to the extent of a commander's material ability to prevent or repress the commission of crimes or to submit the matter to the competent authorities for investigation and prosecution.** Indeed, a commander cannot be blamed for not having done something he or she had no power to do.[13]

Jurists must be attuned to the investigative difficulties and political dynamics that may well inhibit timely and effective investigations. Despite what might be termed the *unique* circumstances of every case, all commanders have the duty to investigate reports of alleged violations committed by persons under their command or against persons who are legally entitled to their protection. Modern multilateral operations pose particular challenges to achieving these objectives. All commanders have wide discretion to order actions or take precautionary measures to ensure efficient and viable investigations. Reforming and streamlining transnational investigative procedures must therefore be a matter of first priority.

As one final observation in passing, commanders must be diligent to discredit media reports or allegations that they deem inappropriate or unsupported. The law of command responsibility should not become a weaponized facet of asymmetric warfare. Social media posts, intentional disinformation efforts, and distorted media accounts, *inter alia*, represent potent avenues for paralyzing the conduct of hostilities. Manufactured media accounts may also seek to polarize domestic populations and degrade nimble strategic or tactical decision-making. Illegitimate exploitation of *jus in bello* norms could permit the legal structure to be portrayed as a mass of indeterminate subjectivity that is nothing more than another weapon in the moral domain of conflict at the behest of the side with the best cameras, biggest microphones, and most compliant media accomplices. Manipulation of the media by parties to

---

13 Prosecutor v. Jean-Pierre Bemba Gombo, Case No. ICC-01/05-01/08 A, Judgment on the Appeal of Mr. Jean-Pierre Bemba Gombo Against Trial Chamber III's "Judgment Pursuant to Article 74 of the Statute", ¶ 167 (AC, June 8, 2018) [hereinafter Bemba Appeals Chamber Judgment] (emphasis added).

the conflict designed to mask genuine war crimes could lead to a cycle of cynicism and second-guessing that weakens the overall commitment of some military members to remain bound by the law. Commanders must be proactive in identifying such abuses and explaining them to the public and to policymakers.

5 A Few Thoughts on Causation in the Context of Article 28

The *Bemba* Appeals Judgment did not address the causation requirement embedded in Article 28. Such analysis was unwarranted on the basis of the actual holdings. Causation is required based on the plain text of the Rome Statute, and at a superficial level this is not a complex matter. If a commander fails to take "necessary and reasonable" preventive action, the very failure to "properly exercise" the inherent duties of command might be said to have "caused" resulting offenses. Causation is a minimum requirement for imputation of individual criminal responsibility for all offenses. Command responsibility charges necessarily entail consideration of both affirmative acts and omissions, and as a theoretical matter both forms of liability should rely upon consistent standards of criminal responsibility. With respect to causality, the standard for affirmative acts and for omissions should be equivalent. Hence, the proximate cause of war crimes in the case of action should simply be inverted to a "but for test" in cases of omission to ensure logical consistency.

In the *lex specialis* of command responsibility, the commander's liability is based on far more than mere negligence or dereliction of duty. Crimes committed by subordinates within her effective control are imputed to the commander. This should require a much higher threshold than a finding that the commander's actions merely increased the risk of resulting offenses. Judge Steiner postulated such a minimal threshold in *dicta*. If future ICC cases establish such a low threshold for the causation standard, the result would create the functional equivalent of strict liability because the very decision to deploy forces to accomplish military mandates can fairly be said to increase the risk of war crimes. Without wars there can be no war crimes. Pacifists around the world would welcome this evolution of command responsibility. It would, however, represent radical departure from the intentions of States Party or accepted customary international law. The important point in the context of causation is that injecting an artificial view of the law rather than sustaining strict fidelity to the intentions of states or the realities of military operations might seriously undermine the credibility of the ICC.

CHAPTER 4

The Bemba Acquittal: A Setback for Superior Responsibility under Article 28

Nadia Carine Fornel Poutou

1 Introduction

Jean-Pierre Bemba Gombo was the highest level commander of the Mouvement de libération du Congo (MLC). The International Criminal Court prosecuted Mr. Bemba for acts committed by MLC forces on the peaceful population in the Central African Republic (CAR) from October 26, 2002 to March 15, 2003. This prosecution relied on Article 28 of the Rome Statute that provides for criminal responsibility for the military commanders and others with superior responsibility over those who commit crimes within the jurisdiction of the Court.

The ICC Trial Chamber III, in its judgment of March 21, 2016, found Mr. Bemba to be criminally responsible, under Article 28(a) of the Rome Statute, for crimes against humanity and war crimes, including murder, rape, and looting committed by MLC troops. The Trial Chamber sentenced him to a total of eighteen years. Faced with this decision, Jean-Pierre Bemba appealed.

On June 8, 2018, the ICC Appeals Chamber decided, by a majority, to reverse the Trial Chamber's holding and acquit Jean-Pierre Bemba of the counts charging war crimes and crimes against humanity.

2 Analysis

As the MLC's military commander during the period charged, Jean-Pierre Bemba was held responsible under Article 28 of the Rome Statute in the decision of Trial Chamber III. The subsequent decision of the ICC Appeals Chamber releasing Jean-Pierre Bemba, set an unfortunate precedent in that it will be difficult to prosecute other officials using similar facts.

The other contradiction in this procedure is that his conviction for witness subordination, subsidiary to the main proceedings, was sustained at the same time that he was acquitted on the much more serious principal charges. It

 | DOI:10.1163/9789004686755_006

raises the question of the seriousness of the approach taken by the judges of the ICC.

The victims of Bemba's crimes were sacrificed due to the negligence of the judges. These victims were not prepared to receive news about Jean-Pierre Bemba's acquittal by the ICC. There is a need to revise this case law, which has no legal basis. The ICC Office of the Prosecutor must explain how it will proceed after this decision to restore the confidence of the victims. Two other cases are currently before the ICC concerning CAR. We wonder whether victims and witnesses will have the courage to cooperate with the Court through the Prosecutor's Office.

On June 13, 2018, the ICC Victims Fund announced the acceleration of its Bemba Victim Assistance Program.[1] This Special Fund stated that "physical and psychological rehabilitation, as well as material support" will be provided within a reasonable time. An amount of €1 million was mobilized for the victims. Victims must be informed as the procedure evolves so as not to cause further harm to victims who have waited more than ten years with the hope of getting redress. Decisions and changes in the form and amount of assistance should be communicated to victims in a timely and transparent manner. Lots of messages must be shared in advance with victims to avoid causing further harm to victims who have waited over ten years to discover that justice remains elusive.

Following the Bemba decision handed down by the ICC Appeals Chamber, most of the civil society organizations that support victims have become discouraged.

3 Recommendations and Conclusion

- We suggest that members of civil society be deeply involved in every step of informing the victims and the public about the evolution of the ICC's procedure. These organizations, in turn, can inform and educate the public and victims in order to restore their confidence.
- Civil society constitutes a bridge between the Court and the victims. This is especially true in the accompaniment and documentation for

1 Press Release, International Criminal Court, Following Mr Bemba's Acquittal, Trust Fund for Victims at the ICC Decides to Accelerate Launch of Assistance Programme in Central African Republic (June 13, 2018), https://www.icc-cpi.int/news/following-mr-bembas-acquittal-trust-fund-victims-icc-decides-accelerate-launch-assistance (last visited June 21, 2023).

the Victim's Fund. This must be proactive and work with the lawyers in CAR.

- Particular emphasis should be placed on the participation of victims, especially by increasing their knowledge of the competence of the ICC and the procedure to be followed through panels and forums.
- Will the victims fund be able to take into account all the victims?

CHAPTER 5

"Judicial-Speculation-Made-Law": More Thoughts about the Acquittal of Jean-Pierre Bemba Gombo

Leila Nadya Sadat

On June 8, 2018, the Appeals Chamber of the International Criminal Court (ICC) reversed the conviction of Jean-Pierre Bemba Gombo and acquitted him on all counts of crimes and humanity and war crimes.[1] The four separate opinions, raising questions about Pre-Trial and Trial Chamber procedures, the standard of Appellate Chamber review, and the scope of command responsibility, revealed sharp disagreements between the judges of the Court and generated considerable confusion over the state of ICC law and procedure. I addressed some of the questions raised by the judgment in a post on *EJILTalk!*[2] just following the release of three of the opinions: The Majority, the Separate Opinion of Judges Van den Wyngaert and Morrison, and the Dissenting Opinion of Judges Monageng and Hofmański. Around the same time, and for several months following, many scholars also commented upon the judgment, either defending it,[3] or critiquing it on other grounds.[4]

1 Prosecutor v. Jean-Pierre Bemba Gombo, Case No. ICC-01/05-01/08 A, Judgment on the Appeal of Mr Jean-Pierre Bemba Gombo against Trial Chamber III's "Judgment pursuant to Article 74 of the Statute" (AC, June 8, 2018) [hereinafter Bemba Appeals Chamber Judgment].

2 Leila Nadya Sadat, *Fiddling While Rome Burns? The Appeals Chamber's Curious Decision in Prosecutor v. Jean-Pierre Bemba Gombo*, EJIL TALK (June 12, 2018), https://www.ejiltalk.org/fiddling-while-rome-burns-the-appeals-chambers-curious-decision-in-prosecutor-v-jean-pierre-bemba-gombo/ (last visited June 21, 2023).

3 For a positive view of the judgment see, e.g., Alexander Heinze, *Some Reflections on the Bemba Appeals Chambers Judgment*, OPINIO JURIS (June 18, 2018), http://opiniojuris.org/2018/06/18/some-reflections-on-the-bemba-appeals-chamber-judgment/ (last visited June 21, 2023); Opinion, *The Bemba Appeals Judgment Warrants Better Investigations and Fair Trials – Not Efforts to Discredit the Decision*, AMNESTY INT'L (June 19, 2018), https://hrij.amnesty.nl/bemba-verdict-warrants-better-investigations-and-fair-trials/ (last visited June 21, 2023).

4 For other critical perspectives see, e.g., Diane Marie Amann, *In Bemba and Beyond, Crimes Adjudged to Commit Themselves*, EJIL TALK (June 13, 2018), https://www.ejiltalk.org/in-bemba-and-beyond-crimes-adjudged-to-commit-themselves/ (last visited June 21, 2023); Joseph Powderly & Niamh Hayes, *The Bemba Appeal: A Fragmented Appeals Chamber Destablises the Law and Practice of the ICC*, PHD STUD. HUM. RTS. (June 26, 2018), http://

 | DOI:10.1163/9789004686755_007

Although the President of the Court[5] and distinguished commentators[6] have suggested that scholars have improperly criticized the ICC for the recent spate of acquittals, which now include the *Gbagbo* case,[7] neither my own nor other academic commentaries can fairly be read as criticisms of the *acquittals* themselves, or of the *judges* issuing them. Rather, they are critical analyses of the *jurisprudence they represent.*

This essay focuses upon two questions raised by the Editor-in-Chief of this Forum regarding the judgment: *first,* what role "remoteness" of the commander should play in assessing liability under Article 28; and *second,* the nature of the precedent formed by a fragmented Appeals Chamber.

The treatment of the commander's "remoteness" by the Appeals Chamber was one of the more curious aspects of the *Bemba* judgment. To begin with, although the issue of remoteness is raised as a legal element informing the Court's appropriate analysis by the Majority Judgment and the Separate Opinion of judges Van den Wyngaert and Morrison, it seems clearly to have been rejected as a relevant factor by the President of the Court in his Separate Opinion, and by the two Dissenting Judges. The Majority found that Trial Chamber had failed to:

---

humanrightsdoctorate.blogspot.com/2018/06/the-bemba-appeal-fragmented-appeals.html (last visited June 21, 2023); Jennifer Trahan, *Bemba Acquittal Rests on Erroneous Application of Appellate Review Standard,* OPINIO JURIS (June 25, 2018), http://opiniojuris.org/2018/06/25/bemba-acquittal-rests-on-erroneous-application-of-appellate-review-standard/ (last visited June 21, 2023); Susana SáCouto, *The Impact of the Appeals Chamber Decision in Bemba: Impunity for Sexual and Gender-Based Crimes?,* INT'L JUST. MONITOR (June 22, 2018), https://www.ijmonitor.org/2018/06/the-impact-of-the-appeals-chamber-decision-in-bemba-impunity-for-sexual-and-gender-based-crimes/ (last visited June 21, 2023); Alex Whiting, Appeals Judges Turn the ICC on Its Head With Bemba Decision, JUST SEC. (June 14, 2018), https://www.justsecurity.org/57760/appeals-judges-turn-icc-head-bemba-decision/ (last visited June 21, 2023).

5 Chile Eboe-Osuji, President, Int'l Crim. Ct., Keynote Address at American Society of International Law Annual Meeting: A Tribute to Robert H. Jackson – Recalling America's Contributions to International Criminal Justice (Mar. 29, 2019), https://www.icc-cpi.int/news/icc-presidents-keynote-speech-tribute-robert-h-jackson-recalling-americas-contributions (last visited June 21, 2023).

6 Richard J. Goldstone, *Acquittals by the International Criminal Court,* EJIL TALK (Jan. 18, 2019), https://www.ejiltalk.org/acquittals-by-the-international-criminal-court/ (last visited June 21, 2023).

7 *See* Prosecutor v. Laurent Gbagbo and Charles Blé Goudé, Case No. ICC-02/11-01/15, Rendering of a Decision (TC I, Jan. 15, 2019) [hereinafter Gbagbo Trial Chamber Judgment] (citing to the video as no written decision has been released as of this writing. These are the decisions on the motions for provisional release and no case to answer). *See also Gbagbo and Blé Goudé Case,* INT'L CRIM. CT., https://www.icc-cpi.int/cdi/gbagbo-goude (last visited June 21, 2023).

> fully appreciate the limitations that Mr. Bemba would have faced in investigating and prosecuting crimes as a remote commander sending troops to a foreign country.[8]

Although joining the Majority, the President apparently disagreed, holding that the "geographic remoteness of a commander" would not necessarily insulate him from criminal responsibility.[9] The Dissent argued that:

> the Majority [seemed to have lost] sight of the focus of Article 28 of the *Statute*, namely holding a commander responsible for his failures and not for his actions.[10]

The dissenters found the Majority's reliance on the fact that the MLC troops were operating in a foreign country to evaluate the actions he took unpersuasive. They criticized the Majority for not conducting its own analysis and for accepting, uncritically, Bemba's own arguments without examining the *bona fides* thereof. The Dissent found the Trial Chamber's analysis to be reasonable, and would have sustained Bemba's conviction on that basis.[11]

Because of the split in the views of the five judges, this issue was not clearly decided. Nonetheless, since it was raised by the Court and two judges clearly thought it important, if not decisive, it is worth examining the issue briefly. We can only guess where the Majority derived the "remote commander" standard from since the Majority's statement on this question is unfootnoted. One possibility is the *Perišić* judgment from the ICTY Appeals Chamber, which, equally controversially,[12] found that "explicit consideration" that the accused had specifically directed the crimes was required for convictions in which the perpetrator was accused of "aiding and abetting" the commission of crimes committed by others, in cases of "remote" perpetrators. The *Perišić* Majority found, Judge Liu dissenting, that prior ICTY appeals judgments had not discussed "specific direction" because those cases:

---

8 Bemba Appeals Chamber Judgment, *supra* note 1, ¶ 191.

9 Prosecutor v. Jean-Pierre Bemba Gombo, Case No. ICC-01/05-01/08-3636-Anx3, Concurring Separate Opinion of Judge Eboe-Osuji (AC, June 14, 2018).

10 Prosecutor v. Jean-Pierre Bemba Gombo, Case No. ICC-01/05-01/08-3636-Anx1-Red, Dissenting Opinion of Judge Sanji Mmasenono Monageng and Judge Piotr Hofmański, ¶ 45 (AC, June 8, 2018) [hereinafter Bemba Appeals Chamber Dissent].

11 *Id.* ¶¶ 54–69.

12 Prosecutor v. Momčilo Perišić, Case No. IT-04-81-A, Judgement (Int'l Crim. Trib. for the Former Yugoslavia AC, Feb. 28, 2013).

> involved relevant acts geographically or otherwise proximate to, and thus not remote from, the crimes of principal perpetrators. Where such proximity is present, specific direction may be demonstrated implicitly through discussion of other elements of aiding and abetting liability, such as substantial contribution [...] Where an accused aider and abettor is remote from relevant crimes, evidence proving other elements of aiding and abetting may not be sufficient to prove specific direction. In such circumstances, the Appeals Chamber, Judge Liu dissenting, holds that explicit consideration of specific direction is required.[13]

Like *Bemba*, *Perišić* was heavily criticized. Although the acquittal was surprising, most of the commentary, including by this author, critiqued the judgment due to concerns that the Chamber had strayed from existing precedent, and did so in a manner that seemed problematic.[14] Neither the *Bemba* nor the *Perišić* majorities cited authority suggesting that "remoteness" is relevant to the legal standards applicable to superiors, commanders, or, in the case of Perišić, aiders and abettors,[15] although obviously remoteness could be a factor (but not a legal criterion) in assessing the reasonableness of a commander's actions in a particular situation. (The unfairness of the *Yamashita* case comes to mind).[16]

In Bemba's case, in particular, his defense was largely predicated upon the notion that he actually knew that crimes were being committed and that he took reasonable measures to investigate and stop those crimes. He received reports and was in regular contact with his troops,[17] convened two commissions to address some of the crimes reported (the effectiveness of which were found to be lacking by a majority of the judges examining them, but not by the

13 *Id.* at 39.

14 *See, e.g.*, James Stewart, *"Specific Direction" is Unprecedented: Results from Two Empirical Studies*, EJIL TALK (Sep. 4, 2013), https://www.ejiltalk.org/specific-direction-is-unprecedented-results-from-two-empirical-studies/ (last visited June 21, 2023); Antonio Coco & Tom Gal, 'Losing Direction: The ICTY Appeals Chamber's Controversial Approach to Aiding and Abetting in Perišić' (May 2014) 12 *J. Int'l Crim. Just.* 345.

15 The *Perišić* Chamber referred to temporal factors as providing relevant precedent, and extrapolated, without discussion, from those to geographic factors.

16 In re. Yamashita, 317 U.S. 1 (Feb. 4, 1946).

17 Prosecutor v. Jean-Pierre Bemba Gombo, ICC-01/05-01/08, Decision Pursuant to Article 61(7)(a) and (b) of the Rome Statute on the Charges of the Prosecutor Against Jean-Pierre Bemba Gombo, ¶ 459 (PTC III, June 15, 2009).

Appeals Chamber Majority), and claimed he had sent a letter to the CAR authorities requesting an investigation.[18] Thus, Mr. Bemba, as would be the case of most modern commanders, clearly had access to information regarding the activities of his troops, making the notion of remoteness seemingly irrelevant to the question whether he had committed a dereliction of duty in failing to prevent further abuses or punishing those that had already occurred.

Turning then to the impact of this fractured – and unfootnoted – finding on the future meaning of Article 28, it would appear to be very little as the "remoteness" standard garnered only two votes.[19] And perhaps, just as *Perišić* was later "reversed" by a differently constituted ICTY Appeals Chamber in *Sainović*,[20] *Bemba's* specific contribution to our understanding of Article 28 may ultimately be *de minimis*. Yet it is not clear that the ICC has the capacity yet to "self-correct" in cases such as this. For this reason, even though the *Bemba* judgment may not be decisive to future cases on the meaning of Article 28, the fact that two judges "discovered" this suddenly dispositive factor on appeal may have a chilling effect on future cases. It incentivizes defense lawyers to raise every conceivable argument, hoping to convince the judges to accept them even if they represent novel or unprecedented theories; it could render trials longer as the law of the ICC becomes increasingly unsettled; it may upset victim communities (as was clearly the case in *Bemba*); and the presence of thinly-footnoted judicial opinions may raise legitimacy questions about the Court's jurisprudence. Judgements that read more like personal opinions, as opposed to carefully constructed arguments resting upon legal precedent, raise the concern that the judges are engaging in what the late U.S. Supreme Court Justice Antonin Scalia called "judicial-speculation-made-law" – involving assumptions about the meaning of the Rome Statute, as opposed to a careful exegesis of the *travaux préparatoires* of the Rome Statute, a systemic examination of existing legal precedent, and the sources of law set out in Article 21 of the *Statute*.

This is deeply worrying, and has been a concern of many close readers of the ICC's judgments for some time. It seems to have been the approach taken

18 Bemba Appeals Chamber Dissent, *supra* note 10, ¶ 68 (The Dissent suggests that the evidence of the letter is questionable, agreeing with the Trial Chamber on that question. Whether or not Bemba actually sent it is not a question this essay addresses; rather, I note only that it seems to indicate that he requested an investigation because he knew crimes were being committed).

19 Miles Jackson, *Geographical Remoteness in Bemba*, EJIL TALK (July 30, 2018), https://www.ejiltalk.org/geographical-remoteness-in-bemba/ (last visited June 22, 2023).

20 Leila Nadya Sadat, 'Can the ICTY Šainović and Perišić Cases Be Reconciled?' (2014), 108 *Am. J. Int'l L.* 475.

by the judges in deciding to import the control of the crime theory into Article 25(3) of the *Statute*, which was both unprecedented and problematic, as I have written elsewhere.[21] It is also evidenced by the controversy regarding the acquittal of Laurent Gbagbo, which resulted once again in a fractured decision (of a Trial Chamber) and, because the standard of review for a "no case to answer" decision is not clear – and weeks after the acquittal, no judgment had been issued – in little guidance to other Chambers or the Prosecutor regarding the appropriate standard to be applied.[22] It also seems apparent in even a superficial reading of Pre-Trial Chamber II's recent decision not to allow the Prosecutor to open an investigation into the Situation in Afghanistan, relying for the first time on a novel – and once again unfootnoted – analysis of the "interests of justice" in Article 53(1) of the Rome Statute.[23] One commentator has described the Afghan decision as a "judicial meltdown"[24] and four distinguished supporters and leaders of the Court have concluded that at this point the ICC "needs fixing," due in part to the poor quality of some of the Court's judgments.[25]

Legal realists may not find any of this surprising. They may assume that politics is at play, or perhaps that "what the judge had for breakfast" explains more about the outcome of a particular case than an analysis of the law.[26] Yet while a well-established court can probably weather criticism of the kind now being directed at the ICC, a young court like the ICC cannot. In a world in which it is struggling to gain a foothold, establish its legitimacy, and win the trust of states and civil society, the missteps of the past year – including the

21 Leila Nadya Sadat & Jarrod M. Jolly, 'Seven Canons of ICC Treaty Interpretation: Making Sense of Article 25's Rorschach Blot' (2014), 27 *Leiden J. Int'l L.* 755.

22 Gbagbo Trial Chamber Judgment, *supra* note 7.

23 Situation in the Islamic Republic of Afghanistan, ICC-02/17, Decision Pursuant to Article 15 of the Rome Statute on the Authorisation of an Investigation into the Situation in the Islamic Republic of Afghanistan, pp. 28–31 (PTC III, Apr. 12, 2019). (The discussion on this point is on pages 28–31. The only source cited in those four pages is the Prosecutor's Policy Paper on the Interests of Justice).

24 Sergey Vasiliev, *Not Just Another 'Crisis': Could the Blocking of the Afghanistan Investigation Spell the End of the ICC? (Part I)*, EJIL TALK (Apr. 19, 2019), https://www.ejiltalk.org/not-just-another-crisis-could-the-blocking-of-the-afghanistan-investigation-spell-the-end-of-the-icc-part-i/ (last visited June 22, 2023).

25 Prince Zeid Ra'ad, et al., *The International Criminal Court Needs Fixing*, ATL. COUNS. (Apr. 24, 2019), https://www.atlanticcouncil.org/blogs/new-atlanticist/the-international-criminal-court-needs-fixing/ (last visited June 22, 2023).

26 *See* Frederick Schauer, *Thinking Like a Lawyer* (Cambridge: Harvard University Press, 2009), p. 129, n. 15 (This quote is often attributed to Jerome Frank, although scholars dispute the likelihood that he actually made this claim).

Bemba decision – suggest a real need for the Court's judiciary to reconsider their approach. They may wish, for example, to stop issuing decisions *seriatim* and with so many crippling dissents, taking instead as their model Chief Justice Marshall of the United States Supreme Court, who built that once frail institution into the powerhouse it is today by insisting upon unity and collegiality on the part of his brethren,[27] and that the Court pay attention to the norm of *stare decisis*.[28] As with the *United States Constitution*, or the *Treaty of Rome* that established the European Economic Community in 1957, the *ICC Statute* is complex, and its interpretation difficult, presenting the ICC's judges with many challenges. However, like the judges of the European Court of Justice and the United States Supreme Court, the judges of the International Criminal Court must find a way to successfully navigate these complexities so as to build trust and confidence in the Institution. Otherwise, the Court may well remain on shaky ground for the foreseeable future. Fortunately, the unanimous, and thoughtfully reasoned judgment in the Appeals Chamber's most recent decision in the controversial Al-Bashir immunities case, suggests that they are beginning to take these ideas on board,[29] although even that case involved a four judge "concurrence" and a two judge "partial dissent" (which has yet to be issued).

27 Charles F. Hobson, 'Defining the Office: John Marshall as Chief Justice' (2006), 154 *U. Pa. L. Rev.* 1421.

28 Jack Knight and Lee Epstein, 'The Norm of Stare Decisis' (1996), 40 *Am. J. Pol Sci* 1018.

29 Prosecutor v. Omar Hassan Ahmad Al-Bashir, Doc. No. ICC-02/05-01/09 OA2, Judgment in the Jordan Referral re Al-Bashir Appeal (AC, May 6, 2019).

PART 2

Completion Strategies for Situations under Investigation

Introduction to Part 2

The following question was featured on www.ICCForum.com from February 2020 to May 2020:

What might be some elements of an ICC completion strategy for situations under investigation?

Investigations are costly and the ICC has limited resources. A long ongoing investigation may also impose costs, pecuniary and psychological, on victims and survivors, as well as nationals that are thought to be subjects of interest, and an endless investigation would not be without problems. A completion strategy for investigation of each particular situation could be useful. More broadly, a comprehensive completion strategy could be devised to maximize the benefits and minimize the costs of ICC action. For reasons similar to these, the International Criminal Tribunal for the former Yugoslavia and the International Criminal Tribunal for Rwanda each adopted completion strategies.

Article 53 of the Rome Statute sets forth conditions for the Prosecutor to initiate an investigation and to inform the Pre-Trial Chamber and the referring state (or the Security Council) of a conclusion that there is no sufficient basis for investigation. However, the Rome Statute does not specify any procedures related to or considerations affecting whether, when, or how to complete an investigation.

What might be some elements of an ICC completion strategy for situations under investigation?

First, how final is "completion"? "Completion" might entail terminating evidence collection, issuance of arrest warrants, and prosecution. Could "completion" include a suspension of those activities, and, if so, under what circumstances? If an investigation were suspended, what factors should trigger revival of an investigation?

Second, what factors should be considered in deciding when completion should take place? Should it matter whether the investigation was based on a Security Council or state referral, or initiated under the Prosecutor's *proprio motu* authority? Should a lack of access to evidence trigger completion? The ICC has authority to try only those "most responsible," but the Rome Statute does not specify how many persons that might include; how should the Prosecutor determine that enough of those "most responsible" have been prosecuted so as to warrant completion? To what extent and on what legal basis should the beginning of domestic criminal proceedings, the establishment of a

 DOI:10.1163/9789004686755_008

truth commission, or other aspects of the situation in the relevant state warrant completion? Should other factors be considered?

Third, what actions should be taken by each of the organs of the Court at completion of an investigation? Should the Prosecutor issue a final report on the status and conclusions of the investigation? Should the Prosecutor refer cases she decides not to prosecute to national courts? If so, what criteria should be used in determining which cases to refer to national courts, and which national courts should be referred to? Should the Registry and other actors under the Statute cease or continue outreach activities, victim reparation activities, or any other activities?

CHAPTER 6

It's a Journey, Not a Destination: Tailored Completion Strategies for ICC Situations under Investigation

Elizabeth Evenson and Alison A. Smith

Done right, a situation-specific ICC completion strategy reverse-engineers the Court's mandate to ensure a clear focus on maximizing the Court's impact. That is, it seeks to define, on a situation-specific basis, what the Court will achieve, how it will know when this is achieved, and what it will need to leave behind "to ensure its ongoing obligations are met and its legacy consolidated."[1] Together this can provide a compelling vision, animating court action and partners. But addressing definitional aspects first are essential to creating this common framework. In our view, broadly speaking, completion will:

> [P]rimarily relate to whether the Court has delivered impartial, independent, and meaningful justice. However, a definition of completion should also consider fulfilment of the Court's mandate as turning as well on whether the domestic jurisdiction is ready to take over the Court's ongoing responsibilities in the situation and resume its primary responsibilities to investigate and prosecute International Criminal Court crimes.[2]

This is admittedly an expansive definition of completion, but it will best orient the Court's work toward a lasting legacy in affected communities. Defining completion on a situation-specific basis requires close consultation and communication between the Court and these communities.

The Office of the Prosecutor's commitment in its 2019–2021 Strategic Plan to developing a policy on the completion of situations under investigation – echoed in the court-wide strategy of the International Criminal Court (ICC) for the same period – has brought renewed and overdue attention back to a

1 Elizabeth Evenson and Alison A. Smith, 'Completion, Legacy, and Complementarity at the ICC', in Carsten Stahn (ed.), *The Law and Practice of the International Criminal Court* (Oxford: Oxford University Press, 2015), pp. 1259, 1261.

2 *Id.* at 1267.

 | DOI:10.1163/9789004686755_009

key topic.[3] As we have argued previously, the fact that the ICC is a permanent institution cannot shield it from the questions confronted by the *ad hoc* tribunals and the Special Court for Sierra Leone when it came to wrapping up their work. While it may be a permanent institution, it will complete its work on a situation-by-situation basis. Nor should these questions be avoided. In fact, as a permanent institution, the ICC is at an advantage when it comes to setting the terms of its own completion strategies. Completion strategies at the *ad hoc* tribunals were developed under considerable pressure to shut down too early.[4]

Although the Office of the Prosecutor poses a number of specific and necessary questions to this Forum that will need to be answered in the implementation of completion strategies, we have chosen to highlight here why a robust definition of completion that is sensitive to the Court's legacy is essential. Greater clarity as to definition and purpose is, in our view, key to determining the when, how, and what of completing the Court's work in a given situation. The ICC remains far behind in addressing these definitional issues. And the context in which current discussions are taking place only underscores the need for the Court to articulate a clear and purposeful understanding of completion.

Earlier efforts arose out of discussions on complementarity within the ICC Assembly of States Parties (ASP). In 2012, states parties called for greater attention to "exit strategies," in the context of intercessional work carried out by the Assembly's focal points on complementarity.[5] In reporting to the ASP the following year, the Court set out an initial framework on completion strategies, tracking the three areas previously outlined by Kevin Jon Heller as components of such strategies: "completion issues," "residual functions," and "leg-

3 Office of the Prosecutor, International Criminal Court, Strategic Plan 2019–2021, ¶¶ 19, 23 (July 17, 2019), https://www.icc-cpi.int/sites/default/files/itemsDocuments/20190726-strategic-plan-eng.pdf (last visited June 22, 2023); Office of the Prosecutor, International Criminal Court, Strategic Plan 2019–2021, pp. 11–12 (July 17, 2019), [hereinafter OTP Strategic Plan] https://www.icc-cpi.int/sites/default/files/itemsDocuments/20190717-icc-strategic-plan-eng.pdf (last visited June 22, 2023).

4 *See* Evenson and Smith, *supra* note 1, at 1260–65 (citing Kevin Jon Heller, 'Completion Strategies and the Office of the Prosecutor', in Luc Reydams, Jan Wouters and Cedric Ryngaert (eds.), *International Prosecutors* (Oxford: Oxford University Press, 2012), p. 887) (Heller's comprehensive study was drawn upon to describe how the development of completion strategies for the ad hoc tribunals and the SCSL took place as a "by-product of the pressure on these tribunals – largely budgetary – to accelerate their conclusion.").

5 *See* International Criminal Court, *ICC-ASP/11/Res.6 Complementarity*, Doc. no. ICC-ASP /11/20, ¶ 7 (Nov. 21, 2012), https://asp.icc-cpi.int/sites/asp/files/asp_docs/Resolutions/ASP11/ICC-ASP–11-Res6-ENG.pdf (last visited June 22, 2023).

acy issues."[6] These discussions highlighted a clear connection between international assistance to strengthen domestic jurisdictions – what has been termed "positive" complementarity – and the Court's completion of its work in a given situation.[7] This was because the prospect of enhanced national capacity could permit the Court to hand over some responsibilities to domestic authorities, allowing it to end certain activities. The clearest example developed in the Court's reporting at the time was witness protection.[8] Indeed, there are several lessons the ICC could learn from the experience of the Residual Special Court for Sierra Leone (RSCSL). While, as likely would be the case with the ICC, the RSCSL remains responsible for oversight of witness protection, it works together with a special unit within the Sierra Leonean police, which was created with the support of the Special Court for Sierra Leone (SCSL).[9]

States parties have included dialogue on completion strategies within the mandate of ASP-appointed focal points on complementarity since 2012. But as the topic of "positive" complementarity became more contentious in the Assembly, state party discussions on completion faded away for several years. The ASP's Committee on Budget and Finance continued to raise the need for attention to completion,[10] and from informal discussions with Court officials, it was clear to us that there remained a strong interest and appetite to explore completion in a more meaningful manner. In 2019, the topic was once again the focus of ASP discussions on complementarity. But

6 Assembly of States Parties, International Criminal Court, *Report of the Court on Complementarity: Completion of ICC Activities in a Situation Country*, Doc. No. ICC-ASP /12/13, ¶ 17 (Oct. 15, 2013), https://asp.icc-cpi.int/sites/asp/files/asp_docs/ASP12/-ICC-ASP-12-32-ENG.pdf; Kevin Jon Heller, Leuven Centre for Global Governance Studies, Completion Strategies (Aug. 5, 2009) (The ASP adapted definitions from Heller's article).

7 ("Positive" complementarity is generally understood to mean initiatives by a range of actors to encourage national prosecutions of international crimes, ranging from legislative assistance to capacity building to political dialogue to counter obstruction. The Court is only one actor in this landscape, which also includes assistance between states, international organizations, and civil society).

8 Assembly of States Parties, *supra* note 6, ¶ 35.

9 Evenson and Smith, *supra* note 1, at 1271 (citing Open Society Justice Initiative, Legacy: Completing the Work of the Special Court for Sierra Leone, pp. 12–13 (2011), https://www.justiceinitiative.org/uploads/12d7b8e9-42db-4b47-a2c8-e9d69dfe8829/legacy-scsl-20111101.pdf (last visited June 22, 2023)); *see also* The Special Court for Sierra Leone and The Residual Special Court for Sierra Leone, https://rscsl.org/ (last visited June 22, 2023).

10 See, e.g., Assembly of States Parties, International Criminal Court, *Report of the Committee on Budget and Finance on the Work of Its Thirty-First Session*, ¶ 59, Doc. no. ICC-ASP /17/15 (Oct. 29, 2018), https://asp.icc-cpi.int/sites/asp/files/asp_docs/ASP17/ICC-ASP-17-15-ENG-CBF-31-Report.pdf.

these discussions, for the first time as far as we are aware, also included completion or closure mechanisms for preliminary examinations, and not only situations under investigation.[11] Discussions on completion or closure of preliminary examination raise, in our view, a different set of issues, and we welcome the emphasis in this Forum on completion strategies for situations under investigation, given that the Court has twelve situations under investigation, many very advanced. Some aspects of the framing for this Forum offer yet another possibility – that completion could also be contemplated for a specific "investigation" within a situation, rather than on a situation-basis.

This history suggests that for real progress to be made in the design and implementation of completion strategies, there is a need for Court officials, its states parties, and other stakeholders to get on the same page as to why talking about situation-specific completion strategies are so important. It is not only about an instruction manual for completing the Court's activities, as the Prosecutor's question for this Forum rightly acknowledges. Contemplating completion is also important for the reasons set out in her question: The Court does have limited resources that need to be purposefully directed and maximized – although, as we discuss below, it would be a mistake to think of completion strategies as a cost-savings tool. And providing closure to victims and survivors as to at least one part of what will be a broader accountability process,[12] and certainty for persons of interest to an investigation, are key goals.

But completion strategies can do more, and the Prosecutor's question seems to nod at this when it suggests they can "maximize the benefits [...] of ICC action." Done right, a situation-specific completion strategy reverse-engineers the Court's mandate. That is, it seeks to define, on a situation-specific basis, what the Court seeks to achieve:

> [W]hether [it] has achieved its mandate and under what conditions the Court will be able to say it has done so. This will primarily relate to whether the Court has delivered impartial, independent, and meaning-

11 *See, e.g.*, Secretariat of the Assembly of States Parties, International Criminal Court, Complementarity: Seminar on Completion Strategies Across the ICC's Activities (Apr. 4, 2019), https://asp.icc-cpi.int/sites/asp/files/complementarity/Documents/4April%20Seminar%20Completion%20Strategies%20Summary%2016May2019%201803.pdf (last visited June 23, 2023).

12 Evenson and Smith, *supra* note 1, at 1261.

> ful justice. However, a definition of completion should also consider fulfilment of the Court's mandate as turning also on whether the domestic jurisdiction is ready to take over the Court's ongoing responsibilities in the situation and resume their primary responsibilities to investigate and prosecute ICC crimes.[13]

Applying this broad concept to a specific situation will take deep consultation with affected communities and national authorities, a lesson learned from the *ad hoc* tribunals and SCSL.[14]

Contemplating completion in this way forces contemplating legacy. By legacy we mean a concern for maximizing the Court's impact in affected communities, its most important stakeholders, "in terms of ending impunity, ensuring accountability and redress, strengthening the rule of law, and contributing to sustainable peace."[15] This concern should animate the Court's work and it requires intentionality. In fact, our argument is that "completion" requires Rome Statute actors to pursue a range of actions from the very outset of an investigation – even in its planning and preparation – and carry right through the Court's involvement in a situation. Again, the experience of other tribunals is instructive. Concern for the SCSL's legacy received dedicated attention in the tribunal's very first annual report, and motivated the Court's approach to the developing the skills of Sierra Leonean staff members and the work of its Outreach Section.[16] The ICTY, assisted by the OSCE, built in assessments to its outreach programming aimed at legacy.[17]

To be sure, as we noted in 2015, this expansive sense of completion is ambitious, particularly when it comes to conditioning completion of the Court's mandate on the reassertion of national authorities of their primary

13 *Id.* at 1267.

14 *Id.* at 1267–68 (citing Heller, *supra* note 4, at 911) (terming the failure to consult with victims regarding the ICTR's closure as "a critical oversight, even if the victim's desires would not have affected the completion strategy: although victim satisfaction may not be a sufficient condition of a tribunal's legitimacy, it is certainly one of its necessary conditions. A tribunal that is not seen as legitimate by the victims of a conflict is unlikely to be seen as legitimate by anyone else.").

15 Evenson and Smith, *supra* note 1, at 1260–61.

16 *Id.* at 1270 (citing Exploring the Legacy of the Special Court for Sierra Leone, https://www.ictj.org/sites/default/files/subsites/scsl-legacy/ (last visited June 22, 2023)) (an overview of SCSL's legacy activities).

17 Evenson and Smith, *supra* note 1, at 1270 (citing Fausto Pocar, 'Completion or Continuation Strategy? Appraising Problems and Possible Developments in Building the Legacy of the ICTY' (2008), 6 *J. Int'l Crim. Just.* 655–665 at 663).

responsibility for the investigation and prosecution of crimes. National justice efforts face many barriers. The Court may fall short in many situations, and may have to conclude that completion will ultimately be premised on moving the goalposts. But setting the goal is essential if we want to take legacy seriously and seek to capitalize on the potentially tremendously influential role of the Court in the situations in which it acts and will be present for a sustained period of time.[18] The Court should be able to rely on its Assembly of States Parties to broker assistance between states parties and other international actors to support these efforts.[19]

The necessity of completion strategies approached from this perspective has become even more acute, as well as provided fresh opportunities.

First, new needs. In 2015, we argued for completion strategies in order to help secure the financial resources the Court needs to robustly carry out its mandate. Making a compelling case for the necessary resources, we thought, would be assisted by a specific definition of the ICC's mission in a given country and a strategy for completing that mission.[20] Since then, the number of situations pending before the ICC has only grown, while state party negotiations on the budget remain distorted by the demand of some governments for zero growth in the Court's resources. This mismatch is forcing a continued over-prioritization of the work of the Office of the Prosecutor – that is, too few cases in each situation – with significant legitimacy costs. Completion strategies alone will not solve this mismatch. And they should not be approached as directed at financial savings, that is, forcing completion in order for the Court's resources to be reallocated to new situations. But, if communicated to all stakeholders, they could provide a framework around which a shared vision of the Court's mission could be built, deepening dialogue between the Court and states parties as to the resources truly needed for the Court to complete that mission responsibly. They could also help direct the Court's resources toward clearly articulated and agreed goals, increasing the efficiency of the use of those resources.

Second, new opportunities. Changes in Court practice have provided new opportunities. First, the Office of the Prosecutor has relatively recently begun referring to its "prosecutorial program" for a given situation, providing a metric against which to measure progress towards completion (as the Office itself indicates in setting out initial ideas regarding completion strategies in its

18 Evenson and Smith, *supra* note 1, at 1268 (citing Pocar, *supra* note 17, at 655).

19 Evenson and Smith, *supra* note 1, at 1273-75.

20 *Id.* at 1261.

2019–2021 Strategic Plan).[21] Second, strengthened country offices in some ICC situation countries and a Country Analysis Unit within the Court's Registry following reorganization of the organ in 2015 provide new opportunities to root the ICC's work nationally and contribute to legacy-sensitive approaches.[22]

These are challenging times for the Court, amidst setbacks for the Prosecutor's office in key cases and hostile actions by the United States government. And an ongoing "Independent Expert Review" – which may touch on completion strategies, but has a much broader mandate addressed to strengthening the Court's effective delivery of justice[23] – and elections later this year of the next Prosecutor, as well as six new judges, will rightfully dominate discourse around the Court, in what could prove to be a monumental year. It may be tempting to think that serious discussion of completion strategies should be shelved in favor of attention to shorter-term priorities. To the contrary, the opportunity should be seized. In defining what the Court seeks to achieve and how it will get there, situation-specific completion strategies can animate court action and partners around a shared vision, increasing the Rome Statute system's resilience and legitimacy.

---

21 *See* OTP STRATEGIC PLAN, *supra* note 3, ¶ 23 ("The Office will aim to identify a prosecutorial program to implement, which will allow it to assess its progress and the obstacles encountered during the implementation.").

22 *See* The Registry, International Criminal Court, Comprehensive Report on the Reorganisation of the Registry of the International Criminal Court (Aug. 2016), https://www.icc-cpi.int/sites/default/files/itemsDocuments/ICC-Registry-CR.pdf.

23 Assembly of States Parties, International Criminal Court, Terms of Reference for the Independent Expert Review of the International Criminal Court, Annex I to Review of the International Criminal Court and the Rome Statute System, Resolution ICC-ASP /18/Res.7 (Dec. 6, 2019), https://asp.icc-cpi.int/sites/asp/files/asp_docs/ASP18/ICC-ASP-18-Res7-ENG-ICC-Review-resolution-17Dec19-1530.cln.pdf.

CHAPTER 7

Articulating a Completion Strategy for Each Situation and Catalyzing Domestic Criminal Justice

Rebecca J. Hamilton

It is fifteen years since the ICC opened its investigations in Sudan and the Central African Republic, and sixteen years since it began its work in the Democratic Republic of Congo and Uganda. The Court was not designed to be a permanent presence in any of the situations it entered, and yet, in the absence of a completion strategy, this is effectively what it has become.

As the Office of the Prosecutor (OTP) noted in its 2019–2021 Strategic Plan, the Court needs a completion strategy as a matter of urgency.[1] The reasons for this are both principled and pragmatic. Endless engagement by the Court in a situation undermines the principle of complementarity that lies at the heart of the Rome Statute. It creates unnecessary additional burdens on victims and witnesses and, at a point when the Court is under enormous reputational and financial pressure, it is neither an effective nor efficient approach to pursuing the Court's mandate.

Designing a completion strategy is a complex endeavor and the task is made more difficult by the fact that the Rome Statute provides no direct guidance on the issue. Still, by looking to both the *Statute* and to the policy work that the OTP has done in recent years, it is possible to develop a set of benchmarks to guide the enterprise.

I offer here an initial framework for thinking through the creation of a completion strategy. Two features of the framework merit emphasis. First, it recognizes that the Court will often have to consider exiting a situation under circumstances of partial success or even failure. The reasons behind such sub-optimal outcomes should shape the completion strategy. Second, completion should be understood as a process, guided by benchmarks, not an event, driven by dates on a calendar.

1 Office of the Prosecutor, International Criminal Court, Strategic Plan 2019–2021, pp. 18–19 (July 17, 2019), https://www.icc-cpi.int/sites/default/files/itemsDocuments/20190726-strategic-plan-eng.pdf (last visited June 23, 2023).

 | DOI:10.1163/9789004686755_010

While the challenges are significant, it is important to understand the development of a completion strategy as a moment of opportunity. Done well, a completion strategy can catalyze domestic investigations and prosecutions, beginning to fulfill the true promise of the ICC. As it stands, the Court is at risk of being a quasi-permanent presence in a handful of African nations. Now is the moment for the Court to reinvigorate the vision that its founders had for it, as a backstop for domestic criminal systems globally, so that survivors of the world's worst crimes are not left without a justice forum.

1 Why Completion Strategies Are Essential

For the Court to be anywhere on a *de facto* permanent basis undermines the principle of complementarity that lies at the heart of the Rome Statute. Designed as a "court of last resort" the Court only enters into situations where the domestic system is "unable or unwilling" to conduct its own genuine investigations or prosecutions.[2] But by staying in situations for well over a decade, the Court has now fostered a moral hazard problem, undermining any incentive for the domestic systems in those situations to become able and willing to undertake prosecutions themselves.[3]

Beyond concerns about the negative impact that such *de facto* permanency has on the ethos of complementarity, there are also practical reasons why the Court should not remain in a situation without a completion strategy in place. First and foremost, such endless engagements take their toll on victims and witnesses. The concern is related but distinct from the psychological toll incurred by the often slow speed of international criminal justice in general. Here, it is not just the victims and witnesses involved in a particular slow-moving case that are affected, but also the many victims and witnesses to crimes that are not part of any current case but, because the Court is still formally engaged with the situation, either hope or fear they will be in the future. With no clarity on if, or when, the Court's engagement will end, those most affected are placed in a permanent state of limbo.

2 International Criminal Court, Rome Statute of the International Criminal Court, art. 17, U.N. Doc. A/CONF.183/9, (July 17, 1998) [hereinafter Rome Statute].

3 *See* Rebecca J. Hamilton, 'The ICC's Exit Problem' (2014) 47 *N.Y.U. J. Int'l L. and Pol.* 1, pp. 11–14.

In addition, endless engagements further the perception of international criminal justice as inefficient. Indeed, by staying in a situation without developing a completion strategy, the Court may, in fact, be fostering inefficiency. Without any sense of an end point, there is little incentive for the Court's staff to increase the speed of their operations, even when they have the capacity to do so.

Finally, there is the pressing problem of resource constraints. The Court's budget has not grown in proportion to the number of situations it has entered, and is unlikely to do so in the future. In a world of limited resources, staying in one situation means not entering another. This then brings us back to the spirit of the Rome Statute. The vision was never to create a court with a quasi-permanent presence in a handful of African nations, but to be a backstop for domestic criminal systems globally.

2 Sources of Guidance on Exit

Recognizing the need for a completion strategy is a necessary first step. But designing such a strategy is a complex endeavor. It is easy enough to say that the ICC should conclude its work in a given situation once it has succeeded in fulfilling its mandate there. But when one's (sweeping) mandate is to "end impunity," any workable definition of success requires significant refinement. And while the Rome Statute provides guidance on when the Court can enter a situation, it provides no such direction regarding when the Court should leave.

The Statute is not, however, irrelevant when thinking through the parameters of a completion strategy. Hypothetically, if the OTP prosecuted all the crimes that rose to an Article 17(d) level of gravity within a given situation, then the Court should consider its work complete. Likewise, if the only reason to stay in a situation was to pursue additional prosecutions on account of the perpetrators' ethnicity or gender, for instance, then the requirement of impartiality in Article 21(3) may well counsel in favor of exit. But such scenarios are so unlikely to arise that, for most practical purposes, any such statutory basis will almost certainly be under-determinative, and so it becomes helpful to also look to the policy guidance that has grown up around the Statute.

As articulated in the OTP's 2016 document on Case Selection and Prioritization, the Prosecution strives to charge those "most responsible" for "a representative sample of [crimes that reflect] the main types of victimization and of the communities which have been affected by the crimes in that situation."[4] This policy guidance is instructive when thinking about a working definition of success. The Court may never "end impunity," but, in a best-case scenario, it could ensure that those most responsible for the main types of victimization in a given situation were prosecuted. And, consistent with the principle of complementarity, success would be as, or even more, meaningful if those prosecutions were undertaken by domestic systems.

The ICC is hardly the first institution with the need to develop a completion strategy. The comparison that most readily comes to mind is from the *ad hoc* tribunals, and certainly there is a body of literature that has emerged around their completion strategies.[5] But, despite the commonality of being an international criminal justice mechanism, the analogy to these tribunals is somewhat attenuated when it comes to exit because the ICC is a permanent institution.

Unlike the ICC, the *ad hoc* tribunals have not had to factor in the impact of their exit on ongoing or future situations. A more apt analogy, then, may be to UN peacekeeping operations, and within this realm there is extensive literature to mine.[6] Some of the key takeaways from work on completion strategies for peacekeeping are instructive as the ICC develops it approach:

1. The most likely scenario involves leaving under conditions short of total success, and the reasons for partial or complete failure should inform a completion strategy.[7]
2. A completion strategy must be flexible enough to respond to changing circumstances. Thus, exiting a situation is a process driven by benchmarks, not an event driven by dates on a calendar.[8]
3. The support of other actors, and in particular, states, are essential to the exit process.[9]

---

4 Office of the Prosecutor, International Criminal Court, Policy Paper on Case Selection and Prioritization, pp. 1, 15 (Sep. 15, 2016), https://www.icc-cpi.int/sites/default/files/items Documents/20160915_OTP-Policy_Case-Selection_Eng.pdf (last visited June 23, 2023).

5 *See, e.g.*, Fausto Pocar, 'Completion or Continuation Strategy? Appraising Problems and Possible Developments in Building the Legacy of the ICTY' (2008), 6 *J. Int'l Crim. Just.* 655–665.

6 U.N. Secretary-General, No Exit Without Strategy: Security Council Decision-Making and the Closure or Transition of United Nations Peacekeeping Operations, Report of the Secretary-General, U.N. Doc. S/2001/394 (Apr. 20, 2001), [hereinafter No Exit Without Strategy] https://digitallibrary.un.org/record/438855 (last visited June 23, 2023).

7 Richard Caplan, *Exit Strategies and State Building*, (Oxford: Oxford University Press, 2012), pp. 3, 8.

8 *See e.g.*, No Exit Without Strategy, *supra* note 6.

9 *Id.* at ¶ 55.

Drawing these sources together in *The ICC's Exit Problem,* I offered the following framework in Figure 7.1 as a starting point for discussions on how the ICC might develop a completion strategy.[10]

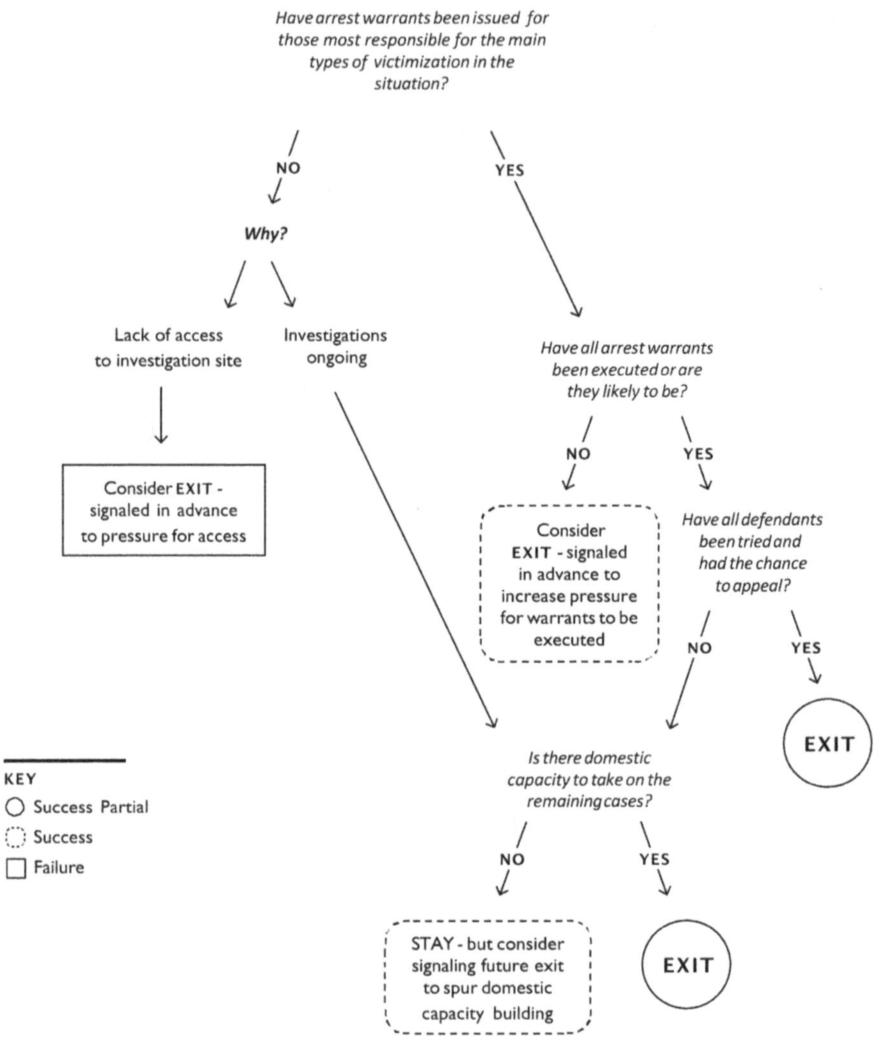

FIGURE 7.1 Exit decision making

10 Hamilton, *supra* note 3, at 49.

3 Completion as Opportunity

The development of a completion strategy, especially under circumstances of partial success or failure, should be seen as a moment of opportunity. First, by publicly articulating the benchmarks guiding its completion strategy, the Court can refocus and rally external actors around the forms of support it needs to fulfill its mandate. Second, a completion strategy can facilitate planning to strengthen domestic systems, where willing, to undertake their own prosecutions.

In terms of having domestic systems take on remaining investigations and prosecutions in a situation, the experience of the International Criminal Tribunal for the former Yugoslavia (ICTY) is useful. As with that tribunal, it is likely that when planning to leave a situation, there will be two basic types of uncompleted cases for the Court to consider. First, there will be those where the Court has charged a defendant and then the domestic system takes the case forward to prosecution once the ICC leaves. Much like the 11 *bis* cases at the ICTY, the Court likely has some responsibility to ensure that the defendant's rights receive the same degree of protection in a subsequent domestic prosecution as they would have if the ICC had completed the case.[11] Second, there will be situations where the ICC has developed an investigative file but not yet filed any charges. Here, the domestic system will take over the investigation. As the OTP's latest strategic document notes, Article 93(10) of the *Statute* provides a mechanism for interested domestic authorities to request access to information including, presumably, an investigative file that it intends to use for a domestic level prosecution.[12] Akin to the ICTY's "category two" cases, the case for the ICC's responsibility toward any future defendant is more attenuated in such a scenario.[13] But, again, if these possibilities are laid out in a completion strategy document, it will facilitate planning by other

11 International Criminal Tribunal for the Former Yugoslavia, Rules of Procedure and Evidence, Rule 11 *bis* (C), U.N. Doc. IT/32/Rev.50, (July 8, 2015), https://www.icty.org/x/file/Legal%20Library/Rules_procedure_evidence/IT032Rev50_en.pdf (last visited June 23, 2023); *See also* Rome Statute, *supra* note 2, at art. 21(3) (Once a defendant is brought to the ICC, he or she can rely on "internationally recognized human rights" standards to protect his or her rights).

12 *See* Strategic Plan, *supra* note 1, at 29–30.

13 Frédéric Mégret, 'Too Much of a Good Thing: Implementation and the Uses of Complementarity', in Carsten Stahn & Mohamed M. El Zeidy (eds.), *The International Criminal Court and Complementarity: From Theory to Practice* (Cambridge: Cambridge University Press, 2011), p. 422.

actors who can provide oversight and help ensure the domestic system has the training and resources needed to conduct a fair trial.

The OTP's 2019–2021 strategic document provided a welcome acknowledgement of the need to start work on completion strategies. But there is no reason for the Court to undertake this daunting task on its own. Both scholars and justice activists, who were actively engaged in helping the Court think through a framework for deciding when to enter a situation, have routinely ignored the parallel question of exit. Hopefully this Forum will kick-start these necessary discussions.

CHAPTER 8

Ongoing Vigilance: The Case for Keeping Investigations Open Indefinitely

Kevin Jon Heller

1 Introduction

Numerous scholars have taken the position that the OTP should eventually close its investigations. This essay offers a (partially) dissenting view, arguing that there are compelling reasons for the OTP to keep its investigations open indefinitely. Sections two and three explain the advantages and disadvantages of not closing investigations. The final section then discusses how the OTP should think about closure if, contrary to the suggestion in this article, it believes that some investigations should be closed instead of kept open indefinitely.

In its Strategic Plan for 2019–2021, the Office of the Prosecutor (OTP) acknowledges "the need to consider, in a strategic manner, the conditions and process by which it can eventually exit situations."[1] All of the scholars who have written on completion strategies at the ICC agree that investigations should eventually be closed.[2]

This article offers a (partially) dissenting view, arguing that there are compelling reasons for the OTP to *never* close an investigation. Section 2 examines the advantages of the OTP hibernating a "completed" or frustrated investigation instead of closing it. Section 3 then acknowledges that, in some circumstances, closure has some advantages of its own. Finally, Section 4 discusses how the OTP should think about closure if, contrary to the suggestion in this

1 Office of the Prosecutor, International Criminal Court, Strategic Plan 2019–2021, ¶ 23 (July 17, 2019), [hereinafter Strategic Plan] https://www.icc-cpi.int/sites/default/files/items Documents/20190726-strategic-plan-eng.pdf (last visited June 23, 2023).

2 *See, e.g.*, Dafna Gozani, 'Beginning to Learn How to End: Lessons on Completion Strategies, Residual Mechanisms, and Legacy Considerations from Ad Hoc International Criminal Tribunals to the International Criminal Court' (2015) 36 *Loy. L.A. Int'l & Compar. L. Rev.* 331, 370; Elizabeth Evenson and Alison A. Smith, 'Completion, Legacy, and Complementarity at the ICC', in Carsten Stahn (ed.), *The Law and Practice of the International Criminal Court* (Oxford: Oxford University Press, 2015), pp. 1259–60.

 | DOI:10.1163/9789004686755_011

comment, it believes that some investigations should be closed instead of kept open indefinitely.

Before proceeding, it is important to clarify terminology. In what follows, "closing" an investigation denotes the legal and factual cessation of all of the OTP's investigative activities in a situation, both in the field and at ICC headquarters. As the OTP notes in its most recent Strategic Plan, this has not happened to date.[3] By contrast, "hibernating" an investigation denotes the cessation of investigative activities in the field and the reallocation of some, but not all, of the resources the OTP previously committed to a situation. This is what the OTP did in Darfur in 2014.[4]

2 Why Close?

According to Evenson and Smith, "[t]he ICC cannot stay in a particular situation in perpetuity."[5] But is that really true? There is no *legal* reason why the OTP has to close an investigation: although the Rome Statute regulates opening investigations, it is completely silent concerning closing them.

Evenson and Smith, of course, don't claim otherwise. They are more concerned with the *practical* implications of never closing investigations, particularly in terms of how such a policy would affect the Court's resources:

> If the ICC's permanence and potential global reach are among its greatest strengths and innovations, they also create a real dilemma regarding how many situations and cases the Court, as a single institution with finite resources, can be expected to handle simultaneously.[6]

There is no question that the OTP lacks the resources to keep full-blown investigations going indefinitely in all situations. But that does not mean the OTP needs to close an investigation completely when it has either completed its initial trial program or has found it too difficult (whether because of government resistance or ongoing violence) to effectively investigate further. It could instead hibernate the investigation, reallocating resources but still

3 Strategic Plan, *supra* note 1, ¶ 23.

4 *Security Council Inaction on Darfur 'Can Only Embolden Perpetrators' – ICC Prosecutor*, UN News (Dec. 12, 2014), https://news.un.org/en/story/2014/12/486172 (last visited June 23, 2023).

5 Evenson & Smith, *supra* note 2, at 1260.

6 *Id.* at 1261.

maintaining a small field presence or situation team at ICC headquarters. Although not completely costless, there is no indication that the OTP cannot sustain a skeletal presence in each situation under investigation. Indeed, the OTP adopted such a cost-saving "maintenance strategy" in Uganda for the four years prior to Ongwen's arrest – a time when it was unclear whether it would ever have anyone to prosecute – by operating with "minimum staff in charge of victims and witness management and protection, outreach, implementation of the Trust Fund for Victims projects and victims participation and reparation matters."[7]

Even this minimal expenditure of resources would be unjustifiable, of course, if there were no practical advantages to keeping investigations open indefinitely. But that is not the case, because never closing an investigation facilitates the OTP's work in numerous ways.

To begin with, it maximizes the OTP's prosecutorial flexibility. As Ongwen's arrest eleven years after the opening of the Uganda investigation indicates, the OTP can never rule out the possibility that a suspect deserving of prosecution will fall into its hands unexpectedly. After all, even the most successful trial program will involve a small fraction of the perpetrators in a particular situation.[8] Closing an investigation would likely not prohibit the OTP from reopening it to prosecute a new suspect, but there is no question that reopening would be much easier under a maintenance strategy.[9] Fabricio Guariglia, Director of the ICC Prosecutions Division, made this point well by contrasting the DRC, where the OTP once closed its investigation in all but name, with Uganda, where it maintained a reduced presence instead:

7 Assembly of States Parties, International Criminal Court, *Report of the Court on Complementarity: Completion of ICC Activities in a Situation Country*, ¶ 42, Doc. No. ICC-ASP/12/32 (Oct. 15, 2013).

8 *See, e.g.*, Mark A. Drumbl, *Atrocity, Punishment and International Law*, (Cambridge: Cambridge University Press, 2007), p. 152 (noting that "selectivity intractably affects, and will continue to affect, the ICC's work" because there will always be "a large disparity between the cases the ICC could potentially prosecute and those that it will effectively prosecute").

9 Evenson & Smith, *supra* note 2, at 1264 ("[W]here possible within the defined limits of the situation open before the Court, the ICC Prosecutor can also intervene again where there may be renewed violence without seeking a new mandate. This flexibility can be essential for responding to crisis situations."). *Cf.* Valerie Oosterveld, 'The International Criminal Court and the Closure of the Time-Limited International and Hybrid Criminal Tribunals' (2010) 8 *Loy. U. Chi. Int'l L. Rev.* 13, 29 ("If the ICC does scale down its presence in a situation country, it must also plan for future rapid scaling up of investigatory, defense and outreach presence if fugitives are captured and transferred to the ICC.").

> Mr. Guariglia noted that there are two main prosecutorial functions after concluding an investigation from an OTP perspective: tracking suspects and maintaining regular contact with local communities and witnesses, including witness protection. This is to help restart an investigation later on. Mr. Guariglia gave two contrasting examples. In the Bosco Ntaganda (DRC) case, OTP had to re-establish contact with witnesses and the victim community after ten years, many of whom felt abandoned, requiring re-engagement to restore trust. Mr. Guariglia contrasted this with the *Ongwen* (LRA) case where the OTP had maintained a field presence in Uganda and it was much easier to resurrect the case.[10]

Re-opening a formally closed investigation also raises difficult legal questions. The Rome Statute says nothing about what, if anything, the OTP must do to re-open a closed investigation. It is quite possible, however, that the OTP would have to formally re-open an investigation that it formally closed. If so, re-opening a *proprio motu* investigation would require new authorization by the Pre-Trial Chamber, while re-opening a state or UNSC-based investigation would require a new referral. It is highly unlikely that such authorization or referral would always be forthcoming.

To be clear, this is the only possible interpretation of the Rome Statute. The judiciary may well treat a "formal" decision to close an investigation as legally equivalent to hibernating one, in which case the OTP could re-open a closed investigation at any time. Nevertheless, the OTP could avoid any possibility of having to litigate the issue by simply leaving its investigations open indefinitely.

Leaving an investigation open indefinitely also has other benefits. Most obviously, an open investigation has more deterrent effect than a closed one. Deterrence is a function not only of severity of punishment, but also of the likelihood of apprehension.[11] Although the odds of being apprehended by the OTP are always low, almost by definition a high-value perpetrator has more to fear from an open investigation – hibernated or not – than from a closed one. And that is true even if the OTP can re-open an investigation

10 Secretariat of the Assembly of States Parties, International Criminal Court, Complementarity: Seminar on Completion Strategies Across the ICC's Activities (Apr. 4, 2019), [hereinafter Secretariat] https://asp.icc-cpi.int/sites/asp/files/complementarity/Documents/4April%20Seminar%20Completion%20Strategies%20Summary%2016May2019%201803.pdf (last visited June 23, 2023).

11 See Drumbl, *supra* note 8, at 169–70.

without the need for judicial authorization or a new referral, because formal closure will mean not only the cessation of investigative activity, but also the closing of any field office and the total reallocation of investigative resources to other situations. A hibernated investigation can thus be restarted much more quickly than a closed one.

This consideration applies to all perpetrators in an investigated situation. The experience of previous international criminal tribunals (ICTs) indicates, however, that leaving an investigation open indefinitely can be particularly advantageous when the primary suspects are government officials. Although states are rarely keen to help an ICT investigate their own officials, non-cooperation in the face of an investigation that will not end merely delays the day of reckoning – it cannot end the threat. By contrast, a state that knows an ICT will eventually cease its investigative activities has a strong incentive to "wait out" the tribunal, refusing to cooperate until the tribunal closes and the threat passes. This is precisely what happened at the ICTY: in 2003, Carla del Ponte told the Security Council that the hard deadlines in the Tribunal's completion strategy, "instead of speeding up cooperation," simply encouraged the Balkan states "to buy time and to place additional obstacles in the way of cooperation with the ICTY."[12]

The OTP could avoid this pitfall, of course, by refusing to close any specific investigation until all of the suspects in its initial trial program have been apprehended and prosecuted. Indeed, as discussed below, that is the approach the OTP should take if it decides to close investigations. Given the OTP's notorious difficulties in obtaining suspects, however, not putting a temporal limit on the length of an investigation will likely mean that the OTP *never* formally closes an investigation. It will instead simply hibernate them until such time as active investigation becomes possible again.

Leaving investigations open indefinitely will also better protect the OTP's reputation when, as has often been the case, the OTP fails to complete its trial program in a particular situation because of lack of resources or state intransigence. Nothing is more harmful to an ICT's reputation than the perception that it did not complete its mandate because of non-legal factors.[13] Previous

12 Press Release, U.N. International Criminal Tribunal for the former Yugoslavia, Address by Ms. Carla Del Ponte, Chief Prosecutor of the ICTY, to the Security Council, at 12, Doc. no. FH/PIS/791-e (Oct. 10, 2003), https://www.icty.org/en/press/address-ms-carla-del-ponte-chief-prosecutor-icty-un-security-council (last visited June 23, 2023).

13 *See generally*, Kevin Jon Heller, 'Completion Strategies and the Office of the Prosecutor', in Luc Reydams, Jan Wouters and Cedric Ryngaert (eds.), *International Prosecutors* (Oxford: Oxford University Press, 2012).

ICTs, all of which focused on one conflict, had no choice but to close when they could not obtain the necessary funding or cooperation from states. The ICC, by contrast, always has the option of hibernating a frustrated investigation instead of closing it. That will not completely insulate the OTP from criticism, as the backlash against the Darfur hibernation indicates.[14] But it seems reasonable to assume that temporarily hibernating an investigation will generally lead to less backlash than abandoning a frustrated investigation entirely.

Finally, there are more quotidian advantages to never closing an investigation, even if doing so requires hibernation and a scaling back of resources. Oosterveld has noted that the continued presence of an OTP field office in a situation country will make it much easier for the Court to deal with a variety of residual issues, such as protecting witnesses and making archival material available to the local population.[15] The same is true for providing a friendly government with evidence, technical assistance, and engaging in general capacity-building efforts.[16] And, of course, the continued presence of a field office will greatly facilitate the Court's ongoing outreach efforts to affected communities. As the SCSL's experience indicates, an ICT's outreach is much more likely to succeed when it has a physical presence in a state: the tribunal was viewed by locals much more positively in Sierra Leone than in Liberia precisely because it was based in the former and not the latter.

3 Advantages of Closing

Taken together, these considerations make a powerful case for the OTP keeping investigations open indefinitely, hibernating instead of closing a particular investigation if the OTP either completes its initial trial program or (more likely) cannot advance the program any further. There is no question, however, that formally closing an investigation does have some advantages.

Most obviously, closing an investigation will better conserve the OTP's limited resources. Although maintaining a field office or team at ICC headquarters for a hibernated investigation is not as resource-intensive as con-

14 *See, e.g.*, Matthew Redding, Darfur ICC Referral Turns 10: Reflections on the Troubled Path to Accountability, COALITION FOR THE INTERNATIONAL CRIMINAL COURT (Mar. 31, 2015), https://www.coalitionfortheicc.org/news/20150331/darfur-icc-referral-turns-10-reflections-troubled-path-accountability (last visited June 23, 2023).

15 Oosterveld, *supra* note 9, at 14–15.

16 Secretariat, *supra* note 10, at 5 (Statement of Rod Rastan).

ducting an active investigation, it does require the OTP to allocate a certain amount of funds and personnel to an investigation that may not lead to additional prosecutions.

Closing an investigation will also better manage the expectations of the victims and the local population in a situation, because it will make clear that – barring exceptional circumstances – the ICC does not intend to prosecute additional suspects. Evenson and Smith make this point well:

> [H]aving one eye on the "end game" is also important from the perspective of the populations affected by conflict. While justice cannot be rushed, there should come a time when the bulk of the accountability work can be considered to be done, so that it does not drag on forever. If the ICC is clear and up-front about when it considers its contribution to accountability has concluded, this will enable local populations to identify what still needs to be done by the national system and also enable them to feel a sense of closure of at least part of the accountability process.[17]

To be sure, closure does not guarantee that the victims and local community will be *satisfied* with the ICC's efforts. That will be a function of how well the OTP designed and executed its trial program. But closing an investigation offers more certainty than hibernating one, because by definition hibernation assumes that the cessation of investigative activities will – or at least may – be temporary.

Relatedly, closing an investigation will encourage states to assume primary responsibility for addressing the international crimes committed on their territory. That may not happen in conflict or post-conflict situations where the government is simply unable to pursue accountability. But closure will send a powerful message to states that have the capacity to hold domestic trials that they can no longer expect the ICC to do the heavy lifting for them. Uganda provides a striking example of this dynamic: Museveni's government always had the ability to prosecute members of the LRA domestically; it simply preferred, for a variety of reasons, to "outsource" accountability to the ICC.[18] Had the OTP closed the Uganda investigation in-

---

17 Evenson and Smith, *supra* note 2, at 1261.

18 *See generally*, Mark Kersten, 'The ICC as an Actor – Negotiating Interests, Selecting Targets, and Affecting Peace', in Mark Kerston, *Justice in Conflict: The Effects of the International Criminal Court's Interventions on Ending Wars and Building Peace* (Oxford: Oxford University Press, 2016).

stead of hibernating it in 2011, perhaps Ongwen would now be standing trial in Uganda's International Crimes Division instead of siphoning off precious OTP resources in an unnecessary international trial.

4 Considerations for Closure

On balance, the OTP would be better off keeping its investigations open indefinitely than formally closing them. The primary exception is where the OTP believes that closing an investigation is the only way to get a capable but intransigent government to pursue accountability itself. In nearly every other situation, the benefits of hibernating an investigation will outweigh the costs.

It is possible, of course, that the OTP does not and will never have the resources to maintain a field office or a small team at ICC headquarters for every situation it investigates. If so, the OTP will be forced to close at least some investigations even if leaving them open would be the better practice. Two questions thus arise: (1) how should the OTP decide which investigations to close, and (2) how should the OTP plan those closures?

4.1 *Determining Closure*

There is no algorithm the OTP can use to decide which investigations to close instead of hibernate. That decision will depend on the balance of costs and benefits in each situation. Nevertheless, at the macro level, two circumstances would seem to strongly support keeping an investigation open indefinitely. The first is where the OTP is investigating crimes committed during an ongoing conflict, as opposed to a post-conflict situation. The need to maintain the deterrent value of an open investigation is obviously much greater during a conflict than after it. Moreover, when violence is ongoing, the need to maintain prosecutorial flexibility is particularly acute, because new high-value suspects can emerge at any time. In a post-conflict situation, the OTP will have a much better idea *ex ante* which important suspects it wants to prosecute and can be more confident that new suspects requiring prosecution will not emerge, making it safer to close the investigation once its initial trial program is completed.

The second circumstance favoring keeping an investigation open indefinitely is where the OTP is investigating current government officials, as opposed to rebels (such as the LRA) or a former head of state (such as Gbagbo). In such a situation, the only way the OTP can prevent the state from "waiting out" its investigation is to refuse to formally close the investigation until all of the relevant suspects have been surrendered to the Court. Similarly, given that the OTP is very unlikely to complete its trial program in a timely fashion when it is investigating government officials – as the investigations in Darfur, Libya, and Georgia demonstrate – the OTP can best protect its reputation by hibernating a frustrated investigation instead of simply closing it. In the latter situation, the government simply "wins." In the former, its victory is only temporary.

Given these considerations, the ideal candidate for closure is an investigation in which violence has ended in the situation country and the OTP is not targeting current government officials. In that context, the need for deterrence and prosecutorial flexibility will be at their nadir while the likelihood of the OTP successfully completing its trial program will be at its apex. Moreover, although the OTP will always find it easier to manage residual issues such as witness protection and outreach when it maintains a field office in a particular situation, those efforts will be less negatively affected by the absence of an office when the OTP is working with a friendly government in a post-conflict situation.

4.2 *Planning Closure*

Although every situation is different, the guidelines above should provide the OTP with a general idea of whether it will be able to eventually close an investigation. The key here is that the OTP needs to make that determination *before* initially opening the investigation, because the single most important lesson concerning completion that can be drawn from the experience of previous ICTs is that a completion strategy adopted *ex ante* is far more likely to be successful than one adopted *in media res*.[19]

The focal point of any such completion strategy must be determining the number of suspects the OTP intends to prosecute before closure – as the OTP is fully aware:

> Mr. Rastan then noted that when the OTP commences work in a situation, there is an OTP integrated team from the outset with team members from all divisions of the OTP. This team then develops not just a case hypothesis, but is also mandated to help the Prosecutor conceive of the OTP's overall prosecutorial programme by mapping all potential cases that meet the OTP's case selection and prioritization criteria. This not only helps to identify which cases the OTP should pursue, but

19 *See* Heller, *supra* note 13, at 917–20.

> also identify one aspect of completion, namely the potential end of the OTP's prosecutorial programme within a given situation.[20]

The OTP should always err on the side of conservatism when deciding the number and kind of suspects it will be able to prosecute, at least insofar as its trial program will be communicated publicly. Experience suggests that nothing is quite as damaging to an ICT's legitimacy than overpromising what it can accomplish. That was clearly the case with the Special Panels for Serious Crimes (SPSC), which was widely rejected by ordinary Timorese, although it was never realistic to expect the SPSC to prosecute those most responsible for atrocities in East Timor – high-ranking members of the Indonesian military. UNTAET unwisely raised Timorese expectations by giving the SPSC universal jurisdiction over anyone who committed a serious crime between January 1, 1999 and October 25, 1999.

Because an incomplete trial program is so devastating to an ICT's legitimacy, the OTP should do everything it can to avoid closing an investigation before it has completed its trial program – even if that means keeping the investigation open, with the concomitant drain on resources, longer than the OTP would like. As Evenson and Smith note, "[p]reparation for the point at which investigations and prosecutions will be complete should not be permitted to devolve into pressure to bring these possibilities to a premature end."[21] Indeed, the need to avoid premature closure is particularly acute at the ICC, where even the most ambitious situation-specific trial program will involve only a small handful of suspects. The ICTR's reputation was not adversely affected by its failure to prosecute the three suspects that remain at large because it was able to convict sixty-one suspects before closing. The OTP's failure to prosecute one of (say) four or five suspects before closing an investigation would obviously be far more delegitimizing.

Finally, because even the most successful OTP investigation will not prosecute all or even most of the deserving suspects in a particular situation, it is particularly critical that the OTP publicly explain – early and often – why it intends to pursue such a limited trial program. Here the SCSL's experience is instructive: because the SCSL's OTP invested considerable resources in explaining to Sierra Leoneans why its mandate extended only to individuals who bore the "greatest responsibility" for the violence in that country, the OTP's limited trial program – thirteen indictments and

20 Secretariat, *supra* note 10, at 5 (Statement of Rod Rastan).

21 Evenson & Smith, *supra* note 2, at 1264.

ten defendants – did not significantly undermine perceptions of the SCSL's legitimacy.[22]

5 Conclusion

In an ideal world, the OTP would keep open all of its investigations indefinitely, even in situations where it was able to complete its trial program. The advantages of hibernating and pursuing a maintenance strategy instead of formally closing a situation are manifold, from maximizing prosecutorial flexibility to promoting deterrence to encouraging effective outreach.

The OTP, of course, combats impunity with the resources it has, not the resources it wishes it had. Budgetary and personnel limitations may well make it impossible for the OTP to keep all of its investigations open indefinitely. If so, the OTP should endeavor to close only those investigations that take place post-conflict and/or focus on crimes committed by rebels and former government officials. When it decides to investigate situations involving ongoing violence and/or crimes committed by current government officials, the costs of closure are simply too high.

---

22 Heller, *supra* note 13, at 918.

CHAPTER 9

ICC Completion Strategy and Prosecutorial Policy: Two Sides of the Same Coin

Fausto Pocar

An ICC completion strategy with respect to investigations over which the Court has jurisdiction presents different features as compared with the completion strategy of the *ad hoc* criminal tribunals (ICTY and the ICTR), and reflects the prosecutorial policy of the ICC. No question arises when the Rome Statute clearly provides for a case to be discontinued under conditions set in the Statute itself. Two main issues arise. First, when the admissibility of a case leaves a margin of appreciation of the position of the state that would be competent in terms of complementarity, a decision should, in principle, be in favor of the jurisdiction of the domestic court. Second, when a decision is based on the gravity of the offense, the level of responsibility of the alleged perpetrator should not be the main criterion to decide whether an investigation should continue or be discontinued, rather the interests of justice should be the main consideration. As to procedural issues (final or temporary discontinuation of investigations; publicity of the decisions) the Prosecutor should enjoy wide discretion, subject to the competence of other ICC bodies, in particular the Pre-Trial Chamber.

The questions raised by the ICC Office of the Prosecutor in connection with the end of the term of office of the second Prosecutor – aiming at identifying some elements of an ICC completion strategy for situations under investigations – are of a great significance, in particular, for the shaping of a future prosecutorial policy of the Office. Cases currently under investigation absorb financial and human resources which are not unlimited and their continuation, if unjustified or unreasonable, may prevent an efficient start and conduct of new investigations and prosecutions that may be required by upcoming situations.

However, referring to a "completion strategy" in this context has to be kept distinct from the use of this expression as initially referred to by the *ad hoc* International Criminal Tribunals established by the UN Security Council in the last decade of last century. After ten years of life, both the ICTY and the ICTR adopted a completion strategy aiming at the closing of the tribunals, which implied the end of new prosecutions, a decision whether to continue

 | DOI:10.1163/9789004686755_012

the prosecution of all pending cases, and the setting of a deadline to conclude all the cases that would remain before the tribunal until its closing. None of these decisions are before the ICC: the Court being permanent, it is not going to close; new prosecutions may start; pending prosecutions and investigations may go on irrespective of the appointment of a new prosecutor; the setting of a deadline to conclude all pending cases may be desirable, but it is not critical. The completion strategy of the *ad hoc* Tribunals was largely imposed by an external decision made by the UN Security Council and only depended to a marginal extent on the policy followed by their prosecutors. In contrast, the envisaged ICC completion strategy is not imposed by external decisions. It is strictly connected with, or is even a part of, the prosecutorial policy followed by the ICC Prosecutor so far, and may impact on that prosecutorial policy in the future. Hence, it would be preferable to refer to it as a completion strategy of pending cases or as a feature of the ICC prosecutorial policy. The expression used by the Prosecutor should be considered with that understanding and in that perspective.

These differences, however, do not mean that there cannot be any similarities between elements of an ICC completion strategy and elements of the *ad hoc* Tribunals completion strategies. In particular, a common feature is the referral of cases to domestic jurisdictions under the principle of complementarity, although such a principle is described in the Rome Statute as conferring primary jurisdiction to national courts while it is described in the Statutes of the *ad hoc* Tribunals as giving priority to international over domestic jurisdiction.[1] It was the ICTY that came to the conclusion that an effective completion strategy had to rely on domestic judiciaries and aimed at transferring cases to them after having ensured that they had become able and ready to deal with such cases, with a view to a continuation of the work of the Tribunal after its closing.[2] In spite of the reasons that may have contributed to its adoption, such a conclusion is not much different from the view expressed by the drafters of the Rome Statute that cases concerning crimes under international law should be prosecuted by domestic jurisdictions unless those jurisdictions are unable or unwilling to genuinely prosecute them.[3]

---

1 International Criminal Court, Rome Statute of the International Criminal Court, arts 17(1), UN Doc. A/CONF.183/9 (July 17, 1998) [hereinafter Rome Statute]; S.C. Res. 827, art. 9 (May 25, 1993); S.C. Res. 955, art. 8(2) (Nov. 8, 1994).

2 Fausto Pocar, 'Completion or Continuation Strategy? Appraising Problems and Possible Developments in Building the Legacy of the ICTY' (2008), 6 *J. Int'l Crim. Just.* 655–665.

3 *See* Rome Statute, *supra* note 1, at art. 17.

Which are, then, the elements that should guide a completion strategy of the ICC for situations under investigation? Which are strictly connected, as stated earlier, with the prosecutorial policy of the Court? External elements substantially affected the *ad hoc* Tribunals completion strategies by imposing deadlines – in particular, the Security Council resolution that called on the ICTY to take all possible measures to complete investigations by the end of 2004[4] – which allowed for no flexibility in terms of prosecutorial policy. The ICC, by contrast, is free to adapt its prosecutorial policy with respect to the completion of pending cases, subject of course to the observance of the provisions of the Rome Statute, and especially of Article 53 concerning the initiation of investigations.

It goes without saying that when it appears during an investigation that any of the required conditions allowing the Prosecutor to initiate an investigation under Article 53 of the Rome Statute have not been met, the investigation should be discontinued. Should it be apparent from a pending investigation that there is no reasonable basis to believe that a crime exists, or that an existing crime belongs to the jurisdiction of the Court, the Prosecutor cannot initiate an investigation and, if it was already initiated, must abandon it. This is just a matter of law, not of prosecutorial policy.

Different situations arise when the Rome Statute allows for a certain flexibility either in the appreciation of the conditions of admissibility of a case or in deciding whether a case over which the Court has jurisdiction should be prosecuted, or rather abandoned, by the Prosecutor.

The first situation concerns the assessment of the admissibility of a case when the state that would be competent to adjudicate it is unable or unwilling to prosecute it. This ground of admissibility is normally characterized as strictly legal and binding on the Prosecutor,[5] and frequently it is so if the inability of a domestic judiciary is manifest or the unwillingness of the state concerned is declared. There are, however, cases where a decision on admissibility on the basis of this ground may imply a margin of discretion.

I do not intend to expressly mention here any specific situation currently investigated by the ICC Prosecutor, but let's imagine a case of a country torn by a domestic conflict where war crimes and crimes against humanity were committed both by armed groups fighting against the state and by state officials in repressing the activity of those armed groups. Let's also assume that, at

4 S.C. Res. 1503 (Aug. 28, 2003).

5 *See, e.g.*, Giuliano Turone, 'Powers and Duties of the Prosecutor', in Antonio Cassese, Paola Gaeta, and John R.W.D. Jones (eds.), *The Rome Statute of the International Criminal Court: A Commentary* (Oxford: Oxford University Press, 2002), p. 1151.

the end of the conflict, the state adopts a peace plan which provides for the establishment of an independent court to prosecute the crimes committed during the conflict, though setting a regime of sentencing that, in most cases, will be somewhat more lenient than the one the ICC will be likely to apply. In such a case, if the local independent court is actually established and starts working, should the ICC Prosecutor continue the investigations or rather yield to the domestic jurisdiction in application of the principle of complementarity? Would the mere likelihood that a prosecution of the crimes by the ICC would lead to more severe punishment of the perpetrators justify the continuation of the investigations with a view to ensuring the retrial of cases already heard be the domestic court, when such retrial would probably lead to the increase by a few years of detention the sentence imposed by the domestic court? In my view, in a case of this kind, it would be wiser for the Prosecutor to drop or at least to suspend the investigations; their continuation should be reserved to the case in which the government's intent is manifestly to shield the accused from prosecution.

Unlike the just mentioned situation, which is partly a matter of interpretation of legal provisions, in particular of Article 17 of the Statute, the second situation described above is essentially a matter of prosecutorial policy. It arises when the jurisdiction of the Court over pending cases is well established and the Prosecutor has to decide how to proceed in prioritizing the cases to be submitted to the Chambers. The issue is delicate because a prioritization may determine not just the sequence of the cases, but also that some of them may eventually be dropped due to an excessive lapse of time before they may be heard. Hence, a decision should take that possibility also into account, and suspend or drop cases when such possibility is close to be a likelihood. In that sense, the prosecutorial policy may also include abandoning investigations which do not deserve to be prioritized.

The Rome Statute itself gives but a limited guidance for such a decision. There are, however, some provisions that may assist. First, there is the general indication in Article 5 that the jurisdiction conferred upon the Court "shall be limited to the most serious crimes of concern to the international community as a whole,"[6] and the specific indication in Article 17(1)(d) that jurisdiction should be declined when "the case is not of sufficient gravity to justify further action by the Court." Second, in a given case, the Prosecutor may conclude under Article 53(2)(c) that there is not a sufficient basis for a prosecution because "a prosecution is not in the interests of justice." All these provisions

6 *See also*, respectively, Rome Statute, *supra* note 1, at preamble ¶ 4, art. 1 (The two sections employ equivalent expressions to define the jurisdiction of the ICC).

offer the Prosecutor some margin of discretion in deciding whether to continue with an investigation or set it aside, although that margin has different degrees and weight.

In particular, the language of the reference to the most serious crimes of concern to the international community in Article 5 of the Rome Statute does not appear to introduce any hierarchy among the crimes listed in the subsequent provisions, but simply to indicate that the listed crimes are indeed the most serious crimes over which the Court has jurisdiction. Nevertheless, that provision has been interpreted as permitting the identification of categories of crimes within those mentioned in the list. As of the beginning of its activity, the first Prosecutor of the ICC wrote in his 2003 Policy Paper that, the Court being an institution with limited resources, it should confine prosecutions to the leaders who bear most responsibility for the crimes.[7] As to lower-ranking perpetrators, the Court should encourage national prosecutions, where possible, or work with the international community to ensure that the offenders are brought to justice by some other means.[8]

Therefore, the Prosecutor expressed the view that there should be a distribution of tasks between the Court and domestic jurisdictions, in terms of a so-called positive complementarity, based on the level of participation in the crimes under the Rome Statute. It is recognized in the Policy Paper that this distribution may leave an impunity gap if lower level perpetrators escape prosecution, but this issue should be left to national courts or to the international community to discover other means. However, since the Statute does not provide for this distribution and only refers to the seriousness of the crimes, the position of the Prosecutor did not simply reflect a legal interpretation but was, rather, the expression of a prosecutorial policy. Although this announced prosecutorial policy was not always followed later in the practice of the Court, it still is an important element for the selection of the cases to be brought before the ICC.[9]

---

7 *See* Office of the Prosecutor, International Criminal Court, Paper on Some Policy Issues before the Office of the Prosecutor, ¶ 2.1 (Sep. 2003), https://www.icc-cpi.int/sites/default/files/NR/rdonlyres/1FA7C4C6-DE5F-42B7-8B25-60AA962ED8B6/143594/030905_Policy_Paper.pdf (last visited June 26, 2023) (According to the Prosecutor, "the concept of gravity should not be exclusively attached to the act that constituted the crime but also to the degree of participation in its commission").

8 *See Id.* at ¶ 2.2.

9 *See* Office of the Prosecutor, International Criminal Court, Policy Paper on Case Selection and Prioritization, ¶¶ 34–46, 47–55 (Sep. 15, 2016), https://www.icc-cpi.int/sites/default/files/itemsDocuments/20160915_OTP-Policy_Case-Selection_Eng.pdf (last visited June 26,

Is this a sound prosecutorial policy when the Rome Statute only mentions the seriousness of the crimes? It certainly has some merits, but also some shortcomings. On one hand, it provides for an objective distribution of tasks between the Court and national jurisdictions, even if the assessment of the rank of the perpetrators may not always be a simple one. On the other hand, however, it fails to take into account the interests of the victims, who, in many cases, expect to get closure from the punishment of the individuals who materially committed the crime, rather than of a distant high rank person with whom they do not have any contact. Additionally, it fails to consider that the task of an international court, and in particular of a criminal court, is not only to pronounce on a specific case, but also to give guidance to domestic jurisdictions to pronounce on similar cases. Consequently, a primary responsibility for an international court is to interpret the law – in this case the Rome Statute, but also customary law when applicable under Article 21 of the Statute[10] – in order to reach a common understanding of the rules governing crimes which are serious and widespread, even when they are rarely materially committed by high rank persons. The value of a judgment rendered by an international court in such a case may even be more significant, in terms of progress of the law and guidance given to domestic courts and to potential perpetrators, than the value that may have a judgment targeting a high rank state official.

The ICTY did not make a distinction based on the rank of the accused at the beginning of its work, although some investigations were also targeting high rank persons.[11] Rather, some cases concerning lower level accused permitted the Tribunal to clarify a number of legal issues and even to render some decisions that remain as leading cases for further international and domestic prosecutions, thus marking a very significant step in the progressive evolution of international criminal law.[12]

2023) (Now, though, there is more flexibility in assessing the gravity of a crime. And there is also an indication of the criteria to be followed for the prioritization of cases).

10 *See* Fausto Pocar, 'Transformation of Customary Law through ICC Practice' (2018) 112 *AJIL Unbound* 182.

11 (In particular, high rank targets included the president and the general of the armed forces of the Republika Srpska, Radovan Karadžić and Ratko Mladić, whose arrest warrants were issued in 1996).

12 Prosecutor v. Duško Tadić, IT-94-1, Decision on the Defence Motion for Interlocutory Appeal on Jurisdiction (Int'l Crim. Trib. for the Former Yugoslavia AC, Oct. 2, 1995); Prosecutor v. Duško Tadić, IT-94-1-A, Judgement (Int'l Crim. Trib. for the Former Yugoslavia AC, July 15, 1999); Prosecutor v. Dragoljub Kunarac, Radomir Kovač and Zoran Vuković, IT-96-23-T, Judgement (Int'l Crim. Trib. for the Former Yugoslavia TC, Feb. 22, 2001) (It is sufficient to mention in that respect the Tadić jurisdiction decision

It is surprising that the ICC, more than eighteen years after the entry into force of the Rome Statute, still does not record any judgment of this kind. Just to make an example, wouldn't it have been more beneficial if the Court, instead of running after some heads of state, had worked for criminally defining slavery, as it is practiced in contemporary world, as a crime against humanity? Article 7(1) and 7(2)(c), dealing with "enslavement," would certainly allow for that approach and a judgment of the Court on such a matter would concern millions of victims[13] and would constitute a significant progress in international law, irrespective of the perpetrators being high rank officials or persons active in criminal organizations. I offer this example here only to show that a sound prosecutorial policy should not exclusively, or even principally, rely on the distinction between high rank and lower rank perpetrators and that, consequently, it should not rely on that distinction at the stage of envisaging a completion strategy with respect to pending cases over which the ICC has jurisdiction.[14]

In light of the above considerations, the only provision on which the Prosecutor may correctly rely to decide whether there is a sufficient basis to continue an investigation with a view to prosecuting a case is Article 53(2)(c) of the Rome Statute which allows her/him to discontinue an investigation when a prosecution is not in the interests of justice. There, too, some elements have to be taken into account under the statutory provi-

---

and the Tadić judgment, which settled the interpretation of the notion of "international armed conflict" in criminal matters and the applicability of a grave breaches regime in non-international armed conflicts or, with respect to specific crimes, the Kunarac Trial judgment, that defined the elements of the crime of rape as a self-standing crime under customary international law).

13 International Labor Office, Global Estimates of Modern Slavery: Forced Labour and Forced Marriage (Sep. 19, 2017), https://www.ilo.org/wcmsp5/groups/public/@dgreports/@dcomm/documents/publication/wcms_575479.pdf (last visited June 26, 2023) (This matter is of public awareness and concern, and it is sufficient to cast a glance at the reports of the ILO to have a better knowledge of its size. According to the ILO report, there are 40 million people in modern slavery and 152 million in child labour around the world).

14 *See* International Criminal Tribunal for the Former Yugoslavia, Rules of Procedure and Evidence, Rule 11 *bis* (C), U.N. Doc. IT/32/Rev.50, rule 11 *bis* (C) (July 8, 2015), https://www.icty.org/x/file/Legal%20Library/Rules_procedure_evidence/IT032Rev50_en.pdf (last visited June 23, 2023); S.C. Res. 1534 (Mar. 26, 2004) (It is true that the ICTY completion strategy relied on the level of responsibility of the accused to refer pending cases to domestic jurisdictions. Rule 11 *bis* (C) refers to the gravity of the crimes charged and the level of responsibility of the accused. However, that rule did not belong to the prosecutorial policy of the Tribunal and was adopted in accordance with Resolution 1534 (2004)).

sion, but additional elements may also play a role. Reference is made to "all the circumstances," which include, but are not limited to, the gravity of the crime, the interests of victims, and the age or infirmity of the alleged perpetrator. The Prosecutor can therefore rely on any circumstances of the crime, which, of course, also includes the rank of the alleged perpetrator. The Prosecutor could consider rank, balancing it against the elements expressly described in the statutory provision, as well as other elements as appropriate.

In conclusion, in shaping a completion strategy with respect to the pending cases under investigation with a view to reducing their number, and assuming these are cases over which the Court's jurisdiction is undisputed, the Prosecutor should not rely specifically on the rank of the alleged perpetrator. He/she should instead stick to Article 53(2)(c) referring to the interests of justice. In light of the flexibility of the provision, it goes without saying that the Prosecutor should give an appropriate reasoning on a case by case basis. As it is intended to be part of prosecutorial policy, it is natural that the Prosecutor should enjoy a wide margin of flexibility in making a decision whether to discontinue an investigation, subject to the above mentioned applicable statutory provisions.

In particular, no special treatment should necessarily be given to the consideration that the investigation was based on a Security Council referral. It is true that the Security Council may have important political motives to refer a situation to the ICC, but, from a legal point of view, its referral simply removes an obstacle to the jurisdiction of the Court by permitting the Prosecutor to investigate alleged crimes connected with a state that has not ratified the Rome Statute. However, in terms of the prosecutorial policy of the Court, no priority is attached to a Security Council referral as such. In the two referrals made by the Security Council so far, the ICC Prosecutor has given those situations priority even beyond the scope of the Security Council resolutions which referred country situations and did not contain a mandate to immediately issue indictments against the two heads of state. This may show an inclination of the Prosecutor to insert the referrals into the Court's prosecution schedule with priority, but it does not constitute a binding precedent *per se*.

In light of the consideration that discontinuing an investigation forms part of the prosecutorial policy, and of the freedom enjoyed by the Prosecutor in shaping such a policy, the Prosecutor should be also free to decide whether abandoning an investigation should be final or temporary. In other terms, an investigation may be suspended if more urgent or compelling cases so require, or if the prospect of arresting alleged perpetrators of the crime or witnesses thereof is limited because the circumstances surrounding the crime so indicate. In any event, it is clear that the discontinuation of an investigation is never absolutely final until there is a final decision concerning the crime alleged.

Should the Prosecutor issue a public report on the decisions taken on a completion strategy concerning cases over which the Court has jurisdiction? There is no obligation to do so, except for what is required under Article 53 (2)(c), which provides that the Prosecutor shall inform the Pre-Trial Chamber, and the state making a self-referral or the Security Council when a situation has been referred by it, of his or her conclusion and the reasons for such conclusion. If the reasons for a decision to discontinue an investigation is because a prosecution is not in the interests of justice, a public report would be desirable. However, any report should be confidential if it may affect further investigations on the same crime, or on related crimes, or if it may have an impact on the security of witnesses or on the interests of victims, which must also be given priority.

CHAPTER 10

Prioritizing Investigations Is Key

Alex Whiting

The Rome Statute sets out several ways to start an investigation, but no mechanism to end one. As open investigations (twelve) and preliminary examinations (nine) pile up, attention is turning to the question: when and how should the International Criminal Court close out an investigation? The answer is that the ICC should terminate investigations only in the narrowest of circumstances – when it turns out there is absolutely no legal or factual basis to continue investigating or when national authorities assume the responsibility for any remaining prosecutions. In the vast majority of situations, however, the problem of having a growing number of open investigations can be addressed through a policy of investigation prioritization that devises a way to select the three to five investigations that are, at any given moment, most urgent or promising. The remaining investigations should not be closed, but can be put on the shelf pending further developments.

The first question is, why do we care about closing investigations? Why does it matter if all of these investigations remain open? One answer might be that we just have a sense that enough is enough. Criminal investigations are meant to be prompt and timely – for the interests of the victims, potential accused, and justice. Moreover, if an investigation drags on for years or even decades, a kind of fatigue inevitably sets in, particularly as new, urgent crises demand our attention. But the core crimes of the ICC carry no statute of limitations, and a central principle of the fight against impunity for these crimes is that while the enforcement efforts may be inadequate and sporadic, they never rest. Perpetrators are reminded again and again that they cannot sleep peacefully, as the long arm of the law might one day catch up with them. For this reason, prosecutions from World War II[1] have continued into the last years, the United Nations Residual Mechanism for Criminal Tribunals[2] is still

1 Thomas Weber, *Time Appears to Have Run Out on the Last Nazi War Crimes Trials. But There Are Other Roads to Justice*, Time (Apr. 3, 2019), https://time.com/5563615/nazi-trials-over/ (last visited June 27, 2023).

2 U.N. Int'l Residual Mechanism for Crim. Tribs., https://www.irmct.org/ (last visited June 27, 2023).

 | DOI:10.1163/9789004686755_013

searching for fugitives from the 1994 Rwanda genocide and is prosecuting cases from the wars in the former Yugoslavia, and the Extraordinary Chambers in the Courts of Cambodia[3] presses on with its cases arising from the crimes committed between 1975 and 1979. The news that Omar al-Bashir and the others the ICC accused in Sudan might be surrendered soon to the ICC,[4] some fifteen years after the investigations began there, is just another reminder that sometimes the wheels of justice can turn slowly.

Another reason to consider closing an investigation might be the interests of the state at issue. A central premise of the principle of "positive complementarity"[5] has been that if the ICC Office of the Prosecutor opens a preliminary examination into a situation, states will motivated to prosecute potential cases themselves to avoid the black cloud of an ICC investigation. On this logic, consideration should also be given to when that "black cloud" gets lifted, when the ICC says that it is no longer investigating in a state. However, the ICC investigates and prosecutes individuals, not states, and so a state's interest in seeing an ICC investigation "terminated" is narrow. Further, even after an investigation commences, states can divest the ICC of jurisdiction by investigating and prosecuting the alleged crimes themselves.

Finally, another reason to bring some investigations to an end is for the sake of the institution itself. There is little prospect that the ICC will gain in resources or power anytime soon which means that if investigations continue to be opened while none are closed, the focus, energy, and authority of the Court could be dissipated. There may, however, be other ways to address this risk aside from terminating investigations by, for example, finding ways to focus the work of the Court.

These are some of the reasons to devise a policy on terminating investigations. What are the risks of closing down investigations? Given how few cases the ICC prosecutes in each situation, the Court will have to consider the risk of reputational harm if it announces that it is terminating an investigation into a particular situation. Victims and other interested parties will likely protest the inadequacy of the prosecutorial response. Further, circum-

---

3 Extraordinary Chambers in the Cts. of Cambodia, https://www.eccc.gov.kh/en (last visited June 27, 2023).

4 Jason Burke, *Sudan Signals It May Send Former Dictator Omar al-Bashir to ICC*, The Guardian (Feb. 11, 2020), https://www.theguardian.com/world/2020/feb/11/sudan-says-it-will-send-former-dictator-omar-al-bashir-to-icc (last visited June 27, 2023).

5 Emeric Rogier, *The Ethos of "Positive Complementarity"*, EJIL TALK (Dec. 11, 2018), https://www.ejiltalk.org/the-ethos-of-positive-complementarity/ (last visited June 27, 2023).

stances can change. What happens if the investigation is closed and then new evidence of crimes suddenly becomes available? This scenario is not fanciful since critical evidence in atrocity investigations has often emerged only years after the events.[6] Could the Prosecutor simply re-open the investigation, or would there need to be a new trigger to do so?

All of these considerations suggest a three-part OTP policy to manage open investigations. First, in a narrow set of circumstances, the OTP could close an investigation if it concluded that there was absolutely *no* possibility of ICC prosecutions arising from a situation. Such terminations would mirror decisions to close a preliminary examination without proceeding to investigation, for example if it were found that a jurisdictional element was missing (e.g. in an investigation of possible war crimes, insufficient evidence of an armed conflict) or the alleged crimes were deemed to be insufficiently grave to warrant ICC prosecution. Given the rigor with which potential situations are analyzed before an investigation is opened, it is expected that these kinds of terminations would occur very infrequently.

Second, the OTP could close an investigation if it assessed that any remaining potential cases would be prosecuted by national authorities. This could occur if the ICC prosecuted senior officials, leaving lower-level perpetrators to the state to prosecute, or if the ICC brought no prosecutions but was confident that the state would proceed against all alleged perpetrators, high and low. In this respect, such terminations would essentially be assessments that remaining cases were no longer "admissible" pursuant to Article 17 of the Rome Statute. The International Criminal Tribunal for the former Yugoslavia (ICTY), succeeded by the Residual Mechanism, is following this path: the alleged most senior perpetrators were prosecuted by the ICTY and the Residual Mechanism, and the expectation is any and all remaining cases can be prosecuted by national authorities.

Third, the OTP could allow the remaining investigations to stay open, but devise a policy prioritizing them that would identify the three to five investigations that would be "active" at any given moment. The other remaining investigations would be put on the shelf, or made "inactive," pending any new developments warranting them to be revisited. The criteria for determining which investigations would be prioritized could track those that the OTP relies upon for prioritizing cases within an open situation, as set out in the

6 Alex Whiting, 'In International Criminal Prosecutions, Justice Delayed Can Be Justice Delivered' (2009) 50 *Harv. Int'l L.J.* 323.

OTP's *Case Selection and Prioritization Policy*.[7] The OTP could assess the urgency of the investigation, the gravity of the situation, and the likelihood of cooperation and success, mindful that these factors are dynamic and that no one factor is necessarily dispositive.

This policy would address all of the concerns raised by the accumulating investigations at the ICC. It would signal to perpetrators and victims that there is no expiration date on justice. It would tell states that, to the extent they perceive the existence of an open ICC investigation as a black cloud, they can lift it by committing to prosecute any outstanding cases themselves. And it would focus the work of the ICC by concentrating its efforts on those investigations that are most pressing and promising. Investigations should be kept open as long as there are perpetrators roaming free, but they should be prioritized to ensure that the efforts of the ICC are effective.

---

7 Office of the Prosecutor, International Criminal Court, Policy Paper on Case Selection and Prioritization (Sep. 15, 2016), https://www.icc-cpi.int/sites/default/files/itemsDocuments/20160915_OTP-Policy_Case-Selection_Eng.pdf (last visited June 27, 2023).

PART 3

The Emerging Use of Cyber Evidence and Open Source Material at the ICC

Introduction to Part 3

The following question was featured on www.iccForum.com from June 2020 to January 2021:

To what extent can cyber evidence repositories, and digital and open-source evidence, facilitate the work of the OTP, and the ICC more generally?

The collection and use of evidence in the course of investigations by the International Criminal Court is regulated by, *inter alia*, Article 54, 68, and 69 of the Rome Statute and Chapter 4, Section 1 of the Rules of Procedure and Evidence. These sources do not specifically address the use of digital evidence available from social media, other open-source websites, other repositories, or organizations or individuals that might provide such evidence.

While there is no specific language on the use of digital, open-source evidence in the Rome Statute or the Rules of Procedure and Evidence , the Court has considered the introduction of such evidence on at least one occasion. On August 15, 2017, the Court issued an arrest warrant for Mahmoud Mustafa Busyaf Al-Werfalli. The ICC relied, in whole or in part, on cyber evidence (for example, videos posted on social media) in issuing an arrest warrant. There remain, however, many procedural, evidentiary, and institutional issues.

As the use of technology increases the availability of digital and open-source evidence, the Court will be faced with various challenges and opportunities. To what extent can cyber evidence repositories, and digital and open-source evidence, facilitate the work of the OTP, and the ICC more generally? The key issues are:

1. its volatile nature and when to strategically preserve,
2. methods of authentication,
3. risk of over-collection,
4. how algorithms and AI influence the ability to objectively search,
5. risks related to crowd sourcing and
6. practical challenges (security, virtual profile maintenance, deep fakes, etc.).

The key questions therefore include:

1. how do national jurisdictions deal with the new challenge of mass volume of data and the evidentiary value of what is collected online,
2. how this differs from material retrieved from digital media carriers,
3. how should such procedures and considerations differ, if at all, from those employed in obtaining non-digital evidence,

 | DOI:10.1163/9789004686755_014

4. and most importantly, how to deal with the internet and related tools that are in constant evolution, while the Office is both constrained in terms of finances and manpower?

Might the ICC partner with an entity that can provide cybersecurity? Should the ICC deal with national or regional courts or law enforcement groups seeking to access this data differently from requests for access to other information or evidence? How much access could the public have to this database, if any? How can the ICC maintain these databases so as to protect privacy rights? To what extent should the ICC respect or comply with national privacy laws?

The issue is further complicated by questions of authentication. How can the ICC protect against "deep-fakes" and other disinformation? Traditionally, evidence is authenticated by the direct source of the evidence. In the digital context, this carries particular dilemmas. How can evidence be authenticated in instances where the direct source is unknown?

Finally, as technology evolves, how can the Court best prepare to evolve with it?

CHAPTER 11

Agility and Openness: Keys to the ICC's Effective Use of Digital Evidence

Jay D. Aronson and Enrique Piraces

Open source evidence will form a core element of almost all grave crimes investigations the International Criminal Court (ICC) undertakes in the near future. The widespread availability of mobile phones with high-quality cameras and GPS-enabled features, and the general acceptance of the notion that interesting, unusual, or shocking events ought to be filmed and uploaded to social media, means that more evidence of human rights violations is publicly available today than ever before. Eyewitnesses, victims, and even perpetrators are all recording and narrating events from their perspectives on a variety of social media platforms, from semi-private Telegram channels to region-specific platforms like Russian-based VKontakte (VK) to US-based giants like Facebook and Instagram, Twitter, and YouTube. Given the private and corporate nature of these platforms, a key challenge for all human rights investigators is that this evidence is often only available online for a short period of time before it is taken down for any number of well-documented reasons. We argue, however, that a savvy and prepared human rights institution can locate and preserve this record of grave crimes in a way that preserves its evidentiary or probative value.

Further, one of the core features of the publicness of this evidence is that a wide range of actors ranging from private citizens to academics to international non-governmental organizations like Amnesty International and Human Rights Watch are collecting and preserving this evidence, leading to a growing ecosystem of digital repositories around the world. This new reality offers a tremendous opportunity for the ICC in general and the OTP in particular because it enables Court investigators to gather relevant information at a distance, cutting costs and reducing the need to put individuals in danger, and also tap into a broader network of non-ICC investigators and first-responders interested in the same situations for a wide variety of reasons. Gathering this digital evidence enables the creation of a factual record that can strengthen and supplement eyewitness testimony. It also allows analysts and investigators to access information about past incidents and monitor ongoing issues in near real time.

 | DOI:10.1163/9789004686755_015

The ability to take advantage of this opportunity requires the development and widespread acceptance of collection and preservation practices that prioritize cooperation with relevant technology partners, an agile and adaptive approach to evidence gathering, and a willingness among all Court staff and leadership to learn new skills and rethink certain aspects of the Court's institutional bureaucracy and professional hierarchy. It also requires a willingness to integrate new analytic tools and methods into the Court's practices in a way that advances the Court's mission.

We want to be clear that we are not writing this essay from the perspective of tech evangelists or tech solutionists. We do not think it is possible for the Court to simply innovate its way to a more effective future. The issues we raise are necessitated by the changing nature of criminal evidence in the 21st century and the budgetary, institutional, and political characteristics of the Court. Each technology-oriented recommendation we make requires a complementary change in practice and outlook among Court staff and leadership.

We should point out that we have both advised the Court and the OTP on technology for more than five years and currently serve on the Court's Technology Advisory Board. One of us (Enrique Piracés) is a human rights practitioner with a long history of developing and adapting information and communication technology (ICT) for human rights documentation and advocacy in both resource-limited and well-resourced contexts. He is the creator of Digital Evidence Vault, a widely-used system for collecting and preserving digital evidence from social media and the internet. The other (Jay Aronson) is a historian and social scientist who has devoted his career to understanding and improving the role that science and technology can play in achieving just outcomes in the domains of law and human rights. He has written extensively on the value of large media collections and first-person video in the investigation of human rights violations, as well as the ways that computer vision, machine learning, and artificial intelligence can (and cannot) be used to analyze this data. Along with a statistician colleague, the authors run the Center for Human Rights Science at Carnegie Mellon University, which was founded in 2011 to facilitate partnerships between scientists and researchers in academia and human rights practitioners with data gathering and analysis challenges that they cannot address on their own. As such, we understand the general issues associated with the collection, preservation, and analysis of cyber evidence and open source intelligence and the unique challenges and opportunities that the Court and the OTP faces in this domain.

As we noted above, we believe that the Court and the OTP have a tremendous opportunity to make use of the content and evidence repositories being built in situations of interest to the Court. We know that tools and methods currently exist for the internal staff of the Court to gather and collect evidence that will positively impact the ability of the Court to investigate crimes against humanity (as we have already seen in the Al-Werfalli case), but that these tools and methods are not currently being used by the Court in the most effective ways. We also believe that computer vision, machine learning, and AI can be used to increase the effectiveness and efficiency of the OTP and the Court. However, the successful implementation of this vision will require changes in the structure and function of the Court and the OTP beyond just the adoption of new technologies.

In what follows, we offer some thoughts on issues the Court and the OTP will need to think through if they are going to make the most of open source human rights media, digital evidence repositories, and artificial intelligence in the future. We do not provide our views on the value of open source evidence here since we have done that elsewhere.[1] Nor do we make the case for open source investigations in human rights accountability efforts more generally or in the context of the ICC (the former has already been done in an extraordinary new volume co-edited by Sam Dubberley, Alexa Koenig, and Darragh Murray,[2] and the latter has been done by Lindsay Freeman in the aforementioned edited volume and by Nikita Mehandru and Alexa Koenig in a recent Harvard Human Rights Journal article[3] and in several reports by them and their UC Berkeley Human Rights Center colleagues). Nor do we address the legal dimensions of admissibility because it is not our area of expertise.

The ICC is the main international institution with the mandate to investigate grave crimes against humanity and prosecute wrong-doers in countries that are unwilling or unable to address them. It is constrained at many

---

1 Jay D. Aronson, 'Computer Vision and Machine Learning for Human Rights Video Analysis: Case Studies, Possibilities, Concerns, and Limitations' (2018) 43 *Law and Social Inquiry* 1188; Jay D. Aronson, McKenna Cole, Alex Hauptmann, Dan Miller and Bradley Samuels, 'Reconstructing Human Rights Violations Using Large Eyewitness Video Collections: The Case of Euromaidan Protester Deaths' (2018), 10 *J. Hum. Rts. Prac.* 159; Jay D. Aronson, 'The Utility of User-Generated Content in Human Rights Investigations', in Molly K. Land and Jay D. Aronson (eds.), *New Technologies for Human Rights Law and Practice* (Cambridge: Cambridge University Press, 2018), p. 129; Jay D. Aronson, 'Preserving Human Rights Media for Justice, Accountability, and Historical Clarification' (2017), 11 *Genocide Studies and Prevention* 82.

2 Sam Dubberley, Alexa Koenig and Darragh Murray (eds.), *Digital Witness: Using Open Source Information for Human Rights Investigation, Documentation, and Accountability*, (Oxford: Oxford University Press, 2020).

3 Nikita Mehandru and Alexa Koenig, *Open Source Evidence and the International Criminal Court*, HARV. HUM. RTS. J. (Apr. 15, 2019), https://harvardhrj.com/2019/04/open-source-evidence-and-the-international-criminal-court/ (last visited June 27, 2023).

levels, not least of which is that it must wait for a request for investigation from the UN Security Council or a party state, or the Prosecutor herself must decide to launch an investigation into a situation in which dire human rights violations are taking place and perpetrators are not being held accountable. This means that the time between crimes against humanity and the start of an investigation is often very long (sometimes years), that the country in which the crimes are being investigated may be hostile to the investigation, or both. These challenges make the job of the investigator incredibly difficult and ensures that ICC officials are never the first to arrive at a crime scene.

In the past, this meant that in order to build a case, the Court was required to find eyewitnesses to the crimes, victims of crimes, or relatives of victims and then make arrangements to get statements from them about events that happened in the past. Such witness statements can sometimes be weak and easy for defense attorneys to discredit. Both critics of the Court and its supporters have long advocated for changes in the way that the OTP makes its case in Court.

At least since the Syria Civil War (and certainly earlier on a limited basis), conflicts and human rights violations have been well-documented on video and in pictures by people on the ground, whether they be bystanders, victims, or the violators themselves. Some of these first responders have been ordinary people, while others are local humanitarian responders, journalists, or human rights advocates. This has made it possible for the Court and its investigators to gain access to evidence produced directly by first responders.

While the Court has been looking for ways of communicating directly with first responders for several years, the most likely means for investigators to gain access to this material is through public social media accounts. In terms of access, the challenge presented by citizen evidence, and overall online content, is not that it *per se* is volatile in nature, but rather that it is held by private third parties that are globally distributed and with different terms of service. This determines what content can be published, removed, or preserved (as well as what the mechanisms are to request removal or preservation). Many organizations, like the UC Berkeley Human Rights Center and WITNESS, have engaged with the private sector to find avenues for materials that may have probative or evidentiary value to be made available to human rights fact-finding efforts, and however valuable they are, they can only satisfy a number of situations.

In the absence of agreements with the main platforms, the only way to ensure that material that is published on social media is available for eventual ICC action is to preserve it as quickly as possible after it is uploaded. However, this opportunistic preservation is often done without a clear focus on what type of information will eventually be needed, leading to too much or too little material being preserved. Further, while there might be a mechanism for working directly with the platform company to do the collection and preservation, the process might be too onerous or inefficient, on the one hand, or lead to a deluge of data on the other. In general, though, platforms have not developed clear guidelines for the human rights community to obtain data from them.

In the absence of the ability to carefully collect just the right media, investigators are often left to ingest as much data as possible in the short term, with the cleaning of the collection and tagging of media for future reference having to wait for later processing. Volume can create a challenge for the ICC OTP as it may burden analysts and lawyers with the need to review content and disclose its findings to the defense.[4] This is where computer vision, machine learning, and AI can have the biggest impact. AI is very good at recognizing patterns in data and looking for these patterns repeatedly in large data sets. It is not very good at developing nuanced interpretations of the meaning of these patterns or placing them in historical, social, and political context. Nor is it particularly good at evaluating the authenticity of the source of the data. Once a dataset has been filtered and tagged automatically, authentication and determination of probative value of relevant material are much better handled by human investigators.

The Court and the OTP cannot be expected to become a scientific institution or employ experts in all relevant emerging technologies. The Court could learn from the experience of other communities of practice where practitioners often find solutions by relying on trusted networks with specialized organizations. The Court should, as much as possible, distribute these connections and knowledge widely across the institution so that no one unit becomes the gatekeeper to accessing technology. Strategically, the Court should also favor systems that are open, both as in source and open for use by all units in the Court, including the defense bar.

The big challenge is how to make this happen in an institution that is not designed for innovation and that has distributed management, as well as ownership, of key responsibilities and resources around technological issues. A sustainable and effective way to approach this is by providing analysts, lawyers, and judges with access to knowledge about the technologies that are behind the growth in digital content as well as the technologies and methods that may have the most potential to address these new challenges. Empower-

4 *See* International Criminal Court, Rules of Procedure and Evidence, Doc. No. ICC-ASP/1/3 (2013).

ing analysts, in particular, by creating opportunities for learning, experimentation, and creativity, may be the best way to adapt to the new challenges.

The OTP could find a good fabric to support such efforts in the myriad of organizations and projects that have been working at the intersection of human rights, science, and innovation over the past decade. For that to be effective, there would need to be a new form of engagement that facilitates rapid response to relevant issues and that also reduces the institutional barriers that traditionally hinder change.

In our invitation to contribute to this Forum, we were given a question to answer. In our conclusion, we wanted to pose a related question for consideration: How can an unique institution, and its particular bureaucracy, create agile mechanisms to stay up to date with the latest forms of evidence and the technology needed to process it; increase the capacity of analysts, lawyers, and judges to understand, adapt, and forecast the use of technology; remove administrative roadblocks to technology adoption when useful; and create spaces for exposure to emerging technologies? We are not suggesting that the Court must adopt new technologies simply because they are available, but it must develop a more robust and less institutionally constrained system for evaluating, adopting, and adapting relevant technologies that make its difficult job easier to accomplish.

CHAPTER 12

Deepfakes and Digital Trust: Authenticating Open Source Evidence

Roisin A. Costello

1 Introduction

The use of open source evidence has increased steadily in the last decade, not least as a result of the increasing prevalence of digital evidence and the predominantly digital record of modern conflict. This has led to an as yet nascent concern over the need to investigate the risks of open source evidence and how it can be preserved.

How to seek out and preserve open source evidence is a significant concern in a context in which a majority of jurisdictions are imposing fines on platforms which fail to remove violent or terrorist related content – and most platforms' own terms of use mean such content is hastily identified and removed. However, mandatory reporting and preservation mechanisms, as well as third party NGO collection of evidence, can go some way towards ameliorating these challenges.[1] But even where open source evidence can be collected and preserved, obstacles to its use remain.

This essay is concerned with a newly emerged risk of open source evidence – authentication and the risk of deepfakes. Given the challenge of keeping pace with the rapid development of the technologies through which deepfakes are created, and the practical obstacles to what Citron has referred to as "immutable life logs" in the contexts in which the ICC operates, this essay argues that a prospective harvesting or collection mechanism of original uncompressed files, potentially in partnership with an external organization, may offer a way forward in dealing with open source evidence.

1 *See* Róisín Á Costello, 'International Criminal Law and the Role of Non-State Actors in Preserving Open Source Evidence' (2018), 7 *Cambridge Int'l L.J.* 268.

 | DOI:10.1163/9789004686755_016

2 Open Source Evidence at the ICC

The International Criminal Court has recognized the need to engage with open source evidence, in particular evidence gathered from social media, which it alluded to in its 2016–2018 Strategic Plan as an imminent challenge which the Court would be called on to face.[2]

Since then, the Court's commitment to engaging with new forms of digital evidence in prosecutions has been encouraging. The Office of the Prosecutor has investigated a series of cases which relied on open source evidence. In the 2015 cases of *Banda Jerbo* and *Abu Garda*, subsequent to the conflict in Darfur, satellite imaging, collected by Google Earth and other open source platforms, was used to track the burning and destruction of villages as well as population and troop movements.[3]

Subsequently, in the case of *Al Mahdi*,[4] the Court was presented with a significant quantity of open source evidence including satellite images taken from Google Earth as well as content from YouTube and audio content sourced online.[5] The conflict in *Al Mahdi* occurred in 2012, and was among the first cases to be tried during a period in which digital recording devices and satellite and drone technology were in common use. In this respect, the case offers an insight into the necessity and prevalence of open source evidence in future international criminal prosecutions. In 2017, the Prosecutor relied on open source evidence in the issuance of the *Al-Werfalli* arrest warrant.[6] The warrant was notable for its reliance on open source evidence drawn from social media, specifically YouTube, as well as five video files drawn from social media generally.[7]

2 Peggy O'Donnell, Alexa Koenig, Camille Crittenden and Eric Stover, UC Berkeley HRC, Beyond Reasonable Doubt: Using Scientific Evidence to Advance Prosecutions at the International Criminal Court, p. 7 (Jan. 2013), https://www.law.berkeley.edu/files/HRC/HRC_Beyond_Reasonable_Doubt_FINAL.pdf (last visited June 27, 2023).

3 Prosecutor v. Abdallah Banda Abakaer Nourain and Saleh Mohammed Jerbo Jamus, ICC-02/05-03/09 OA 4, Judgment on the Appeal of Mr Abdallah Banda Abakaer Nourain and Mr Saleh Mohammed Jerbo Jamus against the Decision of Trial Chamber IV of 23 Jan. 2013 Entitled "Decision on the Defence's Request for Disclosure of Documents in the Possession of the Office of the Prosecutor" (AC, Aug. 28, 2013); Prosecutor v. Bahar Idriss Abu Garda, ICC-02/05-02/09, Decision on the Confirmation of Charges (PTC I, Feb. 8, 2010).

4 Prosecutor v. Ahmad Al Faqi Al Mahdi, ICC-01/12-01/15, Decision on the Confirmation of Charges against Ahmad Al Faqi Al Mahdi (PTC I, Mar. 24, 2016).

5 *Id.*

6 Prosecutor v. Mahmoud Mustafa Busayf Al-Werfalli, ICC-01/11-01/17, Warrant of Arrest, 8 (PTC I, Aug. 15, 2017).

7 *Id.* at 8–9.

However, *Bemba et al.*[8] is perhaps the most concrete example of reliance on social media evidence by the Court to date. In *Bemba*, the defendant was alleged, subsequent to other crimes of which he had been convicted, to have engaged in witness tampering.[9] Specifically, the Prosecution argued that the defendant had bribed witnesses to change their testimony.[10] In support of this allegation, the Prosecution submitted evidence of a wire transfer as well as pictures from Facebook showing the two witnesses alleged to have been bribed together.[11]

3 Authentication of Open Source Evidence

Once open source evidence has been obtained, the issue for the Court is whether such evidence can be used. While open source evidence is by its nature generally already in the public sphere, its use is contingent on authentication.[12] Thus, while there appear to be few practical barriers to the acquisition of such evidence, its collection is troubled by concerns over integrity, compatibility, and standardized authentication procedures.[13]

There is currently no designation of what constitutes admissible evidence within the ICC Rules of Procedure and Evidence. Rather, the Rules establish a framework of evidentiary analysis in accordance with which evidence is admitted or rejected based on its relevance, probative value, and prejudicial impact.[14] In addition, the Court has developed standard procedures for uploading and presenting evidence in the form of the e-Court Protocol.

---

8 Prosecutor v. Jean-Pierre Bemba Gombo, Aimé Kilolo Musamba, Jean-Jacques Mangenda Kabongo, Fidèle Babala Wandu and Narcisse Arido, ICC-01/05-01/13, Public Redacted Version of Judgment pursuant to Article 74 of the Statute (TC VII, Oct. 19, 2016).

9 *Id.*

10 *Id.*

11 *Id.* at 83.

12 *See* Prosecutor v. Vujadin Popović, Ljubiša Beara, Drago Nikolić, Ljubomir Borovčanin, Radivoje Miletić, Milan Gvero, and Vinko Pandurević, ICTY-05-88-T, Decision on Admissibility of Intercepted Communications, 4, 22, 26, 33–35 (Int'l Crim. Trib. For the Former Yugoslavia TC II, Dec. 7, 2007).

13 International Bar Association, Evidence Matters in ICC Trials, 18–20 (Aug. 2016), https://www.ibanet.org/document?id=Evidence-matters-in-icc-trials (last visited June 27, 2023); Aida Ashouri, Caleb Bowers and Cherrie Warden, 'An Overview of the Use of Digital Evidence in International Criminal Courts' (2014), 11 *Digit. Evidence & Elec. Sig. L. Rev.* 115.

14 International Criminal Court, Rules of Procedure and Evidence, Rules 64, 68, 72, ICC-ASP /1/3 (2013).

The Protocol provides for direct disclosure, in-court provision of digital materials, and consistent information exchange.[15] However, it is notable that while the Protocol offers some guidance on authentication, by specifying that metadata should be attached to digital files for example,[16] it is largely limited to harmonizing the format, means of storage, and presentation of digital evidence within the Court system. The Protocol does not address the probative value of digital evidence which, under Rule 63(2), remains flexible, broadly drawn, and subject to the graduated grounds for action under the Rome Statute.

The result is that there seems to be little procedural guidance on the risks and challenges posed by open source evidence and its authentication. Given the minimal involvement of open source evidence in trials previously, this was not a significant issue. But as the events considered by the Court edge into the digital age, as in *Al Mahdi*, the necessity of employing a coherent and consistent approach to authentication will become increasingly necessary. This necessity is now heightened by the emergence of tools for the manipulation of the images, audio, and video which form a crucial part of open source evidence. To date the most potentially problematic of these are deepfake technologies.

4 Deepfake Technologies

Deepfake videos are produced by artificial intelligence and machine-learning tools. Machine learning is a branch of artificial intelligence that permits computer systems to learn from data and "experience" rather than through programmed rules. These tools can merge, combine, replace, and superimpose audio, images, and video onto existing files, creating "fake" content which nevertheless appears authentic. Deepfake videos, for example, allow one person's face to be convincingly superimposed onto a video clip or image of another person. Thus, using deepfake technology, a video of an extra-judicial killing could be manipulated so the face of one individual was superimposed

15 *See* Janet Keddie & Alvaro Flores, International Criminal Court, The Use of eCourt Technology at the International Criminal Court (June 27, 2008), https://aija.org.au/wp-content/uploads/2018/03/KeddieFlores2.pdf (last visited June 27, 2023).

16 Prosecutor v. Germain Katanga and Mathieu Ngudjolo Chui, ICC-01/04-01/07, Prosecution's Communication of eCourt Protocol Metadata to the Defence on 23 June 2008 and Communication of the Original to the Registry (PTC I, June 23, 2008).

over the face of another, or the uniform of a non-state actor was superimposed over that of a militia group.

Concerningly, access to deepfake technology is not limited to the technologically sophisticated or state actors. As Wittes and Blum have noted, even elaborate and ostensibly tightly controlled "dangerous" technologies diffuse rapidly,[17] lagging only where the technology experiences a chokepoint as a result of its tangible and thus limited nature (for example enriched uranium) or institutional controls. In the context of deepfakes, such scarcity is not present, nor is it apparent that institutional awareness of the need to curtail the technologies underlying deepfakes is high. Indeed, at present, the most well-known deepfake technology, Google's Tensorflow, and Adobe which is incorporating AI into its programs (including Scene Stitch), are all available on a direct to consumer basis.

The result, Citron and Chesney argue, is that the capacity to generate deepfakes while already present for those with above average technological capacity will diffuse rapidly as the volume of publicly available deepfake tools increases, extending the reach of such technologies beyond specialized users.[18] Given the fragmentary and incomplete control of the digital environment by states, and the democratization of access to global audiences which social media and online platforms provide, this diffusion carries the potential for such content to reach large and international audiences, and to proliferate to such an extent that the real and the fake are difficult to differentiate.

While the implications of deepfake technologies for the integrity of elections and democratic processes are significant, such technologies pose particular problems for evidential integrity broadly, specifically including international criminal prosecutions. How then to authenticate open source evidence and thus fight against deepfakes and their impact on due process and the administration of justice?

Of course, the manipulation and alteration of photographic and video evidence long predates digital technologies.[19] However, prior to the emergence of digital technologies, a forensic investigator had only to compare an actual photograph with its negative to verify authenticity. In digital imaging, a RAW

17 Benjamin Wittes and Gabriella Blum, *The Future of Violence Robots and Germs, Hackers and Drones-Confronting A New Age of Threat*, (New York: Basic Books, 2015).

18 Bobby Chesney and Danielle Keats Citron, 'Deep Fakes: A Looming Challenge for Privacy, Democracy, and National Security' (2019) 107 *Calif. L. Rev.* 1753.

19 *See generally*, Mia Fineman, *Faking It: Manipulated Photography Before Photoshop*, (New York: Metropolitan Museum of Art, 2012).

file format is the counterpart of this negative. The RAW file is produced by a digital device and constitutes the original or unaffected pixel information of an image. Post-processing alterations of an image leave traces which are thus detectable when the RAW file is examined. Such authentication is complicated by open source deepfakes, however, which are made available in compressed formats that may cancel or fatally compromise RAW files such that the processing history of the associated content is either partially or entirely beyond reach.[20]

Moreover, the machine-learning algorithms and AI on which deepfake technologies rely are designed to constantly improve their performance. As such, authentication tools must constantly evolve alongside deepfake technologies themselves. This was pointedly illustrated by a group of researchers in 2018 who, led by Andreas Rössler, created a dataset using some half million images and developed an algorithm that could detect manipulated or otherwise altered images based on their dataset.[21] However, the same technology could also be used to improve the manipulation of the images such that detection was harder.[22]

In light of such challenges, the US Defense Advanced Research Projects Agency (DARPA) has launched a media forensics research initiative to facilitate the creation of deepfake detection technologies that automatically seek out and assess digital visual media to determine whether images are authentic. However, the resulting technologies remain in development and have not been tested.[23]

In a research context, Citron and Chesney have predicted that such problems with authentication may be ameliorated by the development of what they refer to as "immutable life logs" or authentication trials that permit a possible victim of a deepfake to produce a certified alibi credibly proving

---

20 Andreas Rössler, Davide Cozzolino, Luisa Verdoliva, Christian Riess, Justus Thies, and Matthias Nießner, *FaceForensics: A Large-scale Video Dataset for Forgery Detection in Human Faces* (Mar. 24, 2018), https://arxiv.org/pdf/1803.09179.pdf (last visited June 27, 2023); Paolo Bestagini, Simone Milani, Marco Tagliasacchi and Stefano Tubaro, Local Tampering Detection in Video Sequences, IEEE XPLORE (Nov. 11, 2013).

21 Rössler, *supra* note 20.

22 *This Algorithm Automatically Spots "Face Swaps" in Videos*, MIT TECH. REV. (Apr. 10, 2018) https://www.technologyreview.com/2018/04/10/143999/this-algorithm-automatically-spots-face-swaps-in-videos/ (last visited June 27, 2023).

23 Steven Melendez, *How DARPA's Fighting Deepfakes*, FAST COMPANY (Apr. 4, 2018), https://www.fastcompany.com/40551971/how-darpa-is-fighting-deepfakes (last visited June 27, 2023).

they did not do or say what is depicted.[24] Citron argues such logs are enabled by the introduction of wearable tech, and the internet of things more broadly, but might also be specifically created for the purpose of combatting deepfakes.

In the context of international criminal law, however, the solution based on a life log is problematic. Conflict zones and those in them do not necessarily benefit from the uninterrupted high latency internet connection necessary to produce an unbroken record of an individual's movements. Indeed, those participating in conflicts may actively seek to go "untracked" such that only intermittent and anonymous phone signals are available. This solution, moreover, presumes that individuals can be associated beyond reasonable doubt with a device, and that such devices are present – neither being a given in conflict areas and in less developed countries.

Perhaps the more encouraging avenue towards authentication lies with an industry partnership. Several of the market dominant platforms from which open source evidence is derived now recognize the challenges that deepfakes present. Facebook, for example, is taking measures to combat misleading or false material on its platforms including through verifying the sources of content uploaded to its platforms, while Google and Twitter have announced similar plans and policies against deepfakes.[25] Given the resources necessary to successfully detect deepfakes, it is likely that a partnership with an academic center of industry is the most practical means of ensuring the Court can consistently evolve its authentication methodologies in light of the evolving nature of the AI and machine learning on which deepfakes rely.

---

24 Chesney and Citron, *supra* note 18.

25 *See* Nick Dufour and Andrew Gully, *Contributing Data to Deepfake Detecting Research*, GOOGLE AI BLOG (Sep. 24, 2019), https://ai.googleblog.com/2019/09/contributing-data-to-deepfake-detection.html (last visited June 27, 2023); David McCabe and Davey Alba, *Facebook Says It Will Ban 'Deepfakes,'* N.Y. TIMES (Jan. 7, 2020), https://www.nytimes.com/2020/01/07/technology/facebook-says-it-will-ban-deepfakes.html (last visited June 27, 2023); Mike Schroepfer, *Creating a Data Set and a Challenge for Deepfakes*, META AI (Sep. 5, 2019), https://ai.facebook.com/blog/deepfake-detection-challenge/ (last visited June 27, 2023); Shirin Ghaffary, *Twitter Is Finally Fighting Back Against Deepfakes and Other Deceptive Media*, VOX (Feb. 4, 2020), https://www.vox.com/recode/2020/2/4/21122653/twitter-policy-deepfakes-nancy-pelosi-biden-trump (last visited June 27, 2023).

CHAPTER 13

Digital Video Evidence: Opportunities and Imperatives for the ICC

Dia Kayyali, Raja Althaibani and Yvonne Ng

1 Introduction

This essay discusses how the Office of the Prosecutor (OTP) of the International Criminal Court (ICC) can meaningfully and ethically integrate digital evidence into its work.

Digital evidence refers to videos, photos, text, and other data that is captured and stored electronically. However, the focus here is on how video can be used for justice. Digital evidence can be closed source – for example, a USB stick full of videos provided to an investigator by the person who recorded them. More often, it is open source, collected from public platforms such as Facebook and archived and verified by a third party. This kind of evidence presents myriad challenges: technical, ethical, legal, and practical. It requires expertise to gather, store, and authenticate; and, due to the use of machine learning algorithms to detect so-called "terrorist and violent extremist content," it is being wiped from the face of the Internet at an astounding rate.

Traditional protocols and guidelines have not kept up with the challenges and opportunities digital evidence presents. This essay concludes that to use digital video evidence properly, the OTP must keep in mind the following considerations:

- Video evidence provides only one part of the picture and cannot replace witness testimony and field investigations. It is effective when used to corroborate such evidence, especially where videos are created and shared by the perpetrators themselves.
- Experts in archiving and authentication must oversee the OTP's use of digital evidence. Either the OTP must contract with such experts, or they must adequately train staff in archiving and authentication. In conjunction with such experts, the OTP should update its protocols if necessary.
- The OTP must securely store digital evidence in compliance with GDPR and other relevant legal regimes in an encrypted database. The OTP must control access to digital evidence tightly; it should not be publicly

 | DOI:10.1163/9789004686755_017

available and the OTP should provide the same protections for this evidence as it would for any other sensitive evidence.
- The OTP should publicly acknowledge that digital evidence is of increasing importance, in order to encourage technology companies to take this into account when designing search algorithms as well as tools to detect and remove content from their sites.

Widespread access to technology has transformed the pursuit of human rights and accountability. Platforms like YouTube and Twitter serve as some of the largest repositories of human rights documentation and potential evidence of international crimes, created and shared by eyewitnesses and sometimes perpetrators themselves. This digital content can call attention to atrocities, grant access to closed societies and hard-to-reach places, and provide insight into the intent of perpetrators.

The sourcing and verification of digital content has become central to how journalists and human rights defenders monitor and report on human rights abuses. Increasingly, this content is finding its way into legal proceedings as evidence. When captured, collected, and preserved in ways that meet admissibility standards, digital content can strengthen legal and accountability processes. However, it also presents many challenges. In this comment, we discuss how and to what extent digital evidence, particularly video evidence, can facilitate the work of the OTP.

2 What Is Digital and Open Source Evidence and Who Creates It?

Digital evidence is "information and data of value to an investigation that is stored on, received, or transmitted by an electronic device."[1] It can be closed source, meaning accessible only to some people and stored on devices such as personal cell phones. It can also be based on open source information, which is "publicly available information that can be obtained through observation, request or purchase."[2]

Digital evidence encompasses a wide range of content. In this comment, we primarily focus on video and associated data, including user-generated and machine-generated data. Eyewitness videos taken at the scene of an

1 U.S. Dep't of Just., National Institute of Justice, Electronic Crime Scene Investigation: A Guide for First Responders (2d ed. Apr. 4, 2008), https://www.ojp.gov/pdffiles1/nij/219941.pdf (last visited June 28, 2023).

2 UC Berkeley HRC, Berkeley Protocol on Open Source Investigations (forthcoming 2020) [hereinafter Berkeley Protocol].

incident with mobile phones and cameras are a type of user-generated data. These videos can be created by ordinary people who happen to witness something, human rights defenders who purposefully document abuses, and perpetrators of abuses themselves. These videos are often stored and shared on mobile phones, computers, USB sticks, hard drives, and social media.

Perpetrator video is a term used to describe videos taken at the scene of an incident by a perpetrator of abuse or an accomplice, often with the express intent to do harm. The filmer may create and share the video in order to spark fear, promote hate, dehumanize an individual or community, glamorize violence, recruit new members to an organization, entertain abusers, share tactics, mislead the viewing public, or even simply to document their actions. Ultimately, the distinction between perpetrator video and other eyewitness video is who created the video and for what purpose.[3]

Unlike user-generated data such as a written description of a video, machine-generated data is generated by devices (like mobile phones) or platforms (like Facebook). Devices and platforms collect and generate data for purposes such as providing services and monetization. This machine-generated data can include personal information, usage and transaction data, and technical attributes. For example, one app on your phone could generate a username, a log of location data, and a list of other people you interact with using the app. Such data is typically retained by the service provider for a period of time, and may also be shared with third-parties.

3 How Is Digital Evidence Collected and Stored?

Digital evidence of interest to the OTP resides on various types of electronic devices that are owned or controlled by diverse stakeholders, who determine level and method of access. Closed source information typically resides on devices in the possession of content creators, such as portable hard drives, or on third-party services such as cloud storage providers. Content owners typically control access to their devices or online accounts, although devices and services vary in terms of their vulnerability to unauthorized access.

Open source information resides with the platforms that publish content or allow users to publish content. Content creators or owners typically

3 Raja Althaibani, *New Series Launch: Perpetrator Video in the Middle East and North Africa*, Witness Media Lab (Sep. 2018), https://lab.witness.org/new-series-launch-perpetrator-video-mena/ (last visited June 28, 2023).

upload content to these platforms for the purpose of sharing information publicly or to a closed network. For example, an eyewitness may post a video in a closed Facebook group, or a nontraditional media group may publish a video publicly on their YouTube channel. Users also commonly download and re-upload copies of open source content, creating many duplicates, which can complicate efforts to determine the original source of the content. Platforms display or takedown, and retain or delete uploaded content at their discretion.[4] Most platforms disclose data to law enforcement in accordance with their terms of service and local laws.[5] Platforms may authorize and enable users to download data, sometimes for a fee. In many cases, third-party tools will allow users to download data from platforms without explicit authorization.

Archives and civil society organizations that collect open source information employ both authorized and unauthorized methods of downloading from platforms. They also use different methods to identify, select, ingest, catalogue, preserve, and provide access to content. Some may use their collections for their own research and analysis, and publish the data or reports. These collections can potentially serve as valuable sources of evidence for the OTP, especially for open source content that is no longer available online due to deletions or takedowns.

4 The Role of Civil Society in Digital Evidence

In the case of eyewitness video, there is, by definition, a disconnect between the people who record and publish the content and the people who intend to use it to build cases for court. As with all international justice proceedings, analysts are often trying to understand video content without direct

4 *See, e.g. Terms of Service*, TikTok, ¶ 7, https://www.tiktok.com/legal/page/us/terms-of-service/en (last visited May 23, 2020) ("We have the right to remove, disallow, block or delete any posting you make on our Services if, in our opinion, your post does not comply with the content standards set out at 'Your Access to and Use of Our Services' above. In addition, we have the right – but not the obligation – in our sole discretion to remove, disallow, block or delete any User Content (i) that we consider to violate these Terms, or (ii) in response to complaints from other users or third parties, with or without notice and without any liability to you. As a result, we recommend that you save copies of any User Content that you post to the Services on your personal device(s) in the event that you want to ensure that you have permanent access to copies of such User Content.").

5 *See, e.g., Information for Law Enforcement Authorities,* Facebook, https://www.facebook.com/safety/groups/law/guidelines/ (last visited May 8, 2020).

knowledge of the local context. This situation risks harming accuracy and excluding people and communities affected by rights violations. Local and international stakeholders have been successfully working together to address these gaps and facilitate collaboration with innovative strategies, platforms, and new tools. Currently, some of the richest sources of expertise on digital evidence can be found in civil society organizations. The OTP should collaborate with these stakeholders, as well as legal and academic institutions such as the UC Berkeley Human Rights Center, both for specific cases where appropriate, and for general knowledge and advice on using digital evidence.[6]

4.1 *Civil Society Organizations Working in the Field to Collect Documentation and Evidence Collection in Collaboration with Investigators and Legal Experts*

- Founded in 2011 in Aleppo by a group of lawyers, school teachers, and academics, the Syrian Institute for Justice (SIJ) focuses on human rights and criminal justice.[7] They monitor and document violations and investigate crimes. They also support civil society through programs and training courses. The SIJ is recognized for their quality documentation and investigations, such as their investigation of the Queiq River massacre in Aleppo, Syria.[8]
- Mwatana for Human Rights is an independent organization that defends human rights through field research, creating reports and gathering documentation of violations by all sides to the current conflict in Yemen.[9] Mwatana collaborates with regional and international partners, such as the European Center for Constitutional and Human Rights[10] and the Global Legal Action Network (GLAN)[11] to investigate the potential

---

6 Shakiba Mashayekhi, *The Berkeley Protocol on Open Source Investigations*, UC BERKELEY SOCIAL SCIENCE MATRIX (Jan. 28, 2020), https://matrix.berkeley.edu/research-article/berkeley-protocol-open-source-investigations/ (last visited June 28, 2023) (In particular, the UC Berkeley Human Rights Center will soon be releasing a Protocol on Open Source Investigations that will provide important guidance on "the effective use of open-source information in international criminal and human rights investigations.").

7 Syrian Institute for Justice, FACEBOOK, https://www.facebook.com/Syrianinstituteforjustice/ (last visited May 8, 2020).

8 Luke Mogelson, *The River Martyrs*, The New Yorker (Apr. 22, 2013), https://www.newyorker.com/magazine/2013/04/29/the-river-martyrs (last visited June 28, 2023).

9 Mwatana for Human Rights, https://mwatana.org/en/ (last visited June 28, 2023).

10 European Center for Constitutional Human Rights, https://www.ecchr.eu/en/ (last visited June 28, 2023).

11 Global Action Legal Network, https://www.glanlaw.org/ (last visited June 28, 2023) [hereinafter GLAN].

involvement of various European economic and political actors in alleged war crimes in Yemen.[12]

4.2 *Civil Society Organizations Working on Aggregation, Authentication, (Emergency) Preservation and Analysis in Collaboration with Legal and Technology Experts and Other Relevant Stakeholders Working in the Justice and Accountability Space*

- Mnemonic created the Syrian Archive in 2014 as their first country and issue-specific archive. The Syrian Archive was designed as a proof of concept for future archives, to experiment and establish a working methodology and stable technical workflow.[13] Since 2014, Mnemonic has captured 1.4 million videos of the Syrian conflict, and made them available in a queryable and publicly available database. Mnemonic shares information about their tools and methods publicly. This includes their step-by-step process for identifying, collecting, preserving, and verifying data, as well as the technical tools they use, which are free and available online.[14] The Syrian Archive has partnered and collaborated with myriad international organizations and initiatives in the human rights and citizen journalist sectors. These include the United Nations Office for High Commissioner of Human Rights: Inquiry on Syria, UC Berkeley's Human Rights Center, Bellingcat, WITNESS, and, of course, a diverse network of Syrian journalists, lawyers, and human rights defenders. Findings by the Syrian Archive have been used by international organizations such as Amnesty International and Human Rights Watch, as well as by intergovernmental groups like the Organizations for the Prohibition of Chemical Weapons, and the Independent International Commission of Inquiry on the Syrian Arab Republic. Mnemonic is applying what it has learned together with its infrastructure and networks from the Syrian Archive to its new Yemeni Archive, and other locations and contexts around the world.[15]
- GLAN is a non-profit organization that pursues innovative legal actions across borders, challenging states and other powerful actors involved

12 European Center for Constitutional and Human Rights, Questions and Answers: Accountability for Alleged War Crimes in Yemen – European Arms Exporters' Responsibility Is a Case for the International Criminal Court (Jan. 2020), https://www.ecchr.eu/fileadmin/Q_As/QA_ICC_arms_Yemen_ECCHR_CAAT_Mwatana_Amnesty_Delas_Rete.pdf (last visited June 28, 2023).

13 SYRIAN ARCHIVE, https://syrianarchive.org/ (last visited June 28, 2023).

14 SYRIAN ARCHIVE, *Methods and Tools*, https://syrianarchive.org/en/about/methods-tools (last visited June 28, 2023) [hereinafter Tools and Methods].

15 YEMENI ARCHIVE, https://yemeniarchive.org/ (last visited June 28, 2023).

with human rights violations.[16] Since 2018, GLAN has been building and actively maintaining a database of Saudi/UAE-led Coalition airstrikes and cluster bomb attacks in Yemen.[17] Their user-friendly system enables the cross-referencing of large quantities of evidence and will be available to partner organizations seeking to promote accountability in the future. It brings together key pre-existing technologies to allow online user generated content and private evidence to be stored and viewed together. GLAN is also collaborating with Mnemonic's Yemeni Archive and Bellingcat on a new project that seeks to apply core legal principles to open source investigations, so that it can increase the reliability and usefulness of the evidence.[18] The methodology aims to balance adherence to procedural standards on legal evidence with workability. The information in the database can be made available to litigators, national investigators, and prosecutors, who can use it as primary evidence or as "lead information" for their own investigations.

- Benetech applies advances in technology, including machine learning and computer vision, to help sort, identify, preserve, and analyze evidence of abuses and potential war crimes.[19] The Benetech Initiative works with Syrian civil society organizations and supports the mandate of the United Nations' International, Impartial, and Independent Mechanism on Syrian accountability.

4.3 *Organizations Supporting Documentation and Evidence Collection on a Local Capacity Through Training and Resources*

- WITNESS works with civil society organizations and international experts – including the OTP – to develop guidance so that first responders and non-professional human rights documenters can capture and preserve video that meets the highest admissibility standards. This guidance is published through the *Video as Evidence Field Guide*[20] and *Activists' Guide to Archiving Video*.[21] The guidance, combined with trainings, results

16 GLAN, *supra* note 11.

17 GLAN, *Yemen Airstrike Evidence Database*, https://www.glanlaw.org/airstrike-evidence-database-yemen (last visited June 28, 2023).

18 *Yemen Project*, BELLINGCAT, https://yemen.bellingcat.com/ (last visited June 28, 2023).

19 *JusticeAI: Turning Conflict Data into Actionable Evidence*, Benetech, https://benetech.org/lab/ethical-ai-to-promote-justice/ (last visited June 28, 2023).

20 Kelly Matheson, *Video as Evidence Field Guide*, Witness (Mar. 29, 2016), https://vae.witness.org/video-as-evidence-field-guide/ (last visited June 28, 2023).

21 *Activists' Guide to Archiving Video*, Witness (Aug. 30, 2017), https://archiving.witness.org/archive-guide/ (last visited June 28, 2023).

in better coordination between civil society organizations and international justice institutions and helps provide a more robust evidentiary record.

4.4 *Case Study: Hasiam Omar Sakhanh*

The Swedish Prosecutor's Office and the District Court of Stockholm relied partially on video evidence to find Haisam Omar Sakhanh guilty of a war crime.[22] Sakhnah was sentenced to life in prison for his participation in the killing of seven captured soldiers in Syria in 2012. The rebel group that Sakhanh belonged to documented the execution on video. The video showed nine men posing casually, standing over seven shirtless men with hands tied behind their backs and backs bearing marks of torture. The rebels' commander recites a revolutionary monologue before ordering the killing of the seven men. Sakhanh, appearing on the far left, is shown toting a Kalashnikov with which he used to kill one of the bound men at his feet.

In 2013, the video became public when a former rebel provided the video to The New York Times.[23] The Swedish prosecution was able to build a strong case through collaboration with local stakeholders from Syria as

FIGURE 13.1 Still from a video taken in Syria in 2012, which was introduced as evidence in the Swedish trial of Haisam Omar Sakhanh, who was subsequently convicted of war crimes. Sakhanh appears at the far left.

22 Stockholms Tingsrätt [Stockholm District Court], 2017-02-16, B 3787-16, Case of Haisam Omar Sakhnah, Judgment (Swed.), https://www.ejiltalk.org/wp-content/uploads/2017/03/Stockholms-TR-B-3787-16-Dom-2017-02-16.pdf (last visited June 28, 2023).

23 C.J. Chivers, *Syrian Asylum Seeker Linked to Mass Killing Is Arrested in Sweden*, N.Y. Times (Mar. 14, 2016), https://www.nytimes.com/2016/03/15/world/europe/syrian-asy

well as other countries and institutions. This put the criminal act in the right context, showing that it was not seven cases of murder but rather a war crime. The prosecutors found additional evidence online, including a video taken shortly before the executions in which the rebels appeared posing with their captors and explaining where they had been captured. They also found information online that specified the time and location the prisoners were captured. Some of this information was posted by the rebels themselves. This evidence, and additional information, helped the prosecution establish a timeline, showing only 41 hours passed between the time the soldiers captured and executed the prisoners. The prosecution argued that there couldn't have been any form of quasi-judicial procedure or due process based on the circumstances and rapid timeline. This timeline, and the video evidence of the particularly cruel manner in which the rebels had treated and executed the defenseless prisoners, led to Sakhanh being found guilty.[24]

4.5 *Challenges and Key Considerations for Working with Digital Video Evidence from Closed and Open Sources*

Digital video evidence from closed sources usually resides on an electronic device or user-controlled cloud storage accounts. The biggest challenge for the OTP is identifying and reaching these sources, and obtaining content from them. Local civil society groups can play an important role in this respect, fostering connections between individual eyewitnesses or documenters and large international institutions. In the case of such collections, authenticity can often be established by more standard means – forensics can be applied to the storage device, people who came into contact with the device can be interviewed, etc. Digital open source videos present more challenges, including the staggering volume of content available on social media sites. However, it is that very availability that makes the challenges worth overcoming. Open source videos may be available in situations where corroborating or contextual evidence is essential to building a case but is otherwise impossible to obtain.

lum-seeker-linked-to-mass-execution-is-arrested-in-sweden.html (last visited June 28, 2023).

24 Christina Anderson, *Syrian Rebel Gets Life Sentence for Mass Killing Caught on Video*, N.Y. Times (Feb. 16, 2017), https://www.nytimes.com/2017/02/16/world/europe/syrian-rebel-haisam-omar-sakhanh-sentenced.html (last visited June 28, 2023).

5 Ethics, Security, and Privacy

The OTP must closely consider the related challenges of ethics, security, and privacy. Videos have multiple stakeholders, including the people who created them, the people who may be depicted, the people creating repositories, and the communities the repository is ultimately aimed at supporting. The OTP must consider the potential impact on all of these stakeholders who could be endangered by the creation of collections and use of videos. Videos that depict targets of human rights abuses in a way that makes them identifiable, or that make the location of the filmer identifiable, could lead to retaliation against that person or their family and loved ones. Fortunately, the OTP has experience in risk assessments and shielding victims and is well equipped to integrate these types of concerns into its protocols.

The OTP must also consider the ethical implications of pulling videos out of their original context, processing them, storing them somewhere else, and making them available for uses far beyond what they might have been intended for. This is possible with closed source evidence, for example, if an individual provided a collection to a civil society organization that then provided it to the OTP without communicating the level of consent to the OTP. However, this is a far greater challenge with open source evidence. Of course, the OTP must comply with local laws such as the European Union's General Data Protection Regulation (GDPR). The GDPR may apply to processing of videos and related content that include personal identifying information, and it is important that the OTP do a thorough analysis prior to creating any digital evidence database.

More broadly, it is easy to argue that once something has been posted on a social media site, it is public. It is even possible to look at the terms of use for such sites and argue that people posting there have given up their rights over their content. But this is both incorrect and ethically wrong. First, as noted, it is a far cry from posting a video on Facebook to having that video featured in an international legal proceeding. Second, few people read the terms of use on social media sites, and those terms are famously difficult to understand. Third, even if a video were originally posted online, putting it into a repository may allow it to persist after an owner has deleted it.

Finally, security poses a big challenge. Digital videos may be stored online or offline, directly by the OTP or by a third-party service. Different storage methods present unique security risks. Offline repositories are in many ways the safest method, as access to such collections is naturally limited, but they are still susceptible to physical destruction. Repositories can be self-run or stored on a third party service. Third-party storage relies on the security of whoever is hosting the repository, while self-hosted storage relies on good security knowledge and skills.

The OTP must assess potential risks based on the characteristics of the collection itself and those who might access it. They must consider issues such as how stored data is encrypted, whether to allow remote access at all, and if so under what requirements, i.e. using an OTP-issued laptop. Every person who has access to these collections poses another potential risk. Background checks for working with the Court are the norm, but someone must also vet adherence to minimum security practices, for example having a secure password on any device used to access the OTP's collection.

6 Discovering Digital Evidence

The large volume of videos documenting human rights abuses in conflict zones can be a serious deterrent to finding the right video on social media sites and in private collections. For example, with at least 500 hours of video uploaded to YouTube every minute, it can be difficult to discover relevant content if it lacks an informative and relevant title, description, or tags.[25] Videos that lack sufficient metadata or description to enable users to discover them can be unfindable, both on social media sites and in private collections.

Fortunately, the civil society groups identified in this essay have all created methodologies for finding content. For example, Mnemonic has a large list of trusted sources for video, and Benetech is using new technology to help human rights groups "deduplicate" content.[26] Without collaboration with civil society, most digital video evidence will remain undiscoverable. With collaboration, the OTP will be able to wade through the large volume of videos to find the right content.

---

25 Anmar Frangoul, *With over 1 Billion Users, Here's How YouTube is Keeping Pace with Change*, CNBC (Mar. 14, 2018), https://www.cnbc.com/2018/03/14/with-over-1-billion-users-heres-how-youtube-is-keeping-pace-with-change.html (last visited June 28, 2023).

26 Lale Tekisalp, *How Should Human Rights Advocacy Balance the Opportunities & Risks of Artificial Intelligence?*, PARTNERSHIP ON AI (Dec. 10, 2019), https://partnershiponai.org/how-should-human-rights-advocacy-balance-the-opportunities-risks-of-artificial-intelligence/ (last visited June 28, 2023).

7 Permanence and Availability of Digital Evidence

The permanence and availability of content posted on social media, and any content created by individuals, hosted by a third-party, and accessed on the internet, is precarious. Videos may be voluntarily removed or made private by the person who originally posted them. Most web hosts and social media platforms make no commitment to keep uploaded content available over time. In fact, through the process of content moderation, platforms actively remove content that violates their terms of service (the rules by which a user agrees to abide as a condition of using the platform).

Takedowns especially impact human rights videos, which sometimes contain graphic or violent imagery. Social media sites increasingly deploy machine-learning algorithms, i.e. artificial intelligence (AI), to detect so-called "terrorist and violent extremist content," putting human rights content at risk.[27] AI is not good at telling the difference between content posted to expose or document a human rights abuse, and content posted to incite or glorify human rights abuses. In 2017, YouTube's machine-learning-based algorithm removed hundreds of channels and thousands of videos documenting atrocities in Syria.[28] Mnemonic has documented this removal as much as possible, but there are doubtless innumerable videos that will never be counted because they were deleted so fast.[29]

The increase in AI content moderation is moving forward at a rapid pace due to pressure from policymakers in a number of contexts, including a pending "Preventing the dissemination of terrorist content online" regulation in the European Union, the Christchurch Call to Eradicate Terrorist and Violent Extremist Content Online, and more.[30] These policy conversations do not contemplate the evidentiary and documentary nature of content that could accidentally be captured by AI. They also haven't addressed the biased nature of lists of designated terrorist and violent extremist

27 Hadi al Khatib and Dia Kayyali, *YouTube is Erasing History*, N.Y. TIMES, Oct. 23, 2019, https://www.nytimes.com/2019/10/23/opinion/syria-youtube-content-moderation.html (last visited July 3, 2023).

28 Dia Kayyali and Raja Althabani, *Vital Human Rights Evidence in Syria is Disappearing from YouTube*, Witness (Aug. 30, 2017), https://blog.witness.org/2017/08/vital-human-rights-evidence-syria-disappearing-youtube/ (last visited July 3, 2023).

29 *Tech Advocacy*, Syrian Archive, [https://web.archive.org/web/20200508094114/https://syrianarchive.org/en/tech-advocacy/] (last visited July 3, 2023).

30 Dia Kayyali, *Human Rights Defenders Are Not Terrorists, and Their Content Is Not Propaganda*, Witness (Jan. 21, 2020), https://blog.witness.org/2020/01/human-rights-defenders-not-terrorists-content-not-propaganda/ (last visited July 3, 2023).

groups such as the US State Department's list of Foreign Terrorist Organizations and even the Consolidated United Nations Security Council Sanction List.[31] These lists are disproportionately composed of Islamic extremist groups, to the exclusion of white supremacist and other groups that are responsible for increasing levels of violence around the world. In fact, based on the experience of civil society, it seems that content from conflicts in Yemen, Syria, and other Arabic-speaking and/or Muslim majority places is far more likely to be removed.

Content takedowns are undoubtedly damaging online repositories of evidence. By example, the 2017 ICC arrest warrant for Al-Saiqa commander Mahmoud Mustafa Busayf Al-Werfalli was based largely on video documentation of seven incidents posted on social media. With this evidence, the Court was able to charge Al-Werfalli with committing and ordering murders as a war crime in Libya. However, less than three months after the videos were posted, the first video had already been deleted from Facebook. It would not exist today if it had not been downloaded and saved elsewhere.[32]

Platforms can also go out of business and shut down their services. Justin.tv, Yahoo! Video, and Orkut are just some examples of social media platforms that have shut down in recent years. When services go out of business, they often give a timeframe during which users may download their media content before it is lost.[33] Unfortunately, not all platforms give users adequate warning before they shut down.

While they are operational, many third-party platforms and web hosts create barriers to downloading social media content and its accompanying

---

31 *See, e.g.*, Cat Zakrzewski, *The Technology 202: Instagram Faces Backlash for Removing Posts Supporting Soleimani*, WASH. POST (Jan. 13, 2020), https://www.washingtonpost.com/news/powerpost/paloma/the-technology-202/2020/01/13/the-technology-202-instagram-faces-backlash-for-removing-posts-praising-soleimani/5e1b7f1788e0fa2262dcbc72/ (last visited July 3, 2023); Abdul Rahman Al Jaloud, Hadi Al Khatib, Jeff Deutch, Dia Kayyali and Jillian C. York, EFF, Syrian Archive, and Witness, Caught in the Net: The Impact of "Extremist" Speech Regulations on Human Rights Content (May 30, 2019), https://www.eff.org/files/2019/05/30/caught_in_the_net_whitepaper_2019.pdf (last visited July 3, 2023).

32 *How a Werfalli Execution Site Was Geolocated*, Bellingcat (Oct. 3, 2017), https://www.bellingcat.com/news/mena/2017/10/03/how-an-execution-site-was-geolocated/ (last visited July 3, 2023).

33 *E.g., A Fond Farewell!*, Bambuser (Nov. 30, 2017), [https://web.archive.org/web/20171130001822/https://go.bambuser.com/shutdown-announcement] (last visited July 3, 2023) (Bambuser was a mobile live streaming service that was used widely by activists during conflicts in Syria, Ukraine, and Egypt. When it shut down in 2018, it instructed users to download their videos within two months or lose them).

metadata. Twitter, for example, places limits on its free Search application programming interface (API) for providing access to Twitter data; a full Search API is available but at a monthly cost.

Even when open source information persists online, it remains susceptible to dislocation or so-called "link rot" – a term that applies when external links no longer point to their intended content. This makes information difficult to find over time, as links from web pages or documents are broken.[34]

8 Authentication: Reliability

Authenticating open source information requires significant expertise, time, and labor. Unlike digital content obtained directly from its creator in its original form, the original source of open source content is difficult to clearly establish. Online video platforms and messaging services typically do not make the video available in its original form and with its original metadata. Video posted online can be easily decontextualized or miscontextualized, making it very susceptible to problems of identification and verification, such as establishing the correct time, date, and location of the incident depicted. There is seldom a traceable chain of custody, making it difficult to assert that the information has been handled properly and has not been manipulated or altered.

Those intending to use open source content in criminal investigations and proceedings should approach this content with flexibility and adaptability if traditional means of ascertaining authenticity cannot be applied. They should take advantage of the wide variety of tools and methods created by civil society organizations to determine authenticity, and look to additional forms of media provided by eyewitnesses and other relevant and more closely informed stakeholders (digitally and physically) to help address information gaps.[35] Civil society groups like Mnemonic, for example,

---

34 *See, e.g.*, Jonathan L. Zittrain, Kendra Albert and Lawrence Lessig, 'Perma: Scoping and Addressing the Problem of Link and Reference Rot in Legal Citations' (2014) 127 *Harv. L. Rev. F.* 176, 178 (50% of URLs cited in US Supreme Court decisions since 1996 no longer linked to the originally cited information); Hany M. Salah Eldeen and Michael L. Nelson, 'Losing My Revolution: How Many Resources Shared on Social Media Have Been Lost?' (2012), *arXiv*, https://arxiv.org/pdf/1209.3026.pdf (last visited July 3, 2023) (Within the first year of publishing, nearly 11% of resources shared on social media are lost, and subsequently continue to be lost at a rate of 0.02% per day).

35 *See, e.g.*, *Online Investigation Toolkit*, Bellingcat (v5.1 Mar. 9, 2020), https://bit.ly/bcattools (last visited May 23, 2020) (Bellingcat's freely available online open source

combine both new approaches and traditional ones, to assess the authenticity of open-source information. Mnemonic uses a variety of information and tools to verify videos, such as geolocation and "cross referencing the publishing date on social media platforms (e.g. YouTube and Facebook) with dates from reports concerning the same incident."[36] Importantly, Mnemonic's knowledge of the context and landscape means they can rely on trusted sources, and, when needed, can assess sources' credibility by looking at factors like pre-existing knowledge of the source, past behavior, and location.[37]

Manipulated video in the form of "deepfakes" and "shallowfakes" poses a specific kind of authentication challenge, in addition to generally eroding trust in video evidence.[38] This false or misleading content may be shared on social media for nefarious purposes, or accidentally by well meaning individuals. It is intentionally created to mislead, and must be weeded out for collections to remain reliable. Deepfakes, and other forms of AI-enabled techniques for synthetic media generation, enable the creation of realistic representations of people doing things they never did or saying things they never said. It can make a realistic creation of people or objects that never existed, or of events that never happened.[39] So-called "shallowfakes" are less sophisticated but still highly effective techniques such as mislabeling a real video or lightly editing a real video.

Shallowfakes can usually be detected using well-established authentication techniques. Deepfakes are a bit more complicated. Creators of deepfakes have, until this point, mainly used them to target women for harassment, but their potential for muddying the waters of digital evidence is clear.[40] For-profit organizations are developing sophisticated and effective tools to detect deepfakes. Unfortunately, as outlined in WITNESS's *Ticks or*

investigation toolkit covers "satellite and mapping services, tools for verifying photos and videos, websites to archive web pages, and much more").

36 Tools and Methods, *supra* note 14.

37 *Id.*

38 Sam Gregory, *Deepfakes Will Challenge Public Trust in What's Real. Here's How to Defuse Them*, DEFUSING DISINFO (Feb. 19, 2019), [https://web.archive.org/web/20190222120511/https://defusingdis.info/2019/02/19/deepfakes-will-challenge-public-trust-in-whats-real-online-heres-how-to-defuse-them/] (last visited July 3, 2023).

39 Backgrounder: Deepfakes in 2020, Witness (Apr. 1, 2020), https://lab.witness.org/wp-content/uploads/sites/29/2020/04/Backgrounder-Deepfakes-April-2020.pdf (last visited July 3, 2023).

40 Henry Ajder, Giorgio Patrini, Francesco Cavalli and Laurence Cullen, Deeptrace, The State of Deepfakes: Landscape, Threats, and Impact (Sep. 2019), https://regmedia.co.uk/2019/10/08/deepfake_report.pdf (last visited July 3, 2023).

it Didn't Happen report, there is a real risk that these tools will not be easily available to civil society organizations that create repositories.[41] As this technology becomes more widely available, WITNESS will continue to advocate for solutions that are available to all stakeholders – in particular, groups creating databases of digital video evidence.

9 Managing and Preserving Digital Evidence

As discussed above, digital evidence lives precariously online, necessitating timely capture as a first step if the evidence is to be preserved. If the OTP does not have the capacity to actively monitor and rapidly capture evidence when it appears, it can collaborate with civil society organizations that have dedicated themselves to this effort. The OTP can develop protocols to request and obtain collected content from these groups, and provide guidance to ensure that chain of custody and evidence of authenticity is sufficiently documented.

Once obtained, maintaining collections can be expensive, time consuming, and require constant attention to ensure security and accuracy and keep up with changing technology. This can be challenging for institutions that have less experience using digital evidence. Fortunately, other relevant stakeholders in the justice and accountability space have been working to develop new systems, technologies, and workflows to help navigate the digital deluge of data.

Once the OTP obtains content, it must take on the responsibility for that content's storage and management. The OTP's preservation strategies should be customized to its circumstances, the nature of its collections, and the needs of its intended use. Preservation activities can take place on a spectrum depending on available resources. The key to any approach is that it be planned, consistently applied, and documented to ensure effective long-term preservation. Protocols must ensure data is not improperly altered or mishandled during its access, collection, transmission, and storage.

It would be a mistake to jump directly to thinking about tools and technologies for collecting evidence before first making decisions about *what* the OTP intends to collect and *how* it will be collected and processed, and then codifying these decisions into policies so that they are enacted

41 Gabi Ivens and Sam Gregory, Witness, Ticks or it Didn't Happen: Confronting Key Dilemmas in Authenticity Infrastructure for Multimedia (Dec. 2019), https://lab.witness.org/ticks-or-it-didnt-happen/ (last visited July 3, 2023).

consistently. The case of *The Prosecutor v. Jean-Pierre Bemba Gombo et al.* helps to illustrate the importance of an intentional approach to collecting. During the trial, the prosecution sought to introduce screenshots of a Facebook page as evidence linking Bemba's sister and another witness. The prosecution argued that:

> [The] documents are open source materials from Facebook and, thus, *prima facie* authentic and reliable. The authenticity and reliability of these documents is further corroborated by their general appearance, which bears indicia that they originate from Facebook […].[42]

The defense challenged this assertion, arguing that the screenshots could not be taken as *prima facie* evidence, since screenshots of a Facebook page are neither the Facebook page nor do they "originate from" Facebook. The defense argued that the screenshots neither show whether the images are actually from Facebook, nor who actually created the profile page, nor when and how the screenshots were taken, nor who appears in the screenshots.[43]

The OTP must therefore determine in advance how objects should be captured and preserved in terms of their technical, intellectual, structural, or aesthetic characteristics, to ensure the object's accessibility, usability, interpretability, and authenticity for the Court. By analyzing and identifying the significant properties[44] of the information it is responsible for preserving, the OTP can assess the relative importance of each property for its use in the Court, and to shape its policies with this evaluation in mind.

---

42 Prosecutor v. Jean-Pierre Bemba Gombo, Aimé Kilolo Musamba, Jean-Jacques Mangenda Kabongo, Fidèle Babala Wandu and Narcisse Arido, ICC-01/05-01/13, Prosecution's Fifth Request for the Admission of Evidence from the Bar Table (TC VII, Nov. 30, 2015).

43 Prosecutor v. Jean-Pierre Bemba Gombo, Aimé Kilolo Musamba, Jean-Jacques Mangenda Kabongo, Fidèle Babala Wandu and Narcisse Arido, ICC-01/05-01/13, Defence Response to Prosecution's Third Request for the Admission of Evidence from the Bar Table (TC VII, Sep. 10, 2015).

44 Gareth Knight, InSPECT, Framework for the Definition of Significant Properties (Feb. 14, 2008), https://significantproperties.kdl.kcl.ac.uk/wp33-propertiesreport-v1.pdf (The InSPECT Project usefully classifies significant properties the Court can consider into five general categories: content [e.g. the intellectual material, like words on a page], context [e.g. creator, creation date, and other metadata], rendering [the way the visual or audio elements look and sound], structure [the way pieces of content are related to each other, like pages or attachments], and behavior [the way the object functions or interacts.]).

Considering that the Internet and related tools are in constant evolution, the OTP should also assess how it intends to maintain authenticity of its stored objects in the face of technological change. Transformations like reformatting or media migration can be necessary for preservation or for rendering/playback, and can sometimes involve changing the digital object. The OTP must determine what properties are significant and what evidence of authenticity is sufficient, and choose transformation techniques and workflows that preserve an object's significant properties and authenticity, and document those changes appropriately. Considerations when making transformations might include, for example, the audiovisual quality of the transformed object compared with the original object, the structure of the transformed object compared to the original object, and the transparency or reversibility of the transformation.

Keeping in mind constraints in finances and manpower, the OTP must realistically assess what is involved in collecting and maintaining digital evidence over time. Preserving the availability, identity, persistence, renderability, understandability, and authenticity of a digital object requires much more than just saving its content. Additional information must also be maintained for each object, including reference, provenance, context, access rights, and fixity information. Data management is a key and labor-intensive function. It includes creating and administering databases, performing queries for access purposes, generating reports, keeping the data accurate and up-to-date, and ensuring the associations between stored objects and their metadata are maintained over time.

Unlike with non-digital objects, storage is also not a passive function nor a one-time cost. It involves storage hierarchy management, storage media replacement, error checking, fixity checking, disaster recovery, and locating and returning stored objects. It requires ensuring the persistence of intact and authentic objects, and the ability to find and retrieve them over time, regardless of their physical location.

10 Conclusion

Digital video evidence is not a technological silver bullet, but it is an extremely valuable resource, and worth the trouble it takes to "do it right." In close partnership with affected communities, video evidence has provided insight into atrocities in places like Syria.

The baseline in using digital video evidence has to be "do no harm." That means first assessing the need for digital video evidence in conjunction with people who understand local contexts. In many cases, the OTP will be able to find NGOs and groups of human rights defenders in a country or in a diaspora that can help with this. Next, it means creating a thorough collection and authentication plan and working through the steps to find, process, and store digital evidence, keeping in mind ethics, security, privacy, changing technology, and maintenance of such collections.

The OTP has many impressive examples to work from. Groups like Mnemonic can help the OTP properly handle digital video evidence, opening up new avenues to achieving justice across borders. Finally, as noted, the OTP should make the value of this evidence clear, in order to assist technology companies and policymakers in finding solutions to the problem of "terrorist and violent extremist content," that do not put this evidence in jeopardy.

CHAPTER 14

Cyber Evidence Repositories: Filling Critical Gaps for ICC Investigations

Alexa Koenig

1 Introduction

Over the past twenty years, people around the world have increasingly used online digital technologies to communicate and to document notable moments in their lives. This includes people who witness atrocities. Whether facilitated by the proliferation of the smartphone or the rise of social media, activists frequently share images and commentary about their experiences with others on the Internet – creating, in essence, a decentralized, digital archive of social phenomena, including possible crimes that may be of interest to the ICC.

This shift in documentation and communication towards digital methods has matured in lockstep with the ICC. In many ways, both the Court and a global online community of advocates and activists have grown up alongside each other.

And yet, the Court has historically failed to take full advantage of the vast digital resources at their disposal. This is due to reasons both within and outside the Court's control – ranging from a lack of funding to acquire the personnel and tools needed to efficiently and effectively locate, analyze, and preserve digital data; to a lack of internal and external processes for handling such content; to a lack of cooperation from states and others.

However, the Court has recently been making up for lost time, and – with additional funding and prioritization – is poised to become a global leader in the use of digital data for strengthening legal processes. This is especially true with regards to its investigatory uses of digital open source information – information available online that any member of the public can acquire through observation, purchase, or request.[1]

1 *See* UC Berkeley HRC and U.N. High Commissioner for Human Rights (OHCHR), Berkeley Protocol on Open Source Investigations (forthcoming 2020) [hereinafter Berkeley Protocol].

 | DOI:10.1163/9789004686755_018

In this essay, I explain why digital open source information is an important resource for the Court, how the Court has pivoted to better utilize this resource, what limitations the Court still faces in this work, and how cyber evidence repositories managed by external partners can fill a critical gap to help overcome some of the Court's challenges.

The Office of the Prosecutor (OTP) at the International Criminal Court (ICC) has made significant strides in its use of digital and open source evidence. However, the OTP needs additional capacity to fully realize the potential of digital content for evidentiary purposes – whether that capacity is internal or external to the ICC. Internally, the Court must invest in new technologies, additional personnel, and ongoing training to stay abreast of rapid changes in the digital information ecosystem. Externally, the ICC can benefit from continuing to develop strategic partnerships with states, companies, and civil society organizations to meet some of its capacity needs. Such collaborations should include mining digital archives created by a range of institutions to preserve social media and other online content at risk of removal from the internet.

2 History

Since its inception, an ongoing hurdle for the OTP has been securing sufficient evidence to corroborate witness testimony, in part because of the difficulty of getting to physical and documentary evidence quickly, given its ephemerality in remote regions and sites of conflict. There are several reasons for the delay, some of them outside of the Court's control: the ICC may not have jurisdiction until months or years after an event, delaying investigators from getting on the ground to conduct fact-finding. Additional constraints may be political, such as when a government leader opposes an investigation, or operational, such as security concerns.

This means that digital information that can be accessed remotely from the scene of alleged crimes may have particular utility for the ICC, and especially during the preliminary examination phase of a situation, when the OTP does not yet have full investigatory powers.[2]

2 Office of the Prosecutor, International Criminal Court, Policy Paper on Preliminary Examinations, ¶ 12 (Nov. 2013), https://www.icc-cpi.int/sites/default/files/iccdocs/otp/OTP-Policy_Paper_Preliminary_Examinations_2013-ENG.pdf (last visited July 5, 2023); International Criminal Court, Rome Statute of the International Criminal Court, art. 15, ¶ 2,

The OTP's need to find new ways of securing corroborating information took on a particular urgency in 2011, when the Chambers admonished the OTP that they needed to increase and diversify their acquisition and use of non-testimonial evidence.[3] Soon after, UC Berkeley's Human Rights Center began working with the OTP and a number of other NGOs, including the Open Society Justice Initiative, to host a series of workshops designed to explore potential uses of digital and other scientific content to strengthen the evidentiary foundations of cases. The workshops joined parallel efforts started by the OTP and others to bring together civil society organizations, technologists, and investigators experimenting with new models of fact-finding and verification, including remote sensing, and how to harness user-generated content,[4] such as the photos and videos that people were increasingly capturing with their smartphones.

In 2013, the OTP released its strategic plan for 2012–2015,[5] which underscored the Chambers' request for more "diversified evidence" from the OTP. The OTP explained that it had simultaneously begun "facing an explosive growth in its access to digital data," leading the OTP to "focus on expanding its capabilities to collect different forms of scientific evidence."[6] The document also detailed upcoming changes specific to the Investigations Division,

---

U.N. Doc. A/CONF.183/9 (July 17, 1998) [hereinafter Rome Statute] (describing the powers of the Prosecutor to initiate a preliminary examination).

See also Office of the Prosecutor, International Criminal Court, Report on Preliminary Examination Activites 2019, ¶ 11 (Dec. 5, 2019), https://www.icc-cpi.int/sites/default/files/itemsDocuments/191205-rep-otp-PE.pdf (last visited July 5, 2023); Alexa Koenig, Felim McMahon, Nikita Mehandru and Shikha Silliman Bhattacharjee, 'Open Source Fact-Finding in Preliminary Examinations', in Morten Bergsmo and Carsten Stahn (eds.), *Quality Control in Preliminary Examination: Volume 2* (2018), https://www.legal-tools.org/doc/6706c9/pdf/ (last visited July 5, 2023).

3 *See, e.g.*, Prosecutor v. Mathieu Ngudjolo Chui, ICC-01/04-02/12, Judgment Pursuant to Article 74 of the Statute (TC II, Dec. 18, 2012); Prosecutor v. Callixte Mbarushimana, ICC-01/04-01/10, Decision on the Confirmation of Charges (PTC I, Dec. 16, 2011); Prosecutor v. Bahr Idriss Abu Garda, ICC-02/05-02/09, Decision on the Confirmation of Charges (PTC I, Feb. 8, 2010). *See* Lindsay Freeman, 'Digital Evidence and War Crimes Prosecutions: The Impact of Digital Technologies on International Criminal Investigations and Trials' (2018), 41 *Fordham Int'l L. J.* 283 (excellent discussion of this history and the Court's response). *See also* Office of the Prosecutor, International Criminal Court, Strategic Plan June 2012–2015 (Oct. 11, 2013), [hereinafter Strategic Plan] (noting the chambers requirement that the OTP diversify forms of evidence).

4 *See* Rebecca J. Hamilton, 'User-Generated Evidence' (2018) 57 *Colum. J. Transnat'l L.* 1 (providing an overview of the utility and potential limitations of user-generated content as potential evidence).

5 Strategic Plan, *supra* note 3.

6 *Id.* at 22.

which included "enhancing its capabilities to collect other forms of evidence in addition to witness statements, in particular scientific evidence,"[7] including digital content. Soon after, the OTP began meeting with social media companies such as Facebook, YouTube, and others to figure out how to maximize access to evidence of grave international crimes being posted to those sites.[8] Meanwhile, companies like *SITU* Research and Forensic Architecture were experimenting with creative ways to aggregate open and closed source digital data to help investigators, lawyers, and judges better understand facts on the ground in atrocity cases.[9]

A former ICC investigator, Alison Cole, has played a key role in driving the evolution towards greater collection and use of digital evidence for ICC purposes. She has frequently served as a bridge between the OTP and NGOs, noting the "unique questions" raised by digitally-derived evidence, including the applicability of various rules of procedure and evidence and how they might need to be adjusted to accommodate new forms of digital evidence. As she explained in a 2015 article, figuring out how to effectively integrate digital evidence into investigations has greater importance for the ICC than for most courts. This is due to the barriers the OTP faces in collecting "traditional evidence, such as documents or subpoenaed testimony" given its lack of enforcement powers and its dependency on voluntary cooperation from friendly states.[10] As she explains:

> For the ICC, the 'best evidence' rule is far more likely to involve evidence processed through technological means [than for national courts], particularly evidence generated online and available through open-source investigations. The ICC is therefore most likely to be the first major global jurisdiction to focus predominantly on the newest

7 *Id.* at 7.

8 Alexa Koenig, *The International Criminal Court at RightsCon: Upping its Cyber Game*, HUFFPOST (May 11, 2014), https://www.huffpost.com/entry/the-international-crimina_b_4936346 (last visited July 5, 2023).

9 *See, e.g.*, SITU Research, ICC Digital Platform: Timbuktu, Mali (2016), https://situ.nyc/research/projects/icc-digital-platform-timbuktu-mali (last visited July 5, 2023) (examples of outputs that SITU Research and Forensic Architecture have created to support trials). Forensic Architecture, The Murder of Pavlos Fyssas, https://forensic-architecture.org/investigation/the-murder-of-pavlos-fyssas (last visited July 5, 2023).

10 Alison Cole, *Technology for Truth: The Next Generation of Evidence*, INT'L JUST. MONITOR (Mar. 18, 2015), https://www.ijmonitor.org/2015/03/technology-for-truth-the-next-generation-of-evidence/ (last visited July 5, 2023).

> emerging forms of evidence, including technology-based, cyber, online, and digital evidence.[11]

Cole provided the Libya case as an example of both the pressures the OTP was under to adapt to an increasingly digital world, and how information had changed in ways that were potentially relevant to the Court:

> The legal challenges [to using digital evidence] became most apparent during the opening of the ICC investigations in Libya. The extent of citizen engagement in fact-finding was unprecedented, with an overwhelming deluge of potential evidence uploaded on YouTube, Twitter, and Facebook documenting the conflict in real time. The complexities of social media verification reached crisis mode as high-stake ICC allegations of mass rape, allegedly captured on video and then removed from YouTube, were questioned by the chairman of the UN Commission of Inquiry. It became obvious that it is essential to build ways of managing technology-generated digital evidence and to join the ICC in preparing for the tidal wave of new technology before it hit the ICC and flooded the courtroom with untested evidence.[12]

Cole's comments about the need for, and potential ability of the ICC to pivot, proved prescient. In 2017, the Court reached a milestone with its release of an arrest warrant for Mahmoud Al-Werfalli, commander of the elite Libyan special forces unit, Al Saiqa.[13] As has been widely reported,[14] the warrant was the Court's first to rely heavily on social media content. This had recently been preceded by another open source milestone, the case of *The Prosecutor v. Al Mahdi*,[15] in which a geolocation report that pulled

11 *Id.*

12 *Id.*

13 Prosecutor v. Mahmoud Mustafa Busayf Al-Werfalli, ICC-01/11-01/17, Warrant of Arrest (PTC I, Aug. 15, 2017).

14 See, e.g., Emma Irving, *And So It Begins… Social Media Evidence in an ICC Arrest Warrant*, OPINIO JURIS (Aug. 17, 2017), http://opiniojuris.org/2017/08/17/and-so-it-begins-social-media-evidence-in-an-icc-arrest-warrant/ (last visited July 5, 2023); Alexa Koenig, '"Half the Truth is Often a Great Lie": Deep Fakes, Open Source Information, and International Criminal Law' (2019) 113 *AJIL Unbound* 250.

15 *See* Office of the Prosecutor, International Criminal Court, Report on the Implementation of the OTP Strategic Plan 2016-2018, n.43 (Aug. 23, 2019), https://www.icc-cpi.int/sites/default/files/itemsDocuments/20190823-otp-report-SP-2016-2018-eng.pdf (last visited July 5, 2023) (noting with regards to the use and aggregation of digital data that

together both open and close source digital information was submitted as evidence of the destruction of cultural heritage property by the accused.

Ultimately, this need and resulting capacity building has situated the ICC as a somewhat unexpected and relatively innovative leader in the digital information as evidence space. Given the dearth of national guidance, the OTP has created standard operating procedures for handling digital content – a generic version of which can serve as a guide and support for national courts and others who have yet to similarly pivot. The Court has also played an important role in the development of the *Berkeley Protocol on Digital Open Source Investigations*,[16] a set of international guidelines for using online open source information for evidentiary purposes that will be published this Fall by the United Nations Office of the High Commissioner for Human Rights and the Human Rights Center at Berkeley Law.[17]

3 Barriers to Securing Digital Content and Opportunities for Addressing Those Barriers

Despite this progress, the Court's ability to efficiently utilize digital evidence has limits. Thus, external partnerships are crucial to the ICC's functioning, just as they have been for other international, *ad hoc,* and hybrid tribunals.[18] For example, at the Extraordinary Chambers in the Courts of Cambodia, the NGO community provided diverse support to help meet the needs

"during the presentation of the evidence in the Al-Mahdi trial in August 2016, the OTP utilized an interactive digital platform to present its case. The demonstrative platform displayed 360-degree visuals and incorporated different sets of photographs, satellite imagery and video footage. After the presentation, the platform allowed the judges to further explore the platform and interact with the evidence themselves. Technology-based presentation of evidence was also used in other trial proceedings, such as in the cases of Ntaganda, Ongwen and Bemba et al. Also, the two pending warrants of arrest in the Al-Werfalli case relate to (execution) incidents that were filmed, with graphic videos posted on social media, with this visual record being authenticated and related to other evidence").

16 Berkeley Protocol, *supra* note 1.

17 *Id.*

18 *See, e.g.*, Peggy O'Donnell, Alexa Koenig, Camille Crittenden and Eric Stover, UC Berkeley HRC, Beyond Reasonable Doubt: Using Scientific Evidence to Advance Prosecutions at the International Criminal Court, p. 3 (Jan. 7, 2013), https://www.law.berkeley.edu/files/HRC/HRC_Beyond_Reasonable_Doubt_FINAL.pdf (last visited July 5, 2023) (noting that Court investigators "have frequently relied upon information and assistance from a wide variety of sources including governments, journalists, peacekeepers, human rights researchers, forensic scientists, and intelligence specialists").

of civil parties who participated in the trials or were impacted by historic events.[19] Similarly, the ICC needs and has been receiving state support, as well as assistance from the circle of civil society organizations that hover around it. For example, groups like WITNESS and *Videre est Credere* have been training individuals in situation countries to document atrocities with an eye to meeting the needs of legal investigators, while organizations like eyeWitness to Atrocities, TruePic, and the Whistle have developed tools for secure data collection and storage, and implemented hashing and other digital technologies to help provide some form of chain of custody.

One especially acute challenge that the OTP continues to face is how to manage the vast scale of potentially relevant digital data. As has been famously reported, as of the time of writing, approximately 6000 tweets are created every second[20] and more than 500 hours of video are uploaded to YouTube every minute.[21] However, ironically, at the same time that the OTP risks drowning in data, much of the most powerful information that is relevant to international crimes is at risk of removal from online public spaces, due to its (sometimes) graphic nature.[22]

To help navigate these challenges, over the last few years NGOs have been working with the OTP and social media companies to explore whether there might be a way to create an evidence locker for social media and other user-generated content. To advance that conversation, the UC Berkeley Human Rights Center will soon release a study of the types of digital archives that have been established to collect user-generated content, with the goal of exploring the strengths and weaknesses of these different types of repositories for holding social media content that has relevance to

---

19 *See, e.g.*, Eric Stover, Mychelle Balthazard, and Alexa Koenig, 'Confronting Duch: Civil Party Participation in Case 001 at the Extraordinary Chambers in the Courts of Cambodia' (2011) 93 *Int'l Rev. Red Cross* 503.

20 *See, e.g.*, Kit Smith, *60 Incredible and Interesting Twitter Stats and Statistics*, BRANDWATCH (Jan. 2, 2020), https://www.brandwatch.com/blog/twitter-stats-and-statistics/ (last visited July 5, 2023).

21 *See, e.g.*, Kit Smith, *57 Fascinating and Incredible YouTube Statistics*, BRANDWATCH (Feb. 21, 2020), https://www.brandwatch.com/blog/youtube-stats/ (last visited July 5, 2023); Anmar Frangoul, *With Over 1 Billion Users, Here's How YouTube is Keeping Pace with Change*, CNBC (Mar. 14, 2018), https://www.cnbc.com/2018/03/14/with-over-1-billion-users-heres-how-youtube-is-keeping-pace-with-change.html (last visited July 5, 2023).

22 *See, e.g.*, Avi Asher-Schapiro, *YouTube and Facebook are Removing Evidence of Atrocities, Jeopardizing Cases Against War Criminals*, THE INTERCEPT (Nov. 2, 2017), https://theintercept.com/2017/11/02/war-crimes-youtube-facebook-syria-rohingya/ (last visited July 5, 2023).

international crimes and is at risk of removal. Student researchers have created a typology of archives, which vary across a number of key variables. These include how an archive receives information, who it receives information from, who can access data in the archive, what kinds of content the archive ingests, and whether the social media companies' engagement with the archive is legally-mandated or voluntary.[23]

At one extreme are archives that receive content from the social media companies themselves as required by law, which the research team is calling the "Legal Compulsion Model." Using an example from the United States, Facebook and other social media companies must remove and submit information about child exploitation to the National Center for Missing and Exploited Children, which works with law enforcement and others to "help find missing children, reduce child sexual exploitation, and prevent child victimization."[24]

Another category of repository, which the teams calls the "Voluntary Partnership Model," receives content directly from the social media companies, but on a voluntary basis. A particularly illustrative example is the Global Internet Forum to Counter Terrorism (GIFCT), which was established by a number of tech companies to flag extremist content that their peers might want to know about in order to better detect and remove such content from their platforms. The GIFCT's mandate has recently been expanded and its structure reformulated in the wake of the Christchurch Massacre in New Zealand to "improve the capacity of a broad range of technology companies, independently and collectively, to prevent and respond to abuse of their digital platforms by terrorists and violent extremists," among other goals.[25]

Yet another – the "Aggregated Model" – compiles user-generated and other digital content from a variety of sources. An example is the International, Impartial and Independent Mechanism for Syria (IIIM), that collects information from various organizations and individuals. Sources include "the International Impartial Independent Commission of Inquiry on the Syrian Arab Republic, the UN-OPCW Joint Investigative Mechanism, states, international or regional organizations, entities of the United Nations system, non-governmental organizations, foundations, and individuals."[26]

---

23 *See* UC Berkeley HRC, Digital Lockers: Options for Archiving Social Media Content with Evidentiary Value (forthcoming 2020).

24 *About Us*, NATIONAL CENTER FOR MISSING & EXPLOITED CHILDREN, https://www.missingkids.org/footer/about (last visited July 5, 2023); *see also* Reporting Requirements of Providers, 18 U.S.C. § 2258A (2008).

25 *Evolving an Institution*, GIFCT, https://gifct.org/about/ (last visited May 4, 2020).

26 *Information and Evidence Collection*, IIIM, https://iiim.un.org/what-we-do/information-and-evidence-collection/ (last visited July 5, 2023).

As for its processes and the broader services it provides, the IIIM:

> [R]eviews the information and evidence – both inculpatory and exculpatory – already collected by others and identifies possible gaps [...] [to build] a more complete and nuanced understanding of the crimes and alleged perpetrators, for use in future accountability proceedings.[27]

While the IIIM will likely never provide digital evidence for an ICC case given the Court's lack of jurisdiction over crimes in Syria, it still provides an interesting example of how digital open source information may be aggregated, analyzed, and preserved to support legal accountability. And regardless of jurisdiction and subject matter, IIIM staff engage with the OTP in knowledge exchange that can be used to strengthen the quality of evidence for a diverse array of potential end users, such as national courts and war crimes units,[28] in line with its complementarity function.

On the far opposite end of the spectrum is the "Disaggregated Model," whereby a wide array of civil society groups run a decentralized set of repositories that share a focus on a particular conflict or crisis. One example is the Syrian Archive (now Mnemonic), which proactively identifies, collects, and preserves content from publicly accessible sites. Such disaggregated archives have a defined geographic, temporal, and/or substantive scope (for example, specific to Myanmar between the years of 2016 and 2018, or Syria between 2011 and the present). Under this model, diverse NGO s begin grabbing potentially overlapping data related to atrocities tied to their interests in real time – and in a race against either manual or automatic take down by third party sites (such as Facebook and YouTube) that host that content. At their best, these organizations bring much needed innovation and flexibility to the data collection space, for example, scraping digital content from social media sites and then preserving and indexing that data for future fact-finders, including legal investigators. This is especially needed as a gap filler between the occurrence of potential international crimes and when the OTP gets authorization to investigate atrocities (if ever), since the companies may not be alert to the need and/or incentivized to preserve that content. Just as precious physical evidence may be lost in the interim between crime and courtroom, digital content may prove similarly ephemeral – for example, if alleged perpetrators delete content they've posted

27 *Id.*

28 Elise Baker, et al., 'Joining Forces: National War Crimes Units and the Pursuit of International Justice' (2020) 42 *Human Rights* 594.

once a warrant of arrest is issued, or a social media company removes content that violates its community guidelines. These independent archives may therefore become the sole repositories of precious evidence, filling a critical hole in the digital information-to-evidence lifecycle.

So, in summary, why are these cyber evidence repositories so needed?

First, as discussed above, they are important for addressing temporal lags in acquiring or asserting jurisdiction and the intervening risk of loss.

Second, they can be helpful for mitigating the scale of digital content and making fact-finding more efficient. NGO s can curate user-generated content through digital archives, helping to ensure that relevant information – including exculpatory information – is available to safeguard due process.[29] Through these archives, civil society can play an important role in locating relevant digital data, finding signal in the noise, and creating a first rough cut to minimize the amount of information that the Court has to comb through and preserve. This is especially valuable when that curation honors the investigatory principles of objectivity and completeness. Those external parties ultimately assume the costs of sorting through and tagging that information, as well as providing the server space needed to hold the information, which can be helpful for the under-resourced ICC.

Third, such processes help ensure that legal requirements can be met, including (as mentioned above) obligations to disclose exculpatory information to the defense. If the OTP ingests large quantities of information without the personnel and equipment to adequately comb and index that information, they won't know what they have, and yet could be held responsible for any nondisclosure.[30] Instead, the OTP can make targeted requests of external repositories, limiting the risk of over-ingestion. Ultimately, so long as the digital information is coded and tagged for relatively straightforward retrieval, this "outsourcing" of some of the initial collection avoids the risk of court actors over-collecting information and being burdened with siphoning through large quantities of data that it does not have the capacity to mine.

---

29 *See* Berkeley Protocol, *supra* note 1 (more on key principles related to digital open source investigations). *See also* Alexa Koenig and Lindsay Freeman, 'Open Source Investigations for Legal Accountability: Challenges and Best Practices', in Sam Dubberley, Alexa Koenig and Daragh Murray (eds.), *Digital Witness: Using Open Source Information for Human Rights Investigation, Documentation, and Accountability* (Oxford: Oxford university Press, 2020).

30 *See* Lindsay Freeman and Raquel Vazquez Llorente, *Justice 3.0: International Criminal Evidence and Procedure in the Digital Age* (International Nuremberg Principles Academy, forthcoming 2020).

However, these repositories also come with major challenges. One is knowing that they exist – and thus who may be holding critical information. Another is standardizing what is held and how it is organized, so that the data can "speak" to each other, and so that legal investigators can efficiently locate what they need, when they need it. A third is ensuring that content has been captured and preserved in ways that maximize its value for court processes, for example, by including metadata or preserving some form of chain of custody, so that judges, investigators, and lawyers know how reliable the information is, and can weight it accordingly. This is where the *Berkeley Protocol* and any future public version of the OTP's standard operating procedures may be especially helpful, namely by setting norms and helping standardize collection and organization of digital data in ways that maximize efficiencies for court purposes.

4 What's Needed Next

First, when it comes to accessing information collected by others, the Court should continue establishing and formalizing relationships with external bodies that grab and preserve large quantities of content related to core international crimes as that content comes online. The benefit of this symbiotic practice is that the NGO can become an aggregator of content, while the OTP remains an important – yet nonexclusive – consumer. In order to make this work, however, the OTP needs to continue communicating with those external NGOs in order to:

1. provide critical feedback about how data can be structured in ways that increase its utility and overall value for court processes, and
2. strengthen relationships with organizations and networks that will lead them to relevant datasets in the first place.

Second, funders need to increase their support for these external actors, especially those that have a mission to support international justice. Otherwise, these archives may prove nearly as ephemeral as the content they gather – risking the loss of not only evidence, but the historical record of major world events. Many archives that have sprung up to preserve such content regularly struggle to pay for everything from staff to servers and yet are increasingly recognized as a critical link in the chain of accountability.

Third, the Court should continue exploring how the benefits of digital information extend beyond the OTP. Evidence collection is just one potential objective of digital fact-finding. While the Investigations Division has struggled, at times, to get the information it needs, other units have struggled with effectively communicating with the Court's diverse audiences. One way to think about the potential for utilizing digital open source content is in terms of how to maximize the flow of information in two directions: from users on the ground to the Court, but also from the Court back to users on the ground. Capacity building, which can include strengthening relationships with social media companies, may also be helpful for Outreach, or the Victims Participation and Reparations Section, for example. Such entities could benefit from:

1. working directly with technology companies to facilitate more effective digital communications with survivors in situation countries,
2. conducting online open source investigations to strengthen their analysis of country conditions,
3. providing ongoing training on open source investigations for ICC staff, etc.

Ultimately, all information collection and communication functions can benefit from appropriately tapping into digital resources. Given the rapidly-shifting technological environment, however, the OTP and other units need resources to regularly train personnel and update their capacities – especially with regards to how to verify the authenticity of digital content in light of the increasing risk of "deep fakes."[31] Each unit will also require a deep and broad understanding of:

1. what technologies are being used in locations of interest (for example, Facebook in Myanmar versus Weibo in China); and
2. how use of various platforms differs across everything from age to gender to class to the urban/rural divide.

For example, in the United States, children may use TikTok, while their parents hang out on Facebook. Ultimately, a careful and continual assessment of the technological landscape is key to effectively mining relevant information and deploying technologies to educate populations around the world about the Court's accomplishments.

5 Conclusion

Given an ever-increasing reliance on digital means of communication, the ability to use digital information for fact-finding is more urgent now than ever. While the OTP has come far since 2011, expanding its "expert

31 *See* Koenig, *supra* note 14 (more on strategies for addressing deep fakes).

capabilities in the field of voice communication, electronic data and cyber investigations as well as [their] reliance on partners,"[32] they still have far to go.

Relying on external digital repositories may be a powerful model for overcoming some of the ICC's temporal, legal, and financial limitations. While the ICC generally, and the OTP specifically, have made significant and important strides in their use of digital content, the ICC and the states that support it must continue to invest in such processes for the long haul.

32 Strategic Plan, *supra* note 3.

CHAPTER 15

The Fourth Industrial Revolution Comes to The Hague

Beth Van Schaack

1 Introduction

The information environment has evolved dramatically since the dawn of international criminal law (ICL) in the post-World War II period and even since the field's renaissance in the 1990s. The Fourth Industrial Revolution – which heralds the convergence of digital and physical innovations and the global diffusion of new technologies – is bringing about a transformation in human rights documentation, methodologies, and evidence generation (and manipulation) in a way that will profoundly impact future accountability efforts. Following the near ubiquitous penetration of hand-held camera-equipped technology, expanded broadband access, and the global reach of digital sharing platforms, today's world events are generating terabytes of open-source information – defined as user- or machine-generated data that can be obtained without the necessity of a formal judicial warrant or the use of clandestine or potentially unlawful collection practices (such as hacking).[1]

It is therefore crucial that the Office of the Prosecutor (OTP) of the International Criminal Court (ICC) develops the organizational capacity to fully capitalize on these new sources of potential evidence, particularly in light of the persistent challenges it has encountered in meeting the Court's applicable burdens of proof and the enduring threats faced by percipient witnesses to ICC crimes. The OTP can do this through developing in-house expertise, but also by partnering with trusted external actors motivated by the same

1 United States Office of the Director of National Intelligence, Intelligence Community Directive No. 301, National Open Source Enterprise (Effective July 11, 2006), https://www.hsdl.org/c/abstract/?docid=469452 (last visited July 5, 2023); *Syria Files*, WIKILEAKS (July 5, 2012), https://wikileaks.org/Syria-Files.html (last visited July 5, 2023) (Wikileak's Syria Files provide an example. It is distinct from other forms of intelligence, such as signals intercepts or human intelligence). *See What is Intelligence?*, U.S. OFFICE OF THE DIRECTOR OF NATIONAL INTELLIGENCE, https://www.dni.gov/index.php/what-we-do/what-is-intelligence (last visited July 5, 2023) (outlining the six categories of intelligence).

 | DOI:10.1163/9789004686755_019

quest to instantiate a robust yet fair system of accountability for the world's worst international crimes. This work must be undertaken in a way that anticipates future admissibility challenges (including on privacy grounds),[2] counteracts threats to the fidelity of potential evidence, and foregrounds the need to clearly explain these new investigative methodologies to the Court's judges, who may find it a challenge to adapt the frameworks with which they admit and evaluate evidence to the 21st century data landscape.

The situation in Syria offers an instructive case study for understanding the many new sources of information that exist, the emerging techniques and technologies that are available for exploiting them in the service of accountability, and the potential pitfalls inherent to this endeavor. This essay thus surveys the current organizational ecosystem and documentation efforts devoted to the war in Syria, with an eye toward informing the OTP's investigative, analytical, and prosecutorial practices. While the OTP has, in its recent strategic plans, recognized the need to up its digital game,[3] it is clear that more can be done. And some situations and crime bases in which the OTP is operating may not have generated the same magnitude of digital evidence as the Syrian civil war. In any case, digital evidence is no panacea; nor is it omniscient. Rather, it must be integrated into a comprehensive and rigorous investigative strategy.[4]

2 "Finding a Needle in a Pile of Needles"

The conflict in Syria has become the most documented crime base in human history. Information about today's events on and off the Syrian battlefield has been instantaneously disseminated around the globe through

2 International Criminal Court, Rome Statute of the International Criminal Court, art. 69, ¶ 7, U.N. Doc. A/CONF.183/9 (July 17, 1998) [hereinafter Rome Statute] (excluding evidence obtained by means that violate internationally recognized human rights if the violation undermines reliability or admission would seriously damage the integrity of the proceedings).

3 Office of the Prosecutor, International Criminal Court, Strategic Plan 2016–2018, ¶¶ 54, 96 (July 6, 2015), https://www.icc-cpi.int/sites/default/files/iccdocs/otp/070715-OTP_Strategic_Plan_2016-2018.pdf (last visited July 5, 2023); Office of the Prosecutor, International Criminal Court, Strategic Plan 2019–2021, ¶ 46 (July 17, 2019), https://www.icc-cpi.int/sites/default/files/itemsDocuments/20190726-strategic-plan-eng.pdf (last visited June 22, 2023).

4 Andras Vamos-Goldman, *The Importance of Professional Expertise in Gathering Evidence of Mass Atrocities*, JUST SEC. (Oct. 27, 2017), https://www.justsecurity.org/46355/rules-govern-evidence-gathering-conflict-zones/ (last visited July 6, 2023).

formal and informal media and social networks. From the beginning of the uprising, and in real-time ever since, citizen journalists wielding smartphones from the grassroots began uploading videos and photographs of the revolution, the government's crackdown, and the ensuing armed conflict at a rate never before seen in previous conflicts.[5] Among all this information are millions of video clips purporting to show the targeting of civilians and civilian objects, the execution of captured combatants and perceived opponents, the use of chemical and other indiscriminate weapons, and other international offenses. These have been uploaded onto YouTube and other social media platforms. This degree of citizen activity is particularly remarkable given the heretofore autarkic nature of the Syrian state. The sheer volume of information is overwhelming. Google has estimated that there are "more hours of footage of the Syrian civil war on YouTube then there actually are hours of the war in real life."[6]

Because the current information environment is increasingly internet-based and digital, human rights investigators have had to update their collection, storage, authentication, and analytical protocols.[7] Activists and their allies are thus exfiltrating and digitizing regime documents, taking witness/victim testimonials remotely on new communications platforms, scrubbing social media sites for potential open-source evidence, digitizing gigabytes of data that are then subjected to big-data and statistical modeling techniques, crowdsourcing identification and authentication information, generating three-dimensional crime scene renditions and other forms of data visualization to convey the full horror of the conflict, and securing potential evidence in encrypted digital vaults. All of these efforts are prompting, and benefiting from, innovations in technology around data management, secure storage and communication, optical character recognition or OCR (no

5 *See* Rebecca J. Hamilton, 'User-Generated Evidence' (2018) 57 *Colum. J. Transnat'l L.* 1, 5 (arguing that user-generated evidence is "the most visible sign yet of the fundamental disruption underway within the investigatory ecosystem" of international criminal law).

6 Armin Rosen, *Erasing History: YouTube's Deletion of Syria War Videos Concerns Human Rights Groups*, FAST CO. (Mar. 7, 2018), https://www.fastcompany.com/40540411/erasing-history-youtubes-deletion-of-syria-war-videos-concerns-human-rights-groups (last visited July 6, 2023) (quoting Google executive).

7 *See* Brianne McGonigle Leyh, 'Changing Landscapes in Documentation Efforts: Civil Society Documentation of Serious Human Rights Violations' (2017) 33 *Utrecht J. Int'l & Eur. L.* 44; Els De Busser, 'Open Source Data and Criminal Investigations: Anything You Publish Can and Will be Used Against You' (2014), 2 *Groningen J. Int'l L.* 90, 91; Lindsay Freeman, 'Digital Evidence and War Crimes Prosecutions: The Impact of Digital Technologies on International Criminal Investigations and Trials' (2018) 41 *Fordham Int'l L.J.* 283.

easy feat with Arabic script), machine learning and artificial intelligence, and digital forensics.[8] This includes technologies to de-duplicate, code, and organize reams of data and to make sense of the contents at scale. Journalists, citizen documenters, and advocates are not necessarily well-versed in ICL doctrine, investigative strategies, or the state of the art security protocols, and so NGOs – such as the Institute of International Criminal Investigations, *Videre est Credere*, New Tactics for Human Rights, eyeWitness to Atrocities, and WITNESS – are creating training programs, field guides, and technology tools to help citizen documentarians and others ensure that their collections achieve maximum utility (with manageable risk) in any criminal prosecution or transitional justice process.[9]

Much of the information recorded depicts what purports to be violations of international criminal and humanitarian law. Although this crime base information is valuable, when it comes to legal accountability, it is equally important – if not more so – to collect potential linkage evidence that speaks to individual responsibility. Linkage evidence can help identify not only the direct perpetrator(s), but also his or her confederates, co-conspirators, superiors, subordinates, and enablers, all of whom may be equally liable through doctrines of complicity, aiding and abetting, conspiracy, joint criminal enterprise, common plan, instigation, and superior responsibility, depending on the operative legal framework. Evidence of "key linkage themes" – the order of battle and the objectives of military operations; the functioning of a regime's political, military, police, or paramilitary structures; the procurement and movement of arms; communication patterns and logistical support; command, control, and communications (C3) structures; and the available disciplinary procedures – may be less

---

8 Enrique Piracés, *Collecting, Preserving, and Verifying Online Evidence of Human Rights Violations*, OPENGLOBALRIGHTS (Jan. 30, 2018), https://www.openglobalrights.org/collecting-preserving-and-verifying-online-evidence-of-human-rights-violations/ (last visited July 6, 2023).

9 *See, e.g.*, Craig Silverman (ed.), European Journalism Centre, Verification Handbook for Investigative Reporting (Apr. 27, 2015), http://verificationhandbook.com/downloads/verification.handbook.2.pdf (last visited July 6, 2023); Craig Silverman (ed.), European Journalism Centre, Verification Handbook for Disinformation and Media Manipulation, https://datajournalism.com/read/handbook/verification-3 (last visited July 6, 2023); UC Berkeley HRC and U.N. High Commissioner for Human Rights (OHCHR), Berkeley Protocol on Open Source Investigations (forthcoming 2020); Sam Dubberley, Alexa Koenig and Daragh Murray (eds.), *Digital Witness: Using Open Source Information for Human Rights Investigation, Documentation, and Accountability* (Oxford: Oxford University Press, 2020).

susceptible to open-source research.[10] Instead, prosecutors will still need to collect linkage clues in hard copy documents, electronic intercepts, and testimony (from witnesses, insiders, defectors, and experts). That said, investigators are undertaking social network analyses of social media platforms and other datasets to reveal connections between individuals (and their devices).[11] These sources can be marshalled to prove incitement to violence as well as membership in, or fealty to, an armed group, particularly in the form of enlistment records or allegiance videos.[12]

From the perspective of advancing criminal accountability, these developments present a number of opportunities and challenges. For one, this collection work is often undertaken contemporaneously, before evidence of war crimes can be hidden, tampered with, deliberately or inadvertently destroyed, or removed from public view by corporate entities enforcing their terms of service and community standards against terrorist activity, hate speech, and bigotry.[13] Because far-reaching justice may be years – or even decades – in the making, it is imperative that evidence of crimes is amassed in real time and preserved for when the time is ripe for justice and accountability. Civil society actors – including first responders – will inevitably start to operate well before the OTP can, or is invited to, turn its attention to an unfolding atrocity situation. This speaks to the need for the international community to capacitate digital documentation as soon as the threat of international law violations appears.

Additionally, there is the need to refine these raw data into more structured information and then, ultimately, into admissible evidence. The sheer quantity of documentation collected makes it harder to separate the wheat from the chaff, described as an exercise of "looking for a needle in a pile of

---

10 Ewan Brown and William H. Wiley, *What Can and Should the Next ICC Prosecutor do to Improve the ICC's Investigative Techniques?*, JUST. IN CONFLICT (Apr. 13, 2020), https://justiceinconflict.org/2020/04/13/what-can-and-should-the-next-chief-prosecutor-do-to-improve-the-iccs-investigation-techniques/ (last visited July 6, 2023).

11 Valdis Krebs, *Connecting the Dots: Tracking Two Identified Terrorists*, ORGNET (2008), http://orgnet.com/prevent.html (last visited July 6, 2023); Francesco Calderoni, 'Social Network Analysis of Organized Criminal Groups', in Gerben Bruinsma and David Weisburd (eds.), *Encyclopedia of Criminology and Criminal Justice* (New York: Spring New York, 2018), pp. 4972-4981.

12 Rao Kumar, *How to Digitally Verify Combatant Affiliation in Middle East Conflicts*, BELLINGCAT (Jul. 9, 2018), https://www.bellingcat.com/resources/how-tos/2018/07/09/digitally-verify-middle-east-conflicts/ (last visited July 6, 2023).

13 Ellery Roberts Biddle, *"Envision a new war": The Syrian Archive, Corporate Censorship and the Struggle to Preserve Public History Online*, ADVOX (May 1, 2019), https://advox.globalvoices.org/2019/05/02/envision-a-new-war-the-syrian-archive-corporate-censorship-and-the-struggle-to-preserve-public-history-online/ (last visited July 6, 2023).

needles."[14] Indeed, an abundance of information can paralyze action just as easily as a dearth of information can.[15] That said, this information, even if not fully dispositive, may be important for lead and background purposes. And, even absent an accountability process, the material collected remains vitally important for other transitional justice processes of truth-telling, vetting/lustration, restitution, reparation, memorialization, and institutional reform.

Even with all these documentation efforts underway, we still only have what two statisticians call "snapshots of violence," given the difficulty of gaining access to a complete record of the conflict and all its consequences.[16] As a result, the "dark figure of crime" in ICL – data on those who were killed or mistreated who have not been counted or accounted for – remains disconcertingly high.[17] Open source data is akin to a "convenience sample" that is inherently incomplete and only captures a fraction of that which is observable. In addition, some acts of violence are more likely to be recorded than others (e.g., public incidents with a large number of victims versus custodial abuses in clandestine cells) and conflict dynamics (such as siege warfare) make documentation of some events difficult.[18] All told, different conflicts will have different documentation dynamics, which impact the availability of recorded data.[19] Finally, there is the ever present risk of inadvertently relying upon mis- and dis-information.[20] As the saying goes: "the

14 SAVING PRIVATE RYAN (DreamWorks Pictures 1998); Keith Hiatt, Vice President of Human Rights, Benetech, Stanford University Panel Discussion on Syria (Feb. 13, 2018) (remarks available at https://humanrights.stanford.edu/news/panel-convened-technology-syria-and-human-rights).

15 *See* Patrick Philippe Meier, *Digital Humanitarians: How Big Data Is Changing the Face of Humanitarian Response* (United Kingdom: Routledge, 2015).

16 *See* Megan Price and Patrick Ball, 'Big Data, Selection Bias, and the Statistical Patterns of Mortality in Conflict' (2014), 36 *SAIS Rev. Int'l Affs.* 9 [hereinafter Mortality in Conflict].

17 *See* Megan Price, Anita Gohdes and Patrick Ball, *Documents of War: Understanding the Syrian Conflict*, SIGNIFICANCE, Apr. 2015, at 14, 15 [hereinafter Documents of War], https://rss.onlinelibrary.wiley.com/doi/pdf/10.1111/j.1740-9713.2015.00811.x (last visited July 6, 2023) (The "dark figure" is the number of events not counted in any documentation process).

18 Mortality in Conflict, *supra* note 16, at 10 (discussing event size bias in human rights documentation).

19 Documents of War, *supra* note 17, at 19.

20 Claire Wardle and Hossein Derakhshan, COE, Information Disorder: Toward an Interdisciplinary Framework for Research & Policy Making, 5 (2017), https://rm.coe.int/information-disorder-toward-an-interdisciplinary-framework-for-researc/168076277c (last visited July 6, 2023) (Misinformation is information that is false but not necessarily intended to cause harm. Disinformation is deliberately created to mislead).

first casualty of war is truth." Content creators can easily fabricate information and even metadata can be manipulated. The internet is full of information pollution that can distract or undermine a criminal investigation. The Syrian government, and its the shadowy Syrian Electronic Army,[21] has proven itself quite adept at falsifying and manufacturing information before and during the war.[22]

3 Actors and Action in the Field

When it comes to the Syrian conflict, much of this documentation, verification, forensic, and analytical work is being done in the non-governmental sphere by classic civil society documentation centers (such as the Syrian Archive and the Syria Justice & Accountability Centre); new private and for-profit entities (such as the Commission on International Justice & Accountability (CIJA) and Hala Systems, respectively); and investigative journalists pioneering open source investigations (like Bellingcat). By way of example, the Syrian Archive began as an offshoot of the Tactical Technology Collective with the simple goal of providing a safe information repository for people monitoring peaceful protests in Syria. It now works to support citizen documentarians through the use and dissemination of open source tools and replicable methodologies for collecting, authenticating, and preserving user-generated visual documentation (such as the Electronic Discovery Reference Model commonly used in domestic e-discovery). It maintains public databases of information on a range of international crimes being committed in Syria, including chemical and cluster munition attacks, disappearances, and airstrikes. Each video is given a unique hash value, or digital identification fingerprint, at the point of collection to help with de-duplication, geo-location, and authentication.[23] Cryptographic hashing is like a digital pixel fingerprint that will reveal whether there have been any changes to, or corruption of, the information and metadata and also help establish the chain of custody. The Archive has partnered with Visual

21 Stewart Kenton Bertram, '"Close Enough" – The Link between the Syrian Electronic Army and the Bashar al-Assad Regime, and Implications for the Future Development of Nation-State Cyber Counter-Insurgency Strategies' (2017) 8 *J. Terrorism Rsch.* 1.

22 Maya Abyad, *Regime Wages War of Documents on Syrians*, SYRIAUNTOLD (Mar. 31, 2017), https://syriauntold.com/2017/03/31/regime-wages-war-documents-syrians/ (last visited July 6, 2023).

23 *See* Douglas Carner, *Detecting and Preventing File Tampering*, FORENSIC PROTECTION, http://forensicprotection.com/Education_Authenticate.html (last visited July 6, 2023).

Forensics and Metadata Extraction (VFRAME) to use machine learning with 3D printing and a purpose-built computer vision/object detection program (a subfield of machine learning) to track the use of indiscriminate weapons or weapons remnants, such as cluster munitions.[24]

As another example, CIJA signifies a new model of "privatized" investigations (in the sense of not being sanctioned by any sovereign entity) focused on captured Assad regime and Islamic State in Iraq and the Levant (ISIL) documents with a focus on linking horrific crimes to specific perpetrators. Funded largely by Western governments, CIJA is staffed by veterans of international courts and military intelligence units who are focused less on amassing additional information about the Syrian crime base and more on collecting linkage evidence to the highest criminal law standard to ensure its maximum utility.[25] It produces prosecution-ready files, proto-indictments, and evidentiary briefs on responsible individuals and units, particular crimes, and the structure and functioning of the Assad regime and ISIL.[26] Both organizations have already informed domestic criminal proceedings involving events in Syria.[27]

In the multilateral sphere, numerous United Nations fact-finding efforts are also underway. Most important is an innovative new mechanism created by the UN General Assembly – the International, Impartial and Independent Mechanism to Assist in the Investigation and Prosecution of Persons Responsible for the Most Serious Crimes under International Law Committed in the Syrian Arab Republic since March 2011 (IIIM) – that has been tasked with consolidating and analyzing existing documentation with an eye towards supporting future criminal trials. The IIIM is acting as a central repository of evidence concerning Syria, although it is not necessarily trying

---

24 *See* Jay D. Aronson, 'Computer Vision and Machine Learning for Human Rights Video Analysis: Case Studies, Possibilities, Concerns, and Limitations' (2018), 43 *Law and Social Inquiry* 1188 (Aronson heads the Center for Human Rights Science at Carnegie Mellon University).

25 *See generally* Melinda Rankin, 'Investigating Crimes against Humanity in Syria and Iraq: The Commission for International Justice and Accountability' (2017) 9 *Global Responsibility to Protect* 395 (recounting history of CIJA).

26 Marlise Simons, *Investigators in Syria Seek Paper Trails That Could Prove War Crimes*, N.Y. TIMES (Oct. 7, 2014), https://www.nytimes.com/2014/10/08/world/middleeast/investigators-in-syria-seek-paper-trails-that-could-prove-war-crimes.html (last visited July 6, 2023).

27 Caroline Fehl, *The Partial Return of Universal Jurisdiction: Syrian Torturers on Trial in Germany*, GLOBAL POLICY (May 12, 2020), https://www.globalpolicyjournal.com/blog/12/05/2020/partial-return-universal-jurisdiction-syrian-torturers-trial-germany (last visited July 6, 2023).

to vacuum up all documentation from all sources, which might not only overwhelm the IIIM but also threaten smaller documentation efforts whose holdings are akin to their intellectual property. Rather, it is endeavoring to operate as a hub between multiple stakeholders to index or catalogue what potential evidence is out there and cross-reference it to the information it gathers directly in a gap-filling role. Un-siloing these datasets enables record linkages across the different collections and the construction of a more complete understanding of events.[28] Every piece of evidence is given a unique alphanumeric identifier (the "hash"), which will allow anyone to locate it from the main catalog and identify the "cleanest" version of any particular image or video (e.g., the version devoid of logos or watermarks, and free from tampering, etc.). The result of all this collection work is a massive record of international crimes being committed in Syria; the next question is how to effectively utilize these repositories of data in the service of accountability?

4 New Technologies and Techniques

These actors are all exploiting new technologies and documentation techniques that have revolutionized human rights documentation, reporting, and analysis.[29] For example, eyeWitness, which is affiliated with the International Bar Association, has created a smartphone application that helps users structure the gathering of evidence of atrocity crimes, including key metadata (i.e., data about data that is not necessarily immediately visible in

---

28 *See* Megan Price, Anita Gohdes and Patrick Ball, HRDAG, Updated Statistical Analysis of Documentation of Killings in the Syrian Arab Republic (Aug. 2014), https://www.ohchr.org/sites/default/files/Documents/Countries/SY/HRDAGUpdatedReportAug2014.pdf (last visited July 6, 2023) (In work commissioned by the UN High Commissioner for Human Rights, the Human Rights Data Analysis Group (HRDAG) undertook this with casualty data collected early in the conflict. From these data, HRDAG was able to shed light on the dark figure of victims and estimate the total number of casualties through a process of multiple systems estimation). *See* Amelia Hoover Green, *Multiple Systems Estimation: The Basics,* HRDAG (Mar. 11, 2013), https://hrdag.org/2013/03/11/mse-the-basics/ (last visited July 6, 2023); *See* Documents of War, *supra* note 17, at 16.

29 Eric Reidy, *Technology Exposed Syrian War Crimes Over and Over. Was it for Nothing?*, MIT TECH. REV. (Oct. 18, 2019), https://www.technologyreview.com/2019/10/18/132296/technology-exposed-syrian-war-crimes-over-and-over-was-it-for-nothing/ (last visited July 6, 2023).

a digital artifact).[30] At the source of capture, the app creates a chain of cryptographic and digital fingerprints that render the data resistant to editing. The information assembled using the app is automatically uploaded into a secure evidence vault, which creates a certifiable chain of custody. The platform also allows for verification and analysis by international lawyers with an eye towards enhancing its utility in accountability processes. Similarly, Physicians for Human Rights has created MediCapt, a similar mobile solution, that helps convert a standardized medical intake form into potential forensic documentation to secure evidence of rape and other forms of sexual assault on an encrypted and high-fidelity digital platform. A secure mobile camera facilitates the preservation of evidence of physical injuries, and a mapping feature tracks geographic trends.[31]

Technologists at organizations like Benetech are working to develop software tools to expedite and mechanize processes of collection, verification, prioritization, and analysis. Benetech's Connected Civil Society Initiative is using machine learning algorithms to automate the analysis of videos collected by Syrian documentation organizations, including through clustering, distance mapping, matching, and de-duplicating videos that are related or depict the same event(s). It has also designed a system to extract key metadata and has developed a set of archetypal classifiers to expedite object and audio recognition. These new tools will enable NGOs and the IIIM to compare their holdings, find the "best evidence" of a particular incident, and avoid duplication of efforts. Data visualization tools allow bulk information to be disaggregated along desired characteristics (such as the age and sex of victims or cause of death) and conveyed to multiple audiences – including the general public, policymakers, and judges – in compelling and accessible ways.[32]

Academic institutions are making key contributions to this field. The Syrian Archive has partnered with UC Berkeley's Human Rights Investigations Lab and Amnesty International's Digital Verification Corps to harness student energy around the conflict and train the next generation of human

30 *See* Mark S. Ellis, 'Shifting the Paradigm – Bringing to Justice Those Who Commit Human Rights Atrocities' (2015) 47 *Case W. Rsrv. J. Int'l L.* 265 (discussing the app's origins).

31 *PHR's Mobile App MediCapt Puts Cutting Edge Technology in the Service of Preventing Sexual Violence*, PHYSICIANS FOR HUM. RTS., https://phr.org/issues/sexual-violence/medicapt/ (last visited July 6, 2023).

32 *See* Katharina Rall, Margaret L. Satterthwaite, Anshul Vikram Pandey, John Emerson, Jeremy Boy, Oded Nov and Enrico Bertini, 'Data Visualization for Human Rights Advocacy' (2016) 8 *J. Hum. Rts. Prac.* 171.

rights advocates and investigators.[33] Researchers at Carnegie Mellon University have developed the Event Labeling Through Analytic Media Processing (E-LAMP) system. E-LAMP harnesses dynamic machine learning technologies to identify predefined events and key objects within multimedia images.[34] The system can undertake color, shadow, illumination, and photogrammetry (taking measurements from images) analysis and be "taught" to identify significant semantic concepts ("classifiers") through a user interface. These can be objects (such as weapons, smoke plumes, or vehicles), actions (e.g., tank movements or explosions), text (through OCR), speech acts and sounds (like helicopters or gunfire), human behaviors (such as running, screaming, or crying), and classes of people (including soldiers, corpses, or children).[35] Researchers used over five hundred videos from Aleppo, Syria, to train the system to recognize, with a high degree of accuracy, key munitions being deployed in the Syrian battlespace.

Human rights investigations have become increasingly interdisciplinary, borrowing from tools and techniques developed in other contexts. Forensic Architecture (FA), a multidisciplinary collective of investigators based at the University of London, has employed architectural rendering software to synchronize multimedia information and create groundbreaking computer models of potential crime scenes.[36] These can shed light on the circumstances of particular armed attacks on civilians and civilian objects. When it

33 *See, e.g.*, Anna Banchik et al., Human Rights Investigation Lab, Berkeley HRC, Chemical Strikes on Al-Lataminah, March 25 & 30, 2017 (Jan. 18, 2018), [https://web.archive.org/web/20200414090721/https://humanrights.berkeley.edu/sites/default/files/publications/hama_report-_final_190111.pdf] (last visited July 6, 2023) (analyzing open source visual content regarding attacks in March 2017); Amnesty Int'l, *No Where Is Safe for Us: Unlawful Attacks and Mass Displacement in North-West Syria*, Index No. MDE 24/2089/2020 (May 6, 2020), https://www.amnesty.org/en/documents/mde24/2089/2020/en/ (last visited July 6, 2023).

34 Wei Tong, et al., 'E-LAMP: Integration of Innovative Ideas for Multimedia Event Detection' (2013) 25 *Machine Vision and Applications* 5.

35 Grigorios Kalliatakis, Shoaib Ehsan, Maria Fasli and Klaus D. McDonald-Maier, *DisplaceNet: Recognising Displaced People from Images by Exploiting Dominance Level*, ARXIV (May 3, 2019), https://arxiv.org/pdf/1905.02025.pdf (last visited July 6, 2023); Grigorios Kalliatakis, Shoaib Ehsan, Aleš Leonardis, Maria Fasli and Klaus D. McDonald-Maier, 'Exploring Object-Centric and Scene-Centric CNN Features and their Complementarity for Human Rights Violations Recognition in Images' (2019) 7 *IEEE Access* 10045; Grigorios Kalliatakis, Shoaib Ehsan, Maria Fasli and Klaus D. McDonald-Maier, *GET-AID: Visual Recognition of Human Rights Abuses via Global Emotional Traits*, ARXIV (Feb. 11, 2019), https://arxiv.org/pdf/1902.03817.pdf (last visited July 6, 2023).

36 SITU Research, ICC Digital Platform: Timbuktu, Mali (2016), https://situ.nyc/research/projects/icc-digital-platform-timbuktu-mali (last visited July 5, 2023) (The OTP has

comes to Syria, for example, FA has recreated the sites of chemical attacks and built a three-dimensional rendition of Saydnaya prison where detainees have credibly alleged they were tortured, all by using spatial imagery, computer aided design/architectural software, and acoustic modeling.[37] In addition, FA examined the destruction of the Sayidina Omar Ibn Al-Khattab Mosque in al-Jinah, Syria, which was hit by US airstrikes on March 16, 2017. The United States originally denied having caused multiple civilian casualties and insisted that the venue was a community hall where regional members of Al Qaida were meeting on the night in question. Based on a reconstruction of the building prior to the attack and other data, FA concluded that the building was clearly a mosque being used for religious purposes and that thirty-eight civilians were killed.[38] The United States eventually admitted that the strike had hit part of a "mosque complex" and that "a more deliberative pre-strike analysis should have identified that the target was part of a religious compound,"[39] but continued to argue that appropriate precautions were undertaken.[40]

Human rights advocates are attempting to rehabilitate and augment the utility of satellite imagery for human rights purposes in Syria and elsewhere.[41] Such imagery can support the identification of observables and

---

already explored the potentiality of 3D reconstruction of crime scenes in connection with the destruction of sacred tombs in Mali).

37 Michael Kimmelman, *Forensics Helps Widen Architecture's Mission*, N.Y. TIMES (Apr. 6, 2018), https://www.nytimes.com/2018/04/06/arts/design/forensic-architecture-human-rights.html (last visited July 6, 2023).

38 *See* Christiaan Triebert, *The Al-Jinah Mosque Complex Bombing – New Information and Timeline*, BELLINGCAT (Apr. 18, 2017), https://www.bellingcat.com/news/mena/2017/04/18/al-jinah-new-info-and-timeline/ (last visited July 6, 2023) (Forensic Architecture worked in conjunction with Bellingcat and Human Rights Watch in this investigation). Human Rights Watch, Attack on the Omar Ibn al-Khattab Mosque: US Authorities' Failure to Take Adequate Precautions (Apr. 18, 2017), https://features.hrw.org/features/slider_features/Syria-mosque-mar2017/index.html (last visited July 6, 2023).

39 *Transcript of Pentagon's Al Jinah Investigation Media Briefing*, AIRWARS (Jun. 27, 2017), https://airwars.org/news/transcript-of-al-jinah-investigation-briefing/ (last visited July 6, 2023).

40 *See* Shane R. Reeves and Ward Narramore, *The UNHRC Commission of Inquiry on Syria Misapplies the Law of Armed Conflict*, LAWFARE (Sep. 15, 2017), https://www.lawfaremedia.org/article/unhrc-commission-inquiry-syria-misapplies-law-armed-conflict (last visited July 6, 2023).

41 *See, e.g., Syria: New Satellite Images Show Homs Shelling* HUM. RTS. WATCH (Mar. 2, 2012), https://www.hrw.org/news/2012/03/02/syria-new-satellite-images-show-homs-shelling (last visited July 6, 2023) (discussing evidence of the bombardment of the Baba Amr neighborhood of Homs).

points of interests, the construction of a timeline or before-and-after comparisons, the creation of geographic configurations of a crime scene, and even the development of a narrative of intent where one area or group is singled out for violence.[42] For example, Amnesty International has forged a partnership with the Geospatial Technologies and Human Rights Project of the American Association for the Advancement of Science, and the Standby Volunteer Task Force Satellite Team, an online volunteer community established in 2010 at the International Conference of Crisis Mapping, to provide dedicated live mapping support to organizations in the humanitarian and human rights space, including in Syria.[43] Using high-resolution imagery from DigitalGlobe (now Maxar), this team has employed crowd-tasking to document the presence of regime forces and armored vehicles in civilian areas and identify the commission of potential war crimes, such as the destruction of civilian objects[44] in Aleppo and elsewhere, through before-and-after damage assessment.[45] The project depends largely on volunteers who are recruited through micro-tasking platforms (starting with Tomnod, also succeeded by Maxar), which invite volunteers to solve real-world problems using satellite imagery.

Crowdsourcing (a form of non-probability sampling) offers a useful way to aggregate, verify, and authenticate data of relevance to accountability. It is valuable because it can occur in real-time (or close to real-time) in constrained collection environments.[46] The Syrian Tracker project of Humanitarian Tracker has been crowdsourcing and live mapping the Syrian conflict

42 *See generally* Ben Yunmo Wang, Nathaniel A. Raymond, Gabrielle Gould and Isaac Baker, 'Problems from Hell, Solutions in the Heavens?: Identifying Obstacles and Opportunities for Employing Geospatial Technologies to Document and Mitigate Mass Atrocities' (2013) 2 *Stability* 1, 6–12; Katia Savchuk, *All the Dead We Cannot See: How a Tech Geek Is Using Machine Learning to Hold Human Rights Abusers Accountable*, PACIFIC STANDARD (Dec. 28, 2018), https://psmag.com/social-justice/using-machine-learning-to-hold-human-rights-abusers-accountable (last visited July 6, 2023).

43 *See* Patrick Philippe Meier, *Combining Crowdsourced Satellite Imagery Analysis with Crisis Reporting: An Update on Syria*, IREVOLUTIONS (Sep. 19, 2011), https://irevolutions.org/2011/09/19/crowdsourcing-update-on-syria/ (last visited July 6, 2023).

44 *Satellite Imagery Analysis for Urban Conflict Documentation: Aleppo, Syria*, AAAS (Jun. 27, 2017), https://www.aaas.org/resources/satellite-imagery-analysis-urban-conflict-documentation-aleppo-syria (last visited July 6, 2023).

45 Meier, *supra* note 43.

46 *See generally* The Engine Room, Benetech and Amnesty Int'l, DATNAV: How to Navigate Digital Data for Human Rights Research (Jun. 2016), https://benetech.org/wp-content/uploads/2017/08/en-datnav-report_high-quality_web_1-31-2017.pdf (last visited July 6, 2023).

since April 2011.[47] In an effort to consolidate eye witness accounts and leverage the work of citizen reporters, it accepts anonymous reports – via email, Twitter, phone, the website, and other encrypted means – which are tagged and catalogued by type of attack. Where possible, these contributions are then cross-referenced with media reports and other validation sources using data mining tools. Only a small percentage of submissions are published, given limited resources for de-duplication and verification. The site is built upon the crowdmap technology first developed by Ushahidi to track post-election violence in Kenya.[48]

Crowdsourcing visual images can be used to identify victims and perpetrators. In January 2014, a number of media outlets began circulating gruesome photographs that had been exfiltrated by a former military photographer who worked in Damascus hospitals – an extraordinary cache of government-generated proof of human rights abuses in Syria. The defector, code-named "Caesar" to protect his identity, had smuggled out of the country, on thumb drives and his phone, over fifty thousand images depicting more than eleven thousand victims. Half of the photos depicted cadavers showing signs of torture, starvation, and mistreatment (the other half are likely battlefield deaths).[49] The Syrian Association for Missing and Conscience Detainees posted the entire collection online so that people whose loved ones had disappeared could search for and identify the victims. This approach generated some controversy given the privacy rights of victims and the risk of traumatization to family members.[50] Other Syrian NGOs, such as the Syrian Network for Human Rights, notified the families if they were able to identify the victims.[51] On the other side of the aisle, Adalmaz

47 *See* Lorenzo Franceschi-Bicchierai, *How Data Scientists Are Uncovering War Crimes in Syria*, MASHABLE (Aug. 8, 2014), https://mashable.com/archive/data-scientists-uncover-syrian-war-crimes (last visited July 6, 2023).

48 Will Haydon, *#IndexAwards2015: Digital Activism Nominee Syria Tracker*, INDEX ON CENSORSHIP (Mar. 11, 2015), http://www.indexoncensorship.org/2015/03/indexawards2015-digital-activism-nominee-syria-tracker/ (last visited July 6, 2023).

49 Priyanka Motaparthy and Nadim Houry, Human Rights Watch, If the Dead Could Speak: Mass Death and Torture in Syria's Detention Facilities (Dec. 16, 2015), https://www.hrw.org/report/2015/12/16/if-dead-could-speak/mass-deaths-and-torture-syrias-detention-facilities (last visited July 6, 2023).

50 Syria Justice and Accountability Centre, The Publication of Victims' Photographs Online Jeopardizes Security and Accountability in Syria (Mar. 26, 2015), https://syriaaccountability.org/the-publication-of-victims-photographs-online-jeopardizes-security-and-accountability-in-syria/ (last visited July 6, 2023).

51 Syrian Network for Human Rights, Analytical Study About the Leaked Pictures of Torture Victims in Syrian Military Hospitals: "The Photographed Holocaust" 5 (Oct. 15,

is crowdsourcing photographs of fighters to identify anonymous perpetrators and generate leads for law enforcement. The loved ones of one of the victims depicted in the Caesar photos and their lawyers at the Guernica Center for International Justice initiated the first criminal case against Syrian officials in domestic courts, although the case was dismissed on jurisdictional grounds.

Where these techniques and technologies are potentially game changing is in processing and triaging bulk collections and large datasets. Eventually, however, there can be no doubt that manual analysis by experts – of satellite imagery or the outputs of machine learning algorithms, which are only probabilistic[52] – will be necessary before the OTP can rely on this information for its purposes.[53] Expert testimony will be crucial not only to contextualize the results of these analytical processes but also to offer attestations of validity and to authenticate the technology and methodologies employed. Indeed, according to a recent report from OpenGlobalRights, the key determinant of the admissibility of satellite imagery in human rights litigation is the ability of a human witness to testify credibly about what the images depict.[54]

It is hoped that much of this evidence will be considered self-authenticating such that the original source will not always need to testify in Court (let alone be identified).[55] This can lessen the dependence on witness testimony by offering corroborating evidence and eliminating the need to call multiple witnesses to a single event.[56] There are efforts afoot to

2015), https://snhr.org/wp-content/pdf/english/images_for_victims_of_torture_leaked_from_the_Syrian_military_hospitals_en.pdf (last visited July 6, 2023).

52 Aronson, *supra* note 24, at 1204.

53 Patrick Philippe Meier, *Verifying Crowdsourced Social Media Reports for Live Crisis Mapping: An Introduction to Information Forensics*, IREVOLUTIONS (Nov. 29, 2011), https://irevolution.files.wordpress.com/2011/11/meier-verifying-crowdsourced-data-case-studies.pdf (last visited July 7, 2023).

54 *See* Theresa L. Harris, Jonathan Drake, Jessica M. Wyndham, Susan R. Wolfinbarger, Stephen D. Lott & Michael Lerner, AAAS, Geospatial Evidence in International Human Rights Litigation: Technical and Legal Considerations (Jul. 25, 2018), https://www.aaas.org/sites/default/files/s3fs-public/reports/Geospatial%2520Evidence%2520in%2520International%2520Human%2520Rights%2520Litigation.pdf (last visited July 7, 2023).

55 Hamilton, *supra* note 5, at 55; *Id.* at 45 ("There is a valid legal argument to make that the app itself is the witness" quoting Wendy Betts, Program Director, eyeWitness to Atrocities).

56 *See generally* Keith Hiatt, 'Open Source Evidence on Trial' (2016), 125 *Yale L.J.F.* 323, https://www.yalelawjournal.org/forum/open-source-evidence-on-trial (last visited July 7, 2023) (discussing the promise and perils of open source investigations).

render international trials less dependent on *viva voce* testimony, including through the use of probabilistic methods and other social science research tools – the topic of an earlier issue of the ICC Forum.[57] This reflects the worrisome reality that witnesses are the soft underbelly of any criminal prosecution.[58]

To be sure, no prosecutor worth her salt will mechanically adopt external work product, but this analytical and verification work by trusted partners will jump start and facilitate prosecutorial efforts when suspects are within reach. In particular, the IIIM – as an internationally-mandated organization – can undertake the sort of deep historical, cultural, and contextual research that is necessary to launch a successful war crimes prosecution. This would include gathering proof of the *chapeau* (or circumstantial) elements of war crimes and crimes against humanity, such as the existence of an armed conflict or a widespread and systematic attack against a civilian population. This singular focus on one crime base – coupled with the ability to pursue both structural and target-based investigations – might be difficult for multiple national prosecutors to undertake. The same goes for the OTP, which is already over-stretched with its existing docket of prosecutions, investigations, and preliminary examinations.[59]

5 Conclusion

The Nuremberg proceedings relied heavily on captured Nazi documents – amounting to upwards of three thousand tons of records and photographs – with witnesses playing lesser roles in establishing the commission

57 *See* Anne-Marie de Brouwer, 'Cases of Mass Sexual Violence Can Be Proven Without Direct Victim Testimony', in Richard H. Steinberg (ed.), *Contemporary Issues Facing the International Criminal Court* (Boston: Brill Nijhoff, 2016), p. 282. John Hagan, 'The Use of Sample Survey Interviews as Evidence of Mass Rape', in Richard H. Steinberg (ed.), *Contemporary Issues Facing the International Criminal Court* (Boston: Brill Nijhoff, 2016), pp. 295–299.

58 *See* Press Release, International Federation for Human Rights, The Kenya Cases at the International Criminal Court: Q&A on "Rule 68" and Witness Tampering (Feb. 11, 2016), https://www.fidh.org/en/region/Africa/kenya/the-kenya-cases-at-the-international-criminal-court-q-a-on-rule-68 (last visited July 7, 2023) (The Kenyan cases before the ICC collapsed due to unprecedented witness tampering and intimidation).

59 Patryk I. Labuda, *Less is More: Rediscovering the Prosecutor's Core Mandate*, JUST. IN CONFLICT (Apr. 14, 2020), https://justiceinconflict.org/2020/04/14/less-is-more-rediscovering-the-prosecutors-core-mandate/ (last visited July 7, 2023).

of international crimes.[60] With the revival of the Nuremberg promise in the 1990s, international prosecutors have depended more heavily on *viva voce* testimony, with all that such reliance entails in terms of witness protection, reliability deficits, and persistent problems with interpretation in vernacular languages.[61] The advent of the digital revolution suggests that we may have come full circle when it comes to the ICL evidentiary landscape. Although activating international jurisdiction has proven to be a bridge too far when it comes to Syria,[62] all this documentation on Syria is contributing to episodic cases that are beginning to materialize in domestic courts around the globe – the most promising avenue for justice to date.[63] When it comes to the OTP, a ready judicial forum exists; what is needed is probative and reliable evidence that proves the commission of international crimes beyond a reasonable doubt. New digital repositories and techniques have the potential to make an important contribution in this regard and should be embraced.

---

60 Edna Friedberg, *How the Nuremberg Trial Bore Witness to the Nazis' Worst Crimes*, SLATE (Nov. 20, 2015), https://slate.com/news-and-politics/2015/11/nuremberg-trials-70th-anniversary-the-prosecutors-built-an-unimpeachable-historical-record-of-nazi-crimes.html (last visited July 7, 2023).

61 Chris Stephen, 'Book Review' (2011), 22 *Eur. J. Int'l L.* 602 (reviewing Nancy A. Combs, Fact-Finding Without Facts: The Uncertain Evidentiary Foundations of International Criminal Convictions).

62 Caroline Fehl and Eliška Mocková, *PRIF Spotlight: Chasing Justice for Syria*, PEACE RSCH. INST. FRANKFURT (May 2017), https://www.hsfk.de/fileadmin/HSFK/hsfk_publikationen/Spotlight0517.pdf (last visited July 7, 2023).

63 *See* Beth Van Schaack, *Accountability in the Time of COVID-19: Syria & Iraq*, JUST SEC. (May 6, 2020), https://www.justsecurity.org/69932/accountability-in-the-time-of-covid-19-syria-iraq/ (last visited July 7, 2023); Beth Van Schaack, 'National Courts Step Up: Syrian Cases Proceeding in Domestic Courts' (Feb. 2, 2019), SSRN, https://papers.ssrn.com/sol3/papers.cfm?abstract_id=3327676 (last visited July 7, 2023) (discussing many of these recent cases on Syria).

PART 4

U.S. Sanctions on the Court: Support, Opposition, and Off-Ramps

Introduction to Part 4

The following question was featured on www.ICCForum.com from February 2021 through June 2021:

Is it appropriate or effective for the United States to attempt to influence the actions of the ICC by means of the sanctions set forth in President Trump's June 2020 Executive Order?

On June 11, 2020, U.S. President Donald J. Trump issued Executive Order 13928, seeking "to impose tangible and significant consequences on those responsible for" alleged "ICC transgressions." The Executive Order (EO) was issued under the authority of several U.S. statutes: the *International Emergency Economic Powers Act*, the *National Emergencies Act*, the *Immigration and Nationality Act of 1952*, and Section 301 of Title 3 of the United States Code.

In the EO, President Trump found that:

> [The ICC's] illegitimate assertions of jurisdiction over personnel of the United States and certain of its allies, including the ICC Prosecutor's investigation into actions allegedly committed by the United States military, intelligence and other personnel in or relating to Afghanistan [...] threaten to infringe upon the sovereignty of the United States and impede the critical national security and foreign policy of the United States.

The United States is not a party to the Rome Statute and the President determined that any attempt to investigate, arrest, detail, or prosecute any U.S. personnel without the consent of the United States constitutes an unusual and extraordinary threat to U.S. national security and foreign policy.

Pursuant to the EO, on September 2, 2020, ICC Prosecutor Fatou Bensouda, and Phakiso Mochochoko, Head of the Office of the Prosecutor's Jurisdiction, Complementarity and Cooperation Division, were designated by the U.S. Secretary of State as persons subject to the U.S. Treasury Department's Office of Foreign Assets Control's List of Specially Designated Nationals and Blocked Persons. The designation enabled freezing some of the designees' property and interests in property, denial of their entry and that of their family members into the United States, and other sanctions.

In addition, Section 3(a) of the EO prohibits, in relevant part, any person from "contributing or providing... services... to, or for the benefit of any [designated person]." Section 1(a) contains similar prohibitions. Violation is

 | DOI:10.1163/9789004686755_020

punishable by imprisonment, fines, denial of entry of into the United States of aliens violating the EO, and other penalties.

Are the EO and associated designations appropriate? Does the Office of the Prosecutor's (OTP) investigation of the situation in Afghanistan "threaten to infringe upon the sovereignty of the United States" or "impede the critical national security and foreign policy" of the United States? Is it appropriate to use the EO's underlying authorities for the purposes described in the EO? Is the EO *ultra vires*? Is the scope of the prohibitions in the EO overly broad or too narrow?

What are the consequences or expected consequences of the EO and the designation? To what extent and how might they change the behavior of the designated persons, the OTP, the Court, or others at the ICC, now or in the future? How, and to what extent, might they affect U.S. foreign relations with ICC states parties or non-states parties? Is the EO's approach an appropriate or effective template for future U.S. government disagreements with international organizations or the leaders of those organizations?

Could any of the prohibitions in the EO, particularly its prohibition on the provision of "services" to designated persons, have a chilling effect on the U.S. Constitution's First Amendment rights to freedom of speech or freedom of the press? If so, should that be a basis for voiding or limiting the application or effective scope of the EO?

Assuming the ICC's actions are of concern to the U.S. government, what alternative policies might be available to the U.S. government in reaction the ICC's actions? Should the Biden Administration maintain, modify, or rescind the EO or the designations?

What alternative policies or actions, if any, might be appropriate and available to the Prosecutor, the OTP, or the Court in responding to U.S. government concerns expressed in the EO?

CHAPTER 16

What President Biden and the ICC Prosecutor Should Do to End the United States–ICC Conflict

John B. Bellinger III

One of the numerous foreign policy messes President-elect Biden will inherit from the Trump Administration is the nasty war between the United States and the International Criminal Court. Over the last two years, the Trump Administration has launched a full-scale rhetorical and legal assault on the Court, including issuing Executive Order 13928[1] imposing sanctions on persons associated with the ICC and designating Prosecutor Fatou Bensouda for sanctions, after Bensouda sought and received authorization from the Court to open an investigation of alleged abuse by U.S. personnel of detainees in and relating to Afghanistan. Although Trump's Executive order and sanctions were a gross over-reaction and unworthy of the United States, Bensouda can also be faulted for picking an unnecessary fight. After Biden takes office in January, both he and Bensouda (or her successor) should take steps to de-escalate and end the conflict, which undermines the work of the Court, damages the reputation of the United States, and hurts the cause of international criminal justice.

The Trump Administration's war on the ICC, spearheaded by then National Security Advisor John Bolton, sets the clock back more than a decade to the initial confrontation between the United States and the Court that existed from 2002–2004 in the first term of the Bush Administration, when Bolton (then Under Secretary of State) was the principal architect of U.S. policy towards the Court. During that period, the United States "unsigned" the Rome Statute (in the form of a letter from Bolton to the U.N. Secretary General stating that the United States did not intend to become a party)[2]

1 Exec. Order No. 13928: Blocking Property of Certain Persons Associated with the International Criminal Court, 85 Fed. Reg. 115, 36139 (Jun. 11, 2020) [hereinafter EO 13928], https://www.govinfo.gov/content/pkg/FR-2020-06-15/pdf/2020-12953.pdf (last visited July 7, 2023).

2 Press Release, U.S. Dept. of State, Letter from John Bolton, Under Secretary of State, to Kofi Annan, U.N. Secretary General (May 6, 2002), https://2001-2009.state.gov/r/pa/prs/ps/2002/9968.htm (last visited July 7, 2023).

 | DOI:10.1163/9789004686755_021

and, pursuant to the American Servicemembers' Protection Act of 2002 (ASPA),[3] cut off aid to countries that refused to sign so-called Article 98 agreements committing not to surrender Americans to the Court. (It is worth noting for the historical record that then Senator Biden voted against the ASPA, while then Senators Hilary Clinton and John Kerry voted for ASPA, including its authorization to use all necessary means to secure the release of Americans detained by the ICC.)

I am personally disappointed to see the resumption of hostilities between the United States and the Court because I had worked hard in the Bush Administration's second term, when I was Legal Adviser to the Secretary of State, to develop a more pragmatic *modus vivendi* with the Court, emphasizing the common ground on issues of international justice between the United States and the Court and its supporters, and cases where we could work together, even if the United States did not intend to join the Rome Statute. Starting in 2005, the Bush Administration agreed to support some of the Court's investigations, including the genocide in Darfur. President Bush waived restrictions on counterterrorism assistance to many ICC members after Secretary of State Condoleezza Rice publicly remarked in 2006 that the restrictions were like "shooting ourselves in the foot."[4] And I gave numerous speeches between 2005 and 2008 expressing United States willingness to support the Court's Darfur investigation and other appropriate cases.[5]

By the end of the Bush Administration, ICC watchers had begun to comment on the shift in position. In an article entitled "U.S. Accepts International Criminal Court," the Wall Street Journal quoted lengthy remarks I

3 2002 Supplemental Appropriations Act for Further Recovery from and Response to Terrorist Attacks on the United States, Pub. L. No. 107–206, §§ 2001–2015, 116 Stat. 820, 899–909 (Aug. 2, 2002) (The American Service-Members' Protection Act (ASPA) was passed as Title II of this legislation and codified at 22 U.S.C. §§ 7421–7432).

4 Steven R. Weisman, *U.S. Rethinks Its Cutoff of Military Aid to Latin American Nations*, N.Y. TIMES (Mar. 12, 2006), https://www.nytimes.com/2006/03/12/politics/us-rethinks-its-cut off-of-military-aid-to-latin-american-nations.html (last visited July 7, 2023).

5 John B. Bellinger, III, Legal Advisor, Remarks at George Washington Law School, International Courts and Tribunals and the Rule of Law (May 11, 2006), https://2001-2009.state .gov/s/l/2006/98253.htm (last visited July 7, 2023); John B. Bellinger, III, Legal Advisor, Remarks at the DePaul University College of Law, The United States and the International Criminal Court: Where We've Been and Where We're Going (Apr. 25, 2008) [hereinafter Bellinger's DePaul Remarks], https://2001-2009.state.gov/s/l/rls/104053.htm (last visited July 7, 2023); John B. Bellinger, III, Legal Advisor, Remarks at the Fletcher School of Law and Diplomacy, U.S. Perspectives on International Criminal Justice (Nov. 14, 2008), https://2001-2009.state.gov/s/l/rls/111859.htm (last visited July 7, 2023).

gave on the tenth anniversary of the Rome Statute in 2008 (which John Bolton derided as "pabulum" at the time) in which I urged ICC parties and the United States to "seiz[e] opportunities for cooperative efforts where they exist and avoid [...] pitfalls that risk reigniting past tensions."[6] I concluded:

> The United States and ICC supporters can do more to prevent impunity for serious crimes by working together than either can achieve on their own, and it is in our mutual interest to develop a relationship that recognizes this.[7]

The Obama Administration continued and increased the cooperation between the United States and the Court begun during the Bush Administration. Although President Obama did not seek Senate approval to ratify the Rome Statute, his Administration participated in the Assembly of State Parties and sought to support certain of the Court's investigations, consistent with restrictions in ASPA.

Somewhat surprisingly, given its anti-international bent, the Trump Administration ignored the Court for its first year in office, until the Prosecutor applied to open her investigation of the United States in November 2017. Bensouda was under significant pressure from African countries to show that the Court was not simply an "African Criminal Court" and was willing to investigate powerful countries like the United States.

It is unfortunate for the Court that the Prosecutor chose to pick a fight with the United States, and her timing could not have been worse. The threat by an international court to investigate the U.S. military and the CIA was too much political red meat for the Trump Administration to resist in a U.S. election year. Trump's appointment of John Bolton as National Security Advisor in March 2018 guaranteed a nasty confrontation between the United States and the Court. Although Bolton could easily have focused on Iran, North Korea, China, Russia, or other international adversaries, he chose the ICC as the sole focus of his first major public address. In his speech to the Federalist Society in September 2018,[8] he blasted the Court as "ineffective," "unaccountable," "deeply flawed" and "outright dangerous." He

6 Jess Bravin, *U.S. Accepts International Criminal Court*, WALL ST. J. (Apr. 26, 2008), https://www.wsj.com/articles/SB120917156494046579 (last visited July 7, 2023).

7 Bellinger's DePaul Remarks, *supra* note 5.

8 John Bolton, National Security Advisor, Speech to the Federalist Society (Sep. 10, 2018), https://www.americanrhetoric.com/speeches/johnboltonfederalistsociety2018.htm (last visited July 7, 2023).

said the ICC unacceptably threatens American sovereignty and U.S. national security interests. He criticized the ICC Prosecutor's request as "utterly unfounded" and "unjustifiable." He said that the United States will "use any means necessary to protect our citizens and those of our allies from unjust prosecution by this illegitimate court." Breaking with the previous thirteen years, he insisted that the United States would not cooperate with the ICC and would provide no assistance to the Court. And if the ICC "comes after the United States," he said, the United States would "fight back" by banning its judges and prosecutors from entering the United States, freezing their assets, and prosecuting them in the U.S. criminal justice system. The United States would do the same for "any company or state that assists an ICC investigation of Americans."[9]

I should note here that, while I think the Trump Administration's rhetorical and legal assault on the Court and the Prosecutor were unbalanced and likely counterproductive, any U.S. Administration, Republican or Democratic, would have responded forcefully to an ICC request to open an investigation of the United States. Biden Administration officials can be expected to reject the Afghanistan investigation as outside the scope of the Rome Statute.

Seven months after John Bolton's speech, in April 2019, the Court's Pre-Trial Chamber (PTC) rejected Bensouda's request after concluding that an investigation "would not serve the interests of justice."[10] The PTC noted that the prospects for a successful investigation and prosecution were extremely limited and that the Court should prioritize activities that would have better chances to succeed.[11] Although the PTC's decision was a reasonable interpretation of the Rome Statute, the decision was criticized by many as a cowardly capitulation to the Trump Administration's threats. Undaunted, the Prosecutor appealed to the Court's Appeals Chamber, which in March 2020 reversed the PTC and authorized Bensouda to proceed.[12] Trump promptly retaliated in June with Executive Order 13928[13] and the

9 *Id.*

10 Situation in the Islamic Republic of Afghanistan, ICC-02/17, Decision Pursuant to Article 15 of the Rome Statute on the Authorization of an Investigation into the Situation in the Islamic Republic of Afghanistan (PTC II, Apr. 12, 2019).

11 *Id.*

12 Situation in the Islamic Republic of Afghanistan, ICC-02/17 OA4, Judgment on the Appeal against the Decision on the Authorization of an Investigation into the Situation in the Islamic Republic of Afghanistan (AC, Mar. 5, 2020) [hereinafter *ICC Authorization of Afghanistan Investigation*].

13 EO 13928, *supra* note 1.

Treasury Department subsequently designated Bensouda and another ICC official for sanctions.[14]

Although I argued at the time that the Court and the Prosecutor should avoid a fight with the Trump Administration,[15] it is understandable that neither was willing to back down in the face of Trump's threats. But having now made the ideological point that the Court will not be cowed, and with the inauguration of a new President who undoubtedly would prefer to support the Court for the next four years than fight with it, now would be a very good time for the Prosecutor to act more pragmatically.

Bensouda surely recognizes that an investigation of the United States for actions nearly twenty years ago is unlikely to succeed and will waste the Court's limited resources, already stretched far too thin. Indeed, if the Prosecutor were to go forward, whom should she investigate? Her application lists dozens of offenses allegedly committed by U.S. armed forces and CIA personnel. Should she focus on the military commanders and civilian Defense Department officials responsible for the abuse of detainees in Afghanistan? Should she pursue the Director of Central Intelligence (a Democrat who had been appointed to his position by President Clinton) and numerous CIA officials who proposed and implemented the controversial CIA interrogation program? Should she indict the Attorney General and Department of Justice lawyers who wrote or endorsed the disputed legal opinions upon which executive branch officials relied? (For the record, when I was Legal Adviser, I disagreed in writing with the Department of Justice analysis, arguing that the CIA program was not consistent with Common Article 3 of the Geneva Conventions.)[16] How about the President and Vice President, who accepted the recommendation of the CIA Director and the legal advice of the Attorney General? Or, perhaps, she could go after the dozens of members of Congress from both parties who oversaw and

14 Press Statement, Michael R. Pompeo, Secretary of State, Actions to Protect U.S. Personnel from Illegitimate Investigation by the International Criminal Court, U.S. Dept. of State (Sep. 2, 2020).

15 John B. Bellinger, III, *The Trump Administration Throws Down the Gauntlet to the ICC. The Court Should Decline The Challenge.*, LAWFARE (Sep. 10, 2018), https://www.lawfaremedia.org/article/trump-administration-throws-down-gauntlet-icc-court-should-decline-challenge (last visited July 10, 2023).

16 Letter from John B. Bellinger, III, Legal Advisor, U.S. Dept. of State, to Steven G. Bradbury, Actg. Asst. Atty. Gen., Dept. of Just., Response to OLC Draft Opinion on Enhanced Interrogation Techniques (Feb. 9, 2007), https://www.state.gov/wp-content/uploads/2019/05/44-Bellinger-letter-on-enhanced-interrogation-techniques.pdf (last visited July 10, 2023).

appropriated money for the program? The Prosecutor surely knows there is no possibility that any U.S. official will ever be arrested and prosecuted in The Hague. And if the likelihood of prosecutions is zero, is conducting a multi-year investigation of twenty-year-old offenses worthwhile to prove a point?

Some supporters of the Court will argue an investigation of the United States is necessary to demonstrate that there is no impunity even for powerful countries. This is an understandable argument, but it is not pragmatic. Conducting an investigation of hundreds of senior U.S. officials would be an enormous distraction for the Prosecutor and the Court, both of which are already struggling with many other problems, and would prevent them from concentrating on other more serious cases with higher likelihoods of success. It would prevent a U.S. Administration predisposed to support the Court from helping the Court with other investigations. And it would force countries that are friends of the Court and the United States to choose between the Court or good relations with the United States.

Although Bensouda has received approval from the Appeals Chamber to open an investigation of the United States,[17] she (or her successor) has legitimate reasons under the Rome Statute not to pursue it. First, although the Prosecutor concluded that the allegations of detainee abuse against the United States satisfied the Rome Statute 's gravity requirement, she could also conclude that they are not as serious in number or gravity as the numerous acts of murder and rape committed in other countries that are subjects of ICC investigations. The Court was created to investigate and prosecute the "most serious crimes" of concern to the international community. It simply does not have the capacity to investigate every offense within the scope of the Rome Statute. Second, the Prosecutor could have concluded (and could still conclude) that, under Article 17 of the Rome Statute,[18] the ICC does not have jurisdiction because the United States has conducted investigations of the allegations of detainee abuse by U.S. military personnel and the CIA. Indeed, Bensouda's conclusions with respect to the United States rely primarily on thousands of pages of public findings and conclusions from investigations already conducted by the United States, including the Senate Intelligence Committee, the Senate Armed Services Committee, the Church Report, the Fay Report, the Jacoby Report, the Schlesinger Report, and the Department of Justice's OPR Report. (The

17 ICC Authorization of Afghanistan Investigation, *supra* note 12.

18 International Criminal Court, Rome Statute of the International Criminal Court, art. 17, U.N. Doc. A/CONF.183/9, (July 17, 1998) [hereinafter Rome Statute].

United States conducted other non-public investigations as well, including by Department of Justice Special Counsel John Durham and the CIA Inspector General.) The Prosecutor concluded, however, that these numerous U.S. investigations were not sufficiently comprehensive, in part because President Obama chose not to investigate Executive branch officials that had relied on legal advice from the Department of Justice. Bensouda did state that she would:

> [C]ontinue to assess the existence of national proceedings for as long as the situation remains under investigation, including in relation to any additional information that may be provided by relevant States.[19]

This leaves the door open for her to conclude that the United States has conducted sufficient investigations, even if not every U.S. official has been investigated. Finally, the Prosecutor would also be justified in concluding, under Article 53(1)(c) of the Rome Statute, that in light of the unlikelihood of a successful prosecution by the Court and the need to prioritize the Court's resources, it would not "serve the interests of justice" to proceed with an investigation. The PTC reached this conclusion, and the Prosecutor could make this same determination, especially after factoring in additional information provided by the Biden Administration.

The recommendations of the recent September 2020 report of Independent Experts on the Court support suspending the investigation of the United States.[20] The report states that:

> [The Experts] repeatedly heard concerns that the Court should focus on a narrower range of situations, and limit its interventions to the extent possible, focusing on situations of the highest gravity and on those most responsible for the crimes. While it is a prospect that would be disappointing for many, and further restrict the already limited jurisdiction of the Court, the current situation is unsustainable having regard to the limited resources available.[21]

19 Situation in the Islamic Republic of Afghanistan, ICC-02/17, Request for Authorisation of an Investigation pursuant to Article 15 (PTC III, Nov. 20, 2017) [hereinafter OTP Request for Authorization].

20 Assembly of States Parties, International Criminal Court, Independent Expert Review of the International Criminal Court and the Rome Statute System Final Report (Sep. 30, 2020), https://asp.icc-cpi.int/sites/asp/files/asp_docs/ASP19/IER-Final-Report-ENG.pdf (last visited July 10, 2023).

21 *Id.*

The Experts go on to recommend that:

> The Prosecutor should adopt a higher threshold for the gravity of the crimes alleged to have been perpetrated.[22]

They also argue:

> Feasibility-related factors should be seriously considered after the opening of an investigation. Should more situations reach the investigation stage without sufficient resources available to conduct serious investigations, the OTP should hibernate deprioritized investigations.[23]

Bensouda may be reluctant to change course and announce that she has decided not to pursue her investigation of the United States after all, but it would make sense for her at minimum to hit the "pause" button by announcing that she is suspending her investigation until she receives more information from the United States about the investigations it has already conducted. The Prosecutor apparently held some discussions with Obama Administration officials, and she should allow Biden officials to describe the actions the United States has taken in greater detail.

Bensouda may be tempted to push Biden officials to open new investigations in order to satisfy her desire for perfect complementarity. But the Biden Administration will already have its hands full with investigations of unlawful actions by President Trump and Trump Administration officials. The Prosecutor must recognize that it would not be politically sustainable for a Biden Justice Department to conduct far-reaching and controversial investigations of senior officials (including the Presidents) in both the Bush *and* Trump Administrations. Although she concluded in 2017 that the numerous investigations undertaken by the United States were insufficient,[24] in light of the Court's increasingly stretched resources and the recommendations of the Independent Experts, she would now be justified in reaching a different conclusion.

For his part, President Biden should take the first step towards a *rapprochement* by rescinding President Trump's misguided Executive Order 13928 authorizing the imposition of sanctions on the ICC and by lifting the sanctions on Bensouda. At the same time, Biden Administration officials

---

22 *Id.*

23 *Id.*

24 OTP Request for Authorization, *supra* note 19.

should communicate directly to the Prosecutor and through intermediaries that the United States is prepared to resume support for the Court, but only if the Court ceases its unnecessary investigation of the United States.

The Prosecutor will then have a choice: She could continue an ideological crusade by conducting an investigation of the United States that is likely to go on for years, strain the Court's resources, and ultimately prove unsuccessful, all while antagonizing a U.S. Administration that is prepared to support the Court during a period in which the Court is urgently in need of help and reform. Or she could take a more pragmatic approach by focusing on investigations of greater gravity that are more likely to succeed and resuming the constructive working relationship between the Court and the United States that existed from 2005–2017.

CHAPTER 17

Trump's Sanctions on the International Criminal Court: Inappropriate, Ineffective, and Dangerous

William W. Burke-White

The Trump Administration's imposition of national security sanctions against the International Criminal Court (ICC) and some of the Court's key officials is an inappropriate, legally questionable move that is more likely to backfire on the United States than advance U.S. interests. Far more effective mechanisms are available to the United States to address the potential investigation of U.S. actions in Afghanistan without further undermining the U.S. commitment to human rights around the globe. While recognizing the shortcomings of the ICC, the incoming Biden Administration should quickly lift these sanctions and return to an era of careful, considered, and limited engagement with the Court.

1 From a War in Afghanistan to U.S. Sanctions on the ICC

Trump's sanctions on the ICC must be understood against the backdrop of an evolving investigation of crimes, including those by U.S. citizens, potentially committed in Afghanistan more than a decade ago. In November 2017, nearly fifteen years after those alleged crimes took place, the ICC's Prosecutor, Fatou Bensouda, filed a request with the Pre-Trial Chamber to open an investigation of the situation in Afghanistan, having "determined that there was a reasonable basis to believe" that crimes within the jurisdiction of the Court had been committed by Afghan officials, the Taliban, and U.S. military and intelligence forces.[1] While the United States is not a party to the Rome Statute, Afghanistan is.[2] By virtue of the fact that these alleged

1 Rick Gladstone and Marlise Simons, *Prosecutor's Move in Afghan War Inquiry May Mean Clash with the U.S.*, N.Y. TIMES (Nov. 20, 2017), https://www.nytimes.com/2017/11/20/world/asia/international-criminal-court-afghanistan-united-states.html (last visited July 10, 2023).

2 Parliamentarians for Global Action, *Islamic Republic of Afghanistan: Campaign for the Rome Statute of the International Criminal Court*, https://www.pgaction.org/ilhr/rome-statute/afghanistan.html (last visited July 10, 2023).

 | DOI:10.1163/9789004686755_022

crimes were committed in Afghanistan, the ICC would have jurisdiction over them.

The ICC Prosecutor's request to open an investigation spotlights the conduct of the U.S. military and Central Intelligence Agency (CIA) in Afghanistan in the early 2000s.[3] At the start of the long war in Afghanistan, acts of torture and related war crimes were committed by the U.S. military and the CIA at the Bagram Internment Facility and in so-called "black sites" in eastern Europe.[4] Such actions, even though they were not a standard U.S. practice and were stopped by an Executive order from President Obama in 2009,[5] nonetheless violate basic principles of international humanitarian law. To date, only a few of the direct perpetrators of these abuses have been brought to justice through U.S. military courts-martial.[6] Significantly, U.S. investigations have not worked their way up the chain of command to hold accountable more senior officials who may have ordered or authorized torture and the targeting of civilians in Afghanistan. As a result, an ICC investigation of Afghanistan could, for the first time, result in an investigation, indictment, and possible prosecution of U.S. officials.

The Prosecutor's request to open an investigation made its way through the Court's review process, first before one of the Pre-Trial Chambers. In April 2019, a Pre-Trial Chamber determined that it would not be in the interest of justice to proceed with the case in Afghanistan, observing that due to limited cooperation from governments including the United States:

> [I]t is unlikely that pursuing an investigation would result in meeting the objectives listed by the victims favoring the investigation or otherwise positively contributing to it.[7]

---

3 Situation in the Islamic Republic of Afghanistan, ICC-02/17, Request for Authorization of an Investigation pursuant to Article 15 (PTC III, Nov. 20, 2017).

4 Eliza Grizwold, *Black Hole; The Other Guantanamo*, NEW REPUBLIC (May 6, 2007), https://newrepublic.com/article/63942/black-hole-the-other-guantanamo (last visited July 10, 2023).

5 Exec. Order No. 13491: Ensuring Lawful Interrogations, 74 Fed. Reg. 16, 4893 (Jan. 22, 2010), https://www.govinfo.gov/content/pkg/FR-2009-01-27/pdf/E9-1885.pdf (last visited July 10, 2023).

6 Tim Golden, *Army Faltered in Investigating Detainee Abuse*, N.Y. TIMES (May 22, 2005), https://www.nytimes.com/2005/05/22/world/asia/army-faltered-in-investigating-detainee-abuse.html (last visited July 10, 2023).

7 Situation in the Islamic Republic of Afghanistan, ICC-02/17, Decision pursuant to Article 15 of the Rome Statute on the Authorization of an Investigation into the Situation in the Islamic Republic of Afghanistan, ¶ 96 (PTC II, Apr. 12, 2019).

While the questionable legal reasoning behind this decision is beyond the scope of this essay, the result was to freeze the Prosecutor's attempt to investigate the situation in Afghanistan, pending appeal.[8]

In March 2020, the Appeal's Chamber reversed the decision of the Pre-Trial Chamber, finding that the Pre-Trial Chamber should not have based its review on a determination of the "interests of justice" and that there was a reasonable basis to believe that crimes within the Court's jurisdiction had been committed in Afghanistan.[9] By authorizing an investigation, the Appeals Chamber opened the door for the Prosecutor to investigate potential U.S. war crimes in Afghanistan.[10]

The Trump Administration, not surprisingly, has taken a harsh and escalating line against potential investigation of U.S. conduct. In 2017, when the Prosecutor first sought approval of a potential investigation, a U.S. State Department official noted:

> Our view is clear: an ICC investigation with respect to US personnel would be wholly unwarranted and unjustified.[11]

In September 2018, then National Security Advisor John Bolton issued a scathing critique of the Court in a speech to the Federalist Society. With specific reference to the Afghan investigation, Bolton noted:

> The United States will use any means necessary to protect our citizens and those of our allies from unjust prosecution by this illegitimate court. We will not cooperate with the ICC. We will provide no assistance to the ICC. We will not join the ICC. We will let the ICC die on its own. After all, for all intents and purposes, the ICC is already dead to us.[12]

---

8 Dapo Akande and Talita de Souza Dias, *The ICC Pre-Trial Chamber Decision on the Situation in Afghanistan: A Few Thoughts on the Interests of Justice*, EJIL TALK (Apr. 18, 2019), https://www.ejiltalk.org/the-icc-pre-trial-chamber-decision-on-the-situation-in-afghanistan-a-few-thoughts-on-the-interests-of-justice/ (last visited July 10, 2023).

9 Press Release, International Criminal Court, Afghanistan: ICC Appeals Chamber Authorizes the Opening of an Investigation (Mar. 5, 2020), https://www.icc-cpi.int/news/afghanistan-icc-appeals-chamber-authorises-opening-investigation (last visited July 10, 2023).

10 *Id.*

11 Gladstone and Simmons, *supra* note 1.

12 John Bolton, National Security Advisor, Speech to the Federalist Society (Sep. 10, 2018), https://www.americanrhetoric.com/speeches/johnboltonfederalistsociety2018.htm (last visited July 7, 2023).

When the Prosecutor sought to appeal the Pre-Trial Chamber's rejection of her investigation, the United States revoked her visa, preventing her from traveling to or through the United States. In the words of Secretary Pompeo:

> These visa restrictions will not be the end of our efforts. We are prepared to take additional steps, including economic sanctions if the ICC does not change its course.[13]

In March 2020, Pompeo described the Appeal's Chamber decision allowing the investigation to proceed, as a "truly breathtaking action by an unaccountable, political institution masquerading as a legal body" and pledged that the United States "will take all necessary measures to protect our citizens from this renegade, unlawful, so-called court."[14]

2 Sanctions Strike at the Court and the Rule of Law

The U.S. sanctions imposed on the ICC and its leadership in spring 2020 were intended to fulfill Pompeo's promise and, perhaps, to more actively speed Bolton's prediction of the ICC's death. Given that the Trump Administration's disengagement from the Court significantly decreased United States' ability to shape ICC policy through diplomacy or within the Assembly of States Parties, Trump had few levers of influence remaining. Hence, the Administration turned to the tool kit of sanctions. Through Executive Order 13928 of June 11, 2020, the Trump Administration sought "to impose tangible and significant consequences on those responsible for" alleged "ICC transgressions." The President's Executive order determined that:

> [The ICC's] illegitimate assertions of jurisdiction over personnel of the United States and certain of its allies, including the ICC Prosecutor's investigation into actions allegedly committed by the United States military, intelligence and other personnel in or relating to Afghanistan [...] threaten to infringe upon the sovereignty of the United States and

13 Marlise Simons and Megan Specia, *U.S. Revokes Visa of I.C.C. Prosecutor Pursuing Afghan War Crimes*, N.Y. TIMES (Apr. 5, 2019), https://www.nytimes.com/2019/04/05/world/europe/us-icc-prosecutor-afghanistan.html (last visited July 10, 2023).

14 Elian Peltier and Fatima Faizi, *I.C.C. Allows Afghan War Crimes Inquiry to Proceed, Angering U.S.*, N.Y. TIMES (Mar. 5, 2020), https://www.nytimes.com/2020/03/05/world/europe/afghanistan-war-crimes-icc.html (last visited July 10, 2023).

> impede the critical national security and foreign policy of the United States.[15]

While the United States has had a complicated history with the ICC – from President Bill Clinton's signing of the Rome Statute to President George Bush's early efforts to undermine the Court – the new sanctions go further than any past U.S. actions in their direct attack on the ICC and its staff. Bush's "unsigning" of the Rome Statute was largely symbolic.[16] So, too, was the American Servicemembers' Protection Act that threatened an invasion of the Netherlands to rescue any U.S. citizens that might be prosecuted in The Hague.[17] President Trump's June 2020 sanctions are, however, a much more tangible and direct attack on the ICC and the rule of law more generally. This new sanctions regime draws strong parallels to those imposed by the United States in the past against terrorist groups, dictators, and human rights abusers.[18] In fact, the Executive order on ICC sanctions parrots text directly from an Executive order addressing the Maduro regime in Venezuela and a similar sanctions regime against North Korea.[19] Those same sanctions are now being used not to protect U.S. national security, but to undermine legal institutions, international lawyers, and human rights defenders.

President Trump's sanctions directly target individual lawyers and investigators working for a legitimate international organization undertaking lawful actions under its statute. More specifically, the sanctions authorize the

---

15 Exec. Order No. 13928: Blocking Property of Certain Persons Associated with the International Criminal Court, 85 Fed. Reg. 115, 36139 (Jun. 11, 2020) [hereinafter EO 13928], https://www.govinfo.gov/content/pkg/FR-2020-06-15/pdf/2020-12953.pdf (last visited July 7, 2023).

16 Curtis A. Bradley, *U.S. Announces Intent Not to Ratify International Criminal Court Treaty*, ASIL INSIGHTS (May 11, 2002), https://www.asil.org/insights/volume/7/issue/7/us-announces-intent-not-ratify-international-criminal-court-treaty (last visited July 10, 2023).

17 2002 Supplemental Appropriations Act for Further Recovery from and Response to Terrorist Attacks on the United States, Pub. L. No. 107–206, §§ 2001–2015, 116 Stat. 820, 899–909 (Aug. 2, 2002) (The American Service-Members' Protection Act was passed as Title II of this legislation and codified at 22 U.S.C. §§ 7421–7432).

18 Exec. Order No. 13884: Blocking Property of the Government of Venezuela, 84 Fed. Reg. 152, 38843 (Aug. 5, 2019), https://www.govinfo.gov/content/pkg/FR-2019-08-07/pdf/2019-17052.pdf (last visited July 10, 2023).

19 *Id.*; Exec. Order No. 13810: Imposing Additional Sanctions with Respect to North Korea, 82 Fed. Reg. 184, 44705 (Sep. 20, 2017), https://www.govinfo.gov/content/pkg/FR-2017-09-25/pdf/2017-20647.pdf (last visited July 10, 2023).

seizure of property of to-be-designated ICC officials who undertake investigation or prosecution of U.S. personnel and any other foreign nationals who are deemed to have assisted such efforts. The Executive order authorizes the Secretary of State to designate any foreign persons who have "directly engaged in any effort by the ICC to investigate, arrest, detain, or prosecute any United States personnel without the consent of the United States" as subject to property seizure.[20] The order also allows for the designation of any individual who materially assisted such prosecutions. So too, the new sanctions prohibit the entry into the United States of such individuals and their immediate family members.[21]

While the Executive order only established the legal basis for the imposition of sanctions, nearly three months after its issuance Secretary Pompeo made the first sanctions designations. He designated ICC Prosecutor Fatou Bensouda and Phakiso Mochochoko, Head of the Office of the Prosecutor's Jurisdiction, Complementarity and Cooperation Division (JCCD) of the Office of the Prosecutor. These targets are not surprising given that the Prosecutor has been the driving force behind the Afghanistan investigation and that the JCCD unit within the Office of the Prosecutor is responsible for managing relations between the Prosecutor's office and national governments. These designations represent a direct attack on both the Office of the Prosecutor itself and the individuals who lead that office. Through the serious threat of asset freezing, they seek to influence, interfere with, and undermine the independence of one of the most important branches of a legitimate, treaty-based international institution. It is exactly such interference that the Rome Statute sought to protect against in structuring an Office of the Prosecutor that "shall act independently as a separate organ of the Court."[22]

3 A National Emergency ... Really?

As a matter of U.S. law, the Executive order presents at least two significant problems: the lack of the prerequisite underlying national emergency and an overbroad reach. Trump's sanctions order invoked emergency powers pursuant to the International Emergency Economic Powers Act, the

20 EO 13928, *supra* note 15.

21 *Id.*

22 International Criminal Court, Rome Statute of the International Criminal Court, art. 42(1), U.N. Doc. A/CONF.183/9, (July 17, 1998) [hereinafter Rome Statute].

National Emergencies Act, the Immigration and Nationality Act of 1952, and section 301 of Title 3 of the United States Code. Each of these authorities requires a preliminary determination of a national emergency and/or an extraordinary threat to U.S. national security. Trump's determination that a potential ICC investigation in Afghanistan constitutes a national emergency that poses an "unusual and extraordinary threat to the national security and foreign policy of the United States" is downright farcical.[23] After all, the Administration had already determined, in John Bolton's words, that "the ICC is already dead to us."[24]

In a moment of real national and global crises – ranging from the COVID-19 pandemic, to police misconduct, to the highest unemployment rate in a generation – the fact that President Trump "declare[d] a national emergency to deal with" the threat posed by the ICC investigation in Afghanistan is simply not supported by fact. An underfunded Court with relatively little to show for two decades of work trying to end impunity would likely be surprised to learn that, in Trump's view, it has the power to:

> [I]mpede the critical national security and foreign policy work of United States Government and allied officials, and thereby threaten the national security and foreign policy of the United States.[25]

Admitting that a duly authorized investigation of U.S. conduct in Afghanistan by the ICC constitutes such a threat is both a recognition of the power of international law and a suggestion that the United States has something to hide. While the President does have wide ranging national security authorities, his power to impose sanctions is not unlimited.[26] The lack of any factual predicate whatsoever for the determination that the ICC's investigation constitutes a threat to U.S. national security calls into question the validity of the sanctions regime under the heads of authority invoked in the President's Executive Order.

Beyond the questionable invocation of a national security emergency, Trump's Executive Order presents a second constitutional concern: overbreadth. Pursuant to the Executive order, sanctions can be placed on any person who has "materially assisted, sponsored, or provided financial,

---

23 EO 13928, *supra* note 15.

24 Bolton, *supra*, note 12.

25 EO 13928, *supra* note 15.

26 Jordan Tama, 'Forcing the President's Hand: How the US Congress Shapes Foreign Policy through Sanctions Legislation' (2019), 16 *Foreign Policy Analysis* 397.

material, or technological support for, or goods or services to or in support of" the ICC's investigation of U.S. personnel.[27] The sanctions language is sufficiently broad that it could, in theory, apply to a victim or witness who provided information incidental to the Court's investigation, or an academic whose scholarship the Court relied upon in framing a legal argument. It would certainly seem to apply to a lawyer, fulfilling her duty to represent a client by filing a brief with or making an appearance before the ICC.[28] In so doing, the sanctions regime poses the real risk of chilling the freedom of speech, limiting representation, and undermining, rather than advancing, human rights.

Moreover, even if one could somehow make the case that an ICC investigation of U.S. conduct in Afghanistan were a threat to national security, there is no conceivable way that the kinds of material support for such an investigation, covered by the President's Executive order, themselves constitute such a threat, or that the Executive order is a legitimate response thereto. To deem a victim's truthful testimony a threat to national security is simply inaccurate, no matter how broad the President's authorities. Should further designations be made under the order based on material assistance, there is the very real prospect of a constitutional challenge to the Executive order itself.

4 Empty Threats, Bad Strategy

While the sanctions imposed on ICC officials certainly upped the U.S. rhetorical attack on the ICC, they are unlikely to achieve Trump's objective of blocking the investigation of U.S. conduct in Afghanistan or Bolton's goal of "letting the ICC die on its own." As noted above, the design of Trump's sanctions regime is based almost verbatim on past sanctions targeting terrorists and corrupt dictators. Yet, unlike most corrupt dictators or terrorist organizations, individuals who choose to work for the ICC, or in international human rights more generally, are motivated by conscience, not wealth.[29]

---

27 EO 13928, *supra* note 15.

28 Susan Akram and Gabor Rona, *Why the Executive Order on the ICC is Unconstitutional and Self-Defeating*, OPINIO JURIS (Aug. 13, 2020), https://opiniojuris.org/2020/08/13/why-the-executive-order-on-the-icc-is-unconstitutional-and-self-defeating/ (last visited July 10, 2023).

29 Elena Baylis, 'Tribunal-Hopping with the Post-Conflict Justice Junkies' (2008), 10 *Or. Rev. Int'l L.* 361.

They rarely have significant assets in U.S. bank accounts or meaningful real property for the United States to seize. More than three months after the designation of Bensouda and Mochochoko, there is no indication that the Treasury has found any such assets subject to U.S. jurisdiction. And if the goal of the sanctions is to chill victims or witnesses of crimes in Afghanistan from ultimately testifying before the ICC, that too is unlikely to be successful. How many potential victims or witnesses are likely to have assets subject to seizure?

Ultimately, the threat of asset seizure under the sanctions regime will do little to deter the Court's investigation or individuals' cooperation with the Court. Even blocking ICC employees from entering the United States will have minimal impact. The new sanctions themselves were not responsible for preventing Bensouda from traveling to the United States given that her U.S. visa had already been revoked more than a year earlier. Effective investigation of crimes in Afghanistan more than a decade ago does not require on-the-ground presence of ICC officials in the United States today.

Not only are Trump's sanctions a bad strategy for advancing U.S. interests, they are likely to backfire. Given the moral compass of most human rights advocates and international criminal prosecutors, treating them like terrorists under the sanctions regime will more likely be a call to action under the law than an effective deterrent of legal investigation. The spine of individuals who have chosen careers in international criminal justice – whether at the most junior levels or as ICC judges or prosecutors – essentially immunizes them from the kinds of threats inherent in Trump's sanctions.[30] So too, those called to a career in international criminal justice are likely to channel their frustration with U.S. threats into ever more diligent, methodical investigation, rather than cause them to walk away from a prosecution.

Not only are individuals subject to sanctions likely to redouble their efforts, the Court as an institution is likely to respond to sanctions by asserting its independence from American influence. The decision of the Pre-Trial Chamber to block an Afghanistan investigation was widely criticized in the human rights community, with many suggesting that the Court was buckling to U.S. pressure not to proceed.[31] As Amnesty International observed after the April 2019 decision of the Pre-Trial Chamber:

---

30 *Id.*

31 Jonathan O'Donohue, Opinion, *The Prosecutor's Next Steps on Afghanistan Will Determine the Future of the International Criminal Court*, AMNESTY INT'L (Apr. 17, 2019), https://hrij.amnesty.nl/the-prosecutors-next-steps-on-afghanistan-will-determine-the-future-of-the-international-criminal-court/ (last visited July 10, 2023).

> [T]he OTP must resist any temptation to view this decision as a convenient and largely guilt free way out of conducting a daunting and politically fraught investigation or an opportune basis to close other preliminary examinations that are perceived as too politically sensitive or costly non-priorities.[32]

The subsequent Appeals Chamber's reversal of that decision in March 2020 can be viewed as an effort to assert the Court's independence and willingness to resist U.S. pressure. In the wake of U.S. sanctions, the Court has even less room to drop the Afghanistan case, limit the scope of investigation, or decide not to indict U.S. defendants. If it does so, it will again be seen as succumbing to U.S. pressure, sacrificing both credibility and legitimacy. Hence, if the sanctions have any impact at all, they are likely to lead the Prosecutor and the Court itself to double down on Afghanistan.

Sanctioning the ICC is not just silly, it is also dangerous. In a world in which the use of force is difficult and often ineffective, carefully crafted and strategically applied sanctions are a key tool of U.S. power.[33] For sanctions to work, however, they must be used judiciously and viewed as broadly legitimate.[34] The overuse of sanctions and, particularly, the application of sanctions without broad international support runs the risk of undermining their effectiveness. Overuse of sanctions creates incentives for actors to find workarounds to avoid the economic pain. Sanctions that are seen as illegitimate fail to garner international cooperation for enforcement and compliance. Applying tough sanctions against the personnel of a legitimate and broadly supported international organization undermines the broader efficacy and legitimacy of the tool for times when sanctions could actually advance U.S. national security.

5 Other, Better Tools

So, what should Trump have done instead of authorizing sanctions against the ICC if he wanted to prevent the Court from investigating actions by U.S.

32 *Id.*

33 Jacob J. Lew & Richard Nephew, *The Use and Misuse of Economic Statecraft: How Washington is Abusing its Financial Might*, FOREIGN AFFS. (Oct. 15, 2018), https://www.foreignaffairs.com/articles/world/2018-10-15/use-and-misuse-economic-statecraft (last visited July 10, 2023).

34 Howard Berman et al., *Maintaining America's Coercive Economic Strength: Five Trends to Watch in U.S. Sanctions*, CNAS (Mar. 27, 2019), https://www.cnas.org/publications/reports/maintaining-americas-coercive-economic-strength (last visited July 10, 2023).

personnel in Afghanistan? He could have taken two meaningful steps: a real investigation of potential crimes in Afghanistan and effective diplomacy with the ICC.

First, the Trump Administration (as well as its predecessors) should have investigated and prosecuted any crimes that U.S. personnel may or may not have committed in Afghanistan years ago. The Rome Statute makes clear that the Court is a backstop to national jurisdictions and that it will not investigate or prosecute when national governments have held themselves and their soldiers accountable. Pursuant to Article 17 of the Rome Statute, a case becomes inadmissible if it is or has been "investigated or prosecuted by a state which has jurisdiction over it, unless the state is unwilling or unable genuinely to carry out the investigation or prosecution."[35] In fact, the ICC investigation of U.S. conduct in Afghanistan is only possible because, in the words of the Pre-Trial Chamber:

> As regards [...] investigation efforts at the domestic level in the U.S., [...] the Chamber notes that the information does not show that criminal investigations or prosecutions have been conducted on the incidents referred to and relied upon by the Prosecution.[36]

Had the United States – under Presidents Bush, Obama, or Trump – made justice for past mistakes in Afghanistan a priority, including by investigating and prosecuting senior officials who may have ordered the crimes that occurred in Afghanistan, the ICC would have been stopped in its tracks. Instead, the U.S. military justice system only prosecuted a handful of lower-level soldiers.

If U.S. forces did not commit crimes in Afghanistan within the jurisdiction of the Court, the United States simply must submit to the ICC evidence of a genuine investigation with respect to both military and intelligence agency activities. Under the Rome Statute, states – even those not party to the Statute – have ample opportunity to challenge admissibility by showing a genuine investigation and/or prosecution has occurred.[37] If, on the other hand, there are violations of the laws of war in Afghanistan by U.S. forces that have yet to be adequately investigated and prosecuted, it is not too late for the United States to reverse course. Throughout the course of an investigation, the Court must satisfy itself that national investigations have not

35 Rome Statute, *supra* note 22, art. 17.

36 Decision Pursuant to Article 15, *supra* note 7.

37 Rome Statute, *supra* note 22, art. 19.

been undertaken. In the words of the Pre-Trial Chamber, "it is [...] one of the most compelling duties of the Prosecution to continue verifying the progress of national proceedings during the course of investigations." Should evidence of U.S. investigations and prosecutions that cover "the same individuals and substantially the same conduct as alleged in the proceedings before the Court" begin, the Court will have to declare the case inadmissible and defer to national prosecutions.[38]

A second element of a far more effective strategy involves astute diplomacy and engagement with the ICC. At least until the Trump Administration, there was still room both in Washington and The Hague for productive diplomacy and even cooperation. After all, the United States and the ICC share deep common interests, including a commitment to the rule of law, atrocity prevention, and human rights promotion. Diplomatic engagement around these shared goals, even if circumscribed, creates incentives for the Court to cooperate with the United States, to hear and perhaps even respect U.S. views and interests. Yet, when diplomacy and engagement break down, as they have over the past four years, neither side has any reason to listen to the other, much less accord some deference in choices involving prosecutorial discretion or treaty interpretation.

While the United States and the ICC have long had a troubled past, the Court has sought to retain as productive a working relationship with the United States as possible. That goal was understandable, given the see-saw nature of U.S. engagement with the ICC. Back in 2000, President Clinton signed the Rome Statute establishing the Court.[39] During President Bush's first term, the United States made clear that it would not formally join the Court and actively sought to undermine its work by pressuring other countries to sign agreements barring them from sending Americans to be prosecuted or face aid cutoffs.[40]

But, during President Bush's second term, the United States and the ICC saw a *rapprochement* when the United States allowed the U.N. Security Council to give the Court authority to prosecute the perpetrators of the genocide in Darfur, Sudan.[41] Under President Obama, relations warmed still

---

38 *Id.*

39 Eric P. Schwartz, 'The United States and the International Criminal Court: The Case for "Dexterous Multilateralism"' (2003) 4 *Chi. J. Int'l L.* 223.

40 American Non-Governmental Organizations Coalition for the International Criminal Court (AMICC), *Bush Administration*, [https://web.archive.org/web/20201129035610/https://www.amicc.org/bush-administration-1] (last visited July 10, 2023).

41 John Bellinger and Robert McMahon, *Interview: Bellinger Says International Court Flawed but Deserving of Help in Some Cases*, N.Y. TIMES (Jul. 10, 2007), https://archive

further as the United States engaged more closely with the Court and even offered assistance with evidence collection.[42] In 2010, State Department Legal Advisor Harold Koh announced his intention to meet:

> [With the] Prosecutor at the ICC to examine whether there are specific ways that the United States might be able to support the particular prosecutions already underway in the Democratic Republic of Congo [and] Sudan.[43]

Some such evidence became part of the Prosecutor's investigatory files.[44] While the United States never ratified the Rome Statute, the ICC knew it was better off with tacit support from and a good working relationship with the United States

The ICC's hopes for a productive working relationship with the United States quickly dimmed under the Trump administration. Speaking at the U.N. General Assembly in 2018, President Trump proclaimed:

> As far as America is concerned, the ICC has no jurisdiction, no legitimacy, and no authority.[45]

Not surprisingly after such statements, the Court saw little reason to remain deferential to the United States or to seek its support.

It is often better to have a court on your side than against you. For decades, the institutions of international justice have sought to preserve their relationship with the United States and made prosecutorial and legal choices to avoid direct conflict whenever possible.[46] The Pre-Trial Chamber's decision in April 2019, however legally questionable, may have been a last-ditch

.nytimes.com/www.nytimes.com/cfr/world/slot2_20070710.html (last visited July 10, 2023).

42 Harold Hongju Koh, Legal Adviser U.S. Dept. of State, Speech at Annual Meeting of the American Society of International Law: The Obama Administration and International Law (Mar. 25, 2010), https://2009-2017.state.gov/s/l/releases/remarks/139119.htm (last visited July 10, 2023).

43 Harold Hongju Koh, 'International Criminal Justice 5.0' (2013), 38 *Yale J. Int'l L.* 525.

44 *Id.*

45 Donald J. Trump, President of the United States, Remarks to the 73rd Session of the United Nations General Assembly (Sep. 25, 2018).

46 *See e.g.*, U.N. Int'l Crim. Trib. for the Former Yugoslavia, Final Report to the Prosecutor by the Committee Established to Review the NATO Bombing Campaign Against the Federal Republic of Yugoslavia (June 8, 2000), https://www.icty.org/x/file/Press/nato061300.pdf (last visited July 10, 2023).

effort to do just that. The Appeals Chamber decision makes clear that the Trump administration has now fully squandered whatever good will remained between the United States and the ICC. Instead of seeking U.S. support through diplomacy and shared mutual interest, the ICC has set its sights more actively on the United States

6 A New Administration, a New Approach?

With the election of Joe Biden, there is a real opportunity for a rapprochement between the United States and the ICC. President-Elect Biden has committed to restoring values to American foreign policy, notably through a commitment to human rights and democratic values at home and abroad.[47] The Afghanistan case aside, the ICC fits well with Biden's rights and values agenda. As Presidents Clinton, Bush, and Obama saw, or came to see, the United States and the ICC share many common interests around advancing human rights, preventing atrocities, ending impunity, and ensuring the rule of law. The ICC can be useful to the United States and the United States can be useful to the ICC. It would be naive to suggest that the Biden Administration could – or even should – seek ratification of the Rome Statute. But, reestablishing a productive, diplomatic relationship with the ICC where interests align is possible and should be a priority.

After the damage done by President Trump, repairing the relationship between The Hague and Washington will not be easy, particularly in light of domestic political divides in the United States and the potential for indictments of U.S. personnel in the Afghanistan case. A first key step in rebuilding that relationship must be the revocation of Trump's counterproductive Executive order and the removal of ICC officials from the designated sanctions list. Even without a full embrace of the ICC, the Biden Administration should view these sanctions as a direct affront to international human rights and detrimental to U.S. national interests. They fly in the face of every

47 *The Power of America's Example: The Biden Plan for Leading the Democratic World to Meet the Challenges of the 21st Century*, JOEBIDEN, [hereinafter The Power of America's Example], [https://web.archive.org/web/20201206223501/https://joebiden.com/americanleadership/] (last visited July 10, 2023); Joseph R. Biden, Jr., *Why America Must Lead Again: Rescuing U.S. Foreign Policy After Trump*, FOREIGN AFFS. (Jan. 23, 2020), https://www.foreignaffairs.com/articles/united-states/2020-01-23/why-america-must-leadagain (last visited July 10, 2023).

U.S. and international effort to protect human rights defenders and they offer a powerful example for despots around the world to follow suit.[48]

That said, the Biden Administration will inherit the thorny challenge of a dysfunctional relationship with the ICC and a now authorized Afghanistan investigation. The best approach the Biden Administration can take is not to continue Trump's belligerent statements and ineffective sanctions, but to begin a new era of careful diplomacy and to exercise legal defenses available within the Rome Statute. Through such diplomacy, the new Administration can signal both a willingness to work with the Court and the imperative that the Court avoid indictments of U.S. nationals. At the appropriate time, the new Administration can challenge the admissibility of the case by documenting to the Court investigations and prosecutions that the United States has already undertaken. Hopefully that evidence will suffice to render the case inadmissible. If it turns out, however, that the United States has not undertaken a full investigation of crimes potentially committed by U.S. forces in Afghanistan and subject to ICC scrutiny, we will have to look hard at our own commitment to human rights and accountability. It may, in fact, be time to undertake here at home a more thorough and comprehensive review of our own conduct in Afghanistan. Such a reckoning is, in fact, the ultimate purpose of the ICC and deeply consistent with President-elect Biden's commitment to "repair and reinvigorate our own democracy, even as we strengthen the coalition of democracies that stand with us around the world."[49]

---

48 *US Support for Human Rights Defenders: Fact Sheet*, U.S. DEPT. OF STATE, https://www.state.gov/u-s-support-for-human-rights-defenders/ (last visited July 10, 2023); Organization for Security and Co-operation in Europe (ODIHR), Guidelines on the Protection of Human Rights Defenders (May 28, 2014), https://www.osce.org/files/f/documents/c/1/119633.pdf (last visited July 10, 2023).

49 The Power of America's Example, *supra* note 47.

CHAPTER 18

Rescinding the ICC Sanctions and Signaling America's Commitment to the Rule of Law

Margaret M. deGuzman

1 Introduction

The Biden Administration should rescind President Trump's Executive order attacking the ICC immediately upon taking office. The new administration will have many urgent action items and it may not be immediately apparent why it should give priority to revoking an order that undermines an institution to which the United States is not a party. This essay explains that the importance of this action extends beyond the illegality of the order and the harm it is causing, to the urgent need to signal that the United States is recommitted to the rule of law. By perverting a tool intended to protect people and deter human rights violations, and using it instead to attack an institution devoted to those aims, the Trump Administration has undermined the rule of law in the United States and expressed its disregard for the global rule of law. When President Trump declared ICC efforts to investigate crimes by U.S. personnel to be a "national emergency," he abused the discretion afforded Presidents to keep the United States safe, essentially placing himself above the rule of law. Moreover, by attacking the judicial independence of the ICC, President Trump is seeking to undermine global rule of law. In immediately rescinding the Executive order, President Biden will not only undo an illegal action by his predecessor, he will signal to the world a renewed U.S. commitment to the rule of law.

The Biden Administration will have no shortage of urgent tasks on January 20, 2021. President Trump and his allies have wreaked such havoc on U.S. political, economic, and social systems that it is hard to know where to start seeking to undo the damage. Moreover, the United States, like much of the rest of the world, is under attack by one of the deadliest viruses the world has ever known, which has caused staggering losses of life and shattered the economy. Why then should the new administration focus its attention on an Executive order that seeks to undermine the International Criminal Court (ICC), an institution to which the United States is not a party and whose work does not directly affect the lives of most Americans?

 | DOI:10.1163/9789004686755_023

The answer is not – or not only – that the Executive order is an illegal exercise of executive authority that violates the free speech rights and threatens the livelihoods of people who work for global justice. Rather, it is that the Executive order symbolizes the Trump Administration's disregard for the rule of law within the United States and around the world. As U.S. Senator Patrick Leahy tweeted:

> The Trump Administration's announcement of sanctions against the ICC Prosecutor exposes the fallacy of the White House's professed commitment to the rule of law, and will further undermine U.S. leadership on international justice.[1]

Rescinding the Executive order will thus signal that the United States intends once again to respect and promote global values, including respect for human rights, fairness, accountability, and judicial independence.

2 Background: Executive Orders under the International Emergency Economic Powers Act

The Trump administration has adopted many policies and engaged in many actions that violate human and civil rights and flout international laws and norms. From unleashing federal law enforcement on peaceful protesters to separating children from their families at the U.S. border and essentially imprisoning them, there is no shortage of examples of horrifying policy decisions from the past four years. Even in this climate, however, Executive Order 13928 stands out as particularly concerning. The Executive order perverts a tool intended to protect people and deter human rights abuses, using it instead to attack people who have dedicated their lives to the pursuit of justice for egregious human rights violations, including crimes against humanity and genocide.

The Executive order was issued pursuant to the International Emergency Economic Powers Act (IEEPA), which Congress enacted to enable the president to take extraordinary action in the face of serious threats to U.S. national security constituting national emergencies. Since it was enacted in 1977, IEEPA has most often been used to address national emergencies stemming from the policies of foreign governments. For instance, the first such emergency was declared after the hostage taking at the U.S. embassy

1 Patrick Leahy (@SenatorLeahy), X (Sep. 2, 2020, 2:18 PM), https://twitter.com/SenatorLeahy/status/1301222882433998848 (last visited July 10, 2023).

in Iran in 1979, and remains in effect today. Over the years, IEEPA emergencies have been declared in several dozen countries, including Afghanistan, Iraq, Libya, and Syria. More recently, IEEPA emergencies have been declared with regard to threats that are not linked to particular territories. These address such threats to U.S. security as the proliferation of chemical and biological weapons, terrorism, transnational crime, and malicious cyber-enabled activities.[2] Additionally, IEEPA has sometimes been invoked in response to serious human rights violations in countries such as Sudan and Venezuela.

Executive Order 13928 "Blocking Property of Certain Persons Associated with the International Criminal Court" is the first time the IEEPA has been used to target an international organization, let alone an organization devoted to preventing serious human rights abuses such as genocide, crimes against humanity, and war crimes. In the Executive order, President Trump asserted that ICC efforts to investigate or prosecute U.S. personnel are "an unusual or extraordinary threat to the national security and foreign policy of the United States," and "declare[d] a national emergency to deal with that threat."[3] To address this asserted threat, the Executive order authorizes the Secretary of State, in consultation with the Secretary of the Treasury and Attorney General, to designate for sanctions any foreign person who has engaged in any effort by the ICC to investigate or prosecute personnel of the United States or its allies that are not ICC parties, or who has "materially assisted, sponsored, or provided financial, material, or technological support for, or goods or services to or in support of," such activities.[4] The kinds of assistance prohibited under the order are very broad, including, among other things, contributing funds, goods, or services for the benefit of a designated person. The consequence of designation under the Executive order is that all property and property interests of the designated person in the United States are blocked.

Given the serious consequences of engaging with a designated person, designation leads to what has been described as "civil death."[5] Since the majority of international transactions are conducted in U.S. dollars, they

---

2 Christopher A. Casey, et al., Elsea, Cong. Rsch. Serv., R45618, The International Emergency Economic Powers Act: Origins, Evolution, and Use 20 (2020), https://sgp.fas.org/crs/natsec/R45618.pdf (last visited July 10, 2023).

3 Exec. Order No. 13928: Blocking Property of Certain Persons Associated with the International Criminal Court, 85 Fed. Reg. 115, 36139 (Jun. 11, 2020), https://www.govinfo.gov/content/pkg/FR-2020-06-15/pdf/2020-12953.pdf (last visited July 7, 2023).

4 *Id.* at § 1(a)(i)(C).

5 Adam M. Smith, *Dissecting the Executive Order on Int'l Criminal Court Sanctions: Scope, Effectiveness, and Tradeoffs*, JUST SEC. (Jun. 15, 2020), https://www.justsecurity.org/70779/

involve a bank in the United States Any such transactions by, or on behalf of, designated persons are blocked. Many financial institutions, even outside the United States, refuse to deal with designated persons. As Human Rights Watch has noted, the fear of losing access to U.S. banks causes financial institutions around the world to refuse to engage in transactions involving designated persons.[6]

In addition to consequences for designated persons, the Executive order can be enforced against anyone who interacts with such a person in one of the prohibited ways. Unlike designation, which requires foreign citizenship, any person can be penalized for illegal interactions with a designated person. The consequences of such interactions include civil penalties of the greater of up to $307,922, or twice the value of the transaction that violated the order, and criminal fines of up to $1,000,000 and twenty years in prison.[7]

Since the Trump Administration, in September 2020, designated ICC Prosecutor Fatou Bensouda and Phakiso Mochochoko, head of her office's Jurisdiction, Complementarity and Cooperation Division, they have experienced serious consequences, as has the ICC itself. Bensouda and Mochochoko's travel is severely curtailed and they are unable to access many financial institutions. Additionally, the sanctions have affected the ICC's ability to secure financial resources and services to support its work. Moreover, personnel within the ICC who could be subject to enforcement action for assisting Bensouda and Mochochoko have had to be walled off from working with them. All of these limitations undermine the ICC's ability to fight for justice for international crimes.

3 The Executive Order Is Illegal

On October 1, 2020, I joined the Open Society Justice Initiative and three other law professors in filing a lawsuit challenging the legality of the Executive order and its implementing regulations.[8] Each of the plaintiffs has reason to fear both designation under the Executive order and enforcement of

dissecting-the-executive-order-on-intl-criminal-court-sanctions-scope-effectiveness-and-tradeoffs/ (last visited July 11, 2023).

6 *US Sanctions on the International Criminal Court*, HUM. RTS. WATCH (Dec. 14, 2020), [hereinafter HRW on U.S. Sanctions], https://www.hrw.org/news/2020/12/14/us-sanctions-international-criminal-court (last visited July 11, 2023).

7 International Emergency Economic Powers Act, P.L. 95-223, 91 Stat. 1626 (1977), codified as amended at 50 U.S.C. § 1701 (2018) [hereinafter IEEPA].

8 Press Release, Open Soc'y Just. Initiative, Open Society Justice Initiative Sues Trump Administration over International Criminal Court Executive Order (Oct. 1, 2020), https://

civil and criminal penalties for violating its provisions. First, we are all dual citizens, which may qualify us as "foreign persons" who can be designated for sanctions under the Executive order. Although neither the Executive order nor the regulations define this term, it has been interpreted to include dual citizens in other regulations issued under IEEPA.[9] Second, each of us provides various kinds of assistance to Prosecutor Bensouda and her office. These include, among other things, directly advising the Prosecutor's office, filing amicus briefs supportive of the Prosecutor's positions in cases, engaging in conferences and other exchanges of ideas and information with members of the Prosecutor's office, and publishing books, articles, and other material that provides advice to that office.

As we allege in the complaint, the Executive order and regulations are illegal for several reasons. First, they violate our First Amendment free speech rights by prohibiting us from providing speech-based assistance and services to the ICC Prosecutor and her office. As the law professor plaintiffs have explained in publications about our lawsuit, the Executive order means that we cannot do our jobs effectively.[10] Our professional work focuses on preventing serious crimes such as genocide, war crimes, and crimes against humanity, including by speaking and writing about the work of the ICC Prosecutor and her office. Additionally, one of the plaintiffs, Diane Amann, has had to stop her work as Special Advisor to the Prosecutor on Children In and Affected by Armed Conflict,[11] and the Open Society Justice Initiative has had to limit its engagement in important work to reform the ICC Prosecutor's office, among other initiatives.[12] Other important activities that

---

www.justiceinitiative.org/newsroom/open-society-justice-initiative-sues-trump-administration-over-international-criminal-court-executive-order (last visited July 11, 2023).

9 *See, e.g.*, Narcotics Trafficking Sanctions Regulations, 31 CFR § 536.304 (2004), (defining "foreign person" as "any citizen or national of a foreign state (including any such individual who is also a citizen or national of the United States), or any entity not organized solely under the laws of the United States or existing solely in the United States, but does not include a foreign state.").

10 Diane Marie Amann, Margaret deGuzman, Gabor Rona and Milena Sterio, *Why We Are Suing President Trump*, JUST SEC. (Oct. 8, 2020), https://www.justsecurity.org/72733/why-we-are-suing-president-trump/ (last visited July 11, 2023); Margaret M. deGuzman, *Opinion: For Working to Support Global Justice, I Could Face U.S. Sanctions*, CBC (Oct. 31, 2020), https://www.cbc.ca/news/opinion/opinion-international-criminal-court-sanctions-1.5777753 (last visited July 11, 2023).

11 Diane Marie Amann, *I Help Children in Armed Conflict. The President Is Forcing Me to Stop.*, JUST SEC. (Jun. 29, 2020), https://www.justsecurity.org/71048/i-help-children-in-armed-conflict-the-president-is-forcing-me-to-stop/ (last visited July 11, 2023).

12 Complaint at ¶ 90, Open Soc'y Just. Initiative v. Trump, (S.D.N.Y., 2020) (No. 1:20-cv-08121), 2020 WL 5836982, https://www.justiceinitiative.org/uploads/1a2af879-b89c-4c53-8dd2-6c27f403d0ef/osji-et-al.-v.-donald-trump-et-al_Redactedv2.pdf (last visited July 11, 2023).

we have had to stop include contributing to amicus briefs and speaking publicly about the work of the Prosecutor. Such activities violate the Executive order and could subject us to civil and criminal enforcement penalties, as well as to designation for providing the Prosecutor's office with "material assist[ance]," "support," or "services." Indeed, on January 4, 2021, the court issued an order enjoining the defendants from enforcing IEEPA's civil or criminal penalty provisions against us based on our First Amendment claims.

A second reason the Executive order and regulations are illegal is that they lack the clarity required by the Fifth Amendment regarding what conduct is prohibited, thus permitting arbitrary enforcement. In particular, by failing to define "foreign persons" they lack clarity as to which persons are subject to designation; and by failing to define "materially assisted," "material [...] support," and "services to or in support of", they are ambiguous as to which acts subject a person to designation or enforcement. As a result, the plaintiffs have had to stop engaging in a wide range of activities that support the ICC's global justice efforts for fear of arbitrary enforcement.

Finally, the Executive order and regulations are ultra vires under IEEPA because they seek to regulate activities that are protected by statute. Under 50 U.S.C. § 1702(b)(3), the President may not use IEEPA to "regulate or prohibit [...] the importation from any country, or the exportation to any country, whether commercial or others, [...] of any information or informational materials, including but not limited to, publications, films, posters [...]". Many of the activities in which the plaintiffs have engaged in the past, which they are prohibited from engaging in under the Executive order, constitute such importation and exportation of information and, as such, cannot be regulated under IEEPA.

4 The Executive Order Undermines U.S. Interests, Including the Rule of Law

In addition to being illegal, the Executive Order undermines U.S. interests. First, it is unlikely to accomplish its stated objective of deterring the ICC from investigating and prosecuting personnel from the United States and its non-party state allies. Indeed, the Executive order may increase the ICC's resolve to pursue the situation involving such personnel. For any court, it is important to demonstrate impartiality and independence from political influence. This is particularly true for a court like the ICC that is young and still seeking to establish its legitimacy. If ICC decision-making were influenced, or perceived to be influenced, by political pressure from a powerful state, its legitimacy would be negatively affected, and state support for the Court would likely suffer. The need to avoid a perception of outside influence may encourage the Court to proceed against U.S. personnel. Moreover, as William Burke-White has noted, unlike more typical targets of sanctions such as corrupt government leaders, persons who work for global justice are motivated by conscience rather than wealth.[13] Instead of cowing to bully tactics like the threat of illegal sanctions, they tend to respond to such affronts with renewed determination. Finally, the ferocity of the U.S. attack on the Court may signal that U.S. personnel have "something to hide," further spurring investigation.[14]

Nor has the Executive order undermined support for the Court around the world. Indeed, it has had the oppositive effect. Despite the significant challenges the ICC has faced in recent years, many governments spoke out swiftly and strongly after the Executive order was issued.[15] Within days of the order's promulgation, sixty-seven ICC member countries, including important U.S. allies, issued a statement expressing their "unwavering support for the Court as an independent and impartial judicial institution."[16] Ten members of the Security Council, including France and the United Kingdom, stated their "commitment to uphold the principles and values enshrined in the Rome Statute and to preserve its integrity, undeterred by any threats against the Court, its officials, and those cooperating with it."[17] Again in November 2020, seventy-one ICC member countries reaffirmed their support for the Court in a statement to the U.N. General Assembly, stating: "Any attempt to undermine the independence of the Court should

13 William Burke-White, *The Danger of Trump's New Sanctions on the International Criminal Court and Human Rights Defenders*, BROOKINGS (Jun. 11, 2020), https://www.brookings.edu/articles/the-danger-of-trumps-new-sanctions-on-the-international-criminal-court-and-human-rights-defenders/ (last visited July 11, 2023).

14 Beth Van Schaack, *The Int'l Criminal Court Executive Order: Global Reactions Compiled*, JUST SEC. (Sep. 1, 2020), https://www.justsecurity.org/72256/the-intl-criminal-court-executive-order-global-reactions-compiled/ (last visited July 11, 2023).

15 *See id.*

16 *ICC: Member Countries Rally Around Court*, HUM. RTS. WATCH (Jun. 23, 2020), https://www.hrw.org/news/2020/06/23/icc-member-countries-rally-around-court (last visited July 11, 2023).

17 Press Statement, Permanent Mission of France to the U.N., Statement by States Parties to the Rome Statute in Support of the International Criminal Court on the Occasion of the ICC Report to the General Assembly (Nov. 2, 2020), https://onu.delegfrance.org/We-reiterate-our-commitment-to-uphold-and-defend-the-principles-and-values (last visited July 11, 2023).

not be tolerated."[18] Many other such statements have been made in support of the ICC since the Executive order was issued and the designations were made.[19]

Additionally, as Beth Van Schaack has pointed out, the Executive order undermines any legitimate efforts to preempt the ICC's exercise of jurisdiction over U.S. personnel. Under the ICC's complementarity regime, it may not exercise jurisdiction in cases where a state with jurisdiction is doing so genuinely.[20] The best way to avoid ICC prosecution of U.S. personnel is therefore to conduct credible national investigations and prosecutions. The Trump administration's attacks on the Court would make any such efforts appear disingenuous.

Even more important than the Executive order's negative impact on the objective of avoiding ICC investigation and prosecution of U.S. personnel is the Order's detrimental effect on the rule of law. The United Nations has called the rule of law:

> [A] principle of governance in which all persons, institutions and entities [...] are accountable to laws that are publicly promulgated, equally enforced and independently adjudicated, and which are consistent with international human rights norms and standards.[21]

The Executive order expresses the Trump Administration contempt for the rule of law, both nationally and internationally.

At the national level, the Executive order shows the president's disregard for constraints on the exercise of Executive power. In an effort to ensure presidents have the ability to address a broad range of threats to national security, courts have granted them significant discretion in determining what constitutes an emergency under IEEPA.[22] However, to declare that the threat of ICC investigation rises to the level of a national emergency is

---

18 HRW on U.S. Sanctions, *supra* note 6.

19 Kevin Jon Heller, *Statement Against US Sanctions on ICC Investigations*, OPINIO JURIS (Jun. 30, 2020), available at https://opiniojuris.org/2020/06/30/statement-against-us-sanctions-on-icc-investigations/ (last visited July 11, 2023) (statement against EO 13928 signed by 187 American lawyers).

20 International Criminal Court, Rome Statute of the International Criminal Court, art. 17, U.N. Doc. A/CONF.183/9, (July 17, 1998) [hereinafter Rome Statute].

21 *What is the Rule of Law*, U.N.: U.N. AND THE RULE OF LAW, https://www.un.org/ruleoflaw/what-is-the-rule-of-law/ (last visited July 11, 2023).

22 *See, e.g.*, TikTok Inc. v. Trump, 490 F. Supp. 3d 73, 80 (D.D.C. 2020) ("IEEPA contains a broad grant of authority to declare national emergencies").

so ludicrous that it signals the President considers himself above the law. Unlike typical IEEPA emergencies such as threats from ruthless dictatorships, terrorist organizations, and nuclear proliferation, ICC investigations and prosecutions seek to prevent human rights abuses by punishing those responsible for particularly egregious violations. Sanctioning ICC personnel is such a flagrant violation of discretion as to seek to position the President as outside the rule of law.

Likewise, the Executive order signals that the United States considers itself above the rule of international law. To be sure, U.S. exceptionalism with respect to the ICC pre-dates the Trump administration. Even the Obama administration, which promoted many rule of law efforts around the world, including supporting ICC investigations, never sought to join the Court. It also declined to prosecute U.S. personnel responsible for torture, extraordinary rendition, and other serious human rights violations. However, in using sanctions to target persons who fight human rights violations rather than those who commit them, the Trump administration expressed a new level of contempt for the application of international law to the United States

Ironically, one of the few positive actions the Trump Administration has taken with respect to rule of law promotion overseas is the expansion and use of sanctions against foreign personnel suspected of serious human rights violations. The Administration has made active use of the Global Magnitsky Human Rights Accountability Act, designating numerous suspected human rights violators for sanctions, and has adopted an Executive order that expands the scope of such sanctions.[23] The juxtaposition of these actions with the Executive order highlights the extent to which the Administration sees the United States as beyond the reach of international law. As Mark Kersten has written, the Administration's view seems to be: "If you're American, look like an American, or are a friend of America, international criminal justice must not apply to you."[24]

This extreme exceptionalism both positions the United States and its allies outside the reach of justice efforts, and, relatedly, signals that they are free to commit human rights abuses. Dictators and others around the world

---

23 Exec. Order No. 13818: Blocking the Property of Persons Involved in Serious Human Rights Abuse or Corruption, 82 Fed. Reg. 246, 60839 (Dec. 20, 2017), https://www.govinfo.gov/content/pkg/FR-2017-12-26/pdf/2017-27925.pdf (last visited July 11, 2023).

24 Mark Kersten, *Trump's Sanctions Against International Criminal Court Staff Aren't Just 'Bad', They're Racist*, JUST. IN CONFLICT (Sep. 10, 2020), https://justiceinconflict.org/2020/09/10/trumps-sanctions-against-international-criminal-court-staff-arent-just-bad-theyre-racist/ (last visited July 11, 2023).

who know that U.S. political or economic interests align with their own are likely emboldened by the Executive order to engage in repressive actions that violate human rights. The order gives them comfort that the world's most powerful government may protect them from accountability efforts.

Finally, the Executive order vitiates the rule of law by seeking to undermine the independence of a judicial institution. The clear intent of the Executive order is to coerce the ICC to stop investigating persons from the United States and its allies. In an interview with the American Enterprise Institute, Ambassador-at-Large for Global Criminal Justice Morse Tan threatened that unless the ICC Statute is revised to preclude such investigations, the United States will seek to shutter the institution.[25] Such bullying of a judicial institution is a tactic typically employed by dictators to undermine rule of law.

Many states and governmental and non-governmental organizations have reacted with outrage to U.S. efforts to undermine the ICC's independence.[26] The International Bar Association declared itself "appalled by the United States Government's continued campaign to intimidate ICC staff;" and asserted that "[t]he unprecedented punitive application of sanctions on a legitimate judicial institution is a shameful move to undermine the Court's authority […]"[27] The American Bar Association adopted a policy "urg[ing] all national governments to observe, respect, and protect the independence of the International Criminal Court,"[28] and noted:

> In a time when democracy is in retreat globally, such an attack against the ICC and its professional staff by the United States – historically the leading exemplar of democracy and a just rule of law, of which an independent judiciary is an indispensable part – gives fodder to those

25 *The International Criminal Court and Global Criminal Justice: A Conversation with Amb. Morse H. Tan*, AMERICAN ENTERPRISE INSTITUTE (Oct. 26, 2020), https://www.aei.org/events/the-international-criminal-court-and-global-criminal-justice-a-conversation-with-amb-morse-h-tan/ (last visited July 11, 2023).

26 Van Schaack, *supra* note 14.

27 Press Release, Int'l Bar Ass'n, IBA Condemns US President's Executive Order Authorising Sanctions Against International Criminal Court Personnel, (Jun. 12, 2020), https://www.ibanet.org/article/91b435ac-2ab3-4dad-b8b2-2f6c18d8aecd (last visited July 11, 2023).

28 *ABA Adopts Policy Condemning Threats Against the ICC and Its Officers*, INT'L CRIM. JUST. TODAY (Aug. 3, 2020), https://www.international-criminal-justice-today.org/news/aba-adopts-policy-condemning-threats-against-the-icc-and-its-officers/ (last visited July 11, 2023).

> who cite such attacks as a legitimate basis to undermine judicial independence in their countries.[29]

In sum, the Executive order undermines the rule of law both inside the United States and abroad by positioning the United States and its President above the law, and by attacking the independence of a judicial institution.

5 Conclusion

According to the United Nations, respect for rule of law requires:

> [M]easures to ensure adherences to the principles of supremacy of the law, equality before the law, accountability to the law, fairness in the application of the law, separation of powers, participate in decision-making, legal certainty, avoidance of arbitrariness, and procedural and legal transparency.[30]

By rescinding the Executive order on day one, the Biden Administration can signal a recommitment to these principles. This signal will be important to U.S. allies who have watched with dismay for four years as the United States pursued policies more in line with those of a corrupt dictatorship than a beacon of democracy and justice.

---

29 Am. Bar Ass'n Ctr. for Hum. Rights, Resolution (2020), https://www.americanbar.org/content/dam/aba/administrative/news/2020/08/2020-am-resolutions/114.pdf (last visited July 11, 2023).

30 What is the Rule of Law, *supra* note 21.

CHAPTER 19

Rescinding ICC Prosecutor's "Designation" as Part of a Broader Strategy

Luis Moreno-Ocampo

President Trump designated the International Criminal Court's Prosecutor "for having directly engaged in an effort to investigate U.S. personnel."[1] The consequences of being designated include, but are not limited to, freezing their assets and blocking any persons or entities, including financial institutions, from providing services to the designated individual. The measure is typically used against terrorists and narcotics traffickers.

President Biden has the legal authority to cancel the designation of Fatou Bensouda, the ICC Prosecutor, and he should do it. But rescinding the designation is not just a legal issue; it's also a charged political decision.

Imagine U.S. media comments about an isolated decision to repeal the designation: 'Biden supports Prosecutor who's seeking to imprison U.S. soldiers fighting to protect us from terrorists.' In war, those who support the opponent are seen as the enemy.

Protecting U.S. officers involved in the War on Terror from judicial investigations is popularly supported in the United States. And the three previous Presidents did so. But the ICC Prosecutor's designation was unprecedented.

The Trump Administration adopted the decision a few weeks before election day, cornering the Democratic Party. Joseph Biden, the opposition candidate, did not mention the issue during his campaign.

Considering the U.S. political context, it is clear that revoking the ICC Prosecutor's designation could not be a measure adopted in isolation. It should be a piece of a new general strategy to end the Afghanistan military intervention. But the expert community is not proposing options that allow President Biden to make a rational choice to address the Afghanistan problem.

1 Press Statement, Michael R. Pompeo, Secretary of State, U.S. Dept. of State, Actions to Protect U.S. Personnel from Illegitimate Investigation by the International Criminal Court (Sep. 2, 2020), https://web.archive.org/web/20200903052842/https://www.state.gov/actions-to-protect-u-s-personnel-from-illegitimate-investigation-by-the-international-criminal-court/ (last visited July 11, 2023).

 | DOI:10.1163/9789004686755_024

In 2015, Stephen Walt denounced a collective failure of the entire U.S. foreign-policy establishment, including both Democrats and Republicans, to propose new strategies to deal with international terrorism in the Middle East.[2] Since then, there has been little to address that failure.

In this comment, I invite the ICC Forum to be the platform to develop a comprehensive exit strategy from Afghanistan for President Biden, which includes rescinding the ICC Prosecutor's designation.

The exit plan should not capitulate to the Taliban, and the new U.S. Administration would need a legal strategy to avoid an ICC investigation against U.S. officers.

My perspective as a foreigner might illuminate some possibilities, but this should be an urgent conversation and a collective exercise led by U.S. scholars.

In my opinion, it is possible to create a special "International Antiterrorist System," a unique law enforcement model that would remain in place in Afghanistan without military intervention. It could combine an ad hoc international criminal system, using intelligence that should not be disclosed, and special forces operations. This essay presents the idea in general terms to open a discussion.

The presentation of such a model by President Biden would offer the perfect opportunity to end the Prosecutor's designation.

1 The Facts

On November 20, 2017, ICC Prosecutor Fatou Bensouda requested authorization to open an investigation in Afghanistan.[3] The crimes to be investigated included allegations of torture committed by members of the CIA and the U.S. Army in Afghanistan.[4]

Afghanistan ratified the Rome Statute[5] and provided jurisdiction to the ICC from May 1, 2003, onwards. The United States never ratified the Rome

2 Stephen M. Walt, *Just Say No: Why the United States Can't Kick the Bad Habit of Repeating Failed Campaigns in its War Against Terror*, FOREIGN POL'Y (Mar. 31, 2015), https://foreignpolicy.com/2015/03/31/just-say-no-us-war-on-terror-yemen-iraq/ (last visited July 11, 2023).

3 Situation in the Islamic Republic of Afghanistan, ICC-02/17, Request for Authorisation of an Investigation pursuant to Article 15 (PTC III, Nov. 20, 2017).

4 *Id* at 23.

5 International Criminal Court, Rome Statute of the International Criminal Court, U.N. Doc. A/CONF.183/9 (July 17, 1998) [hereinafter Rome Statute].

Statute and considered that a non-ratified treaty does not apply to U.S. citizens.

The crimes under investigation by the ICC were committed under the Bush Administration and recognized by different U.S. authorities. In December 2012, the Senate Intelligence Committee led by Sen. Dianne Feinstein produced a confidential report. It would take two years to issue a redacted report for the public to read in December 2014, presenting significant evidence that U.S. personnel engaged in acts of torture.[6]

President Obama recognized that "we tortured some folks."[7]

Neither the Bush nor the Obama Administration investigated those who authorized the crimes. Since the beginning of his term, President Obama had "a belief that we need to look forward as opposed to looking backward."[8]

There are no national investigations against those most responsible for the alleged tortures and, under the principle of complementarity, the cases could be admissible before the ICC. On March 5, 2020, the ICC Appeals Chamber authorized the Prosecutor to commence an investigation into Afghanistan.[9]

On June 11, 2020, President Trump reacted in the face of an inherited problem and issued an Executive order considering that the ICC investigation "constitutes an unusual and extraordinary threat to the national security and foreign policy of the United States."[10]

On September 2, 2020, the Trump Administration "designated" ICC Prosecutor Fatou Bensouda and the Head of the Office of the Prosecutor's Jurisdiction, Complementarity and Cooperation Division Phakiso Mochochoko. Anyone who materially assists the designated individual can themselves be designated.

---

6 SENATE SELECT COMM. ON INTEL., COMMITTEE STUDY OF THE CENTRAL INTELLIGENCE AGENCY'S DETENTION AND INTERROGATION PROGRAM, S. DOC. NO. 113–288 (2014).

7 Josh Gernstein, *Obama: 'We tortured some folks'*, POLITICO (Aug. 1, 2014), https://www.politico.com/story/2014/08/john-brennan-torture-cia-109654 (last visited July 11, 2023).

8 David Johnston and Charlie Savage, *Obama Reluctant to Look into Bush Programs*, N.Y. TIMES (Jan. 11, 2009), https://www.nytimes.com/2009/01/12/us/politics/12inquire.html (last visited July 11, 2023).

9 Situation in the Islamic Republic of Afghanistan, ICC-02/17 OA4, Judgment on the Appeal against the Decision on the Authorization of an Investigation into the Situation in the Islamic Republic of Afghanistan (AC, Mar. 5, 2020).

10 Exec. Order No. 13928: Blocking Property of Certain Persons Associated with the International Criminal Court, 85 Fed. Reg. 115, 36139 (Jun. 11, 2020), https://www.govinfo.gov/content/pkg/FR-2020-06-15/pdf/2020-12953.pdf (last visited July 7, 2023).

Even U.S. professors and this Forum halted the provision of "services" to the ICC's designated persons.

2 The Protection to U.S. Officers Provided by Previous Presidents

George W. Bush, Barack Obama, and Donald Trump's ideas and personalities are very different. However, the three of them protected U.S. officers involved in the War on Terror from any judicial investigation. The War on Terror rewarded loyalty to the United States over respect for legal norms.

President Bush supervised and legally protected those who designed "enhanced interrogation techniques."

President Obama banned the use of torture, but he did not encourage investigations. On the contrary, he wanted to make sure that CIA people, "who are working very hard to keep Americans safe," should not spend "all their time looking over their shoulders."

During a small seminar at Harvard, a member of the Obama Administration explained that the Bush Administration's leaders who authorized enhanced interrogation techniques could have been prosecuted. But he described the political reasoning behind the decision not to do so. To fulfill his promise that "quality and affordable health care would not be a privilege, but a right," President Obama needed to build support in Congress. Considering the political consequences of alienating the Republican Party, the decision adopted was to stop any effort to investigate high-ranking personnel.

President Trump followed a similar path but went beyond that. He neutralized even U.S. justice investigations against military personnel. He pardoned two army officers charged by the U.S. military justice system with war crimes and restored the rank of a Navy Seal officer previously acquitted by a military jury on all but a minor count.[11] At a December 2019 political rally, Trump brought two men on stage, claiming that he had "stuck up for three great warriors against the deep state."[12]

The three Presidents' decisions to cover U.S. officers' crimes indicate that U.S. voters demand to protect those who are protecting them. There is no

11 Dave Philipps, *Trump Clears Three Service Members in War Crimes Case*, N.Y. TIMES (Nov. 15, 2019), https://www.nytimes.com/2019/11/15/us/trump-pardons.html (last visited July 11, 2023).

12 Maggie Haberman, *Trump Brings 2 Officers He Cleared of War Crimes Onstage at Fund-Raiser*, N.Y. TIMES (Dec. 8, 2019), https://www.nytimes.com/2019/12/08/us/politics/trump-war-crimes-pardons.html (last visited July 11, 2023).

U.S. empathy for aliens in foreign countries who are the victims of the actions of U.S. personnel.

John Tirman wrote an entire book analyzing: "One of the most remarkable aspects of American wars is how little we discuss the victims who are not Americans."[13]

President Biden cannot ignore such national political realities.

3 The Failure of the Expert Community to Propose New Solutions

After nineteen years, U.S. politicians, legal experts, and other scholars have failed to propose alternative solutions to manage the new challenges posed by international terrorism.

The specialized knowledge developed by diverse disciplines, namely international relations, political science, international law, international criminal law, humanitarian law, and military strategy, protects each field's boundaries and rejects other paradigms. Consequently, scholars are not proposing new integrated solutions to deal with international terrorism, and the three previous Presidents had to improvise their options.

As Jack Goldsmith explained: "For decades, the U.S. government had officially viewed terrorism as a law enforcement problem." Still, it took President Bush just a few minutes on the very morning of 9/11 to decide "that the conflict with Islamist terrorists must be viewed as a war."[14]

President Bush accepted that he had to improvise a solution: "There is no textbook on how to steady a nation rattled by a faceless enemy. I relied on instincts and background."[15] As a consequence, the United States was not able to learn from previous counterinsurgency experiences.

The U.S. Army concluded in 1989 that the Soviet invasion was "the strongest unifying factor for the insurgents" in Afghanistan. Similar to what would happen after U.S. intervention in 2001, the Afghans "had invading infidels against whom to unite."[16]

---

13 John Tirman, *The Deaths of Others: The Fate of Civilians in America's Wars* (New York: Oxford University Press, 2011), p. 3.

14 Jack Goldsmith, *The Terror Presidency: Law and Judgment Inside the Bush Administration* (W.W. Norton and Company, 2007), p. 103.

15 George W. Bush, *Decision Points* (New York: Crown Publishers, 2010), p. 140.

16 U.S. Dept. of the Army Declassification Release, U.S. Army, Lessons from the War in Afghanistan (May 1989), https://nsarchive2.gwu.edu/NSAEBB/NSAEBB57/us11.pdf (last visited July 11, 2023).

The initial phase of military operations in Afghanistan followed the Bush Administration's improvised plan. The removal of the Taliban government and the bombing of Al Qaeda's training camps was a small and successful operation executed by four hundred U.S. personnel in coordination with Afghan militias. "That war proved, in the short term, to be one of the easiest, cheapest, and most successful campaigns in American military history."[17]

After, the U.S. military faced a different problem: an increased insurgency. The U.S. Army was not prepared for such a challenge.

The only new strategy was counterinsurgency (COIN), developed in 2006 by the U.S. Army and Marines, an effort led by General David Petraeus and Marine General James Mattis. The COIN manual considers that:

> Soldiers and Marines are expected to be nation builders as well as warriors. They must be prepared to help reestablish institutions and local security forces and assist in rebuilding infrastructure and basic services. They must be able to facilitate establishing local governance and the rule of law.[18]

COIN was considered a success in the Iraq "surge" in 2007.

From the beginning of his term, President Obama learned that Al Qaeda had almost no presence in Afghanistan, and the anti-terrorist focus must shift to Pakistan. The mission should be targeting Al Qaeda in Pakistan and not the Taliban in Afghanistan.[19]

For months, President Obama was resisting the military advice to deploy thirty thousand additional troops in Afghanistan. As the Vice President, Joseph Biden participated in the Afghanistan strategy discussions and proposed a different approach.

---

17 Michael Mandelbaum, *Mission Failure: America and the World in the Post-Cold War Era* (Oxford: Oxford University Press, 2016), p. 162 ("The American government made common cause with the Northern Alliance. [...] Two weeks after the September 11 attacks a handful of CIA operatives arrived in Afghanistan carrying cash for their new allies. JSOC personnel also arrived in small numbers to identify Taliban military and political targets for American planes to strike. Altogether, only about 400 Americans set foot in the country in the final months of 2001. In the war against the Taliban it was the Northern Alliance that supplied the ground forces; the United States provided the airpower. The tribes that had accepted Taliban rule, sometimes grudgingly, because there had seemed to be no alternative, now deserted them.").

18 U.S. Dept. of the Army and U.S. Marine Corps, Field Manual No. 3–24 and Marine Corps Warfare Pub. No. 3–33.5 Counterinsurgency at Foreword (2006), https://www.hsdl.org/?view&did=468442 (last visited July 11, 2023).

19 Bob Woodward, *Obama's Wars* (New York: Simon & Schuster, 2010), p. 99.

But, at the Secretary of Defense Robert Gates and Generals Petraeus and McChrystal's insistence, President Obama reluctantly adopted COIN for another couple of years.

President Obama understood that it was not possible to transform Afghanistan into Denmark and changed his policy. He concluded that "a military can't create a political culture or build a society."[20]

Since then, President Obama resolved to return responsibilities to the Afghan government while pursuing a strategy of attrition. He provided instructions "to carry out a singular, ruthless mission of killing suspected terrorists and keeping the country from spiraling out of control."[21]

In July 2010, the American Civil Liberties Union (ACLU) raised its voice against President Obama's policy and stated that: "The Obama administration will preside over the creation of a 'new normal.' "[22]

The war on terror became the "forever war." Obama's CIA Director, John Brennan, warned the U.S. people to expect the war on terror "to continue for millennia."[23]

Jack Goldsmith, in 2012, largely agreed with the ACLU's analysis and explained that the strategy to confront terrorism as a war and not as a crime created the "new normal." He ascribed the lack of new ideas to "a persistence in the interests and outlook of the national security leadership and especially of the national security bureaucracy."[24]

Similarly, Stephen Walt attributed the lack of alternative proposals to a U.S. foreign policy elite operating "in a system that rewards conformity, penalizes dissent, and encourages its members to remain within the prevailing consensus."[25]

President Obama made efforts to end the Afghanistan intervention. Speaking from Afghanistan in February 2012, he announced: "A future in

20 Mark Landler, *The Afghan War and the Evolution of Obama*, N.Y. TIMES (Jan. 1, 2017), https://www.nytimes.com/2017/01/01/world/asia/obama-afghanistan-war.html (last visited July 11, 2023).

21 *Id.*

22 ACLU, *Establishing a New Normal: National Security, Civil Liberties, and Human Rights Under the Obama Administration* (July 2010), https://www.aclu.org/sites/default/files/field_document/EstablishingNewNormal.pdf (last visited July 11, 2023).

23 Micah Zenko, *CIA Director: We're Winning the War on Terror, But It Will Never End*, COUNCIL ON FOREIGN REL. (Apr. 8, 2015), https://www.cfr.org/blog/cia-director-were-winning-war-terror-it-will-never-end (last visited July 11, 2023).

24 Jack Goldsmith, *Power and Constraint: The Accountable Presidency after 9/11* (New York: W.W. Norton and Company, 2012), p. 27.

25 Stephen M. Walt, *The Hell of Good Intentions: America's Foreign Policy Elite and the Decline of U.S. Primacy* (New York: Farrar, Straus and Giroux, 2018), p. 60.

which war ends, and a new chapter begins."[26] Obama signed a strategic partnership agreement with President Hamid Karzai that set the terms for relations after the departure of American troops in 2014, showing that he was "winding down a costly and increasingly unpopular war."[27]

Mr. Obama sought to portray the withdrawal as an unalloyed achievement, though it remains far from certain that the Afghan government can hold its own against the Taliban with reduced American support, or that what were once considered critical American goals here can still be met.[28]

President Obama had no new strategy to replace COIN, and he could not end the Afghanistan war.

Even Marine General James Mattis abandoned COIN. Donald Trump interviewed him as a candidate to be his first Secretary of Defense. Mattis confronted Trump's proposal to return to the torture method, but he suggested the need to move from President Obama's low attrition policy to a war of annihilation. Mattis was appointed.

In December 2018, President Trump concluded that the military efforts were not producing good results and announced his intention to withdraw all American troops from Syria and half of the U.S. forces in Afghanistan.[29] Landler, writing in the New York Times, said that such a resolution united the U.S. left and right against his plan.[30]

In any case, President Trump received no alternative suggestions on what to do. Marine General Mattis strongly disagreed with President Trump's decision and resigned as the Secretary of Defense.[31]

President Trump continued with his effort to end the Afghanistan intervention. On February 19, 2020, the United States and the Taliban signed an "agreement for bringing peace" to Afghanistan after more than eighteen years of conflict. The United States promised to withdraw all troops within

---

26 Mark Landler, *Obama Signs Pact in Kabul, Turning Page in Afghan War*, N.Y. TIMES (May 1, 2012), https://www.nytimes.com/2012/05/02/world/asia/obama-lands-in-kabul-on-unannounced-visit.html (last visited July 11, 2023).

27 *Id.*

28 *Id.*

29 Mark Landler, *Trump Unites Left and Right Against Troop Plans, But Puts Off Debate on War Aims*, N.Y. TIMES (Dec. 27, 2018), https://www.nytimes.com/2018/12/27/us/politics/trump-syria-afghanistan-withdraw.html (last visited July 11, 2023).

30 *Id.*

31 Helene Cooper, *Jim Mattis, Defense Secretary, Resigns in Rebuke of Trump's Worldview*, N.Y. TIMES (Dec. 20, 2018), https://www.nytimes.com/2018/12/20/us/politics/jim-mattis-defense-secretary-trump.html (last visited July 11, 2023) ("My views on treating allies with respect and also being cleareyed about both malign actors and strategic competitors are strongly held.").

fourteen months if the militants uphold the deal. President Trump said: "It's time after all these years to bring our people back home."[32]

The negotiation:

> [V]irtually excluded a divided Afghan central government from the negotiating process. It set no clear conditions for a broad ceasefire or for reaching an actual peace settlement. It did not define how the negotiations would take place, and it seemed far more focused on establishing a clear date for United States withdrawal.[33]

President Biden urgently needs new options.

4 Exploring Alternatives

The problem could create an opportunity for change. Any plan should be based on three principles:

a) no continued United States military presence;
b) non-exclusive reliance on the Afghan national government; and
c) a renewed focus on the control of international terrorism that motivated U.S. intervention in 2001.

A broader policy ending the military effort and defining a reasonable exit strategy from Afghanistan should include a new mechanism to investigate, punish, and control international terrorism.

It is time to return to addressing terrorism as a crime to be fought by law enforcement rather than a war to be faced exclusively with military troops. But the law enforcement model should be equipped to deal with the specific problems posed by terrorism.

The new model should include:

a) a central investigation unit, with personnel working in Afghanistan, but analysts and leaders based outside to provide them with full protection;

---

32 Lyse Doucet, *Afghan Conflict: US and Taliban Sign Deal to End 18-Year War*, BBC NEWS (Feb. 29, 2020), https://www.bbc.com/news/world-asia-51689443 (last visited July 11, 2023).

33 Anthony H. Cordesman, *Afghanistan: The Peace Negotiations Have Become an Extension of War by Other Means* (Ctr. for Strategic Int'l Studies, Working Draft, 2020), https://csis-website-prod.s3.amazonaws.com/s3fs-public/publication/201028_Cordesman_Afghan_War_Other_Means.pdf (last visited July 11, 2023).

b) strong cooperation between the relevant intelligence services, something that is already starting to happen on the ground;
c) the possibility of arresting a suspect for a limited time using intelligence information without disclosure as happens during grand jury investigations;
d) establishing some special courts with the ability to order coercive measures, following the model of the U.S. Foreign Intelligence Surveillance Court; and
e) an independent and robust enforcement arm, combining local authorities and special forces dedicated to that task.

A Trial Chamber should be included to convict individuals following due process.

Furthermore, the investigations should include a vital money tracking component. Financial investigations are a crucial part of any effort to disrupt a criminal organization. Surprisingly, no one is sanctioning those who finance terrorism in the Middle East. The U.S. Treasury, President Obama, and President Trump mentioned specific states financing terrorism, and there was no action against them or their banks. The war framework protects them; they are friends, not enemies. Those states financing terrorism are covered because they support the United States and help fund U.N. programs to control terrorism financing.

The "Anti-terrorist System" could be an exclusive U.S. exercise in agreement with the Afghan government. It could be better if adopted by the U.N. Security Council, reestablishing a global order based on some international consensus. Such an international mechanism could be tested in Afghanistan and eventually exported to investigate Al Qaeda in Pakistan, and other terrorist groups operating in Yemen, Libya, and Somalia.

5 The ICC Admissibility of the Cases against U.S. Personnel

President Biden should also have a legal plan to stop the ICC investigation against U.S. officers.

Complementarity is the legal solution to avoid an ICC investigation, and there are different ways to invoke national primacy. Still, in my opinion, former President Bush assuming responsibility for the actions of his subordinates could provide the best option.

The Rome Statute defines when a case would be admissible before the ICC.

If the national state did not investigate the same case or is "unwilling" or "unable" to conduct investigations, or they are not genuine, the case would be admissible.[34]

Many experts suggest that the United States has to conduct new investigations. Harold Koh went further and proposed to relaunch prosecutions and accept pending Freedom of Information requests "to get the full story."[35] As Koh mentioned, the New York Times had invoked the Freedom of Information Act to request the disclosure of documents from a Justice Department investigation into CIA interrogations, including summaries of interviews with about a hundred witnesses and documents explaining why in the end no charges were filed. But the Obama administration urged the court to reject the request.[36] The Biden Administration would not behave differently.

ACLU Director Anthony Romero proposed a different way. He considered it clear that President Obama was "not inclined to pursue prosecutions." Instead, he suggested pardoning George W. Bush and his administration officials for the authorization of the torture practice.[37]

Romero's idea could be further developed. Former President George W. Bush could accept his responsibility as the supervisor of those involved in the authorization of torture practices. He could do it confidentially or publicly. Bush has the character to assume responsibility and to protect his subordinates. He does not need to go to jail. Analogously, the Office of the Prosecutor accepted that the FARC guerrillas in Colombia could receive an alternative punishment that included helping the victims and other measures.[38]

34 Rome Statute, *supra* note 6, Arts. 53(1)(b), 17.

35 Harold Hongju Koh, *The Torture Report Is Only the First Step*, FOREIGN POL. (Dec. 12, 2014), https://foreignpolicy.com/2014/12/12/the-torture-report-is-only-the-first-step/ (last visited July 11, 2023).

36 Charlie Savage, *U.S. Tells Court That Documents From Torture Investigation Should Remain Secret*, N.Y. TIMES, (Dec. 10, 2014), https://www.nytimes.com/2014/12/11/us/politics/us-tells-court-that-documents-from-torture-investigation-should-remain-secret.html (last visited July 11, 2023).

37 Anthony D. Romero, Editorial, *Pardon Bush and Those Who Tortured*, N.Y. TIMES (Dec. 8, 2014), https://www.nytimes.com/2014/12/09/opinion/pardon-bush-and-those-who-tortured.html (last visited July 12, 2023).

38 Statement, Fatou Bensouda, ICC Prosecutor, On the Conclusion of the Peace Negotiations Between the Government of Colombia and the Revolutionary Armed Forces of Colombia – People's Army (Sep. 1, 2016), https://www.icc-cpi.int/news/statement-icc-prosecutor-fatou-bensouda-conclusion-peace-negotiations-between-government (last visited July 12, 2023).

If Bush accepted such responsibility, it would be an enormous service for his party, his country, and the international rule of law.

6 Conclusion

Can this Forum create the space to prepare alternative strategies? There is no time to lose. The entire program should be announced during the first one hundred days of Biden's Presidency.

CHAPTER 20

The ICC: A Political Institution That Promotes Double Standards

John Choon Yoo and Ivana Stradner

The International Criminal Court (ICC) authorized an investigation of alleged war crimes and crimes against humanity by U.S., Afghan, and Taliban troops in Afghanistan, as well as alleged crimes committed at CIA black sites operated in Poland, Lithuania, and Romania.[1] While the prosecution will likely fail, it represents another effort by a global elite – consisting of European governments, international organizations, and their supporting interest groups, academics, and activists – to threaten American sovereignty.

The Rome Statute,[2] which established the ICC in 1998, was originally supported by 120 states. It had the worthy goal of preventing the world's most horrific crimes. The U.N. Secretary General, Kofi Annan, called the establishment of the ICC "the promise of universal justice."[3] Today the ICC can exercise jurisdiction over war crimes, crimes against humanity, aggression, and genocide. Its founders believed that an international organization in the form of a court could replace the customary role of nation-states to punish those who violate the rules of civilized warfare.

The Clinton administration signed the treaty in 2000, but did not submit it for Senate ratification. American support for the Court later dissolved after 9/11, as American officials worried that the ICC would become an anti-American kangaroo court used by certain countries to constrain nation-state sovereignty, which proved to be correct. In 2002, the Bush administration announced that it would not sign the agreement, and empowered then-State Department official John Bolton to lead a U.S. campaign to sign bilateral immunity agreements with more than a hundred countries to protect both parties from the ICC's jurisdiction.

1 *Afghanistan*, INT'L CRIM. CT., https://www.icc-cpi.int/Afghanistan (last visited July 12, 2023).

2 International Criminal Court, Rome Statute of the International Criminal Court, U.N. Doc. A/CONF.183/9 (July 17, 1998) [hereinafter Rome Statute].

3 Kofi Annan, 'Advocating for an International Criminal Court' (1997) 21 *Fordham Int'l L.J.* 363.

 | DOI:10.1163/9789004686755_025

Ever since then, the ICC has labored ineffectually. To date, the Court has spent more than two billion dollars and yielded only eight successful convictions and four acquittals, focusing only on African countries. While there are 123 member states, nations that still might have to wage war, such as the United States, Israel, India, South Korea, China, and Russia, have refused to join. In doing so, these states expressed that they would preserve the Court's "integrity and independence undeterred by any measures or threats against the Court, its officials and those cooperating with it."

America's Western European allies, perhaps still hoping for a utopian future where war has disappeared and meager conventional forces are all that is needed, lend the ICC its greatest support.

Most ICC officials have long hoped to achieve international relevance by attacking the ICC's greatest critic: the United States. Since November 2017, ICC Prosecutor Fatou Bensouda has sought to use alleged crimes in Afghanistan to bring charges against the U.S. military and intelligence community. The ICC Pre-Trial Chamber later ruled against an investigation (and possible prosecution) of the United States for alleged crimes in Afghanistan because both would most likely fail. However, the ICC's Appellate Chamber reversed this ruling of the Court's lower Pre-Trial Chamber and allowed Bensouda to continue her investigations of American activities in Afghanistan and elsewhere after 9/11.

America's response has been tough towards the Court, and after numerous threats by the ICC, U.S. Secretary of State Mike Pompeo ordered the revocation of the ICC Prosecutor's U.S. entry visa. In June 2020, President Donald Trump issued an Executive order on Blocking Property of Certain Persons Associated with the International Criminal Court, criminalizing those who work at the ICC.[4] The Executive Order explained the situation as "illegitimate assertions of jurisdiction over personnel of the United States and certain of its allies" and described an attempt by the ICC to investigate the United States as a "threat to the national security and foreign policy of the United States." In September 2020, Secretary of State Pompeo announced new sanctions against ICC Prosecutor Fatou Bensouda and Phakiso Mochochoko.[5] As a result of the U.S. Executive Order, close U.S. allies, such

4 Exec. Order No. 13928: Blocking Property of Certain Persons Associated with the International Criminal Court, 85 Fed. Reg. 115, 36139 (Jun. 11, 2020), https://www.govinfo.gov/content/pkg/FR-2020-06-15/pdf/2020-12953.pdf (last visited July 7, 2023).

5 *Phakiso Mochochoko*, INTERNATIONAL CRIMINAL COURT, https://www.icc-cpi.int/about/otp/who-s-who/phakiso-mochochoko (last visited July 12, 2023).

as Australia, Canada, the UK, and France, offered their "unwavering support for the Court as an independent and impartial judicial institution."[6]

The ICC judge Chile Eboe-Osuji claimed that American sanctions constituted coercion, which is illegal under international law, as well as U.S. domestic law. In his words:

> In any liberal democracy, or even not so liberal democracies, you pick up a statute book and it will tell you that it is against the law to coerce a court of law in order to have justice the way you want it.

This analysis is incorrect because the U.S. response was not coercion. Instead, American sanctions had a deterrent role (which is not contrary to international law) to protect its sovereignty, which is the main principle in international law.

Speaking at the U.N. General Assembly, President Trump stated: "As far as America is concerned, the ICC has no jurisdiction, no legitimacy, and no authority" and he is correct. The ICC has no jurisdiction to investigate the U.S. military for two main reasons. First, the United States is not a state party to the Rome Statute. The ICC lacks jurisdiction over crimes occurring before the Rome Statute entered into force on July 1, 2002 or over crimes occurring before ratification for those member states after that date. This rule prevents the Court from prosecuting individuals for new crimes. However, nationals of nonparties can be subject to prosecution no matter when new crimes are included or where they are situated, which is contrary to the main principle of sovereignty. Second, the ICC is based on "the principle of complementarity"[7] and it is a court of last resort and can only step in where national legal systems fail to undertake prosecutions. Given that the U.S. government already investigated multiple alleged crimes in Afghanistan and prosecuted several individuals,[8] the ICC should not be in charge of any further investigation. The United States is a democratic country and a

6 Press Statement, Permanent Mission of France to the U.N., Statement in Support of the International Criminal Court Following the Release of the US Executive Order of 11 June 2020 (Jun. 23, 2020), https://onu.delegfrance.org/We-remain-committed-to-an-international-rules-based-order (last visited July 12, 2023).

7 Darryl Robinson, et al., *Informal Expert Paper: The Principle of Complementarity in Practice*, INTERNATIONAL CRIMINAL COURT (2003), https://www.icc-cpi.int/sites/default/files/NR/rdonlyres/20BB4494-70F9-4698-8E30-907F631453ED/281984/complementarity.pdf (last visited July 12, 2023).

8 William Burke-White, *The Trump Administration Misplayed the International Criminal Court and Americans May Now Face Justice for Crimes in Afghanistan*, BROOKINGS (Mar. 11, 2020), https://www.brookings.edu/articles/the-trump-administration-misplayed-the-international-criminal-court-and-americans-may-now-face-justice-for-crimes-in-afghanistan/ (last visited July 12, 2023).

supranational judicial court is only necessary in countries where a domestic judicial system fails.

The Prosecutor maintained that her Office's sole objective was to investigate and prosecute alleged war crimes and crimes against humanity "independently, impartially and objectively." The ICC claims to be an independent judicial institution not subject to political control.[9] However, the politicization of the Afghanistan case, and the ICC's history of targeting only African countries, demonstrate a markedly different picture. Although Israel has never joined the ICC, the Court found "a reasonable basis" to believe that "war crimes have been or are being committed in the West Bank, including East Jerusalem and the Gaza Strip."

The ICC recently rejected a case charging the People's Republic of China with genocide. Brought by two Uighur advocacy groups, the complaint was tossed by Prosecutor Fatou Bensouda on the grounds that China is not an ICC member state. The abdication of the world's nominal premier guardian of justice notwithstanding, the cases for both ICC jurisdiction and for the claim of genocide are clear. Numerous evidence shows that the existence of "re-education" camps, which detained more than a million Uighurs. There are credible allegations of torture, rape, and brainwashing.[10] Outside of China, Uighurs are harassed, surveilled, and intimidated by the Chinese state. These grotesque violations of human rights fits the United Nations' legal definition of genocide.[11] Bensouda's shyness towards China contradicts her zeal in going after the United States for war crimes. Indeed, the very logic used by the ICC to establish its jurisdiction to investigate crimes allegedly committed by U.S. forces in Afghanistan should theoretically apply equally when it comes to Chinese genocide. In this instance, an ICC mandate for Beijing exists (and is supported by precedents from 2018 and 2019)[12] because of illegal mass deportations of Uighurs from ICC member states Tajikistan and Cambodia into Xinjiang.[13]

9 International Criminal Court, Understanding the International Criminal Court (2013), https://www.icc-cpi.int/sites/default/files/Publications/understanding-the-icc.pdf (last visited July 12, 2023).

10 *Uyghurs*, N.Y. TIMES, https://www.nytimes.com/topic/subject/Uyghurs (last visited July 12, 2023).

11 Convention on the Prevention and Punishment of the Crime of Genocide, Dec. 9 1948, 78 U.N.T.S. 277.

12 Tia Sewell, *Unpacking the Recent Uighur ICC Complaint Against Chinese Leaders*, LAWFARE (Jul. 21, 2020), https://www.lawfaremedia.org/article/unpacking-recent-uighur-icc-complaint-against-chinese-leaders (last visited July 12, 2023).

13 Marlise Simons, *Uighur Exiles Push for Court Case Accusing China of Genocide*, N.Y. TIMES (Jul. 6, 2020), https://www.nytimes.com/2020/07/06/world/asia/china-xinjiang-uighur-court.html (last visited July 12, 2023).

There, they were detained and subjected to further crimes. Although Bensouda found a way to establish the ICC jurisdiction for the Afghanistan case, she said that China is not an ICC member state and refused to scrutinize Beijing's grotesque genocide. Though the U.S. government already investigated the situation in Afghanistan, Bensouda found these efforts inadequate – but seems to have nothing to declare of Chinese courts' active collaboration in Uighur oppression. And while the U.S. case allegedly relates to about eighty victims for war crimes more than fifteen years ago, China stands accused of atrocities against hundreds of thousands of victims in an ongoing genocide.

The ICC has also been reluctant to bring justice to Venezuela.[14] In September 2018, Argentina, Canada, Chile, Colombia, Paraguay, and Peru referred the human rights situation in Venezuela to the ICC for investigation over allegations of "crimes against humanity." After the Organization of American States accused the Court of failing to investigate Maduro's regime for committing torture, rape, politically motivated detentions, and extrajudicial executions, the ICC Prosecutor announced that she believes there is "reasonable basis" to believe Venezuela committed crimes against humanity and will determine in 2021 whether to open a full investigation.[15]

The Prosecutor also stated that she might complete a case between Russia and Georgia by the end of 2020, but this case still remains incomplete.[16]

The United States should continue to challenge the Court's jurisdiction and protect the rights of nations that are bound only by rules to which they consent. Rumor has it that the Biden administration will lift Trump's sanctions,[17] but that would be a grave mistake. The Trump sanctions offer an opportunity to the Biden administration, and Biden should not lift the sanctions without first negotiating with the Court. He should be clear that unless

---

14 Ivana Stradner and Ryan Berg, Editorial, *The International Criminal Court Needs to Investigate Venezuela*, NEWSWEEK (Dec. 17, 2020), https://www.newsweek.com/international-criminal-court-needs-investigate-venezuela-opinion-1555353 (last visited July 12, 2023).

15 *ICC Prosecutor Sees 'Reasonable Basis' to Believe Venezuela Committed Crimes Against Humanity*, REUTERS (Dec. 14, 2020), https://www.reuters.com/article/us-venezuela-politics-court/icc-prosecutor-sees-reasonable-basis-to-believe-venezuela-committed-crimes-against-humanity-idUSKBN28O2ZS (last visited July 12, 2023).

16 *Int'l Criminal Court May Complete the Investigation of the Russia-Georgia War by End of 2020*, AGENDA.GE (Dec. 4, 2019), https://agenda.ge/en/news/2019/3303 (last visited July 12, 2023).

17 Colum Lynch, *Biden Likely to Lift Sanctions on ICC Chief Prosecutor*, FOREIGN POL. (Nov. 25, 2020), https://foreignpolicy.com/2020/11/25/biden-likely-lift-sanctions-icc-prosecutor-fatou-bensouda/ (last visited July 12, 2023).

the ICC opens an investigation against China for committing genocide, finishes the case between Russia and Georgia, and starts an investigation for Venezuela, lifting U.S. sanctions will not be an option.

The ICC is at a turning point as elections for the next Prosecutor loom near and the winning candidate will direct the agenda of the Court for years to come. Given that the election of the Prosecutor has been postponed several times, the United States should strike at the ICC through its supporters. Japan, the United Kingdom, France, Italy, Canada, Spain, Mexico, and Australia are all major Court funders. The United States should warn countries that contribute substantially to the ICC while simultaneously depending utterly on the United States for their defense (such as Japan) that they cannot expect American troops to protect any nation seeking to prosecute and imprison them. It should weaken defense ties with ICC member countries, and cut foreign aid to any nation that cooperates with the Court. The United States should continue to deny ICC officials and any government officials (such as any military or law enforcement officers) that assist them from entering the United States or using its financial system.

With these actions, the Biden administration will defend the rights, not just of the United States, but of all sovereign nations. America did not join the Rome Statute and thus it remains unfettered by its requirements. To protect international law, it should refuse to recognize any ICC probe. International rules should only bind nations that consent to them. Allowing the ICC to claim power over the United States, which does not consent to its jurisdiction, will erode any incentive to obey any international rules at all. The ICC's actions threaten the only true mechanism for deterring human rights abuses.

Subjecting U.S. forces to an after-the-fact and idealistic human rights barometer will only discourage Washington from intervening to end massive human rights abuses in difficult world hotspots. If the global elite want the United States to lead efforts to end killings in places such as Syria, Yemen, or Sudan,[18] the last thing it should do is prosecute American troops when they take on the difficult jobs that no other nation can or will do.

---

18 Ralph Ranalli, *The "Next Rwanda" Will Look Different: Samantha Power Reflects on What We've Learned and Forgotten 25 Years After the Genocide*, HARV. KENNEDY SCH. (Apr. 4, 2019), https://www.hks.harvard.edu/faculty-research/policy-topics/human-rights/samantha-power-reflects-what-weve-learned-and (last visited July 12, 2023).

PART 5

The Gravity Threshold

Introduction to Part 5

The following question was featured on www.ICCForum.com from July 2021 through February 2022:

What is the universe of cases upon which the ICC should focus? Should the Prosecutor investigate and prosecute a large number of cases whenever Rome Statute legal criteria have been met, or focus on only a small number of those situations, when crimes of the most gravity have taken place? In selecting cases to investigate and prosecute, what should be the threshold for the gravity that warrants investigation of a situation or prosecution of those most responsible?

The Office of the Prosecutor's (OTP) 2016 Policy Paper on Case Selection and Prioritization (Policy) outlines current practice. Cases considered for prosecution must first meet the legal criteria of jurisdiction, admissibility, and interests of justice. Of those cases, the Policy directs that the OTP decide which to select based on three factors: the gravity of the crime(s), the degree of responsibility of alleged perpetrators, and whether the charges would reflect the extent of the criminality that has occurred. "Gravity of crime(s)" refers to "the most serious crimes within a given situation that are of concern to the international community as a whole." The OTP aims to prosecute all cases that are selected according to the criteria above, but it prioritizes cases for prosecution based on such factors as a comparative assessment across the selected cases, the impact of investigations and prosecutions on ongoing criminality, and other factors.

The OTP has limited resources and may be unable to investigate and prosecute all crimes that meet the legal criteria set forth in the Rome Statute. Some have argued that if the OTP were to adopt a stricter approach to the gravity of a situation, concentrating on only a few of the gravest situations where crimes have been perpetrated on a massive scale, then it might be able to do more complete investigations and prosecute more perpetrators in those particularly grave situations. In addition, in those situations, the Registry could execute deeper and wider outreach, and the Trust Fund for Victims could provide more reparations per capita. In short, the argument goes, the ICC could have a bigger impact on the gravest situations. The tradeoff, or course, would be the absence of ICC intervention in situations with crimes of less gravity, even though crimes have taken place, the ICC has jurisdiction, and other legal criteria have been met.

What gravity threshold is appropriate for OTP action? On what scale must crimes be perpetrated to trigger an investigation or prosecution? Is

 | DOI:10.1163/9789004686755_026

the "concern of the international community as a whole" an appropriate criterion? If so, then what constitutes the "international community" and how should the OTP assess whether that community is concerned "as a whole"? Should the OTP focus only on the most serious crimes and perpetrators within a given situation, or cast a wider net and prosecute many perpetrators when particularly grave crimes have been committed?

Is it appropriate for the OTP to refrain from investigation or prosecution in some situations where all the legal criteria have been met and where the gravity of the crimes is alarming, but not of extreme gravity or not perpetrated on a large scale? In such a situation, should the potential precedential value of a prosecution be considered in deciding whether to move forward, even though the gravity of the crime(s) would not otherwise warrant doing so? Does the failure to prosecute in situations where crimes have not yet been committed on a large scale, or not otherwise committed with the requisite gravity, undermine deterrence and increase the risk that the situation will develop into one where criminality multiplies?

CHAPTER 21

The Aperture of the ICC: More than Just the Issue of Gravity

Todd F. Buchwald

What is the aperture issue? On a camera, the aperture is the opening through which light passes for the camera to process. It can be widened or narrowed, depending on the desired result. Light is essential, but different people will have different perceptions of what settings are optimal.

So too with the ICC. The ICC has no "lens" as such, but various dials regulate the size of the opening and how the Court goes about selecting the situations and cases on which it will focus. Questions about the aperture will be at the forefront of issues confronting the Court as the ICC enters its third decade. The Independent Expert Report, completed in September 2020, underscored the central importance of getting these issues right,[1] as has the newly-elected ICC Prosecutor.[2] As discussed below, much of the aperture discussion has been about possible re-calibration of the way the ICC approaches the issue of gravity, but it would be prudent for the Court and the new Prosecutor to broaden their thinking in the way they analyze these issues.

1 How Does the Rome Statute Set the Aperture?

The Rome Statute controls the aperture in numerous ways but the two most basic are its provisions on jurisdiction and admissibility.

1 Assembly of States Parties, International Criminal Court, Independent Expert Review of the International Criminal Court and the Rome Statute System Final Report (Sep. 30, 2020), https://asp.icc-cpi.int/sites/asp/files/asp_docs/ASP19/IER-Final-Report-ENG.pdf (last visited July 10, 2023).

2 *See, e.g.*, Shehzad Charania, *Delivering the ICC Vision Through Deeds not Words: An Interview with Karim Khan QC*, OPINIO JURIS (May 21, 2021) [hereinafter Charania Interview with Karim Khan], http://opiniojuris.org/2021/05/21/selling-the-icc-vision-through-deeds-not-words-an-interview-with-karim-khan-qc/ (last visited July 12, 2023) ("To have impact, you need to prioritise against the greatest need").

 | DOI:10.1163/9789004686755_027

1.1 *Jurisdiction*

First, the Rome Statute tells us the types of cases over which the ICC can and cannot exercise jurisdiction. Article 11, for example, tells us that the ICC has jurisdiction only over crimes committed after the Rome Statute entered into force. More fundamentally, Article 5 tells us that the ICC has jurisdiction only over four specific types of crimes. The negotiators of the Statute considered, but ultimately rejected, proposals to include numerous other crimes but, in the end, created a Court with jurisdiction over genocide, crimes against humanity, war crimes, and the crime of aggression, and – indeed – only as those four crimes are defined in the Rome Statute.[3] Thus, no matter how heinous, de-stabilizing, or shocking to the conscience they may be, crimes like airplane hijacking, the murder of diplomats, killing of peacekeepers outside of armed conflict, mass shootings, systemic corruption, staging of a military coup, drug-trafficking, and terrorism do not fall within the Court's jurisdiction unless in particular cases they somehow manage to fit into the definitions of these four crimes.

The Rome Statute also established preconditions to the exercise of jurisdiction. Thus, within the universe of crimes described in Article 5, the Court may not exercise jurisdiction unless the conduct in question occurred on the territory of a state that is a party to the Rome Statute or the accused is a national of such a state.[4] Once again, no matter how heinous, de-stabilizing, or shocking to the conscience they may seem to the international community, the Court may not exercise jurisdiction unless these preconditions are satisfied. The distinction between situations in which the Court has jurisdiction and those in which the Court is able to "exercise" jurisdiction need not be addressed here. The relevant point for present purposes is that, taken together, these provisions circumscribe the kinds of cases over which the exercise of ICC jurisdiction is possible.

---

3 *See, e.g.*, Office of the Prosecutor, International Criminal Court, Situation in the Republic of Korea: Article 5 Report ¶ 55 (Jun. 2014), https://www.icc-cpi.int/sites/default/files/icc docs/otp/SAS-KOR-Article-5-Public-Report-ENG-05Jun2014.pdf (last visited July 12, 2023) (The Rome Statute "does not impose criminal liability for all violations of the laws of armed conflict" but rather only those codified in Article 8).

4 (There are exceptions if the crime was committed on board a vessel or aircraft that is registered with a Rome Statute party, if the relevant state became a party to the Rome Statute after its entry into force, if a non-party has accepted the Court's jurisdiction through a declaration under Article 12(3), or if the Security Council refers a situation to the ICC Prosecutor under Article 13(b) – but they do not affect the points that I am trying to make here. Also note that, for purposes of this comment, I am putting aside questions involving the Court's jurisdiction over the crime of aggression, which is subject to a different jurisdictional regime).

There is another provision – the first sentence of Article 5 – that also warrants mention. It precedes the sentence that specifies that the Court has jurisdiction over the four crimes listed above and says that the jurisdiction of the Court "shall be limited to the most serious crimes of concern to the international community as a whole." At least on its face, this first sentence of Article 5 leaves room for debate whether it is intended to convey that any commission of these four crimes are considered ipso facto to be "the most serious crimes of concern to the international community as a whole," or whether the intent is to limit the Court's jurisdiction to that subset of these four crimes that is in fact of "most serious concern." The Preamble of the Rome Statute vows that whatever crimes are included in this category are crimes that "must not go unpunished."[5]

1.2 *Admissibility*

In addition to the questions about the Court's jurisdiction, there is an additional issue of admissibility. Specifically, under Article 17(1) of the Rome Statute, a case over which the Court could otherwise exercise jurisdiction is inadmissible if either:

1. a State satisfies the complementarity principles described in subsections (a), (b), or (c) of that provision, or
2. under subsection (d), "the case is not of sufficient gravity to justify further action by the Court."

Article 17 is written to apply to the admissibility of a specific "case," but the same general ideas are relevant when, under Article 53, the Prosecutor decides whether to initiate an investigation of a "situation" in the first place. However, at the point at which he or she is deciding whether to commence an investigation, the Prosecutor will not have identified particular cases to bring to trial and will look instead to potential cases that might be brought.[6]

There is also an additional admissibility-like provision – set out in Article 53(1)(c) – which provides that the Prosecutor, in deciding whether to commence an investigation, should also consider whether there are "substantial reasons to believe that an investigation would not serve the interests of

---

5 International Criminal Court, Rome Statute of the International Criminal Court, Preamble, ¶ 4, U.N. Doc. A/CONF.183/9 (July 17, 1998) [hereinafter Rome Statute].

6 Situation in the Republic of Kenya, ICC-01/09-19-Corr, Corrigendum of the Decision pursuant to Article 15 of the Rome Statute on the Authorization of an Investigation into the Situation in the Republic of Kenya, ¶ 48 (PTC II, Mar. 31, 2010) [hereinafter Kenya Investigation Authorization].

justice." Taken together, these three elements – complementarity, gravity, and the interests of justice – narrow what would otherwise pass through the aperture as a suitable matter for the Court to take up.

Are there crimes that that fall outside these jurisdictional and admissibility rules that warrant the attention of the international community? Of course. Are there victims of other crimes whose plights should not be forgotten and whose rights deserve to be vindicated? Of course. So why create an ICC that is so limited? The framers of the Rome Statute needed to balance many considerations. Some kinds of cases – perhaps terrorist attacks – may be every bit as egregious, but less amenable to prosecution before a new international court, or in comparatively less need of a fail-safe mechanism to guard against states pursuing cases with insufficient zeal. Others were excluded to help ensure that states have confidence "that their sovereign right to try crimes [...] would not be encroached upon"[7] and to frame the Court's mandate in a way that would help it develop and maintain the support from other international actors that it requires in order to thrive. In a more general sense, the Court, like all international (and indeed domestic) institutions, has finite resources. It must compete for those resources with other priorities – global health, environmental, and development, just to name a few – and needs to make decisions about the kinds of situations and cases to which its resources and energies are best directed. These are the kinds of considerations to which the inclusion of the various aperture-control provisions in the Rome Statute were implicitly responding.

2 Concerns about the Aperture

All these provisions were of course agreed upon at Rome. At least in some quarters, however, there is lively debate about their interpretation and application, and about the number of preliminary examinations and investigations in which they have led the Court to become involved. Thus, although the Independent Experts Report did not use the word, "aperture" was a key point of departure for their analysis. They reported that, in the course of their consultations, they "repeatedly heard concern that the Court should focus on a narrower range of situations, and limit its interventions to the extent possible, focusing on situations." In the face of concern that the Court is spread too thin to operate successfully, they concluded:

---

7 William A. Schabas, *The International Criminal Court: A Commentary on the Rome Statute* (Oxford: Oxford University Press, 2016), p. 447.

> While it is a prospect that would be disappointing for many, and further restrict the already limited jurisdiction of the Court, the current situation is unsustainable having regard to the limited resources available.[8]

For their part, the Independent Experts recommended that the Prosecutor consider adjusting the aperture by raising the gravity threshold when considering what situations to investigate (though they did not make clear how they would calculate either the existing gravity threshold or their recommended replacement).[9]

The OTP appears to have accepted the Experts' logic at least in part. "It is true," said the OTP in responding to the Experts' recommendations, "that, in order to succeed, the OTP must connect the ends it wishes to achieve with the means it has available to achieve them."[10] It said, however, that "insofar as [gravity] is applied as a legal threshold under the Statute, [it] cannot be addressed unilaterally by the OTP, since it will be subject to judicial review."[11]

3 Admissibility and Jurisdiction in Practice

Lying beneath the surface of all this are questions about the manner in which the Rome Statute provisions on admissibility and jurisdiction have been interpreted and applied in practice.

3.1 *The Gravity Threshold*

The Chambers that have addressed the issue do not appear to have assigned gravity a significant filtering role. For example, according to the Appeals Chamber in last year's Al Hassan decision, the four crimes over which the Court has jurisdiction are by definition the most serious crimes of

8 IER Report, *supra* note 1, ¶ 646.

9 *Id.* at ¶ 650, R. 227.

10 International Criminal Court, Overall Response of the International Criminal Court to the "Independent Expert Review of the International Criminal Court and the Rome Statute System – Final Report" Preliminary Analysis of the Recommendations and Information on Relevant Activities Undertaken by the Court ¶ 404 (Apr. 14, 2021) [hereinafter ICC Response], https://asp.icc-cpi.int/sites/asp/files/asp_docs/ASP20/Overall%20Response%20of%20the%20ICC%20to%20the%20IER%20Final%20Report%20-%20ENG%20-%2014April21.pdf (last visited July 12, 2023).

11 *Id.* at ¶ 405.

international concern and these crimes "are, in principle, of sufficient gravity to justify further action."[12] In the view of the Appeals Chamber, it thus follows that the gravity test aims only at excluding "rather unusual cases" and that the purpose of the gravity requirement "is not to oblige the Court to choose only the most serious cases."[13] The Pre-Trial Chamber in the Comoros case was even more emphatic, saying that gravity "is not a criterion for the selection of the most serious situations and cases," but rather is only "a requirement for the exclusion of (potential) cases of marginal gravity." It further said that the gravity test is met if a situation gives rise even "to only one potential case that is not of marginal gravity."[14]

Such a conception of gravity, and such an approach to selecting situations, could involve the Office of the Prosecutor in far more situations than those in which it is currently involved. It certainly seems a far cry from "the holocaust, the killing fields of Cambodia, and the genocide in the former Yugoslavia and Rwanda" that the newly-elected Prosecutor has reminded us those present in Rome invoked as warranting the Court's creation.[15] For each of these, the selection of the situations that would be subjected to the scrutiny of the tribunal reflected an assessment of the overall level of atrocities that had been perpetrated and not simply the existence of particular cases.

This approach is particularly striking when combined with the Court's jurisprudence interpreting and applying Article 53, which has regularly emphasized that – at least in situations that are referred – the mandatory nature of the wording of Article 53 ("the Prosecutor shall [...] initiate an

12 Prosecutor v. Al Hassan Ag Abdoul Aziz Ag Mohamed Ag Mahmoud, Case No. ICC-01/12-01/18-601-Red, Judgment on the Appeal of Mr Al Hassan against the Decision of Pre-Trial Chamber I Entitled "Décision relative à l'exception d'irrecevabilité pour insuffisance degravité de l'affaire soulevée par la défense" ¶¶ 55–56 (AC, Feb. 19, 2020).

13 *Id.* at ¶ 59.

14 Situation on the Registered Vessels of the Union of the Comoros, the Hellenic Republic and the Kingdom of Cambodia, Case No. ICC-01/13-111, Decision on the "Application for Judicial Review by the Government of the Comoros" ¶¶ 96–97 (PTC I, Sep. 16, 2020) [hereinafter Comoros] ("Thus, if a situation gives rise to at least one potential case that is not of marginal gravity, the requirements of articles 53(1)(b) and 17(1)(d) of the Statute are met.").

15 Charania Interview with Karim Khan, *supra* note 2; *see also* David Scheffer and Ashley Cox, 'The Constitutionality of the Rome Statute of the International Criminal Court' (2008) 98 *J. Crim. L. and Criminology* 983, 992 (The very nature of the exercise around which the international community circled was "to prosecute the masterminds of complex and massive atrocity crimes before an international court in The Hague"). Rome Statute, *supra* note 5, Preamble, ¶ 2 (The Rome Statute itself talks about the "millions of children, women and men [that] have been victims of unimaginable atrocities that deeply shock the conscience of humanity.").

investigation")[16] leaves the Prosecutor without discretion to decline to investigate if the conditions under the Rome Statute are met.[17] Thus, the Pre-Trial Chamber in the Comoros case concluded that, if the conditions are met, "the Prosecutor is duty-bound to open an investigation." According to the Chamber, the Prosecutor would then have discretion to refrain from going forward only if he determines "that such an investigation would not serve the interests of justice," which the Court treats as a policy factor rather than a factor going to the issue of admissibility.[18] The result of all this has been a gravity test that plays a less robust role than it might in the process of filtering what situations will progress from preliminary examinations to investigations. Indeed, once there is found to be a single case that justifies the opening of an investigation, other incidents need not be "closely linked" to that one case in order also to be subject to that investigation. The result is an even wider aperture opening in terms of what the OTP can then choose to pursue.[19]

One reason so much attention flows to the issue of gravity is that the Rome Statute is worded in a way that would seem to make it an inviting target for playing a stronger role in aperture adjustment. Thus, Article 17 of the Statute simply says that a case must be "of sufficient gravity to justify further action by the Court." The word "sufficient" can readily be interpreted as involving an assessment that takes into account the resources that an investigation of the situation would be expected to consume, and the alternative uses to which the Court might otherwise put those resources, in determining whether the gravity of a specific situation of case is "sufficient." To give an admittedly over-simplified example: if the Prosecutor has resources for only one investigation, a situation involving one hundred atrocity victims may well not entail sufficient gravity if there is an alternative situation involving one million victims, but it might well do so if the alternative situation involved ten victims.

3.2 *Complementarity and the Interests of Justice*

Although not addressed by the Independent Experts in these terms, one can also imagine the principles of complementarity and the interests of justice as playing stronger roles in filtering than they presently do.

16 Rome Statute, *supra* note 5, Article 53 (emphasis added).

17 (See discussion in this essay at Section IV(B)).

18 Comoros, *supra* note 14, ¶ 15.

19 Situation in the Islamic Republic of Afghanistan, Case No. ICC-02/17 OA4, Judgment on the Appeal against the Decision on the Authorisation of an Investigation into the Situation in the Islamic Republic of Afghanistan ¶¶ 61–63 (AC, Mar. 5, 2020) [hereinafter Afghanistan Appeals Chamber Decision].

3.2.1 Complementarity

Much about complementarity is enigmatic. The basic principle is simple enough – the ICC should only step in where states are unable or unwilling to do so in a genuine manner – though at least arguably the words of the Rome Statute do not quite match this basic principle. Among other things, the principle of complementarity can help conserve the Court's resources, defer to local actors who may well have a better understanding of local circumstances, promote local ownership of the process and development of local justice institutions, encourage states to implement their responsibilities to address these problems, allow and encourage states to self-correct, and reduce the number of situations in which the ICC might clash with states in ways that states would likely see as intruding on their sovereign rights. Questions about deferral under the principle of complementarity issues can, however, be particularly thorny, including because the same local actors to whom the Court would defer may well be aiming their efforts at shielding rather than prosecuting those responsible for alleged crimes. Nevertheless, one could easily imagine the principle of complementarity being applied in a manner so as to concentrate on – to allow to pass through the aperture – those situations in which the shielding is the most egregious or the most systematic, on the principle that this represents the heart of what the ICC was created to safeguard against.

In practice, the application of the complementarity principle, including the use of "same person/same conduct" and "inactivity" tests, has led to at least some criticism that the principle is being applied in a too "mechanistic" manner.[20] The "inactivity" test was developed in the context of early self-referrals in the DRC and Uganda, and helped avoid the need to show that those states were "unwilling" to prosecute in order for the ICC to exercise jurisdiction as the states had requested. Would it be palatable to assert that Uganda was at the time "unwilling" to investigate or prosecute members of the LRA who had perpetrated atrocities? The question could be avoided if the simple fact that Uganda had not done so was sufficient to make the matter admissible. At least from a policy perspective, however, situations in which a state has self-referred may present a poor model when

20 *See* Todd Buchwald, *Part II: What Kinds of Situations and Cases Should the ICC Pursue? The Independent Expert Review of the* ICC *and the Question of Aperture*, JUST SEC. (Dec. 1, 2020), https://www.justsecurity.org/73622/part-ii-what-kinds-of-situations-and-cases-should-the-icc-pursue-the-independent-expert-review-of-the-icc-and-the-question-of-aperture/ (last visited July 12, 2023).

figuring out how to balance the various equities that the Court must confront when facing a state that is contesting the need or propriety of ICC involvement. A different balancing may thus be appropriate in cases in which a state is not requesting the Court's assistance, with greater deference given a state's decision not to pursue criminal cases, at least if its failure to do so does not establish that it is driven by an intent to shield the perpetrators.

Beyond questions like this, there are also broader policy questions about whether the ICC might adjust its aperture to take into account responses that do not involve traditional criminal prosecutions, or that involve other forms of genuinely coming to terms with the past, in determining whether a state's response is so inadequate that an ICC investigation of the situation should be pursued.

The more mechanistic approach to complementarity that the Court has applied can also interplay with the logic of the Court's decision in the Comoros case that an investigation should be commenced – indeed that the Prosecutor may be required to commence an investigation – if there is even one potential case that would be admissible. Under a version of these principles, in which greater reliance is placed on complementarity-related principles for filtering, the Court might look more broadly to the actions of the state in question, as opposed to the existence of particular cases, more squarely zero in on shielding and non-genuineness, and take account also of forms of accountability and coming to terms with the behavior in question that do not involve traditional criminal prosecutions or that otherwise involve other forms of genuinely coming to terms with the past.

3.2.2 Interests of Justice

The Rome Statute's "interests of justice" language was unclear from the outset, and there appears to have been no clear agreement about what it was intended to encompass. There are of course different things that it could be understood as encompassing. At least some in Rome intended it to provide a basis for not pursuing investigations and prosecutions in situations where – as in the then-recent case of the truth and reconciliation commissions in South Africa – a society had made a good-faith decision to utilize alternatives to traditional modes of criminal accountability in order to come to terms with its past. Indeed, speaking shortly after the Rome Conference, then-U.N. Secretary-General Kofi Annan dismissed as a "travesty" any argument that the unwillingness or inability to pursue criminal accountability as part of such a reconciliation process could be a basis for ICC action:

> No one should imagine that it would apply to a case like South Africa's, where the regime and the conflict which caused the crimes have come to an end, and the victims have inherited power. It is inconceivable that, in such a case, the Court would seek to substitute its judgement for that of a whole nation which is seeking the best way to put a traumatic past behind it and build a better future.[21]

In practice, the OTP has essentially read the interests of justice language as playing virtually no role as a filtering mechanism. This is reflected in its September 2007 policy paper in which the OTP reasoned that the "interests of peace" is not part of the assessment of the interests of justice that the Prosecutor should take into consideration in deciding whether to pursue an investigation.[22] One can readily understand the reluctance of the OTP to take on responsibility for assessing these kinds of considerations that might be involved in evaluating the "interests of peace" – e.g., on what basis could the OTP claim a superior ability to assess such questions than other international actors involved in pursuing peace in a region? But this does result in an outcome that risks an under-filtering in which, from a policy perspective, crimes are too readily able to pass through the aperture. The "interests of justice" test may present the Prosecutor and the Court with politically difficult questions, but the fact that they are difficult does not mean they are unimportant.

The interests of justice test could also be interpreted to address the issue of infeasibility – i.e., where the prospects for success in a particular situation were sufficiently remote that it would not serve the broader cause of justice to devote limited resources to it. This was of course the approach taken by the Pre-Trial Chamber in its April 2019 decision declining to authorize an investigation in Afghanistan.[23] That decision, coming in the wake of strident U.S. attacks on the Court, provoked a storm of criticism and was reversed by

21 Press Release, Secretary General, Secretary-General Urges "Like-Minded" States to Ratify Statute of the International Court of Justice, U.N. Press Release SG/SM/6686 (Sep. 1, 1998).

22 Office of the Prosecutor, International Criminal Court, Policy Paper on the Interests of Justice (Sep. 2007), https://www.icc-cpi.int/sites/default/files/NR/rdonlyres/772C95C9-F54D-4321-BF09-73422BB23528/143640/ICCOTPInterestsOfJustice.pdf (last visited July 12, 2023).

23 Situation in the Islamic Republic of Afghanistan, Case No. ICC-02/17-33, Decision pursuant to Article 15 of the Rome Statute on the Authorisation of an Investigation into the Situation in the Islamic Republic of Afghanistan (PTC II, Apr. 12, 2019).

the Appeals Chamber,[24] but the idea that feasibility is a factor that needs to figure in decisions about where to direct resources is hard to simply dismiss out of hand. It may be unfortunate that the Court will never have the resources needed to pursue investigations and prosecutions of all of the otherwise-unpunished crimes that deserve attention, but it is at the same time inevitable.

4 Other Ways in Which the Aperture Opening Is Wide

There are a variety of other elements that affect the Court's aperture in ways we might not ordinarily think about, three of which I will describe here.

4.1 *Contextual Factors*

The reliance upon contextual elements in the definitions of Rome Statute crimes plays an essential part in distinguishing between the type of conduct to which the Prosecutor and the Court should, and the type of conduct to which they should not, direct their attention and resources. As an obvious example, an "ordinary" murder is a horrifying crime, but it would not amount to a "crime against humanity" over which the Court has jurisdiction unless committed as "part of a widespread or systematic attack directed against [a] civilian population." It is the contextual elements that tell us that the conduct is not only horrific, but that we are dealing with a crime against humanity that potentially warrants the involvement of the ICC.

Given the practical reality that almost all of the ICC's actual prosecutions will continue to be for war crimes or crimes against humanity, it is worth comparing the contextual elements of the two crimes.

For crimes against humanity, a significant amount of filtering is at least in principle built into the definition of the crime by virtue of the requirement that the relevant act must have been committed as part of a widespread or systematic attack against a civilian population, and the associated requirement that the attack have been undertaken in furtherance of a state or organizational policy.[25] Much of course depends on how the Prosecutor and the Court interpret these contextual elements and strong differences of view have in fact been expressed about how they should be interpreted and

24 Afghanistan Appeals Chamber Decision, *supra* note 19.

25 Rome Statute, *supra* note 5, Article 7(2)(a).

how strong a filtering role they should be expected to play,[26] but at least the basic idea of a substantial filter is built into the definition.

The late Judge Kaul spoke to the importance of the aperture-setting function of the contextual elements in his famous dissent in the Situation in Kenya case, in which he described the risk of what he considered the setting of too low a standard for what qualified as crimes against humanity:

> It is my considered view that the existing demarcation line between those crimes must not be marginalized or downgraded, even in an incremental way. I also opine that the distinction between those crimes must not be blurred.
>
> Furthermore, it is my considered view that this would not be in the interest of criminal justice in general and international criminal justice in particular. It is neither appropriate nor possible to examine and explain in this opinion all the potential negative implications and risks of a gradual downscaling of crimes against humanity towards serious ordinary crimes. As a Judge of the ICC, I feel, however, duty-bound to point at least to the following: such an approach might infringe on state sovereignty and the action of national courts for crimes which should not be within the ambit of the Statute. It would broaden the scope of possible ICC intervention almost indefinitely. This might turn the ICC, which is fully dependent on state cooperation, in a hopelessly overstretched, inefficient international court, with related risks for its standing and credibility. Taking into consideration the limited financial and material means of the institution, it might be unable to tackle all the situations which could fall under its jurisdiction with the consequence that the selection of the situations under actual investigation might be quite arbitrary to the dismay of the numerous victims in the situations disregarded by the Court who would be deprived of any access to justice without any convincing justification.[27]

In contrast to crimes against humanity, the contextual elements for war crimes carry virtually no such water. The only real contextual element for war crimes is that the relevant acts must have the requisite nexus with an armed conflict. Article 8 – the provisions that contains the Rome Statute

26 Compare Kenya Investigation Authorization, *supra* note 6, (majority decision) with *Id.* (Hans-Peter Kaul dissenting).

27 Kenya Investigation Authorization, *supra* note 6, ¶¶ 9–10 (Hans-Peter Kaul dissenting).

definition of "war crimes" – does provide that the Court has jurisdiction over the war crimes listed therein "in particular when committed as part of a plan or policy or as part of a large-scale commission of such crimes." But the Court has made clear that the use of the phrase "in particular" means that jurisdiction is not in fact limited to cases involving a plan or policy or large-scale commission. Indeed, the Appeals Chamber has said that "a single act could also amount to a war crime within the jurisdiction of the Court if it was committed in the context of and was associated with an armed conflict."[28]

4.2 *Article 53 Standard of Proof for Commencing an Investigation*

The standard of proof that must exist in order to commence an investigation also affects the aperture.

How clear must it be that jurisdiction exists? The answer in practice has been: not very. I have mentioned above the language of Article 53 under which the Prosecutor shall "initiate an investigation unless he or she determines that there is no reasonable basis to proceed under the Statute." This, various chambers have pointed out, is "the lowest evidentiary standard provided in the Statute" – requiring merely "a sensible or reasonable justification for a belief that a crime falling within the jurisdiction of the Court has been or is being committed." The information available to the Prosecutor is not "required to point towards one conclusion," and the existence of facts that are "unclear" is identified as an affirmative reason to commence an investigation.[29] There has thus been an underlying tilt towards opening an investigation, reflecting a seeming premise that "we won't know unless we investigate," but also perhaps an unstated (though not self-evidently correct) premise that the resource, political, and credibility costs to the Court of commencing investigations are relatively small.

---

28 Prosecutor v. Callixte Mbarushimana, Case No. ICC-01/04-01/10, Decision on the Confirmation of Charges ¶¶ 94–96 (PTC I, Dec. 16, 2011); Situation in the Democratic Republic of the Congo, ICC-01/04-169, Judgment on the Prosecutor's appeal against the decision of Pre-Trial Chamber I entitled "Decision on the Prosecutor's Application for Warrants of Arrest, Article 58" ¶ 71 (AC, Jul. 13, 2006) [hereinafter DRC Arrest Warrants Appeal].

29 Situation in the Republic of Burundi, Case No. ICC-01/11-17-X, Decision pursuant to Article 15 of the Rome Statute on the Authorization of an Investigation into the Situation in the Republic of Burundi ¶ 30 (PTC III, Oct. 25, 2017); *see also* Comoros, *supra* note 14, ¶ 16 ("Facts which are difficult to establish or unclear, or the existence of conflicting accounts, call for the opening of an investigation (rather than the opposite), since it is the very purpose of such an investigation to properly assess the facts and provide clarity.").

In proprio motu situations – i.e., those in which neither a state nor the Security Council has referred the situation – there are of course provisions under which the Prosecutor must persuade an ICC Pre-Trial Chamber of her conclusion that "there is a reasonable basis to proceed with an investigation and that the case appears to fall within the jurisdiction of the Court." This requirement is designed to act as a check on the discretion of the Prosecutor and thus stands as another way in which the Court's aperture might be regulated. In practice, however, the lowness of the standard and the way the Court applies it have resulted in little by way of filtering. Indeed, the ICC judges have recently said that, when the Prosecutor has concluded that an investigation should be commenced, the Prosecutor's assessment of complementarity or gravity, or the interests of justice, is unreviewable.[30] Following this, the Prosecutor accordingly provided no explanation whatsoever for her conclusion that the gravity, complementarity, and interests of justice tests had been met in the recent request for authorization to commence an investigation in the situation in the Philippines that she recently submitted to the judges.[31]

On the other hand, in its recent decision not to commence an investigation of UK forces in Iraq, the OTP appears to have subjected itself to a higher standard – moving away from a "we don't know and therefore need to investigate" approach to a decision not to move forward because the OTP was not in a position affirmatively to substantiate that the UK had not proceeded in a genuine manner. It is hard to know whether this may be the beginning of a trend, but it at least potentially represents a move toward aperture adjustment efforts that could narrow the universe of situations on which the ICC would focus.[32]

---

30 Afghanistan Appeals Chamber Decision, *supra* note 19, ¶ 40 (decision of the judges to authorize an investigation should not incorporate issues of admissibility). *Id.* at ¶ 41 (there is no basis for the pre-trial chamber to consider the issue of admissibility). *But see* Kenya Investigation Authorization, *supra* note 6, ¶ 24 (Moreover, if the purpose of the article 15 procedure is to provide the Chamber with a supervisory role over the proprio motu initiative [then] the Chamber must equally consider whether the requirements set out in article 53(1)(a)–(c) of the Statute are satisfied for the sake of meeting the "reasonable basis to proceed" test before deciding whether to authorize the Prosecutor to commence an investigation).

31 Situation in the Republic of the Philippines, Case No. ICC-01/21-7-Red, Request for Authorization of an Investigation pursuant to Article 15(3) ¶ 130 (PTC I, Jun. 14, 2021).

32 *See* Office of the Prosecutor, International Criminal Court, Situation in Iraq/UK – Final Report ¶ 409 (Dec. 9, 2020), https://www.icc-cpi.int/sites/default/files/itemsDocuments/201209-otp-final-report-iraq-uk-eng.pdf (last visited July 12, 2023) (taking as sufficient explanations of decisions not to prosecute that are "generally reasonable" and

How much leeway does the OTP have to set the aperture control in proprio motu situations as it sees fit? There is room for debate whether the language of Article 15 permits OTP to decline to move forward with a request for an investigation as a matter of complete discretion. For example, on the one hand, Article 15(3) of the Rome Statute says that the Prosecutor "shall" submit a request for authorization if she concludes there is a reasonable basis to proceed, and the OTP Policy Paper on Preliminary Examinations states that "[i]f the Office is satisfied that all the criteria established by the Statute for this purpose are fulfilled, it has a legal duty to open an investigation into the situation."[33] On the other hand, the OTP had suggested that the decision to seek authorization in a proprio motu situation is discretionary[34] and the Appeals Chamber appears to have embraced this view in the Afghanistan case.[35] Perhaps most importantly, there is no apparent enforcement mechanism built into the Rome Statute to compel the OTP to move forward, as one might expect if there were an obligation to do so.

4.3 *The "Situation as a Whole" Principle*

When the Government of Uganda referred the situation "concerning the Lord's Resistance Army" in northern Uganda to the ICC Prosecutor in 2003,[36] the Prosecutor notified Uganda that the referral would be interpreted as covering "all crimes under the Statute committed in northern Uganda, and that [its] investigation would be impartial."[37] This episode

---

justifying OTP's decision not to pursue an investigation on basis that "the evidence available to it [...] does not allow [the OTP] to conclude that there was intent on the part of the UK authorities to shield persons [...] from criminal responsibility.").

33 Office of the Prosecutor, International Criminal Court, Policy Paper on Preliminary Examinations ¶ 2 (Nov. 2013) [hereinafter OTP Policy Paper], https://www.icc-cpi.int/sites/default/files/iccdocs/otp/OTP-Policy_Paper_Preliminary_Examinations_2013-ENG.pdf (last visited July 12, 2023).

34 *See* ICC Response, *supra* note 10, ¶ 412.

35 Afghanistan Appeals Chamber Decision, *supra* note 19, ¶ 31 (emphasizing the "discretionary nature of the power accorded to the Prosecutor under Article 15" and that it would be contrary to the nature of this power "to suggest that a duty to investigate could be imposed by the pre-trial chamber in the absence of a request for authorisation of an investigation by the Prosecutor").

36 Press Release, President of Uganda Refers Situation Concerning Lord's Resistance Army (LRA) to International Criminal Court, U.N. Press Release AFR/821-L/3055 (Jan. 29, 2004).

37 *See* Statement, Luis Moreno-Ocampo, Prosecutor, Int'l Crim. Ct., Statement on the Uganda Arrest Warrants (Oct. 14, 2005), https://www.icc-cpi.int/sites/default/files/NR/rdonlyres/3255817D-FD00-4072-9F58-FDB869F9B7CF/143834/LMO_20051014_English1.pdf (last visited July 12, 2023).

embodies the essence of the "situation as a whole" principle, and the desirability of preventing a sitting government from instrumentalizing the ICC by empowering the OTP to proceed only against the forces of the government's adversaries and not those of the government. At least in proprio motu cases, however, the Rome Statute requires the Prosecutor to persuade a Pre-Trial Chamber that the conditions warranting an investigation have been met before the investigative tools of the Prosecutor can be deployed against the personnel of a state that believes an investigation is unwarranted. The need for approval from the judges was a built-in check designed to protect states from the risk of being subject to the burden of an investigation absent a conclusion that the standards set out in the Rome Statute had been met. At least arguably, the fact that a state can – under the "situation as a whole" principle – be enmeshed in an investigation based on the conduct of other parties erodes the value of such assurances, and represents a kind of further opening of the aperture.

5 Observations

The sections above suggest various ways in which the ICC's aperture is set. Each of the aperture settings affects the extent to which Court actors must bear the political responsibility for seeming to favor one kind of situation over another – even in such basic ways as precluding the need for the Court to address whether a crime beyond the four listed in Article 5 should contend for the Court's attention. Some of the aperture settings may be easier to adjust and some less easy, depending for example on the extent to which they are grounded in the wording of the Rome Statute, and for each of the settings there can be legitimate questions about the extent to which it is the Prosecutor or the Court that is best positioned to widen or narrow the aperture.

All that said, the description above does not tell nearly the whole story because, in fact, there is an enormous amount of filtering that takes place behind the scenes via the exercise of prosecutorial discretion. One way this can occur is through the decisions made, after the Prosecutor commences an investigation, to prioritize or de-prioritize particular investigations, parts of investigations, or potential cases against particular individuals. Thus, there are easily hundreds – probably thousands – of cases that would fit through the aperture as the Court and the Prosecutor have to this point set it, yet only a small handful of actual prosecutions. Whatever the legal constraints that might be seen as requiring the Prosecutor to commence an investigation, there are few discernible standards that the OTP is required to apply in deciding how, or even whether, to actually proceed once an investigation is launched.[38]

Should not the de facto aperture narrowing that this kind of prosecutorial discretion supplies be good enough to ensure that the Court is not over-extended? My answer to that question is: I am not so sure. First, unless the Prosecutor can keep a matter bottled up interminably in the preliminary examination stage, this approach only works for dealing with matters after an investigation is commenced, and it will be the judgment of the Prosecutor rather than the application of rules laid out in the Rome Statute that will actually be decisive in what is actually pursued. To be sure, some discretion – indeed, a significant amount of discretion – is both unavoidable and desirable. But it is virtually inevitable that even the fairest choices by the Prosecutor will be criticized and attacked, and it may do the Prosecutor no real favor to saddle him with political responsibility for so vast a portion of the filtering process.

One can sense the way these issues both pull and tug the OTP. On the one hand, the OTP has published an extensive Policy Paper that in principle is supposed to give more substance to the criteria it applies in selecting and prioritizing cases.[39] This is a way to elaborate in advance basic principles that can be visible to the public, and better position the OTP to be seen as applying these principles in an objective manner rather than simply exercising discretion. On the other hand, the paper is ultimately quite opaque in that it ultimately does little to clarify what the OTP will actually decide to pursue when facing real life situations and cases. For example, the Policy Paper includes an extensive discussion of gravity, with the OTP saying that the assessment "includes both quantitative and qualitative factors," and that it is guided by "the scale, nature, manner of commission and impact of the crimes." At the end of the day, however, it provides little real insight,

38 OTP Policy Paper, *supra* note 33, ¶ 14. (Another way this can occur is through decisions not to make decisions about whether to move from a preliminary examination to an investigation. As the OTP has noted, "[t]here are no timelines provided in the Statute for bringing a preliminary examination to a close." By "parking" a matter as a preliminary examination, the Prosecutor can, at least for a time and probably an extended period of time, avoid the need to commence an investigation of a situation that could pass through the aperture but that the OTP believes does not really justify the use of the limited OTP resources that would be needed to conduct a proper investigation).

39 *See* Office of the Prosecutor, International Criminal Court, Policy Paper on Case Selection and Prioritisation (Sep. 15, 2016), https://www.icc-cpi.int/sites/default/files/itemsDocuments/20160915_OTP-Policy_Case-Selection_Eng.pdf (last visited July 12, 2023).

sprinkled as it is with explanations like the "[t]he nature of the crimes refers to the specific factual elements of each offence." In other places the Policy Paper sets out seemingly important principles (e.g., the OTP will consider "the extent to which the crimes were systematic or resulted from a plan or organised policy or otherwise resulted from the abuse of power or official capacity"), but never quite informs us how all these factors will actually be weighed against each other, how cases within a situation will actually be compared, or how the rules are supposed to apply in assessing cases across different situations. In the words of William Schabas:

> The Policy Paper pretends to clarify and inform but in reality it only serves to obscure things, perpetuating the fiction that the process is fundamentally objective rather than one that is inevitably steeped in subjectivity.[40]

That said, the indefiniteness of the policy paper is not without an important rationale. Unstated is the understandable reluctance of any Prosecutor to voluntarily rule out in advance any cases, or to bind the Prosecutor to a formula that he or she may later regret, particularly in a realm where it is so difficult to predict the many different situations that might arise in the future. More explicit is the fear that a more definite rule about what constitutes sufficient gravity "would hamper the deterrent role of the Court."[41] Better to have an enormous universe of conduct that might be prosecuted so as not to encourage would-be perpetrators to commit crimes that would fall outside a narrowed universe of crimes that the OTP would be saying in

---

40 William A. Schabas, *Feeding Time at the Office of the Prosecutor*, INT'L CRIM. JUST. TODAY: ARGUENDO (Nov. 23, 2016), https://www.international-criminal-justice-today.org/arguendo/icc-prosecutors-perpetuation-of-the-fiction-of-objectivity/ (last visited July 12, 2023). (In his note, Schabas imagines an analogous OTP "Policy Paper on Meal Selection" that would explain how OTP staff members would choose menu items at a restaurant, including for example:

"When selecting within a category, members of the Office take into account the following factors: (a) appearance; (b) the name of the dish; (c) anticipated taste and texture; (d) availability; (e) variety; (f) cost; (g) caloric intake. There is no hierarchy, however, and one or more of these factors may be of particular importance, depending upon the circumstances."). (The point is not that the list of factors is wrong, but that it offers no actual insight into how the factors will be applied, or whether the staff members "will be eating fish, chicken, or beef, or drinking still water, sparkling water or diet Coke").

41 Policy Paper on Case Selection and Prioritisation, *supra* note 39, ¶ 32, citing DRC Arrest Warrants Appeal, *supra* note 28, ¶¶ 69–79.

advance it would be willing to pursue. And, to be sure, it is hard to be unsympathetic to the idea that perpetrators of all serious crimes should be held to account.

But what does such an approach mean in practice? Is the goal to deter individuals who the ICC will not in fact pursue on the theory that the ICC might in fact pursue them? It is fair to ask whether such a strategy is sustainable over time. What is the effect of such an approach as the world comes to see, time and again, that conduct that the Rome Statute says we should treat as crimes that must not go unpunished do in fact go unpunished, or the risk that the ICC will be increasingly seen as an institution making a promise that it avows is sacred but does so little to vindicate?

This terrain is filled with conundrums for which there are no fool-proof answers, but there are two thoughts that might benefit from more discussion. First, we may be misconceiving the aperture issue if we place exclusive or too much focus on gravity. If it is true, as the report of the Independent Experts suggests, that the OTP and the Court will need to narrow the aperture in order for the Court to succeed, we should look to the various different ways that the aperture is controlled. In some ways, it is worth considering an approach in which the aperture-control mechanism can be applied in a more holistic manner – for example, an approach in which gravity is considered not solely in relation to the underlying conduct, but in relation to how egregious any failure to investigate or prosecute, or any decisions not to pursue conventional criminal responsibility, may be. Second, with respect to gravity as traditionally conceived, it is worth considering ways for tying its application to more tangible standards, so that the evaluation of gravity is seen more as an application of rules identified and agreed in advance, and less as a simple exercise of discretion. To be sure, the task of developing more concrete rules is a formidable one, particularly with respect to what the OTP calls the qualitative factors that go into its assessments. At the end of the day, both quantitative and qualitative factors will be important, but this may be an argument in favor of according greater weight to the quantitative factors, which can be applied in a manner that can more readily be seen as objective.

CHAPTER 22

Defining Gravity: The ICC's Struggle to Establish Selection Criteria

Ray Murphy

1 Introduction

Gravity has a fundamental role to play in informing the Office of the Prosecutor (OTP) in the situation and case selection process. Policy and practice have dictated that international prosecutions be selective and limited to the most serious crimes of international concern. Although the core crimes within the jurisdiction of the International Criminal Court (Court or ICC) are all serious in nature, the gravity threshold is intended to filter the cases that come before the Court and thereby prevent it from being overwhelmed. This does not mean that perpetrators other than leaders should not be brought before the Court, even if it seems implicit that only leaders should be. The policy and practice of the ICC has been subject to criticism and it is legitimate to question the basis on which the OTP is making an evaluation and whether it is a comprehensive, objective analysis based on sound criteria.

The OTP Policy Paper on Case Selection and Prioritisation (Policy)[1] marked an important advance in transparency surrounding the policy criteria being adopted in the selection of cases, i.e. whom to prosecute and for what crimes. It also provides an important mechanism to make the OTP's approach to selection and prioritization of cases more transparent. It should be read in conjunction with the more recent Draft Policy on Situation Completion[2] which also references many of the same themes but in the context of a wider situational strategy. The completion policy seeks to illustrate the considerations leading to a decision, in the exercise of prosecutorial

1 Office of the Prosecutor, International Criminal Court, Policy Paper on Case Selection and Prioritisation (Sep. 15, 2016), https://www.icc-cpi.int/sites/default/files/itemsDocuments/20160915_OTP-Policy_Case-Selection_Eng.pdf (last visited July 12, 2023).

2 Office of the Prosecutor, International Criminal Court, Draft Policy on Situation Completion (Mar. 24, 2021), https://www.icc-cpi.int/sites/default/files/itemsDocuments/2021-03-24-otp-draft-policy-situation-completion-eng.pdf (last visited July 12, 2023).

 | DOI:10.1163/9789004686755_028

discretion, that sufficient prosecutions have been brought in a situation to satisfy the OTP's mandate under the Rome Statute and goes hand in hand with case selection policy.

In addition to the gravity test, the OTP is obliged to consider the principle of complementarity in deciding whether or not to start an investigation. Crimes that are not of sufficient gravity will be left to possible domestic investigation and prosecution. In order to maintain a manageable workload for both the OTP and the Court, prioritization is a necessity. A central focus of the OTP in assessing gravity should also be the impact for victims and those communities affected by the crimes. The OTP has significant latitude and discretion when it comes to case selection and prioritization. At the same time, Article 53 of the Rome Statute, dealing with the initiation of an investigation and selection choices, ensures that the exercise of such discretion is not unlimited. The process outlined in the Policy facilitates prioritization of cases, completion strategies, and the adoption of a holistic approach while clearly setting out the case strategic and operationalization criteria.

When the OTP determines that certain cases are not of sufficient gravity in the context of an overall situation, it is imperative that it outline how this decision was arrived at. Failure to do so may alienate victims and discredit the Court. The Court will continue to face challenging resource constraints given the high number of situations opened. This has become a key theme over the last year, with the OTP repeatedly raising the issue of budget constraints.[3] This situation renders prioritization between cases a matter of necessity.

3 *See* Statement, Fatou Bensouda, Prosecutor, Int'l Crim. Ct., Statement on the Conclusion of the Preliminary Examination of the Situation in Nigeria (Dec. 11, 2020), https://www.icc-cpi.int/news/statement-prosecutor-fatou-bensouda-conclusion-preliminary-examination-situation-nigeria (last visited July 12, 2023); Statement, Fatou Bensouda, Prosecutor, Int'l Crim. Ct., Statement on the Conclusion of the Preliminary Examination in the Situation in Ukraine (Dec. 11, 2020), https://www.icc-cpi.int/news/statement-prosecutor-fatou-bensouda-conclusion-preliminary-examination-situation-ukraine (last visited July 12, 2023); Fatou Bensouda, Prosecutor, Int'l Crim. Ct., Remarks at the 19th Session of the Assembly of States Parties, Presentation of the 2020 Annual Report on Preliminary Examination Activities (Dec. 15, 2020) [hereinafter 2020 Annual Report], https://www.icc-cpi.int/sites/default/files/itemsDocuments/201216-otp-statement-report-pe.pdf (last visited July 12, 2023); Statement, Fatou Bensouda, Prosecutor, Int'l Crim. Ct., Statement Regarding the Situation in Palestine (Oct. 17, 2018) [hereinafter Situation in Palestine], https://www.icc-cpi.int/news/statement-prosecutor-international-criminal-court-fatou-bensouda-regarding-situation-palestine (last visited July 12, 2023); Statement, Fatou Bensouda, Prosecutor, Int'l Crim. Ct., Remarks at the 18th Session of the Assembly of States Parties, Presentation of the 2019 Annual Report on Preliminary Examination Activities (Dec. 6, 2019), https://

2 Background

The duties and powers of the Prosecutor outlined in the Statute of the International Criminal Court (Rome Statute) bestows a central role to the OTP in the functioning of the ICC, and in the selection and prioritization of situations and cases.[4] The OTP is responsible for both the primary selection of situations and the subsequent determination of what cases to examine. Impartial selection of cases and their prosecution, along with effective communication, are critical in fulfilling the Court's role in ending impunity for serious international crimes.[5] The OTP Strategic Plan 2019–2021 acknowledged a period of mixed results and significant setbacks as well as unprecedented external challenges.[6] A central challenge for the Court has consistently been to develop a sound approach to gravity, both as a threshold requirement for admissibility and as a discretionary relative consideration in the selection of situations and cases.[7]

Crimes within the jurisdiction of the ICC are outlined in the Rome Statute Articles 6, 7, 8, 8 *bis* (genocide, crimes against humanity, war crimes, and aggression), but Article 17 also requires that, in addition, the case must be of sufficient gravity to justify action by the Court.[8] While this

www.icc-cpi.int/sites/default/files/itemsDocuments/191206-otp-pe.pdf (last visited July 12, 2023).

4 International Criminal Court, *Regulations of the Office of the Prosecutor*, Doc. No. ICC-BD /05-01-09, R. 54, 34–35 (Apr. 23, 2009), https://www.icc-cpi.int/sites/default/files/NR/rdonlyres/FFF97111-ECD6-40B5-9CDA-792BCBE1E695/280253/ICCBD050109ENG.pdf (last visited July 12, 2023); *see also* Olympia Bekou, et al., 'Article 54: Duties and Powers of the Prosecutor with Respect to Investigations', in Otto Triffterer and Kai Ambos (eds.), *The Rome Statute of the International Criminal Court: A Commentary* (3d. ed., Oxford: Hart, 2016) p. 1381; William A. Schabas, *The International Criminal Court: A Commentary on the Rome Statute* (New York: Oxford University Press, 2010), pp. 672–82.

5 International Criminal Court, Rome Statute of the International Criminal Court, Preamble ¶ 4, U.N. Doc. A/CONF.183/9 (July 17, 1998) [hereinafter Rome Statute] (affirming that "the most serious crimes of concern to the international community as a whole must not go unpunished" and refers to the millions of children, women and men who have been victims of unimaginable atrocities that deeply shock the conscience of humanity). *See also* Margaret M. deGuzman, 'Gravity and the Legitimacy of the International Criminal Court' (2008), 32 *Fordham Int'l L.J.* 1400.

6 Office of the Prosecutor, International Criminal Court, Strategic Plan 2019–2021, ¶¶ 3, 5 (July 17, 2019), https://www.icc-cpi.int/sites/default/files/itemsDocuments/20190726-strategic-plan-eng.pdf (last visited June 23, 2023).

7 *See* deGuzman, *supra* note 5, at 1449.

8 Rome Statute, *supra* note 5, Article 17(1)(d) ("The case is not of sufficient gravity to justify further action by the Court"). *See also* Schabas, *supra* note 4, at 347–49 (Article 1 and the

admissibility threshold is important in determining prosecutorial policy,[9] according to Schabas, the "insignificance of article 17(1)(d) was confirmed by the Appeals Chamber" when it overturned an earlier ruling on issuance of an arrest warrant.[10] The Pre-Trial Chamber had held that as all crimes within the jurisdiction of the Court were in principle serious, there was an additional gravity dimension to be assessed in determinations of admissibility.[11] It required that the conduct be either systematic or large scale, and provoke what it referred to as "social alarm." This test was rejected by the Appeals Chamber. It considered that the criterion of "social alarm" depended upon "subjective and contingent reactions to crimes rather than upon their objective gravity" and that crimes within the jurisdiction of the Court are "the most serious crimes of international concern" and "the subjective criterion of social alarm" was not an appropriate test.[12]

The Pre-Trial Chamber had also expressed the view that the deterrent effect of the Court would be strongest if it focused on the highest ranking perpetrators only.[13] The Appeals Chamber found this to be "questionable" and "that the deterrent effect of the Court is highest if no category of perpetrators is per se excluded from potentially being brought before the Court."[14] Unfortunately, the Appeals Chamber failed to provide an alternative test and did not offer any further guidance on the interpretation of Article 17 (1)(d).

Gravity also remains a potentially contentious issue to be considered before initiating an investigation or prosecution under Article 53.[15] This was

---

Preamble to the Rome Statute also limit the Court's jurisdiction to "the most serious crimes").

9 Policy Paper on Case Selection and Prioritisation, *supra* note 1, ¶ 6 ("Gravity is the predominant case selection criteria adopted by the Office and is embedded also into considerations of both the degree of responsibility of alleged perpetrators and charging.").

10 Schabas, *supra* note 4, at 348.

11 Prosecutor v. Thomas Lubanga Dyilo, Case No. ICC-01/04-01/06-2, Decision on the Prosecutor's Application for Warrants of Arrest, Article 58, ¶¶ 42–64 (PTC I, Feb. 10, 2006) [hereinafter Lubanga Warrant Decision].

12 Situation in the Democratic Republic of the Congo, Case No. ICC-01/04-169, Judgment on the Prosecutor's Appeal against the Decision of Pre-Trial Chamber I Entitled "Decision on the Prosecutor's Application for Warrants of Arrest, Article 58", ¶ 70 (AC, Jul. 13, 2006) [hereinafter Arrest Warrants Appeal].

13 Lubanga Warrant Decision, *supra* note 11, ¶¶ 54–55.

14 Arrest Warrants Appeal, *supra* note 12, ¶¶ 73–74.

15 William A. Schabas and Mohamed M. El Zeidy, 'Article 17: Issues of Admissibility', in Otto Triffterer and Kai Ambos (eds.), *The Rome Statute of the International Criminal Court: A Commentary* (3d. ed., Oxford: Hart, 2016) pp. 794, 811–16.

evident in the OTP's decision not to proceed to investigate the Gaza flotilla incident on the basis of lack of gravity, which was later subject to Article 53(3) review.[16] Although the core crimes within the jurisdiction are all very serious in nature, the gravity threshold is intended to filter the seriousness of cases that come before the Court and thereby prevent it from being overwhelmed. Despite the concept of gravity being a central tenet of international criminal justice, the Rome Statute provides little by way of explanation into what this actually means in practice.

Policy and practice have dictated that international prosecutions be selective and limited to the most serious criminals.[17] This does not mean that perpetrators other than leaders should not be brought before the Court. The Appeals Chamber disagreed with the Pre-Trial Chambers' focus on only the most senior leaders.[18] It considered that assessing the role of a suspect will vary "considerably depending on the circumstances of the case" and should

16 *See* Situation on Registered Vessels of the Union of the Comoros, the Hellenic Republic and the Kingdom of Cambodia, Case No. ICC-01/13-98, Judgment on the Appeal of the Prosecutor against Pre-Trial Chamber I's 'Decision on the "Application for Judicial Review by the Government of the Union of the Comoros"', (AC, Sep. 2, 2019) (rejecting the appeal filed by the OTP of the ICC Pre-Trial Chamber I's decision on the November 15, 2018 "Application for Judicial Review by the Government of the Union of Comoros." The Appeals Chamber confirmed the Pre-Trial Chamber's decision, directing that the OTP must reconsider its decision regarding the Comoros referral. The Appeals Chamber did maintain that the "ultimate decision" regarding whether or not to initiate an investigation remains with the OTP). *See also* Press Release, Int'l Crim. Ct., Situation on the Registered Vessels of Comoros, Greece and Cambodia: ICC Appeals Chamber Rejects the Prosecutor's Appeal (Sep. 2, 2019), https://www.icc-cpi.int/news/situation-registered-vessels-comoros-greece-and-cambodia-icc-appeals-chamber-rejects (last visited July 14, 2023)

("[A] referral was received by the OTP from the authorities of the Union of the Comoros, a State Party to the Rome Statute, in relation to an attack on 31 May 2010 by the Israeli Defence Forces on the Humanitarian Aid Flotilla bound for the Gaza strip. On 6 November 2014, the Prosecutor issued her decision not to investigate the attack. On 16 July 2015, Pre-Trial Chamber I, by majority, requested Prosecutor to reconsider the 6 November 2014 decision not to investigate the attack. Subsequently, on 29 November 2017 the Prosecutor filed her decision, which she considered to be final, reaffirming her previous decision not to investigate the attack. On 15 November 2018, Pre-Trial Chamber I directed the Prosecutor to reconsider her decision of 6 November 2014 not to investigate the attack in light of the specific directions of the Pre-Trial Chamber's 16 July 2015 decision. The Prosecutor then appealed this decision.").

17 M. Cherif Bassiouni, *Introduction to International Criminal Law* (Boston: Martinus Nijhoff Publishers, 2013), p. 706.

18 Arrest Warrants Appeal, *supra* note 12, ¶ 73.

not be based on "excessively formalistic grounds."[19] At the same time, the ICC was never intended to deal with all cases coming within its jurisdiction. Low-level perpetrators may be best dealt with by national courts. However, the decision whether to focus on a low-level perpetrator falls within prosecutorial strategy.[20] Identifying precisely the criteria adopted by international prosecutors in the exercise of their discretionary powers was described as a real challenge and the lack of transparency as "occult or secret in nature."[21] According to the OTP, experience showed that the situations faced by the Court tended to involve large-scale commission of crimes, with an untold number of victims as well as many alleged perpetrators.[22] For this reason, one of the most important elements of the strategy, considering the global nature of the ICC and the need to handle several situations concurrently, was to focus investigative and prosecutorial efforts on those who bore the greatest responsibility for the most serious crimes. Selection of cases was said to be based on "objective and impartial analysis in accordance with the criteria set out in article 53 of the Statute."[23] Amongst the most important of these criteria is the gravity of the crime. The methodologies for determining gravity were not clear, but included the number of persons killed, the number of victims, and the impact of the crimes.[24] In the past, the OTP did not necessarily limit investigations to situations where killing had been the predominant crime.[25] Furthermore, the concept of gravity was not exclusively attached to the act that constituted the crime but also to the degree of participation.[26]

The policy and practice of the OTP has been subject to criticism. It has been accused of "missteps in the selection of cases" that "created significant credibility gaps for the Court [and] led to perceptions of bias."[27] This in turn was said to have undermined its potential positive impact in affected

19 *Id.* at ¶ 76.

20 Schabas and El Zeidy, *supra* note 15, at 815.

21 *See* Luc Côté, 'Reflections on the Exercise of Prosecutorial Discretion in International Criminal Law' (2005) 3 *J. Int'l Crim. Just.* 162, at 167, 171.

22 Statement, Luis Moreno-Ocampo, Prosecutor, Int'l Crim. Ct., Informal Meeting of Legal Advisors of Ministries of Foreign Affairs, p. 5 (Oct. 24, 2005), https://www.icc-cpi.int/sites/default/files/NR/rdonlyres/9D70039E-4BEC-4F32-9D4A-CEA8B6799E37/143836/LMO_20051024_English.pdf (last visited July 14, 2023).

23 *Id.* at 6.

24 *Id.*

25 *Id.*

26 *Id.*

27 Human Rights Watch, *Comments on the ICC Office of the Prosecutor Draft Policy Paper on Case Selection and Prioritisation* (May 3, 2016), https://www.hrw.org/sites/de

communities and, in some cases, "led to a loss of trust and confidence in the Court as an independent and impartial judicial institution."[28] Another criticism was that, in the past, the OTP's case selection choices were seemingly driven by a somewhat ad hoc approach, involving the selection of one or two cases, followed by additional cases if and when resources permitted.[29]

While the ICC is neither mandated nor designed to prosecute all perpetrators of serious international crimes, the controversy in the early days regarding the selective investigation and prosecution of rebel or similar forces only, has probably been overtaken by events in later situations where attempts have been made (sometimes unsuccessfully) to investigate both sides.[30] Such a policy created a danger of perceived political selectivity in the situations referred to the Court. However, there is a pre-investigation prosecutorial and judicial review, and, in theory at least, "situations" encompass all participants in a conflict and are not limited to particular groups or individuals.[31] The question is, on what basis is the Prosecutor making her evaluation and is it a comprehensive, objective analysis based on sound criteria?[32]

---

fault/files/supporting_resources/hrw_comments_on_case_selection_policy.pdf (last visited July 14, 2023).

28 *Id.*

29 *Id.*

30 *See, e.g.*, *Kenya*, INT'L CRIM. CT., https://www.icc-cpi.int/kenya (last visited July 14, 2023); *Central African Republic II*, INT'L CRIM. CT., https://www.icc-cpi.int/carII (last visited July 14, 2023); *Georgia*, INT'L CRIM. CT., https://www.icc-cpi.int/georgia (last visited July 14, 2023); *People's Republic of Bangladesh/Republic of the Union of Myanmar*, INT'L CRIM. CT., https://www.icc-cpi.int/bangladesh-myanmar (last visited July 14, 2023); Situation in the Islamic Republic of Afghanistan, Case No. ICC-02/17-33, Decision pursuant to Article 15 of the Rome Statute on the Authorisation of an Investigation into the Situation in the Islamic Republic of Afghanistan (PTC II, Apr. 12, 2019); Situation in Palestine, *supra* note 3.

31 *See* Situation in the Islamic Republic of Afghanistan, Case No. ICC-02/17 OA4, Judgment on the Appeal against the Decision on the Authorisation of an Investigation into the Situation in the Islamic Republic of Afghanistan, ¶¶ 57–61 (AC, Mar. 05, 2020); *see also* Payam Akhavan, 'The Lord's Resistance Army Case: Uganda's Submission of the First State Referral to the International Criminal Court' (2005), 99 *Am. J. Int'l L.* 403, 411.

32 *See* Office of the Prosecutor, International Criminal Court, Policy Paper on Preliminary Examinations (Nov. 2013) [hereinafter Policy Preliminary Examinations], https://www.icc-cpi.int/sites/default/files/iccdocs/otp/OTP-Policy_Paper_Preliminary_Examinations_2013-ENG.pdf (last visited July 12, 2023) (describing the process and criteria for the opening of an ICC investigation in a situation).

3 Policy Paper on Case Selection and Prioritisation

In September 2016, the OTP published the Policy Paper on Case Selection and Prioritisation which outlines current practice.[33] This marked an important advance in transparency surrounding the policy criteria being adopted in the selection of cases (i.e., whom to prosecute and for what crimes). It also provides an important mechanism to make the OTP's approach to selection and prioritization of cases more transparent while at the same time providing significant general guidance to all those involved in case selection and management.

The Policy draws on many of the same principles and criteria that are applied at the preliminary examination stage.[34] According to the Policy, the jurisprudence of the Court distinguishes between "situations," which are generally defined in terms of temporal, territorial, and in some cases personal parameters, and "cases," which comprise specific incidents within a given "situation" during which one or more crimes within the jurisdiction of the Court may have been committed.[35] Cases considered for prosecution must first meet the legal criteria of jurisdiction, admissibility, and interest of justice.[36] The OTP must then decide which of those cases to select based on three factors: the gravity of the crime(s), the degree of responsibility of alleged perpetrators, and whether the charges would reflect the extent of the criminality that has occurred.[37] The OTP aims to prosecute all cases that are selected according to the criteria above, but it prioritizes cases for

33 Policy Paper on Case Selection and Prioritisation, *supra* note 1 (describing the selection of cases for investigation in a situation, and their prioritization in light of the multiple situations under investigation in the OTP. It is part of a trilogy of policy papers describing the life cycle of the OTP's operations in a situation, and must be read with the recent Draft Policy on Situation Completion, *supra* note 2).

34 *Id.*

35 Situation in the Democratic Republic of the Congo, Case No. ICC-01/04, Decision on the Applications for Participation in the Proceedings of VPRS 1, VPRS 2, VPRS 3, VPRS 4, VPRS 5 and VPRS 6, ¶ 65 (Jan. 17, 2006); Prosecutor v. Thomas Lubanga Dyilo, Case No. ICC-01/04-01/06-8-Corr, Decision Concerning Pre-Trial Chamber's Decision of February 10, 2006 and the Incorporation of Documents into the Record of the Case against Mr Thomas Lubanga Dyilo, ¶ 21 (Feb. 24, 2006).

36 Policy Paper on Case Selection and Prioritisation, *supra* note 1, at 4, 9–12; *see also* Office of the Prosecutor, International Criminal Court, Policy Paper on the Interests of Justice (Sep. 2007), https://www.icc-cpi.int/sites/default/files/NR/rdonlyres/772C95C9-F54D-4321-BF09-73422BB23528/143640/ICCOTPInterestsOfJustice.pdf (last visited July 14, 2023).

37 Policy Paper on Case Selection and Prioritisation, *supra* note 1, at 5, 12–15.

prosecution based on such factors as a comparative assessment across the selected cases, the impact of investigations and prosecutions on both ongoing criminality and victims, and other factors.[38]

The history of the ICTR and ICTY demonstrates that some of the most serious international crimes may not in practice be prosecuted at an international level. This was reflected in the requirement to affirm in the Preamble to the Rome Statute that "the effective prosecution must be ensured by taking measures at the national level and by enhancing international co-operation."[39] Thus, in addition to the gravity test, the Prosecutor is obliged to consider the principle of complementarity in deciding whether or not to start an investigation.[40] It is the primary responsibility of states to investigate and prosecute international crimes.[41] This has important implications for self-referrals by states.[42] The gravity of the crime is one of the express considerations to be taken into account in ascertaining the existence of a reasonable basis to proceed. Its inclusion in the Preamble may be seen as a reflection of the concern that the interests underlying the complementarity principle sufficiently permeate the Rome Statute.

The Preamble and Article 1 of the Rome Statute reinforce each other and confirm that the Court's jurisdiction covers "the most serious crimes of international concern." Crimes that are not of sufficient gravity will be left to possible domestic investigation and prosecution.[43] The reference in Article 8 to war crimes committed "as part of a plan or as part of a large-scale commission of such crimes" may also be seen in this light and may imply that less serious war crimes should be prosecuted domestically. The final paragraph of the Preamble resolves to guarantee both lasting respect for international justice and its enforcement. It is of utmost significance in the prosecutorial policy to be adopted by the OTP and refers to the enforcement

---

38 *Id.* at ¶ 50.

39 Rome Statute, *supra* note 5, Preamble ¶ 4.

40 *Id.* at art. 17(1)(a); *see also* Schabas and El Zeidy, *supra* note 15, at 781–831. (Policy Paper on Case Selection and Prioritisation, *supra* note 1, ¶ 8 provides: "The overall aim of the Office is to represent as much as possible the true extent of the criminality which has occurred within a given situation, in an effort to ensure, jointly with the relevant national jurisdictions, that the most serious crimes committed in each situation do not go unpunished."). *See also* Rod Rastan, 'What is 'Substantially the Same Conduct?' Unpacking the ICC's 'First Limb' Complementarity Jurisprudence' (2017), 15 *J. Int'l Crim. Just.* 1.

41 Rome Statute, *supra* note 5, Preamble ¶¶ 4, 6.

42 Ray Murphy, 'Gravity Issues and the International Criminal Court' (2006), 17 *Crim. L.F.* 281, 286.

43 Bekou, et al., *supra* note 4, at 1373.

of international criminal law in international and national criminal jurisdictions.

The cornerstone of the Rome Statute is Article 17 dealing with admissibility.[44] The Pre-Trial Chambers and the OTP have adopted a unified approach in the assessment of gravity and this is reflected in paragraphs 32, 34 and 37 of the Policy.[45]

> 32. In relation to gravity as a criterion for admissibility under article 17 (1)(d), the Appeals Chamber has dismissed the setting of an overly restrictive legal bar that would hamper the deterrent role of the Court.[46] The factors that guide the Office's assessment of gravity include both quantitative and qualitative considerations, relating to the scale, nature, manner of commission and impact of the crimes.[47]
>
> 34. The Office will select cases for investigation and prosecution in light of the gravity of the crimes, the degree of responsibility of the alleged perpetrators and the potential charges. The weight given to each criterion will depend on the facts and circumstances of each case and each situation, and the stage of development of the case hypothesis and investigation.[48] The Case Selection Document will be reviewed as investigations proceed, by applying the same case selection criteria.[49]
>
> 37. The Office's assessment of gravity includes both quantitative and qualitative considerations. As stipulated in regulation 29(2) of the Regulations of the Office, the factors that guide the Office's assessment include the scale, nature, manner of commission, and impact of the crimes.[50]

---

44 *Id.* at 786.

45 *Id.* at 815.

46 Arrest Warrants Appeal, *supra* note 12, ¶¶ 69–79.

47 Regulations of the Office of the Prosecutor, *supra* note 4, R. 29(2); *see also* Policy Preliminary Examinations, *supra* note 32, ¶¶ 59–66; Situation in Georgia, Case No. ICC-01/15-12, Decision on the Prosecutor's Request for Authorization of an Investigation, ¶ 51 (PTC I, Jan. 27, 2016) [hereinafter Georgia Investigation Authorization]; Schabas and El Zeidy, *supra* note 15, at 815–16.

48 Rome Statute, *supra* note 5, Preamble ¶¶ 4, 10; *see also* Office of the Prosecutor, International Criminal Court, Paper on Some Policy Issues Before the Office of the Prosecutor (Sep. 2003), https://www.icc-cpi.int/sites/default/files/NR/rdonlyres/1FA7C4C6-DE5F-42B7-8B25-60AA962ED8B6/143594/030905_Policy_Paper.pdf (last visited July 14, 2023).

49 Policy Paper on Case Selection and Prioritisation, *supra* note 1, ¶¶ 13, 51, 53.

50 Prosecutor v. Bahar Idriss Abu Garda, Case No. ICC-02/05-02/09-243-Red, Decision on the Confirmation of Charges, ¶ 31 (PTC 1, Feb. 8, 2010). Situation in the Republic of

The Policy drew on strategy papers, and other policy papers addressing particular fundamental issues on which the OTP wanted to provide more clarity and transparency.[51] At the same time, the need for selection and prioritization remains owing to size and capacity restraints[52] in the OTP and the

Côte d'Ivoire, Case No. ICC-02/11-14-Corr, Corrigendum to "Decision Pursuant to Article 15 of the Rome Statute on the Authorization of an Investigation into the Situation in the Republic of Côte d'Ivoire", ¶ 203–04 (PTC III, Nov. 15, 2011) [hereinafter Côte d'Ivoire Investigation Authorization]. For further understanding of the issues in paragraph 37, *see* Situation in the Republic of Kenya, Case No. ICC-01/09-19-Corr, Corrigendum of the Decision Pursuant to Article 15 of the Rome Statute on the Authorization of an Investigation into the Situation in the Republic of Kenya, ¶¶ 62, 188 (PTC II, Mar. 31, 2010) [hereinafter Kenya Investigation Authorization]. "In making its assessment, the Chamber considers that gravity may be examined following a quantitative as well as a qualitative approach. Regarding the qualitative dimension, it is not the number of victims that matter but rather the existence of some aggravating or qualitative factors attached to the commission of crimes, which makes it grave. When considering the gravity of the crime(s), several factors concerning sentencing as reflected in rule 145(l)(c) and (2)(b)(iv) of the Rules, could provide useful guidance in such an examination. These factors could be summarized as: (i) the scale of the alleged crimes (including assessment of geographical and temporal intensity); (ii) the nature of the unlawful behavior or of the crimes allegedly committed; (iii) the employed means for the execution of the crimes (i.e., the manner of their commission); and (iv) the impact of the crimes and the harm caused to victims and their families. In this respect, the victims' representations will be of significant guidance for the Chamber's assessment." Georgia Investigation Authorization, *supra* note 47, ¶ 51; Regulations of the Office of the Prosecutor, *supra* note 4, Article 29(2); Policy Preliminary Examinations, *supra* note 32, ¶¶ 9, 71.

51 Policy Preliminary Examinations, *supra* note 32; Policy Paper on the Interests of Justice, *supra* note 36; Office of the Prosecutor, International Criminal Court, Policy Paper on Victims' Participation (Apr. 2010), https://www.icc-cpi.int/sites/default/files/NR/rdonlyres/9FF1EAA1-41C4-4A30-A202-174B18DA923C/281751/PolicyPaperonVictimsParticipationApril2010.pdf (last visited July 17, 2023); Office of the Prosecutor, International Criminal Court, Policy Paper on Sexual and Gender-Based Crimes (Jun. 2014), https://www.icc-cpi.int/sites/default/files/iccdocs/otp/OTP-Policy-Paper-on-Sexual-and-Gender-Based-Crimes–June-2014.pdf (last visited July 17, 2023); Office of the Prosecutor, International Criminal Court, Strategic Plan 2016–2018 (Jul. 6, 2015), https://www.icc-cpi.int/sites/default/files/iccdocs/otp/070715-OTP_Strategic_Plan_2016-2018.pdf (last visited July 17, 2023); *see also* Rod Rastan, 'Case Selection and Prioritisation at the International Criminal Court', in Morten Bergsmo (ed.), *Criteria for Prioritizing and Selecting Core International Crimes Cases* ¶ 7.3.2 (3d ed. forthcoming, Oslo: Torkel Opsahl) [hereinafter Prioritisation Criteria].

52 Assembly of States Parties, International Criminal Court, *Report of the Court on the Basic Size of the Office of the Prosecutor*, Doc No. ICC-ASP /14/21 (Sep. 17, 2015) [hereinafter Basic Size], https://asp.icc-cpi.int/sites/asp/files/asp_docs/ASP14/ICC-ASP-14-21-ENG.pdf (last visited July 14, 2023) (referred to in Policy Paper on Case Selection and Prioritisation, *supra* note 1, ¶ 11).

need for "prioritization of activities."[53] In order to maintain a manageable workload for both the OTP and Court, prioritization is a necessity.[54] The situation of work overload, according to Ambos:

> [L]eaves the Court/the OTP no other choice than to deliver mere distributive (instead of retributive) criminal justice, where the main challenge is not so much the fair or just delivery of sanctions to individual defendants, but the fair distribution of justice to a selected number of suspects and/or perpetrators.[55]

An important focus of the OTP and Court as a whole should also be the impact for victims and those communities affected by the crimes.[56] In that regard, the commitment to pursue charges that are "a representative sample of the main types of victimization and of the communities which have been affected" marked a progressive development.[57]

4 Prosecutor's Discretion

The Policy recognizes the importance of the general principles of independence, impartiality, and objectivity to building the ICC's legitimacy.[58] In that context, the OTP has significant latitude and discretion when it comes to case selection and prioritization subject to limited judicial review.[59] In the discharge of its mandate, the OTP exercises its discretion in determining which cases should be selected and prioritized for investigation and prosecution.[60] The OTP also has discretion to define how many cases will make up the Prosecutorial Program for a situation.[61]

53 *Id.* ¶ 5.

54 Policy Paper on Case Selection and Prioritisation, *supra* note 1, ¶¶ 11–12 (referring to the "overall basic size and capacity constraints" and the limited "resources available").

55 Kai Ambos, 'Office of the Prosecutor: Policy Paper on Case Selection and Prioritisation (Int'l Crim. Ct.)' (2018), 57 *International Legal Materials* 1131.

56 Rome Statute, *supra* note 5, Article 53(1)(c) (referring to the "interests of victims" while at the same time recognizing that there are factors that may outweigh that interest). *See also* Kenya Investigation Authorization, *supra* note 50, ¶ 62.

57 Policy Paper on Case Selection and Prioritisation, *supra* note 1, ¶ 45.

58 *Id.* ¶ 16; *see also* Draft Policy Situation Completion, *supra* note 2, ¶¶ 11–15.

59 Rome Statute, *supra* note 5, Article 53.

60 *Id.* Articles 14(1), 42(1), 58(1) (reflecting the Prosecutor's discretion).

61 *See id.* at Arts. 53(2), 54, 48; *see also* Policy Paper on Case Selection and Prioritisation, *supra* note 1, ¶¶ 25–26, 29, 33; Situation in Darfur, Sudan, Case No. ICC-02/05-185,

The Policy retains this discretion in the OTP while attempting to provide guidance and objective criteria by which to assess case selection and prioritization. It was intended to ensure that the exercise of such discretion "is guided by sound, fair and transparent principles and criteria."[62] It also emphasized that it is not the responsibility or role of the OTP to investigate and prosecute all alleged criminal acts within a given situation or every person allegedly responsible for such crimes. This would be impractical and run counter to the notion of complementary action at the international and national level, as highlighted in the Preamble and Article 1 of the Rome Statute. Given the importance of the role of the OTP under the Statute, it is difficult to envisage how the Court would otherwise be able to function effectively.

Applying discretion in the selection process remains the prerogative of the OTP. At the same time, Article 53, dealing with the initiation of an investigation and selection choices, ensures that the exercise of such discretion is not unlimited. The Prosecutor is bound by the criteria outlined in the Statute, especially with regard to issues involving some discretion and relating to "gravity" and "those bearing the greatest responsibility." In this way, the exercise of a limited review power by the Pre-Trial Chamber is possible. Such a process, based on checks and balances between the OTP and the Pre-Trial Chamber and combined with a transparent selection strategy, should facilitate achieving coherence in the practice of the OTP and Court as a whole.

The shift in the attention of the OTP from African states to other regions is to be welcomed. Nevertheless, a major challenge for the Court is to avoid giving the impression that it only prosecutes nationals of weak states, and in so doing reinforces existing structural inequalities between states, while exposing itself to accusations of bias.[63] Such perceptions may have been mitigated somewhat after the sanctions imposed by the U.S. during the Trump administration.[64] The situation is further complicated by the fact

---

Decision on Application under Rule 103 ¶ 24 (PTC I, Feb. 4, 2009) (holding that "States Parties have granted the Prosecution discretion to decide whether to request the initiation of a case through the issuance of an arrest warrant or a summons to appear," subject to the Pre-Trial Chamber's verification of reasonable grounds to believe that the person in question is responsible for a crime under the Statute).

62 Policy Paper on Case Selection and Prioritisation, *supra* note 1, ¶ 5.

63 *See* Birju Kotecha, 'The Art of Rhetoric: Perceptions of the International Criminal Court and Legalism' (2018), 31 *Leiden J. Int'l L.* 929.

64 *US Sanctions on the International Criminal Court: Questions and Answers,* HUM. RTS. WATCH (Dec. 14, 2020), https://www.hrw.org/news/2020/12/14/us-sanctions-international-criminal-court (last visited July 14, 2023).

that suspects may be selected as representative of certain categories of perpetrators, as opposed to individuals, to which a degree of collective blame may be attached.

5 Case Selection Document

The Policy introduces a significant innovation in the form of a Case Selection Document which identifies in broad terms the potential cases across all situations that the OTP intends to focus on.[65] As each new situation is opened for investigation, the OTP will include the potential cases arising from that situation into the Case Selection Document. This is a "dynamic document"[66] that will be reviewed as investigations proceed, by applying the same case selection criteria.[67] This process is confidential until a person has been arrested or appears voluntarily before the Court.[68]

The process outlined in the Policy facilitates prioritization of cases,[69] completion strategies, and the adoption of a holistic approach. The commitment to "investigate and prosecute all cases that are selected pursuant to the case selection criteria"[70] is especially welcome and should address past criticism while establishing a clear strategic goal. However, this also creates a de facto tiered system which has the potential to undermine the commitment to investigate all cases that are selected.

The Policy clearly sets out the case strategic and operationalization criteria.[71] It provides that these criteria stand in no hierarchical order to each other and that the specific weight to be given to individual criterion will depend on the circumstances of each case.[72] This proposes a pragmatic approach taking into account quantity and quality of evidence, the nature of cooperation to support the OTP, and capacity and security issues as the

---

65 Policy Paper on Case Selection and Prioritisation, *supra* note 1, ¶ 10; *see also* Rastan, *supra* note 51, ¶ 7.3.3.

66 Policy Paper on Case Selection and Prioritisation, *supra* note 1, ¶ 10; Regulations of the Office of the Prosecutor, *supra* note 4, R. 33, 34; Draft Policy Situation Completion, *supra* note 2, ¶ 24.

67 Policy Paper on Case Selection and Prioritisation, *supra* note 1, ¶¶ 13, 51, 53.

68 *Id.* at ¶ 15.

69 *Id.* at ¶ 11; Basic Size, *supra* note 52; Policy Paper on Case Selection and Prioritisation, *supra* note 1, § 6; Prioritisation Criteria, *supra* note 51, ¶ 47–53; Draft Policy Situation Completion, *supra* note 2, ¶¶ 33–35.

70 Policy Paper on Case Selection and Prioritisation, *supra* note 1, ¶ 47.

71 *Id.* at ¶¶ 50–51.

72 *Id.* at ¶¶ 51–52.

overriding criteria when determining prioritization, with the more normative strategic case prioritization criteria outlined in paragraph 50 being a secondary consideration. However, while deprioritization is not "deselection," this may in fact turn out to be the de facto consequence.[73]

The Policy on case selection should be read in conjunction with the recently published Draft Policy on Situation Completion, which also references many of the same themes but in the context of a wider situational strategy. The latter also acknowledges the need to manage selected cases which have been effectively de-prioritized.[74] The completion policy seeks to illustrate the considerations that lead to a decision, in the exercise of prosecutorial discretion, that sufficient prosecutions have been brought in a situation to satisfy the OTP's mandate under the Rome Statute.

The current situation is that neither the ICC, nor any other international criminal tribunal, can hold corporations criminally liable for core international crimes.[75] Among the reasons for this is that business activity, however serious, rarely reaches the gravity threshold required for international crimes within the jurisdiction of the ICC. However, while the Policy Paper on Case Selection and Prioritisation does not expand the ICC's jurisdiction, it does provide a mechanism to focus on individuals responsible for business-related crimes.[76] Furthermore, in assessing the gravity of crimes, which is one of the fundamental case selection criterion, the document emphasizes that the OTP will give particular consideration to:

> [C]rimes that are committed by means of, or that result in, inter alia, the destruction of the environment, the illegal exploitation of natural resources or the illegal dispossession of land.[77]

In this way, the OTP is now more likely to consider crimes committed with the complicity of the private sector.[78] However, there are potential disadvantages to this as it may create the false impression that the ICC can simply start proceedings following the filing of a communication, which may, in turn, lead to accusations of failure when it does not do so.[79]

73 Human Rights Watch, *supra* note 27.

74 Draft Policy Situation Completion, *supra* note 2, ¶¶ 33–35.

75 Nadia Bernaz, 'An Analysis of the ICC Office of the Prosecutor's Policy Paper on Case Selection and Prioritization from the Perspective of Business and Human Rights' (2017) 15 *J. Int'l Crim. Just.* 527, 532.

76 *Id.* at 535.

77 Policy Paper on Case Selection and Prioritisation, *supra* note 1, ¶ 41.

78 Bernaz, *supra* note 76, at 533.

79 Megan A. Fairlie, 'The Hidden Costs of Strategic Communications for the International Criminal Court' (2016) 51 *Tex. Int'l L.J.* 281, 292–96.

The Report on Preliminary Examination Activities 2020 provides insights into the process and outlines that in order to distinguish the situations that warrant investigation from those that do not, and in order to manage the analysis of the factors set out in Article 53(1), the OTP has established a filtering process comprising four phases.[80] Phase 1 consists of an initial assessment of all information on alleged crimes received under Article 15 (Communications). Although the nature of this assessment has generally tended to focus on questions of subject-matter jurisdiction, it may also consider questions of gravity and complementarity where they appear relevant.[81]

In practice, the assessments that require the most time and resources are those situations where alleged crimes are not manifestly outside the jurisdiction of the Court, but do not clearly fall within its subject-matter jurisdiction.[82] In such situations, the OTP will first consider whether the lack of clarity applies to most, or a limited set of allegations, and in the case of the latter, whether they are nevertheless of such gravity to justify further analysis. The OTP will then consider whether the exercise of the Court's jurisdiction may be restricted due to factors such as a narrow geographic and/or personal scope of jurisdiction and/or the existence of national proceedings relating to the relevant conduct.[83]

6 Conclusion

Gravity has a fundamental role to play in informing the OTP in the situation and case selection process.[84] This may require the OTP to prioritize selected ICC goals, thus gravity factors, over others. At the same time, a distinction must be drawn between the gravity threshold for admissibility under Article 17 and considerations of gravity for the purposes of determining which situations or cases will be investigated or prosecuted as a matter of prosecutorial discretion under Article 53.[85] The Policy provides greater clarity with regard to the criteria used for case selection.[86] It also attempts to reflect

80 2020 Annual Report, *supra* note 3.

81 *Id.* at ¶¶ 15, 27–29.

82 *Id.* at ¶ 28.

83 *Id.*

84 deGuzman, *supra* note 5, at 1465.

85 Susana SáCouto & Katherine A. Cleary, 'The Gravity Threshold of the International Criminal Court' (2007) 23 *Am. U. Int'l L. Rev.* 807, 814.

86 Kai Ambos and Ignaz Stegmiller, 'Prosecuting International Crimes at the International Criminal Court: Is There a Coherent and Comprehensive Prosecution Strategy?' (2013) 58 *Crime, L. & Soc. Change* 415.

and respond to the experience and needs of victims.[87] It is imperative that these needs be respected in practice.

Taking into account the large number of communications and referrals to the Court, a focused strategy setting out the criteria for situation and case selection and prioritization is necessary. In this regard, the positive complementarity approach emphasizing cooperation with national jurisdictions while enhancing OTP prosecutorial capacity is a welcome and realistic policy approach.[88] In this way, close and effective cooperation with national jurisdictions will enhance the Court's capacity to end impunity.

In the past, the policy of identifying and pursuing the most senior leaders did have a certain pragmatic appeal. Nonetheless, such a policy should not be an overriding consideration in deciding whom to investigate and prosecute. The consequence of such an approach was problematic as it could mean the exclusion of others equally culpable of heinous crimes, but who did not hold positions of authority. The Rome Statute does not refer to the most senior leaders, it specifically refers to the "perpetrators" of "the most serious crimes."[89] The current Policy reflects this and provides that the overall aim of the OTP is to represent as much as possible the true extent of the criminality in an effort to ensure that the most serious crimes committed do not go unpunished.[90] In so doing, the Policy requires that particular attention be paid to crimes that have been traditionally under-prosecuted.[91]

A consequence of this overall OTP strategy, which was first introduced in the 2012 OTP Strategic Plan,[92] and this policy, is that very few cases brought under Prosecutor Bensouda have been leadership cases (other than cases she inherited), and most have involved mid-level perpetrators, some notorious, and a few in senior leadership positions. The "new" policy reflects the pragmatic reality that prosecutors need to retain some degree of flexibility based on the actual evidence available. Sometimes there is insufficient evidence to bring a prosecution against those alleged to be most responsible, but it may be useful to build a case based on insiders and/or lower to mid-level perpetrators, or there may be some symbolic value to going after a

87 *See Id.* at ¶¶ 9, 33, 38, 40–41, 45, 50.

88 *Id.* at 415–37.

89 Rome Statute, *supra* note 5, at Preamble, art. 5.

90 Policy Paper on Case Selection and Prioritisation, *supra* note 1, at ¶¶ 8, 45.

91 Policy Paper on Case Selection and Prioritisation, *supra* note 1, at ¶ 45 (focusing attention on crimes affecting children, rape and other sexual and gender-based crimes, attacks against cultural, religious, historical and other protected objects, as well as against humanitarian and peacekeeping personnel).

92 Strategic Plan 2016–2018, *supra* note 51.

notorious perpetrator such as Al-Werfalli[93] and Al Mahdi.[94] Another danger with the adoption of a selective strategy focusing on those who bear the greatest responsibility is that it is discriminatory and by its very nature requires making value judgments that may be influenced by political or resource factors. Conducting impartial investigations does not mean prosecuting all groups in a given situation. Impartiality means applying the "same criteria for all, in order to determine whether the high thresholds of the Statute are met and our policy of focusing on the persons most responsible is satisfied."[95]

It was said to be an open secret that international prosecutors, in selecting a potential accused, may take into account criteria relating to belonging to or affiliation with a certain group in order to present more balanced cases involving all parties to the conflict.[96] It seems that the OTP was initially influenced by the experience of the ad hoc tribunals, the success of which depended on not exceeding the bounds of what is politically acceptable to the prevailing balance of power.[97] The adoption of a policy based on the maxim "let justice be done, though the heavens fall"[98] may not seem like a pragmatic recommendation in the "realpolitik world of international affairs," but it encapsulates a fundamental principle of international justice.[99] In this context, it would help if the OTP outlined a clear articulation

93 *Al-Werfalli Case*, INT'L CRIM. CT., https://www.icc-cpi.int/libya/al-werfalli (last visited July 17, 2023).

94 *Al Mahdi Case*, INT'L CRIM. CT., https://www.icc-cpi.int/mali/al-mahdi (last visited July 17, 2023).

95 Moreno-Ocampo, *supra* note 22, at 6.

96 *See* Luc Côté, *supra* note 21, at 175.

97 David P. Forsythe, 'Politics and the International Tribunal for the Former Yugoslavia', in Roger S. Clark and Madeleine Sann (eds.), *The Prosecution of International Crimes: A Critical Study of the International Tribunal for the Former Yugoslavia* (New Brunswick: Transaction Publishers, 1996), p. 186; *see also* Rod Rastan, 'Comment on Victor's Justice and the Viability of Ex Ante Standards' (2010) 43 *J. Marshall L Rev.* 569.

98 (The latin phrase *fiat justitia ruat coelum*, ascribed to Lucius Calpurnius Piso Caesoninus (d. 43 B.C.), translates to "Let justice be done, though heaven should fall.").

99 *Contra*, U.N. Secretary General, Report of the International Tribunal for the Prosecution of Persons Responsible for Serious Violations of International Humanitarian Law in the Territory of the Former Yugoslavia Since 1991, ¶ 18, UN Doc. A/49/342, S/1994/1007 (Aug. 29, 1994) ("In sum, it would be wrong to assume that the Tribunal is based on the old maxim fiat justitia et pereat mundus (let justice be done, even if the world were to perish). The Tribunal is, rather, based on the maxim propounded by Hegel in 1821: fiat justitia ne pereat mundus (let justice be done lest the world should perish). Indeed, the judicial process aims at averting the exacerbation and aggravation of conflict and tension, thereby contributing, albeit gradually, to a lasting peace.").

of policy and reflection of that policy in practice in a way that generates perceptions of legitimacy. When the OTP decides not to bring any cases on the basis of insufficient gravity within an overall "situation," it is important that it explain how this decision was arrived at. Failure to do so may alienate victims and undermine the legitimacy of the Court. Unfortunately, some degree of alienation is inevitable given the mismatch between resources/capacity and expectations, and the practical dilemma that any selection process creates. In this way, according to Rastan, the requirement for selection when prosecuting serious international crimes represents the most pressing and ethically challenging imperative in the task of applying the law to situations of large scale violence.[100] Selection choices must not result in arbitrariness or bias.

The OTP's strategy remains a work in progress. The importance of the general principles of independence, impartiality, and objectivity cannot be overstated.[101] There was an urgent need for the OTP to publish its criteria for initiating an investigation and prosecution in order to create as transparent a process as possible. This should also help clarify any uncertainty arising from the Appeals Chamber decision in relation to Lubanga and subsequent decisions.[102] The publication of the Policy brought enhanced transparency and accountability as the general policies relating to prosecutorial selection are known and can thus be subject to public scrutiny. There will always be some degree of controversy surrounding decisions by the OTP. The criterion for determining gravity was far from settled jurisprudence and required fine-tuning.[103] The OTP continues to retain significant latitude and discretion when it comes to case selection and prioritization, subject to limited judicial review.[104] The Policy will help ensure that the exercise of discretion is based on appropriate principles and criteria.[105]

100 Rastan, *supra* note 51, at 589–93.

101 Policy Paper on Case Selection and Prioritisation, *supra* note 1, ¶ 16.

102 Arrest Warrants Appeal, *supra* note 12; Kenya Investigation Authorization, *supra* note 50, at 188; Côte d'Ivoire Investigation Authorization, *supra* note 50, ¶ 203; Abu Garda, *supra* note 50, ¶ 31; Georgia Investigation Authorization, *supra* note 47, ¶ 51; Regulations of the Office of the Prosecutor, *supra* note 4, Article 29(2); Policy Preliminary Examinations, *supra* note 32, ¶¶ 9, 71.

103 *See* Ignaz Stegmiller, 'The Pre-Investigation Stage' in *The Pre-Investigation Stage of the ICC: Criteria for Situation Selection* (Berlin: Duncker Humblot GmbH, 2011), vol. 8, pp. 329–330.

104 Rome Statute, *supra* note 5, art. 53.

105 Policy Paper on Case Selection and Prioritisation, *supra* note 1, ¶ 5.

According to Human Rights Watch, the current Basic Size assumption regarding active cases per year is limited.[106] For this reason, the ICC's intervention in its situation countries in the past has likely been too limited to fully achieve the general principles and the specific legal and case selection criteria articulated in the Policy. These limits have intensified as the number of situations open before the Court has increased, without sufficient increases in funding to support its mandate.[107] The Court will continue to face challenging resource constraints given the high number of situations opened. This renders prioritization between cases a matter of necessity. For this reason, "available resources" was included in the Policy as a prioritization criteria governing the roll-out of selected cases. While the OTP should be cautious in any over-reliance on prioritization,[108] a recent independent expert review repeatedly heard concerns that the Court should raise the gravity threshold and focus on a narrower range of situations.[109] It acknowledged that this was a prospect that would be disappointing for many as it would further restrict the already limited jurisdiction of the Court, but that the current situation is unsustainable, having regard to the limited resources available. In response to the expert review, the OTP noted that the OTP cannot unilaterally do this as it would go against established jurisprudence of the Court and it would be subject to potential judicial review.[110] Moreover,

---

106 Basic Size, *supra* note 52.

107 *See* Policy Paper on Case Selection and Prioritisation, *supra* note 1.

108 Human Rights Watch, *supra* note 27.

109 Assembly of States Parties, International Criminal Court, Independent Expert Review of the International Criminal Court and the Rome Statute System Final Report, ¶ 646, R. 227 (Sep. 30, 2020), https://asp.icc-cpi.int/sites/asp/files/asp_docs/ASP19/IER-Final-Report-ENG.pdf (last visited July 10, 2023) ("In order to address the disparity between the OTP resources and the high number of PEs resulting in investigations, the Prosecutor should consider adopting a higher threshold for the gravity of the crimes alleged to have been perpetrated. Gravity should also be taken into account at Phase 1 of PEs.").

110 International Criminal Court, Overall Response of the International Criminal Court to the "Independent Expert Review of the International Criminal Court and the Rome Statute System – Final Report" Preliminary Analysis of the Recommendations and Information on Relevant Activities Undertaken by the Court, p. 94 (Apr. 14, 2021), https://asp.icc-cpi.int/sites/asp/files/asp_docs/ASP20/Overall%20Response%20of%20the%20ICC%20to%20the%20IER%20Final%20Report%20-%20ENG%20-%2014April21.pdf (last visited July 12, 2023)

([Regarding Recommendation 411:] "However, as the Experts themselves appear to recognise, there is a difference between gravity as a legal threshold respecting the opening of investigations, with the ICC's jurisprudence so far setting a relatively low gravity threshold, and gravity as a policy factor, where the OTP might raise the gravity threshold where it has broad discretion, such as in case selection or prioritisation

any raising of the gravity threshold at the start of investigations would result in raising of threshold also for individual cases, since both are applied on the basis of the same provision of the Rome Statute, Article 17(1)(d).

State parties are bound to co-operate with the OTP irrespective of any agreement or understanding reached in relation to a situation or investigation. While the OTP does need the co-operation of state parties in order to carry out investigations, this should be based on obligations flowing from ratification of the Rome Statute, not some understanding that certain perpetrators of atrocities will not be pursued. This is the real dilemma for the Prosecutor – how to work closely with the members of the international community and yet remain independent. The paradox is to be independent and interdependent at the same time. Ending impunity and deterring further serious crimes irrespective of who the alleged perpetrators are and where the crimes occurred must remain the overriding consideration.

---

decisions. It should be recognized that the OTP cannot unilaterally raise the legal threshold of gravity, although it can exercise its discretion in selecting which cases to investigate or prosecute.").

CHAPTER 23

Gravity of Crimes by Low-Ranking Perpetrators and Peacekeepers

Melanie O'Brien

1 Introduction

In decisions about cases, the ICC is restricted by resources, and thus will make decisions within the parameters of jurisdiction and admissibility in order to keep the number of situations and cases realistic within the Court's capacity. One of the ways the OTP limits situations and cases is by applying the required gravity threshold found in the Rome Statute, Articles 17(1)(d), 53.

The OTP has noted that, when assessing gravity, it will be guided by "quantitative and qualitative considerations, relating to the scale, nature, manner of commission and impact of the crimes," and does not want to set "an overly restrictive legal bar that would hamper the deterrent role of the Court." In its 2016 Policy Paper on Selection of Cases Selection and Prioritisation, the OTP expands on what is included in the factors relevant to "gravity": "the scale, nature, manner of commission and impact of the crimes," outlining suggested elements that would constitute each of these factors.[1] The elements provided do not represent an exhaustive list, leaving it open for the OTP to consider other elements that fall within these four broad factors.

This essay argues that two categories of overlooked perpetrators need to be considered for prosecution by the ICC, because they still fit the Rome Statute's gravity threshold: low-ranking perpetrators, and peacekeepers (regardless of rank).

1 Office of the Prosecutor, International Criminal Court, Policy Paper on Case Selection and Prioritisation (Sep. 15, 2016), https://www.icc-cpi.int/sites/default/files/itemsDocuments/20160915_OTP-Policy_Case-Selection_Eng.pdf (last visited July 12, 2023).

 | DOI:10.1163/9789004686755_029

2 Who Is "Most Responsible"?

There is a focus in international criminal courts and tribunals, including the ICC, on prosecuting "those most responsible" for international crimes, where "those most responsible" means high-ranking perpetrators, such as political leaders and military commanders.[2] However, it can be argued that crimes by lower ranking perpetrators, and by specific categories of perpetrators, would fall within the scope of gravity. Prosecuting low-ranking perpetrators would follow the ruling of the ICC Appeals Chamber, which strongly pointed out that "[f]rom the head of a state downwards every person is personally accountable for the commission of every crime categorized in the Statute" and that "[l]iability is not limited to any category of persons guilty of conduct that constitutes a crime under the Statute."[3] The Appeals Chamber pointed out that if "the jurisdiction of the Court was confined to crimes committed by the top leadership of the state or organization that plan them," this would render Article 33 of the Rome Statute (superior orders are no defense) superfluous and contradictory to the Statute.[4]

When thinking about the idea of "those most responsible," I keep returning to a quote from Catherine MacKinnon: "to every woman who is raped, the fish who did it is plenty big."[5] As an example, take the Ongwen case, in which victims provided testimony about their experiences of forced marriage.[6] These experiences included abduction, forced labor, beatings, and rape: years of brutal, repeated violence. The victims relayed consistent experiences, whether they were direct victims of Ongwen (taken to be his "wife") or indirect (taken as a "wife" of other, subordinate soldiers). While it is appropriate and justified that Ongwen is punished for the crimes he committed, why should his subordinates not be punished for their commission of the same forced marriage crimes? Myriad Lord's Resistance Army (LRA) soldiers took or were given girls and women as forced "bush wives," physically

2 Asymmetrical Haircuts, *Episode 41 – Fatou Bensouda Bows Out at the ICC*, JUSTICEINFO.NET (May 19, 2021), https://www.asymmetricalhaircuts.com/episodes/episode-41-fatou-bensouda-bows-out-at-the-icc/ (last visited July 17, 2023).

3 Situation in the Democratic Republic of Congo, Case No. ICC-01/04-169, Judgment on the Prosecutor's Appeal against the Decision of Pre-Trial Chamber I Entitled "Decision on the Prosecutor's Application for Warrants of Arrest, Article 58", ¶ 35 (AC, Jul. 13, 2006).

4 *Id.*

5 Catharine A. MacKinnon, 'The ICTR's Legacy on Sexual Violence' (2008) 14 *New Eng. J. Int'l & Compar. L.* 101, 106.

6 Prosecutor v. Dominic Ongwen, Case No. ICC-02/04-01/15, Trial Judgment, pp. 738–830 (TC IX, Feb. 4, 2021).

abusing and raping them. Why should the standard be set that only Ongwen is punished, but for all the other girls and women, their abuser faces no accountability simply because of their lower rank?

The crimes of forced marriage committed by the LRA satisfy numerous elements of the gravity factors as listed by the OTP:

- **Scale** includes "the number of direct and indirect victims, the extent of the damage caused," especially physical or psychological harm, and their geographical or temporal spread (in the case of the LRA the number of victims was extensive, with crimes committed over a lengthy period of time; the physical and psychological harm was extreme).
- **Nature** includes rapes and other sexual offences, and crimes committed against or affecting children (rapes were an integral part of the forced marriages; most "wives" were abducted as children).
- **Manner of Commission** includes systematic crimes, crimes resulting from a plan, the use of rape, cruelty, and vulnerability of victims (the Trial Chamber found a plan of forced marriages across the LRA; rape and cruelty were common in these "marriages" and victims were vulnerable due to youth and inability to escape).
- **Impact** includes increased vulnerability of victims (youth, repeated physical punishment, and rape).

There is need for empirical research amongst victims, to explore whether atrocity crime victims are happy to see only the main leaders prosecuted for atrocity crimes – or whether victims also need to see justice done for themselves, against those who carried out the atrocities on the ground. However, a study undertaken of the general United States population (i.e. average persons) by Stuart Ford shows that, for the average person, the number of victims and abuse of power or official capacity are seen as only moderate indicators of crime gravity, and that strong indicators are seen to be the physical harm suffered, the type of crime, and the particular cruelty of the crime.[7] This indicates that it is the crime and its impact that the average person finds grave, rather than number of victims or rank of perpetrator.

3 War Crimes by Peacekeepers: Grave Enough for ICC Jurisdiction

The "big fish," the one to catch and prosecute, is generally seen as being the political or military leader. However, who is a "big fish" should be a flexible

7 Stuart Ford, 'The Meaning of Gravity at the International Criminal Court: A Survey of Attitudes about the Seriousness of Mass Atrocities' (2018) 24 *U.C. Davis J. Int'l L. & Pol'y* 209.

concept, looking beyond leadership for other types of perpetrators that could be considered "big." An example of this kind of perpetrator that I have proposed in my research is peacekeepers. Peacekeepers do commit crimes that could amount to war crimes or crimes against humanity, depending on the circumstances (and for the purposes of this comment, we assume the relevant chapeau elements are met).[8] While much peacekeeper misconduct would not rise to the level of war crimes (e.g., false medical claims), crimes that would be considered war crimes include physical assault, torture, and sexual exploitation and abuse (SEA). SEA is by far the most common form of reported misconduct by peacekeepers, with an average of 69 allegations reported each year over the past decade. In 2019, there were 80 allegations; in 2020, 66 allegations. These are down from an all-time allegation high of 357 in 2005. The range of SEA offenses committed by peacekeepers includes sexual exploitation (demanding sexual favors in return for service or goods) and rape, including of children.[9] It is important to note, however, that the figures are only those cases that are reported to the United Nations. It is generally agreed by scholars in the field that the actual instances of SEA by peacekeepers are much higher.

The U.N. has been working hard, particularly under Secretary-General Antonio Guterres, to work with troop and police contributing countries (TCCs/PCCs) to ensure criminal accountability for the peacekeepers who commit such crimes. However, accountability remains elusive for many victims, with U.N. reports demonstrating that after the U.N. refers misconduct to TCCs/PCCs, it often does not receive any further communication. With regard to allegations received between July 1, 2007 and February 15, 2021, 219 have been referred to TCCs/PCCs with no information received, indicating that disciplinary action was unlikely to have been taken.[10] These allegations include serious assault and SEA. While there has been some response by some states in recent years, due to the pressure of the U.N., these figures demonstrate that other states still do not take peacekeeper crimes seriously, including sexual exploitation and abuse.[11] In addition, it is difficult to

---

8 Melanie O'Brien, 'Protectors on Trial? Prosecuting Peacekeepers for War Crimes and Crimes Against Humanity in the International Criminal Court' (2012) 40 *Int'l J.L., Crime & Just.* 223.

9 Melanie O'Brien, 'Sexual Exploitation and Beyond: Using the Rome Statute of the International Criminal Court to Prosecute UN Peacekeepers for Gender-based Crimes' (2011) 11 *Int'l Crim. L. Rev.* 803.

10 U.N. Secretary-General, *Criminal Accountability of United Nations Officials and Experts on Mission*, U.N. Doc A/75/217 (Jul. 23, 2020).

11 U.N. Secretary-General, *Special Measures for Protection from Sexual Exploitation and Abuse*, U.N. Doc A/75/754 (Feb. 15, 2021) (*See* the Annexes to this report, U.N.

ascertain whether appropriate accountability is taking place. Details of state action remain vague, noted as "TCC Dismissal" or "TCC Administrative," "PCC Demotion," with a rare "TCC Jail." The U.N. documentation demonstrates that jail is a rare outcome, even when the perpetrator has committed sexual abuse of a child.[12] Overall, it is clear that, despite the positive progress made over the past decade by the U.N. in preventing SEA, many states are still unwilling or unable to hold peacekeepers accountable for criminal misconduct, particularly SEA, and thus it still occurs.

How does this connect to the ICC's gravity threshold? I argue that a peacekeeper should be considered a "big fish," and therefore crimes by peacekeepers, even if they are not committed on a mass scale, should satisfy the ICC's gravity requirement.[13] The reason for this is that peacekeepers are specifically tasked with protecting the vulnerable civilian population in times of conflict and post-conflict. They are by default highly trusted by the local population (and the international community more broadly) and thus, by committing SEA, they are violating their very purpose and breaching the trust of the people they are supposed to protect. Therefore, their crimes should be considered grave enough to fall within ICC jurisdiction, if TCCs/PCCs are unwilling or unable to ensure accountability.

This should also fit with the OTP's move away from the "magic number" approach adopted under Moreno-Ocampo, and towards both "quantitative and qualitative considerations," where the decision is no longer just about the number of victims.[14] Likewise, such a decision would also fit with the OTP's focus on investigating and prosecuting crimes of sexual and gender-based violence.[15]

Secretary-General, Supplementary Information to the Report of the Secretary-General on Special Measures for Protection from Sexual Exploitation and Abuse (A/75/754), https://conduct.unmissions.org/sites/default/files/supplementary_information_to_the_secretary-general_report_a74754.pdf (last visited July 17, 2023)).

12 *Id.*

13 Melanie O'Brien, 'Prosecutorial Discretion as an Obstacle to Prosecution of United Nations Peacekeepers by the International Criminal Court: The Big Fish/Small Fish Debate and the Gravity Threshold' (2012) 10 *J. Int'l Crim. Just.* 525.

14 Prosecutor v. Bahar Idriss Abu Garda, Case No. ICC-02/05-02/09, Decision on the Confirmation of Charges, ¶ 31 (PTC I, Feb. 8, 2010) [hereinafter Prosecutor v. Abu Garda]; Situation on Registered Vessels of the Union of the Comoros, the Hellenic Republic and the Kingdom of Cambodia, Case No. ICC-01/13-34, Decision on the Request of the Union of the Comoros to Review the Prosecutor's Decision Not to Initiate an Investigation, ¶ 26 (PTC I, Jul. 16, 2015) [hereinafter Comoros PTC Rejection Decision].

15 Office of the Prosecutor, International Criminal Court, Policy Paper on Sexual and Gender-Based Crimes (Jun. 2014), https://www.icc-cpi.int/sites/default/files/iccdocs/

The commission of SEA by peacekeepers qualifies as an abuse of power or official capacity, an example of the gravity factor "manner of commission of the crimes" specifically identified by the OTP in its policy paper. In addition, this fits under several of the OTP's interpretations:

- **Manner** of Commission also includes the vulnerability of victims (protected civilians in conflict and post-conflict zones) and the use of rape and sexual violence;
- **Nature** includes specific reference to rapes and other sexual or gender-based crimes, and crimes committed against or affecting children (which fits peacekeeper SEA); and
- **Impact** includes the social and economic damage inflicted on communities (local and global communities lose trust in peacekeepers, thus damaging the ability of peace operations to function effectively; high levels of SEA can create conflict and post-conflict sex economies; in some communities, the ostracism of girls and women survivors).

Thus, multiple elements of the factors of gravity are fulfilled by the parameters of these SEA crimes when committed by peacekeepers. The crimes by peacekeepers should be considered to fulfill the gravity requirement, by virtue of the status of the perpetrators (as peacekeepers), regardless of the rank of the individual peacekeeper perpetrator. This status – a protector abusing their protectees – should be seen as what the Pre-Trial Chamber has referred to as an "aggravating factor" attached to the commission of the crimes, thereby satisfying the gravity requirement.[16] In addition, applying the Pre-Trial Chamber's finding that, when assessing gravity, the OTP "should have recognised the possibility that the events at issue had an impact going beyond the suffering of the direct and indirect victims," including "the international concern caused by the events at issue,"[17] peacekeeper SEA has significant impact beyond the direct victims. This impact, as noted, causes international concern: it damages the trust in and reputation of peace operations, thereby jeopardizing the ability of peace operations to function effectively, consequently endangering peace and security in the operation region. This may also equally imperil the ability of other peace operations to function effectively, as other communities lose trust in

otp/OTP-Policy-Paper-on-Sexual-and-Gender-Based-Crimes–June-2014.pdf (last visited July 17, 2023).

16 Situation in Republic of Kenya, Case No. ICC-01/09-19-Corr, Corrigendum of the Decision pursuant to Article 15 of the Rome Statute on the Authorization of an Investigation into the Situation in the Republic of Kenya, ¶ 62 (PTC II, Mar. 31, 2010).

17 Comoros PTC Rejection Decision, *supra* note 14, ¶ 48.

peacekeepers. In its (satisfied) assessment of gravity in the Abu Garda Confirmation of Charges, the Pre-Trial Chamber took into account the negative impact of the crimes on the functionality of peacekeeping and thus the protection of civilians in the region.[18] The same reasoning should be applied to peacekeeper SEA crimes.

I use the example of peacekeepers in the gravity discussion for three reasons. Firstly, to emphasize that crimes by peacekeepers, particularly SEA, are ongoing, serious, and lacking accountability, and thus remain a situation the ICC should consider. Secondly, to present a concept of gravity that on face value may seem "outside the box," because the perpetrators do not fit the usual perpetrator image and the (recorded) victim numbers are not high, but, upon analysis, wholeheartedly fit the gravity requirement, thus setting a precedent for "outside the box" application of the gravity threshold. Thinking "outside the box" would not be inconsistent with the OTP's track record, considering its creativity in sculpting jurisdiction over crimes against the Rohingya. Thirdly, peacekeepers are a category of perpetrator who reinforce the need to reconsider a focus on only high- or even medium-ranking perpetrators, demonstrating that crimes by a low-ranking perpetrator should be considered grave enough for ICC jurisdiction, through applying the broader factors of gravity.

Waschefort observes that we do not want to see those who fall "between the petty crimes of little people, and the evils of men of great power [...] remain beyond the reach of the law."[19] deGuzman argues that gravity should be framed in terms of the values and goal of international criminal law, seeking to protect human dignity.[20] Ensuring that individual perpetrators of atrocities – not just those who ordered them – and those who violated their role of protector, are held accountable would certainly fit within the values of international criminal law and ensure the reach of the law is far enough. After all, it certainly cannot be denied that these crimes shock the conscience of humanity.

---

18 Prosecutor v. Abu Garda, *supra* note 14, ¶ 33.

19 Gus Waschefort, 'Gravity as a Requirement in International Criminal Prosecutions: Implications for South African Courts' (2014) 47 *Compar. & Int'l L.J. S. Afr.* 38, 63.

20 Margaret M. deGuzman, *Shocking the Conscience of Humanity: Gravity and the Legitimacy of International Criminal Law* (Oxford: Oxford University Press, 2020).

CHAPTER 24

Higher Gravity Threshold? A Plea for Caution

Carsten Stahn

1 Introduction

After almost two decades of practice and a mixed record in investigations and prosecutions, the ICC needs to reconsider some of its investigative policies and strategies. This is no secret. The publicity and prospect of ICC engagement triggers a large amount of communications – more than the Court can handle. States have adopted self-referrals, collective referrals (Venezuela), or Art. 12(3) declarations, in order to enable the Court to intervene. NGOs are keen to involve the Court in any possible atrocity situation, even if the jurisdictional link of the Court is thin or remote.[1] The Office of the Prosecutor (OTP) has a large docket of preliminary examinations or situations under investigation.[2] Some of them have been pending for decades. Others have made only modest progress. This large pool of situations contrasts with the limited amount of cases that the Court can take on in each situation. This discrepancy requires the OTP to be careful in its situation and case selection. The OTP needs to bring thoroughly investigated cases, which have a sufficient success rate at trial, based on the evidentiary standards. At the same time, it must represent main patterns of crimes or criminality, or capture different layers of responsibility, in order to provide a meaningful justice response to complex conflicts.

The Independent Expert Review has viewed this dilemma. It has made a number of recommendations in order to enable the Court to navigate the tension between its broad mandate and its selectivity. One of the most controversial proposals is the idea to limit the number of situations through a higher gravity threshold. The experts argued that the OTP should "consider

1 Megan A. Fairlie, 'The Hidden Costs of Strategic Communications for the International Criminal Court' (2016) 51 *Tex. Int'l L.J.* 281.

2 Carsten Stahn, 'Damned If You Do, Damned If You Don't: Challenges and Critiques of Preliminary Examinations at the ICC' (2017) 15 *J. Int'l Crim. Just.* 413; Morton Bergsmso and Carsten Stahn (eds.), *Quality Control in Preliminary Examinations* (Brussels: Torkel Opsahl Academic ePublisher, 2018).

 | DOI:10.1163/9789004686755_030

the application of a higher gravity threshold in deciding whether to open or continue a PE" in order to allocate the Court's limited resource to situations "that are the most serious, and for those most responsible for the commission of the crimes."[3] This is clearly reflected in Recommendation 227, which states that "the Prosecutor should consider adopting a higher threshold for the gravity of the crimes alleged to have been perpetrated," in order to address "the disparity between the OTP resources and the high number of PEs resulting in investigations."[4] It justifies this higher gravity threshold by the alleged foundational purpose of the Court, namely its establishment "to investigate and prosecute the most serious crimes of concern to the international community as a whole" and to "focus on those most responsible for the commission of such crimes."[5] This is complemented by a proposal to reconsider case selection criteria, namely to establish "a hierarchy" of "criteria of highest importance," including: (i) "the gravity of the crimes," (ii) "the strength and diversity of the evidence" and (iii) "the degree of responsibility of potential suspects."[6]

The policy reasons for such a proposal are appealing. The accountability architecture is changing. With growing institutional and normative critiques of ICC justice, such as its physical or cultural remoteness from crimes, superficial engagement in atrocity contexts, ICC-centric readings of complementarity, fragility of cases or lack of meaningful completion strategy, and a turn to new investigative mechanisms, supporting the exercise of domestic jurisdiction, targeted hybrid or specialized courts or emerging regional mechanisms, it becomes central to re-think how the ICC can make the most meaningful impact with the limited means at its disposal. As a matter of policy, it is tempting to argue that "less is more," namely that the Court should engage in lesser situations, but do them well, rather than trying to fix all accountability problems that come its way, without leaving a lasting impact in the respective context. As the Independent Expert Review notes, some ICC engagements have had limited impact:

3 Assembly of States Parties, International Criminal Court, Independent Expert Review of the International Criminal Court and the Rome Statute System Final Report, ¶ 650 (Sep. 30, 2020), [hereinafter IER Report] https://asp.icc-cpi.int/sites/asp/files/asp_docs/ASP19/IER-Final-Report-ENG.pdf (last visited July 10, 2023).

4 *Id.* at R. 227.

5 *Id.* at ¶ 650.

6 *Id.* at R. 230.

> In several situations to date, only one case has been prosecuted and thereafter de facto closed. It is questionable whether a single prosecution is sufficient to address the justice needs of a whole situation.[7]

However, it is doubtful whether a higher gravity threshold for situations or selection of cases is the proper remedy to address the underlying problems. It might do more harm than good. It is preferable to search for alternative solutions, in order to address some of the valid concerns raised by the review process. Gravity should not be read as the overriding factor for the selection of situations, but rather as a minimum threshold, in order to keep sufficient flexibility and contextualize crimes. As Pre-Trial Chamber I noted in Comoros, the purpose is "not to oblige the Court to choose only the most serious cases, but merely to oblige it not to prosecute cases of marginal gravity."[8] According to the drafting history, gravity under Art. 17(1)(d) of the Rome Statute was deemed to protect the Court from "being overwhelmed with less serious cases," particularly with regard to the so-called treaty crimes, which have lesser inherent thresholds than core crimes.[9]

Neither states parties nor the Court have given any serious consideration to develop the deeper social or criminological meanings or gravity. As Stuart Ford has shown, there is very limited empirical research as to what renders a situation or crime grave across different audiences, i.e. those affected by crimes, directly or indirectly affected states, or civil society more broadly.[10] Margaret deGuzman has helpfully clarified that gravity cannot be considered in isolation of the goals of the Court.[11] The proposal puts the cart before the horse. Based on the existing lack of understanding, it is premature to raise the bar through a different interpretation of gravity. Instead of

7 *Id.* at ¶ 683.

8 Situation on the Registered Vessels of the Union of the Comoros, the Hellenic Republic and the Kingdom of Cambodia, Case No. ICC-01/13-111, Decision on the "Application for Judicial Review by the Government of the Comoros" (PTC I, Sep. 16, 2020) [hereinafter Comoros].

9 *See* Prosecutor v. Al Hassan Ag Abdoul Aziz Ag Mohamed Ag Mahmoud, Case No. ICC-01/12-01/18-601-Red, Judgment on the Appeal of Mr Al Hassan against the Decision of Pre-Trial Chamber I Entitled "Décision relative à l'exception d'irrecevabilité pour insuffisance degravité de l'affaire soulevée par la défense", ¶ 57, n. 103 (AC, Feb. 19, 2020) [hereinafter Al Hassan Appeal].

10 Stuart Ford, 'The Meaning of Gravity at the International Criminal Court: A Survey of Attitudes about the Seriousness of Mass Atrocities' (2018) 24 *U.C. Davis J. Int'l L. & Pol'y* 209.

11 Margaret M. deGuzman, *Shocking the Conscience of Humanity: Gravity and the Legitimacy of International Criminal Law* (Oxford: Oxford University Press, 2020).

trying to give new normative content to gravity, which may be impossible to achieve in light of the diversity of opinion, it may be more helpful to directly target the dilemmas that the expert review has identified. The policy to focus on the "most responsible," which has been advocated in early prosecutorial strategy, turned out to be a Trojan horse. Experiences with cases, such as Bemba, Gbagbo, or Al-Bashir, suggest that it may be overly ambitious to target the highest political or military leaders, without a line of cases establishing command structures, hierarchies, or specific fact patterns, particularly in circumstances in which there has been no political transition and ICC cases are directed against state officials who remain in power. The rhetoric on targeting leadership crime only creates unhelpful expectations and needs to be differentiated. As more recent strategies indicate, it may be necessary to be more modest, pragmatic, and realistic.

2 Gravity in Context: A Plea for Caution

International law has an uneasy relationship to gravity. The notion plays a role across different areas. Systemically, gravity is not only a technical notion, which determines the applicability of norms or jurisdictional or admissibility thresholds, but a relational concept, which provides legitimacy to institutions.[12] The discursive association with grave situations, grave crimes or violations, or the "most responsible persons" provides moral authority or symbolic importance to institutions. Gravity is like a magic spell. The cause pursued by institutions is deemed to create solidarity and compassion. Gravity is a means to increase the expressive potential of international courts and tribunals. It creates an aura that provides weight to their decisions. The institutions become too important to fail from a moral point of view.

Gravity serves at the same time to draw boundaries and distinctions. It organizes processes of inclusion and exclusion. For instance, it determines which issues deserve global attention, what constitutes an international or a domestic crime, or what scenarios come within the ambit of specific areas of law (e.g., use of force). Rachel López has provided an excellent

12 Gus Waschefort, 'Gravity as a Requirement in International Criminal Prosecutions: Implications for South African Courts' (2014) 47 *Compar. & Int'l L.J. S. Afr.* 38, 43 ("Gravity, as a foundational philosophy for the actual establishment of the ICC, as opposed to gravity in relation to the other listed spheres, exists to give legitimacy to the existence of the Court.").

comparative survey, showing how the concept of gravity is used to determine relations of affect and possible reactions to breaches of law. She has argued that the "gravity of a violation" may not only provide a cause for common concern, but trigger "obligations erga omnes," or determine "the severity of coercive measures that are permitted to enforce international law."[13] Gravity thus organizes legal gray zones and seeks to order or clarify permissible response schemes to violations.

The basic dilemma of gravity is its attempt to square the circle. The concept introduces dividing lines, labels, categorizations, or responses to diffuse social phenomena. It may create false binaries or hierarchies which contrast with normative complexity. For instance, the connection between international and domestic crimes is fluid. It is over-simplistic to assume that international crimes necessarily carry a greater degree of gravity than domestic crimes. Many crimes against humanity have a double face: they are both international and domestic crimes. The indeterminacy of the notion of "other inhumane acts" reflects this fluidity. Formally, the notion of gravity may not even be needed to distinguish international and domestic crime. One may simply say that a crime becomes international when it is defined in international legal instruments or triggers rights and obligations under international law.[14]

Gravity is a social construct. Its construction depends on cultural contexts and normative evaluation. The ICC Pre-Trial Chamber recognized this quite early in the Court's jurisprudence when, in order to determine gravity, it relied on the social alarm test in the arrest warrant against Ntaganda.[15] However, it drew the wrong conclusions from this point of departure. Gravity relies heavily on social awareness, consciousness, and perception.[16] The Chamber did not try to determine the constituents of social alarm, but simply put forward a number of legal criteria, drawn from parallels of ad hoc

13 Rachel López, 'The Law of Gravity' (2020) 58 *Colum. J. Transnat'l L.* 565.

14 *See* Carsten Stahn, *A Critical Introduction to International Criminal Law* (Cambridge, Cambridge University Press, 2018), pp. 20–21.

15 Prosecutor v. Thomas Lubanga Dyilo, Case No. ICC-01/04-01/06-2, Decision on the Prosecutor's Application for Warrants of Arrest, art. 58, ¶¶ 42–60, 63 (PTC I, Feb. 10, 2006).

16 *See generally* Émile Durkheim, *The Division of Labour in Society*, George Simpson (trans.), (London: Collier Macmillan Publisher, 1964) (Sociologist Émile Durkheim has referred to the collective conscience in its justification of punishment. Durkheim argued that the evil nature of criminality lies not so much in the crime itself, but rather in its destructive effect on common beliefs. He claimed that judicial institutions are guardians of public conscience which are entitled to express social condemnation of crimes through punishment).

tribunal jurisprudence under Rule 11 *bis*, without developing a methodology to take into account the social dimensions or the perception of gravity by those affected. Gravity was solely determined by the voice of the interpreter, i.e. the Chamber.

In the aftermath of the Lubanga decision, gravity was construed in a more flexible way.[17] It has become a truism in decisions to argue that gravity involves both quantitative and qualitative elements. Gravity became everything and nothing at the same time. This approach created a circular logic. The Court did not determine gravity, but rather created it. In essence, a Court finding that something merits investigation and prosecution rendered it grave, rather than the other way around. Subsequent decisions, such as Al Mahdi or Comoros have relied on the international impact of crimes to highlight gravity. However, this is a very internationalist reading of social alarm, which reduces perspectives and marginalizes less internationally visible voices. It makes the ICC vulnerable to socio-legal or imperial critiques which postulate that international criminal justice entrenches existing inequalities and focuses predominantly on spectacular violence.[18]

Overloading the very concept of gravity with legal meaning may have counterproductive effects. It may feed into critiques of legalism, overstretch the limits of law,[19] or reduce social complexity in artificial ways. There is thus some merit in the minimalist reading of the ICC which held that gravity should only:

> [E]xclude from the purview of the Court those rather unusual cases when conduct that technically fulfills all the elements of a crime under the Court's jurisdiction is nevertheless of marginal gravity only.[20]

---

17 For a survey, *see* Marco Longobardo, 'Everything is Relative, Even Gravity' (2016), 14 *J. Int'l Crim. Just.* 1011; Kevin Jon Heller, 'Situational Gravity under the Rome Statute', in Carsten Stahn and Larissa van den Herik (eds.), *Future Directions in International Criminal Justice* (The Hague: T.M.C. Asser Press, 2010), p. 227.

18 John Reynolds and Sujith Xavier, '"The Dark Corners of the World": TWAIL and International Criminal Justice' (2016) 14 *J. Int'l Crim. Just.* 959; Frederick Cowell, 'Inherent Imperialism: Understanding the Legal Roots of Anti-imperialist Criticism of the International Criminal Court' (2017) 15 *J. Int'l Crim. Just.* 667; Christine Schwöbel-Patel, *Marketing Global Justice: The Political Economy of International Criminal Law* (Cambridge: Cambridge University Press, 2021).

19 Mark J. Osiel, 'When Law "Expresses" More Than It Cares to Admit: Comments on Heller', in Carsten Stahn and Larissa van den Herik (eds.), *Future Directions in International Criminal Justice* (The Hague: T.M.C. Asser Press, 2010).

20 Comoros, *supra* note 8, ¶ 22; *see also* Al Hassan Appeal, *supra* note 9, ¶ 59.

3 Risks and Dilemmas of a Higher Gravity Threshold in the Selection of Situations

The proposal to apply a higher gravity threshold to the selection of situations creates a number of problems and potential unintended consequences which deserve critical review.

3.1 *Dynamic Nature of Situations*

A first problem of a higher gravity threshold is the unpredictability of gravity at the situation stage. Gravity is not an absolute, but a relative concept. In physics, it is a force that ties things together. In law, it builds on interconnectedness. It is challenging to determine a firm gravity benchmark, since it is dependent on purposes and variables, such as scale, nature, impact, or manner of commission, which need to be balanced against each other. Many of these factors only become apparent through examination or investigation. The Rome Statute lacks guidance as to what would render a situation sufficiently grave. As ICC jurisprudence has clarified, at the situation stage, gravity is assessed against the "potential cases" arising from the situation.[21] Gravity involves thus hypothetical assessment.

Many conflicts are dynamic. A fundamental difference of the ICC to the ad hoc tribunals for the former Yugoslavia or Rwanda is that the ICC intervenes in contexts of ongoing conflict rather than after the fact. Situations such as Libya or Afghanistan show that the level of violence or the nature of the conflict may change over time. International armed conflicts are often followed by internal turmoil or violence. Low intensity conflicts or civil wars can easily take on international or transnational features, based on the involvement of third parties. Applying a burdensome gravity threshold at the start may compromise the ability of the ICC to act early on, namely when atrocities unfold. Both prevention, and investigation and adjudication, rely on instant response, i.e. the possibility of quick reaction in situations of urgency. The proposal may compromise this ability, since it would require the ICC to stay inactive in dynamic conflict situations. This may affect the ability to gather material and evidence immediately after atrocity, and ultimately hamper the prospects of potential cases.

3.2 *Legal Black Holes and Blind Spots*

A higher gravity threshold may also reinforce selectivity and compromise the perception of independence and impartiality. Modelling gravity at the

21 Comoros, *supra* note 8, ¶ 18.

ICC after the example of the ad hoc tribunals may render the ICC even more suspect in the eyes of those who view it as a tool of Western nations or the powerful. It would make it more difficult to deflect critiques that the ICC focuses predominantly on accountability dilemmas in states that suffer from governance flaws or political crises, while turning a blind eye on accountability deficits in stable democracies or their broader contributions to such conditions.[22] This may reinforce geopolitical critiques, such the ICC's focus on certain parts of the world, or even prompt further pushback or backlash from those who are at the receiving end of ICC investigations or prosecutions.

A stricter gravity test might exclude situations with a narrower focus, such as the U.K. crimes in Iraq or the Comoros situation, which encompassed only a limited number of incidents. This may ultimately create greater legal black holes and perpetuate the impression that the Court goes after easy targets or "the weak," or leaves the more complex or subtle contributions to conflict aside. If the argument of complementarity is taken seriously, the Court may need to take up such situations in the absence of domestic investigations or prosecutions, precisely because other states will be reluctant to pursue them. Rightly understood, gravity derives not only from the number of incidents, crimes, or victims, but also from a culture of failing to prevent abuse, deception by institutions, or factors related to the authors of violations.

Another critical side effect of the adoption of a higher gravity threshold is the impact on prevention and cooperation, namely its potential to limit the capacity of the Court to contribute to prevention of crimes or support local investigations or prosecutions. The effect would reach far beyond the Rome Statute. For instance, U.N. fact-finding or investigative mechanisms would lose part of their leverage, since the prospects of ICC engagement would become more remote. This will ultimately reduce pressure on domestic jurisdictions to act and make international justice even more dependent on the U.N. Security Council, or hybrid tribunals, or "private" investigations, which are often highly donor-driven.

3.3 *Problems of Judicial Assessment*

A third problem is judicial assessment.[23] Gravity under Art. 17(1)(d) is an admissibility requirement that needs to be examined ex officio from the early

22 *See* William A, Schabas, 'The Banality of International Justice' (2013), 11 *J. Int'l Crim. Just.* 545.

23 *See generally* Priya Urs, 'Judicial Review of Prosecutorial Discretion in the Initiation of Investigations into Situations of "Sufficient Gravity"' (2020) 18 *J. Int'l Crim. Just.* 851.

stages of proceedings by the prosecution and judges. Gravity decisions do not involve only legal, but also contextual and political assessment. Introducing a higher threshold would introduce a high degree of uncertainty. As the situations in relation to Bangladesh/Myanmar or Palestine indicate, the OTP is unlikely to proceed with extended preliminary examinations or investigations in cases where fundamental issues of jurisdiction or admissibility are unsettled. Starting proceedings on an uncertain basis involves risks. The OTP would likely seek early clarification from the Pre-Trial Chamber in order to avoid a waste of resources. The Rome Statute lacks clear procedures authorizing the OTP to seek guidance on admissibility, including the determination of the gravity threshold, at the situational stage.[24] Even if such an option was provided or accepted as part of the inherent jurisdiction of Chambers, the following adjudication may not only delay justice intervention, but confront the judges with difficult predictions and contextual assessments that do not easily lend themselves to judicial review.

In existing practice, judges have largely shied away from detailed gravity assessments. The fluidity of gravity criteria has allowed judges to refrain from such determinations. The OTP as quasi-judicial body, with political expertise and a closer nexus to facts and circumstances, is better equipped to make delicate gravity assessments. Awarding greater power to judges to determine the appropriate threshold may not only create complex and lengthy litigation, but involve the Pre-Trial Chamber, and potentially the Appeals Chamber, in issues of social relevance or political impact which go to limits of the judicial mandate.

3.4 *Exclusionary Effects*

Most importantly, a higher gravity threshold may deprive the ICC of the flexibility to take on some of the most pressing cases of our time. Situation selection is the symbolic capital of the Court. Many atrocity crimes contain speech acts which violate norms and require denunciation to demonstrate the equality of perpetrators before the law or to affirm the violation of rights of victims and survivors.[25] The success of the mandate of the ICC depends

24 International Criminal Court, Rome Statute of the International Criminal Court, art. 19, U.N. Doc. A/CONF.183/9 (July 17, 1998) [hereinafter Rome Statute].

25 *See* Carsten Stahn, *Justice as Message: Expressivist Foundations of International Criminal Justice* (Oxford: Oxford University Press, 2020); Carsten Stahn, *Justice as Message Symposium: Message from the Author*, OPINIO JURIS (Dec. 14, 2020), http://opiniojuris.org/2020/12/14/justice-as-message-symposium-message-from-the-author/ (last visited July 17, 2023).

not only on the record of its own investigations and prosecutions, but also on its expressive effects,[26] namely its ability to communicate and signal what types of crimes deserve prosecution or punishment. International criminal justice is far more than a means to provide retribution, inflict suffering, or protect society from the offender. Its strength lies partly in its ability to publicly denounce wrongdoing, affirm the legal order, send messages to future offenders, or communicate wrongdoing to the convicted person. The selection of situations should thus not only be driven by gravity factors, but also by the expressive potential of the Court, i.e., its ability to shape accountability practices in areas which are neglected and in need of greater attention. For instance, a Prosecutor may have valid reasons to engage with criminal behavior that is not currently perceived to be as grave as existing atrocity crimes, but which is in need of further attention or public action.[27]

The current framework of atrocity crime has striking gaps in relation to cyber-crime, environmental crime, historical injustices such as colonial crimes, the intersection between economic and atrocity crime, or corporate criminal responsibility. Prompting accountability in contexts where states do not currently act is precisely one of the added advantages of the ICC as global institution. A technical gravity threshold, modeled after classical atrocity crimes, may prevent the ICC from engaging with such phenomena.

For example, Rachel López has tried to map determinants of gravity, based on a comparative study of institutions. She has found that gravity is associated with violations that are:

> [U]niversally condemned as grave, done deliberately, and either acutely harm a limited number of individuals or are so widespread and systematic that the cumulative harm is severe.[28]

If such "laws of gravity" were applied to selection of ICC situations, they might exclude a broad range of contexts, such as slow forms of violence,

26 On international criminal justice, *see* Barrie Sander, 'The Expressive Turn of International Criminal Justice: A Field in Search of Meaning' (2019) 32 *Leiden J. Int'l L.* 851 (Since the 1960s, expressive theories have been invoked in general theories of law to explain public regulation and domestic justifications of punishment. Expressive theories suggest that law has value because of its ability to convey social meaning, in addition to its ability to control behavior).

27 Nirej Sekhon, 'The Pedagogical Prosecutor' (2014) 44 *Seton Hall L. Rev.* 1.

28 Rachel López, *The Law of Gravity: A Newtonian Proposal for Public International Law*, OPINIO JURIS (Jul. 24, 2020), http://opiniojuris.org/2020/07/24/the-law-of-gravity-a-newtonian-proposal-for-public-international-law/ (last visited July 17, 2023).

including environmental or socio-economic harms; non-intentional forms of wrongdoing, such as reckless, negligent, careless, or even thoughtless behavior; or non-anthropocentric forms of harm. Preserving the ability of the Court to select situations not merely based on existing gravity perceptions, but also by reference to expressive rationales, is key to its relevance, its capacity to react to changing patterns and perceptions of criminality, and its need to respond to structural critiques of international criminal justice.

4 Risks and Dilemmas of a Higher Gravity Threshold in the Selection of Cases

The proposal to apply a higher gravity threshold to case selection faces similar critiques. The idea to "focus on those most responsible for the commission of such crimes" has proved to be unrealistic in practice and faces certain policy objections. Some flexibility is necessary, in order to allow the ICC to include certain expressive rationales in case selection. A hierarchization of criteria, based on factors such as "the gravity of the crimes" or the "degree of responsibility of potential suspects,"[29] may unduly constrain the reach of the ICC and limit its ability to pursue more remote causes of criminality.

While it is feasible to broaden the number of cases per situation and develop strategic planning, "especially if mid-level perpetrators are to be prosecuted,"[30] it may be counterproductive to theorize case selection predominantly based on evidence relating to political or military elites. The social roles and contributions enabling crime are more diffuse.

Given the existing experiences, the ICC will likely continue to struggle to bring cases against leaders who remain in power. However, the Court is well equipped to trace the global interconnections of crimes. A compelling example is corporate involvement in crime. The absence of corporate criminal responsibility is one of the structural deficits of the ICC regime.[31] Tribunals, like the Special Tribunal for Lebanon, have made a start by holding companies accountable for contempt of court. In resource-driven conflicts or corruption-fueled violence, the ICC may benefit from bringing complicity cases against corporate representatives, even though they may not belong to

29 IER Report, *supra* note 3, R. 230.

30 *Id.* ¶ 683.

31 *See* Carsten Stahn, 'Liberals vs Romantics: Challenges of an Emerging Corporate International Criminal Law' (2018) 50 *Case W. Rsrv. J. Int'l L.* 91.

social elites or be the immediate perpetrators of atrocity crimes. Such cases may have a more limited nexus to the crimes, but carry great benefit in terms of social alarm, prevention, or revealing the structural causes of violations. In specific circumstances (e.g. historical violations), there may also be merit in targeting bystanders, who become complicit in the enduring consequences of crimes.

The drafters of the Rome Statute foresaw this flexibility in the conception of modes of liability. They are adverse to a strict hierarchy, based on "degree of responsibility of potential suspects." Depending on the circumstances, both commission and participation may potentially entail similar sentencing. This flexibility should not be artificially curtailed through the backdoor of hierarchized gravity criteria.

5 Some Alternative Paths

The notion of gravity has become one of the cornerstones of controversy over the policies and orientations of the ICC. In practice, the imprecise contours of the legal notion have been used as strategic argument by different actors in order to advance their interests. Judges have tried to give new normative content to gravity in order to enhance their control over investigative or prosecutorial choices. The OTP relied on the contested methodology of comparing situations in order to justify its initial decision not to proceed with a request for an authorization of an investigation relating to Iraq.[32] Powerful states or non-states parties push for stricter gravity requirements in order to avoid interference by the OTP. The Independent Expert Review has proposed a modified gravity threshold to transform the selection policy and record of the Court, including the prospect of success of cases. Others advocate for higher gravity in order to maintain budgetary control over the activities of the OTP.

A common trend is the use of gravity as an argumentative tool to solve specific normative conflicts, without full consideration to the implications that such choices have across situations or on the long term. Gravity has turned partly into a normative site or surrogate for underlying battles, which are far less clearly articulated.

---

32 Letter from Luis Moreno-Ocampo, Chief Prosecutor, Int'l Crim. Ct., Regarding Situation in Iraq (Feb. 9, 2006), https://www.icc-cpi.int/sites/default/files/NR/rdonlyres/04D143C8-19FB-466C-AB77-4CDB2FDEBEF7/143682/OTP_letter_to_senders_re_Iraq_9_February_2006.pdf (last visited July 17, 2023).

5.1 *Articulating Dilemmas: Less Rather than More Gravity*

The methodology needs to be reversed. In order to address existing problems, it may be helpful to rely less, rather than more, on gravity. A better way to reform Court practices may be to make dilemmas more apparent and explain choices and constraints more thoroughly and openly, rather than trying to fill the notion of gravity with further substantive criteria. Changes in practice depend on organizational factors, including changes in organizational culture.[33] For instance, decisions by the OTP require greater transparency and motivation in order to understand selectivity dilemmas. The OTP needs to better articulate specific goals and priorities for each situation in order to justify its choices towards states, victims, and affected communities. Gravity may be a part of this, but its meaning should not be overstretched. Otherwise, the Court will easily apply inconsistent or incoherent approaches. In particular, decisions not to proceed under Art. 15 of the Rome Statute, decisions not to start investigations, or decisions to close situations require better motivation. Many of these dilemmas are silenced by mere recourse to gravity language.

5.2 *Better Discursive Structures*

The structures, which permit dialogue over situation or case selection, should be revisited. Gravity is often a means to end debate rather than to open dialogue. Stakeholders of the Court are confronted with outcomes rather than implicated in decision-making processes. Communication is one-sided rather than dialogical. In particular, affected communities are often left aside, since their interests are mediated through the prosecution, the state, or victim representatives. Court policies claims that "people most affected by the crimes should have the right to understand, to participate in, but also to have a sense of ownership of the justice process."[34] However, this is still partly lip-service. Engagement with these communities remains highly selective and is often one-dimensional, i.e. framed as outreach rather than open consultation. As Margaret deGuzman has argued, gravity requires more "dialogical approaches" and openness towards alternate views of Court audiences in the decision-making process.[35] The Court needs to

---

33 Birju Kotecha, 'The International Criminal Court's Selectivity and Procedural Justice' (2020) 18 *J. Int'l Crim. Just.* 107, 123.

34 *See Interacting with Communities Affected by Crimes*, INT'L CRIM. CT., https://www.icc-cpi.int/about/interacting-with-communities (last visited July 17, 2023).

35 deGuzman, *supra* note 11, 196–197.

develop its capacity to actively listen to others, including ideas that it might find difficult to engage with (radical listening).

5.3 *Political Structures*

Most importantly, many disputes over gravity are political in nature. They cannot be solved through abstract legal criteria, but require concrete and targeted political strategies and structures. It is important to respect prosecutorial discretion and expertise, while creating political channels to solve impasses. This requires investment in the governance structures of the Assembly of States Parties and the ability of states to mediate conflicts over the exercise of the Court's mandate. For instance, I have elsewhere argued for a targeted forum inside the Assembly of States Parties to promote dialogue with non-states parties and strengthen complementarity on a political level, including in completion strategies for situations.

> [It] could serve as a collective platform to create leverage for effective investigations or prosecutions, channel knowledge and expertise to facilitate domestic justice efforts, engage with states that face impediments or serve as a broader sounding board for concerns.[36]

Voices of the Global South need to be listened to more carefully. Such initiatives may be a better way forward than a restriction of the Court's reach, based on shaky and malleable gravity considerations.

---

36 Carsten Stahn, *Revitalizing Complementarity a Decade After the Stocktaking Exercise* 1, 4 (Brussels: Torkel Opsahl Academic EPublisher, Pol'y Brief Series No. 115, 2020), https://www.toaep.org/pbs-pdf/115-stahn/ (last visited July 17, 2023).

CHAPTER 25

Assessing Gravity: Should the ICC Consider the Impact of Crimes on the International Community?

Maartje Weerdesteijn and Lachezar Yanev

1 Introduction

The concept of "gravity" plays a central role in the procedural framework of the International Criminal Court (ICC). It is contained in Articles 17(1)(d) and 53(1)(c) of the ICC's Rome Statute and, as Pre-Trial Chamber III noted, is "an additional safeguard, which prevents the Court from investigating, prosecuting and trying peripheral cases."[1] The Office of the Prosecutor (OTP) is, thus, required to select for investigation and prosecution only those situations (and cases) which are sufficiently grave. In this sense, the core function of this concept is to limit the case load of the ICC and help determine where its resources should be directed.[2]

Filtering "peripheral" situations or cases from those that are grave enough to warrant an ICC investigation has proven to be an exceptionally challenging and controversial task. In part, the difficulty lies with the nebulous meaning of gravity, seeing as neither the Rome Statute nor its travaux préparatoires establish a clear definition of this notion, or state which factors should be taken into account when determining the gravity of a situation or case.[3] In the early years of the Court's functioning, therefore, there was little

1 Situation in the Republic of Kenya, Case No. ICC-01/09-19-Corr, Corrigendum of the Decision pursuant to Article 15 of the Rome Statute on the Authorization of an Investigation into the Situation in the Republic of Kenya, ¶ 56 (PTC II, Mar. 31, 2010) [hereinafter Kenya Investigation Authorization]; Situation in the Republic of Côte d'Ivoire, ICC-02/11-14-Corr, Corrigendum to "Decision pursuant to Article 15 of the Rome Statute on the Authorisation of an Investigation into the Situation in the Republic of Côte d'Ivoire", ¶ 201 (PTC III, Nov. 15, 2011) [hereinafter Côte d'Ivoire Investigation Authorization].

2 Margaret M. deGuzman, 'Gravity and the Legitimacy of the International Criminal Court' (2008) 32 *Fordham Int'l L.J.* 1400, 1403. Ghazia Popalzai and Hiba Thobani, 'The Complexities of the Gravity Threshold in the International Criminal Court: A Practical Necessity or an Insidious Pitfall?' (2017) 20 *Max Planck Y.B. U.N. L. Online* 150, 151–53.

3 Popalzai and Thobani, *supra* note 2, at 153.

 | DOI:10.1163/9789004686755_031

to guide the OTP's gravity analyses, which tended to focus on quantitative factors, as evidenced in, e.g., the OTP's decision in 2006 not to investigate the situation in Iraq.[4] This changed when, in 2009, the Regulations of the Office of the Prosecutor entered into force, specifying that the "scale, nature, manner of commission and impact" of the crimes are factors that should be taken into account when evaluating gravity.[5] Further explanation of these factors was subsequently provided in the OTP's Draft Policy Paper on Preliminary Examinations from 2010,[6] which was finalized in 2013.[7] One notable difference between these two versions of the Policy Paper is the importance that the OTP seemed to attach to the impact that the crimes had on the international community when evaluating their gravity. In particular, this impact was originally included as a relevant consideration in the 2010 Draft, only to be removed from the final version of the Policy Paper.

This essay examines the extent to which the ICC accepts the impact of crimes on the international community as a relevant factor for assessing the gravity of the situation where they are committed and then further discusses the merits of this factor through the prism of the ongoing preliminary examination into the situation in Venezuela.[8] The Venezuelan situation is the first time a group of states referred a situation to the ICC, thus expressing their concern over the crimes that seem to have been perpetrated by the Venezuelan government. The situation had already been under

4 Letter from Luis Moreno-Ocampo, Chief Prosecutor, Int'l Crim. Ct., Regarding Situation in Iraq, pp. 8–9 (Feb. 9, 2006), https://www.icc-cpi.int/sites/default/files/NR/rdonlyres/04D143C8-19FB-466C-AB77-4CDB2FDEBEF7/143682/OTP_letter_to_senders_re_Iraq_9_February_2006.pdf (last visited July 17, 2023).

5 International Criminal Court, *Regulations of the Office of the Prosecutor*, Doc. No. ICC-BD/05-01-09, R. 54 (Apr. 23, 2009), [hereinafter OTP Regulations] https://www.icc-cpi.int/sites/default/files/NR/rdonlyres/FFF97111-ECD6-40B5-9CDA-792BCBE1E695/280253/ICCBD050109ENG.pdf (last visited July 12, 2023).

6 Office of the Prosecutor, International Criminal Court, Draft Policy Paper on Preliminary Examinations (Oct. 4, 2010) [hereinafter OTP Draft Policy Paper], https://www.icc-cpi.int/sites/default/files/NR/rdonlyres/E278F5A2-A4F9-43D7-83D2-6A2C9CF5D7D7/282515/OTP_Draftpolicypaperonpreliminaryexaminations04101.pdf (last visited July 18, 2023).

7 Office of the Prosecutor, International Criminal Court, Policy Paper on Preliminary Examinations (Nov. 2013) [hereinafter OTP Policy Paper], https://www.icc-cpi.int/sites/default/files/iccdocs/otp/OTP-Policy_Paper_Preliminary_Examinations_2013-ENG.pdf (last visited July 18, 2023).

8 Dapo Akande, Payam Akhavan and Eirik Bjorge, 'Economic Sanctions, International Law, and Crimes Against Humanity: Venezuela's Referral to the International Criminal Court' (2021) 115 *Am. J. Int'l L.* 493 (We will focus only on the situation in Venezuela I in this essay since it currently does not seem likely Venezuela II will lead to an investigation).

preliminary examination and, although the referral would mean the Prosecutor does not need to seek judicial authorization from the Pre-Trial Chamber, the significance of the referral is more symbolic and political than legal.[9] The OTP decided in 2020 that there is a reasonable basis to believe that "crimes within the jurisdiction of the Court have been committed in Venezuela since at least April 2017" and the admissibility requirements, including gravity, are now being assessed.[10]

Given the current focus in the OTP's Policy Paper on the crimes' impact on victims and their immediate communities, it seems unlikely that the OTP would also take into account the concerns of the referring states, or the impact that the crimes had on these and other states, in analyzing the gravity of the situation. This is particularly troubling because the deep crisis in which the country has found itself has caused millions of people to flee to neighboring states that struggle to accommodate them.[11] In those circumstances, where the consequences of the crimes spill across borders, the OTP may no longer be able to do justice to the full scope of harm that is caused by the crimes when evaluating the gravity of the situation only by reference to the victims and their community.

2 The Collapse of Venezuela

Venezuela has descended into authoritarianism since Hugo Chavez took power in 1999. After Nicolas Maduro succeeded him, repression became more pervasive as the government clung to power.[12] After the Venezuelan

9 Nicholas E. Ortiz, *Understanding the State Party Referral of the Situation in Venezuela*, EJIL TALK (Nov. 1, 2018), https://www.ejiltalk.org/understanding-the-state-party-referral-of-the-situation-in-venezuela/ (last visited July 18, 2023).

10 Office of the Prosecutor, International Criminal Court, Report on Preliminary Examination Activities 2020, ¶ 202 (Dec. 14, 2020), https://www.icc-cpi.int/sites/default/files/itemsDocuments/2020-PE/2020-pe-report-eng.pdf (last visited July 18, 2023).

11 Mauricia John, 'Venezuelan Economic Crisis: Crossing Latin American and Caribbean Borders' (2019) 8 *Migration & Dev.* 437; Alec Waid, 'Nicolás Maduro's Impunity is a Foregone Conclusion: A Case Replacing the Treaty-Based Rule of Law Model with Universal Jurisdiction' (2020) 51 *U. Mia. Inter-Am. L. Rev.* 107, 109.

12 Javier Corrales, 'Autocratic Legalism in Venezuela' (2015) 26 *J. Democracy* 37, 37, 44; Luisa Feline Freier and Nicholas Parent, 'The Regional Response to the Venezuelan Exodus' (2019) 118 *Current Hist.* 56, 57; *See also* Letter from Luis Moreno-Ocampo, Chief Prosecutor, Int'l Crim. Ct., Regarding Situation in Venezuela, pp. 4–5 (Feb. 9, 2006), https://www.icc-cpi.int/sites/default/files/NR/rdonlyres/4E2BC725-6A63-40B8-8CDC-ADBA7BCAA91F/143684/OTP_letter_to_senders_re_Venezuela_9_February_2006.pdf

Supreme Justice Tribunal decided to dissolve the opposition-dominated National Assembly on March 29, 2017, protests broke out.[13] Months of unrest followed in which the protestors clashed with the Venezuelan armed forces. The political unrest came on top of an economic crisis, during which food shortages had increased rapidly and health care deteriorated as inflation skyrocketed and the country was quickly running out of cash.[14]

In November of that year, former Venezuelan prosecutor Luisa Ortega petitioned the ICC to start investigating the Venezuelan situation claiming that more than 8000 people were killed between 2015–2017 and arguing that thousands more had been subjected to torture and arbitrary arrests.[15] Subsequently, on February 8, 2018, Prosecutor Bensouda announced that her Office was opening a preliminary examination for crimes allegedly committed "since at least April 2017, in the context of demonstrations and related political unrest."[16]

In September 2018, a group of states parties to the Rome Statute referred the situation in Venezuela to the ICC, citing also the findings of a report by a panel of experts of the Organization of American States (OAS).[17] The referral stated that:

(last visited July 18, 2023) (During this time, the OTP received communications about alleged crimes that were perpetrated by the Venezuelan government but the Prosecutor concluded that "the available information did not provide a reasonable basis to believe that the requirement of a widespread or systematic attack against any civilian population had been satisfied.").

13 Ayumary M. Fitzgerald, 'Crimes Against Humanity in Venezuela: Can the ICC Bring Justice to Venezuelan Victims?' (2018) 26 *U. Mia. Int'l & Compar. L. Rev.* 127, 129; Rafael Romo and Marilia Brocchetto, *Venezuela Protests: What You Need to Know*, CNN (Apr. 20, 2017), https://edition.cnn.com/2017/04/18/americas/venezuela-protest-explainer/index.html (last visited July 18, 2023).

14 Romo & Brocchetto, *supra* note 13.

15 Fitzgerald, *supra* note 13, at 130; *Venezuela's Ex-Chief Prosecutor Asks International Court to Try Maduro*, THE GUARDIAN (Nov. 16, 2017), https://www.theguardian.com/world/2017/nov/16/venezuelas-ex-chief-prosecutor-asks-international-court-to-try-maduro (last visited July 18, 2023).

16 Statement, Fatou Bensouda, Chief Prosecutor, Int'l Crim. Ct., Statement on Opening Preliminary Examinations into the Situations in the Philippines and in Venezuela (Feb. 8, 2018), https://www.icc-cpi.int/news/statement-prosecutor-international-criminal-court-fatou-bensouda-opening-preliminary-0 (last visited July 18, 2023).

17 Organization of American States, Report of the General Secretariat of the Organization of American States and the Panel of Independent International Experts on the Possible Commission of Crimes Against Humanity in Venezuela (May 29, 2018) [hereinafter OAS Crimes Report], https://reliefweb.int/sites/reliefweb.int/files/resources/Informe-Panel-Independiente-Venezuela-EN.pdf (last visited July 18, 2023).

> The analysis of the panel of experts includes a detailed evaluation of how a situation of commission of crimes against humanity in Venezuela would have been configured, based on generalized or systematic attacks against a part of the civilian population of that country, constituted by the opposition to the government of President Nicolás Maduro [...]. A particularly dramatic aspect are the alleged arbitrary detentions, murders, extrajudicial executions, torture, sexual abuse and rape, as well as flagrant attacks against due process, to the detriment of people of both sexes, including minors. At the same time, a systematic action would be carried out against young men between 15 and 30 years old, who, without justification, would be arrested or taken away from their homes to accuse them of acts they would not have committed, or to kill them on the grounds that they resisted[18]

These allegations were given more weight the following year when the UN accused the Venezuelan government of using death squads to instill fear in the population,[19] with an estimated 18,000 to 19,000 people falling victim to extrajudicial executions.[20] The Lima Group, established in 2017 to allow for regional collaboration to find a peaceful solution to the Venezuelan crisis,[21] issued a statement backing the notion that Venezuela should be subject to an investigation by the ICC.[22]

---

18 Letter from Mauricio Macri, President, Republic of Arg., et al., to Fatou Bensouda, Chief Prosecutor, Int'l Crim. Ct., Regarding a Referral of Venezuela (Unofficial Translation) (Sep. 26, 2018), https://www.icc-cpi.int/sites/default/files/itemsDocuments/180925-otp-referral-venezuela_ENG.pdf (last visited July 18, 2023).

19 *Venezuela's Rulers Accused by UN of Death Squads and Policy of Fear,* BBC NEWS (Jul. 5, 2019), https://www.bbc.com/news/world-latin-america-48873500 (last visited July 18, 2023); *See also* G.A., 45th Sess., Hum. Rts. Council, Report of the Independent International Fact-Finding Mission on the Bolivarian Republic of Venezuela, UN Doc. A/HRC/45/33 (Sep. 25, 2020); G.A., 45th Sess., Hum. Rts. Council, Detailed Findings of the Independent International Factfinding Mission on the Bolivarian Republic of Venezuela, UN Doc. A/HRC/45/CRP.11 (Sep. 15, 2020).

20 *World Report 2021: Venezuela: Events of 2020*, HUM. RTS. WATCH, https://www.hrw.org/world-report/2021/country-chapters/Venezuela (last visited July 18, 2023); Organization of American States, Fostering Impunity: The Impact of the Failure of the Prosecutor of the International Criminal Court to Open an Investigation into the Possible Commission of Crimes Against Humanity in Venezuela (Dec. 2, 2020), http://www.oas.org/documents/eng/press/Crimes-Against-Humanity-in-Venezuela-II-ENG.pdf (last visited July 18, 2023).

21 Freier and Parent, *supra* note 12, at 61.

22 *Statement from the Lima Group* (Oct. 13, 2020), https://www.international.gc.ca/world-monde/international_relations-relations_internationales/latin_america-amerique_latine/2020-10-14–lima_group-groupe_lima.aspx?lang=eng (last visited July 18, 2023).

Conditions in Venezuela continue to be grave as the economic crisis has deepened, corruption has soared,[23] and the government has clamped down even harder, using the COVID-19 crisis as an excuse.[24] Moreover, this situation has had far reaching consequences for the broader region. Out of a population of 32 million, some 5 million Venezuelans have sought refuge in other countries.[25] While those fleeing Venezuela are not necessarily seen as refugees, Freier argues that the reasons for not applying the Cartagena definition,[26] which expanded on the 1951 Refugee Convention and offers protection to victims of generalized violence, are generally political, not legal.[27] Most Venezuelans fled to other Latin American countries and Caribbean nations which are ill-equipped to accommodate the large influx of people and are experiencing significant socioeconomic and cultural transformations because of it.[28] Some of these countries are having their own difficulties with high levels of crime and economic instability, and are fearful of the spillover effect the Venezuelan crisis may have.[29]

In 2020, the OTP came to the conclusion that "there is a reasonable basis to believe that crimes within the jurisdiction of the Court have been committed in Venezuela since at least April 2017."[30] The preliminary examination is thus now in Phase III of the OTP's evaluation on whether to open an investigation into the Venezuela situation: i.e., the phase where the Prosecution examines the admissibility of the potential cases arising from this situation and falling within the Court's jurisdiction.[31] With reports of the UN and OAS arguing that crimes against humanity have been perpetrated, neighboring states having to deal with a displacement crisis, and a referral to the ICC

23 Naomi Roht-Arriaza and Santiago Martínez, 'Grand Corruption and the International Criminal Court in the "Venezuela Situation"' (2019) 17 *J. Int'l Crim. Just.* 1057.

24 *Venezuela: Events of 2020*, *supra* note 20.

25 *Id.*

26 UNHCR: The UN Refugee Agency, Cartagena Declaration on Refugees, p. 36 (Nov. 22, 1984), https://www.unhcr.org/media/cartagena-declaration-refugees-adopted-colloquium-international-protection-refugees-central (last visited July 18, 2023) ("Persons who have fled their country because their lives, safety or freedom have been threatened by generalized violence, foreign aggression, internal conflicts, massive violation of human rights or other circumstances which have seriously disturbed public order").

27 Luisa Feline Freier, *Understanding the Venezuelan Displacement Crisis*, E-INT'L REL. (Jun. 28, 2018), https://www.e-ir.info/2018/06/28/understanding-the-venezuelan-displacement-crises/; Freier and Parent, *supra* note 12, at 57–58.

28 John, *supra* note 11, at 437; Waid, *supra* note 11, at 109.

29 John, *supra* note 11, at 441.

30 Report on Preliminary Examination Activities 2020, *supra* note 10, ¶ 202.

31 *Id.* ¶¶ 207–09.

by regional states, the situation in Venezuela has sparked international concern and has had an impact beyond the primary victims of the alleged crimes by the Venezuelan government. Uncertain, however, is to what extent and how this impact will and should be taken into account by the OTP in the gravity assessment.

3 Gravity and the Crimes' Impact on Victims

As the preliminary examination of the situation in Venezuela now enters into Phase III, the admissibility phase, the OTP must address two core questions, one of them being that of gravity.[32] Is the Venezuela situation sufficiently grave – as per Articles 17(1)(d) and 53(1)(c) of the Rome Statute – to warrant the opening an ICC investigation?

When assessing the gravity of a situation, the ICC Chambers have come to consistently hold that this evaluation "should be conducted in a general sense, as regards the entire situation, but also against the backdrop of the potential case(s)" arising from it.[33] This means that – before an actual investigation has actually been conducted – the OTP is expected to already carry out a generic assessment of the (group of) individuals that are likely to become the object of future ICC trials, as well as of all the crimes committed in this situation that are likely to be charged in the said future trials. Once these two parameters are known, the gravity of the situation can be assessed by determining:

---

32 *See, e.g.*, Côte d'Ivoire Investigation Authorization, *supra* note 1, ¶¶ 192–94. (The other question is that of complementarity, namely whether Venezuela – or any other State with jurisdiction – is conducting or has conducted national proceedings in relation to the person and crimes that are likely to constitute the potential future case at the ICC).

33 Côte d'Ivoire Investigation Authorization, *supra* note 1, ¶ 202; *see also* Kenya Investigation Authorization, *supra* note 1, ¶¶ 60–61; Situation in the Islamic Republic of Afghanistan, Case No. ICC-02/17-33, Decision pursuant to Article 15 of the Rome Statute on the Authorisation of an Investigation into the Situation in the Islamic Republic of Afghanistan, ¶ 80 (PTC II, Apr. 12, 2019). Situation in the Republic of Burundi, Case No. ICC-01/17-X, Decision pursuant to Article 15 of the Rome Statute on the Authorization of an Investigation into the Situation in the Republic of Burundi, ¶ 184 (PTC III, Oct, 25, 2017), [hereinafter Burundi Authorization Decision]; Situation in Georgia, Case No. ICC-01/15-12, Decision on the Prosecutor's Request for Authorization of an Investigation, ¶ 51 (PTC I, Jan. 27, 2016) [hereinafter Georgia Investigation Authorization].

i. in relation to the identified individuals over whom the ICC has jurisdiction, whether they include "those who may bear the greatest responsibility for the alleged crimes committed;"[34] and
ii. in relation to the identified crimes over which the ICC has jurisdiction, by looking into qualitative and quantitative factors, including the "nature, scale and manner of commission of the alleged crimes, as well as their impact on victims."[35]

For the purposes of the present research, it is the meaning of the last factor for assessing the gravity of crimes – i.e., "their impact on victims" – that is of particular interest. Specifically, one outstanding question is whether the assessment here is supposed to be limited to the crimes' impact on the direct victims alone, or could it also involve broader impact considerations, such as impact on the international community?

It was in its 2009 Regulations that the Office of the Prosecutor coined, for the very first time, the expression that the "scale, nature, manner of commission, and impact" of crimes have to be considered when evaluating gravity.[36] Then, in its 2010 Draft Policy Paper on Preliminary Examinations, the OTP explained its interpretation of the impact-factor in the following terms:

> The impact of crimes may be assessed in light of, inter alia, their consequence on the local or international community, including the long term social, economic and environmental damage; crimes committed with the aim or consequence of increasing the vulnerability of civilians; or other acts the primary purpose of which is to spread terror among the civilian population.[37]

Originally, thus, the OTP was certainly not of the opinion that assessments of the impact-factor must be limited to examining the effect of crimes committed on their (direct) victims. However, when the final version of that

34 Côte d'Ivoire Investigation Authorization, supra note 1, ¶ 204; *See also* Kenya Investigation Authorization, *supra* note 1, ¶ 60; Burundi Authorization Decision, *supra* note 33, ¶ 184.

35 Situation on Registered Vessels of the Union of the Comoros, the Hellenic Republic and the Kingdom of Cambodia, Case No. ICC-01/13-34, Decision on the Request of the Union of the Comoros to Review the Prosecutor's Decision Not to Initiate an Investigation, ¶ 21 (PTC I, Jul. 16, 2015) [hereinafter Comoros Situation Pre-Trial Chamber Decision]; *See also* Kenya Investigation Authorization, *supra* note 1, ¶ 62; Georgia Investigation Authorization, *supra* note 33, ¶ 51.

36 OTP Regulations, *supra* note 5, R. 29(2).

37 OTP Draft Policy Paper, *supra* note 6, ¶ 70(d), (emphasis added).

Policy Paper was issued in 2013, the OTP's interpretation of the impact-factor appeared to be narrower, shifting the focus on the crimes' impact on victims and "affected communities:"

> The impact of crimes may be assessed in light of, inter alia, the sufferings endured by the victims and their increased vulnerability; the terror subsequently instilled, or the social, economic and environmental damage inflicted on the affected communities.[38]

One can speculate what prompted the OTP to exclude the reference to consequences on "the international community" from its explanation of the impact-factor in the final version of the Policy Paper on Preliminary Examinations. The reason for this may be certain findings that the ICC judges had made when they first evaluated gravity in the context of two specific cases: Lubanga and Ntaganda.[39] When deciding whether to issue warrants of arrest against these two accused, the Pre-Trial Chamber held that, in order to determine if a case is sufficiently grave to be admissible under Article 17(1)(d) of the Rome Statute, "due consideration should also be given to the social alarm caused to the international community by the relevant type of conduct."[40] The definition that the OTP originally provided of the impact-factor in its Draft Policy Paper on Preliminary Examinations is, at first glance, very similar to this "social alarm" criterion, which the Pre-Trial Chamber defined. However, the OTP actually disagreed with the Pre-Trial Chamber's analysis on this point and appealed it, arguing that assessing the social alarm caused to the international community would be a criterion that not only lacks legal basis in the Rome Statute, but is "related to subjective and contingent reactions [to crimes], rather than the objective gravity of the crime."[41] The Appeals Chamber fully agreed with the Prosecution and rejected the criterion of "social alarm."[42]

---

38 OTP Policy Paper, *supra* note 7, ¶ 65.

39 Prosecutor v. Bosco Ntaganda, Case No. ICC-01/04-02/06-20-Anx2, Annex 2 to "Decision on the Prosecutor's Application for Warrants of Arrest, Article 58" (Pretrial Chamber I, Feb. 10, 2006) [hereinafter Annex 2].

40 *Id.* ¶ 64(i); *See also* Annex 2, *supra* note 39, ¶ 63.

41 Situation in the Democratic Republic of Congo, Case No. ICC-01/04-169, Judgment on the Prosecutor's Appeal against the Decision of Pre-Trial Chamber I entitled "Decision on the Prosecutor's Application for Warrants of Arrest, Article 58", ¶ 66 (AC, Jul. 13, 2006).

42 *Id.* at ¶ 72.

One conclusion that can be drawn from the above analysis is that the OTP and the Pre-Trial Chamber both agreed – at least originally – that the effect that crimes may have on the international community is also a relevant factor for evaluating gravity. The difference seemed to be that, for the OTP, this effect/impact referred to objectively verifiable, material harms that the said crimes caused to the international community (such as, e.g., "long term social, economic and environmental damage"),[43] while the Pre-Trial Chamber was focusing more on the emotive effect of the crimes, measured in the degree of public outrage/alarm caused on the international community. So how should the removal of any reference to "consequences on the international community" from the final version of the OTP's Policy Paper be interpreted? It could be that the OTP did this simply to avoid any conflation of its interpretation with that of the Pre-Trial Chamber, while still very much keeping the idea that material consequences inflicted on the international community is a relevant factor to be considered when assessing the impact of crimes. However, it could also be that the OTP changed its mind altogether and decided to completely exclude any considerations of crimes' impact on the international community as a relevant factor for assessing gravity. In this respect, it is helpful to look at how the OTP has assessed the impact-factor in its subsequent decisions (not to) open an investigation into a situation, as well as when requesting the Pre-Trial Chamber for authorization to this effect.

The notion of gravity, and in particular the impact-factor, was most extensively litigated in the Comoros situation. As is well known, the OTP refused to open an investigation into that situation after finding that it was not sufficiently grave.[44] When evaluating the impact of all the crimes committed by the Israeli Defense Forces on-board the flotilla, the OTP focused solely on the consequences which the identified war crimes (killing, causing serious bodily harm, and committing outrages upon personal dignity) had on the direct victims and their families, as well as more broadly on the civilian population in Gaza.[45] Upon reviewing the OTP's analysis, the Pre-Trial Chamber, however, went on to also emphasize the impact that the said crimes had on the international community as a whole, noting to this effect:

43 *See* OTP Draft Policy Paper, *supra* note 6.

44 Office of the Prosecutor, International Criminal Court, Situation on Registered Vessels of Comoros, Greece and Cambodia, Article 53(1) Report, ¶¶ 150–51 (Nov. 6, 2014), https://www.icc-cpi.int/sites/default/files/iccdocs/otp/OTP-COM-Article_53(1)-Report-06Nov2014Eng.pdf (last visited July 18, 2023).

45 *Id.* at ¶ 141.

> [T]he Prosecutor should have recognised the possibility that the events at issue had an impact going beyond the suffering of the direct and indirect victims. [...] Also the international concern caused by the events at issue, which, inter alia, resulted in several fact finding missions including by the UN Human Rights Council and the UN Secretary General, is somehow at odds with the Prosecutor's simplistic conclusion that the impact of the identified crimes points towards the insufficient gravity of the potential case(s) on the mere grounds that the supplies carried by the vessels in the flotilla were ultimately later distributed to the population in Gaza.[46]

Seeing as the Pre-Trial Chamber was measuring the crimes' impact on the international community in terms of the reactions ("international concern") they prompted within the United Nations, it can be concluded that the judges were effectively using the "social alarm" criterion here. The OTP understood this dictum in such terms, which is why it concluded the following in its subsequent renewed evaluation of the gravity of the Comoros situation:

> As to the moral or political effect of the events aboard the Mavi Marmara, the Prosecution is "in no position to assess" the majority's view of the "symbolic importance of the identified crimes" on "an objective basis." This is for the same reasons previously identified by the Appeals Chamber when it observed that "the criterion of 'social alarm' depends upon subjective and contingent reactions to crimes rather than upon their objective gravity."[47]

The Prosecution thus clearly rejected once again (just like it did in Lubanga and Ntaganda) the idea that crimes' effect on the international community – measured purely in terms of moral outrage, social alarm, etc. – is a relevant factor for assessing gravity. The Prosecution's position on this point, however, has not been entirely consistent. In the Mali situation, for instance, the

46 Comoros Situation Pre-Trial Chamber Decision, *supra* note 35, ¶ 48.

47 Office of the Prosecutor, International Criminal Court, Final Decision of the Prosecutor Concerning the "Article 53(1) Report" (ICC-01/13-6-AnxA), Dated 6 November 2014, as Revised and Refiled in Accordance with the Pre-Trial Chamber's request of 15 November 2018 and the Appeals Chamber's Judgment of 2 September 2019, ¶ 49 (Dec. 2, 2019), https://www.icc-cpi.int/sites/default/files/RelatedRecords/CR2019_07299.PDF (last visited July 18, 2023).

OTP motivated its decision to open an investigation by pointing out in its impact-analysis that one of the central crimes committed in this situation – i.e., the destruction of historical and religious World Heritage sites in Timbuktu – "appears to have shocked the conscience of humanity."[48] To support its analysis on this point, the Prosecution cited solemn declarations and resolutions by the United Nations and the African Union, which condemned the destruction of the holy sites in Timbuktu.

Leaving aside the social alarm that the crimes in the Comoros situation caused in the international community, it is also unclear whether the OTP would have been willing to include in its impact-analysis any tangible negative effects (harms), which the crimes may have caused beyond the direct victims and their immediate community. Indeed, the Prosecution skirted any reference to the international community in its assessment of the impact criterion. This can very well be because the limited range of crimes committed aboard the Mavi Marmara probably did not cause significant tangible consequences for the international community. It does show, however, that even in situations where such impact could be identified objectively, the OTP's analysis has remained limited to the crimes' impact on the victims and their communities. For instance, when requesting authorization to open an investigation into the Bangladesh situation, the OTP assessed the impact that the waves of violence against Rohingya Muslims in Myanmar had "on both individual victims and the entire Rohingya community of Rakhine State."[49] The Prosecution did not deem it necessary to also point out the broader impact which the identified crimes also had on the international community, seeing as the waves of violence resulted in mass migration, with more than 700,000 Rohingya Muslims seeking refuge in neighboring Bangladesh, as well as in other states, including Malaysia, India, Pakistan, Thailand, Indonesia, Saudi Arabia, and the United Arab Emirates.[50] The UN Development Programme reported that the influx of Rohingya refugees in Bangladesh had a calamitous impact on its economy and

48 Office of the Prosecutor, International Criminal Court, Situation in Mali: Article 53(1) Report, ¶¶ 157–60 (Jan. 16, 2013), https://www.icc-cpi.int/sites/default/files/itemsDocuments/SASMaliArticle53_1PublicReportENG16Jan2013.pdf (last visited July 18, 2023).

49 Situation in the People's Republic of Bangladesh/Republic of The Union of Myanmar, Case No. ICC-01/19-7, Request for Authorisation of an Investigation pursuant to Article 15, ¶¶ 287–89 (PTC III, Jul. 4, 2019).

50 Public International Law and Policy Group, Documenting Atrocity Crimes Committed Against the Rohingya in Myanmar's Rakhine State: Factual Findings Report, pp. 7–8 (Sep. 2018), https://static1.squarespace.com/static/5900b58e1b631bffa367167e/t/5bd8bdabf950b7e10b575111/1540930993999/PILPG+-+Documenting+Atrocity+Crimes+Against

infrastructure, including a drastic rise of unemployment and prices, falling wages of low-skilled workers, etc.[51] In view of all the above, one could only speculate whether the OTP did not include such considerations in its impact-analysis because it did not consider them relevant, or because it thought that its analysis of the consequences that the harms had on the individual victims, and on the Rohingya community, sufficed on its own to confirm the impact factor.

4 Finding Middle Ground: From Social Alarm to an Objective Assessment of the Consequences for Other States

It remains unclear to what extent the OTP rejects the notion of "social alarm" as a criterion for assessing the impact of crimes, seeing as its decisions in Comoros and Mali appear somewhat inconsistent in that respect. Overall, the OTP seems to have been hesitant and inclined to reject social alarm as a consideration due to its subjective nature. However, there may be objective indicators, such as declarations, reports, or referrals by international bodies and organizations that clearly signal the impact (in terms of alarm and moral outrage) that crimes committed in a given situation may have on the international community.

Beyond the question of whether the OTP is willing to interpret the extent to which the crimes shocked the conscience of humanity, it remains to be seen whether the OTP is also unwilling to take into account the crimes' tangible impact beyond the direct victims and their communities, as the 2013 Policy Paper on Preliminary Examinations seems to indicate. There is a real risk that the OTP might be throwing away the baby with the bathwater by refusing to consider the crimes' broader impact on the international community when assessing the gravity of situations. Taking into consideration the spillover effect that international crimes may have, for instance, on neighboring countries or on a particular region, is not necessarily consideration of "subjective and contingent reactions" to the crimes.

The situation in Venezuela and its destabilizing influence on the entire region are exemplary in that respect. If the "international community" is not meant to signify the UN in its entirety, but is interpreted to also include countries beyond the state in which the crimes are perpetrated, we clearly

51 U.N. Development Programme, Impacts of the Rohingya Refugee Influx on Host Communities (Nov. 2018), https://reliefweb.int/sites/reliefweb.int/files/resources/Impacts%20of%20the%20Rohingya%20Refugee%20Influx%20on%20Host%20Communities.pdf (last visited July 18, 2023).

see serious consequences for the region that can be objectively assessed and taken into account when determining gravity. The social and economic consequences – that were originally mentioned in the 2010 Draft Policy Paper – are significant for many regional states that need to accommodate the millions of Venezuelans that fled from the political violence and the dire conditions in which they found themselves. Many of these countries are ill-equipped to take so many people in and there is a real risk that the Venezuelan crisis can have a destabilizing political, economic, and social effect on countries in the region.[52]

A middle ground can be found between the initial Pre-Trial Chamber's position that the "social alarm" of the international community needs to be taken into account and the OTP and Appeal Chambers' notion that this has no place in an objective determination of gravity. This can be done by acknowledging that the "social alarm" may stem from serious consequences of the crimes for neighboring states, a particular region, or the broader "international community"[53] that can be assessed objectively to determine the gravity of a situation.

The situation in Venezuela is likely to meet the gravity threshold[54] even without taking into account the impact of the crimes on other states (i.e., by looking solely at the scale, nature, and manner of commission of the concerned crimes), yet this may not always be the case in every situation. As such, while the OTP understandably would want to be cautious about considering the reactions of other states only, it would be wise to keep the door open to include an analysis of the direct consequences of crimes for other states in its gravity assessment. As the Venezuelan crisis shows, international crimes may have spillover effects that deserve to be recognised as adding to the gravity of a particular situation.

5 Conclusion

The Preamble of the Rome Statute notes that states parties are:

> Conscious that all peoples are united by common bonds, their cultures pieced together in a shared heritage, and concerned that this delicate mosaic may be shattered at any time,

52 John, *supra* note 11, at 437–41; Waid, *supra* note 11, at 109; Freier, *supra* note 27.

53 Some consequences, like environmental damage, might indeed have broader implications for any number of states.

54 OAS Crimes Report, *supra* note 17, at 383.

> Mindful that during this century millions of children, women and men have been victims of unimaginable atrocities that deeply shock the conscience of humanity,
>
> Recognizing that such grave crimes threaten the peace, security and well-being of the world

It is, therefore, acknowledged that states are not isolated, that what occurs in one state impacts another, and that international crimes may not only shock the conscience of humanity, but threaten the well-being of citizens beyond the state in which these crimes are committed. As such, it would seem logical that these considerations should be taken into account when determining the gravity of a situation, yet the manner and extent to which the OTP has been willing to consider the crimes' impact on the international community in its gravity determination has been inconsistent and ambiguous. While in Mali the OTP referred to the idea that the crimes shocked mankind, it has rejected such notions of "social alarm" on other occasions, most recently in Comoros.

In addition, whether the OTP might consider the impact that international crimes may have on other states in its gravity determination remains an open question. The 2013 Policy Paper provides a non-exhaustive list of factors to be taken into consideration, and the OTP, therefore, has the possibility to also consider the impact on neighboring states or on the region in its gravity determination. In some of its decisions, most notably Bangladesh, where the crimes clearly had a negative impact on neighboring states, the OTP has been silent on the issue.

The upcoming gravity assessment in the Venezuela situation opens up new possibilities to clarify and explain the role that the concern of the international community, and the impact on the region, play in the determination of gravity. Given the destabilizing effects of the Venezuelan crises, given the large flows of refugees and the negative impact it had on the countries of refuge, we encourage the OTP to keep an open mind about taking objective measures of adverse effects on other states into consideration.

PART 6

Cyber Operations and Cyberwarfare under the Rome Statute

Introduction to Part 6

The following question was featured on www.ICCForum.com from March 2022 through July 2022:

To what extent and under what conditions might cyber operations or cyberwarfare constitute crimes specified in the Rome Statute?

In its 2019 report, the World Economic Forum warned that "offensive cyber capabilities are developing more rapidly than our ability to deal with hostile incidents." Increasingly, states and non-state actors have employed cyber attacks to disrupt or manipulate economic, social, political, and humanitarian activities. Social media sites have been used to incite violence. And the major militaries of the world now routinely plan for, develop, and maintain offensive and defensive cyber capacities.

Article 5 of the Rome Statute defines Genocide, Crimes Against Humanity, War Crimes, and the Crime of Aggression as within the ICC's jurisdiction. The elements of these crimes are detailed in Articles 6, 7, 8, Article 8 *bis*, Article 15 *bis*, and Article 15 ter. Could cyber attacks fall within the Rome Statute's definition of these crimes? In what contexts? What types of cyber attacks might fall within the scope of each of the crimes defined in the Rome Statute?

In general, what are the biggest challenges in employing the Rome Statute to address grave cyber crimes? States may attempt to disguise or outsource their cyber activity, and some cyber operations may involve many actors. What challenges are faced in attributing responsibility for a cyber attack? Cyber operations may have unintended consequences, so how can it be determined whether a specific target was intended or merely incidental civilian damage? Under what conditions would incapacitating vital infrastructure (e.g., water processing, hospitals) via a cyber operation be equivalent to physical destruction of that infrastructure? In the case of cyber operations, how should the gravity threshold be assessed?

With respect to the crime of genocide, how should the ICC treat cyber conduct that causes psychological harm? In applying Article 6(b), what should be the threshold for finding that serious mental harm caused by cyber activities constitutes a genocidal act? What kinds of cyber operations might serve as evidence of genocidal intent?

With respect to crimes against humanity, how should the Court look at exclusively non-physical effects of cyber operations, such as exclusively psychological or mental harm?

 | DOI:10.1163/9789004686755_032

With respect to war crimes, can a cyber operation itself trigger an international armed conflict and, therefore, the application of international humanitarian law? Does the Office of the Prosecutor possess the requisite investigative powers to obtain information necessary to determine whether a cyber-related conflict exists, particularly at the Preliminary Examination stage? Should civilian data, particularly civilian medical data, be considered a civilian object within the meaning of Article 8(2)? How should the principles of distinction and proportionality apply to cyber attacks?

With respect to the crime of aggression, when does a cyber operation amount to a manifest violation of the U.N. Charter? How should the character, gravity, and scale of a cyber attack be assessed? How directly must loss of life be connected to a cyber operation to be considered a result of the attack? Might a lower scale attack warrant a crime of aggression prosecution if it compromised critical infrastructure, military systems, caused a grave impact on an economic system, or deleted crucial medical data? What other cyber attack scenarios might constitute a crime of aggression?

Article 2(4) of the U.N. Charter provides:

> All Members shall refrain in their international relations from the threat or use of force against the territorial integrity or political independence of any state, or in any other manner inconsistent with the Purposes of the United Nations.

Under what circumstances, if any, might Article 2(4) accommodate cyber attacks under its definition of "force"? To what extent might such an accommodation be relevant to the ICC's jurisdiction? What would be the implications for the Court if the Security Council were to deem a cyber attack an unlawful use of force?

The Tallinn Manual, the ICRC's Commentary on Cyberwarfare, and the Council of Advisers' Report on the Application of the Rome Statute to Cyberwarfare each suggest ways to conceptualize cyberwarfare and how international law might relate to it. How might these works guide the inclusion of cyberwarfare into the scope of the Rome Statute? To what extent should they be considered authoritative?

Is the Rome Statute adequate for addressing grave cyber crimes? Should it be amended for that purpose? Should a new institution be created for that purpose?

CHAPTER 26

Cyber Attacks as International Crimes under the Rome Statute of the International Criminal Court?

Kai Ambos

Introduction

In this short essay,[1] I argue that cyber operations in the form of cyber attacks may entail individual criminal responsibility under international criminal law, especially when they amount to war crimes. In Section 1, I start with some conceptual remarks regarding the umbrella terms "cyber operations" and "cyberwarfare," then, in Section 2, I argue that cyber attacks may amount to "attacks" in the legal sense of the term on the basis of an effects approach. In Section 3, I apply this approach to the international core crimes within the meaning of Article 5 of the Rome Statute, focusing mainly on war crimes. I then conclude in Section 4 with some remarks on the law on individual criminal responsibility.

1 Preliminary Conceptual Remarks: Cyber Operations and Cyber Warfare

"Cyber operation" is an umbrella term referring to "employment of cyber capabilities to achieve [certain] objectives in or through cyberspace."[2] The term

1 This essay draws upon the following two sources. The research assistance of Luca Petersen is gratefully acknowledged. Kai Ambos, 'International Criminal Responsibility in Cyberspace', in Nicholas Tsagourias and Russell Buchan (eds.), *Research Handbook on Cyberspace and International Law*, 2d ed., (Cheltanham, UK: Edward Elgar Publishing, 2021), p. 118; Kai Ambos, 'Individual Criminal Responsibility for Cyber Aggression' (2016) 21 *J. Conflict & Sec. L.* 495.

2 Michael N. Schmitt (ed.), *Tallinn Manual 2.0 on the International Law Applicable to Cyber Operations* (Cambridge: Cambridge University Press, 2017), p. 564 [hereinafter Tallinn Manual]; *accord* Paul A.L. Ducheine, 'The Notion of Cyber Operations', in Nicholas Tsagourias and Russell Buchan (eds.), *Research Handbook on Cyberspace and International Law* (Cheltenham, UK: Edward Elgar Publishing, 2015), later version with Peter B.M.J. Pijpers (Apr. 14, 2020), https://papers.ssrn.com/sol3/papers.cfm?abstract_id=3575755 (last visited July 18, 2023).

 | DOI:10.1163/9789004686755_033

is more specific than the broader "cybercrime"[3] and covers inter alia cyber espionage, cyber manipulation, and cyber attacks.[4] Thinking of cyber operations in terms of international criminal law, the focus shifts to cyber attacks given that they constitute the strongest, most aggressive form of a cyber operation and are as such the only possible candidates serious enough to qualify as international crimes (see, infra, Section 3).[5]

"Cyberwarfare" is, more narrowly, the conduct of a cyber operation by military means in order to achieve military objectives.[6] Means of cyberwarfare "are cyber weapons and their associated cyber systems."[7] Given that cyber attacks can reasonably be expected to cause injury or death to persons or damage or destruction to objects, they can be fairly described, together with the device and/or software employed, as cyber weapons and thus as means of cyberwarfare.

---

3 Philipp Kastner and Frédéric Mégret, 'International Legal Dimension of Cybercrime', in Nicholas Tsagourias and Russell Buchan (eds.), *Research Handbook on Cyberspace and International Law* (Cheltenham, UK: Edward Elgar Publishing, 2015), p. 190 ("Cybercrime" refers to any criminal activity involving computer technology, committed by means of or against a computer). Convention on Cybercrime, Nov. 23, 2001, E.T.S. No. 185 [hereinafter Budapest Convention] (At the international level, the most comprehensive regulation of Cybercrime has been the Budapest Convention, said to have influenced the criminal law legislation of about 120 States). *Cf.* Council of Europe, Cybercrime Programme Office, The Global State of Cybercrime Legislation 2013–2021: A Cursory Overview (Jun. 30, 2021), https://rm.coe.int/3148-1-3-4-cyberleg-global-state-jun2021-v5-public/1680a302be (last visited July 18, 2023).

4 *See* Ducheine, *supra* note 2. (In a profound analysis, Ducheine demonstrates the similar strategic objectives and common operational means and methods of State and Non-State actors and set out six typical phases of a cyber operation, i.e., reconnaissance, design, intrusion, action, camouflage, and exfiltration).

5 *See* Marco Roscini, 'Cyber Operations as Use of Force', in Nicholas Tsagourias and Russell Buchan (eds.), *Research Handbook on Cyberspace and International Law* (Cheltenham, UK: Edward Elgar Publishing, 2015). (In contrast, the previously mentioned cyber espionage or manipulation is, as a rule, non-destructive and only employed to enter a computer system to extract information).

6 Tallinn Manual, *supra* note 2, at 564 (This is a military extension of the definition of "cyber operation"). Ducheine, *supra* note 2, 290 n. 112 (offering a critical discussion, but also, however, create the impression that the Tallinn Manual, quoting the first edition from 2013, provides a definition of "cyber warfare"). Heather Harrison Dinniss, *Cyber Warfare and the Laws of War* (Cambridge: Cambridge University Press, 2012), p. 294 (referring to "electronic warfare" as "Military action involving the use of electromagnetic and directed energy to control the electromagnetic spectrum or to attack the enemy.").

7 Tallinn Manual, *supra* note 2, at 452.

2 Cyber Attacks as "Attacks" due to Their Effects

The main difference between cyber and conventional attacks is the lack of the exertion of kinetic force of the former. In contrast to conventional kinetic attacks, cyber attacks regularly do not cause damage through direct kinetic force, but rather indirectly through the alteration or destruction of data. "Kinetic" means, in this regard, that the damage is related to or results from the motion or the dynamic of the attack. Kinetic weaponry is weaponry that acts through mechanical transmission.

However, kinetic and cyber-attacks may be comparable in their effects or consequences. The conventional physical bombardment of a military base or causing a complete loss of function through a cyber attack may have the same effect, that is, the temporary suspension of the use of the military base. Still, even though the attacks are comparable in their effect, they are achieved in fundamentally different ways: while physical damage occurs in the case of conventional attacks, it is usually absent in the case of cyber attacks. Notwithstanding, a cyber operation may well trigger and/or cause kinetic damage, e.g., widespread flooding caused by the deactivation of the regulating system of a large dam. For these scenarios of cyber attacks with indirect kinetic effects, the notion of "cyber-kinetic-attacks" has been coined.[8] The term is somewhat misleading, though, since it lumps together apparently contradictory – cyber vs. kinetic – notions. It is thus clearer to speak of indirect, secondary or even reverberating effects of cyber attacks.[9]

At any rate, given the fundamental difference between a conventional (kinetic) and a cyber (non-kinetic) attack, it has been argued that only the former amounts to an attack in the legal sense of the term since such an attack presupposes physical damage and the ensuing replacement of physical components of the attacked object.[10] The opposing view holds that damage to an operating system (with the ensuing need to reinstall it) or destruction of particular data may suffice to be qualified as an "attack" if similar harmful con-

8 *See, e.g.*, Scott D. Applegate, 'The Dawn of Kinetic Cyber', in Karlis Podins, Jan Stinissen and Markus Maybaum (eds.), *5th International Conference on Cyber Conflict* (Tallinn: NATO CCD COE Publications, 2013), https://ccdcoe.org/uploads/2018/10/10_d2r1s4_applegate.pdf (last visited July 19, 2023).

9 *Cf.* Karine Bannelier-Christakis, 'Is the Principle of Distinction Still Relevant in Cyberwarfare?', in Nicholas Tsagourias and Russell Buchan (eds.), *Research Handbook on Cyberspace and International Law* (Cheltenham, UK: Edward Elgar Publishing, 2015), p. 343 (with further references).

10 Tallinn Manual, *supra* note 2, at 417 ("a majority"). *See also* William H. Boothby, *Weapons and the Law of Armed Conflict*, 2d ed. (Oxford: Oxford University Press, 2016), p. 239.

sequences (loss of functionality, etc.) ensue.[11] This latter view is, in principle, more convincing.[12] While physical objects and mere data are certainly different, they are inseparably connected and interrelated. For this reason, cyber attacks may have an effect comparable to physical damage through functionally producing data corruption, which, in turn, has a significant negative impact on cyber infrastructures. Indeed, in today's cyber world, the traditional concepts of "use of force," "armed attack," or "acts of violence"[13] need to be reconsidered, focusing on their effects instead of overemphasizing the means (the kind of weapon) used to bring about these effects. This is even more true in the case of damage to so-called critical infrastructures.[14] Thus, in sum, interpreting cyber attacks in the light of existing international (humanitarian) law, the effect-based approach focusing on the effects or consequences of a cyber attack with regard to a concrete target is to be preferred over a mere means or instruments approach.[15]

---

11 Tallinn Manual, *supra* note 2, at 417–18 ("Some of the experts"). *See also* Julia Dornbusch, *Das Kampfführungsrecht im internationalen Cyberkrieg* (Nomos, 2018), pp. 97–98; *see also* Terry D. Gill, 'International Humanitarian Law Applied to Cyber-Warfare: Precautions, Proportionality and the Notion of "Attack" Under the Humanitarian Law of Armed Conflict', in Nicholas Tsagourias and Russell Buchan (eds.), *Research Handbook on Cyberspace and International Law* (Cheltenham, UK: Edward Elgar Publishing, 2015) (discussing effects which may turn data destruction into an attack). *See* Bannelier-Christakis, *supra* note 9 (discussing loss of functionality).

12 Roscini, *supra* note 5 (for a narrower view with regard to attacks on data as use of force). *See also* Bannelier-Christakis, *supra* note 9 (on the opposing views regarding data).

13 *Cf.* Roscini, *supra* note 5 (on the synonymity of these concepts).

14 Exec. Order No. 13636: Improving Critical Infrastructure Cybersecurity, 78 Fed. Reg. 11739 (Feb. 12, 2013), https://obamawhitehouse.archives.gov/the-press-office/2013/02/12/executive-order-improving-critical-infrastructure-cybersecurity (last visited July 19, 2023) (According to § 2, a "critical infrastructure" "means systems and assets, whether physical or virtual, so vital to the United States that the incapacity or destruction of such systems and assets would have a debilitating impact on security, national economic security, national public health or safety, or any combination of those matters." This definition is still valid). Exec. Order No. 14028: Improving the Nation's Cybersecurity, 86 Fed. Reg. 26633 (May 12, 2021), https://www.whitehouse.gov/briefing-room/presidential-actions/2021/05/12/executive-order-on-improving-the-nations-cybersecurity/ (last visited July 19, 2023); *A Proclamation on Critical Infrastructure Security and Resilience Month, 2021*, THE WHITE HOUSE (Oct. 29, 2021), https://www.whitehouse.gov/briefing-room/presidential-actions/2021/10/29/a-proclamation-on-critical-infrastructure-security-and-resilience-month-2021/ (last visited July 19, 2023) (confirming the Biden administration's commitment to secure the critical infrastructure, focusing, inter alia, on critical software).

15 *See* Bannelier-Christakis, *supra* note 9 (For the same view with several further references but rightly pointing to the evidentiary problems with regard to the proof of damage caused by a cyber operation and the precise extent of this damage). *See also* Roscini, *supra* note 5. (A combination of the instruments (weapons) and effects (of these weap-

3 Cyber Attacks as International Crimes

International crimes may be committed through cyber attacks alone or in combination with kinetic acts. At any rate, such attacks must be of a sufficient gravity to fall under the ICC's mandate as a consequence of the (autonomous) gravity threshold within the framework of the complementarity regime of Article 17(1)(d) of the Rome Statute. While no cyber situations have yet been the object of analysis of the ICC's Prosecutor,[16] cyber attacks surely have the potential to reach the necessary gravity threshold due to their effects and the associated external impact in line with the criteria of "scale, nature, manner of the commission, and impact".[17]

Let us now have a look at the crimes under the Rome Statute, focusing in particular on war crimes.

3.1 *War Crimes (Article 8 of the Rome Statute)*

The basic requirement for the application of the war crime regime is that an armed conflict exists (common Article 2 of the Geneva Conventions (GC)), i.e., that armed force has been employed between parties to a conflict and it can be attributed to one of them.[18] As argued above, the question of whether a pure cyber attack can be qualified "armed force" needs to be answered from

---

ons) approaches, as advocated by, does not yield different results since ultimately the decisive question is whether the cyber attacks cause a significant (physical) damage or a significant loss of functionality affirming a use of force in these cases while only seeing a violation of the principle of non-intervention in case of "other" cyber attacks).

16 However, while the issue did not give rise, so far, to a preliminary examination or even investigation, it is likely to increasingly come up in Article 15 communications and appears to be considered as part of overall investigative/protection strategies and information security management.

17 International Criminal Court, *Regulations of the Office of the Prosecutor*, Doc. No. ICC-BD/05-01-09, Reg. 29(2) (Apr. 23, 2009), https://www.icc-cpi.int/sites/default/files/NR/rdonlyres/FFF97111-ECD6-40B5-9CDA-792BCBE1E695/280253/ICCBD050109ENG.pdf (last visited July 12, 2023); *see* Jennifer Trahan, 'The Criminalization of Cyber-operations Under the Rome Statute' (2021) 19 *J. Int'l Crim. Just.* 1133, 1138–46; *see also* Marco Roscini, 'Gravity in the Statute of the International Criminal Court and Cyber Conduct That Constitutes, Instigates or Facilitates International Crimes' (2019) 30 *Crim. L.F.* 247.

18 *Cf.* Prosecutor v. Dusko Tadić, Case No. IT-94-1-AR, Decision on the Defence Motion for Interlocutory Appeal on Jurisdiction, ¶ 70 (Int'l Crim. Trib. for the Former Yugoslavia AC, Oct. 2, 1995); *see* Michael Cottier and Matthias Lippold, 'Article 8: War Crimes', in Kai Ambos (ed.), *Rome Statute of the International Criminal Court: Article-by-Article Commentary*, 4th ed., (München, Germany: Beck, 2022) (detailed discussion with further case law).

the perspective of the effects of such attacks as compared to traditional kinetic attacks. This effect-based reading is also in line with the definition of "armed attacks" as "acts of violence" in the sense of Article 49(1) of the Additional Protocol [AP] I GC, provided that a cyber attack produces violent effects, for example, by harming a physical part of a computer network that results in its replacement. In contrast, if a cyber attack does not produce any (lasting) physical or serious functional damage, it does not reach the armed conflict threshold. At any rate, generally it can be said that cyber attacks hardly reach the armed conflict threshold on their own but only in combination with traditional kinetic attacks; yet, cyber means of warfare may be employed in the context of a traditional armed conflict.[19]

It is more difficult to meet the second element of the armed conflict requirement, namely the attribution of a cyber attack to one of the parties to the conflict. While there are rules of attribution which may serve as guidance, e.g. in the International Law Commissions's Draft on State Responsibility[20] or, more specifically, in the Tallinn Manual,[21] the difficulties are mainly of a factual and evidentiary nature. They lie in the identification of the attacker and/or the attribution of the attack to a party to the respective armed conflict. On the one hand, the attack may come out of the anonymity of the Internet and thus may not be traceable to a specific person or group; or it may be traced to the wrong person or group. At best, it may be possible to identify the computer responsible for the attack via its IP address and thus establish its territorial location. Yet, while this may arguably allow one to presume the responsibility of the territorial state, such a presumption may be rebutted by this state, for example, by pointing to a group of non-state actors which it does not control.[22] On the other hand, the attacker may be identified, but s/he may not belong to or be affiliated with a party to the conflict and thus the attack may not be attributable to such a group; in addition, the attackers themselves may

19 *Cf.* Gill, *supra* note 11; *see also* Bannelier-Christakis, *supra* note 9 (stating that "it has never been proven" that the use of cyber operations during armed conflict had the same harmful consequences as the use of kinetic weapons); *but see* Trahan, *supra* note 17, at 1155 (considering the (Russian) cyber attacks on Eastern Ukraine as "possible" war crimes).

20 G.A., 53rd Sess., Int'l L. Comm'n., Articles on State Responsibility, Arts. 4–9, UN Doc. Supplement No. 10 (A/56/10) (Aug. 2001) (establishing the rules of attribution of acts of State organs or private groups or agents to a State).

21 Tallinn Manual, *supra* note 2, Rules 15–18.

22 *See* Constantine Antonopoulos, 'State Responsibility in Cyberspace', in Nicholas Tsagourias and Russell Buchan (eds.), *Research Handbook on Cyberspace and International Law* (Cheltenham, UK: Edward Elgar Publishing, 2015) (for a discussion).

not qualify as an armed group within the meaning of International Humanitarian Law (IHL) – lacking the necessary degree of organization, i.e., command, control, discipline, and hierarchy – and thus would not, on their own, constitute an autonomous party to the conflict. For example, groups of hackers usually lack the IHL criteria just mentioned; a spontaneous collective attack, e.g., a denial-of-service attack, does not comply with the organization requirement either. One may avoid these problems of attribution invoking a due diligence obligation of the (territorial) state to prevent cyber-attacks from happening in the first place or to intervene to stop them, since such an approach focuses on the primary obligation of due diligence and its breach.[23] However, this approach entails other problems. In particular, to establish a fair control standard – what can be fairly expected from a state in terms of control of cyber activities on its territory – and a sufficiently precise mental or cognitive standard.[24]

In line with the effects approach, it is conceivable that cyber attacks that disrupt the function of critical infrastructure – e.g., the health care system – cross the armed conflict and attack thresholds and amount to war crimes under Article 8 of the Rome Statute by "wilfully causing great suffering, or serious injury to body or health," "attacks against the civilian population as such or against individual civilians not taking direct part in hostilities," or "[i] ntentionally directing attacks against [...] medical units." Any person acting on behalf of a party to the conflict may commit such a war crime and thus be a responsible agent. In the cyber context, the participation of civilians is of particular relevance, since the reliance on civilian expertise is indispensable. These civilians may be members of formal armed forces but also of non-state actors and thus be targetable according to the (highly controversial) general rules of participation in hostilities. Here, too, certain particularities are to be noted, above all how cyber active civilians are to be distinguished from ordinary civilians in terms of their participation in hostilities. Generally, it can be said that the decision about the participation (with the ensuing loss of immunity from attacks) depends on the importance of the cyber civilian's contribution and his/her expertise. Thus, if an attack would not have been possible without this contribution, a participation is to be affirmed while a mere support function, e.g., maintenance of a computer network, does not justify such an affirmation. While the decision depends ultimately on the circumstances of

23 *Cf. id.*

24 *Id.* (While a strict knowledge standard would make it difficult if not impossible to establish the territorial State's responsibility, lower standards, like the infamous constructive knowledge, are highly controversial and thus difficult to agree on).

the concrete case, it is clear that a (too) broad reading of the participation requirement may undermine the protective purpose of IHL,[25] as especially expressed by the principle of distinction to which we now turn.

The usual IHL principles, i.e., humanity, necessity, proportionality,[26] precaution, and distinction,[27] also apply to cyber attacks if they amount to "attacks" under IHL.[28] Take, for example, the war crime of "[i]ntentionally directing attacks against civilian objects, that is, objects which are not military objectives" from Article 8(2)(b)(ii) of the Rome Statute. This provision constitutes a concrete implementation of the principle of distinction, embodied in Article 48 AP I GC and part of customary international law applicable in both international and non-international armed conflicts. Civilian objects are (only) defined negatively in delimitation to "military objectives" and these are "limited to those objects which by their nature, location, purpose or use make an effective contribution to military action and whose [...] neutralization [...] offers a definitive military advantage" (Article 52 AP I GC). While it is fairly uncontroversial that the principle of distinction also applies to cyber attacks, its concrete application is shrouded by controversy and uncertainty.[29] Apart from the usual difficulties to distinguish between civilian and military objects pursuant to the just mentioned blurred definition, the situation is even more complicated in the cyber area given that any computer system can be used for both civilian and military purposes at the same time or interchangeably – the dual-use problem.[30] Thus, ultimately, the decision

25 *See* Bannelier-Christakis, *supra* note 9 ("kind of Trojan horse" leading to a "total cyber war").

26 Gill, *supra* note 11 (on proportionality in particular, Gill argues that the principle largely applies in the same way in case of cyber attacks).

27 *Cf.* U.N. Secretary General, *Group of Governmental Experts on Development in the Field of Information and Telecommunication in the Context of International Security*, ¶ 28(d), U.N. Doc. A/70/174 (Jul. 22, 2015) (mentioning the principles of humanity, necessity, proportionality, and distinction).

28 *Cf.* Tallinn Manual, *supra* note 2, at 422 ("Only when a cyber operation [...] rises to the level of an attack it is prohibited by the principle of distinction"). Bannelier-Christakis, *supra* note 9 (providing a more nuanced, dynamic interpretation, arguing that IHL principles may also apply to cyber operation below the attack threshold).

29 *See* Bannelier-Christakis, *supra* note 9. (In a recent, profound analysis, Bannelier-Christakis stresses the uncertainty and examines State practice and non-State/academic views in detail).

30 *Id.* (In a deeper analysis, Bannelier-Christakis concludes that it is "rather illusory" to strictly limit attacks to military objects given that the "interconnection between civilian and military networks is so deep").

whether a certain object is "military" and can therefore be targeted is very much case-based on the specific circumstances.

3.2 *Other International Core Crimes*

In line with the effects approach, it is easily conceivable that cyber attacks may produce the objective effects of a genocidal attack on a protected group pursuant to Article 6(a)–(e) of the Rome Statute, or bring about the results of the underlying crimes of crimes against humanity pursuant to Article 7 of the Rome Statute. In the former case it will, as always, be difficult to overcome the high subjective threshold in the form the specific intent to destroy one of the protected groups. In the latter case, the cyber-attack would have to be carried out pursuant to a certain policy and, further, to be widespread or systematic. With regard to the organizational requirement in Article 7(2)(a) of the Rome Statute, similar questions as under war crimes, with a view to a minimum organizational threshold, arise.

Last but not least, the crime of aggression under Article 8 *bis* is only of limited, if any, relevance in the cyber context. This is so mainly for three reasons. First, Article 8 *bis* does not cover non-state actors but these are often behind cyber attacks. Secondly, a cyber attack may only exceptionally amount to a "use of armed force" within the meaning of Article 8 *bis* (2).[31] Third, it is even less conceivable that such attacks constitute "a manifest violation" of the U.N. Charter as required by Article 8 *bis* (1).

4 Individual Criminal Responsibility

Individual criminal responsibility presupposes the existence of international crimes and the relevant participation in these crimes by natural persons. The Tallinn Manual 2.0 now explicitly recognizes individual and superior (criminal) responsibility, albeit limited to war crimes, in line with Articles 25 and 28 of the Rome Statute;[32] as to superiors, it additionally provides a responsibility for "ordering cyber operations that constitute war crimes."[33]

31 *Cf.* Andreas Zimmermann and Elisa Freiburg-Braun, 'Article 8 *bis*', in Kai Ambos (ed.), *Rome Statute of the International Criminal Court: Article-by-Article Commentary*, 4th ed. (München, Germany: Beck, 2022) (Note that the drafters preferred a narrow understanding focusing on kinetic force, notwithstanding, in line with the effects approach defended above, "the use of computer networks as weapons" may be qualified as the use of armed force within the meaning of the provision).

32 *Cf.* Tallinn Manual, *supra* note 2, Rules 84, 85.

33 *Id.* at Rule 85(a).

Participants in cyber attacks are criminally responsible, under various subsections of Articles 25 and 28 of the Rome Statute, according to the nature and degree of involvement in the attack either as perpetrators acting alone, jointly with another, or through another person – or as secondary participants – inducing the attack or collaborating in it. Superiors may order the attack or fail to properly supervise subordinates carrying out such an attack. Liability for ordering is based on the general provision of Article 25(3)(b) of the Rome Statute, i.e., it is not limited to superiors within the meaning of Article 28, although there is, in factual terms, good reason to argue that only such superiors are in the position to order. At any rate, the just mentioned Tallinn Manual's specific Rule 85(a) turns out to be redundant in light of the ordering alternative in Article 25(3)(b) of the Rome Statute. Apparently, the Tallinn drafters wanted to incorporate both the superior's active conduct and failure to act in one specific Rule, i.e., Rule 85.[34]

In the case of the crime of aggression, criminal responsibility only arises, pursuant to the so-called leadership clause in Article 8 *bis* (1) of the Rome Statute, with regard to "a person in a position effectively to exercise control over or to direct the political or military action of a state." This means that the persons effectively carrying out a cyber attack would not be criminally liable but, at best, their superiors would be, if they belong to the leadership level and can be held responsible for the acts of the actual "cyber warriors".

34 *Cf. Id.* at 397 n. 958. (In fact, the commentary to Rule 84 on Individual Criminal Responsibility omits to mention the ordering alternative when discussing Article 25(3)(b) and moves this discussion to Rule 85(a)).

CHAPTER 27

Cyber Behavior: Gray Areas and Attribution Difficulties

Gary D. Brown

1 Introduction

Cyber activities continue to harass and confound governments and citizens alike. Although, under some circumstances, cyber operations constitute a welcome alternative to military force for advancing state interests, some disruptive cyber activities that don't constitute a use of force under the U.N. Charter are nevertheless serious enough to cause concern. Some of these non-destructive cyber activities could constitute the crime of aggression under the Rome Statute. However, given the growing practice of states in cyberspace, the generally muted reactions to transgressive cyber behavior, and the difficulty in attributing cyber aggression to states, the Rome Statute is unlikely to have a significant deterrent effect on disruptive cyber behavior.[1]

2 Clear Cases

States, the U.N., and other international organizations struggle to determine which state-sponsored cyber operations violate international law. Although it seems intuitively clear that cyber operations disrupting normal civilian life or interfering with the conduct of government business should constitute violations of international law, the law itself can be difficult to interpret in the virtual context. International law governing aggression is geared toward kinetic (physical) effects. International aggression has been closely aligned with military force, and military force results in physical destruction, injuries, and deaths. A body of law designed to deal with kinetic options is a poor fit for cyberspace, where effective operations can result in widespread

1 The views expressed in this essay are those of the author and are not an official policy or position of the National Defense University, the Department of Defense, or the U.S. Government.

 | DOI:10.1163/9789004686755_034

effects that, while effective in advancing strategic interests, may not directly result in damage or injury. Despite scholarly attempts to address this gap in the law by generous interpretation of the applicability of sovereignty and discussion of the nonintervention principle, it remains an ambiguous and hotly debated area of law. Some states appear to carefully structure their cyber activities to ensure that the effects remain below the traditional understanding of a use of force in violation of the U.N. Charter. In other cases, states use cyber capabilities to undertake massive espionage campaigns which, although exponentially larger in scale than more traditional espionage, remain just espionage and therefore currently beyond the reach of international law.

The international law applicable to the top and bottom of the range of state cyber activities is relatively clear. At the top end, cyber activities that cross the use of force threshold violate Article 2(4) of the U.N. Charter.[2] There is room for discussion about exactly where this line falls, but cyber actions directly resulting in physical damage or destruction of objects, or injury or death to people, clearly violate the Charter, just as their analogs in physical space would. At the bottom end, it is well-established that espionage, while not likely to win any friends, does not violate international law – or at least constitutes a "no-go" zone for the law.

3 The Gray Zone

Between these two limits there is a vast gray zone where the legality of state-sponsored cyber activities remains unclear. Two examples of these difficult categories are dual-purpose implants on critical systems and large-scale disruption of non-critical systems.

State operations conducted in the virtual environment can quickly step back and forth between espionage and more aggressive activities. Software surreptitiously implanted on systems can provide states continuing, long-term access to any computer network.[3] Such access can potentially give

---

2 U.N. Charter art. 2, ¶ 4 ("All Members shall refrain in their international relations from the threat or use of force against the territorial integrity or political independence of any state, or in any other manner inconsistent with the Purposes of the United Nations.").

3 *What Is an Advanced Persistent Threat* (APT)?, KASPERSKY, https://www.kaspersky.com/resource-center/definitions/advanced-persistent-threats (last visited July 19, 2023). (An advanced persistent threat requires significant resources, and is often state-sponsored). ("[A]n advanced persistent threat (APT) uses continuous, clandestine, and sophisticated

operators who control it the ability to gather information, manipulate or delete information, or even physically damage electronic systems. Given the appropriate access, any of these activities may be the intent and culmination of a particular cyber operation. It can be nearly impossible for victim states to determine exactly what the intent is. These operations are troublesome enough on nonessential systems. The real challenge arises when states are able to gain access to critical systems. Particularly sensitive targets of this type of dual operation include power grids, national intelligence systems, or even systems connected to nuclear power plants, or nuclear command and control. Given the criticality of these systems, it would be appropriate to take steps to ensure they are not penetrable by malicious actors. Unfortunately, it seems that whatever steps have been taken to defend them have, on some occasions, proven insufficient. States are understandably reluctant to discuss vulnerabilities in these systems, but successful incursions and threats have been reported in the press.[4] Even systems considered to be "air-gapped," i.e., completely disconnected from the internet, seem to be vulnerable to skilled and tenacious cyber actors.[5]

It is also possible that, beyond the access provided to human operators, implanted malware itself can be dual-use, and could even be artificially intelligent, allowing the malware to determine an appropriate time and situation to convert from gathering intelligence to wreaking havoc on the affected system.[6] This stacked ambiguity combined with the sensitivity of

hacking techniques to gain access to a system and remain inside for a prolonged period of time, with potentially destructive consequences.").

4 *See, e.g.*, William J. Lynn III, *Defending a New Domain: The Pentagon's Cyberstrategy*, FOREIGN AFFS. 97 (Sep. 2010), https://www.foreignaffairs.com/articles/united-states/2010-09-01/defending-new-domain (last visited July 19, 2023); Herbert Lin, 'Cyber Risk Across the U.S. Nuclear Enterprise' (2021) 4 *Tex. Nat'l Sec. Rev.* 107; Michael Riley, *What Happens When Russian Hackers Come for the Electrical Grid*, BLOOMBERG NEWS (Jan. 26, 2022), https://www.bloomberg.com/news/features/2022-01-26/what-happens-when-russian-hackers-cyberattack-the-u-s-electric-power-grid (last visited July 19, 2023); Danny Yadron, *Iranian Hackers Infiltrated New York Dam in 2013*, WALL ST. J. (Dec. 20, 2015), https://www.wsj.com/articles/iranian-hackers-infiltrated-new-york-dam-in-2013-1450662559 (last visited July 19, 2023).

5 Raymond Pompon, *Attacking Air-Gap-Segregated Computers*, F5 LABS (Sep. 5, 2018), https://www.f5.com/labs/articles/cisotociso/attacking-air-gap-segregated-computers (last visited July 19, 2023).

6 Paul Kraus, *Will AI Malware Change the Game?*, SECURITY (Mar. 5, 2021), https://www.securitymagazine.com/articles/94757-will-ai-malware-change-the-game (last visited July 19, 2023). (Artificial intelligence in malware is currently employed to avoid detection, but will certainly be adapted to other uses in the future).

certain systems creates the potential for aggression that was simply not contemplated as the international legal system developed.

The second gray-zone activity to be addressed here is using cyber capabilities to disrupt, but not damage, non-critical civilian systems.[7] In addition to those listed above, examples of such civilian systems are web conferencing services, financial institutions, and entertainment streaming services. Using kinetic capabilities to disrupt such systems – for example by severing communications cables or physically attacking banks or server farms – would meet the traditional definition of aggression, and the application of international law in those cases is well-established. By contrast, a state-sponsored cyber operation could disrupt the same systems with malware programmed to make them unavailable or unusable at unpredictable and inconvenient times, for unknown periods of time, without actually damaging or destroying the systems. As soon as the aggressive state's goals are met, it could return the affected systems to normal operations. The effects of these operations are considered "temporary," so they may be considered less important, but such effects can be long-term and devastating to affected individuals, and they can play a significant role in advancing a state's strategic interests.

The examples above, currently falling into a much-exploited "gray zone," could be better deterred if states accepted that they were crimes of aggression under the Rome Statute. Under Article 8 *bis*(2), the crime of aggression requires a use of armed force in an "act of aggression which, by its character, gravity and scale, constitutes a manifest violation of the Charter of the United Nations."

Of course nothing is as simple as it seems. There is even a question of whether cyber activities could ever constitute "armed force," but that question is beyond the scope of this short essay. Here, we will assume that aggressive state-sponsored cyber actions meet this requirement, and focus on which of such cyber activities constitute a manifest violation of the Charter based on their character, gravity, and scale.

As noted above, states have been quite hesitant to discuss cyberspace operations in an official context. That reluctance extends to both discussions of offensive cyber operations they may have undertaken, as well as

7 *See, e.g.*, Colleen M. Newbill, 'Defining Critical Infrastructure for a Global Application' (2019) 26 *Ind. J. Glob. Legal Stud.* 761 (Here I use the term "non-critical" to distinguish systems from those necessary to sustain life, such as systems directly providing food, water, medical care, etc. I consciously avoided using the U.S. (or any other state's) overbroad definitions of "critical infrastructure").

fully open discussions of incidents where they might find their systems victimized by malicious cyber activities of other states. The reasons for states' recalcitrance in the area include protecting intelligence sources and methods, avoiding further exploitation of vulnerable systems, and the desire to maintain their own operational prerogatives. However justifiable, this lack of a meaningful official dialogue about state cyber operations has left the field open for individuals and organizations to control the conversation.[8] Fortunately, a clear-eyed assessment of the application of international law in the cyber context is provided in Tallinn Manual 2.0 on the International Law Applicable to Cyber Operations (Tallinn Manual 2.0).[9]

4 Efforts at More Clarity

Rule 68 in Tallinn Manual 2.0 notes the applicability of U.N. Charter Article 2(4) to cyber operations. It goes on to explain the straightforward application of the rule in situations involving kinetic (i.e., physical) effects resulting from aggressive cyber activities. The manual suggests that under some circumstances cyber activities below the kinetic threshold might violate Article 2(4), but does not argue that there is unambiguous law on the matter. Instead, Tallinn Manual 2.0 sets out a complex, eight-part test to determine whether a particular cyber operation is a use of force.[10] The test is perfectly reasonable, but the very notion that such a test is needed weighs heavily against any argument that such incidents are "manifest" violations of the Charter.

---

8 GLOB. COMM'N ON THE STABILITY OF CYBERSPACE, https://web.archive.org/web/20220224014116/https://cyberstability.org/ (last visited July 20, 2023); Kurt John, *Critical Infrastructure Security and a Case for Optimism in 2022*, SIEMANS (Jan. 28, 2022), https://www.siemens.com/us/en/company/press/siemens-stories/smart-infrastructure/critical-infrastructure-security-case-optimism-2022.html (last visited July 19, 2023); Joseph Guay and Lisa Rudnick, *What the Digital Geneva Convention Means for the Future of Humanitarian Action*, UNHCR: POL'Y LAB (Jun. 25, 2017), https://www.unhcr.org/innovation/digital-geneva-convention-mean-future-humanitarian-action/ (last visited July 19, 2023).

9 Michael N. Schmitt (ed.), *Tallinn Manual 2.0 on the International Law Applicable to Cyber Operations* (Cambridge: Cambridge University Press, 2017), p. 564 [hereinafter Tallinn Manual 2.0].

10 *Id.* art. 69(9). (The test suggests such factors as severity, immediacy, and invasiveness are relevant in determining whether a particular cyber activity is a use of force).

One way to address the potential gap in international law coverage is to simply interpret the law in a creative way that eliminates the gap. In other words, to consider whether:

> [D]isruptive cyber operations also fall under the scope of U.N. Charter Article 2(4) if the disruption caused is significant enough to affect state security.[11]

Although scholars continue to make arguments that this might be the case, states are not acting in ways that suggest this is an accepted interpretation of the law.[12] Additionally, such a significant expansion of the definition of a key term of art is inconsistent with the normal development of international law, in that it would create a cyber-specific rule that would be more broadly restrictive than the rule used in cases of international aggression involving physical means.

Another line of effort in the legal community has been the notion that virtual activities alone can violate a state's sovereignty. So far, this argument has not been particularly successful. There is also the point that states have very different views on how cyberspace and sovereignty intersect. For example, even states with friendly relations can have wildly different views on how minor cyber effects on cyber infrastructure in a state's territory impacts sovereignty.[13] Discussions about sovereignty in this

---

11 Marco Roscini, *Cyber Operations and the Use of Force in International Law* (Oxford: Oxford University Press, 2014), p. 55.

12 Paul M. Nakasone, Commander, U.S. Cyber Command, *An Interview with Paul M. Nakasone* (2019), *in* 92 *Joint Force Q.* 4 ("In the last 10 years, our adversaries have been operating below the threshold of armed conflict, stealing our intellectual property, leveraging our personally identifiable information, or attempting to influence our elections – again, all below the threshold of armed conflict."). *See also* Lin, *supra* note 4; Riley, *supra* note 4; Yadron, *supra* note 4.

13 *See* Jeremy Wright, UK Att'y Gen., Speech at Chatham House: Cyber and International Law in the 21st Century (May 23, 2018), https://www.gov.uk/government/speeches/cyber-and-international-law-in-the-21st-century (last visited July 19, 2023); *see also* Michael N. Schmitt, *France's Major Statement on International Law and Cyber: An Assessment*, JUST SEC. (Sep. 16, 2019), https://www.justsecurity.org/66194/frances-major-statement-on-international-law-and-cyber-an-assessment/ (last visited July 19, 2023) ("France contends that a hostile cyber operation against French cyber infrastructure or one causing "effects" on French territory violates French sovereignty if it has been launched by another State's organs, persons or entities exercising elements of government authority, or by persons or entities operating under the instruction or direction or control of another State.").

context seem more academic than practical and, in any event, it's unclear whether a naked violation of sovereignty through the use of non-damaging cyber capabilities would be of sufficient character, gravity, and scale to violate the Rome Statute.

A potentially more useful – and certainly more creative – trail was blazed in 2021 by scholars with the Oxford Process on International Law Protections in Cyberspace.[14] They suggest that focusing solely on the effects of cyber operations ignores the possibility that even cyber operations lacking specific effects might violate Art 2(4) by constituting a threat to use force.[15]

The possibility of this approach is suggested at Tallinn Manual 2.0, Rule 70. After establishing that U.N. Charter Article 2(4) prohibits threats to use force, the rule notes:

> [T]here is no requirement that a specific 'demand' accompany the threat. The essence of a threat is that it must be communicative in nature, that is, it must be intended to be conveyed to the target State.[16]

The Oxford experts put forward that some cyber espionage operations could violate the threat of a use of force prohibition because:

> [1] The same activity necessary to conduct espionage against a target is necessary to use force against it, [2] many cyber operations have [...] much larger footprints than their authors may intend, [and 3] these operations regularly go beyond the acquisition or demonstration of a capacity to its actual deployment [inside a state's borders].[17]

---

14 *The Oxford Process on International Law Protections in Cyberspace*, OXFORD INST. ETHICS, L., ARMED CONFLICT, https://www.elac.ox.ac.uk/the-oxford-process/ (last visited July 19, 2023) (Convened by well-regarded international law experts Dapo Akande and Duncan Hollis, the Oxford Process is sponsored by Oxford's Institute for Ethics, Law, and Armed Conflict; the Government of Japan; and Microsoft. Because the vast majority of cyber infrastructure is privately owned, the involvement of the private sector is essential for ensuring success in establishing a normative framework. This is yet another unique challenge in applying international law to cyberspace).

15 Duncan B. Hollis and Tsvetelina van Benthem, *What Would Happen If States Started Looking at Cyber Operations as a "Threat" to Use Force?*, LAWFARE (Mar. 30, 2021), https://www.lawfaremedia.org/article/what-would-happen-if-states-started-looking-cyber-operations-threat-use-force (last visited July 19, 2023).

16 Tallinn Manual 2.0, *supra* note 9, Rule 70(4).

17 Hollis and van Benthem, *supra* note 15.

These three observations are addressed below.

Taken separately, none of the three arguments is sufficient to demonstrate a manifest violation of the prohibition against the threat to use force. Although there are often striking similarities between cyber capabilities used for espionage and those used for aggression, that similarity alone does not evidence violation of the Charter. Normally, it would be self-defeating for a cyber espionage operation to be disruptive or destructive, since it would then likely interrupt a potential source for acquiring further strategic information. Also, espionage operations are usually conducted with the intent that they not be discovered, which would fail the required "communicative in nature" portion of the test.[18]

The second observation, that a cyber operation might create a presence on an unintentionally large number of systems is similarly insufficient to demonstrate an intentional communication of a threat. In addition, it requires a rather ambitious leap of logic to use an unintentional effect as proof of intent to communicate a threat.

Even the third observation, that deploying malicious, potentially destructive code in another state's territory constitutes a threat to use force is perilously close to the so far unsuccessful suggestion that states consider such presence alone to be an act of aggression. The New York Times reported that the U.S. has engaged in malware prepositioning operations, which would suggest the U.S. doesn't consider the activity to be unlawful.[19] Russia reportedly went a step farther in Ukraine, actually taking down a power grid for a time, but refraining from engaging in the kind of destructive attack that would have been possible, perhaps with the intent to send a message.[20]

---

18 François Dubuisson and Agatha Verdebout, *Espionage in International Law*, OXFORD BIBLIOGRAPHIES (Sep. 25, 2018), https://www.oxfordbibliographies.com/display/document/obo-9780199796953/obo-9780199796953-0173.xml (last visited July 19, 2023) ("International espionage consists of the access, on behalf of a state, to information that is held by another state and considered as confidential or strategic, in the military, security, or economic field."). (Although the definition doesn't require it, espionage is ordinarily thought to be carried out secretly).

19 David E. Sanger and Nicole Perlroth, *U.S. Escalates Online Attacks on Russia's Power Grid*, N.Y. TIMES (Jun. 15, 2019), https://www.nytimes.com/2019/06/15/us/politics/trump-cyber-russia-grid.html (last visited July 19, 2023); David E. Sanger and Mark Mazzetti, *U.S. Had Cyberattack Plan if Iran Nuclear Dispute Led to Conflict*, N.Y. TIMES (Feb. 16, 2016), https://www.nytimes.com/2016/02/17/world/middleeast/us-had-cyberattack-planned-if-iran-nuclear-negotiations-failed.html (last visited July 19, 2023).

20 Kim Zetter, *Inside the Cunning, Unprecedented Hack of Ukraine's Power Grid*, WIRED (Mar. 3, 2016), https://www.wired.com/2016/03/inside-cunning-unprecedented-hack-uk

The strongest case can be made by combining all three factors in a single case. In other words, if a state implants potentially destructive code on an important system in another state, and the aggressor state intends that the targeted state discover the implanted capability and understand that there is a threat associated with the presence of the malware, it might be enough to constitute a clear violation of the Charter's prohibition of the threat to use force in violation of the Rome Statute. This could be the case even if the malware is or could be used for espionage, if the malware has a destructive capability.

5 The Attribution Problem

At this point, states don't appear to be ready to go that far, however. Even if states agreed the law is sufficient to establish a case that prepositioned malware could constitute a threat to use force, building a factual case would require dealing with a constantly looming issue in the cyber arena – attribution.

Discussions of law and cyber activities inevitably raise questions about attribution. Even if certain cyber activities constitute unlawful aggression as argued here, the International Criminal Court (ICC) would be left to determine what level of certainty would be required to attribute an unlawful cyber activity to a state. As a matter of course, cyber operators obfuscate their operations, routing activities through any number of states while using various systems that may be commercially leased or accessed without the owner's consent – but are almost certainly not obtained by the sponsoring state openly.

Given how cyber operations are conducted, even with near perfect information, it can be difficult to establish state responsibility. Knowing the location and identity of networks and systems used to launch or facilitate malicious activities is only part of the case; the critical step is the necessity of determining the intent, identity, and sponsorship of those putting the systems to work. And unfortunately, analyzing responsibility for operations with near perfect information is rarely an option. Sifting through network

raines-power-grid/ (last visited July 19, 2023). (One expert quoted in the article interpreted Russia's actions as, "We want to be seen, and we want to send you a message." The alleged Russian activity took place in the context of the continuing armed conflict with Ukraine over disputed territory, so its relevance here is by analogy to state actions outside armed conflict).

traffic, intelligence reports, intercepted communications, technical “tells,” clues contained in computer code, etc. requires time and highly-skilled personnel to arrive at the most basic conclusions.[21] Even when states have the resources and willingness to commit to such a difficult undertaking, they have rarely been willing to speak openly about what they discover, fearing the disclosure of classified sources and methods of collecting intelligence. Even if state positions were to modify sufficiently to make it possible to apply the Rome Statute, the attribution issue must be addressed.

6 Conclusion

The spirited debate around the adoption of the crime of aggression amendment has generally focused on large-scale aggression – such as military invasion and occupation – where the issue is mostly the justification for the action. This essay has focused rather on the activity itself, especially on whether strategic cyber operations that might have no direct physical effects could possibly have the character, gravity, and scale to constitute a manifest violation of the U.N. Charter. The likelihood of actual prosecution is another issue entirely. Still, just defining these offenses rationally under international law would be a huge step forward.

The Rome Statute has relevance in the cyber arena, but like much (or all) of international law, merely saying it applies to cyber operations is only the first step. The devil is in the details, and determining precisely how it applies will be the key to making progress toward a more stable and predictable international system. So far, states seem more serious about conducting operations in cyberspace than they are about limiting them. That fact, coupled with the ever-present challenge of cyber attribution, is likely to prevent prosecution of disruptive cyber operations at the ICC.

21 Office of the Director of National Intelligence, A Guide to Cyber Attribution (Sep. 14, 2018), https://dl.icdst.org/pdfs/files3/db004a6f55f96c056a23fc4efc6a23ac.pdf (last visited July 19, 2023).

CHAPTER 28

Cyber Operations, Cyberwarfare, and the Crime of Aggression

Oona A. Hathaway

1 Introduction

This essay will focus on one of the four crimes in the Rome Statute: the crime of aggression. This crime, and whether it should be included in the Rome Statute, has of course been the subject of intense debate and discussion. This essay puts that debate to one side to focus on the question of whether the crime of aggression – whatever one may think of it – applies to cyber operations or cyberwarfare and under what conditions.

2 Does the Crime of Aggression Apply to Cyber Operations?

An initial question is whether the crime of aggression applies to cyber operations at all. Article 8 *bis*(1) defines a "crime of aggression" to include:

> [T]he planning, preparation, initiation or execution, by a person in a position effectively to exercise control over or to direct the political or military action of a State, of an act of aggression which, by its character, gravity and scale, constitutes a manifest violation of the Charter of the United Nations.[1]

Nothing in this definition limits the crime to a particular set of weapons or tools. Article 8 *bis*(2) goes on to define an "act of aggression" as:

> [T]he use of armed force by a State against the sovereignty, territorial integrity or political independence of another State, or in any other manner inconsistent with the Charter of the United Nations.[2]

1 International Criminal Court, Rome Statute of the International Criminal Court, art. 8 *bis* (1), U.N. Doc. A/CONF.183/9 (July 17, 1998) [hereinafter Rome Statute].

2 *Id.* at art. 8 *bis* (2).

 | DOI:10.1163/9789004686755_035

It then includes a list of acts that "regardless of a declaration of war" qualify as an act of aggression.

This presents two questions: First, can a cyber operation constitute a manifest violation of the Charter of the United Nations ? Second, is the list of actions that qualify as an "act of aggression" exhaustive or merely illustrative?

On the first question – whether a cyber operation can constitute a manifest violation of the Charter of the United Nations – the answer is clearly yes. When the possibility of aggressive cyber incidents first emerged, there was an initial debate over whether international law applied to cyber operations. Some scholars thought that it did not. Those who took what is sometimes referred to as an "instrument-based approach," argued that:

> [A] cyber-attack alone will almost never constitute an armed attack for purposes of Article 51 'because it lacks the physical characteristics traditionally associated with military coercion' – in other words, because it generally does not use traditional military weapons.[3]

That view, however, has largely given way to the view that, though the technology is relatively new and certainly post-dates the Charter, the U.N. Charter nonetheless can be applied to cyber incidents.[4]

States affirmed this conclusion in the 2013 and 2015 Reports of the Group of Governmental Experts on Developments in the Field of Information and Telecommunications in the Context of International Security. They concluded that states are obligated to follow their U.N. Charter obligations in their use of information and communications technologies, including cyber operations.[5] The 2018 "Paris Call for Trust and Security in Cyberspace,"

3 Oona A. Hathaway, et al., 'The Law of Cyber-Attack' (2012) 100 *Calif. L. Rev.* 817, 823 (citing Duncan B. Hollis, 'Why States Need an International Law for Information Operations' (2007) 11 *Lewis & Clark L. Rev.* 1023, 1042). *See also* Legality of the Threat or Use of Nuclear Weapons, Advisory Opinion, 1996 I.C.J. 226, ¶ 39 (Jul. 8) (Article 2(4) applies to "any use of force, regardless of the weapons employed").

4 *See, e.g.*, Hathaway et al., *supra* note 3; Michael N. Schmitt (ed.), *Tallinn Manual 2.0 on the International Law Applicable to Cyber Operations* (Cambridge: Cambridge University Press, 2017) [hereinafter Tallinn Manual 2.0].

5 *See, e.g.*, G.A., 70th sess., Note by the Secretary-General, Group of Governmental Experts on Developments in the Field of Information and Telecommunications in the Context of International Security, p. 12, U.N. Doc. A/70/174 (Jul. 22, 2015), https://documents-dds-ny.un.org/doc/UNDOC/GEN/N15/228/35/PDF/N1522835.pdf?OpenElement (last visited July 19, 2023) ("The 2013 report stated that international law, and in particular the Charter of the United Nations, is applicable and is essential to maintaining peace and stability and

signed by a number of states and private organizations and actors, similarly affirmed that international law applies to cyber operations:

> We also reaffirm that international law, including the United Nations Charter in its entirety, international humanitarian law and customary international law is applicable to the use of information and communications technologies (ICT) by States.

It continued:

> We reaffirm that international law, together with the voluntary norms of responsible state behavior during peacetime and associated confidence and capacity-building measures developed within the United Nations, is the foundation for international peace and security in cyberspace.[6]

Hence the clear consensus is that cyber operations are governed by international law, including the prohibition on the use of force in the United Nations Charter.

On the second question – is the list of actions that qualify as an "act of aggression" in the Rome Charter exhaustive or illustrative? – there remains some disagreement, but the better view is that it is illustrative. The Council of Advisers' Report on the Application of the Rome Statute of the International Criminal Court to Cyberwarfare, convened by the Permanent Mission of Liechtenstein to the United Nations, considered this question directly.[7] It

---

promoting an open, secure, stable, accessible and peaceful ICT [Information and communications technologies] environment. Pursuant to its mandate, the present Group considered how international law applies to the use of ICTs by States.").

6 The French Ministry for Europe and Foreign Affairs, Paris Call for Trust and Security in Cyberspace (Nov. 12, 2018), https://www.diplomatie.gouv.fr/IMG/pdf/paris_call_text_-_en_cle06f918.pdf (last visited July 20, 2023) (Even more recently, the U.N. Open-Ended Working Group stated that "States reaffirmed that norms do not replace or alter States' obligations or rights under international law, which are binding, but rather provide additional specific guidance on what constitutes responsible State behaviour in the use of ICTs. Norms do not seek to limit or prohibit action that is otherwise consistent with international law."); G.A., Open-Ended Working Grp. on Devs. in the Field of Info. and Telecomms. in the Context of Int'l Sec., Final Substantive Report, p. 5, U.N. Doc. A/AC.290/2021/CRP.2 (Mar. 10, 2021).

7 Permanent Mission of Liechtenstein to the United Nations, The Council of Advisers' Report on the Application of the Rome Statute of the International Criminal Court to Cyberwarfare (Aug. 2021) [hereinafter Council of Advisers' Report], https://www.regierung.li/

concludes that there are two ways in which cyber operations could fit into the specific list of acts of aggression enumerated in Article 8 *bis*. First, the list is non-exhaustive; hence it allows the ICC to find other uses of armed force that constitute an act of aggression. Second, many of the acts in the list could be interpreted to apply to cyber operations. Hence it is clear that the crime of aggression as defined in the Rome Statute can apply to cyber operations.

3 When Does a Cyber Operation Constitute a "Crime of Aggression"?

Having established that a cyber operation can constitute a crime of aggression under the Rome Statute, the next question is to what extent and under what conditions does it do so.

There are two different scenarios in which this question may arise: First, it may arise where the cyber operation is a part of a broader aggressive war; second, it may arise where the cyber operation is a stand-alone event.

As to the first, it is clear that a cyber operation carried out in concert with a conventional kinetic act of aggression in manifest violation of the United Nations Charter can constitute a part of an overall crime of aggression. For example, the Russian government has used cyber operations in direct connection with its war of aggression against Ukraine that is currently under way.[8] Those cyber operations are part of the overall act of aggression and thus part of the overall crime of aggression that is being committed.

The much harder questions come in the second scenario, where a cyber operation takes place in the absence of conventional kinetic military force. It is important to note that to establish that a stand-alone cyber operation constitutes a crime of aggression under the Rome Statute, it is not sufficient that the cyber operation violate Article 2(4) of the U.N. Charter. The violation must be manifest, as justified by its "character, gravity, and scale."

---

files/medienarchiv/The-Council-of-Advisers-Report-on-the-Application-of-the-Rome-Statute-of-the-International-Criminal-Court-to-Cyberwarfare.pdf (last visited July 19, 2023) (I was one of the advisers who was consulted in the preparation of the report).

8 *Ukraine Computers Hit by Data-Wiping Software as Russia Launched Invasion*, REUTERS (Jan. 24, 2022), https://www.reuters.com/world/europe/ukrainian-government-foreign-ministry-parliament-websites-down-2022-02-23/ (last visited July 19, 2023).

This is a very high threshold to meet. Indeed, to date, there is disagreement as to whether any stand-alone cyber operation has constituted a "use of force" in violation of Article 2(4), much less a manifest violation. Nearly or perhaps all cyber operations to date have been what are referred to as "below the threshold" operations – meaning they fall below the Article 2(4) use of force threshold.

The test most commonly applied to assess whether a cyber operation is an illegal use of force is to look at its effects. As my coauthors and I explained in 2012:

> [W]e conclude that the best test of when a cyber-attack is properly considered cyber-warfare is whether the attack results in physical destruction – sometimes called a 'kinetic effect' – comparable to a conventional attack.[9]

For a cyber incident to be a use of force in violation of Article 2(4), it must cause a tangible physical effect – for example, causing something to explode or a dam to open above a populated area.[10] It may also do so through an incident where the immediate and direct effect is loss of life or serious physical injury – for instance shutting down air control systems when airplanes are in flight, causing fatal accidents as a result.

As already noted, there remains significant debate about whether any cyber incident to date constitutes an act of cyber war. Thomas Rid, in his 2013 book, Cyber War Will Not Take Place, argues that "So far there is no known act of cyber 'war,' when war is properly defined."[11] The 2017 Tallinn Manual 2.0 asserts that the use of the Stuxnet malware on Iranian nuclear facilities – causing centrifuges to malfunction, in the process destroying 984 uranium enriching centrifuges, one fifth of Iran's total centrifuges reportedly

---

9 Hathaway et al., *supra* note 3, at 841 (2012).

10 *See, e.g.*, Paul C. Ney, Jr., Gen. Couns., Dept. of Def., Remarks at U.S. Cyber Command Legal Conference (Mar. 2, 2020), https://www.defense.gov/News/Speeches/Speech/Article/2099378/dod-general-counsel-remarks-at-us-cyber-command-legal-conference/ (last visited July 19, 2023); Harold Hongju Koh, U.S. Dept. of State, Legal Adviser, Speech at U.S. Cyber Command Inter-Agency Legal Conference (Sep. 18, 2012), *in Harold Koh on International Law in Cyberspace*, OPINIOJURIS (Sep. 19, 2012), http://opiniojuris.org/2012/09/19/harold-koh-on-international-law-in-cyberspace/ (last visited July 19, 2023).

11 Thomas Rid, *Cyber War Will Not Take Place* (New York: Oxford University Press, 2013), p. 10.

by the U.S. and Israel[12] – was a use of force.[13] This is in some tension, however, with its conclusion that, "To date, no international armed conflict has been publicly characterized as having been solely precipitated in cyberspace."[14]

What is clear is that a cyber operation that causes an effect comparable to a conventional kinetic weapon could constitute a "use of force" in violation of Article 2(4) of the U.N. Charter and could even constitute a manifest violation, if of sufficient "character, gravity, and scale." Thankfully, no violation has yet occurred that might meet this stringent test. In part as a result, exactly what a "manifest" violation of the U.N. Charter means in the context of cyber operations has not yet been established.

Illustrating the current lack of consensus, Members of the Council of Advisers on the Application of the Rome Statute to Cyberwarfare reached different conclusions about what would constitute a "manifest" violation.[15] Some advisers, including myself, took the position that only cyber operations resulting in loss of, or injury to, human life would reach the level of a "manifest" violation. Others maintained that cyber operations with large-scale physical destruction might also reach the level of a manifest violation. Others suggested loss of functionality or incapacitation, without physical destruction, could even be sufficient. Suffice it to say that there are, as of this writing, significant differences among experts on the matter. There is agreement, however, that cyber operations with mere economic effects would not be sufficient to constitute a crime of aggression.[16] There is agreement, as well, that it is important to be cautious about an expansive interpretation of what constitutes a cyber operation in violation of Article 2(4), because doing so could open the door to actions in self defense under Article 51 of the U.N. Charter – actions that need not be limited to the cyber realm.

---

12 William J. Broad, John Markoff and David E. Sanger, *Israeli Test on Worm Called Crucial in Iran Nuclear Delay*, N.Y. TIMES (Jan. 15, 2011), https://www.nytimes.com/2011/01/16/world/middleeast/16stuxnet.html (last visited July 19, 2023).

13 Tallinn Manual 2.0, *supra* note 4, at 342 (The consulted experts were "divided as to whether the damage [inflicted by Stuxnet] sufficed to meet the armed criterion." *Id.* at 384).

14 *Id.* at 384.

15 Council of Advisers' Report, *supra* note 7, at 13–14.

16 *Id.* at 14.

4 Conclusion

There is significant agreement about core principles when it comes to application of the Rome Statute's crime of aggression to cyber operations: International law prohibiting the use of force applies in the cyber context, and cyber operations can constitute a crime of aggression. Whether a particular cyber operation constitutes a crime of aggression must be determined by examining its effects – whether the operation has an effect comparable to a conventional attack that would itself constitute a "manifest" violation of the U.N. Charter's prohibition on use of force. While there remains disagreement about precisely what stand-alone cyber operations would be sufficient to meet this stringent test, the next several years will likely bring greater clarity, as the world inevitably confronts increasingly destructive cyber operations.

CHAPTER 29

When Cyber Operations Constitute War Crimes Under the Rome Statute

Marco Roscini

1 Introduction

The use of cyber technologies as a new means to commit, instigate, or facilitate crimes under the ICC's jurisdiction has so far received little attention in international criminal law scholarship. Even the Tallinn Manual 2.0 on the International Law Applicable to Cyber Operations, published by a group of experts in 2017, devotes only two rules (out of 154) to cyber international criminality.[1] This essay explores when cyber operations can constitute war crimes under the ICC's jurisdiction. This can occur when:

1. They have been committed in the context of and in association with an armed conflict, kinetic or otherwise;
2. They involve the elements of the war crimes listed in Article 8 of the Rome Statute;
3. They have been committed on the territory of a state party or by a national of a state party; and
4. The case involving them is sufficiently grave.

The next sections address these points in turn.

2 The Cyber Operation Must Be Conducted in the Context of and in Association with an Armed Conflict

There obviously is no "war crime" if there is no "war." Contemporary international humanitarian law (IHL), however, has dropped the use of this expression in favor of the more objective "armed conflict," the existence of which depends on the factual occurrence of armed violence and not on the

1 Michael N. Schmitt (ed.), *Tallinn Manual 2.0 on the International Law Applicable to Cyber Operations* (Cambridge: Cambridge University Press, 2017), rules 84, 85 [hereinafter Tallinn Manual] (Rules 84 and 85 are respectively titled "Individual criminal responsibility for war crimes" and "Criminal responsibility of commanders and superiors").

 | DOI:10.1163/9789004686755_036

intention of the belligerents (animus bellandi). IHL treaties do not provide a definition of "armed conflict" but according to the International Criminal Tribunal for the former Yugoslavia:

> [A]n armed conflict exists whenever there is a resort to armed force between States or protracted armed violence between governmental authorities and organized armed groups or between such groups within a State.[2]

There is now broad consensus that this definition reflects customary international law. An (international) armed conflict also occurs in

> [A]ll cases of partial or total occupation of the territory of a High Contracting Party, even if the said occupation meets with no armed resistance.[3]

Cyber operations can be employed during an existing traditional international armed conflict as "force multipliers." An illustration is the 2008 armed conflict between Georgia and the Russian Federation, during which Georgia's governmental and media websites were taken off-line or defaced during the initial phases of the conflict, allegedly by Russian hackers, thus affecting Georgia's ability to communicate and possibly also the operability of its armed forces.[4] Russia has also been accused of conducting cyber operations against Ukraine since 2014.[5] In neither case, however, has Russia's responsibility been conclusively established: indeed, the anonymity that characterizes cyberspace is the main obstacle to the application of IHL.

Cyber operations can trigger an armed conflict themselves when they involve the use of cyber means or methods of warfare in support of a

2 Prosecutor v. Dusko Tadić, Case No. IT-94-1, Decision on the Defence Motion for Interlocutory Appeal on Jurisdiction, ¶ 70 (Int'l Crim. Trib. for the Former Yugoslavia AC, Oct. 2, 1995).

3 Geneva Convention for the Amelioration of the Condition of the Wounded and Sick in Armed Forces in the Field, 6 U.S.T. 3114, 75 U.N.T.S. 31, art. 2 (adopted Aug. 12, 1949, entered into force Oct. 12, 1950).

4 Independent Fact-Finding Mission on the Conflict in Georgia, Report Vol. II, pp. 217–18 (Sep. 2009), [https://web.archive.org/web/20200802082113/https://www.mpil.de/files/pdf4/IIFFMCG_Volume_II1.pdf] (archived Aug. 2, 2020).

5 Marco Roscini, 'Cyber Operations as a Use of Force', in Nicholas Tsagourias and Russell Buchan (eds.), *Research Handbook on Cyberspace and International Law*, 2d ed., (Cheltanham, UK: Edward Elgar Publishing, 2021), pp. 296, 314.

belligerent to the detriment of another. Such use must result, or be reasonably likely to result, in military harm to the adversary, physical damage to property, loss of life or injury to persons, or significant disruption of critical infrastructures. If the cyber operations are conducted between states, international armed conflict breaks out, otherwise the conflict is of a non-international character. In the latter case, however, it is highly unlikely that a loose online collective like Anonymous will ever meet the organization requirement necessary for the existence of a non-international armed conflict (NIAC) under the Tadić definition of armed conflict and Article 8(2)(f) of the Rome Statute. Nothing precludes, however, that a "traditional" armed group can conduct cyber operations (followed or not by kinetic hostilities) capable of triggering a NIAC.

It is arguably only those cyber operations that exceed mere inconvenience and significantly disrupt the correct functioning of military or civilian critical infrastructures that can potentially qualify as resort to armed force/violence and thus initiate an armed conflict, as it is only in this case that the effects of disruption can be equated to those of destruction caused by kinetic armed force. Hence, even if it were demonstrated that Russia was behind the operations, the 2007 Distributed Denial of Service (DDoS) attacks on Estonia would not qualify as an international armed conflict between the two states: although they targeted critical infrastructures – banking and communications – no property damage or personal injury occurred and no serious disruption ensued. A different conclusion would likely be reached with regard to a cyber attack that takes down the national electrical grid for a prolonged time, given likely severe negative repercussions on the provision of medical services, transport, financial markets, and security.

The Elements of Crimes under Article 8 of the Rome Statute require that a war crime be committed in the context of and in association with an armed conflict. This nexus requirement distinguishes war crimes from domestic offenses committed during an armed conflict, although the distinction might not always be easy to make, especially in the cyber context.[6] Taking into account the relevant case law, it appears that a sufficient belligerent nexus exists if the conduct is committed when and where armed hostilities are taking place or, if it occurs at a time and place where no combat activities are occurring, it was "shaped or dependent upon the environment"

6 Guénaël Mettraux, 'Nexus with Armed Conflict', in Antonio Cassese (ed.), *The Oxford Companion to International Criminal Justice* (New York: Oxford University Press, 2009), p. 435.

of the armed conflict.[7] The Ntaganda Trial Chamber has suggested certain indicators in order to establish the existence of the nexus requirement for war crimes, including:

1. the status of the perpetrator and victim, and whether they had a role in the fighting;
2. whether the act may be said to serve the ultimate goal of a military campaign; and
3. whether the crime is committed as part of, or in the context of, the perpetrator's official duties.[8]

From the above considerations it can be evinced that IHL applies to cyber operations, and potential war crimes can be committed in case of its violation, in the following cases:

1. when the cyber operations are conducted in the context of and in association with an existing kinetic international or non-international armed conflict;
2. if the exchange of cyber operations between states amounts in itself to "resort to armed force," i.e., it entails the use of cyber means or methods of warfare resulting or reasonably likely to result in military harm to the adversary, physical damage to property, loss of life or injury to persons, or significant disruption of critical infrastructures;
3. if an organized armed group conducts cyber operations amounting to protracted armed violence against a state or against another organized armed group;[9]
4. if the cyber operations are conducted by the occupying power in the exercise of its policing and governance powers in occupied territory, or are part of the mounted resistance by the local population to the exercise of such powers; or
5. if the cyber operations accompany the resumption or continuation of kinetic hostilities in occupied territory and are conducted in the context of and in association with them, or themselves amount to the initiation, resumption, or continuation of an international or non-international armed conflict in occupied territory.

---

7 Michael Cottier and Matthias Lippold, 'Article 8: War Crimes', in Kai Ambos (ed.), *Rome Statute of the International Criminal Court: Article-by-Article Commentary*, 4th ed., (München, Germany: Beck, 2022), pp. 317, 351–52.

8 Prosecutor v. Bosco Ntaganda, Case No. ICC-01/04-02/06-2359, Judgment, ¶ 732 (TC VI, Jul. 8, 2019).

9 Whether a NIAC falls under Common art. 3 of the Geneva Conventions or Protocol II Additional to the Geneva Conventions depends on their respective thresholds of applications.

3 The Cyber Operation Must Be Committed on the Territory or by a National of an ICC State Party

This requirement is prescribed by Article 12(2) of the Rome Statute.[10] The territorial jurisdictional link does not cause insurmountable problems in the cyber context: contrary to what it might seem at first sight, cyberspace is not a domain where state territorial sovereignty and jurisdiction do not apply. Indeed, it consists both of a physical and syntactic (or logical) layer: the former includes the physical infrastructure through which the data travel wired or wireless, including servers, routers, satellites, cables, wires, and the computers; while the latter includes the protocols that allow data to be routed and understood, as well as the software used and the data itself. The ICC, therefore, could exercise territorial jurisdiction when the attacked physical component is located on the territory of a state party.[11] Still debated, however, is whether all types of prejudicial effects are relevant to establish jurisdiction or only physical damage: the ICC case law will clarify this point.

With regard to the second jurisdictional link (nationality of the perpetrator), it could be challenging to obtain sufficient evidence to attribute the cyber operation to a specific individual, especially at the preliminary examination stage, as anonymity is one of the main characteristics of cyberspace. The internet, in particular, is a decentralized system where the communications protocol divides the sent data into several packets that take different unpredictable pathways to reach their destination before being reassembled. An IP address identifies the origin and the destination of the data: with the cooperation of the Internet Service Provider through which the system corresponding to the IP address is connected to the internet, it could be associated with a person, group, or state. The IP address, however, could be "spoofed," or the corresponding computer system may only be a "stepping stone" for an attacker located elsewhere.[12] Providing

10 International Criminal Court, Rome Statute of the International Criminal Court, art. 13 (b), U.N. Doc. A/CONF.183/9 (July 17, 1998) [hereinafter Rome Statute] (This requirement, however, does not apply when a situation is referred to the ICC Prosecutor by the U.N. Security Council acting under Chapter VII).

11 Anne-Laure Chaumette, 'International Criminal Responsibility of Individuals in Case of Cyberattacks' (2018) 18 *Int'l Crim. L. Rev.* 1, 23; *see also* Council of Europe, Explanatory Report to the Convention on Cybercrime, E.T.S. No. 185, ¶ 233 (Nov. 8, 2001), https://rm.coe.int/16800cce5b (last visited July 19, 2023).

12 Scott J. Shackelford and Richard B. Andres, 'State Responsibility for Cyber Attacks: Competing Standards for a Growing Problem' (2011) 42 *Geo. J. Int'l L.* 971, 982.

sufficient evidence of the identity of the hacker, then, might be a difficult task for the ICC Prosecutor and may require the cooperation of the states from which the cyber operation was conducted.

Having said that, at the preliminary stage the standard of proof is not "beyond reasonable doubt," a standard which is only necessary for convictions:[13] it suffices that there is a "reasonable basis to proceed," as there is still no accused to protect and the Prosecutor acts only on the basis of publicly available information.[14] The evaluation of admissibility, however, is stricter at the post-investigation stage and lack of sufficient evidence might be a significant obstacle to the identification and prosecution of those involved in cyber war crimes. Importantly, in 2013, the Office of the Prosecutor hired an expert in digital forensics for its Scientific Response Unit to improve its ability to collect and analyze digital evidence.[15]

4 The Cyber Operation Must Involve the Elements of the ICC War Crimes

In spite of the fact that, by 1998, states had already started to address cyber criminality, cyber issues were completely ignored during the negotiations of the crimes to be included in the Rome Statute. Conduct in cyberspace, however, might fall under the jurisdiction of the Court either because it constitutes a new means to commit a crime already incorporated in the Statute, or because it instigates or facilitates the commission of such crime.[16] If cyber crimes were considered new crimes and not new means to commit existing ones, on the other hand, their investigation or prosecution by the ICC would be barred by the *nullum crimen sine lege* principle incorporated in Article 22 of the Statute.

Of the war crimes contained in Article 8 of the Rome Statute, it is mainly those related to targeting, rather than those concerning mistreatment, that are relevant for cyber operations. Only cyber operations amounting to "attacks" as defined in Article 49(1) of the 1977 Protocol I additional to the 1949 Geneva Conventions on the Protection of Victims of War ("acts of violence

13 Rome Statute, *supra* note 10, at Article 66(3).

14 *Id.* at Article 53(1).

15 UC Berkeley HRC, Digital Fingerprints: Using Electronic Evidence to Advance Prosecutions at the International Criminal Court, p. 5 (Feb. 2014), https://www.law.berkeley.edu/files/HRC/Digital_fingerprints_interior_cover2.pdf (last visited July 19, 2023).

16 Rome Statute, *supra* note 10, Article 25(3).

against the adversary, whether in offence or in defense") are the object of the law of targeting and of the corresponding war crimes. When does a cyber operation amount to an "attack"? There is broad agreement that cyber operations that foreseeably result in physical damage to property or persons qualify as "acts of violence": cyber operations are able to produce damaging physical consequences in the analog world by corrupting the operating systems of physical infrastructures such as Supervisory Control and Data Acquisition (SCADA) systems, which could result in the malfunction of such infrastructures and possible loss of life or destruction of property. An example is a belligerent's cyber attack against the adversary which shuts down the cooling system of a nuclear power reactor located in enemy territory, thus causing the release of radioactive substances that indiscriminately reach civilians.

On the other hand, it is controversial whether cyber operations which negatively affect the functionality of infrastructure without physically damaging them also constitute "acts of violence." It is submitted that the definition of "attack" under Article 49(1) of Additional Protocol I should be interpreted to take into account recent technological developments and that the concept of "violence" should be expanded to include not only material damage to objects, but also the loss of functionality of infrastructures without destruction. Indeed, the dependency of modern societies on computers, computer systems, and networks has made it possible to cause significant harm through non-destructive means. After all, if the use of graphite bombs, which spread a cloud of extremely fine carbon filaments over electrical components, thus causing a short-circuit and a disruption of the electrical supply, would undoubtedly be considered an "attack" even though it does not cause more than nominal physical damage to the infrastructure, one cannot see why the same conclusion should not apply to the use of viruses and other malware that achieve a similar effect.

With the above in mind, the elements of the crimes contained in Article 8 of the Rome Statute can be transposed to the cyber context without significant obstacles. Cyber attacks intentionally aimed at causing civilian casualties or at destroying protected objects, or which are expected to result in "incidental loss of life or injury to civilians or damage to civilian objects or widespread, long-term and severe damage to the natural environment which would be clearly excessive in relation to the concrete and direct overall military advantage anticipated," would, for instance, amount to war crimes under Article 8(2)(b)(i), (ii) and (iv), and Article 8(2)(e)(i) of the Rome Statute. When the cyber operation aims to cause material damage to property or persons or incapacitation of infrastructures, the attacked "object" is not only, and not mainly, the information itself, but rather the persons, property, or infrastructure attacked through cyberspace. In the case of Stuxnet, for instance, the relevant "object" was not the Siemens software that operated the centrifuges at the Natanz uranium enrichment facility in Iran, but the centrifuges themselves. When a cyber operation aims solely at deleting or altering data stored in computer systems, however, the question arises whether such data are per se an "object" for the purpose of the definition of military objective contained in Article 52(2) of Additional Protocol I (and thus the application of the principle of distinction) if no physical damage or loss of functionality result from it. The problem should not be overestimated. If the cyber operation only causes the corruption, deletion, or alteration of data without consequences in the analog world, in most cases it will not be an "attack" in the sense indicated above and the law of targeting and the definition of "military objective" will therefore not apply, whether or not the data are an "object." The only exceptions may be cyber operations targeting data convertible into tangible objects, such as bank account records, so that if the data are destroyed so are the tangible objects; intellectual property that exists only online and that, if attacked and destroyed, cannot be recovered; or data that have an intrinsic value, as in the case of digital art.[17] It is only in such and similar exceptional situations that the cyber operation may be an attack even without consequences on physical infrastructures or persons.

Other problems related to the application of existing IHL rules in the cyber context are also overestimated. Take, for instance, the case of the application of the principle of proportionality in attacks. On the one hand, the potentially less damaging character of cyber operations may offer a more effective means to minimize incidental damage on civilians and civilian property. Cyber operations also present advantages for the attacking state, as they virtually entail no risk for its forces thanks to their remote character and the difficulties with regard to identification and attribution. On the other hand, the problem with calculating proportionality in the cyber context resides in the speed and covert nature of cyber attacks: it may be difficult for the parties to the conflict to readily establish their magnitude and consequences. Furthermore, as with biological weapons, some kinds of malware sent through cyberspace might spread uncontrollably because of the malware's characteristics and the interconnectivity of information systems.

---

17 Michael N. Schmitt, 'Cyber Operations and the Jus in Bello: Key Issues' (2011) 87 *International Law Studies* 89, 96.

All in all, however, meeting the proportionality criterion is essentially a technical issue: customized proportionate cyber reactions are possible if the software is written with this purpose in mind and the targeted system is sufficiently known. The code could, for instance, be designed in a way as to be activated only by the presence of certain characteristics, as in the case of Stuxnet. This requires a high degree of information on the targeted systems, which it may be possible to obtain through traditional intelligence collection and/or cyber espionage.

Another overestimated problem concerns the dual-use nature of most cyber infrastructures, namely the fact that they are, at the same time, used by civilians and the military. This is not unique to the cyber context. The fact that an object is also used for civilian purposes does not affect its qualification under the principle of distinction: if the two requirements provided in Article 52(2) of Additional Protocol I are present, the object is a military objective and is thus targetable, but the neutralization of its civilian component needs to be taken into account when assessing the incidental damage on civilians and civilian property under the principle of proportionality. What is prohibited is to attack the dual-use cyber infrastructure because of its civilian function or to attack a dual-use facility where the incidental civilian damage expected from the attack is excessive in relation to the anticipated concrete and direct military advantage.

Cyber technologies can also be used to instigate or facilitate the commission of crimes under the ICC jurisdiction. Accessory liability, for instance, could be engaged through an act preparatory of genocide like:

> [A] network intrusion to acquire the names of individuals registered as a certain race in a state census in order to engage in genocide.[18]

Individuals could also incite others to commit crimes by posting comments to that aim on blogs, Twitter, or other social media, as noted by the International Independent Fact-Finding Mission on Myanmar established by the U.N. Human Rights Council.[19] In September 2012, Azerbaijan also denounced cyber attacks conducted by a self-styled "Armenian Cyber Army" under the direction and control of Armenia that were:

18 Tallinn Manual 2.0, *supra* note 1, at 66.

19 G.A., 39th sess., Hum. Rts. Council, Report of the Independent International Fact-Finding Commission on Myanmar, U.N. Doc. A/HRC/39/64, ¶ 74 (Sep. 12, 2018).

> [A]imed at glorifying terrorists and insulting their victims, as well as at advocating, promoting and inciting ethnically and religiously motivated hatred, discrimination and violence.[20]

5 The Case Involving the Cyber Operation Must Be Sufficiently Grave

Article 17(1)(d) of the Rome Statute provides that a case is inadmissible, and must then be rejected, if it "is not of sufficient gravity to justify further action by the Court." Article 53 also provides that the Prosecutor may not initiate an investigation or, after an investigation, proceed to a prosecution if he considers the case inadmissible under Article 17. Leaving aside the fact that the persons who are likely to be the object of the investigation or prosecution should include those "most responsible" for the alleged crimes, an issue which faces the already mentioned evidentiary problems,[21] ICC case law has indicated that an evaluation of gravity must be made on the basis of both quantitative and qualitative factors, including, but not limited to, the scale, nature, manner of commission of the crimes, as well as their impact. These factors have been applied by the Office of the Prosecutor and the Pre-Trial Chamber (PTC) to assess the gravity of both situations and cases.

5.1 *Scale*

As already noted, cyber attacks can potentially cause significant physical damage to persons and objects. One could think of a cyber attack that shuts down an electrical power station in the middle of a harsh winter with consequent deaths among the civilian population due to the low temperatures, or a cyber attack that incapacitates computers controlling waterworks and dams, thus generating flooding of inhabited areas, or that disables the air traffic control system with consequent downing of civilian aircraft.[22] Scale includes, among others:

---

20 G.A., 66th sess., Letter dated September 6, 2012 from the Chargé d'affaires a.i. of the Permanent Mission of Azerbaijan to the United Nations addressed to the Secretary-General, U.N. Doc. A/66/897-S/2012/687, at 1 (Sep. 7, 2012).

21 On this aspect, *see* Marco Roscini, 'Gravity in the Statute of the International Criminal Court and Cyber Conduct That Constitutes, Instigates or Facilitates International Crimes' (2019) 30 *Crim. L.F.* 247, 256–59.

22 Some of these examples are contained in Jeremy Wright, UK Att'y Gen., Speech at Chatham House: Cyber and International Law in the 21st Century (May 23, 2018),

> [T]he number of direct and indirect victims, the extent of the damage caused by the crimes, in particular the bodily or psychological harm caused to the victims and their families, or their geographical or temporal spread (high intensity of the crimes over a brief period or low intensity of crimes over an extended period).[23]

Cyber operations might have a significant geographical spread but still result in limited physical damage. The malicious worm Stuxnet, for instance, spread to computers across several countries, including Iran, Indonesia, India, Azerbaijan, United States and Pakistan, but only caused physical damage to the Iranian uranium enrichment facility in Natanz while causing little harm to computers that did not meet certain specific characteristics. DDoS attacks also often involve millions of botnets across several countries hijacked by a botmaster, but they only result in temporary and reversible harm to the target by shutting down the servers and systems overflooded with requests: this might lead to the temporary interruption of services, but not physical damage to persons or property. It is unlikely, therefore, that, even assuming for the sake of argument that they amounted to crimes under the jurisdiction of the Court, operations like the 2007 DDoS attacks on Estonia, which disrupted banking and communications infrastructures in the Baltic country, would be grave enough from a scale point of view in spite of their geographical spread, unless they also result in loss of life or destruction of physical property.

5.2 *Nature*

It is not essential that a situation or case concerns an extensive number of casualties in order to justify investigation and prosecution.[24] Indeed, qualitative factors also need to be taken into account. Nature, in particular:

> [R]efers to the specific elements of each offence such as killings, rapes and other crimes involving sexual or gender violence and crimes

---

https://www.gov.uk/government/speeches/cyber-and-international-law-in-the-21st-century (last visited July 19, 2023).

23 Office of the Prosecutor, International Criminal Court, Policy Paper on Preliminary Examinations, ¶ 62 (Nov. 2013), [hereinafter Policy Paper] https://www.icc-cpi.int/sites/default/files/iccdocs/otp/OTP-Policy_Paper_Preliminary_Examinations_2013-ENG.pdf (last visited July 5, 2023).

24 Situation in the Republic of Burundi, Case No. ICC-01/17-9-Red, Decision Pursuant to Article 15 of the Rome Statute on the Authorization of an Investigation into the Situation in the Republic of Burundi, ¶ 184 (PTC III, Oct. 25, 2017).

> committed against children, persecution, or the imposition of conditions of life on a group calculated to bring about its destruction.[25]

This implies that certain crimes are by definition graver than others: for instance, national and international sources suggest that murder is considered the most serious crime from a sentencing point of view. Crimes of sexual violence and those involving torture and physical/psychological suffering are also considered serious, while – as recalled by the Trial Chamber[26] – crimes against property are considered comparably less serious.[27] The argument according to which there is a hierarchy among crimes within the jurisdiction of the ICC, and among war crimes in particular, is controversial, as it does not find an explicit basis in the letter of the Rome Statute. If it is accepted, however, cases involving cyber attacks that only cause damage to physical property (like the case of Stuxnet) might not be considered grave enough by their nature especially if compared to other cases involving killing or physical suffering.

5.3 *Manner of Commission*

Criteria to assess this factor include, inter alia:

> [T]he means employed to execute the crime, the degree of participation and intent of the perpetrator (if discernible at this stage), the extent to which the crimes were systematic or result from a plan or organized policy or otherwise resulted from the abuse of power or official capacity, and elements of particular cruelty, including the vulnerability of the victims, any motives involving discrimination, or the use of rape and sexual violence as a means of destroying groups.[28]

The means employed to execute the crimes, in our case, are malware and cyber infrastructures like computers and servers, which are unlikely to be an aggravating factor as such (differently, for instance, from the use of electrocution, machetes, and prohibited weapons). Intent might be difficult to discern in the cyber context, as malware can function unpredictably due to

25 Policy Paper, *supra* note 23, ¶ 63.

26 Prosecutor v. Ahmad al-Faqi al-Mahdi, Case No. ICC-01/12-01/15-171, Judgment and Sentence, ¶ 77 (TC VIII, Sep. 27, 2016).

27 *Id.*

28 Policy Paper, *supra* note 23, ¶ 64.

technical errors or insufficient knowledge of the targeted systems. Cyber operations, however, can be characterized by cruelty, for instance in the case of a cyber operation that changes the medical data of patients so that they receive the wrong, painful, or unnecessary treatment.

5.4 *Impact*

Impact can result from, among other things:

> [T]he sufferings endured by the victims and their increased vulnerability; the terror subsequently instilled, or the social, economic and environmental damage inflicted on the affected communities.[29]

Impact, then, has two aspects: the direct impact on the victims and the broader impact on the community. According to the PTC, the impact beyond the victims can be relevant in order to determine sufficient gravity, but its absence does not necessarily negate it.[30]

The inclusion of this factor in the assessment of gravity entails that even cases that result in a low number of victims on the basis of quantitative requirements might be grave enough from a qualitative perspective if they have a significant impact. For instance, cyber attacks resulting in the death of peacekeepers and humanitarian workers could have a substantial impact because of the importance of peacekeeping missions and of the deterrent effect they could have on them.[31] Cyber attacks committed to influence political elections might also have a significant impact on the community. In August 2017, for instance, the Kenyan opposition claimed that hackers had manipulated the results of the recent elections by breaking into the database of Kenya's electoral commission so to acquire data on the elector-

29 *Id.* ¶ 65; *see also* Situation in the Republic of Kenya, Case No. ICC-01/09-3, Request for Authorisation of an Investigation pursuant to Article 15, ¶¶ 56, 59 (PTC II, Nov. 26, 2009).

30 Situation on the Registered Vessels of the Union of the Comoros, the Hellenic Republic and the Kingdom of Cambodia, Case No. ICC-01/13-34, Decision on the Request of the Union of the Comoros to Review the Prosecutor's Decision Not to Initiate an Investigation, ¶ 47 (PTC I, Jul. 16, 2015).

31 *See* Prosecutor v. Bahr Idriss Abu Garda, Case No. ICC-02/05-02/09-243-Red, Decision on the Confirmation of Charges, ¶ 33 (PTC I, Feb. 8, 2010); Situation in Georgia, Case No. ICC-01/15-12, Decision on the Prosecutor's Request for Authorization of an Investigation, ¶ 55 (PTC I, Jan. 27, 2016).

ate and draft a targeted campaign strategy.[32] This is, as such, not an international crime, but at least twenty-four people were killed in the violence that erupted after the contested re-election of President Kenyatta. Certain cyber attacks might also have repercussions on a country's economy, as in the case of the 2007 DDoS attacks against Estonia. In general, cyber attacks that target national critical infrastructures, thus disrupting the provision of essential services to the society, will have more significant impact on the broader community than those on other infrastructures, especially if their effects are long-term. Not only social and economic damage should be considered in this context, however, but also damage to the natural environment: one could imagine, for instance, a cyber attack on a chemical plant intended to cause the release of hazardous substances into the ocean during an armed conflict.

---

32 Talita De Souza Dias, *Propaganda and Accountability for International Crimes in the Age of Social Media: Revisiting Accomplice Liability in International Criminal Law*, OPINIOJURIS (Apr. 4, 2018), http://opiniojuris.org/2018/04/04/propaganda-and-accountability-for-international-crimes-in-the-age-of-social-media-revisiting-accomplice-liability-in-international-criminal-law/ (last visited July 20, 2023).

CHAPTER 30

Amending the Rome Statute to Cover Cyberwarfare as Aggression

David Scheffer

1 Introduction

During the negotiations leading to the establishment of the International Criminal Court (ICC),[1] there was no discussion that I recall of cyber attacks as illegal conduct or prohibited weaponry under Article 8 (war crimes) of the Rome Statute governing the ICC.[2] Nor was cyberwarfare factored into the discussions concerning the crime of aggression, either during the 1990s or thereafter in the talks leading up to and including the Kampala Review Conference in 2010, when the definition and implementation procedures of the crime of aggression were codified as amendments to the Rome Statute, subject to ratification by Member States.[3] While in the lexicon of some pleading before the ICC, judges might be able to interpret the Rome Statute as covering cyber measures including cyber attacks and cyberwarfare, cyber measures are essentially a novel, uncodified, but hugely impactful means of assaulting governments, international institutions, business, and peoples and violating the sovereignty and territorial integrity of a country. Labeling serious injurious cyber measures as criminal, even at the domestic level, much less the international level, remains a work in progress.

Nonetheless, there is good reason to consider how the Rome Statute could be amended to prosecute cyber measures within at least the context of the crime of aggression. In 2017, I published a book chapter in The Crime of Ag-

1 International Criminal Court, Rome Statute of the International Criminal Court, U.N. Doc. A/CONF.183/9 (July 17, 1998) [hereinafter Rome Statute]; *see also* David Scheffer, *All the Missing Souls: A Personal History of the War Crimes Tribunals* (Princeton, N.J.: Princeton University Press, 2012), pp. 163–247.

2 Rome Statute, *supra* note 1, Article 8.

3 Assembly of States Parties, International Criminal Court, *The Crime of Aggression*, Doc. No. RC/Res.6 (Jun. 11, 2010); The amendments to the Rome Statute were circulated by the U.N. Secretary General in U.N. Secretary General, Depositary Notification, U.N. Doc. No. C.N.651.2010.TREATIES-8 (June 11, 2010).

 | DOI:10.1163/9789004686755_037

gression – A Commentary,[4] and an article in the Harvard International Law Journal,[5] wherein I proposed amendments to the Rome Statute to accommodate the rapidly rising threat of cyber measures. This essay draws from those publications and I refer the reader to all of the footnotes therein.

War during the twenty-first century often will not be fought conventionally between nations. Non-state actors like the Islamic State of Iraq and Syria (ISIS), Al Qaeda, Boko Haram, the Lord's Resistance Army, and al-Shabab, to name only a few past and present, will dominate the theaters of conflict and hostilities. Unfortunately, because it is grounded in General Assembly Resolution 3314 (XXIX) of December 14, 1974,[6] Article 8 *bis*(2) of the Rome Statute, defining an "act of aggression," is already exceptionally antiquated. The definition is relevant only for the actions of states (including "armed bands, groups, irregulars or mercenaries" sent by or acting on behalf of a state).

Article 8 *bis*(1) of the Rome Statute defines the "crime of aggression" in terms of what a person does in holding a "position effectively to exercise control over or to direct the political or military action of a State." There is no opportunity for the ICC to prosecute an individual for aggression when he acts in a leadership capacity to guide a non-state entity. The ICC Prosecutor thus is disarmed in connection with vast exercises of aggressive warfare waged by non-state entities across national boundaries. Internal aggression, which has been a favorite tactic of ISIS and other non-state actors determined (sometimes successfully) to seize territory within a state, also escapes the Article 8 *bis* definition.

The many manifestations of cyber measures have become a common staple of international affairs, and yet the entire concept is absent from the Article 8 *bis* definition. This is unsurprising given the fact that cyber measures, and particularly cyberwarfare, essentially did not exist in 1974 when the General Assembly defined acts of inter-state aggression. But its absence from Article 8 *bis* is a glaring omission in modern times and will cripple the ICC in how it will investigate aggression that may consist solely or largely of cyberwarfare tactics.

4 David Scheffer, 'Amending the Crime of Aggression under the Rome Statute', in Claus Kreβ and Stefan Barriga (eds.), *The Crime of Aggression: A Commentary* (Cambridge: Cambridge University Press, 2017).

5 David Scheffer, 'The Missing Pieces in Article 8 *bis* (Aggression) of the Rome Statute' (2017) 58 *Harv. Int'l L.J. Online* 83.

6 G.A. Res. 3314 (XXIX), Definition of Aggression (Dec. 14, 1974).

Cyberwarfare refers, at least by one definition, to:

> [T]he actions by a nation state or international organization to attack and attempt to damage another nation's computers or information networks through, for example, computer viruses or denial-of-service attacks.[7]

Another useful definition is as follows:

> Cyberwarfare is the word used to define the most aggressive form of attack by a foe or rival over the internet. It largely applies to actions by states and involves denying internet services to communities or countries, or, at worst, destroying critical infrastructure or industrial facilities.
>
> One other use of the term is to describe activity by a national army that might accompany its invasion of another country using conventional forces. Most major states would today be expected to use cyberwarfare to attack another country's computer infrastructure as part of an invasion or aggression.
>
> Cyberwarfare tends to be distinguished from other forms of hostile cyber activity. Cybercrime involves activities like raiding bank accounts. Cyber espionage describes the stealing of secrets. Cyberwarfare tends to describe an assault that affects the national security of the state that is victimized.[8]

The U.S. Department of Defense has identified cyber attacks as having the capacity to constitute acts of war.[9] Since 2010, the Pentagon has operated a

---

7 *Cyber Warfare*, RAND CORP., https://www.rand.org/topics/cyber-warfare.html (last visited July 20, 2023).

8 Cybersecurity Ventures, *Cyberwarfare.com Acquired by Cybersecurity Ventures*, EIN PRESSWIRE (Jan. 16, 2017), https://www.einnews.com/pr_news/362191170/cyberwarfare-com-acquired-by-cybersecurity-ventures (last visited July 20, 2023) (quoting the definition for "cyberwarfare" which used to be on the "Lexicon" section of the Financial Times' website, but is no longer available).

9 David E. Sanger and Elisabeth Bumiller, *Pentagon to Consider Cyberattacks Acts of War*, N.Y. TIMES (May 31, 2011), https://www.nytimes.com/2011/06/01/us/politics/01cyber.html> (last visited July 20, 2023); William J. Lynn III, *Defending a New Domain: The Pentagon's Cyberstrategy*, FOREIGN AFFS. 97 (Sep. 2010), https://www.foreignaffairs.com/articles/66552/william-j-lynn-iii/defending-a-new-domain (last visited July 20, 2023) ("As a doctrinal matter, the Pentagon has formally recognized cyberspace as a new domain of warfare.").

U.S. Cyber Command to confront cyber threats to the national security of the United States.[10] Other countries have also been focusing on cyber attacks and cyberwarfare as part of the modern threat environment.[11] There is not much of a leap from the cyber attacks and cyberwarfare described in most reports and scholarship about cyberspace to the reality of cyber aggression. The distinction of the latter is one of "character, gravity, and scale" that "constitutes a manifest violation of the Charter of the United Nations."[12]

The description of cyberwarfare, however, continues to evolve and, in my view, certainly involves actions by non-state actors such as ISIS, other terrorist organizations, paramilitaries, insurgencies, and even rogue corporate interests that might one day engage in such actions to disrupt part of a nation's infrastructure in a manner that imperils the national security or democratic integrity of that country.

Cyberwarfare typically would be executed with far greater secrecy than conventional uses of force. Thus, the challenge for the Prosecutor would be to identify the source of the cyber attack and then assess whether it meets the jurisdictional conditions for designation as the crime of aggression. But, in many respects, that is the challenge in evaluating conventional acts of aggression already described in Article 8 *bis*(2) of the Statute, so this task should not be regarded as insurmountable. It is entirely plausible, indeed logical, to classify cyberwarfare as an act of aggression under some circumstances, particularly as cyber capabilities exponentially expand into the future. Ignoring the reality of cyber measures would be similar to ignoring the utility of tanks, aircraft bombers, and V2 rockets as major implements of aggression during the Second World War.

For example, if a state or a non-state entity were to use cyber measures to seriously undermine the democratic processes of a target state and significantly influence the outcome of elections, that action should not be immune from ICC investigation as an act of aggression. The same could be said of cyber

10 U.S. CYBER COMMAND, https://www.cybercom.mil/ (last visited July 20, 2023); *see also* U.S. Cyber Command, Achieve and Maintain Cyberspace Superiority: Command Vision for U.S. Cyber Command (Apr. 2018), https://www.cybercom.mil/Portals/56/Documents/USCYBERCOM%20Vision%20April%202018.pdf (last visited July 20, 2023)

("Military superiority in the air, land, sea, and space domains is critical to our ability to defend our interests and protect our values. Achieving superiority in the physical domains in no small part depends on superiority in cyberspace.").

11 Richard A. Clarke and Robert K. Knake, *Cyber War: The Next Threat to National Security and What to Do About It* (New York: Ecco, 2010); Newton Lee, *Counterterrorism and Cybersecurity: Total Information Awareness* (New York: Springer, 2013), pp. 77–118.

12 Rome Statute, *supra* note 1, Article 8 *bis*(1).

attacks that shut down a nation's power grid or disable vital communications or transportation networks or military capabilities. All of this is currently the subject of intense speculation, protective measures, and action by governments. One must recognize, however, that the United States and its allies reportedly use cyber measures to defend against major threats, including nuclear, from such adversaries as North Korea and Iran. The distinction between waging cyber aggression and engaging in cyber self-defense measures would rest upon the "character, gravity, and scale" that "constitutes a manifest violation of the Charter of the United Nations."[13] This would surely be a complex calculation for the ICC to adjudicate, but to ignore it would be to miss the elephant in the room.

2 Revising the Definition of the "Crime of Aggression"

Article 8 *bis*(1) of the Rome Statute defines the "crime of aggression" by relegating it only to acts of aggression that have been planned, prepared, initiated, or executed "by a person in a position effectively to exercise control over or to direct the political or military action of a State[.]" Adding offensive cyber measures to the acts of aggression, as proposed here, would require amending the text to include individuals who can exercise control over or direct cyber attacks. One would want to avoid the contention that a cyber attack is neither political nor military in character, and thus outside the realm of leadership culpability under Article 8 *bis*(1). Adding the possibility of a non-state entity committing an act of aggression, also proposed here, would require that the relevant leader of the non-state entity be subjected to the jurisdiction of the ICC. Thus, the text of Article 8 *bis*(1) should be revised to read as follows:

> For the purpose of this Statute, "crime of aggression" means the planning, preparation, initiation or execution, by a person in a position effectively to exercise control over or to direct the political, or military, or cyber action of a state or non-state entity, of an act of aggression which, by its character, gravity and scale, constitutes a manifest violation of the Charter of the United Nations.

Since the crime of aggression is so integrally tied to the definition of an act of aggression, the role of any non-state entity in the commission of an act of

13 *Id.*

aggression would be critical to establish and thus is addressed immediately below.

Article 8 *bis*(2) of the Rome Statute sets forth, in its preambular component, the umbrella definition of an "act of aggression." This is followed in seven subsections thereunder with a listing of explicit actions qualifying as acts of aggression. The entire wording is drawn from 1974 G.A. Resolution 3314. It is thus of limited relevance for certain modern developments in the use of force that would be understood to be acts of aggression as a matter of common sense, such as actions by non-state entities and cyber measures.

In approaching a revision of Article 8 *bis*(2), I am also mindful that two uses of military force and even of cyber measures actually should be preserved with much greater clarity than currently exists in the Rome Statute. Defensive or protective responses to cross-border transgressions aimed at territorial acquisition, and to the relentless commission of atrocity crimes against civilian populations related to such actions, remain critical options and grow in importance with every passing year. Carefully calibrated and proportional cyber counter-measures may also be legitimate acts of self-defense to a cyber attack. There are potential uses of military force or cyber measures undertaken for defensive purposes or to protect civilians at risk that should not be prohibited as a matter of criminal law under the Statute. Indeed, such uses should be explicitly shielded from liability under Article 8 *bis*(2).

The existing wording in Article 8 *bis*(2) of "in any other manner inconsistent with the Charter of the United Nations" may technically preserve the inherent right of self-defense under Article 51 of the Charter. However, modern challenges to state sovereignty from multiple threats, including international terrorism, resurgent empire-building, and the tactics of cyberwarfare, require a stronger acknowledgement of the right of self-defense than currently exists in Article 8 *bis*(2).

I propose revision of the preambular segment of Article 8 *bis*(2) of the Statute to read as follows:

> For the purpose of paragraph 1, 'act of aggression' means the use of armed force or cyber measures by a state or non-state entity against the sovereignty, territorial integrity or political independence of another state, or in any other manner inconsistent with the Charter of the United Nations, exclusive of acts that are in exercise of the right of self-defense under Article 51 of the Charter of the United Nations. Any of the following acts, regardless of a declaration of war, shall, in accordance with United Nations General Assembly Resolution 3314 (XXIX) of 14 December 1974 or part (h) hereunder, qualify as an act of aggression:

The reference to "part (h)" points to cyber measures as a new act of aggression added to the 1974 G.A. Resolution 3314 list of acts of aggression already set forth in Article 8 *bis*(2) of the Rome Statute. This is addressed below.

3 Adding Cyber Measures as an Act of Aggression

Adding cyber measures to the list of acts of aggression would be appropriate as the crime of aggression has been operationalized. The capacity for cyberwarfare already has arrived and is recognized by the military, governments, corporations, civil society, and scholars as a real threat to international peace and security. Cyber measures should be added to the acts of aggression listed in Article 8 *bis*(2) of the Statute. So new subsection (h) of Article 8 *bis*(2) would read as follows:

> (h) The use of cyber measures for an offensive purpose that significantly disrupts or degrades governmental, military, commercial, cultural, or media entities or other societal activities in another State.

The Prosecutor and judges of the ICC would have to determine whether the contextual "character, gravity and scale" requirements for an act of aggression and, by extension, of a crime of aggression are met. That tight-knit filter will leave only the most egregious cyber attacks across borders within the scrutiny of the ICC. Nonetheless, I have established, within the defining character of this act of aggression, a magnitude test of "significantly disrupts or degrades" so as to reinforce the presumably narrow category of cyber measures that would constitute an act of aggression for the purposes of the Rome Statute. The fact that the General Assembly did not foresee this type of aggression in 1974 should not prevent the states parties to the Rome Statute from recognizing the reality of the threat today; cyber measures that are used for offensive purposes to inflict significant damage on another state's public or private infrastructure should be subject to criminal prosecution before the ICC.

PART 7

Non-Western Law at the ICC: What Is Its Place?

Introduction to Part 7

The following question was featured on www.ICCForum.com from July 2022 through December 2022:

To what extent has the ICC under-represented non-Western laws, principles, rules, procedures, practices, or traditions in its legal structure and system?

The ICC has faced criticism for under-representation of non-Western legal laws, principles, rules, procedures, practices, or traditions in its legal structure and system. To what extent is this criticism justified? How could the organs of the Court address this criticism? To what extent might non-Western principles, rules, procedures, practices, or traditions be incorporated into the substantive, procedural, or evidentiary law or practice of the Court?

Rome Statute Article 21(1) prescribes the Court's applicable law, which includes:

> (a) "In the first place, the Statute, Elements of Crimes and its Rules of Procedure and Evidence;
> (b) In the second place, where appropriate, applicable treaties and the principles and rules of international law, including the established principles of the international law of armed conflict;
> (c) *Failing that, general principles of law derived by the Court from national laws of legal systems of the world including, as appropriate, the national laws of States that would normally exercise jurisdiction over the crime, provided that those principles are not inconsistent with this Statute and with international law and internationally recognized norms and standards.* (italics added)

Article 21(2) specifies that the "Court may apply principles and rules of law as interpreted in its previous decisions," and Article 21(3) provides, in relevant part:

> *The application and interpretation of law pursuant to this article must be consistent with internationally recognized human rights, and be without any adverse distinction founded on grounds such as gender,...age, race, colour, language, religion or belief, political or other opinion, national, ethnic or social origin, wealth, birth or other status.* (italics added)

 | DOI:10.1163/9789004686755_038

How should the Article 21(1)(c) proviso and Article 21(3) be applied? How broadly or narrowly should the conditions be construed? Where a non-Western legal system, code, provision, procedure, or practice makes an adverse distinction founded on impermissible grounds, could that law be applied by severing the adverse distinction, or should that law be disregarded entirely?

To what extent does "national laws of legal systems of the world" include traditional legal and quasi-legal principles, rules, and practices that might not be codified in national laws? To what extent should the ICC consider laws of regional legal systems, such as regional human rights courts or tribunals?

Under what conditions, if any, should the Prosecutor determine that a case is inadmissible under Article 17 because traditional, non-Western legal practices, laws, or procedures have been employed to address criminal behavior, thus satisfying the complementarity principle? Or because a regional legal system or a regional human rights system has addressed criminal behavior? Where traditional, non-Western legal practices, laws, or procedures have been employed to address criminal behavior, or where a regional system has done so, would it be appropriate for the Prosecutor to determine that an investigation or prosecution is not "in the interests of justice" within the meaning of Article 53? To what extent should non-Western legal norms or practices be used to assess whether a situation "is not of sufficient gravity to justify further action by the Court"?

What would be appropriate means by which the Office of the Prosecutor, Chambers, or the Registry could become more regularly and reliably informed of the national laws of legal systems of the world?

CHAPTER 31

The International Criminal Court, Islamic Legal Tradition, and the Arab World: Quo Vadis?

Mohamed Elewa Badar

1 Introduction

Almost twenty-five years after the conclusion of the Rome Statute, a groundbreaking international treaty which established the world's first permanent and (intended) universal International Criminal Court (ICC), the Court appears to have reached a quagmire, whereby its reach and jurisdiction is far from universal. The intended universal reach of the Court that was envisioned in 1998 has been undermined throughout the past quarter of a century by a singular operation of the Court and narrow interpretation of the Rome Statute that have placed Western international law principles and institutions on a pedestal, and largely neglected the alternative visions of law that exist in the world, particularly Islamic Law. The implication of this has been to alienate Islamic law countries from reach of the Court, notwithstanding that many of prosecutions that have been brought before the ICC have related to the Muslim world in one way or another. It is therefore critical that steps are taken to redirect the course towards a more inclusive, pluralistic Court, which acknowledges the legal traditions of the whole world, and not just those belonging to the West. In light of this, this essay seeks to provide some solutions for the Court, by illuminating the historical development of the Court and its place in the Muslim world, and exploring the points of contact and tension between international criminal law as it is traditionally conceived by Western international law institutions and Islamic law.

The Court is viewed as a Westernized adjudicator of international criminal law (ICL), which has alienated the East. This essay seeks to examine the extent to which the ICC has under-represented non-Western laws, traditions, principles, rules, and practices in its legal structure and system, and more importantly to propose solutions for the Court to address this issue. As Fraser has warned, "despite the salience of Islamic law for the ICC, recognition, engage-

 | DOI:10.1163/9789004686755_039

ment and understanding is only nascent."[1] This essay explores this issue in the specific context of the Islamic legal tradition across the Arab world. The majority of populations in Arab countries, apart from Lebanon, are Muslims, and their constitutions place Islamic – or Sharia – law at the heart of their legal and political administration. Thus, it is important to clarify that this essay refers only to Arab states, and not to all Muslim majority states in the Muslim world.

Arab states refer to those post-colonial societies whose present realities have been significantly influenced by the colonial experience. This necessarily underpins their view of the imperialistic structures that persist within international criminal law (ICL), which, as this essay demonstrates, is central to the tension that exists between the Westernized, or Eurocentric, conception of ICL that dominates international legal institutions, and Islamic law. The timely nature of this question cannot go unacknowledged, with many investigations under consideration by the ICC relating to Muslim-majority states, and the prominence of conflict in Islamic contexts.[2] It is time for an international court that is truly universal in its jurisdiction. More particularly, this essay addresses the extent to which Muslim majority states are skeptical of the ICC and its reliance on Western systems of justice, and the extent to which Islamic law aligns with the principles of the ICC and could be better incorporated into the ICC's jurisprudence.

As the next section of this essay outlines, the broader context in which Arab states exist underpins and explains their lack of engagement with ICL. This was apparent in the process of enacting the Rome Statute establishing the ICC, which highlighted the definitional discrepancies that exist between ICL and Islamic – or *Sharia* – law, particularly in the realm of international human rights law and the prohibition of torture, a *jus cogens* norm alongside the international crimes contained within the Rome Statute. This was exacerbated by the preclusion of reservations being made by signatory states to the Rome Statute, in order to avoid interpretations of the Statute that are inconsistent with Sharia being enforced upon those states that follow Sharia law.

The subsequent section explores the extant relationship between the Arab world and the ICC, and in particular highlights the sovereignty concerns

---

1 Julie A. Fraser, 'Exploring Legal Compatibilities and Pursuing Cultural Legitimacy: Islamic Law and the ICC', in Julie A. Fraser and Brianne McGonigle Leyh (eds.), *Intersections of Law and Culture at the International Criminal Court* (Edward Elgar, 2020), p. 379, https://doi.org/10.4337/9781839107306.00029; *see also* Mohamed Elewa Badar, 'Is There a Place for Islamic Law Within the Applicable Law of the International Criminal Court?', in Tallyn Gray (ed.), *Islam and International Criminal Law and Justice* (Brussels: Torkel Opsahl Academic EPublisher, 2018), p. 201.

2 Fraser, *supra* note 1, at 378.

raised by Arab states about the ICC, especially given the power afforded to the United Nations Security Council (S.C.) to refer and defer cases to the ICC. This power has operated unequally against Western states on one hand, and Muslim majority states on the other. That section also demonstrates the unequal operation of the ICC itself, through actions of the Office of the Prosecutor (OTP) and the abuse of the principle of complementarity by powerful Western states to avoid accountability for the commission of international crimes. This concern has again very recently resurfaced with allegations of extra-judicial killings by the British elite Special Air Services (SAS) in Afghanistan during joint British-American occupation. This section does, however, highlight a certain hope regarding the ruling on the Court's competence over Palestine.

The final section examines the way forward for the ICC, exploring the various points of tension and contact that exist between ICL and Islamic law and proposes solutions that the ICC could implement in order to move forward with a more inclusive development of ICL.

2 Islam, Arab States, and the Rome Statute

Despite Islamic Law (Sharia) being applied differently in Arab states, the compatibility of treaty law with Sharia has been one of the determining factors for Arab states when deciding whether to ratify a treaty or not. This is reflected in the practice of Arab states to make reservations – known as the Sharia reservations – to human rights treaties, by which they arguably intend to avoid any incompatibilities between the treaty provisions and Sharia rules and principles.[3] Therefore, it is reasonable to conclude that one of the reasons preventing most of the remaining Arab states from ratifying the Rome Statute is their persisting concern that the Rome Statute is prone to being implemented in a manner incompatible with Sharia.[4]

3 This is not to assert the validity of Sharia reservations with the object and purpose of human rights treaties. *See generally* Nora Salem, 'Sharia Reservations to Human Rights Treaties', in Rüdiger Wolfrum (ed.), *Max Planck Encyclopedia of International Law* (Oxford: Oxford University Press, 2020), https://opil.ouplaw.com/display/10.1093/law-epil/9780199231690/law-9780199231690-e2149.

4 *Cf.* Shaheen Sardar Ali and Satwant Kaur Heer, 'What is the Measure of "Universality"? Critical Reflections on "Islamic" Criminal Law and Muslim State Practice vis-à-vis the Rome Statute and the International Criminal Court', in Tallyn Gray (ed.), *Islam and International Criminal Law and Justice* (Brussels: Torkel Opsahl Academic EPublisher, 2018), p. 175.

Arab states expressed their concerns during the Rome Conference about specific provisions in the Statute and their incompatibility with Sharia. They expressed concern regarding the inclusion of forced pregnancy as a separate act constituting crimes against humanity. In the opinion of Arab states,[5] forced pregnancy was related to rape and does not warrant separate mentioning. They expressed fear that its inclusion would impact their national legislations regarding abortion.[6] To accommodate their concerns, paragraph 7(2)(f) was added to stipulate that the definition of forced pregnancy "shall not in any way be interpreted as affecting national laws relating to pregnancy." The revival of debates regarding the definition of torture as a crime against humanity suggests that Arab states were also concerned that the definition of torture in the Statute could be interpreted to include certain forms of punishments in Islamic law. Two alternatives were presented: the first was to exclude from the definition of torture "pain or suffering arising only from, inherent in or incidental to, lawful sanctions [in conformity with international law]"; the second alternative was to employ the definition of torture in Article 1 of the United Nations Convention Against Torture and Other Cruel, Inhuman or Degrading Treatment (Convention Against Torture) which excludes "pain or suffering arising only from, inherent in or incidental to, lawful sanctions" without qualifying the lawful sanctions as being in conformity with international law.[7] It was then accepted that article 7(2)(e) retains the language of the Convention against Torture.[8]

Furthermore, Arab states expressed their preference of allowing reservations to the Rome Statute.[9] Nevertheless, this proposal was rejected by

5 *See* U.N. Diplomatic Conference of Plenipotentiaries on the Establishment of an International Criminal Court, *Summary Records of the Plenary Meetings and of the Meetings of the Committee of the Whole*, U.N. Doc. A/CONF.183/13 (Vol. II), at 72 (Jul. 17, 1998) [hereinafter Summary Records] (Jordan was not among those Arab States).

6 *Id.* at 160 ¶ 63 (Comment of Libyan Arab Jamahiriya); *Id.* at 160 ¶ 66 (Comment of United Arab Emirates); *Id.* at 164 ¶¶ 30–33 (Comment of Egypt).

7 U.N. Diplomatic Conference of Plenipotentiaries on the Establishment of an International Criminal Court, *Report of the Preparatory Committee on the Establishment of an International Criminal Court*, U.N. Doc. A/CONF.183/2/Add.1, at 27 (Apr. 14, 1998) [hereinafter Preparatory Committee].

8 *See* Bureau of the Committee of the Whole, *Discussion Paper*, U.N. Doc. A/CONF.183/C.1/L.53, at 204 (Jul. 6, 1998).

9 *See* Preparatory Committee, *supra* note 7, at 27 (There were four alternatives for reservations. Most Arab States expressed preference for option four that suggests that no reservation clause should be inserted and that it should be left to the general rules of reservations in international law.); *see also* United Nations Diplomatic Conference of Plenipotentiaries on the Establishment of an International Criminal Court, *Summary Record of the 19th Meeting*

other states, and Article 120 was included in the Statute, stipulating that "no reservations may be made to this Statute." Arab states expressed concern about this and the Sudanese representative – speaking on behalf of the Arab Group – stated that "the right to express reservations should also have been granted. The removal of that right by Article 120 would be an obstacle to accession."[10] Although there was no explicit reference to Sharia, it is reasonable to conclude – based upon their practice – that Arab states are in favor of allowing reservations to avoid incompatible interpretations with Sharia.

Although there have been elaborated studies on the compatibility of Sharia and ICL,[11] those studies do not seem to constitute a strong catalyst for abolishing Arab states' concerns about the Rome Statute. One reason for that seems to be the functioning of the ICC itself, and its non-engagement with Islamic law.[12] Although the ICC could resort to Islamic law under Article 21(1)(c) of the Rome Statute,[13] the Court has not, to date, conducted a deep analysis of Islamic principles of criminal law, despite establishing its jurisdiction over situations in states whose national laws have been enacted on the basis of Islamic law.[14] Ignoring Islamic principles affects the Court's legitimacy by affirming the view that international criminal law is a "distinctly Western venture."[15] This lack of engagement with Islamic law has even driven several scholars to call for the establishment of a hybrid court

of the Committee of the Whole, U.N. Doc. A/CONF.183/C.1/SR.19, at 252 ¶ 10 (Jun. 29, 1998) [hereinafter 19th Meeting]; *Id.* at 256 ¶ 57 (Comments of Iraq); *Id.* at 254 ¶ 29 (Comments of Kuwait).

10 *See* United Nations Diplomatic Conference of Plenipotentiaries on the Establishment of an International Criminal Court, *Summary Record of the 9th Meeting of the Committee of the Whole*, U.N. Doc. A/CONF.183/C.1/SR.9, at 126–27 ¶ 78 (Jul. 17, 1998) (Comments of Sudan).

11 Mohamed Elewa Badar, 'Islamic Law (Shari'a) and the Jurisdiction of the International Criminal Court' (2011) 24 *Leiden J. Int'l L.* 411.

12 *See* Summary Records, *supra* note 5, at 102 ¶ 83 (Previously, during the Rome negotiations, Libya pointed out that "Western values and legal systems should not be the only source of international instruments. Other systems were followed by a large proportion of the world's population.").

13 Fraser, *supra* note 1, at 387.

14 Except for a reference to Islamic law in Situation in the Democratic Republic of the Congo, Doc. No. ICC-01/04-168, Judgment on the Prosecutor's Application for Extraordinary Review of Pre-Trial Chamber I's 31 March 2006 Decision Denying Leave to Appeal, ¶¶ 25–31 (AC, Jul. 2006).

15 John Reynolds and Sujith Xavier, 'The Dark Corners of the World: TWAIL and International Criminal Justice' (2016) 14 *J. Int'l Crim. Just.* 959, 962.

for the prosecution of members of the Islamic State for crimes committed in Iraq and Syria.[16]

The ICC's latest decision on the situation in Mali could amplify Arab and Muslim states' concerns. In that decision, the Pre-Trial Chamber upheld the Prosecutor's conclusion that the installation and implementation of Sharia law in Timbuktu proves the existence of an organizational policy to commit a widespread or systematic attack against a civilian population.[17] Not only this, but the Pre-Trial Chamber also accepted the Prosecutor's contention that applying different forms of Sharia punishments amounted to torture under Article 7(2)(e) of the Rome Statute. It explicitly stated that cultural relativism was rejected in international criminal law. The ramifications of this decision have been highlighted by the defense for Al Hassan, the latter stating that "the allegation that Sharia law constitutes a policy to commit an attack against a civilian population is problematic on many legal and evidential levels." It also pointed out that upholding the Prosecutor's contentions:

> [W]ould have catastrophic effects as concerns the potential universalization of the Rome Statute: clearly, States will not ratify the *Statute* if the mere fact that *Sharia* law is practiced in their territory renders them liable to be prosecuted for war crimes and crimes against humanity.[18]

Regarding the Court's interpretation of torture, it stated that pain or suffering arising from, inherent in or incidental to, lawful sanctions can only be excluded from the definition of torture when "in conformity with international law." Consequently, the Court considered that the different forms of punishments in Sharia law were not in conformity with international law and were thus considered acts of torture. The Court based its decision on recommendations and statements made by the Committee against Torture and other human rights bodies and legal scholars. However, the Court neither took

---

16 Sergey Sayapin, *A "Hybrid" Tribunal for Daesh?*, EJIL TALK (May 4, 2016), https://www.ejiltalk.org/a-hybrid-tribunal-for-daesh/ (last visited September 11, 2023).

17 On these points, among others, *see* Prosecutor v. Al Hassan Ag Abdoul Aziz Ag Mohamed Ag Mahmoud, Doc. No. ICC-01/12-01/18-394-Red, Submissions for the Confirmation of Charges, ¶ 82 (Jun. 4, 2019) [hereinafter June 4th Submission]; Prosecutor v. Al Hassan Ag Abdoul Aziz Ag Mohamed Ag Mahmoud, Doc. No. ICC-01/12-01/18, Defence's Final Submissions Regarding the Confirmation of Charges, ¶¶ 11–14 (Jul. 31, 2019) [hereinafter July 31st Submission].

18 *See* June 4th Submission, *supra* note 17, ¶ 208.

into consideration the preparatory works of the Article 7(2)(e) of the Rome Statute nor those of Article 1 of the Convention Against Torture. By referring to both, the Court would have recognized that there was no consensus reached among the states regarding the interpretation of the term "lawful sanctions" and thus states had accepted to resort to constructive ambiguity in that respect.

In the drafting history of the Convention Against Torture, a proposal was presented to exclude from the definition of torture "pain or suffering arising only from, inherent in or incidental to, lawful sanctions to the extent consistent with the Standard Minimum Rules for the Treatment of Prisoners."[19] However, Western states refused to refer to the "Standard Minimum Rules for the Treatment of Prisoners" as this would render the latter a binding instrument.[20] At the same time, those states expressed their concern that excluding lawful sanctions without any qualification would weaken the definition of torture and thus argued for the limitation of the exception only to lawful sanctions that are in conformity with international law.[21] Nevertheless, a compromise was reached among the negotiating states to delete any limitation to the lawful sanctions. This compromise was made to ensure the ratification of Arab and Muslim majority states applying Sharia punishments.[22] Nor did the Court examine whether there is any subsequent state practice establishing the agreement of the parties regarding the interpretation of the term "lawful sanctions."[23] By this, the Court decided to give supremacy to the

19 Commission on Human Rights, Swedish Draft International Convention against Torture and Other Cruel, Inhuman, or Degrading Treatment or Punishment, U.N. Doc. E/CN.4/1285, (Jan. 23, 1978), https://digitallibrary.un.org/record/556717/files/E_CN.4_1285-EN.pdf.

20 Commission on Human Rights, U.N. Doc. E/1978/34-E/CN.4/1292, Report of the Thirty-Fourth Session, 31 (Mar. 10, 1978), https://digitallibrary.un.org/record/220211/files/E_1978_34_E_CN.4_1292-EN.pdf. *See also* Gerrit Zach, 'Art. 1 Definition of Torture', in Manfred Nowak, Moritz Birk and Giuliana Monina (eds.) *The United Nations Convention against Torture and its Optional Protocol: A Commentary* (Oxford: Oxford University Press, 2020), ¶¶ 42–53.

21 Commission on Human Rights, U.N. Doc. E/CN.4/L.1470, Report of the Working Group on a Draft Convention against Torture and Other Cruel, Inhuman or Degrading Treatment or Punishment, ¶ 21 (Mar. 12, 1979), https://digitallibrary.un.org/record/6761/files/E_CN.4_L.1470-EN.pdf.

22 Herman Burgers and Hans Danelius (eds.), *Annotations on the Provisions of the Convention, in The United Nations Convention against Torture: A Handbook on the Convention against Torture and Other Cruel, Inhuman or Degrading Treatment or Punishment* (Norwell: Kluwer Academic Publishers, 1998), p. 119.

23 Vienna Convention on the Law of Treaties, art. 31(3)(b), *opened for signature* May 23, 1969, 1155 U.N.T.S. 331.

law *de lege ferenda* over the law *de lege lata*. Furthermore, the Court implicitly granted to the statements of the Committee against Torture and the other human rights bodies a binding character; a character long rejected by states. Such a flawed decision that fails to conduct a thorough examination of different state opinions and does not take into consideration non-Western traditions and cultures would further undermine the legitimacy of the ICC in the eyes of the Arab world. As Cherif Bassiouni has highlighted:

> ICL is proscriptive, whereas IHRL is prescriptive. In other words, ICL criminalizes, while IHRL does not. One of the consequences of this essential distinction is that ICL is at least theoretically bound by principles of legality, which requires its terminology to be more specific, whereas international human rights law, which is not bound by such a requirement, tends to be more general.[24]

3 An Overview of the Relationship between the Arab World and the ICC

As previously mentioned, the Arab states' role in the establishment of the ICC is generally recognized as a positive one.[25] Nonetheless, this has not guaranteed their accession to the Rome Statute. At the end of the Rome Conference, six Arab states, namely Libya, Iraq, Yemen, Qatar, Syria, and Sudan, joined the United States (U.S.) in opposition to the Statute.[26] By the time the Statute was opened for signature, only two Arab states ratified it, namely Jordan and Djibouti. Other Arab states followed, becoming signatories in 2000, yet Qatar, Libya, Lebanon, and Iraq neither signed nor ratified the Rome Statute at that

---

24 M. Cherif Bassiouni, *Crimes Against Humanity: Historical Evolution and Contemporary Application* (Cambridge: Cambridge University Press, 2014), pp. 208–09. This position was upheld by Mr. Al Hassan's defense team, *see* June 4th Submission, *supra* note 17; July 31st Submission, *supra* note 17.

25 *See* Hossam ElDeeb, The Ratification and Implementation of the Rome Statute of the International Criminal Court by the Arab States: Prospects and Challenges (Dec. 2015) (Ph.D. thesis, University of Brunel) (on file with the Brunel University Research Archive).

26 Michael P. Scharf, *Results of the Rome Conference for an International Criminal Court*, ASIL INSIGHTS (Aug. 11, 1998), https://www.asil.org/insights/volume/3/issue/10/results-rome-conference-international-criminal-court (last visited October 1, 2023).

date.[27] As of today, five Arab countries have ratified or acceded to the Rome Statute, namely Jordan, Djibouti, Tunisia, Palestine, and Comoros.

The current world legal order has developed from the Western legal systems of great European powers,[28] meaning most of the modern world is expected to rely on the oversight of Westernized institutions such as the United Nations (U.N.). Indeed, many of the "Great Powers" that sit as permanent members on the S.C. often do not feel obliged by the rules under the U.N. Charter and, as a result, use force under the cover of, for example, war against terrorism.[29] This alleged protective oversight, therefore, is rightly perceived by other nations as imperialistic – something that remains an obstacle for universal acceptance. Although the Rome Statute was compromised to accommodate some of the Arab states' concerns, sovereignty remains one of the main issues pulling them back from ratifying the Statute. Due to the role granted to the S.C. in referring and deferring situations to the ICC, Arab states feared that the ICC would be a political tool in the hands of Western countries to pursue their interests and infringe upon the sovereignty of Arab states.[30] So far, the only two situations referred to the ICC by the S.C. have been Sudan and Libya. Indeed, Gissel highlights that this could be seen to pull "the entire doctrine of equality before the law in a sphere which ought to be insulated from such extraneous influences."[31] These concerns have not diminished through the functioning of the ICC but, rather, have been buttressed. The ICC's engagement with Sudan meant other Arab states became involved, particularly with regard to Al Bashir's arrest warrant. Its issuance in 2009 spurred the Arab League's support for Sudan, which was propelled further when Jordan, a state party to the Rome Statute, failed to arrest the former Sudanese President during his attendance at the 28th Summit of the Arab League in Amman, in March 2017. In contrast to how the ICC handled South

---

27 *Status of Treaties: Rome Statute of the International Criminal Court*, UNITED NATIONS TREATY COLLECTION, https://treaties.un.org/Pages/ViewDetails.aspx?src=TREATY&mtdsg_no=XVIII-10&chapter=18&clang=_en (last visited Jul. 17, 2022).

28 Thilo Marauhn and Heinhard Steiger (eds.), *Universality and Continuity in International Law* (The Hague: Eleven Intl Pub, 2011), p. 18; Julie A. Fraser, 'A Seat at the Table: Islamic Law's Neglected Potential in Universalising International Humanitarian Law', in Norman Weiss and Andreas Zimmermann (eds.), *Human Rights and International Humanitarian Law: Challenges Ahead*, 225, 238.

29 Marauhn and Steiger, *supra* note 28, at 18.

30 ElDeeb, *supra* note 25, at 160-62.

31 Line Engo Gissel, 'Nomos and Narrative in International Criminal Justice: Creating the International Criminal Court' (2022) 20 *J. Int'l Crim. Just.* 117, 137.

Africa's failure to arrest, the ICC referred Jordan's inaction to the S.C. and the Assembly of States Parties.[32] Both Jordan and the League of Arab States contended that these referrals "constituted an abuse of discretion."[33] Further, the Court's differential treatment of Jordan from South Africa meant that the Court had not relied on the specific facts of the case but rather on "the situation of a different state party."[34] Instances such as these create the "ambivalence towards universal justice [that] defines the relationship between the Arab League and the [ICC, which is] perceived as a neo-colonial instrument of power."[35]

Not only did the indictment of the then Sudanese President receive opposition from the Arab Governments, public opinion in Arab states also opposed it. According to a survey, conducted by WorldPublicOpinion.org in seven Muslim majority and African states (namely Egypt, Turkey, Kenya, Nigeria, Pakistan, Iraq, and the Palestinian territories) regarding charging Al Bashir before the ICC, a majority disapproved the indictment: the Palestinian territories (70% with 25% approving) and Egypt (52%, with 47% approving). Iraqis were evenly divided (35% approved, 37% disapproved).[36] This adds to the extant negative public opinion generated by the trial of the former Iraqi President Saddam Hussein. Arab public opinion viewed the trial "as an American-backed enterprise intended to justify an unpopular war."[37] It is without doubt that public resentment strengthens the prevailing reluctance to engage with the institutional framework of ICL.

---

32 Prosecutor v. Omar Hassan Ahmad Al Bashir, Doc. No. ICC-02/05-01/09-309, Decision under Article 87(7) of the Rome Statute on the Non-Compliance by Jordan with the Request by the Court for the Arrest and Surrender o[f] Omar Al-Bashir (Dec. 11, 2017).

33 Prosecutor v. Omar Hassan Ahmad Al Bashir, Doc. No. ICC-02/05-01/09-367, The League of Arab States' Observations on the Hashemite Kingdom of Jordan's Appeal against the "Decision under Article 87(7) of the Rome Statute on the Non-compliance by Jordan with the Request by the Court for the Arrest and Surrender [of] Omar Al-Bashir", ¶ 37 (Jul. 16, 2018).

34 *Id.* at ¶ 44.

35 Annette Weber, FRIDE, Bridging the Gap Between Narrative and Practices: The Role of the Arab League in Darfur 16 (Mar. 2010), https://www.swp-berlin.org/publications/products/fachpublikationen/03._Arab_League_Weber1_ks.pdf (last visited October 3, 2023).

36 *Many Approve of ICC Indictment of Bashir: Poll of 7 Muslim and African Nations*, WORLDPUBLICOPINION.ORG (Jul. 16, 2009) https://worldpublicopinion.net/many-approve-of-icc-indictment-of-bashir-poll-of-7-muslim-and-african-nations/ (last visited October 15, 2023).

37 Shibley Telhami, *Arab Public Opinion and the Trial of Saddam Hussein*, BROOKINGS INST. (May 11, 2006), https://www.brookings.edu/articles/arab-public-opinion-and-the-trial-of-saddam-hussein/ (last visited October 15, 2023).

However, the Arab Spring in 2011 was thought to be a turning point in the Arab-ICC relationship.[38] After ousting President Ben-Ali, Tunisia's interim government ratified the Rome Statute.[39] Along the same lines, the Egyptian Ministry of Foreign Affairs pledged to ratify the Statute.[40] Morocco, on its part, included Article 23 in its constitution which criminalizes three core crimes of the Rome Statute (crimes against humanity, genocide, and war crimes).[41] Moreover, the ICC held its first regional conference in Qatar, sponsored by Qatar and the Arab League, a step recognized as a "a dramatic and impressive shift in the attitudes of the Arab world towards international criminal justice generally, and the International Criminal Court, in particular."[42] During the conference, the ICC launched a campaign, entitled "Calling Arab Lawyers," to encourage Arab counsels to participate in the Court's proceedings, highlighting the importance of language and culture in understanding the conflicts from which cases arise before the Court.[43]

Soon, it became recognized that the Arab Spring was not a strong enough catalyst for improving Arab engagement with the ICC. While there was thirst for accountability in the wake of the Arab Spring, this – as rightly highlighted by Frédéric Mégret and Nidal Nabil – is not the same as "questions of accountability that the international community has emphasized through its investment in international criminal law."[44] Furthermore, the functioning of the ICC

38 Mark Kersten, *The Arab World and the ICC: A New Chapter or Smoke and Mirrors?*, JUST. IN CONFLICT (May 30, 2011), https://justiceinconflict.org/2011/05/30/the-arab-world-and-the-icc-a-new-chapter-or-smoke-and-mirrors/ (last visited October 15, 2023); *see also* Maryam Jamshidi, 'The International Criminal Court and the Arab Spring: Overcoming Bias, Increasing Engagement', in Saul Takahashi (ed.) *Human Rights, Human Security, and State Security: The Intersection* (Praeger, 2014), p. 43.

39 *Tunisia Becomes First North African Nation to Join International Criminal Court*, UN NEWS (Jun. 24, 2011), https://news.un.org/en/story/2011/06/379632 (last visited October 14, 2023).

40 *Egypt: Important Commitment to Ratify Rome Statute: Meaningful Cooperation with the International Criminal Court Should Follow*, HUM. RTS. WATCH (Apr. 29, 2011), https://www.hrw.org/news/2011/04/29/egypt-important-commitment-ratify-rome-statute (last visited Oct. 14, 2023).

41 al-Dustūr [Constitution] Jul. 30, 2011, art. 23 (Morocco), translated in *Morocco's Constitution of 2011*, CONSTITUTE PROJECT, https://www.constituteproject.org/constitution/Morocco_2011.pdf.

42 Kersten, *supra* note 38.

43 International Criminal Court, 'ICC Launches Campaign to Encourage Arab Counsel to Practice Before the Court' (2011) 79 *ICC Weekly Update* 6, https://asp.icc-cpi.int/sites/asp/files/NR/rdonlyres/1534A997-44A5-41F6-85E1-FE6C95A44618/283383/Ed79Eng1.pdf.

44 Frédéric Mégret and Nidal Nabil Jurdi, 'The International Criminal Court, the "Arab Spring" and its Aftermath' (2016) *Diritti umani e diritto internazionale* 2.

both prior to the Arab Spring and afterwards seems to hold back the remaining Arab states from ratifying the Rome Statute. Although Egypt pledged to ratify the Statute, its political relations with Sudan have delayed this step.[45] Arab states also raised concern, during the Qatar Conference, about the ICC's delay in responding to Palestine's declaration to accede to the Court's jurisdiction over events taking place in the Occupied Palestinian Territories after July 1, 2002.[46] It took the ICC Prosecutor three years to decide that he was not competent to decide on the validity of Palestine's declaration.[47]

While reluctant to ratify accession to the ICC, Arab states did not reject the referral of the situation in Libya by means of Security Council Resolution 1970.[48] However, the NATO intervention in Libya and the killing of former President Mu'ammar Gaddafi revealed the instrumentalization of the ICC by Western states to pursue regime change.[49] After using the ICC "to frame the intervention in the name of justice and to marginalise and pressure Gaddafi,"[50] Western powers quickly abandoned the Court by tacitly supporting the right of the new government to try those responsible for the commission of grave crimes. Similarly, Arab states became more inclined to support domestic prosecutions rather than prosecutions at the ICC.[51] The Arab League explicitly supported Libya's quest to try Saif El Islam domestically.[52] Mauritania has surrendered El Senussi to Libya, refusing the ICC's repeated calls for

45 Mark Kersten, *Egypt to Join the ICC but Also Guarantee Bashir Immunity*, JUST. IN CONFLICT (Feb. 20, 2013), https://justiceinconflict.org/2013/02/20/egypt-to-join-the-icc-but-also-guarantee-bashir-immunity/ (last visited October 15, 2023).

46 Kersten, *supra* note 38.

47 Office of the Prosecutor, International Criminal Court, Situation in Palestine (Apr. 3, 2012), https://www.icc-cpi.int/sites/default/files/NR/rdonlyres/9B651B80-EC43-4945-BF5A-FAFF5F334B92/284387/SituationinPalestine030412ENG.pdf (last visited October 16, 2023).

48 *See* U.N. SCOR, 66th Sess., 6491st mtg. at 4, U.N. Doc. S/PV.6491 (Feb. 26, 2011) (Lebanon stated that voting in favor of the resolution was in line with the Arab Consensus).

49 Mark Kersten, 'Between Justice and Politics: The ICC's Intervention in Libya', in Christian De Vos, Sara Kendall and Carsten Stahn (eds.), *Contested Justice: The Politics and Practice of International Criminal Court Interventions* (Cambridge: Cambridge University Press, 2015), pp. 466-69.

50 *Id.* at 468.

51 *See* U.N. SCOR, 73d Sess., 8388th mtg. at 10-11, U.N. Doc. S/PV.8388 (Nov. 2, 2018) (See Kuwait's statement on the occasion of the ICC Prosecutor Fatou Bensouda's briefing on the situation in Libya where it stressed that Libya has the primary responsibility in prosecuting perpetrators of international crimes and that the international community shall assist it in that respect).

52 Prosecutor v. Saif Al-Islam Gaddafi, Doc. No. ICC-01/11-01/11-130-Red, Application on Behalf of the Government of Libya Pursuant to Article 19 of the ICC Statute (May 1, 2012).

his extradition.[53] The newly appointed ICC Prosecutor, Karim Khan, seems to have received little support during his first briefing on the situation in Libya to the Security Council, as Western states merely called upon the national authorities to secure the arrest and surrender of those wanted by the ICC.[54]

The instrumentalization of the ICC in the Libyan conflict was a mistake not to be repeated in the Syrian conflict. This has been reflected by the number of Arab states supporting a referral by the Security Council of the situation in Syria to the ICC. Although Saudi Arabia and the Arab Group presented a proposal, which later became a U.N. General Assembly Resolution, calling for the accountability of those responsible for the commission of international crimes and calling upon the S.C. to consider appropriate measures in that regard,[55] proposals at the S.C. for an actual referral were explicitly supported by only a few Arab States (namely Libya, Jordan, Qatar, UAE, and Saudi Arabia).[56]

The perception of the ICC as a neo-colonial Court seems to be reinforced by its decision regarding crimes committed by U.K. military forces in Iraq and its decision regarding the situation in Afghanistan. Although the OTP decided that there is reasonable basis to believe that crimes were committed by members of British forces against Iraqi civilians in detention, the OTP decided to close the preliminary examination into the situation in Iraq because the

53 Kevin Jon Heller, *Mauritania Extradites Al-Senussi to Libya*, OPINIO JURIS (Sep. 5, 2012), https://opiniojuris.org/2012/09/05/mauritania-extradites-al-senussi-to-libya/ (last visited October 16, 2023).

54 *See* Meeting Coverage, Security Council, International Criminal Court Prosecutor, Outlining Vision, Calls for New Era of Engagement with Security Council to End Atrocity Crimes in Libya, U.N. Doc SC/14710 (Nov. 23, 2021).

55 Nabil Abi Saab, *Arab League Draft Resolution on Syria in the General Assembly*, UN DRAFTS (Jul. 27, 2012), https://un-report.blogspot.com/2012/07/arab-league-draft-resolution-on-syria.html.

56 United Nations Security Council, Draft Resolution, U.N. Doc. S/2014/348 (May 22, 2014). In a proposal to refer the situation in 2013, only two states, Tunisia and Libya, explicitly supported it. *See* United Nations General Assembly, Security Council, U.N. Doc. A/67/694, S/2013/19, Letter Dated 14 January 2013 from the Chargé D'Affaires a.i. of the Permanent Mission of Switzerland to the United Nations Addressed to the Secretary-General (Jan. 16, 2013); Kristyan Benedict, *The Countries That Support Referring Syria to the International Criminal Court-and Some Absent "Friends"*, AMNESTY INT'L U.K. CAMPAIGNS BLOG (Sep. 20, 2013), https://www.amnesty.org.uk/blogs/campaigns/syria-icc-international-criminal-court (last visited October 15, 2023) (This remark was also made by a report issued by Amnesty International United Kingdom); *see also* Richard Dicker & Sarah Leah Whitson, *Letter to Egyptian Foreign Minister on Syria and the ICC*, HUM. RTS. WATCH (Jan. 13, 2013), https://www.hrw.org/news/2013/01/13/letter-egyptian-foreign-minister-syria-and-icc (last visited October 16, 2023) (urging him to support the referral to the ICC).

U.K. has been conducting its own investigations into allegations of crimes committed by its military forces. Despite having concerns about the comprehensiveness of those investigations, the OTP stated that there was no evidence to conclude that:

> [The] UK authorities have been unwilling genuinely to carry out relevant investigative inquiries and/or prosecutions (Article 17(1)(a)) or that decisions not to prosecute in specific cases resulted from unwillingness genuinely to prosecute (Article 17(1)(b)).[57]

This decision has spurred strong criticism and sustained Arab states' concerns that the principle of complementarity is applied so as to provide leeway for powerful states to avoid accountability for the commission of international crimes.[58]

Not only this, but the decision also paints a false picture of said crimes being prosecuted adequately at U.K. national courts. The worst part of the report in terms of narrative, however, is that it perpetuates falsehoods from the lead up to the invasion of Iraq. It describes the events in the following paragraph:

> After the January 1991 Gulf War, the Security Council adopted a resolution setting out ceasefire terms, including ending production of weapons of mass destruction and permitting inspection teams on the territory of Iraq. In September 2002, the US and UK argued that Iraq was in material breach of the relevant resolutions and was seeking to develop weapons of mass destruction. UN weapons inspectors stated they had not found any 'smoking gun' in their search for weapons of mass destruction but noted that this was 'no guarantee that prohibited stocks or activities could not exist at other sites, whether above ground, underground or in mobile units.' The US gathered a coalition of 48 countries,

---

57 *See* Office of the Prosecutor, International Criminal Court, Situation in Iraq/UK: Final Report (December 2020), https://www.icc-cpi.int/sites/default/files/itemsDocuments/201209-otp-final-report-iraq-uk-eng.pdf (last visited November 5, 2023) [hereinafter Iraq/U.K. Report].

58 *ICC Decision on UK Military in Iraq Rewards Obstructionism*, AMNESTY INT'L (Dec. 10, 2020), https://www.amnesty.org/en/latest/news/2020/12/icc-decision-on-uk-military-in-iraq-rewards-obstructionism/ (last visited October 15, 2020); *see also* Thomas Obel Hansen, *Complementarity (in)action in the UK?*, EJIL TALK (Dec. 7, 2018), https://www.ejiltalk.org/complementarity-inaction-in-the-uk/ (last visited October 16, 2023).

> including the UK, for the stated purpose of searching and destroying alleged weapons of mass destruction in Iraq.[59]

This misleading description implies that S.C. Resolution 699 of 1991 authorized the invasion and does not mention that the S.C. itself never endorsed this view, or that this has been a highly disputed question in international law. The cited inspectors' report detailed that no evidence of weapons of mass destruction (WMDs) had been found and that Iraqi authorities were cooperating with the inspectors, yet the above paragraph chooses to focus on a sentence of the report allowing for the hypothetical existence of WMDs.[60] Moreover, in a footnote, the report relies on The Assessment of the British Government on Iraq's Weapons of Mass Destruction, a document now known as the "dodgy dossier," a piece of pro-war propaganda that has long been discredited.

Furthermore, the OTP's Report labels the Iraqis who resisted the foreign occupation as "insurgents" throughout the document. As historian Craig Murray notes:

> The idea that the invaders were the respectable power and the locals were 'insurgents' may be the language of the British MOD and may be adopted by the Daily Mail, but it should not be the language of the International Criminal Court.[61]

This biased narrative further contributes to delegitimizing the ICC in the Arab world. Additionally, the U.S. would not allow the Iraqi government any attempt to become a state party to the Rome Statute because of the atrocities and numerous violations of international law, in particular the law of armed conflict, committed by its soldiers against the Iraqi civilians and those placed *hors de combat* during their invasion of Iraq in 2003 and its aftermath period, until their withdrawal in 2011. Furthermore, a number of cases, such as Abu

59 Iraq/U.K. Report, *supra* note 57, ¶ 36.

60 Hans Blix, *Notes for Briefing the Security Council*, UN.ORG (Jan. 9, 2003), https://www.un.org/depts/unmovic/bx9jan.htm (last visited October 15, 2023) (Hans Blix was Executive Chairman to UNMOVIC); *see also* United Nations Security Council, *Twelfth Quarterly Report of the Executive Chairman of the United Nations Monitoring, Verification and Inspection Commission in Accordance with Paragraph 12 of Security Council Resolution 1284*, U.N. Doc. S/2003/232, (Feb. 28, 2003).

61 Craig Murray, *The International Criminal Court: Now Simply Indefensible*, CRAIG MURRAY (Dec. 29, 2020), https://www.craigmurray.org.uk/archives/2020/12/the-international-criminal-court-now-simply-indefensible/ (last visited October 16, 2023).

Ghraib prison and the so called Nisour Square Massacre, were never subject to a transparent and impartial trial. This has enhanced the belief that the international community is paralyzed and silent towards such violations.

In addition to that, the Pre-Trial Chamber II (PTC) decision on the situation in Afghanistan raises many legitimacy concerns. In that decision, the PTC rejected the request of the OTP to open an investigation into the situation in Afghanistan because it would not "serve the interests of justice."[62] This decision was subject to criticism[63] and resulted in alarming calls for reform.[64] Refusing to open an investigation in Afghanistan that could have ended in investigating crimes committed by U.S. troops and the Central Intelligence Agency (CIA) was regarded as an act of succumbing to pressure from the Trump administration,[65] affirming Arab states' concerns that the ICC is only a court for the weak states and never a tool for achieving universal international justice. Cautious hope arose when the PTC decision was reversed by the Appeals Chamber.[66] However, the following sequence of events was not promising. The Government of Afghanistan – led by then-President Ashraf Ghani – was granted the request to defer the investigation to the Afghan Na-

62 Situation in the Islamic Republic of Afghanistan, Doc. No. ICC-02/17-33, Decision Pursuant to Article 15 of the Rome Statute on the Authorisation of an Investigation into the Situation in the Islamic Republic of Afghanistan (Apr. 12, 2019).

63 Christian De Vos, *No ICC Investigation in Afghanistan: A Bad Decision with Big Implications*, INT'L JUST. MONITOR (Apr. 15, 2019), https://www.ijmonitor.org/2019/04/no-icc-investigation-in-afghanistan-a-bad-decision-with-big-implications/ (last visited October 16, 2023).

64 Kai Ambos, *Interests of Justice? The ICC Urgently Needs Reforms*, EJIL TALK (Jun. 11, 2019), https://www.ejiltalk.org/interests-of-justice-the-icc-urgently-needs-reforms/ (last visited October 10, 2023); Todd F. Buchwald, *The International Criminal Court Decision on Afghanistan: Time to Start a New Conversation*, JUST SEC. (Apr. 13, 2019), https://www.justsecurity.org/63622/the-international-criminal-court-decision-on-afghanistan-time-to-start-a-new-conversation/ (last visited October 10, 2023).

65 Press Release, Amnesty International, Afghanistan: ICC Refuses to Authorize Investigation, Caving into USA Threats (Apr. 12, 2019), https://www.amnesty.org/en/latest/press-release/2019/04/afghanistan-icc-refuses-to-authorize-investigation-caving-into-usa-threats/ (last visited October 10, 2023); *ICC: Judges Reject Afghanistan Investigation*, HUM. RTS. WATCH (Apr. 12, 2019), https://www.hrw.org/news/2019/04/12/icc-judges-reject-afghanistan-investigation (last visited October 10, 2023).

66 Situation in the Islamic Republic of Afghanistan, Doc No. ICC-02/17-138 OA4, Judgment on the Appeal against the Decision on the Authorization of an Investigation into the Situation in the Islamic Republic of Afghanistan (AC, Mar. 5, 2020). On that decision, *see* Aldo Zammit Borda, *The Situation in Afghanistan, US Sanctions and the Historical Narratives Emerging From the ICC*, EJIL TALK (Jun. 24, 2020), https://www.ejiltalk.org/the-situation-in-afghanistan-us-sanctions-and-the-historical-narratives-emerging-from-the-icc/ (last visited October 16, 2023).

tional Authorities. Then, on September 27, 2021, the Prosecutor filed an application before the Pre-Trial Chamber seeking authorization to resume investigation in Afghanistan because "there is no longer the prospect of genuine and effective domestic investigations."[67] Nevertheless, he emphasized that his investigation will focus "on crimes allegedly committed by the Taliban and the Islamic State – Khorasan Province and to deprioritise other aspects of this investigation."[68] This implies that crimes committed by U.S. Troops and the CIA will be outside the scope of his investigation. This decision has been criticized.[69] The decision to deprioritize investigations against the U.S. troops was regarded as a "bow to political as well as resource pressure,"[70] and constitutes another decision that will contribute to delegitimizing the ICC in the eyes of the Arab world amid concerns about its double standards and its selectivity.

Concerns surrounding the ability of the ICC to investigate alleged crimes committed by U.K. troops in a Muslim majority state have recently resurfaced, with the revelations by investigative journalists at the BBC of extra-judicial killings committed against Afghan detainees by British soldiers, with apparent impunity, during the period of 2010 to 2013, when Afghanistan was under American-British occupation.[71] The reported failures of the British military to investigate and report such allegations goes to the very heart of Arab states' concerns over apparent inapplicability of ICL to Western, imperial powers. Indeed, in response to the allegations, the U.K. Ministry of Defense accused the journalists of jumping to "unjustified conclusions from allegations that have already been investigated" and indicate they would only investigate the

67 Statement, Karim A. A. Khan, ICC Prosecutor, Statement Following the Application for an Expedited Order Under Article 18(2) Seeking Authorisation to Resume Investigations in the Situation in Afghanistan (Sep. 27, 2021), https://www.icc-cpi.int/news/statement-prosecutor-international-criminal-court-karim-khan-qc-following-application (last visited October 16, 2023).

68 *Id.*

69 Kelebogile Zvobgo, *The ICC's Flawed Afghan Investigation: Why the Court Shouldn't Let America Off the Hook*, FOREIGN AFFS. (Nov. 3, 2021), https://www.foreignaffairs.com/articles/afghanistan/2021-11-03/iccs-flawed-afghan-investigation (last visited October 15, 2023); Jennifer Trahan, *Prosecutor De-Prioritizes ICC Investigation of US Torture Program*, OPINIO JURIS (Oct. 1, 2021), https://opiniojuris.org/2021/10/01/prosecutor-de-prioritizes-icc-investigation-of-us-torture-program/ (last visited October 15, 2023).

70 *Afghanistan: ICC Prosecutor's Statement on Afghanistan Jeopardises His Office's Legitimacy and Future*, AMNESTY INT'L (Oct. 5, 2021), https://hrij.amnesty.nl/afghanistan-icc-prosecutors-statement-on-afghanistan-jeopardises-his-offices-legitimacy-and-future/ (last visited October 16, 2023).

71 Hannah O'Grady & Joel Gunter, *SAS Unit Repeatedly Killed Afghan Detainees, BBC Finds*, BBC NEWS (Jul. 12, 2022), https://www.bbc.com/news/uk-62083196 (last visited October 10, 2023).

allegations if new evidence comes to light.[72] This is worrying, given the track record of impunity for U.K. actors in the Iraq and Afghan conflicts, and will likely exacerbate the distrust harbored by Muslim majority states and Arab countries towards the ICL framework and institutions.

Nevertheless, the Court's very recent decision affirming its jurisdiction over crimes committed in Palestine raises hope that there could be light at the end of the tunnel in the relationship between the Arab states and the ICC.[73] The Arab League has welcomed – in Resolution 8594 adopted by the Council of the Arab League at the ministerial level at its extraordinary session held in Cairo on February 8, 2021[74] – the ICC decision regarding Palestine. It has also emphasized in its 155th Extraordinary Session held in Cairo on March 3, 2021, that any peace plan inconsistent with the terms of reference for the Middle East peace process will be rejected and cannot succeed; and called for rejection of any political or financial pressure brought to bear on the Palestinian people or its leadership in an attempt to impose unjust solutions to the question of Palestine.[75] The ICC's continued engagement in the situation in Palestine will certainly contribute to enhancing the legitimacy of the Court in the Arab world, if it is able to overcome pressure exerted from powerful states.[76]

---

72 *Id.*

73 Situation in the State of Palestine, Doc. No. ICC-01/18-143, Decision on the "Prosecution Request pursuant to Article 19(3) for a Ruling on the Court's Territorial Jurisdiction in Palestine" (PTC I, Feb. 5, 2021).

74 *See* United Nations General Assembly, Security Council, U.N. Doc. A/75/761, S/2021/137, Letter Dated 12 February 2021 from the Permanent Representative of Egypt to the United Nations Addressed to the Secretary-General (Feb. 19, 2021).

75 *Resolutions adopted by the League of Arab States at its 155th Extraordinary Session held in Cairo on 3 March 2021*, UNITED NATIONS: THE QUESTION OF PALESTINE (Apr. 3, 2013), https://www.un.org/unispal/document/resolutions-adopted-by-the-league-of-arab-states-at-its-155th-extraordinary-session-held-in-cairo-on-3-march-2021/ (last visited October 16, 2023).

76 *See* Press Statement, Antony J. Blinken, U.S. Secretary of State, The United States Opposes the ICC Investigation into the Palestinian Situation, U.S. DEPT. OF STATE (Mar. 3, 2021), https://www.state.gov/the-united-states-opposes-the-icc-investigation-into-the-palestinian-situation/. Several Western states have explicitly opposed the ICC decision on Palestine. *See* Balkees Jarrah, *The United Kingdom's Brazen Assault on ICC Independence: Prime Minister's Letter at Odds with Rule of Law*, HUM. RTS. WATCH (Apr. 16, 2021), https://www.hrw.org/news/2021/04/16/united-kingdoms-brazen-assault-icc-independence (last visited October 16, 2023) (British Prime Minister Boris Johnson issued a letter strongly opposing the ICC decision.); Press Statement, Marise Payne, Australian Minister for Foreign Affairs, ICC Pre-Trial Chamber Decision on Jurisdiction in Relation to the 'Situation in Palestine' (Feb. 6, 2021), https://www.foreignminister.gov.au/minister/marise-payne/media-release/icc-pre-trial-chamber-decision-jurisdic

Before concluding this overview, it must be mentioned that the failure on the part of the Arab states to engage with the institutional framework of ICL does not mean that the connection is lost between the Arab world and the normative framework of this field of international law. In various forms, national legislations of Arab states have incorporated international crimes. According to the International Committee of the Red Cross's Eighth Periodic Report on the implementation of international humanitarian law at the level of Arab States (2015–2018), Arab states' incorporation of international crimes into national legislation could be grouped in four categories. Incorporation has either taken the form of stand-alone legislation on international crimes,[77] or the form of generally integrating some aspects of those crimes into military codes, or incorporation has taken the form of generally including some international crimes in penal codes, or it has taken the form of a legislation establishing a special domestic tribunal, or fact finding commission, related to international crimes.[78] Proposals for stand-alone legislation for international crimes is still pending in Egypt,[79] Kuwait,[80] Morocco,[81] Tunisia, and Palestine.[82] In that context, it is noteworthy that adopting those pieces of legislation has been incentivized by the importance of evading the jurisdiction of the ICC.[83]

4 Overcoming the Residual Barriers to Universal Acceptance of ICL

This essay has covered a substantial part of the history of international law, including its origins, its overall development in the modern world, and, more

77 Union Des Comoros, President de l'Union, Décret No 12-022/PR, Loi n°11-022/AU (Dec. 13, 2011) (implementing the Rome Statute), available online (Fr.) (As the report mentions only UAE and Bahrain, I would like to add Comoros).

78 *See* International Committee for the Red Cross, Eighth Periodic Report on the Implementation of International Humanitarian Law at the Level of Arab States 2015–2018, 26–27 (2019), https://www.icrc.org/en/document/eighth-periodic-report-implementation-international-humanitarian-law-level-arab-states-2015 [hereinafter Eighth Periodic Report].

79 On the pending Egyptian draft, *see* ElDeeb, *supra* note 25, at 304–08.

80 Eighth Periodic Report, *supra* note 78, at 26.

81 *See Morocco and the Rome Statute*, PARLIAMENTARIANS FOR GLOBAL ACTION, https://www.pgaction.org/ilhr/rome-statute/morocco.html (last visited Jul. 17, 2022).

82 Eighth Periodic Report, *supra* note 78, at 26.

83 *See* Muhannad Al-Ghandour and Ahmed Al-Khattab, The Law of Serious International Crimes Between UAE Reality and the Egyptian Mamluk 10 (Oct. 15, 2019) (Arabic); The authors also examine Federal Decree Law No. 12 of 2017 on International Crimes (Sep. 18, 2017) (U.A.E.); Decree Law No. 44 of 2018 on International Crimes (Sep. 25, 2018) (Bahr.).

importantly, the inherent flaws it continues to carry. However, the only way to progress modern international law away from the aforementioned issues is to suggest a way forward, in order to bridge the gap between the ICC and the Arab world. Indeed, the structural differences between both legal systems, arising from the traditional and religious foundations of Islamic law, on one hand, and the secularity of ICL[84] on the other, contain a certain flexibility in both legal systems which can prove useful to developing a sustainable and complementary relationship between them. For instance, just as international judges assume the responsibility of interpretation, so too does Islamic law rely on doctrinal interpretation.[85] The laws in both systems are not strictly stagnant, but instead are capable of some evolution to accommodate more present and relevant social needs. There is a necessity, therefore, to promote rigor in both research and study of Islamic legal norms, as well as dialogue within and between the two traditions.[86]

Scholars such as Mashood Baderin have advanced a number of suggestions to support the argument that modern international law must be further developed to create a more inclusive system. To begin with, Baderin develops the argument that the majority of the academic questions posed to general international law are often dealt with by strict Western, Eurocentric legal scholars, who naturally have limited knowledge of the effect it will have on other legal systems.[87] To exacerbate the problem, there is also little consideration of relevant contributions that have been made by other legal systems, such as Islamic law. If these contributions are given fair notice, then it may encourage

84 *See* Hossein Esmaeili and Jeremy Gans, 'Islamic Law Across Cultural Borders: The Involvement of Western Nationals in Saudi Murder Trials' (2000) 28 *Denver J. Int'l L. & Pol'y* 145; *see also* Adel Ibrahim Maged, Gender Violence Prohibition in IHL and in Sharia Law, 2nd Conference on Islam, Politics, and Law 59 (Nov. 27, 2009) (Presentation Abstract), http://www.asser.nl/upload/documents/2222010_53102Reader%20final.docx.

85 Butti Sultan and Butti Ali Al-Muhairi, 'Islamization and Modernization Within the UAE Penal Law: Shari'a in the Pre-Modern Period (1995) 10 *Arab L. Q.* 308.

86 Corri Zoli, M. Cherif Bassiouni and Hamid Khan, 'Justice in Post-Conflict Settings: Islamic Law and Muslim Communities as Stakeholders in Transition' (2017) 33 *Utrecht J. Int'l and Eur. L.* 38, 40, 44

("[Within Muslim societies,] the barriers to such research and dialogue are many: lack of support for such work, censorship and rigid or homogenous approaches to studying Islamic law, even profound misunderstandings circulated by authorities in public spaces.").

87 Mashood A. Baderin, 'Islamic Socio-Legal Norms and International Criminal Justice in Context: Advancing an 'Object and Purpose' cum 'Maqáṣid' Approach' in Tallyn Gray (ed.) *Islam and International Criminal Law and Justice* (Brussels: Torkel Opsahl Academic EPublisher, 2018).

an increase in the universal acceptance of international law.[88] The first argument, therefore, is to tailor the response to academic questions to involve better inclusion of more than one legal perspective in order to create a more accurate response – a multi-disciplinary approach.[89] Another suggestion that is advanced by Baderin is that there must be an allowance for international law to be developed further. While the theory of legal pluralism is the picture of an ideal international legal system, there must be a recognition of what Baderin refers to as the pluralistic reality.[90] While the concept of legal pluralism is good, the development of current modern international law must include the consideration of other legal systems around the world as well as an understanding of what role other legal systems can play in the overall development.

To begin with, there must be an understanding that there are three types of legal pluralism: combative legal pluralism, competitive legal pluralism, and co-operative legal pluralism.[91] As co-operative legal pluralism is more centered around the notion of complementarity, naturally this is what modern international law should aim for. Co-operative legal pluralism will complement other domestic legal systems within the international criminal justice system in order to encourage universal acceptance.[92] The goal is co-operative legal pluralism, and in order to achieve this, we must move on from the primarily exclusive Eurocentric approach taken towards modern international law, and begin to encourage inclusive analysis. There have been suggestions as to how this can be achieved. For example, as already mentioned, there is an obligation to change the exclusively Eurocentric approach to transform the overall narrative of ICL and the overall judicial interpretation and recognized principles of ICL, as well as its political manipulations.[93] Similarly, there is also an obligation on Muslim-majority states to fulfil their primary obligation of prosecuting domestically where necessary, fulfilling their secondary obligation of regional responsiveness, and maintaining co-operation with the ICC if they fail in their obligations.[94]

88 *Id.*

89 Gideon John Boas, 'What is International Criminal Justice?', in Gideon John Boas, William A. Schabas and Michael P. Scharf (eds.) *International Criminal Justice: Legitimacy and Coherence* (Northampton: Edward Elgar, 2012), p. 1.

90 Baderin, *supra* note 87.

91 Geoffrey Swenson, 'Legal Pluralism in Theory and Practice' (2018) 20 *Int'l Stud. Rev.* 438.

92 Baderin, *supra* note 87.

93 *Id.*; Fraser, *supra* note 28, at 227.

94 Baderin, *supra* note 87.

The inherent difference between traditional ICL and Islamic law is undeniable – ICL being rooted in principles of secularism and legal positivism, in contrast to Islamic law – yet not insurmountable. For example, the chasm between the embrace of modernity by the two legal traditions creates division, whereby religious states feel they are unrepresented in the developing world order that is dominated by secular institutions and frameworks. This tension manifests through the so-called "sword of Damocles that is the conflict of Islamic doctrine with 'universal' human rights."[95] Although international treaties and conventions are acknowledged by many states, and indeed many Muslim majority states, the violation and infringement of said human rights are still occurring in varying degrees of intensity.[96] Steiger demonstrates that the likely reason behind the inconsistency of human rights implementation is primarily because many nations perceive the notion of democracy and liberalism as Western conceptions that only take into account European thought in an attempt to increase international dominance.[97] It is often the case, therefore, that based on the belief that public international law is too Western-focused, many nations go further than refusing its implementation by also questioning its validity in the first place.[98] It follows that many Arab nations are adverse to the process of modernity within their legal systems, viewed as an imperialistic, colonial process imposed by the militarily and economically dominant West.[99] In relation to the role of modernity alongside the implementation of Sharia law, Mohamed Khalil demonstrates the friction between Islam and modernity being caused by the issue, *inter alia*, of proper interpretation of Islamic law, and the compatibility of Islam with democracy and human rights (modernity from a Western perspective advocates the encouragement of a democracy that may not align with Islamic values).[100]

95 Markus Peter Beham, 'Islamic Law and International Criminal Law' in Marie-Luisa Frick and Andreas Th. Müller (eds.), *Islam and International Law: Engaging Self-Centrism from a Plurality of Perspectives* (Leiden: Brill, 2013), p. 360.

96 *Id.* at 19.

97 *Id.*

98 *Id.*; *see also* Julie A. Fraser, *Social Institutions and International Human Rights Law Implementation: Every Organ of Society* (Cambridge: Cambridge University Press, 2020), pp. 6-7, 273.

99 Ebrahim Afsah, 'An Islamic Law of Nations? The Weight of History and Tormented Modernization in Muslim Nations' in Thilo Marauhn and Heinhard Steiger (eds.), *Universality and Continuity in International Law* (The Hague, Eleven Intl Pub, 2014) p. 189.

100 *See* Mohamed Ibrahim Khalil, 'Islam and the Challenges of Modernity' (2004) 5 *Geo. J. Int'l Affs*. 97.

Corporal punishments laid out in Islamic law are inherently contrary to modern, universal human rights standards, and particularly, as outlined above, the prohibition of torture.[101] This highlights a certain irreconcilability between the two systems, which is rooted in maxims of ICL, such as the one contained in Article 22 of the Rome Statute, which prohibits derogation from a minimum human rights standard. This creates a perception among Islamic systems of Western human rights as an imposition.[102] Furthermore, the dearth of Muslim judges sitting on benches of international tribunals in proportion to the fifty-seven Muslim majority states that are members of United Nations exacerbates this problematic perception in the Muslim world that Western legal principles, and Western justice, are also being imposed upon them.[103]

In light of this, to further encourage universal acceptance, Baderin suggests adopting an object and purpose paradigm approach towards the analysis of international treaties. In adopting this approach, one must analyze the object and purpose of the treaty that is often outlined in its preamble.[104] If only the substantive content of the treaty is focused on, it will naturally lead to the argument of imposed hegemonic dominance and will not be willingly applied on an international scale.[105] If steps such as these are taken into consideration and, ideally, enacted, then it may encourage future universal acceptance and a better designed universal international legal system that is more inclusive of more than one legal system.

In relation to designing a system that encourages better inclusivism, other legal perspectives must be included in the discussion. This can be achieved through inviting experts of different legal systems to the drafting of present and future international treaties, allowing an open-table discussion of how current modern international law can be improved, and inviting more legal experts of different backgrounds into the ICC itself. In relation to the first advancement of inviting experts of different legal backgrounds, the inclusion of Third World Approaches to International Law (TWAIL) scholars is crucial in this respect. While TWAIL scholars have typically focused on the difficulties of

101 *Id.* (The prohibition of torture as well as cruel, inhuman, or degrading treatment is enshrined in the Universal Declaration of Human Rights, art. 5, International Covenant on Civil and Political Rights, art. 7, and the United Nations Convention against Torture, arts. 1, 16. The prohibition is generally considered to form part of jus cogens).

102 Khalil, *supra* note 100, at 361.

103 *Id.*

104 Baderin, *supra* note 87, at 45–82.

105 *Id.*

the foundations of modern international law, there have been some suggestions provided that could improve the situation.[106]

For example, as already mentioned, there have been some scholars of various backgrounds, such as those from Asia, that have criticized the Eurocentric approach towards the historiography of international law. These filtered versions of history have been utilized by European scholars to create an international system that is far from an accurate representation of other legal systems. This discussion is similar to that advanced by Baderin, aforementioned, in that this naturally creates combative legal pluralism – one version of events versus another. If this method of narrative continues unchecked, universal acceptance of international law will always waiver.

A similar discussion can be had over the notion of cultural difference. Ronald Dworkin advances the argument that if we continue to emphasize the cultural differences between nations without attempting to find some form of middle ground, there will always be an obstacle against modern acceptance of universality.[107] The primary focus on scholars that deliberately dismiss the inclusion of religion in public and political life has automatically framed the matter entirely as one of religious irrationality versus modern secular rationality.[108] If narratives such as this continue to dominate the conversation of modern international law, any notion of religious influence will be disregarded as irrational and so will not be afforded sufficient consideration. To create a system that is centered around the notion of co-operation, there cannot continue to be a pattern of selectivity with what is considered to be suitable inclusion.

In taking the time to develop an understanding of Islamic legal systems, we can arrive at a number of similarities that can be utilized to develop a more inclusive system. For example, Kamari Clarke demonstrates that the foundations of most Islamic legal systems are based on the authority and teachings of the Prophet Muhamed – similar to Western-centric legal systems that are historically based on the foundations of Christian-Judeo principles.[109] While

106 Usha Natarajan, John Reynolds, Amar Bhatia and Sujith Xavier, 'Introduction: TWAIL-On Praxis and the Intellectual' (2016) 37 *Third World Q.* 1946; Bhupinder S. Chimni, 'Third World Approaches to International Law: A Manifesto' (2006) 8 *Int'l Cmty. L. Rev.* 3.

107 Ronald Dworkin, *Sovereign Virtue: The Theory and Practice of Equality* (Cambridge, Massachusetts: Harvard University Press, 2002), pp. 153-55.

108 Baderin, *supra* note 87, at 153–55.

109 Kamari Maxine Clarke, *Fictions of Justice: The International Criminal Court and the Challenge of Legal Pluralism in Sub-Saharan Africa* (Cambridge: Cambridge University Press, 2010), p. 161.

each system is centered around its own particular regime of truth, and arguably its own religious perspectives, it is only the Western-centric legal systems that narrate the history and future of international law, while regarding alternative viewpoints as irrational.[110]

While a substantial argument can be made for the incompatibility of modern international law and its implementation at the ICC with Islamic law, it is important to highlight that it was not an idea that was entirely rejected by many Islamic nations. For the majority of Islamic nations, there was no objection to the introduction of the ICC.[111] To provide an example of the support for the ICC from some Muslim states, a delegate from the Islamic Republic of Iran declared that "the establishment of an international criminal court, independent, universal, effective and impartial, would be a milestone towards achieving peace with justice."[112] There was a general consensus of satisfaction with the idea of international justice that drafters of the Rome Statute were proposing. However, it is questionable whether this agreed upon principle became a point of friction through the method in which the ICC operates and implements international criminal law. Other evidence provides that there was still plenty of support provided from nations that still had some reservations about the idea.

However, while there was a general consensus of satisfaction, this is not necessarily well reflected into unanimity over signatures and ratifications.[113] As outlined above, there were some concerns over the apparent threat to national sovereignty. The foundations of ICL, enforced by the ICC, were built on the principle of complementarity. The ICC should not be able to step in and take charge of a prosecution unless the concerned state is proven to be unwilling or unable to carry out effective proceedings. In theory, this method upholds the principle of complementarity as it allows the opportunity for a case to be handled domestically. However, as mentioned, many states were uncomfortable with the role and powers handed to the OTP to initiate proceedings where it deemed necessary.[114] While some states were in favor of an independent prosecutor having the power to pursue prosecution where it was

110 Dworkin, *supra* note 107, at 161–62.

111 Sardar Ali and Kaur Heer, *supra* note 4.

112 *Summary Records*, *supra* note 5, ¶¶ 23–27.

113 Siraj Khan, 'Arab and Islamic States' Practice: The Shari'ah Clause and its Effects on the Implementation of the Rome Statute of the International Criminal Court', in Tallyn Gray (ed.), *Islam and International Criminal Law and Justice* (Brussels: Torkel Opsahl Academic EPublisher, 2018), p. 145.

114 Sardar Ali and Kaur Heer, *supra* note 4, at 191.

necessary, many nations believed this to be a threat to their state sovereignty and so remained wary of the role of the ICC. As Siraj Khan demonstrates, therefore, the reluctance surrounding the ICC was not necessarily relevant to Islamic law or Sharia. The concerns were primarily centered around an ineffective principle of complementarity that could be overlooked to threaten state sovereignty.[115]

However, while there is an important note to make that the inclusion of Sharia law is not always one of the primary obstacles towards ratification, there are some discussions to examine that emphasize the role of Sharia law. In situations where there is a choice to accept ratification of the Rome Statute, there can be a general reluctance to do so. The issue is often relevant to the subject of international human rights. As discussed in detail above, there are different ideals that are advanced from differing cultures on topics such as human rights – its implementation often varies according to local religious practice and belief. An act that is committed in Saudi Arabia, for example, may be of no concern in the state itself. However, from the point of view of a European nation, for example, the act could be one that warrants investigation and potential prosecution. If the understanding of certain concepts such as human rights continues to vary, there will always be a potential disagreement in relation to its implementation. It is this possibility of disagreement that often leaves some states concerned that if they were to ratify the Rome Statute and incorporate it into domestic legislation, the ICC would pursue prosecution against that state for certain acts which were previously not deemed to be unlawful.

Finally, having Islamic expertise participate in the Court process can illuminate the historical, political, social, and even geographical context in which Arab societies exist, which can improve Arab states engagement with ICL. This could empower the Court to truly engage with, and apply, Islamic legal concepts, where applicable, to matters that come before it, while ensuring principles of ICL remain strictly adhered to. This could apply particularly to a matter that concerns alleged offenses that occurred in Islamic jurisdictions, by alleged perpetrators who are Muslims, and in apparent pursuance of Islamic laws, as was the context of two recent prosecutions brought before the ICC in the cases of *Al Mahdi* and *Al Hassan* (ongoing).

115 *Id.* at 191–92.

5 Conclusion

To conclude the aforementioned suggestions and discussions, the overall takeaway is that there must be a more effective method of taking into consideration alternative viewpoints of different legal systems that does not primarily focus on a Western perspective. While the Rome Statute was built on a Western perspective, as during its development there was not necessarily an open discussion or consideration of alternative legal systems, there is still an opportunity to adopt more inclusive methods of developing a future international legal system that can truly be applied internationally.

The message must be conveyed to the ICC that interpretation by its judges of the provisions of the Rome Statute should benefit from the plurality of legal traditions that occupy our world, in order to make the adjudication of ICL a truly universal and far-reaching mechanism of justice. The undeniable differences that exist between the foundations and operation of ICL and Islamic law respectively do not justify the Court simply setting Islamic law to one side, in favor of traditional ICL. Indeed, as this essay has demonstrated, such differences are not wholly irreconcilable.

In the context of Islamist militant groups who stand before the ICC, it is submitted that the legality of their acts must be examined through the lens of Islamic legal principles, and not solely through that of Western ICL principles, in order to legitimize such legal scrutiny in the eyes of Muslim majority states.

The ignorance of Islamic law by the ICC is counter-productive, serving only to further alienate the Arab world from its jurisdiction, thus weakening its own legitimacy and outreach. The implications of this unfamiliarity with other legal traditions are already evidenced through the Court's lack of reach to Arab countries, manifested through feelings of distrust and refusals to cooperate with ICC warrants, and the distortion of Islamic law by extremist militant groups to justify their contravention of ICL. This appears particularly reckless on the part of the Court in light of the submissions made in this essay concerning the potential for these legal traditions to collaboratively implement the most fundamental laws in our universal society and uphold the most important of humanity's values.

In order to develop more inclusive legal pluralism, we must adopt a cooperative stance rather than a combative one. Combative legal pluralism has played a substantial part in the history of international law by consistently highlighting the strong cultural differences that has long justified a single-minded development. Provided that the concerned cultural differences can be examined and settled in an open discussion between scholars and legal practitioners from multiple backgrounds, there is a better chance that future international law can be developed from a more co-operative perspective. As long as scholars and legal practitioners continue to sit down with one another and continue to discuss how things can be improved through a more inclusive consideration, we may at some point achieve the idealistic reality of an international legal system that operates fairly on the international stage.[116] The Court will undoubtedly be presented with ample new opportunity to work towards this reality, as it will likely be confronted with matters from various Muslim majority states, including Myanmar/Bangladesh, Palestine (as mentioned above), Iraq, Nigeria, Sudan, and perhaps even Syria or Yemen.[117] Let us hope this can mark an end to Islamic exclusion from the ICC, and usher in a new era of true universality of ICL. As Rudolph Schlesinger put it nearly seventy-five years ago:

> The time has come, perhaps, to discard or limit the visionary goal of 'one law' or 'one code' for the whole world and to substitute for it the more realistic aim of crystallizing a common core of legal principles.[118]

---

116 *See Conference on Legal Pluralism and Its Significance to the Work of the International Criminal Court*, NORTHUMBRIA UNIVERSITY NEWCASTLE (May 14, 2022), https://www.northumbria.ac.uk/about-us/news-events/events/2022/05/legal-pluralism-and-its-significance-to-the-work-of-the-international-criminal-court/ (This recent conference was organized by the present author and co-sponsored by the International Bar Association War Crimes Committee and Northumbria Law School. The author is currently working together with Professor Morten Bergsmo, Director of CILRAP, and a Team of Editors from the MENA region (academics and practitioners) on the Lexsitus-CLICC commentary (covering both the ICC Statute and RPE) which will be fully translated into Arabic and become available online before the end of 2022. Arabic-speaking lawyers, academics, and students, can now have free access to Lexsitus-Lectures, an audio-visual service where the subtitles of 234 films by leading ICL-experts from around the world are already available in Arabic. The Arabic subtitles are also available as separate transcript PDF files in the ICC Legal Tools Database. In the words of Bergsmo:

"CILRAP is not only a 'disseminator', but a knowledge – and discourse-actor. Lexsitus-Lectures and Lexsitus-CLICC not only seek to disseminate information about the ICC Statute and RPE, but to foster independent knowledge-generation in international criminal law. The Arabic versions seek to do that among Arabic-speaking actors.").

117 Fraser, *supra* note 1, at 396.

118 Rudolf B. Schlesinger, 'Research on the General Principles of Law Recognized by Civilized Nations' (1957) 51 *Am. J. Int'l L.* 734; *see also* Kai Ambos, 'International Criminal Law at the Crossroads: From Ad Hoc Imposition to a Treaty-Based Universal System', in Carsten Stahn and Larissa van den Herik (eds.), *Future Perspective on International Criminal Justice* (T.M.C. Asser Press, 2010) (noting that a purely Western approach must be complemented by non-Western concepts of crime and punishment, such as Islamic law, to establish and develop a universal system).

CHAPTER 32

Beyond Prosecution: Lessons for the ICC from Regional Human Rights Systems

James Cavallaro and Jamie O'Connell

The International Criminal Court (ICC) has much to learn from other human rights systems – non-Western and Western alike. The lessons, though, are less about tensions between Western and non-Western approaches to law and more about the role of prosecution in response to mass atrocity. We argue that the ICC has overemphasized prosecution and underemphasized complementarity. Regional mechanisms, by contrast, have struck a much more effective balance, especially those in the Americas and Europe. The approach of these mechanisms may have been influenced by non-Western understandings of societal goals after mass atrocity. We counsel the ICC to learn from these bodies and move beyond its excessive focus on prosecution.

The ICC has faced, and continues to face, a devastating array of critiques, many legitimate, others less so. With an annual budget approaching $200 million,[1] and total expenditures to date of well over $2 billion dollars, the Court has managed to successfully prosecute only a half dozen defendants in two decades of existence. To be fair, the Office of the Prosecutor (OTP) has opened some seventeen preliminary investigations in as many countries (virtually all of them in the Global South).[2] But even those numbers make the ICC a costly investment with little concrete return.

Critiques that focus on the Western bias of the ICC – for example, that, to date, only African nationals have been brought to trial and the vast majority of investigations concern situations in Africa – constitute a significant subset of the universe of commentary on the Court. These critiques, while sometimes valid, can distract from the most important challenges the institution faces.

1 *See* Assembly of States Parties, International Criminal Court, *Resolution of the Assembly of States Parties on the Proposed Programme Budget for 2022, the Working Capital Fund for 2022, the Scale of Assessment for the Apportionment of Expenses of the International Criminal Court, Financing Appropriations for 2022 and the Contingency Fund*, Doc. No. ICC-ASP/20/Res.1, § A.1. (Dec. 9, 2021).

2 These figures are drawn from the ICC's website. For the investigation on the Philippines, for example, *see Republic of the Philippines*, ICC, https://www.icc-cpi.int/philippines (last visited September 5, 2023).

 | DOI:10.1163/9789004686755_040

Our research and analysis find that these are tied to the fundamentally mistaken understanding that criminal prosecution by the ICC should be the Court's primary means for advancing its objectives.[3] To be sure, the Court on the whole has more rigorously investigated and prosecuted individuals from less powerful countries (Global South, primarily Africa) than more powerful states (European countries, the United States and their close allies). Even after Biden succeeded Trump in office, Prosecutor Khan seems to have accepted the limits of his position, opting to continue the exclusion of possible U.S. war crimes from the OTP's Afghan investigation.[4] By contrast, the rapid – and justified – response to Russia's criminal invasion of Ukraine provides fodder for claims that the ICC serves the interests of the powerful at the expense of the weak. While Russia, with its vast nuclear arsenal, is certainly more powerful than the African states whose nationals comprise the bulk of the ICC docket, the ongoing war in Ukraine has demonstrated the former super-power's weakness. The ICC appears to have assessed as much. And Russia is the lone state outside the Global South among the OTP's investigations. But all this is a topic for another essay.

Although the ICC purports to be a purely legal entity that engages only in the realm of law, it is in fact a body embedded in an international legal system that is highly unequal and deferential to the interests of powerful actors. The consequence to date has been a docket of investigations and prosecutions that has focused on peripheral states (mostly African) and which provides little or no oversight of powerful states. As Morehouse Professor Oumar Ba has argued, even referrals involving African nationals conform to regional and subregional power politics: in many cases, these referrals, rather than involving other states, have involved political opponents or guerrilla groups within the very states that have referred situations against their enemies.[5]

---

3 James L. Cavallaro and Jamie O'Connell, 'When Prosecution Is Not Enough: How the International Criminal Court Can Prevent Atrocity and Advance Accountability by Emulating Regional Human Rights Institutions' (2020) 45 *Yale J. Int'l L.* 1.

4 Agence France-Presse, *ICC Prosecutor Defends Dropping US From Afghan War Crime Probe*, AL JAZEERA (Dec. 6, 2021), https://www.aljazeera.com/news/2021/12/6/icc-prosecutor-defends-dropping-us-from-afghan-investigation; *see also* Cavallaro and O'Connell, *supra* note 3, at 65. (The ICC's reluctance to pursue the most powerful state in the world is either an unconscionable ethical compromise – or a necessary acknowledgment of the limits of the Court's power and authority. At a minimum, though, the Court should not have acknowledged that it was curtailing the investigation because it was weak).

5 Oumar Ba, *States of Justice: The Politics of the International Criminal Court* (Cambridge: Cambridge University Press, 2020); *see also* Payam Akhavan, 'Self-Referrals Before the International Criminal Court: Are States the Villains or the Victims of Atrocities?' (2010) 21 *Crim. L.F.* 103 (finding such self-referrals consistent with the Rome Statute).

Thus, within the African continent, situations investigated reflect power dynamics on the continent and within particular states. On the whole, the caseload of the ICC has responded to global and regional hierarchies in which Western states remain at the top of the pyramid.

It is valuable to ask if these problems might be resolved, or at least mitigated in substantial measure, by ensuring greater representation of non-Western laws, traditions, principles, rules, and practices in the legal structure and system of the ICC. Our inclination is to believe that diversifying the personnel and practices of the ICC are likely to be valuable goals,[6] but these measures are unlikely to bring about the kind of significant change the Court needs.

Nonetheless, we will endeavor to engage this question on its terms. To do so, we suggest dividing the possible non-Western-inspired changes into two broad categories: first, changes to the ICC's rules and legal practices and, second, changes to the Court's broader understanding of how political and social change work and what role it can play in those processes. We will say relatively little about rules and legal practices. First, neither of us is an expert in substantive or procedural international criminal law. More importantly, in our view, what ails the ICC is not fundamentally a matter of legal procedure.

Our critique is more profound and involves the institution's understanding of itself and its role – the second category of possible changes. The ills which

---

6 International Criminal Court, List of Counsel Before the ICC, https://www.icc-cpi.int/sites/default/files/2022-04/list-of-counsel-eng_0.pdf (last visited June 25, 2022) (At the level of counsel appearing before the ICC, the majority come from states in the Global North despite the absolute lack of defendants from those countries. Counsel that appear before the ICC, in accordance with Rule 22 of the Rules of Procedure and Evidence and Regulation 27 of the Regulations of the Court, may be divided as follows: 599 are from Developed Western States comprised of 24 Countries – Australia, Austria, Belgium, Canada, Denmark, France, Germany, Greece, Hungary, Ireland, Israel, Italy, Japan, Luxembourg, Monaco, the Netherlands, New Zealand, Norway, Portugal, Spain, Sweden, Switzerland, United Kingdom, United States. 416 are from Global South States comprised of 82 Countries – Algeria, Angola, Argentina, Armenia, Bangladesh, Benin, Bissau, Bolivia, Bosnia and Herzegovina, Botswana, Brazil, Bulgaria, Burkinabe, Burundi, Cameroon, Central African Republic, Chad, Chile, China, Colombia, Croatia, Cyprus, Czech Republic, Democratic Republic of the Congo, Egypt, Estonia, Fiji, Former Yugoslav Republic of Macedonia, Gabon, Gambia, Ghana, Guinea, India, Iran, Ivory Coast, Jamaica, Jordan, Kenya, Kosovo, Kuwait, Lebanon, Liberia, Macedonia, Malaysia, Mali, Mauritania, Mexico, Moldova, Mongolia, Morocco, Niger, Nigeria, Pakistan, Palestine, Peru, Philippines, Poland, Republic of the Congo, Romania, Russia, Rwanda, San Marino, São Tomé e Príncipe, Senegal, Serbia, Sierra Leone, Singapore, Slovenia, South Africa, Sri Lanka, Sudan, Syria, Togo, Trinidad and Tobago, Tunisia, Turkey, Uganda, Ukraine, Uruguay, Venezuela, Yemen, Zimbabwe).

we believe must be addressed concern the Court's selection of situations to investigate, the nature and extent of its efforts to promote national-level prosecution and political and social change, and the ICC's excessive focus on its own prosecutions. The problems the Court faces are about its priorities, in particular its overemphasis on its own investigation and prosecution of individual cases. Relatively little would be gained by modifying the laws or rules of procedure in those prosecutions, including the incorporation of non-Western elements.

However, depending on what one understands to be non-Western understandings of social and political change, and the possible role of an international court in it, those might well improve the Court's effectiveness. We would wish to tread cautiously in generalizing about "non-Western" societies, concerned about effacing the vast diversity among billions of people spread across most of the world. At the same time, we recognize that common historical experiences – such as under Western colonial rule – may have created some similarities. We thus see efforts (such as this Forum) to explore such questions as invaluable. Some analysts have argued that centering criminal investigation and prosecution as a means to respond to mass atrocity is a distinctively "Western" approach. If that is true – a question we feel underqualified to judge – then incorporating non-Western approaches into transitional justice might de-center investigation and prosecution. That approach would dovetail somewhat with our analysis of how the ICC has gone wrong, although it would diverge as well, as we generally support national level investigation and prosecution of crimes within the ICC's jurisdiction. Non-Western approaches might also overlap with the methods of regional human rights institutions, such as the Inter-American Commission on Human Rights and the European Court of Human Rights. Those bodies are not fundamentally concerned with individual criminal responsibility, but instead with the overall human rights situation in countries over which they exercise jurisdiction.

We have written about these issues relatively recently in the *Yale Journal of International Law* (YJIL).[7] Below, we summarize our essential findings and analysis.

We suggested that the ICC could learn from regional human rights systems. We focused on two of the ICC's many goals: securing criminal accountability for mass atrocity and preventing its recurrence. We comprehensively surveyed and analyzed research on the effectiveness of the ICC and of regional human rights institutions – the European Court of Human Rights, the Inter-

7 Cavallaro and O'Connell, *supra* note 3.

American Court and Commission on Human Rights, and the African Court and Commission on Human and Peoples' Rights – in advancing those two goals.[8] We concluded that the accumulated experience of regional systems provides a roadmap that the ICC might adopt and adapt to enhance its effectiveness. In terms of the question presented in this dialogue, by embracing the traditions, principles, and practices of other human rights systems, we contend the ICC could advance this agenda. In particular, we argued that the ICC has understood its role in a limited and legalistic fashion. Of course, the International Criminal Court is a court and exercises judicial functions. But the Court has the potential to do much more – to stimulate processes in countries around the world by taking its complementary role much more seriously. This, we explained, is what regional rights bodies have done – applying traditions, principles, and practices that focus less on accountability through individual prosecution and more on policy, engagement with civil society, media, and social movements, as well as by working with some authorities.

> The ICC [...] has focused narrowly on choosing cases and investigating, prosecuting, and judging them – and compiled a record of many failures and few successes. While the International Criminal Court's prosecutors and judges should improve their performance of these core judicial tasks, they – along with the ICC's state parties, who oversee and guide its priorities – also must rethink the Court's strategy for pursuing its goals. The methods developed by the regional bodies provide invaluable guidance. We contend that the ICC should devote less attention and fewer resources to directly investigating and prosecuting cases and more to catalyzing and supporting actions within States – by investigators, prosecutors, judges, executive-branch actors, and civil society – that yield criminal accountability for perpetrators and reduce the chances that mass atrocity will occur.[9]

The question posed in this debate seeks to remedy the limitations and failures of the Court through consideration of possible legal flaws derived from an

---

8 *Id.*
("The ICC and other international criminal tribunals have not been the only supranational institutions working to stop mass atrocity: regional human rights commissions and courts in the Americas, Europe, and Africa have used a variety of tools to successfully pressure governments and, through them, non-State actors to halt abuses and hold violators accountable.").

9 *Id.* at 6-7.

excessively Western legal approach. To the extent that one considers the Court's excessive focus on prosecution to be Western in nature and non-prosecutorial approaches to be non-Western, then integrating non-legal approaches could help transform the ICC. But we believe that such an approach would be tangential. As we diagnosed in YJIL:

> The Court's leaders and staff have succumbed to a lawyerly temptation to view their role as narrowly judicial and technical, detached from complicated, often politicized, processes on the ground. The ICC must reconceive its place in the multilevel legal and political realm, as a player that exercises influence through a variety of political and legal channels and whose impact depends on its interaction with others.[10]

Our contention that the Court sees itself as a body focused nearly exclusively on prosecutions is supported by the data. In particular, the priorities of the OTP (until recently, at least) have manifested this priority:

> The OTP Situation Analysis Section, which conducts preliminary examinations, had just five to six staff members until 2011 – and devoted half its time to work on investigation-stage situations. [Former Prosecutor Fatou] Bensouda has improved matters: by 2018 the unit had thirteen staff who appeared to be focused almost entirely on preliminary examinations. However, Human Rights Watch's analysis of their workload concluded that this was too few even for the research and analysis tasks necessary in that stage – such as determining whether crimes within the Court's jurisdiction had been committed – "let alone the steps that may be necessary to engage national authorities in a way that can catalyze national prosecutions." For 2019, the OTP requested approximately one-fifteenth as much funding for preliminary examinations as for investigations and prosecutions.[11]

A central element of the approach of regional bodies has been a multi-dimensional view of the role of law in political and social change and a creative and sophisticated understanding of how the bodies themselves can advance such change. The Inter-American Court and Commission, the European Court, and to some degree the African Commission and Court approach their respective mandates with a clearer sense of the political nature of their

10 *Id.* at 7.
11 *Id.* at 25.

engagement. This leads them to engage in a far more expansive set of actions, extending far beyond promoting criminal prosecution. To be fair, these bodies are not empowered to prosecute individuals directly. But they could take a narrow view of their function as essentially to adjudicate state responsibility for human rights violations and order a narrow range of remedies. Instead, they have used their powers more creatively to promote accountability and prevent mass atrocity in the future. The Inter-American human rights system and its African counterpart retain Commissions with broad mandates and extensive competencies beyond adjudicating cases. The Inter-American system has been particularly adept at leveraging its many competencies to advance prosecutions in states themselves, as well as truth commissions, reparations programs, museums and other sites of historical memory, and other measures designed to foster truth-telling, accountability, and to create barriers to recurrence of mass violence. The European Court has begun to order a similarly wide range of remedies and has for decades carefully built its authority and influence over states, to the point where the latter have embedded respect for human rights throughout their executive, legislative, and judicial processes to a striking – if still incomplete – extent.

Even if we were to consider the success rate on the dimension of promoting successful prosecutions alone, the regional systems far outpace the ICC on a cost-per-case basis. Alexandra Huneeus has examined the effect of decisions of the Inter-American system, for example, analyzing the connection between sentences ordering investigation and prosecution and subsequent domestic investigations and prosecutions. A comparison of the impact of these court sentences demonstrates that they have resulted in nearly as many prosecutions as carried out by the ICC, the ICTY and ICTR combined, though with a far more limited budget. Huneeus wrote in 2013:

> [T]he Inter-American Court of Human Rights has made national prosecution of gross, state-sponsored crimes a centerpiece of its regional agenda. The Court [...] regularly orders states to investigate, try, and punish those responsible for gross human rights violations as a form of equitable relief. Then, through another interpretive twist, it supervises states' implementation of its orders: it holds mandatory hearings and issues compliance reports that aspire to hasten and guide the progress of national criminal processes. The Court has decreed and is actively monitoring prosecutions of international crimes in roughly fifty-one cases across fifteen states. Pursuant to its orders in these cases, states have launched new criminal investigations, exhumed mass graves, moved cases from military to civil jurisdiction, overturned amnesties,

> bypassed statutes of limitations, and created new institutions and working methods to facilitate prosecution of such crimes. Indeed, at least thirty-nine prosecutions launched pursuant to the Court's orders have yielded convictions.[12]

Far from undermining their work, this appreciation of the politics inherent in international law has led the Inter-American human rights system and other regional bodies to develop processes that seek to leverage their limited power by engaging a broad range of actors in the countries in which they operate as well as in their broader regions.[13] Our analysis in YJIL goes into some detail on their successes.[14]

In fact, as we have noted, the ICC has, in some instances, taken measures to promote accountability through means other than prosecutions. When it has done so, we argue, it has been most effective:

> The ICC's greatest potential impact is indirect, through its support of and pressure on national-level actors who gather evidence of crimes, prosecute perpetrators in national courts, and punish them at the domestic level, and other contributions to dynamics that reduce atrocity or increase accountability. Less promising is the Court's conventional judicial work of direct investigation and prosecution of particular perpetrators. Its indirect exercise of influence resembles the process by which regional human rights systems work, and matches the philosophy of complementarity that guided the ICC's creators.[15]

---

12 Alexandra V. Huneeus, 'International Criminal Law by Other Means: The Quasi-Criminal Jurisdiction of the Human Rights Courts' (2013) 107 *Am. J. Int'l L.* 1, 1–2.

13 Cavallaro and O'Connell, *supra* note 3, at 6.

([T]he ICC should reconceive its strategy and overhaul its operations to act more like a regional human rights institution. Both theory and evidence from practice show that prevention and accountability result primarily from political and legal processes and norms within States, sometimes catalyzed or supported by international institutions, rather than from the actions of international bodies in isolation. Evidence suggests these local processes tend to have more profound and durable effects, provoke less resistance, and cost less than purely international legal processes. The regional human rights mechanisms – especially the Inter-American Commission and Court and the European Court – have learned to play this complementary role with great effectiveness. Through decades of experimentation and practice, they have devised tactics that contribute to the political and legal dynamics that generate accountability and prevention.).

14 *See id.* at 30–57.

15 *Id.* at 13.

The kinds of changes the ICC should make are less about non-Western understandings of law and more about understanding – from a Western or non-Western perspective – the role of courts and the dynamics of change in societies that have experienced mass atrocity. Indeed, in a few rare but important situations, the OTP has engaged in this way with significant success. As we observed in YJIL, in the case of the conflict in Colombia, engagement by the OTP followed this logic to great success.

> The ICC's role in Colombia's peace negotiations with right-wing paramilitaries and the Fuerzas Armadas Revolucionarias de Colombia – Ejército del Pueblo (FARC) illustrates how ICC activities other than building and prosecuting individual cases can contribute to reducing atrocities and achieving criminal accountability. The ICC Prosecutor has kept the Court's examination of Colombia in the preliminary examination stage for fifteen years, since 2004, rather than upgrading it to an investigation and issuing indictments. Moreno Ocampo, then Bensouda, and their staff have engaged regularly in public and private with the Colombian government, judiciary, and civil society, and modulated their positions as the peace talks have progressed. This flexible, strategic approach has allowed the ICC some influence in a complex, high-stakes peace process. The Court has supported the conclusion of a landmark agreement that could end a four-decade civil war characterized by rampant atrocities, while preserving the possibility of criminal accountability in Colombian courts. As Courtney Hillebrecht and Alexandra Huneeus conclude in their exceptionally subtle study, the ICC's and Inter-American Court's effect on the Colombian peace process suggests that " 'shadow effects' [may be] the most important way courts exert influence," rather than through indicting and prosecuting individual cases.[16]

The blueprint for successful engagement exists. It requires less emphasis on prosecution and far more on complementarity, incorporating as much as possible, the lessons from regional mechanisms.

---

16 *Id.* at 26.

CHAPTER 33

Inter-jurisdictional Dialogue with Non-Western Traditions

Alexandra Huneeus

In a series of ground-breaking resolutions, Colombia's transitional justice mechanism has declared that the territories of indigenous peoples and Black Colombian communities were victims of the fifty-year internal armed conflict, and thus have rights to truth, reparation, and participation in the transitional justice process. The resolutions are the fruit of Colombia's constitutional commitment to legal pluralism, which is also reflected in the 2016 Peace Accord between the government and the FARC-EP guerrilla. This essay will argue that the JEP's inter-jurisdictional work, and the concept of the "territory as victim," provide an opportunity for the ICC to enrich its engagement with non-Western law. When the ICC closed its Preliminary Examination in Colombia in October of 2021, it committed to continued engagement through "exchanges of lessons learned and best practices."[1] Moving forward, the ICC should highlight the JEP's inter-jurisdictional work as a useful model for other transitional justice processes that include non-Western law. The concept of territory as victim, with its emphasis on the relation of a people to their place and to the non-human beings with whom they share it, also has implications for debates over adding the crime of ecocide to the Rome Statute.

1 Territory as a Victim with Rights: Why Legal Pluralism in Colombia's 2016 Peace Accord Matters

Colombia's Special Jurisdiction for the Peace (hereinafter JEP for its Spanish acronym) was created pursuant to the 2016 peace agreement between the Colombian government and the FARC-EP. It is a unique transitional justice mechanism that seeks to render justice for the crimes of Colombia's fifty year

1 *See* International Criminal Court, *Cooperation Agreement Between the Office of the Prosecutor of the International Criminal Court and the Government of Colombia*, art. 7 (Oct. 28, 2021), https://www.icc-cpi.int/sites/default/files/itemsDocuments/20211028-OTP-COL-Cooperation-Agreement-ENG.pdf (last visited September 6, 2023).

 | DOI:10.1163/9789004686755_041

conflict through a mix of retributive and restorative measures. Since opening its doors in 2018, one of the JEP's main tasks has been delineating and investigating ten emblematic "macro-cases," each of which encompasses hundreds of individual crimes.

In 2019, JEP judge Belkis Izquierdo issued a resolution granting the request of the Awá people that their territory, the Katsa Su, be declared a victim of the armed conflict in the context of the JEP's macro-case 02.[2] Judges have followed suit in two other JEP macro-cases, granting victim status to the Cxhab Wala Kiwe and the Eperara Euja, which are the territories of the Nasa and the Sia people, as well as to the territories of two Black communities of Tumaco.[3]

The resolutions reflect the JEP's commitment to acknowledging that the armed conflict had differential impact on differently situated groups.[4] Indigenous and Black Colombians were particularly hard hit by the armed conflict, suffering high levels of displacement from their territories, direct attacks on the general populations, and strategic attacks on leaders.[5] Of the ten macro-cases, three focus on regions where indigenous peoples and Black Colombian communities reside (Cases 02, 04, and 05), and a fourth will be focused entirely on the conflict's impact on all of Colombia's ethnically identified peoples (Case 09).

In a prior article, co-author Pablo Rueda Sáiz and I show that the JEP's accreditation of territories as victims gives legal expression to the idea that:

2 Jurisdicción Especial Para la Paz, *Auto Sala de Reconocimiento de Verdad Belkis Izquierdo Torres* 079 (Nov. 12, 2019) (Colom.) [hereinafter Awá Resolution], http://files.harmonywithnatureun.org/uploads/upload904.pdf.

3 *See* Jurisdicción Especial Para la Paz, *Auto Sala de Reconocimiento de Verdad Raúl Sánchez* 002 (Jan. 17, 2020) (Colom.) [hereinafter Nasa Resolution], https://www.coljuristas.org/observatorio_jep/documentos/documento.php?id=142 (accrediting Cxhab Wala Kiwe territory as victim); *See also* Jurisdicción Especial Para la Paz, *Auto Sala de Reconocimiento de Verdad Belkis Izquierdo Torres* 079 (Jun. 10, 2020) (Colom.), https://vlex.com.co/vid/auto-n-7995-tribunal-862789496 (accrediting Eperara Euja territory as victim).

4 Congress of Colombia, *Estatuaria de la Administración de Justicia en la Jurisdicción Especial Para la Paz*, Law 1957, art. 18 (Jun. 6, 2019).

5 *Los Impactos del Conflicto en los Territorios de los Pueblos Indígenas de la Región Andina y sus Luchas por la Pervivencia y Reexistencia*, COMISIÓN DE LA VERDAD (Oct. 20, 2020) (Colom.), https://comisiondelaverdad.co/actualidad/noticias/impactos-del-conflicto-en-los-territorios-pueblos-indigenas-region-andina; *see also Más De 1,2 Millones de Víctimas Étnicas Dejó El Conflicto Armado en Colombia*, UNIDAD VÍCTIMAS (Oct. 10, 2017) (Colom.), https://www.unidadvictimas.gov.co/es/asuntos-etnicos/mas-de-12-millones-de-victimas-etnicas-dejo-el-conflicto-armado-en-colombia/39543.

> [I]t is not just human lives and relationships that are upended by armed conflict, but also relations with non-humans, including animals, plants, ecosystems and natural entities [...] such as rivers and mountains, and the spiritual world.[6]

The theme that runs through these resolutions, in other words, is that the armed conflict severed the ties between a people and its territory.[7] In the words of the Nasa people, as quoted by the JEP:

> Our ancestral and sacred territory has suffered violations, alterations, mutilations, occupations and harms, product of the armed internal conflict, which have negatively transformed the bond that the indigenous communities had with their territory, violating the balance, harmony, and autonomy of the Nasa indigenous people.[8]

The JEP and its interlocutors are only just beginning to figure out how to bring these ideas about harm to life through legal procedures. The accreditation of the territories means that they have the same rights as any other victim under the 2016 peace agreement: rights to truth, reparation, justice, and participation in the JEP's processes. But the Katsa Su cannot appear in court to convey the harm it has suffered or the reparation it seeks. Thus, the JEP has allowed the organization that represents the Awá before the JEP to speak for the Katsa Su.[9] The JEP has held special hearings in situ to learn of the harm of the Katsa Su, with special attention to how this harm affects the Awá people in turn.[10] In a later stage, the JEP will have to create reparatory measures to redress the harm suffered by the victimized territories.[11]

---

6 Alexandra Huneeus and Pablo Rueda Sáiz, 'Territory as a Victim of Armed Conflict' (2021) 15 *Int'l J. Transnat'l Just.* 210, 222; *see also* Belkis Izquierdo and Lieselotte Viaene, 'Decolonizing Transitional Justice From Indigenous Territories' (2018) 34 *Per La Pau* 1; *Katsa Su: Ecologías de la Guerra en la Pervivencia del Gran Territorio Awá: Derecho Propio, Coordinación Interjurisdiccional y Violencia Estructural*, DEJUSTICIA (Mar. 25, 2022), https://www.dejusticia.org/wp-content/uploads/2022/03/Brief-Informe-Caso-02_Katsa-Su-y-Ecologias-de-la-Guerra.pdf.

7 Huneeus and Rueda Sáiz, *supra* note 6, at 211.

8 Nasa Resolution, *supra* note 3, ¶ 13.5 (my translation).

9 Awá Resolution, *supra* note 2.

10 Jurisdicción Especial Para la Paz, *Prioriza la situación territorial de Ricaurte, Tumaco y Barbacoas* (Nariño) (Colom.) [hereinafter Prioritizing the Territorial Situation], https://www.jep.gov.co/macrocasos/caso02.html (last visited Jun. 22, 2022).

11 *See* Huneeus, *supra* note 6; *see also* Dejusticia, *supra* note 6.

2 Lessons for the ICC and for Ecocide Advocates

In closing its seventeen-year Preliminary Examination, the ICC signed a cooperation agreement with the Colombian government which depicts the transitional justice process as "a valuable experience that may be replicated in other situations around the world."[12] The two parties committed to ongoing dialogue and "exchanges of lessons learned and best practices."[13] The concept of "territory as victim" provides just such a "lessons learned" opportunity for the ICC. First, it provides a model of how an institution that is rooted in Western law can conduct an inter-jurisdictional dialogue with non-Western law in the context of transitional justice. Second, the concept has implications for those considering how to write the crime of ecocide into the Rome Statute.

2.1 *On How to Conduct Inter-jurisdictional Dialogue*

The JEP's openness and ongoing commitment to dialogue with indigenous legal systems could serve as a model for other transitional justice processes. The ICC should use it as an example of a legally plural process when it engages with other situations which include people from non-Western traditions.

The legal concept of territory as victim is a hybrid legal product – it is the fruit of a long-standing dialogue between Colombia's national legal system, rooted in Western traditions, and the justice systems of its indigenous peoples. However, as argued by Daniel Ruiz Cerda, the concept of territory as victim takes this dialogue to a new level.[14] By recognizing territory as a legal subject, the Colombian legal system goes beyond merely recognizing that the Awá have a distinct worldview and a different way of understanding their territory. The JEP's resolutions adopt this way of viewing the Awá's territory as their own: they bring the Katsa Su into being as a legal subject in Colombian law.[15] In this way, the Colombian legal system is not acting as a neutral arbiter between different cultural views but allowing itself to be changed through its dialogue with indigenous legal systems.[16]

---

12 Cooperation Agreement, *supra* note 1.

13 *Id.* art. 4.

14 Daniel Ruiz-Serna, 'El Territorio Como Víctima. Ontología Política y Las Leyes de Víctimas Para Comunidades Indígenas y Negras en Colombia' (2017) 53 *Revista Colombiana de Antropología* 85.

15 Huneeus, *supra* note 6.

16 Ruiz-Serna, *supra* note 14; *Id.*

The JEP is also a model in how closely it collaborates with victims to understand their perspective. In the context of Case 02 alone, the JEP reports that is has conducted over eighty inter-jurisdictional hearings with indigenous justice actors.[17] Additionally, the JEP is a model of diversity. Of the fifty-one SJP judges, over half are women; over 10% identify as indigenous and over 10% identify as Afro-descendent Colombians; and a majority hail from outside the capital city of Bogotá. It is not a coincidence that Judge Belkis, who first accredited the Katsa Su, is herself an indigenous woman who understands and is committed to moving between cultures, or *cosmovisions*.[18] Her work suggests that inter-jurisdictional dialogue is more likely to succeed in systems that give leadership roles to indigenous peoples alongside non-indigenous actors.

The JEP as a model of legally plural practice comes with a caveat. Colombia's legal pluralism is the product of the decades-long activism of indigenous groups in Colombia, and in Latin America more generally. These groups have pushed successfully for legal recognition of their territories and for greater autonomy and recognition within national legal systems, frequently turning to the Inter-American Human Rights System to advance their claims. Further, the Colombian constitution commits the government to the task of inter-jurisdictional dialogue. It is a practice with which Colombian judges and lawyers are familiar. Together these factors create a legal context that is more open to and familiar with indigenous legal thought than may be available in most of the situations before the ICC.

Also, while I am recommending that the JEP's practice serve as a model of interjurisdictional dialogue with non-Western peoples, I am not recommending that the ICC adopt the practice of accrediting territories as victims as a general practice. The territory as victim is a culturally specific legal idea. It would not have made sense, for example, to declare the mausoleums and other protected buildings of Timbuktu to be victims in the Ahmad Al Faqi Al Mahdi case. Such a practice should only come at the request of the victims and should reflect the way in which the victims experience the harm.

2.2 *Ecocide and the Concept of Territory*

The concept of territory as victim foregrounds the ties – cultural, spiritual, social, and moral – of a people to their particular place. This emphasis could inform how we conceive of the elements of the ecocide and should be studied by those who seek to add the crime of ecocide to the Rome Statute.

---

17 Prioritizing the Territorial Situation, *supra* note 10.

18 *See* Izquierdo, *supra* note 6.

In July 2021, a working group organized by Stop Ecocide released a draft of the language that they are advocating should be added to the Rome Statute.[19] In delineating the harm threshold necessary for an unlawful act to qualify, they require that the damage caused be either "severe and widespread" or "severe and long-term."[20] By widespread, they refer to:

> [D]amage which extends beyond a limited geographic area, crosses state boundaries, or is suffered by an entire ecosystem or species or a large number of human beings.[21]

The definition is focused on the geographical and physical features of the land, not on its cultural and spiritual meaning. It speaks to space, not place. This definition fails to attend to the ideas expressed by the territory as victim: a territory can be of limited geographical reach, and yet its destruction has deep meaning that could impede the cultural survival of a people.[22] This can be the case even if the destruction does not meet the threshold for long-term.[23]

An international law that that is in dialogue with indigenous peoples could mean giving weight to the relationship of a people to their territory, either by adding an exception as regards indigenous people's territory, or by shifting the focus of the definition to include not only physical but cultural attributes of what it calls "the environment." But such a revision must be made with care. As noted above, the territory as victim concept is the product of the long-term activism of indigenous group fighting for more autonomy and control of their territories, and the claim rests on their special relationship to their territory – on its distinctiveness. It is important not to dilute the political leverage of their

19 Stop Ecocide Found., Independent Expert Panel for the Legal Definition of Ecocide: Commentary and Core Text (Jun. 2021), https://static1.squarespace.com/static/5ca2608ab914493c64ef1f6d/t/60d7479cf8e7e5461534dd07/1624721314430/SE+Foundation+Commentary+and+core+text+revised+%281%29.pdf (last visited September 7, 2023).

20 *Id.* at 5.

21 *Id.*

22 *See, e.g.*, David R. Goyes, Nigel South, Mireya Astroina Abaibira, Pablo Baicué, Angie Cuchimba, and Deisy Tatiana Ramos Ñeñetofe, 'Genocide and Ecocide in Four Colombian Indigenous Communities: The Erosion of a Way of Life and Memory' (2021) 61 *Brit. J. Criminology* 965 (drawing connections between ecocide and genocide in the Colombian context); *see also* Lauren J. Eichler, 'Ecocide Is Genocide: Decolonizing the Definition of Genocide' (2020) 14 *Genocide Stud. & Prevention* 104.

23 Stop Ecocide Found., *supra* note 19 ("'Long-term' means damage which is irreversible, or which cannot be redressed through natural recovery within a reasonable period of time.").

claim which is of a differential harm. We must take care to learn from an indigenous concept in a way that does not appropriate, expropriate, or weaken it, but rather in a way that acknowledges and bolsters the autonomy of indigenous peoples.

3 Conclusion

There is a paradox here. The ICC was created as a way of imposing a top-down regime that would push states to respond to international crimes in a particular way. The whole point was to construct a universal, one-size-fits-all paradigm. Now, as the prompt to this Forum suggests, the ICC is being asked to consider the nuances of transitional justice, and in particular to engage in the complexity of inter-jurisdictional dialogue with non-Western peoples. The ICC's openness to the JEP, with its unique mix of restorative and retributive measures, is a sign that it is starting to be able to approach transitional justice systems with nuance. It is to be hoped that the ICC also will be able to learn from the JEP's deep engagement with indigenous and Black Colombian people.

CHAPTER 34

Recognizing Broader, Deeper, and Longer Conceptions of Justice

Ray Nickson

Concerns that the ICC disproportionately emphasizes Western, European approaches to justice are not new.[1] Nor are arguments that the ICC, with its exclusive use of prosecutions and trials, emerging largely from African locations, is a neo-colonial enterprise.[2] While there may be merit to these critiques, there does not have to be. What is required from the ICC to avoid these critiques is greater institutional humility and an acceptance by the ICC and its staff of justice in national jurisdictions that is broader, deeper, and longer than currently conceived.[3] This does not require any legal reform of the ICC. Indeed, while Article 21(1) of the Rome Statute might provide scope for the more formal adoption of non-Western laws, traditions, rules and practices by the ICC, we do not have to wait for formal inclusion.[4] Instead, recog-

1 Jennifer Llewellyn, 'A Comment on the Complementarity Jurisdiction of the International Criminal Court: Adding Insult to Injury in Transitional Contexts?' (2001) 24 *Dalhousie L.J.* 192, 215 (This is a theme of early critiques and questions about the ICC's relationship with alternative justice mechanisms in national jurisdictions. For example, Llewellyn raises concerns about the ICC and its view of truth commissions and amnesties, and suggests:

> Where, then, does this leave states wanting to preserve the truth commission option? It seems states are left with two obvious choices – do not sign or ratify the treaty, or refuse to cooperate with the Court should it request extradition of an individual who has received amnesty.).

2 *See Is the International Criminal Court (ICC) Targeting Africa Inappropriately?*, ICC FORUM (Mar. 17, 2013), https://iccforum.com/africa (The question of whether the ICC unduly focuses on Africa, for example, was previously examined in this forum.); *see also* Mahmood Mamdani, *Darfur, ICC, and the New Humanitarian Order: How the ICC's "Responsibility to Protect" is Being Turned Into an Assertion of Neocolonial Domination*, PAMBAZUKA NEWS (Sep. 17, 2008), https://www.pambazuka.org/governance/darfur-icc-and-new-humanitarian-order (last visited October 28, 2023); For a recent overview of postcolonial critiques, *see* Lea Ina Schneider, 'The International Criminal Court-A Postcolonial Tool for Western States to Control Africa?' (2020) 1 *J. Int'l Crim. L.* 90.

3 Ray Nickson and John Braithwaite, 'Deeper, Broader, Longer Transitional Justice' (2014) 11 *Eur. J. Criminology* 445.

4 International Criminal Court, Rome Statute of the International Criminal Court, art. 21(1), U.N. Doc. A/CONF.183/9 (July 17, 1998) [hereinafter Rome Statute].

 | DOI:10.1163/9789004686755_042

nizing non-Western laws, traditions, rules, and practices simply requires a more embracive approach to complementarity under Article 17.[5] By recognizing justice efforts conceived more broadly, deeply, and longer as satisfying complementarity, the ICC provides the space for non-Western, traditional, indigenous, restorative, and other justice mechanisms to be employed at the national and local level. The ICC can buttress such an approach to complementarity by noting that when national justice initiatives are genuine attempts to address wrongs and harms caused by contravention of international criminal law, it is not in the interests of justice under Article 53 to proceed with investigation and prosecution merely because those justice initiatives do not resemble justice as the ICC would pursue it. This avoids postcolonial critiques of the ICC by incorporating into the ICC's function a recognition of the myriad ways in which a meaningful justice to local communities can be pursued when opting for something other than an adversarial model from Western legal traditions. The ICC, its representatives, and its supporters must be champions of broader, deeper, and longer justice initiatives, and not merely invoke Western retributive justice as the only way to respond to international crimes in the wake of mass violence.

The ICC could be considered to perform multiple functions, but I am interested here in its role as part of transitional justice. Transitional justice is "the process that seeks to address the abuses and crimes of prior regimes or conflicts in transitions to more democratic policies."[6] There is no consensus among scholars or practitioners of an exhaustive or definitive list of the goals or aims of transitional justice.[7] Such goals and aims, however, typically exceed what a trial, or trials, focusing on individual guilt or innocence can achieve.[8] As currently constituted, the ICC itself can only perform and deliver a limited type of justice: trials and punishment.[9] While trials may be significant in some contexts, they will not be the most important mechanism for achieving meaningful justice in all contexts.

---

5 *Id.* art. 17.

6 Ray Nickson and Alice Neikirk, *Managing Transitional Justice: Expectations of International Trials* (Cham: Palgrave MacMillan, 2018), p. 3.

7 *Id.*

8 *Id.*

9 Ray Nickson, 'Participation as Restoration: The Current Limits of Restorative Justice for Victim Participants in International Criminal Trials', in Kerry Clamp (ed.), *Restorative Justice in Transitional Settings* (Abingdon: Routledge, 2016), p. 95 (It is possible that victim participation at the ICC could deliver broader justice outcomes for victims, but this is limited by how participation has been conceived at the ICC).

Due to the nature of complementarity in the Rome Statute, however, the ICC can (and indeed should) recognize, empower, and support other forms of justice as conceived and pursued within national jurisdictions. Article 17 of the Rome Statute established the relationship between national and international jurisdictions. It states that cases are inadmissible where the state that has jurisdiction carries out a genuine investigation or prosecution and not merely an attempt to shield the perpetrator from accountability with a sham proceeding. Almost immediately after the Rome Statute that established the ICC was finalized, questions were raised about complementarity and the relationship between the ICC and national justice initiatives that did not follow the ICC's model of adversarial trials. Llewellyn posed the question early in this debate: "[whether] the ICC's jurisdiction [would] add insult to injury in transitional contexts by precluding truth commissions as a viable means of dealing with the past?"[10] Llewellyn, in analyzing Article 17 of the Rome Statute, noted that the issue is whether investigation and prosecution are distinct and separate actions, and if an alternative approach to justice that included investigation but did not anticipate prosecutions, would be enough to satisfy state jurisdiction and prevent the ICC from invoking its own jurisdiction.

Two decades on and the question of alternative justice mechanisms and complementarity with the ICC is still debated. In a thorough examination of the question of complementarity, Minow, almost twenty years after Llewellyn, asks "whether the ICC and the project of international criminal justice it represents, leave room for alternative conceptions of justice beyond the Western adversarial model."[11] Minow suggests a possible understanding of Article 17 where the ICC must leave space for such alternatives, because if the ICC only recognized Western-style prosecutions as satisfying complementarity then post-colonial critiques of the ICC would have merit.[12] Minow concludes that:

> Greater acceptance of alternatives to formal criminal prosecution at the local level may be wise, given both the symbolic and real benefits of deferring to domestic and culturally resonant responses to mass violence, and the exigencies that make formal and criminal prosecution unavailable in a domestic context.[13]

10 Llewellyn, *supra* note 1, at 196.

11 Martha Minow, 'Do Alternative Justice Mechanisms Deserve Recognition in International Criminal Law?: Truth Commissions, Amnesties, and Complementarity at the International Criminal Court' (2019) 60 *Harv. Int'l L.J.* 1, 7.

12 *Id.*

13 *Id.* at 37.

An interpretation of the Rome Statute that permits recognition of alternative justice mechanisms, and not solely adversarial trials, is to be preferred because we should prioritize the idea that international justice should reflect the diversity of justice models internationally, while also being open to innovation. Innovation, for example, might mean the "rediscovery" of lost or moribund traditional or indigenous justice practices. It may also mean the development of a novel justice mechanism, suited to the context and culture of the communities it serves. The ICC, when evaluating whether an alternative justice practice satisfies for the purposes of complementarity, should consider broader, deeper, and longer conceptions of justice. In particular, we must eschew the Western criminal law's obsessive attachment to retribution and punishment when conceiving of a justice that is more international.[14] If it is the *International* Criminal Court, then it must allow diverse approaches to satisfy the complementarity principle. Indeed, "the hard sell for the myopically legal approach that preceded establishment of the International Criminal Court must now be put in its box."[15]

Minow notes that statements from the ICC's Prosecutors suggest that only criminal investigations with the possibility of criminal trials are considered to satisfy complementarity in the Rome Statute and therefore exclude jurisdiction of the ICC.[16] A broader, deeper, and longer conception of justice provides more space for survivors to be vindicated by some justice. The real strength of the ICC should be in how it empowers national and local justice initiatives that genuinely seek to address past harms and advance peace and healing through its complementary role, invoking jurisdiction only when genuine local efforts, including non-prosecutorial alternative justice efforts, are absent. Alternative justice initiatives at the national and local level should not fall short of satisfying complementarity principles simply because they do not employ Western models of criminal justice and do not emphasize retribution as the primary justice outcome. Communities affected by crimes against humanity and war crimes may prioritize other justice goals. Therefore, we should not elevate trials that provide limited justice outcomes over potential alternative justice mechanisms that may deliver justice outcomes seen as more relevant by post-conflict communities.

In this essay, I wish to focus on broadening and deepening our conceptions of justice, with specific reference to how the ICC considers complementarity.

---

14 Nickson, *supra* note 3, at 448.

15 *Id.*

16 Minow, *supra* note 11.

Discussions of lengthening justice are elaborated elsewhere and are not as relevant to this discussion of complementarity.[17] That does not mean, however, that lengthening our conception of justice is irrelevant when considering the jurisdiction of the ICC. Indeed, Article 17 makes plain that an unjustified delay in bringing someone to justice may be enough to trigger ICC jurisdiction.[18] Yet, we should allow temporal space for affected communities to define their own justice goals and pursue them. A rush by the ICC to invoke jurisdiction because a nation exiting conflict does not immediately pursue justice could be counterproductive. Speedy investigations and trials do, of course, have their advantages and a delay may result in the loss of crucial evidence for pursuing justice, or the flight or death of potential defendants. Advantages of swift justice may be outweighed, however, by the advantages of providing stakeholders in affected communities the opportunity to design and pursue a justice that is most meaningful to them.

If we conceive of transitional justice more broadly, it may be possible to deliver more justice.[19] Nickson and Braithwaite explain, "[t]his response grows from valorizing the idea that international law should have a more international, less narrowly Western, character, because it is international."[20] What we ought to include in our vision for transitional justice are alternative forms of justice to the retributive model: forms such as traditional justice;[21]

---

17 For a full discussion, *see* Nickson and Braithwaite, *supra* note 3; *see also* Nickson and Neikirk, *supra* note 6.

18 Rome Statute, *supra* note 4, art. 17(2)(b) (The Rome Statute states that in determining whether an unwillingness to investigate or prosecute has occurred, the ICC can consider whether: "[t]here has been an unjustified delay in the proceedings which in the circumstances is inconsistent with an intent to bring the person concerned to justice." Caution should be taken when determining when a delay is "unjustified" and "is inconsistent with an intent to bring the person to justice." A hasty judgment may not provide sufficient opportunities for nations to collectively engage their affected communities to determine the best course for pursuing justice).

19 Nickson and Braithwaite, *supra* note 3.

20 *Id.* at 448.

21 *See* Luc Huyse, Bert Ingelaere, et al., Inst. for Democracy and Electoral Assistance, Traditional Justice and Reconciliation After Violent Conflict: Learning from African Experiences (2008), https://www.idea.int/sites/default/files/publications/traditional-justice-and-reconciliation-after-violent-conflict-learning-from-african-experiences_0.pdf (last visited September 15, 2023) (providing a fuller discussion of the role of traditional forms of justice in transitional justice and peacebuilding).

indigenous justice;[22] restorative justice[23] and so on. In this way, it is recognized that justice is holistic and ought to be practiced that way. For the world's largest religions, the holism of justice is a constant theme.[24] Zehr has pointed out that Judaism and Christianity share the Hebrew word *shalom* for holistic peace with justice.[25] Llewellyn and Philpott state that the word *salam* in Arabic has a similar meaning.[26] *Shalom* and *salam* resonate with the concept of ubuntu. Ubuntu is a Zulu, Xhosa and pan-African concept of justice. The holism of an ubuntu-informed understanding of justice was outlined in a 2011 hate speech trial in South Africa:[27]

> Ubuntu is recognized as being an important source of law within the context of strained or broken relationships amongst individuals or communities and as an aid for providing remedies which contribute towards more mutually acceptable remedies for the parties in such cases. Ubuntu is a concept which:

---

22 James W. Zion, 'Navajo Therapeutic Jurisprudence' (2002) 18 *Touro L. Rev.* 563 (As Zion notes, indigenous justice may be described as "the pre-state form of justice. It is not necessarily a separate development, confined to indigenous thought, but the original political arrangement." Indigenous justice systems will obviously vary according to local traditions and understandings); Ada Pecos Melton, 'Indigenous Justice Systems and Tribal Society' (1995) 79 *Judicature* 126, 126 (For example, the following explanation of indigenous justice in North America may differ from an Aboriginal Australian concept of indigenous justice:

> The indigenous justice paradigm is based on a holistic philosophy and the world view of the aboriginal inhabitants of North America. These systems are guided by the unwritten customary laws, traditions, and practices that are learned primarily by example and through the oral teachings of tribal elders.).

23 Tony F. Marshall, Home Office of Research Development and Statistics Directorate, Restorative Justice: An Overview 5 (1996) (Restorative justice has been defined as: "[A] process whereby all the parties with a stake in a particular offence come together to resolve collectively how to deal with the aftermath of the offence and its implications for the future."); Howard Zehr, *The Little Book of Restorative Justice* (Intercourse: Good Books, 2002) (Zehr provides an excellent overview of the diverse restorative justice literature. Multiple understandings of the concept exist).

24 Nickson, *supra* note 3.

25 Howard Zehr, *Changing Lenses: A New Focus for Crime and Justice* (Scottsdale: Herald Press, 1990).

26 Jennifer J. Llewellyn and Daniel Philpott, 'Restorative Justice and Reconciliation: Twin Frameworks for Peacebuilding', in Jennifer J. Llewellyn and Daniel Philpott (eds.), *Restorative Justice, Reconciliation, and Peacebuilding* (Oxford: Oxford University Press, 2014), pp. 14–36.

27 *Afri-Forum and Another v. Malema and Another*, 2011 (12) BCLR 1289 (EqC).

1. is to be contrasted with vengeance;
2. dictates that a high value be placed on the life of a human being;
3. is inextricably linked to the values of and which places a high premium on dignity, compassion, humaneness and respect for humanity of another;
4. dictates a shift from confrontation to mediation and conciliation;
5. dictates good attitudes and shared concern;
6. favors the re-establishment of harmony in the relationship between parties and that such harmony should restore the dignity of the plaintiff without ruining the defendant;
7. favors restorative rather than retributive justice;
8. operates in a direction favoring reconciliation rather than estrangement of disputants;
9. works towards sensitizing a disputant or a defendant in litigation to the hurtful impact of his actions to the other party and towards changing such conduct rather than merely punishing the disputant;
10. promotes mutual understanding rather than punishment;
11. favors face-to-face encounters of disputants with a view to facilitating differences being resolved rather than conflict and victory for the most powerful;
12. favors civility and civilized dialogue premised on mutual tolerance.

Ubuntu broadens (Western) justice by incorporating different paths for addressing wrongs. A conception of transitional justice informed by ubuntu may well serve to enhance the justice that stakeholders receive. It does this by enabling responses that would otherwise be overlooked or dismissed in an approach to complementarity privileging Western legal traditions.

A way to broaden transitional justice would be to consider more actively a focus on harms and needs when assessing complementarity. Current transitional justice as practiced by the ICC focuses primarily on crimes. This focus is not unique to transitional justice or international criminal justice. It is also a dominant feature of most Western conceptions of criminal justice. The adoption of a focus on harms rather than crimes could assist the realization of a greater number of aims for justice.[28] Many aims relate more to the victim/survivor experience of mass violence and their needs for recovery. Currently,

28 *See* Zehr, *supra* note 25, at 40. (For example, as Zehr explains, restorative justice shifts the focus from crimes to harms).

these aims are not well-addressed in official retributive expressions of transitional justice. When we focus on crimes, recovery is rarely considered directly. A crime focus seeks to respond to a wrong, frequently by punishing the wrongdoer. These efforts do hope to provide some redress for those harmed directly by the wrongdoer – yet only for those whose harms are prosecuted. This leaves the victims whose harms have not been prosecuted, or perhaps even investigated, without redress. A focus on crimes can only ever hope to recognize symbolically the harms suffered by others whose offenders have not had their crimes investigated and prosecuted. This is a relevant consideration for the ICC, an institution that can only ever provide a handful of symbolic prosecutions.

There are several distinct benefits to transitional justice adopting a focus on harms.[29] The ICC can contribute to this through recognition and support for such initiatives through complementarity under Article 17. For societies in transition, the prior human rights abuses were most likely widespread. Hence, offending is similarly widespread. Transitional justice, as it is practiced through trials, has come to accept that the vast majority of offenders will not be prosecuted. This leaves the vast majority of crimes unattended by official efforts. Consequently, the victims of those crimes will not be directly engaged or invested in the transitional justice process. This means that the majority of victims are excluded, which can equate to the majority of a transitional society being excluded. Many of the intended goals of transitional justice can only be realized with the participation and investment of local communities. For this reason, recognizing as legitimate alternative justice mechanisms that focus on harms is beneficial, as it can include a far greater number of community members in the transitional justice process. When such efforts take place and ICC investigations and prosecutions might undermine those efforts, it is clearly not in the interests of a justice conceived more broadly, deeply, and longer to intervene.

A problematic concept with trials after periods of mass violence is that judging takes place from an entirely different moral order than that which existed during conflict.[30] Human rights abuses often take place in societies

29 *See* Joel Feinberg, *The Moral Limits of the Criminal Law: Harm to Others*, 4 vols. (Oxford: Oxford University Press, 1987) vol. I (for a full discussion of harms).

30 Miriam J. Aukerman, 'Extraordinary Evil, Ordinary Crime: A Framework for Understanding Transitional Justice' (2002) 15 *Harv. Hum. Rts. J.* 39, 59 (This difficulty is observed by Aukerman: "Radical evil involves horrific acts committed by average people who would never commit ordinary crime. How can one understand intent in such circumstances?"); James Cockayne, 'Hybrids or Mongrels? Internationalized War Crimes Trials as Unsuccessful Degradation Ceremonies' (2005) 4 *J. Hum. Rts.* 455 (Cockayne argues that this

with an absence of law and order and skewed moral frames as a result of conflict. In these conditions, crimes are frequently encouraged, rewarded, supported, and condoned by leaders, military and religious authorities, and even the offenders' communities. Under these circumstances, it may be difficult for many to avoid participation in human rights abuses. It may be common for human rights abusers to face a tough choice between demonstrating solidarity with their own group by participating in abuses, or risk the safety and security of themselves and their family. Judging such conduct when hostilities have abated and a different normative frame is in place may raise questions of legitimacy. A focus on crimes encourages judging from a legal framework. That framework is unlikely to sufficiently account for the moral quandaries some offenders faced during conflict. This in turn may discourage participation by those who are most likely to be in a position to repair harms: offenders, for instance, who know the fate and location of deceased loved ones. A focus on harms does not face this challenge. A focus on harms redirects attention towards recognizing the humanity of those who have suffered.

This is not to dismiss entirely the value of a focus on crimes, a focus designed to designate offensive conduct as abhorrent. The label of crime carries authority and weight: to describe something as a crime is to forcefully declare it outside the boundaries of accepted conduct. The application of the label crime is a powerful form of censure for criminals and provides a degree of acknowledgment for (some) victims. This is as true in transitional justice as it would be in domestic criminal justice. Similarly, a focus on crimes may promote the expressivist function of transitional justice described by Drumbl: "the messaging value of punishment to affirm respect for law, reinforce a moral consensus, narrate history and educate the public."[31] While the censure that follows from labelling something as criminal may be severe, the acknowledgment is likely to end at this point. It does not require that we examine the extent of the crime or its ongoing effects. It certainly does not require that we acknowledge the continuing impact of the crime on the victim. It may be a superficial form of acknowledgment for victims when genuine efforts at repair may do more to acknowledge the harms caused by the crime. For these reasons, there is limited scope to the acknowledgement victims receive by labelling the conduct that harmed them as criminal. In contrast, a focus on harms requires a commensurate focus on needs. The needs of individuals and com-

---

confrontation of moral orders, that forces transitional societies to reflect on their past, is a distinct benefit of trials in transitional justice).

31 Mark A. Drumbl, *Atrocity, Punishment, and International Law* (Cambridge: Cambridge University Press, 2007), p. 12.

munities after mass violence will correspond to what we might otherwise express as many of the aims of transitional justice: reparation, acknowledgment, truth.[32] Acknowledging alternative justice mechanisms that focus on harms rather than crimes as sufficient to exclude ICC jurisdiction is a fundamental way the ICC can be less Eurocentric and promote international law that is more authentically international.

Broadening our conception of responsibilities in transitional justice may provide another way to achieve a greater number of transitional justice goals. The term *responsibilities,* as it is used here, is distinct from *responsibility.* This proposal does not seek to broaden our understanding of who is criminally responsible. That would be a problematic suggestion. Criminal responsibility for crimes against humanity is a well-developed area of jurisprudence. Rather, it is proposed that we broaden our understanding of responsibilities in the wake of mass violence and as a component of transitional justice. If the ICC recognizes alternative justice efforts that focus on responsibilities, the scope for what justice might be delivered to post-conflict communities is enhanced. Responsibilities, in this sense, are steps that individuals, communities, businesses, industries, governments, militias, and others ought to take to rectify past wrongs and contribute to ongoing justice and rebuilding efforts. An oft-cited justification for the use of criminal trials in transitional justice is that they individualize guilt. The benefit of this, it is claimed, is to alleviate the burden of collective guilt from communities and to encourage communities to see crimes as having been perpetrated by individuals, not groups or entire communities, thereby promoting reconciliation. The true extent that this has taken place in post-conflict societies is difficult to assess. It appears, however, to have been more of a dream than a reality.[33] For instance, Nettlefield's research shows that members of the Armed Forces of Bosnia and Herzegovina were more likely to believe that other ethnicities, not their own, were most

32 Nickson, *supra* note 6.

33 *See* Laurel E. Fletcher and Harvey M. Weinstein, 'Violence and Social Repair: Rethinking the Contribution of Justice to Reconciliation' (2002) 24 *Hum. Rts. Q.* 573 (We should also be careful because a focus on individual guilt can contribute to misunderstandings and deliberate fictions about wider complicity and collaboration. This is problematic, as masking broader responsibility for crimes against humanity can be an impediment to justice and reconciliation. A justice that prosecutes relatively few senior leaders but leaves direct perpetrators of violence untouched, often among communities that include their victims, may not feel like much justice to those communities and victims).

responsible for atrocities, despite international and domestic trials.[34] In my own research, interviewees in Cambodia spoke of discrimination against the children of Khmer Rouge cadre by their non-Khmer Rouge teachers.[35] Such evidence suggests that trials have not been successful in removing collective guilt from communities. In response, it is proposed that to broaden transitional justice, we also need to conceive of responsibilities that stem from mass violence more broadly. There is a benefit in avoiding the attachment of guilt to communities in transitional societies, as outlined by the advocates for individualizing guilt. What should be encouraged is collective ownership of harms. This means that communities, government agencies or departments, businesses and industries, militias and security forces would accept responsibility to perform acts that will address the impact of conduct or complicity by such groups during conflict. Recognizing alternative justice mechanisms that respond to harms may result in more meaningful justice for those most affected by conflict, than from distant trials of a few leaders.

The notion advanced here of collective responsibility builds upon and draws from successful practices of group reconciliation efforts in Bougainville,[36] where reconciliation between groups was observed to create paths to reconciliation between individuals.[37] The rebuilding of houses and places of worship is not a new manifestation of collective efforts at reconciliation: such activities occurred in Indonesian peacebuilding and were seen to encourage the return of victims to former communities.[38] Activities conducted under this rubric are likely to go a long way in achieving many goals of transitional justice that are often neglected in a focus on prosecutions and trials. Of course, such initiatives could be pursued with trials, but where post-conflict communities elect for an alternative to prosecution, and where ICC involvement

---

34 Lara J. Nettlefield, 'From the Battlefield to the Barracks: The ICTY and the Armed Forces of Bosnia and Herzegovina' (2010) *Int'l J. Transnat'l Just.* 87.

35 Nickson, *supra* note 6.

36 John Braithwaite and Ray Nickson, 'Timing Truth, Reconciliation, and Justice After War' (2012) 27 *Ohio State J. Disp. Res.* 443, 460; *see also* John Braithwaite, Hilary Charlesworth, Peter Reddy and Leah Dunn, *Reconciliation and Architectures of Commitment: Sequencing Peace in Bougainville* (Canberra: Australian National University E Press, 2010).

37 Braithwaite, *supra* note 36, at 460 (Only later, after individuals who murdered or raped specific individuals had attended that collective reconciliation and realized that forgiveness was genuine, would they consider individual reconciliation.).

38 John Braithwaite, Valerie Braithwaite, Michael Cookson and Leah Dunn, *Anomie and Violence: Non-Truth and Reconciliation in Indonesian Peacebuilding* (Canberra: Australian National University E Press, 2010).

would interfere with this, the ICC should prioritize local choices through its complementary role.

A practical reason to recognize alternative justice is that trials can be counterproductive. Offenders may find living with their crimes difficult and employ techniques of rationalization and neutralization to justify their behavior.[39] In a domestic criminal setting, offenders will argue that: their victims deserved it or invited the offense; the victims could afford to be deprived of their property or rights; the criminal conduct was not particularly harmful; or the offender themself is the true victim of the situation.[40] Such techniques are used to diminish feelings of guilt that would otherwise be experienced as a result of criminal conduct. Trials are said to address such rationalization and neutralization quite poorly.[41] Instead of encouraging offenders to dispense with rationalization and neutralization techniques – to accept the harms committed and recognize the impact of their behavior and the suffering of victims – prosecutions and trials have quite the opposite effect. The adversarial nature of criminal proceedings encourages the maintenance of rationalization and neutralization techniques. Similarly, the removal of – or limited role for – victims from the process does little to facilitate any realization of the impact of offending on them. There is very little in prosecutions and trials that confronts the offender directly with the harm of their offending and that consequently challenges their rationalizations and neutralizations.

This is directly relevant to transitional societies. In such societies, rationalization and neutralization techniques are manifested in the process of othering. Here, groups are divided by some form of identity (such as ethnicity) and encouraged to view others in opposition to that identity. These "others" are the enemy and atrocities and human rights abuses against them are both

39 Gresham M. Sykes and David Matza, 'Techniques of Neutralization: A Theory of Delinquency' (1957) 22 *Am. Socio. Rev.* 664, 666 ([M]uch delinquency is based on what is essentially an unrecognized extension of defences to crimes, in the form of justifications for deviance that are seen as valid by the delinquent but not by the legal system or society at large. These justifications are commonly referred to as rationalizations. They are viewed as following deviant behaviour and as protecting the individual from self-blame and blame of others after the fact.);

See also Zehr, *supra* note 23 (Also noted by Zehr, who sees a possible solution in restorative justice).

40 Sykes, *supra* note 39 (describing these as the denial of responsibility, the denial of injury, the denial of the victim, the condemnation of the condemners, and the appeal to higher loyalties).

41 Zehr, *supra* note 23.

rationalized and neutralized by reference to this identity framework.[42] Problematically, in international criminal trials, these rationalizations and neutralizations continue. It has been common for defendants to maintain their neutralization fictions during international criminal trials. In many trials, the actions are still maintained as saving, liberating, reforming, or protecting the perpetrator's in-group.[43] Or the extent and nature of the abuses is denied. Such conduct during trials can further entrench social division in transitional societies. This is because the various sides still see the enemy-other; there is nothing to bring communities together in this landscape. It is an impediment to peaceful co-existence and reconciliation.

An approach that directly confronted these rationalization and neutralization techniques could go much further in aiding shared aims of peaceful co-existence and reconciliation. What may be required is a process that re-humanizes the victim who has become the enemy-other through rationalization and neutralization. Although such re-humanization must take place from the offender's (and preferably also the offender community's) perspective, it places the dignity and inviolability of the victim at its center. A shift from viewing the victim as the enemy-other to considering them a fellow citizen worthy of the same respect and rights is an important step towards reconciling individuals and communities. One way would be to focus on harms, but it also requires greater inclusivity. Even if reconciliation is too hopeful, there is still the prospect of contributing to an easing of tensions and the reduction of embedded violence by fostering a climate of greater mutual respect.

Deepening our conception of transitional justice means providing greater opportunities for meaningful engagement in the process. When an ICC investigation and prosecution would disrupt local justice initiatives or undermine the integrity of local, democratic institutions pursuing justice, the ICC should defer to these initiatives under its complementary role. Recognizing deeper conceptions of justice can mean empowering local, contextually and culturally relevant designs for pursing justice. This method of institutional

42 *See* Elizabeth Stanley, 'Torture, Silence and Recognition' (2004) 16 *Current Issues Crim. Just.* 5, 15 (Stanley, in discussion of the Chilean experience of transitional justice, notes:

> The distancing thesis proposes that perpetrators and victims of torture share no commonalities, no human connection – they are essentially 'othered'. Of course [...] the 'othering' or 'monstering' of political opponents in Chile was part of state techniques to suppress dissent against violations. The construction of 'victims' as being troublesome threats to the state ensured compliance from individual officers assigned to participate in violence.).

43 Nickson, *supra* note 6.

design, "outside-in" design,[44] is a more participatory and stakeholder inclusive method. An "outside-in" approach to the design of an institution is where the design reflects the needs and preferences of users rather than administrators.[45] Braithwaite notes, in relation to tax systems and risk management, that institutions designed inside-out (designed with administrative purposes in mind) can often be too inflexible.[46] A similar practice exists in transitional justice: mechanisms are often designed to reflect the capacities of donors or goals of elites. The ICC is such an institution, not designed by post-conflict communities, but pre-existing and inflexible in adapting its practices to local contexts and needs, except when it utilizes complementarity with a broader, deeper, longer conception of justice. An "outside-in" design for transitional justice would incorporate many more justice goals in this process.[47] There are several benefits for transitional justice from this. It makes transitional justice far more inclusive than its current practice at the official level. Recognizing alternative justice initiatives designed outside-in means communities would be aware that they have involvement in the process and that their ideas are considered.

A broader conception of transitional justice is a more holistic and multidimensional understanding of what justice can mean and be.[48] The ICC exemplifies how legalism has come to dominate the theory and practice of transitional justice. This dominance of legalism, especially Western adversarial trials, constrains the positive contributions other understandings of justice can make in transitional societies. In a broadened conception of transitional justice, prosecutorial responses would be problematized to a greater extent and various other responses would be considered in tandem with, or in place of, trials. A significant and straightforward way to achieve this is for the ICC and its Prosecutors to take a more humble view of investigation and prosecution in the Western legal sense and accept broader, deeper, and longer understandings of alternative justice mechanisms as genuine national efforts at justice that exclude further ICC involvement.

---

44 John Braithwaite, *Markets in Vice, Markets in Virtue* (New York: Oxford University Press, 2005), p. 156.

45 *Id.*

46 *Id.*

47 Jaya Ramji-Nogales, 'Designing Bespoke Transitional Justice: A Pluralist Process Approach' (2010) 32 *Mich. J. Int'l L.* 1, 56 (noting the success of a similar approach – "surveying the preferences of local populations and of thorough integration of traditional systems of justice" – to designing transitional justice in Timor-Leste).

48 Nickson, *supra* note 3.

The ICC was only ever conceived as a supplementary institution to national jurisdiction for international criminal law – it complements, but does not usurp the authority of national courts to pursue justice in the wake of breaches of international criminal law. It is precisely because of the ICC's complementary role that it can perform a more inclusive approach to non-Western legal traditions, and support traditional, restorative, and other more contextually appropriate justice measures when nations exiting conflict and transitioning to peace and democracy elect to utilize them. This will require for many, particularly for the international legal and NGO communities invested in conceptions of international criminal justice premised on Western, retributive justice, a reimagining of how justice is understood. I argue that nothing, in particular, must change about the rules of the ICC, but that those within the ICC and its advocates must be more embracive of broader, deeper, and longer conceptions of justice. To this end, the ICC must be more humble about what it can contribute, and recognize where appropriate alternative justice mechanisms are satisfactory without a further need for investigation and prosecution. This will permit far greater recognition of the myriad ways that justice can be sought – and achieved – in the wake of mass violence and crime against humanity.

CHAPTER 35

The ICC and Global Constitutionalism as Western Hegemony: Reconceptualizing Criminal Conduct and Structures

Theresa Sophia Reinold

The success of the ICC – an institution which forms an integral part of the global constitutionalist project – depends upon a complex interplay of factors. Yet, as I shall argue in this essay,[1] the Court's most precious and, at the same time, most precarious resource – and therefore the most important determinant of its success – is its legitimacy. Legitimacy is not a quantity that can simply be created and then left to operate by itself; it needs to be constantly renewed and is easily wasted through bias, arrogance, and/or neglect. States from the global periphery have long accused the ICC of just these failures, many going as far as calling the Court a tool of neocolonial interference, a Trojan horse designed to subjugate the global South once more to the rule of the North – this time, however, not through military means or other forms of outright coercion, but through the more subtle and insidious mechanisms offered by hegemonic international law. This erosion of the Court's legitimacy in the Global South has undermined its ability to induce compliance from those addressed normatively and thus represents a grave danger to the ICC's ability to successfully discharge its mandate. In this essay I will therefore engage with the critique articulated by representatives of the global South in more detail – a critique which has been voiced not only by states from the global periphery but equally by scholars representing Third World Approaches to International Law (TWAIL). I will discuss to what extent the ICC – both on paper and in practice – has indeed under-represented the norms, traditions, and interests of the Global South, and at the same time suggest ways to counteract the ICC's erosion of legitimacy.

Law, such is the fundamental premise underlying this comment, implies a political choice. The material content of the law, the way it is applied,

1 This essay reuses material from Theresa Reinold, 'Constitutionalization? Whose Constitutionalization? Africa's Ambivalent Engagement with the International Criminal Court' (2012) 10 *Int'l J. Const. L.* 1076.

 | DOI:10.1163/9789004686755_043

interpreted, and enforced – all of this involves decisions which in turn are shaped by political ideologies, power imbalances, and hegemonic influence. This, however, does not imply that the law has no autonomy from politics, that it is simply a tool used by the powerful and central to subjugate the weak and peripheral. In both the disciplines of International Law and International Relations, theories have been developed that seek to account for the ways in which the powerful seek to usurp the law to universalize their own interests;[2] or, alternatively, to explain how the law may resist such attempts at usurpation, how it can maintain its autonomy in the face of attempted political interference.[3] In this essay, I posit that power and law are deeply intertwined, that the law is at the same time partly autonomous from and an instrument of political power. This perspective is inspired by a theoretical approach that has been labeled "realist constructivism" which addresses the myriad ways in which political power and law interact.[4]

Now, just like general international law is at the same time an instrument of power and a constraint upon this exercise, so is international criminal law (ICL). The ICC reflects this tension very well, as it embodies a fundamentally Western (or Northern) understanding of international criminal justice and has therefore frequently come under fire for allegedly being biased against the Global South. Elsewhere I have argued that the ICC forms part of an emerging global constitutionalist architecture,[5] and that constitutionalism tends to evoke the idea of taming politics through the force of law – which suggests that less powerful actors should welcome the supposedly equalizing force of ICL. It turns out, however, that states from the Global South are continuously contesting the ICC's legitimacy, as they see constitutionalism as an essentially hegemonic project, which condenses Western notions of good governance, human rights, and the rule of law into the nucleus of an emerging global constitutional order.

This point of view is associated with a school of thought which has become known as TWAIL.[6] Rather than seeing international law as an emancipatory project, which enabled self-determination, de-colonization, and independent statehood for the Global South, TWAIL scholars tend to

2 *See, e.g.*, Balakrishnan Rajagopal, *International Law from Below: Development, Social Movements and Third World Resistance* (Cambridge: Cambridge University Press, 2003).

3 *See, e.g.*, Theresa Reinold, 'Cynicism and the Autonomy of International Law, in Cynical International Law? Abuse and Circumvention', in Björnstjern Baade et al. (eds.), *Public International and European Law* (Berlin: Springer, 2020), p. 15.

4 J. Samuel Barkin, 'Realist Constructivism' (2003) 5 *Int'l Stud. Rev.* 325.

5 Reinold, *supra* note 1.

6 *See, e.g.*, Makau W. Mutua, 'What is TWAIL?' (2000) 94 *Proc. ASIL Ann. Meeting* 31.

view international law as a fig leaf for the pursuit of particularistic hegemonic interests. Their goal is therefore to turn international law into a weapon wielded by the powerless and peripheral against the strong and central. As Makau Mutua famously wrote:

> TWAIL is driven by three basic, interrelated and purposeful objectives. The first is to understand, deconstruct, and unpack the uses of international law as a medium for the creation and perpetuation of a racialized hierarchy of international norms and institutions that subordinate non-Europeans to Europeans. Second, it seeks to construct and present an alternative normative legal edifice for international governance. Finally, TWAIL seeks through scholarship, policy, and politics to eradicate the conditions of underdevelopment in the Third World.[7]

TWAIL scholarship's basic conception of international law as a hegemonic project has time and again also surfaced in controversies involving the ICC and states of the Global South. Taking these controversies to a more abstract level, one could argue that they revolve around two major themes, one regarding substance, the other one regarding process: in terms of substantive law, the ICC has often been criticized for failing to take into account non-Western values, traditions, and historical grievances. Secondly, at a procedural level, the ICC has been accused of being politicized by the Western-dominated institutions of global governance, notably the U.N. Security Council, which was given a prominent role in activating (or suspending) the ICC's jurisdiction.

I will address each of these critiques in turn. Before, however, I will briefly reflect upon some of the basic theoretical propositions underlying these controversies, as they raise fundamental questions about the global normative order, questions which touch upon international law's relationship with its most important ally (or enemy), namely powerful states.

International law is in constant need of legitimation. To the extent that it is being "upgraded" into a law of subordination which makes increasingly intrusive demands upon the internal make-up of nation-states, a need for justification arises: why must states follow this blueprint of legitimate governance and not another? While constitutions confer legitimacy upon political systems, in order to retain their compliance pull towards those addressed normatively, constitutions simultaneously require an ongoing

---

7 *Id.* at 31.

process of legitimation. This process is contested and disruptive, however, as different actors hold diverging conceptions of the "good life." The concept of constitution is here defined as a framework composed of primary and secondary norms – the former being a set of fundamental rules that directly regulate the behavior of the legal subjects, whereas the latter govern the (trans)formation, interpretation, application, and enforcement of these primary norms. The primary norms enshrined in a given constitution stipulate a particular version of the "good life," a core set of values, which, in the Global North, typically includes fundamental civil and political rights. Second or even third generation human rights are generally considered to be less relevant in the North; at the same time, however, these categories of rights feature much more prominently in the legal discourse and practice of the Global South.

While primary norms directly regulate behavior, secondary rules regulate how primary norms are made, and how different public authorities involved in the making and application of primary norms relate to one another. The litmus test for the constitutionalization of international law is therefore the emergence of overarching secondary rules that govern the relationship between different layers of law and regulate the competencies of the various bodies involved in the making and application of international law.

If the project of global constitutionalism is thus informed by a core value system that seeks to universalize a particular concept of the good life, this naturally begs the question of whose vision of the good life is being universalized and whose worldviews are being marginalized. The global normative order rests on a corpus of mainly Western norms, which, over time, came to be regarded as universal by the international community at large. The semblance of universality has not made existing geopolitical cleavages, ideological struggles, and Third World grievances disappear, however. On this view, the project of global constitutionalism thus ought to be treated with considerable skepticism. If the nascent global constitutional order is seen not as reflecting universal interests, but rather as a particularistic project launched by powerful actors seeking to cement their hegemony in world politics, this perception will undermine the law's compliance pull towards actors from the periphery.

The International Criminal Court's establishment in 1998 represented an important step towards the constitutionalization of international law, as the Rome Statute not only universalizes a set of fundamental primary norms, but also lays down important secondary rules clarifying the Court's position in the broader global system of checks and balances. The ICC is not just an organization dedicated to the protection of a core set of human rights, but is simultaneously nested in a broader framework of global governance institutions whose relationships are regulated through various instruments, such as the U.N. Charter, the Rome Statute, and the Vienna Convention on the Law of Treaties.

It has frequently been pointed out that negotiations at Rome cut across the usual geopolitical fault lines, bringing together actors from the Global North as well as representatives of the Global South. Many African states pushed for a strong and independent court, much like their European counterparts within the so-called like-minded group. Yet a few years after the entry into force of the Rome State, the relationship between non-Western states and the ICC turned sour, when it became clear that the ICC was focusing primarily on what many saw as "easy prey," that is, weaker states from the Global South, all the while shielding powerful Northern actors from prosecution. The AU-ICC standoff is a well-documented example of this North-South cleavage. The controversy sparked by the U.N. Security Council's referral of the Al-Bashir case to the ICC raised thorny legal (and political) issues that affect the global constitutional architecture as a whole. When the controversy erupted, the African Union not only sought to influence the interpretation of fundamental primary norms of international law (in this case, the principle of immunity), but also targeted the secondary rules of international law, namely those norms regulating the allocation of authority for the maintenance of international peace and security. Since the AU-ICC standoff has been analyzed in much detail elsewhere, I will not revisit this debate here.

Rather, I would like to take a step back, and explore the broader theoretical question of hegemonic bias in the global constitutionalist architecture, of which the ICC is an integral part. According to many voices from the global periphery, the ICC – in terms of both material jurisdiction and procedure (or, to use constitutionalist language, in terms of both primary and secondary norms) – is biased against the Global South.

Regarding the first criticism addressing the Court's subject-matter jurisdiction, one must concede that present-day ICL was indubitably inspired Western (or Northern) legal traditions, with the Nuremberg principles informing subsequent projects of international criminal justice, including the adoption of the Rome Statute. Non-Western sources of law, such as principles of African customary law, Islamic law, Chinese law, etc. are not represented in the ICC's normative framework. In particular, criticism has been leveled against the ICC's exclusive focus on direct violence, as exemplified by the Rome Statute's definition of core crimes, namely aggression, genocide, war crimes, and crimes against humanity. This definition of core crimes has been criticized for allegedly blinding the Court to the underlying root causes of direct violence, namely the colonial legacy which gave rise to inter-ethnic grievances, fragile states, and abusive regimes in the first place, and thus created powder kegs that were bound to explode at some point. Johan Galtung famously distinguished between three types of violence:[8] direct physical violence (e.g. a Russian soldier shooting an unarmed civilian in the town of Bucha); structural violence, that is, the avoidable non-fulfillment of basic human needs (e.g. a child starving to death in Bangladesh because of the global food crisis triggered by Russia's invasion of Ukraine); and, finally, cultural violence, that is, the attitudes and practices that make us unable to see that structural or physical violence is being perpetrated (e.g. Western media disproportionately covering the suffering of white Ukrainians, while underreporting humanitarian tragedies suffered by non-white, non-Western victims).

Inspired by Galtung's typology, scholars writing from a TWAIL perspective have maintained that the ICC's narrow focus on exercising jurisdiction over various forms of direct violence affecting the enjoyment of fundamental civil and political rights is limiting and one-sided, and that the Rome Statute should recognize the significance of structural and cultural violence,[9] which, of course, are forms of violence much more difficult to address in a criminal trial. ICC trials specifically, and proceedings in Western or Western-style courts more generally, typically criminalize and usually individualize certain forms of violent conduct that takes place under often chaotic and complex circumstances. The root causes of such criminal conduct, such as colonialism, racism, etc. are not addressed in the course of such trials, leaving important and devastating forms of mass violence unaddressed. Rajagopal thus laments that ICL's prevailing focus on violations of fundamental civil and political rights renders other types of violence, "such as that generated by development, invisible to the discourse."[10]

Courts in the Global South have unsurprisingly been more open to including such forms of indirect violence in their subject-matter jurisdiction – consider, for instance, the list of crimes over which the Criminal Chamber in the African Court of Justice and Human Rights (ACJHR) seeks jurisdiction. Even though not without flaws, the scope of material jurisdiction of the chamber has been welcomed by TWAIL scholars as it broadens the list

8 Johan Galtung, 'Violence, Peace, and Peace Research' (1969) 6 *J. Peace Rsch.* 167-91.

9 Asad G. Kiyani, 'Third World Approaches to International Criminal Law' (2016) 109 *Am. J. Int'l L. Unbound* 258.

10 Rajagopal, *supra* note 2, at 231.

of crimes to include conduct that the ICC has neglected, including unconstitutional changes of government, corruption, the illicit exploitation of natural resources, money laundering, and trafficking in human beings, drugs, and toxic waste.[11] This expansion of material jurisdiction addresses the concern articulated by TWAIL scholars about Western-style courts' exclusive focus on direct physical violence, as it also extends to forms of structural violence, arising, for instance, out of the corruption of public officials, crimes against the environment, etc.

To make the ICC more responsive to the interests of the Global South, TWAIL scholars have therefore suggested a radical reconstruction of the Rome Statute. Recognizing that the ICC does criminalize certain forms of neocolonial practices (with Article 7 of the Rome Statute criminalizing forcible population transfer and apartheid, and Article 8 prohibiting the settlement of occupied territory by an occupying power), TWAIL scholars nonetheless believe that these provisions do not go far enough. Since their envisaged reconstruction of ICL is quite radical, it deserves being quoted at length:

> [M]ore importantly, a TWAIL perspective would prescribe reconceptualization of the material conduct and structures that are criminalized in the first instance. While the existing population transfer crimes [...] might at least begin to get at some of the land control and migration issues that go to the structural conditions underlying socio-economic inequality, where they are rooted in the Geneva Conventions they will remain limited to traditionally defined and bracketed settings of armed conflict and belligerent occupation. Any meaningful reconstructionist approach to international criminal law will need to go beyond the problems of unequal enforcement and operational selectivity to the essence of the actions and forms of violence criminalized at the design level. If international criminal law is to take seriously its claim to be part of a project of global justice, it must at some point begin to tackle the economic contexts of war, exploitation and scarcity.[12]

According to these scholars, there is nothing novel about positing such a significant reconstruction of ICL – after all, beginning in the 1950s, the

11 Protocol on Amendments to the Protocol on the Statute of the African Court of Justice and Human Rights, art. 28A, June 27, 2014.

12 John Reynolds and Sujith Xavier, '"The Dark Corners of the World": TWAIL and International Criminal Justice' (2016) 14 *J. Int'l Crim. Just.* 980.

International Law Commission had already engaged in efforts at defining an expanded list of international crimes. Initially, the list was quite extensive and mentioned twelve core crimes, yet due to the opposition of Western states to including crimes such as colonialism, apartheid, and severe environmental damage, the list was ultimately reduced to the four core crimes nowadays codified in the Rome Statute.[13]

Now, while I agree that it is imperative to address the structural and cultural forms of violence that are the root causes of the more direct forms of violence criminalized by the Rome Statute and other international legal instruments, I do not think that the ICC is the right institution to take on this challenge. Handing such an expansive wish-list to a Court whose resources are already stretched thin (and which, as a result, is confronting multiple charges of selectivity and bias) would only make matters worse, and further undermine the ICC's ability to effectively discharge its mandate. In theory, it would certainly be desirable for the ICC to dispense justice to all victims of violence of whatever form, but this is simply not feasible. We live in a decidedly non-ideal world and the ICC's jurisdiction rules as well as prosecutorial decisions have to take this into account. While, as discussed above, the ACJHR's founding mothers and fathers have been engaged in an innovative attempt at criminalizing structural violence, I am quite doubtful that the ACJHR will be able to deliver on this promise. Like any other international court, the ACJHR has limited resources, and overburdening the court with an extremely ambitious mandate will likely undermine its ability to bring justice to either category of victims – those suffering physical violence as well as those experiencing structural or cultural violence.

Therefore, rather than expanding its subject-matter jurisdiction, the ICC should demonstrate its responsiveness to the interests of the Global South in a different way. As argued earlier, the global constitutionalist project requires not only agreement on a core set of substantive values but equally implies the emergence of secondary rules. Thus, apart from the controversy over which primary norms should be included in the material jurisdiction of the ICC, the Rome Statute has also frequently been criticized for laying down secondary rules that strongly disfavor weaker states and perpetuate the hegemonic privileges of the Global North. This criticism has focused on three provisions in particular: the U.N. Security Council's referral and deferral powers enshrined in Rome Statute Articles 13 and 16 respectively, and Article 98 on bilateral agreements. The U.N. Security Council's role in

13 *Id.* at 981.

activating or suspending the ICC's jurisdiction has been the subject of the ongoing controversy between the AU and the ICC. The perception of hegemonic bias was further reinforced by powerful states' frequent use of Article 98, which allows the conclusion of bilateral agreements that would prevent the ICC from demanding the arrest or extradition of individuals from one state who are in the jurisdiction of the second. The United States has concluded numerous Article 98 agreements to shield its own nationals from prosecution. In so doing, it has made ample use of its preponderant material power to "induce" other states into signing these agreements in order to safeguard America's hegemonic privileges. This inevitably creates a perception that despite the assumption of sovereign equality, some states are more equal than the rest, and that the Global North – by virtue of its economic prowess and political clout – may easily escape accountability, while peripheral states lacking these material resources will be disproportionately targeted by the ICC.

Criticizing this imbalance does not imply that perpetrators from the Global South who are brought before the ICC are in any way less culpable and should not be prosecuted – just because justice cannot be achieved everywhere this does not mean that it should not be sought anywhere.

It does imply, however, that if the secondary rules governing the application of international criminal justice are so obviously and blatantly skewed in favor the Global North, the ICC – if it wants to maintain its legitimacy as the universal face of international criminal justice – needs to urgently rethink its prosecutorial decisions: even in those cases where the ICC could potentially exercise jurisdiction over powerful Northern actors – the Afghanistan situation is a case in point – the Prosecutor decided to set aside war crimes committed by U.S. forces in Afghanistan and instead prioritized crimes committed by the Taliban and the Islamic State. While the latter's misconduct clearly deserves to be investigated, prosecuted, and punished, letting the United States off the hook once again only reinforces existing grievances in the Global South and inevitably creates the impression that equality before the law is an illusion, that what matters most in international (criminal) law is money and weapons, thus reaffirming a basic tenet of realist International Relations theory according to which international law is merely an epiphenomenon of the underlying distribution of (hard) power in world politics.

While I am in full agreement that the secondary rules governing the deferral and referral of situations before the ICC are outdated, hegemonic, and harmful to the Court's legitimacy, I also think that a modification of these rules is highly unlikely in the near future. I therefore do not want to issue yet another (futile) call for disempowering the U.N. Security Council. I do want to conclude, however, by calling upon the Office of the Prosecutor to rethink its prosecutorial strategy in order to correct the imbalances that have characterized the ICC's previous interventions. There are ways to reduce the ICC's hegemonic bias which do not require modifying the Rome Statute, with all the difficulties this entails. Correcting or at least reducing this bias essentially lies within the discretion of the Prosecutor, who decides what crimes to focus on once the Court has indeed asserted jurisdiction. The Prosecutor should use his discretion to focus on emblematic cases involving crimes committed by powerful Northern actors (such as war crimes committed by U.S. troops in Afghanistan) in order to demonstrate to the international community in general and the Global South in particular that no one is above the law. Evidently, such courage does not come without political cost – after all, the ICC is dependent on Western donors and turning against some of these donors risks losing the financial and political support they have to offer. Yet while donor support is an incredibly important resource for the ICC, there is one resource that is even more precious, namely legitimacy. If the ICC squanders this valuable resource by continuing to go after the easy prey all the while avoiding the tough cases, it puts its own existence at risk.

PART 8

Decentralized Accountability: ICC Prosecutorial Engagement with State Courts and Regional Entities

Introduction to Part 8

The following question was featured on www.ICCForum.com from September 2023 through January 2024:

How, and to what extent, should the ICC's Office of the Prosecutor engage with national, regional, or other authorities or organizations to support accountability for those accused of grave crimes?

The Rome Statute and its principle of complementarity contemplate potential accountability for grave crimes via a range of possible authorities, including not only the International Criminal Court, but also national authorities (which might prosecute their own nationals, or non-nationals under various theories, including universal jurisdiction), special tribunals or procedures established by the United Nations, or entities established on a regional or plurilateral basis.

Given its limited resources, mandate, and authority, the OTP is able to prosecute a limited number of those accused of being most responsible for grave crimes. Increasingly, some have suggested expanding global accountability at the national level, via exercise of universal jurisdiction, or through entities that might be established on a regional, plurilateral, or other international level. We refer to this approach as "decentralized accountability."

In this expanded issue of the ICC Forum, we ask four sets of questions.

FIRST, how, and to what extent, should the ICC's Office of the Prosecutor engage with national authorities exercising universal jurisdiction?

With more states now exercising universal jurisdiction, how can the Office of the Prosecutor (OTP) of the International Criminal Court (ICC or the Court) make itself a more effective partner, including by expanding its provision of information or evidence to national authorities pursuant to Article 93(10) of the Rome Statute?

The expanded exercise of universal jurisdiction by national authorities presents increased opportunities for accountability. Positive complementarity may entail a coordinated approach to the prosecution of crimes by the ICC and national authorities, one that could be employed in cases where the exercise of universal jurisdiction is contemplated or engaged. It has been suggested that the OTP might encourage national trials via the exercise of universal jurisdiction, where possible, for some crimes. In some cases, it has been suggested that positive complementarity might involve: the use and admission of evidence collected by the OTP before national courts; OTP training or workshops for state prosecutors on issues specific to the

 | DOI:10.1163/9789004686755_044

prosecution of international crimes; OTP assistance, as appropriate, with drafting national laws that codify or enable assertion of universal jurisdiction over international crimes; or the Court's Chambers offering training of, or workshops for, national judges on challenges particular to the prosecution of international crimes in universal jurisdiction cases. As the Court has limited financial resources and is not a development agency, some suggest the costs of any such trainings should not be assumed by the Court.

To what extent and how should the ICC, and the OTP in particular, engage in such efforts? How could consistency in the application of the law and standards of investigations and prosecutions be maintained? What difficulties do national authorities confront in attempting to prosecute pursuant to universal jurisdiction, and how might the OTP best assist in overcoming those difficulties?

Given security and confidentiality concerns related to information and evidence collected by the OTP, what limits may or should be placed on the sharing and use of any such information or evidence by the OTP with national authorities exercising universal jurisdiction? To the extent that the OTP, or the Court more broadly, could offer training, workshops, or technical assistance to national investigators, prosecutors, or judges that might be engaging in universal jurisdiction cases, how should such activities be structured? To what extent and under what conditions might the OTP assist national authorities in their drafting of national statutes to deter international crimes via universal jurisdiction?

What are the crimes with respect to which the OTP may offer assistance? Article 93(10)(a) of the Rome Statute provides:

> The Court may, upon request, cooperate with and provide assistance to a State Party conducting an investigation into or trial in respect of conduct which constitutes a crime within the jurisdiction of the Court or which constitutes a serious crime under the national law of the requesting State.

In considering OTP assistance to national authorities exercising universal jurisdiction, how should a "serious crime under the national law of the requesting State" be defined or evaluated? To what extent should the OTP assist national authorities exercising universal jurisdiction where crimes are being charged both within and outside the parameters of Article 93(10)(a)?

Could and should the ICC assist in national cases of civil accountability?

SECOND, how, and to what extent, should the ICC's Office of the Prosecutor engage with regional organizations to support accountability for those accused of grave crimes?

What potential role could be envisioned for regional organizations in implementation of the principle of complementarity? What remedies or mechanisms adopted by regional courts or organizations would satisfy the Rome Statute's principle of complementarity?

What kinds of support from the ICC or the Office of the Prosecutor might regional organizations want or need in pursuit of accountability?

Pursuant to Rome Statute Articles 54(3)(d) and (e), 87(1)(b), and 87(6), the Court may conclude agreements and arrangements to cooperate with international organizations, including regional organizations, courts, tribunals, or other mechanisms. What kinds of cooperative agreements or arrangements with regional organizations or entities might be advisable in support of accountability?

With what types of regional organizations should the Court or the Office of the Prosecutor conclude such agreements or arrangements? Regional courts or tribunals? Regional commissions? Regional investigations? Regional development banks? Regional non-governmental organizations?

To what extent, under what circumstances, and subject to what limitations should the ICC work with regional organizations to share or collect evidence? What technical assistance, if any, should the ICC or the Office of the Prosecutor provide to regional organizations in pursuit of accountability for grave crimes?

THIRD, how, and to what extent, should the ICC's Office of the Prosecutor engage with specialized international criminal tribunals or commissions, with jurisdiction over a particular crime or conflict, established by an international body, such as the United Nations or an organ thereof, to support accountability for those accused of grave crimes?

What kinds of support from the ICC or the Office of the Prosecutor might such a tribunal or commission want or need in pursuit of accountability? What kinds of cooperative agreements or arrangements with such a tribunal or commission might be advisable in support of accountability?

Given security and confidentiality concerns related to information and evidence collected by the OTP, what limits may or should be placed on the sharing and use of any such information or evidence by the OTP with such a tribunal or commission?

What are the crimes with respect to which the OTP may offer assistance to such a tribunal or commission?

FINALLY, what are the strengths and weaknesses, and prospects and risks, of decentralized accountability?

CHAPTER 36

Proactive Complementarity (Revisited)

William W. Burke-White

Some fifteen years ago, I argued that the International Criminal Court should implement a strategy of "proactive complementarity" or, as some have called it, "positive complementarity."[1] Under this model, the ICC would take an active approach in encouraging and supporting domestic prosecutions of international crimes, particularly in the state in which those crimes occurred. A significant consideration in my argument was that the mere threat of prosecution by an international tribunal could incentivize territorial states to prosecute such crimes so as to avoid international intervention and supervision. Initial evidence, from cases including Bosnia (where the ICTY was actively undertaking prosecutions) and Congo (where the ICC was active) supported this pathway to domestic accountability.[2]

When I put those arguments forward, the ICC was still a brand-new institution, building its capacities and opening its first investigations. Attention was focused far more on how the ICC might get cases and apprehend suspects than it was on how the ICC might get rid of cases and send suspects back to national jurisdictions. Fifteen years later, the question has flipped. With 17 situations under investigation and more than 50 individuals indicted,[3] it has become clear that the ICC – no matter how efficient or well-resourced it becomes – cannot prosecute all the cases currently before it, much less the full range of serious international crimes occurring in the

1 William W. Burke-White, 'Proactive Complementarity: The International Criminal Court and National Courts in the Rome System of Justice' (2008) 49 *Harv. Int'l L.J.* 53–108.

2 William W. Burke-White, 'The Domestic Influence of International Criminal Tribunals: The International Criminal Tribunal for the Former Yugoslavia and the Creation of the State Court of Bosnia and Herzegovina' (2008) 46 *Colum. J. Transnat'l L.* 279–350; William W. Burke-White, 'Complementarity in Practice: The International Criminal Court as Part of a System of Multilevel Global Governance in the Democratic Republic of Congo' (2005) 18 *Leiden J. Int'l L.* 557–590.

3 *Defendants*, INTERNATIONAL CRIMINAL COURT, https://www.icc-cpi.int/defendants (last visited September 4, 2023).

 | DOI:10.1163/9789004686755_045

world today. Some have described it as a "capacity crisis" that "threatens not only the ICC's effectiveness, but also its legitimacy."[4]

While the case overload at the ICC is problematic, the broader structural considerations that limit the Court's capacity are not. In fact, those structural limitations should be embraced. During the negotiation of the Rome Statute in 1998, the ICC was conceived of as a court of limited jurisdiction, secondary to national courts. After all, the preamble to the Rome Statute makes clear that it is the duty of states "to exercise its criminal jurisdiction over those responsible for international crimes" and that the Court is "complementary to national criminal jurisdictions."[5]

While the young ICC – particularly under its first two Prosecutors – focused on building its own capacities, it was reluctant to actively engage with national jurisdictions to encourage their own prosecutions of international crimes. ICC officials did, of course, take part in consultations and trainings in some states in which it was undertaking investigations. But it did not make it an institutional priority to systematically advance and support national prosecutions of international crimes, especially those under active ICC investigation. The time has come for it to do so. In fact, today's more mature ICC has far more capacity and influence to actually catalyze national prosecutions than it did back in 2005.

1 The ICC's Ability to Catalyze National Prosecutions

Generally speaking, domestic prosecutions of international crimes fail for two key reasons: lack of political will and lack of capacity.[6] The ICC has the ability to assist states in overcoming both of these limitations. The Rome Statute specifically authorizes and envisions the Court to play a role in moving domestic prosecutions forward. Article 93(10)(a) provides:

> The Court may, upon request, cooperate with and provide assistance to a State Party conducting an investigation into or trial in respect of conduct which constitutes a crime within the jurisdiction of the Court

4 Elizabeth Evenson and Jonathan O'Donohue, *The International Criminal Court at Risk*, OPEN DEMOCRACY (May 6, 2015), https://www.opendemocracy.net/en/openglobalrights-openpage/international-criminal-court-at-risk/ (last visited September 4, 2023).

5 International Criminal Court, Rome Statute of the International Criminal Court, Preamble, U.N. Doc. A/CONF.183/9, (July 17, 1998) [hereinafter Rome Statute].

6 *Id.* at art. 17.

> or which constitutes a serious crime under the national law of the requesting state.[7]

The modalities of that assistance, however, will differ with respect to domestic prosecutions undertaken by the territorial state and those that would be based on universal jurisdiction. In both scenarios, however, there is much the ICC can and should do to advance domestic efforts at accountability. There are also limits to what the Court can and should offer states that must inform its efforts.

1.1 *Territorial Prosecutions*

Given that it remains the primary international legal duty of territorial states to prevent and punish the most serious crimes in international law and that there are recognized benefits from locating prosecutions as close to the events and victims as possible, the ICC's priority should be to incentivize the state in which the relevant crimes occurred to prosecute.[8] The single most powerful tool available to the ICC to catalyze such territorial prosecutions remains the threat of ICC prosecution. As I argued back in 2005:

> [ICC] intervention into otherwise exclusively domestic criminal processes imposes considerable sovereignty costs on national governments that states may seek to avoid by undertaking their own investigations and prosecutions.[9]

In short, most states do not want the ICC to step in and supplant their own domestic judicial processes, so they may become more willing to undertake prosecutions themselves in the face of a pending international prosecution.

In 2005, it was understandable that many states might be skeptical of whether the ICC would, in fact, open an investigation of events on their territories, much less actually prosecute the perpetrators of such crimes. At the time, the Court's track record was limited and many of its early high-profile indictees – such as Joseph Kony and Omar al-Bashir – were still at large. Eighteen years later, however, the ICC has a proven (albeit imperfect) track record of indictments, arrests, and prosecutions. That track-record is now a

---

7 *Id.* at art. 93(10)(a).

8 *Id.* at Preamble.; G.A. Res. 60/1, ¶ 138 (Sept. 16, 2005); Casten Stahn, 'The Future of International Criminal Justice' (2009) 4 *Hague Just. J.* 257–66.

9 See above 1108.

form of political capital that the ICC can rely on to show national governments that when the Court decides to prosecute, it will actually do so. The near certainty of the ICC following through on its commitments to exercise jurisdiction will be sufficient to motivate at least some states to prosecute domestically.

When seeking to catalyze prosecutions by territorial states, the ICC's leverage vis-a-vis a national government increases the closer the ICC is to undertaking its own prosecution. In some cases, naming a country as part of a situation under investigation may be sufficient. The actual indictment of specific individuals generates even more leverage to encourage domestic judicial action. Apprehension of a suspect subject to potential transfer to The Hague likely generates the most international pressure for a country to investigate and prosecute a particular individual. This phenomenon has proved true in Kosovo (with respect to potential ICTY prosecution) and led to the establishment of the Kosovo Specialist Chambers.[10] In the DR Congo, similar external pressure by the ICC and a subsequent judicial reform led to the prosecution of some military leaders in Congolese courts.[11]

More recently, the ICC's long and difficult negotiations with the government of Sudan over the transfer or trial of Omar-al-Bashir is indicative of both the influence it may have with national governments and the limits thereof. The closer the ICC came to actually being able to arrest Bashir, the more willing the Sudanese government became to consider domestic prosecution as an alternative. As Sudan's Justice Minister explained in 2000:

> [O]ne possibility is that the ICC will come here so they will be appearing before the ICC in Khartoum, or there will be a hybrid court maybe, or maybe they are going to transfer them to The Hague. That will be discussed with the ICC.[12]

10 Sarah Williams, 'The Specialist Chambers of Kosovo: The Limits of Internationalization' (2016) 14 *J. Int'l Crim. Just.* 25–51.

11 *Accountability for Atrocities Committed in the Democratic Republic of Congo: Supporting the Governments Proposal to Establish Specialized Mixed Chambers and Other Related Judicial Reforms*, HUM. RTS. WATCH (Apr. 1, 2014), https://www.hrw.org/news/2014/04/01/accountability-atrocities-committed-democratic-republic-congo (last visited Sep. 16, 2023).

12 Mark Kersten, *The ICC Inches Closer to Bashir as Sudan and Israel Normalize Relations*, JUST. IN CONFLICT (Oct. 28, 2020), https://justiceinconflict.org/2020/10/28/the-icc-inches-closer-to-bashir-prosecution-as-sudan-and-israel-normalize-relations/ (last visited Sep. 16, 2023); *Omar Bashir: ICC Delegation Begins Talks in Sudan Over Former Leader*, BBC NEWS (Oct. 17, 2020), https://www.bbc.com/news/world-africa-54548629 (last visited Sep. 16, 2023).

The ICC should use exactly this sort of pressure to nudge territorial states toward domestic prosecutions.

Where, in light of an ICC indictment, a territorial state becomes open to undertaking a genuine domestic investigation, the Office of the Prosecutor should use that indictment as leverage both for the arrest of the suspect and transfer to The Hague and for the initiation of a domestic prosecution. Even where the ICC has already issued an indictment or apprehended a suspect, its legal obligation is and policy goal should be to prioritize domestic prosecution, rather than exercise jurisdiction itself. Ultimately, such a warrant must be understood as a step toward accountability – international or domestic – and not as an indication that a case is now exclusively within the ICC's jurisdiction. Articles 18 and 19 of the Rome Statute allow admissibility to be challenged throughout procedural phases at the ICC. Where a national government begins its own prosecution, the ICC must defer.

So too, the ICC must be open to the reality that such domestic prosecutions may take different forms and may not follow ICC rules and procedures. In some cases, a territorial state may be willing to establish a semi-internationalized special tribunal; in others it may demand a purely domestic trial based on its own national approaches to justice. For a model of proactive complementarity to be viable, the ICC, as well as the international justice community, will need to become more comfortable with variation in the procedures and processes of accountability.[13] That is precisely why the Rome Statute's admissibility requirements define acceptable domestic prosecutions broadly under the rubric of genuineness.

Political pressure to change a state's willingness to undertake the prosecution of international crimes is only one piece of the puzzle. In addition, territorial states undertaking such prosecutions may need a range of other assistance, including expertise, evidence, resources, and perhaps even the handover of the accused. Each of these forms of assistance are at least theoretically plausible under Article 93 of the Statute. Nonetheless, the ICC is not and should not become a judicial development organization – that is not part of its mandate nor its expertise.[14] Hence, the ICC must be judicious in its efforts to support – as opposed to incentivize – national prosecutions.

13 Alexander Greenawalt, 'The Pluralism of International Criminal Law' (2011) *Ind. L.J.* 1063–1129; Jean Galbraith, 'The Pace of International Criminal Justice' (2009) 31 *Mich. J. Int'l L.* 79–142.

14 Jane Stromseth, 'Justice on the Ground: Can International Criminal Courts Strengthen Domestic Rule of Law in Post-Conflict Societies?' (2009) 1 *Hague J. on Rule L.* 87–97;

Expertise is by far the easiest and most appropriate form of support the ICC can offer to territorial states undertaking prosecutions of international crimes. Such expertise can come in many forms ranging from training sessions to the short-term secondment of ICC personnel. Where countries are genuine in their efforts to undertake domestic prosecutions and willing to learn from the Court's expertise, the ICC should actively prioritize such efforts and build them into the mission and budget of the OTP. Regular secondments of ICC personnel to countries that are engaged in investigations and prosecutions should become routine.

The ICC's provision of evidence to a national government elevates the stakes of its involvement in a domestic prosecution and raises potential pitfalls. Any provision of evidence under Article 93 of the Statute should be predicated on concrete steps by the national government that demonstrate its commitment to a genuine prosecution. Such evidentiary support should be based on a written agreement with the government as to how that evidence will be used and protected. Some forms of evidence may be easy to provide to national governments, particularly where they reflect the ICC's compilation of open-source data and information. In contrast, other forms of evidence that may implicate victims, reveal witness information, or compromise sources and methods of evidence collection may simply be inappropriate for handover to national government.[15] In such circumstances, the national government may build parts of its case without ICC support.

Generally speaking, the ICC is not a donor organization and should not provide direct transfers of financial resources to national governments. The Court's own resources are limited, and the Assembly of States Parties has not made financial transfers a priority within the Court's budget. Countries seeking to undertake domestic prosecutions of international crimes will need to look to other funding sources, including their own national budgets, bilateral development aid, and philanthropic support to fund their efforts.[16] That said, the ICC may be able to encourage such financial support through the signals it sends to the donor community by training national judicial

Morten Bergsmo, Olympia Bekou, and Annika Jones, 'Complementarity After Kampala: Capacity Building and the ICC's Legal Tools' (2010) 2 *Goettingen J. Int'l L.* 791–811.

15 Markus Eikel, 'Witness Protection Measures at the International Criminal Court: Legal Framework and Emerging Practice' (2012) 23 *Crim. L.F.* 97.

16 *Towards a New Consensus on Access to Justice: Summary of Brussels Workshop, 29–30 April 2008*, OPEN SOC'Y FOUND. JUST. INITIATIVE, https://www.justiceinitiative.org/publications/new-reports-urge-donors-enhance-and-improve-criminal-justice-investments.

officials, seconding personnel, or reaching an agreement on the provision of evidence.

Perhaps the most important – but also the most potentially problematic – step the ICC could take to support a domestic prosecution would be the transfer of an indictee from the Court to the national jurisdiction. Ultimately, such transfers may be necessary to address the ICC's current case backlog and are a necessary element of prioritizing domestic prosecutions. But the hand-back of indictees should only occur where a national government has been determined by the Pre-Trial Chamber to satisfy the complementarity requirements under Article 17 of the Statute and the Court has appropriate assurances as to the genuineness and fairness of the national prosecutions that will result. Such a step should not be undertaken lightly, but it must be understood not as a failure of the ICC, but as the successful realization of the goals of the Rome Statute.[17]

Of course, in any case in which the ICC considers deferring to national prosecutions and, particularly in cases in which it might hand an indictee back to a territorial state, it will need to remain vigilant that prosecutions are in fact genuine. So too, the Court will need to ensure that a minimum level of human rights protections is in place and that a trial is fair. To that end, the Office of the Prosecutor should negotiate and memorialize an agreement with a national government prior to the handover of an indictee, ensuring the genuineness of a subsequent prosecution. The resulting trial may not be procedurally identical to an ICC prosecution, but it will still advance the goal of ending impunity while relieving the Court of some of its judicial burden. The time has come to recognize that imperfect justice – at least according to international standards – may be better than justice delayed, as long as basic human rights are respected.

1.2 *Prosecutions under the Principle of Universal Jurisdiction*

The ICC may also have a role to play in assisting national courts undertaking prosecution of international crimes under the principle of universal jurisdiction. While universal jurisdiction has existed with respect to international crimes for centuries, there appears to be a growing willingness among at least some national governments to undertake such prosecutions.[18] Universal jurisdiction prosecutions must be understood as an integral part of

17 Rome Statute, *supra* note 5 at Preamble.

18 *Universal Jurisdiction Annual Review 2020*, TRIAL INT'L (Mar 30, 2020), https://trialinternational.org/latest-post/universal-jurisdiction-annual-review-2020-atrocities-must-be-prosecuted-soundly-and-rigorously/.

the overall Rome system of justice and an important piece of the broader effort to end impunity. While the ICC cannot and should not be expected to coordinate a mosaic of domestic courts prosecuting international crimes, it can incentivize and support such prosecutions.[19] It could also serve as an information and expertise hub in a decentralized system of domestic justice for international crimes.[20]

The logic behind the ICC's ability to catalyze non-territorial states to prosecute international crimes under universal jurisdiction differs from the ways it can influence territorial states to prosecute crimes domestically. Third states exercising universal jurisdiction do not fear the sovereignty costs of international intervention. In fact, the threat of ICC prosecution might actually give third states reason not to prosecute. After all, the prosecution of international crimes is often expensive and may divert resources from a country's domestic justice system. Third states might well prefer to defer to the ICC if it is willing to prosecute. Hence, when working with states considering exercising universal jurisdiction, the ICC must emphasize not the threat of ICC prosecution, but rather its own limited capacity, the dangers of impunity, and the need for action by national governments.

Most states considering the exercise of universal jurisdiction are committed to the broader goal of ending impunity. Some may have a historical or other ties to the perpetrator or territorial state where the crime occurred, giving them particular incentive to ensure justice is realized.[21] Rather than sending such states a signal that the ICC will undertake prosecutions itself, the Court should make clear to third states that its own capacity is limited, that it remains the primary obligation of national governments to end impunity, and that if a prosecution is not undertaken based on universal jurisdiction, the perpetrator may well avoid accountability. Appropriately calibrated diplomatic messaging can and should be part of the work of the Office of the Prosecutor, encouraging universal jurisdiction prosecutions whenever possible.

Beyond political pressure and diplomatic messaging, the ICC may also be able to offer evidentiary and technical assistance to national governments

19 Louise Arbour, 'Will the ICC Have an Impact on Universal Jurisdiction' (2003) 1 *J. Int'l Crim. Just.* 585.

20 William W. Burke-White, 'A Community of Courts: Toward a System of International Criminal Law Enforcement' (2000) 24 *Mich. J. Int'l L.* 1.

21 Jeremy Rabkin and Craig S. Lerner, 'Criminal Justice is Local: Why States Disregard Universal Jurisdiction for Human Rights Abuses' (2022) 55 *Vand. J. Transnat'l L.* 375.

exercising universal jurisdiction. The same broad objectives and considerations discussed above with respect to territorial prosecutions will apply in this context as well. The Court can and should provide technical assistance and expertise when needed. It may consider evidence sharing, if appropriate safeguards are in place. Finally, in appropriate circumstances and with written assurances about the terms and procedures of a universal jurisdiction prosecution, it may consider handing over already apprehended suspects for domestic prosecution. It should not, however, finance domestic prosecutions – whether territorial or based on universal jurisdiction.

The Court's involvement in cases brought under universal jurisdiction may present fewer concerns than its support for territorial states undertaking domestic prosecutions. Generally speaking, the interests and objectives of countries exercising universal jurisdiction will be more clear-cut and hopefully aligned with the goals of the Rome Statute. Such countries are also likely to have more developed domestic judiciaries and require less assistance from ICC. The sharing of evidence may be facilitated by the existence of adequate legal protection of both evidence and witnesses under the requesting state's domestic judicial system. Where the ICC is able to share evidence, it may reduce the burdens on the prosecuting state, perhaps allowing that state to prosecute where it would not have had the resources to do so without ICC support.

Nonetheless, the ICC must remain vigilant when cooperating even with states exercising universal jurisdiction. There may well be states seeking to exercise universal jurisdiction that have mixed motives for prosecuting, or other states that seek to exercise universal jurisdiction, but lack adequate domestic legal frameworks to protect evidence or the rights of victims or the accused. In such circumstances, the ICC should play a more limited role (perhaps offering trainings and expertise) or no role at all. The Court may wish to remind states diplomatically that where a case under universal jurisdiction fails to meet the tests of genuineness, the ICC may decide to act on its own.

Beyond active support for domestic prosecutions under universal jurisdiction, the ICC can easily position itself as a hub in a broader system of justice for the most serious international crimes. At the very least, the ICC can serve as a repository of information on the prosecution of crimes within its jurisdiction undertaken by states based on universal jurisdiction. Cataloguing and sharing such information would allow the Court to show the broader movement toward ending impunity and perhaps highlight for governments the potential of universal jurisdiction to contribute to those efforts.

2 The Limits of Positive Complementarity

This essay has focused on how the ICC can do more to catalyze domestic prosecutions of international crimes, either by territorial states or by states exercising universal jurisdiction. While the time is right for the Court to make such efforts a central part of its mission and, thereby, relieve some of its caseload, there are limits both to what the Court can do to incentivize such prosecutions and what it is appropriate for national governments to do in undertaking such prosecutions. Those limitations on domestic justice are precisely why the ICC was established in the first place: to prosecute the most serious crimes when national governments are unable or unwilling to do so. There are a variety of circumstances in which the Court should not pursue a strategy of proactive complementarity.

2.1 *Where Domestic Prosecutorial Efforts Lack Genuineness*

Any efforts to catalyze domestic prosecutions of international crimes must be predicated on the willingness of states to undertake genuine prosecutions. The genuineness requirement is enshrined in Article 17 of the Rome Statute and is essential for ensuring rights, justice, and accountability. As outlined in this essay, the ICC can and should push states toward meeting those requirements. Initially, the Court may need to accept the good faith of such governments, until their actions call such good faith into question.[22] Where genuineness is in doubt, the Court may be advised to take only small steps to assist states with domestic prosecutions, while carefully monitoring the actions and motivations of the national government interested in prosecuting the case. When and if it becomes clear that a government does not intend to undertake a genuine prosecution, the ICC must cease its efforts to catalyze that government forward. In such cases, the Court itself may decide to prosecute, may seek to encourage third states to act under universal jurisdiction, or may simply have to recognize that, given resource limitations, accountability may not be presently feasible.

2.2 *Where Crimes Fall Outside the ICC's Jurisdiction or Gravity Thresholds Are Not Met*

The ICC must remain focused on the most serious crimes that fall within its jurisdiction. There are a range of crimes subject to universal jurisdiction, but that are not within the Court's jurisdiction. Some crimes (such as

22 Vienna Convention on the Law of Treaties, art. 26, *opened for signature* May 23, 1969, 1155 U.N.T.S. 331.

piracy) may be subject to universal jurisdiction, but not included expressly in the Rome Statute. Similarly, national governments may seek assistance with the prosecution of crimes that do not meet the nationality or territoriality requirements for ICC prosecution. The ICC should not actively assist such prosecutions given its limited mandate and resources.

Even with respect to crimes within the Court's jurisdiction (such as crimes against humanity), there may be circumstances in which national governments prosecute crimes under universal jurisdiction that do not meet the ICC's gravity thresholds.[23] While such prosecutions should be lauded as part of the broader effort of ending impunity, the ICC should not prioritize assisting national governments with such prosecutions. Again, the ICC is not a judicial development or capacity-building mechanism.[24] Of course, the ICC's assistance to states exercising universal jurisdiction over crimes within the Court's jurisdiction and that satisfy its gravity threshold may have knock-on effects of enhancing that country's domestic justice capability. Such side effects should be viewed positively, but not prioritized.

2.3 *Where Crimes Involve the Prosecution of Sitting Government Officials with Immunity before Domestic Courts*

The drafters of the Rome Statute recognized the need to hold even sitting senior government officials accountable for international crimes. To that end, they gave the Court the power to prosecute such officials even while they remain in office by providing that official capacity would be irrelevant before the ICC.[25] In contrast, national courts can not prosecute senior sitting government officials under universal jurisdiction.[26] The ICC should not endeavor to support such prosecutions domestically, but instead should seek to exercise jurisdiction itself.

2.4 *Where a Prosecution Has High Symbolic Value or Poses Systemic Risks*

Some cases present unique political challenges for the prosecuting state or the international community as a whole. While all prosecutions of international crimes are complex and most are politically charged in the state in

---

23 Rome Statute, *supra* note 5 at art. 17(1)(d); Stuart Ford, 'The Meaning of Gravity at the International Criminal Court' (2018) 24 *U.C. Davis J. Int'l L. & Pol'y* 209.

24 Rome Statute, *supra* note 5 at Preamble.

25 *Id.* at art. 17.

26 Case Concerning the Arrest Warrant of 11 April 2000 (Dem. Rep. Congo v. Belg.), Judgement, 2002 I.C.J. 3 (Feb 14, 2002).

which the crimes occurred, certain cases may pose a greater degree of political risk. The 2023 indictment of sitting Russian president Vladimir Putin is a prime example. As President of Russia, Putin is, of course, immune from prosecution in the domestic courts of any third state. However, if he were to leave office – or be forced out of office – a domestic prosecution could be plausible. The ICC should not attempt to catalyze or support such a prosecution. The prosecution of Putin in Ukraine or in any G7 member country would run the risk of being seen as victor's justice or it could exacerbate or rekindle military conflict. Similarly, in some post conflict states, a domestic prosecution might destabilize a fragile peace agreement or prompt a new wave of violence and retribution.[27] Once again, these are circumstances in which the ICC should undertake its own prosecutorial efforts, rather than encourage domestic prosecutions.

3 Conclusion

The ICC has made great progress in the past 23 years. But its success also highlights its limitations. The Court presently has before it more cases and suspects than it can reasonably handle. Unfortunately, events the world over continue to expand its docket. The solution to the ICC's capacity challenge is actually found in its Statute – that the Court can and should encourage and support the domestic prosecutions of international crimes. By catalyzing and, at times, supporting national prosecutions both by territorial states and by states acting under universal jurisdiction, the ICC can maximize its ability to end impunity while slimming its own caseload. Caution must be exercised in the process and new techniques and tools will need to be developed by the Court. Ultimately, more active efforts to catalyze domestic prosecutions may contribute to ending impunity more broadly than just through its own prosecutions.

27 Cyanne E. Loyle and Benjamin Appel, 'Conflict Recurrence and Post Conflict Justice: Addressing Motivations and Opportunities for Sustainable Peace' (2017) 61 *Int'l Stud. Q.* 690.

CHAPTER 37

Safeguards for Complementarity

Douglass Cassel

What safeguards should be implemented by the International Criminal Court (ICC) Prosecutor to assist national authorities in the exercise of universal jurisdiction? The best example I know of is the set of safeguards that evolved during the ICC's longest running preliminary examination in any state – Colombia.

From 2004 to 2021, the ICC conducted a preliminary examination[1] of crimes against humanity in Colombia.[2] In 2009, Colombia's transitional declaration which excluded ICC jurisdiction over war crimes expired.[3] Thereafter, the preliminary examination covered war crimes as well, until it was closed in 2021. Throughout the preliminary examination and continuing today under a Cooperation Agreement with the state which ended the examination (without prejudice to renewing it if necessary),[4] the ICC Prosecutor adopted – and the state acquiesced or agreed to – an important set of safeguards. Although not "always readily transferable to other situations,"[5] the ICC safeguards in Colombia nonetheless constitute a "valuable experience that may be replicated in other situations around the world."[6]

1 International Criminal Court, Rome Statute of the International Criminal Court, art. 15(6), U.N. Doc. A/CONF.183/9, (July 17, 1998) [hereinafter Rome Statute].

2 *See Colombia: Preliminary Examination*, INTERNATIONAL CRIMINAL COURT, https://www.icc-cpi.int/colombia (last visited September 28, 2023).

3 Rome Statute, *supra* note 1, art. 124.

4 Office of the Prosecutor, International Criminal Court, Cooperation Agreement Between the Office of the Prosecutor of the International Criminal Court and the Government of Colombia (2021), https://www.icc-cpi.int/sites/default/files/itemsDocuments/20211028-OTP-COL-Cooperation-Agreement-ENG.pdf [hereinafter Cooperation Agreement].

5 Office of the Prosecutor, International Criminal Court, Situation in Colombia: Benchmarking Consultation, ¶ 10 (June 2021) https://www.icc-cpi.int/sites/default/files/itemsDocuments/20210615-COL-Benchmarking-Consultation-Report-eng.pdf [hereinafter Benchmarking Consultation].

6 Cooperation Agreement, *supra* note 4, Preamble.

 | DOI:10.1163/9789004686755_046

The safeguards in Colombia supplement the ICC Prosecutor's more general policy on complementarity adopted in 2013.[7] That policy addresses mainly the substantive standards for complementarity, such as whether a state is "genuinely" willing to prosecute.[8] In contrast, most of the safeguards agreed to in Colombia are more procedural in nature, governing the relationship between the ICC Prosecutor and the national authorities.

The ICC safeguards in Colombia are summarized below. However, they were (and remain) focused on investigations of alleged crimes committed in Colombia by Colombians. At times, alleged perpetrators sought refuge in neighboring Ecuador and Venezuela. Yet Colombia did not exercise "universal jurisdiction" in the pure sense of a state prosecuting foreign citizens for crimes against foreign victims on foreign territory, based solely on the gravity of the crime. Nor did Colombia exercise universal jurisdiction even in the hybrid sense of prosecuting heinous foreign criminals based solely on their passing presence in its territory.[9]

Whether in the exercise of true or hybrid universal jurisdiction, additional safeguards beyond those implemented in Colombia may need to be adopted, as suggested two decades ago by three members of the International Court of Justice.[10] Section 1 below addresses the Colombia safeguards. Section 2 considers additional safeguards where a state party to the ICC undertakes to exercise universal jurisdiction (whether pure or hybrid) over foreign citizens.

1 Colombia Safeguards

The seventeen-year-long ICC preliminary examination of crimes against humanity (and later war crimes) may be the leading example of the value of

---

7 Office of the Prosecutor, International Criminal Court, Policy Paper on Preliminary Examinations, (November 2013) https://www.icc-cpi.int/sites/default/files/OTP-Policy_Paper_Preliminary_Examinations_2013-ENG.pdf [hereinafter Preliminary Examinations].

8 *Id.* at ¶¶ 46–55.

9 *See* Case Concerning the Arrest Warrant of 11 April 2000 (Dem. Rep. Congo v. Belg.), Judgment, 2002 I.C.J. 3 (Feb 14, 2002) [hereinafter Arrest Warrant Case]; *Id.* at 63, ¶ 41 (joint separate opinion by Judges Higgins, Koojimans and Buergenthal).

10 *Id.* ¶¶ 59–60.

"positive" complementarity.[11] The ICC is designed to prosecute Rome Statute crimes only where the national state is unwilling or unable to do so.[12] In the case of Colombia, rather than take a "negative" complementarity posture and advocate an ICC prosecution because of Colombian prosecutorial shortfalls, the ICC Prosecutors sought to use a potential prosecution in The Hague to incentivize Colombia to prosecute in its own courts.

That made good sense. The ICC does not have the human or budgetary resources to prosecute large numbers of cases in The Hague. Developed judicial systems like those of Colombia have far greater quantitative capacity. And even the limited numbers of cases that can be tried in The Hague face higher costs of transportation and translation, legal barriers of jurisdictional obstacles (e.g., complementarity) not faced in national prosecutions, and less direct access to the trial by victims, witnesses, the concerned public, and the national media. All things being equal, national trials are preferable to international trials.

Of course, all things are not equal. National prosecutors and courts may be less prone to pursue local potentates. They may be more vulnerable to corruption. They may be less likely to apply international substantive standards on matters such as command responsibility, on which local variants, subjected to local legislative pressures, may make it more difficult to secure convictions.

None of this should make an ICC trial the default position. There are advantages and disadvantages of trials in The Hague. The task of positive complementarity should be to encourage the national state, not merely to prosecute, but to conduct a serious criminal investigation in a genuine effort to pursue justice through a fair trial that meets international norms of due process.

If the ICC Prosecutor were to set the bar for acceptable national prosecutions too high, more cases than the ICC could realistically and properly investigate and adjudicate would be sent to The Hague. If the bar were set too

---

11 *See* OFFICE OF THE PROSECUTOR, INTERNATIONAL CRIMINAL COURT, REPORT ON PROSECUTORIAL STRATEGY 5 (2014), https://www.icc-cpi.int/sites/default/files/ProsecutorialStrategy20060914_English.pdf.

(A Court based on the principle of complementarity ensures the international rule of law by creating an interdependent, mutually reinforcing international system of justice. With this in mind, the Office has adopted a positive approach to complementarity, meaning that it encourages genuine national proceedings where possible; relies on national and international networks; and participates in a system of international cooperation.)

12 Rome Statute, *supra* note 1, art. 17.

low, too many cases would be left to national trials destined to end in impunity, thereby frustrating justice for "the most serious crimes of concern to the international community as a whole."[13]

Positive complementarity, then, must strike a balance. It should be neither too demanding nor too lenient. It demands what the ICC Prosecutor calls the "twin principles of partnership and vigilance" to guide the Prosecutor's interactions with a state with respect to complementarity.[14] Achieving that balance calls for the exercise of informed judgment. In arguable situations, reasonable observers may differ on whether an appropriate balance has been struck.

In Colombia, critics can – and do – argue that the balance struck by the ICC was skewed against justice, one way or the other. On the left (and elsewhere), critics argue that the ICC allowed far too much time before Colombian prosecutions of high-ranking military officers and that, even now, too few have been prosecuted. On the right (and elsewhere), critics decry that punishments for guerrilla leaders who committed horrendous crimes are too lenient.

Each observer can make her or his own call. Whatever call is made for the Colombian situation, one point strikes me as indisputable: far fewer investigations and prosecutions of serious crimes in Colombia would have been conducted without the constant possibility, reinforced by periodic public and private warnings, that if Colombia utterly defaulted on justice, the ICC Prosecutor would step in and bring to The Hague cases that matter greatly to Colombia.

I experienced this impact of positive complementarity reality firsthand, while serving as one of Colombian President Juan Manuel Santos' advisers and negotiators on transitional justice with FARC guerrilla leaders in 2015 and 2016. As I later recounted:

> [The ICC] helped us in negotiating an agreement on transitional justice […] I believe that not a single negotiating session of our juridical subcommittee went by without mention and consideration of the impact of the ICC on whatever we might agree to.[15]

---

13 *Id.* art. 1.

14 Benchmarking Consultation, *supra* note 5, ¶ 9.

15 Doug Cassel, 'Buscando la paz con la mayor justicia posible: un recuerdo personal de la negociación de la JEP [Searching for Peace with the Most Justice Possible: A Personal Recollection of the Negotiation of the JEP]', in Danilo Rojas Betancourth (ed.), *La JEP vista por sus jueces (2020–2021)* (Bogotá: Jurisdicción Especial para la Paz-

In addition, I wrote that:

> [T]hroughout the peace negotiations in Colombia, as well as before and after, the ICC Prosecutor or her office issued declarations and public reports, and held meetings with Colombian officials, at times during visits to the country, expressing concern about the necessity of justice for certain war crimes and crimes against humanity in Colombia, without ever closing the door either to national justice or to international justice.
>
> For us, the government negotiators in the juridical subcommittee, this posture of the ICC permitted us to insist with the FARC-EP on a degree of justice, without depriving us of the flexibility to negotiate creative means of transitional justice. Even the lawyers of the FARC-EP in the juridical subcommittee accepted the realities of the jurisprudence of the Inter-American Court of Human Rights and of the possible intervention of the ICC. These realities conditioned all our negotiations on transitional justice.[16]

Furthermore, in my role of assessing the international legitimacy of the transitional justice accords, I wrote a letter dated September 25, 2015,

---

Fundación Konrad Adenauer, 2022), pp. 377–95 (This is my English translation of my article. The Spanish original states that an institution which "nos ayudó en negociar un acuerdo sobre la justicia de transición fue la Corte Penal Internacional (CPI). Creo que no pasó ni una sesión de negociación en nuestra subcomisión jurídica sin mención y consideración del impacto de la CPI en lo que podríamos acordar." *Id.* at 385. JEP are the Spanish initials of the Special Jurisdiction for Peace.).

16 *Id.* at 386 (My English translation of the following:
"Además, a lo largo de las negociaciones para la paz en Colombia, así como antes y después, la fiscal de la CPI o su despacho emitió declaraciones e informes públicos, y sostuvo reuniones con oficiales colombianos, a veces durante visitas al país, expresando preocupación sobre la necesidad de justicia para varios crímenes de guerra o crímenes de lesa humanidad en Colombia, sin nunca cerrar la puerta, ni a la justicia nacional, ni a la justicia internacional." "Para nosotros, los negociadores del Gobierno en la subcomisión jurídica, esta postura de la CPI nos permitió insistir con las FARC-EP sobre un grado de justicia, sin quitarnos la flexibilidad de negociar modalidades creativas de justicia de transición. Hasta los mismos abogados de las FARC-EP en la subcomisión jurídica aceptaron las realidades de la jurisprudencia de la Corte IDH y de la posible intervención de la CPI. Estas realidades condicionaron todas nuestras negociaciones de justicia de transición.").

> [A]t the request of President Santos, for him to take to the United Nations in New York and show to whomever he pleased. The letter detailed my judgment that the document on transitional justice drafted by the subcommittee satisfied the norms of international law [including the public statements of the ICC Prosecutor].
>
> Second, in late September [2015], Manuel José [Cepeda] and I traveled to The Hague to meet with the Office of the ICC Prosecutor.... We explained why the concept of the JEP [Special Jurisdiction for Peace] was consistent with international law and the Rome Statute [of the ICC]. I believe the meeting was successful. After hearing our argument, they had an open mind on the JEP, pending the final agreement.[17]

The transitional justice accords were only one aspect of Colombian justice that benefited from the supporting stimulus of the ICC preliminary examination. Also included in the mix evaluated by the ICC were Colombia's ordinary courts and its Justice and Peace Law Tribunals for paramilitary crimes.[18]

By June of 2021, ICC Prosecutor Fatou Bensouda was sufficiently satisfied that Colombia justice appeared to meet the bar of complementarity that she convened a "Benchmarking Consultation" to solicit the views of civil society and other stakeholders on the role of an ICC preliminary examination that faces a "long-term, multi-layered domestic accountability processes

17 *Id.* at 391 (My English translation of the following:
"escribí una carta fechada 25 de septiembre de 2015, a solicitud del presidente Santos, para que él la llevara a las Naciones Unidas en Nueva York y allí mostrarla a quien fuera. La carta detalló mi juicio jurídico de que el documento sobre la justicia de transición, elaborado por la subcomisión, cumplía con las normas del derecho internacional. Segundo, para fines de septiembre, viajamos Manuel José y yo a La Haya para reunirnos con la fiscalía de la CPI. (Yo conocía a la gente de la fiscalía desde hacía tiempo, de otros casos.) Les explicamos por qué el concepto de la JEP era coherente con el derecho internacional y con el Estatuto de Roma. Creo que la reunión fue exitosa. Oído nuestro argumento, ellos quedaron con la mente abierta sobre la JEP, pendientes del acuerdo final.").

18 Press Release, International Criminal Court, ICC Prosecutor, Mr Karim A. A. Khan QC, Concludes the Preliminary Examination of The Situation in Colombia with a Cooperation Agreement with the Government Charting the Next Stage in Support of Domestic Efforts to Advance Transitional Justice (Oct. 28, 2021), https://www.icc-cpi.int/news/icc-prosecutor-mr-karim-khan-qc-concludes-preliminary-examination-situation-colombia (last visited October 3, 2023).

where national proceedings were likely to extend over a considerable period of time."[19]

The Prosecutor commented on both the benchmarks and the indicators of progress against the benchmarks. She explained that the "benchmarks must be concrete, measureable and realistic. Similarly, indicators should also be simple to understand and apply, timely and few in number, reliable, based on transparent and verifiable methodology, and conform with relevant international standards."[20]

Applying these criteria to an assessment of whether to continue the preliminary examination, the Prosecutor identified three indicators on which to focus:[21]

- "*Structural indicators*: focusing on the nature of domestic law in relation to criminal accountability for conduct constituting Rome Statute crimes, whether it incorporates the required international standards, as well as the institutional mechanisms competent to investigate, prosecute and adjudicate those crimes."
- "*Process indicators*: measuring ongoing efforts by competent institutional mechanisms to promote and protect accountability for these crimes, including policies, budgetary resources and measures taken to ensure implementation."
- "*Outcome indicators*: capturing specific individual and collective accountability outcomes in specific proceedings."

Following the consultation, and applying these benchmarks, the new ICC Prosecutor Karim Khan Q.C. decided to close the preliminary examination of crimes against humanity and war crimes in Colombia, by means of a "Cooperation Agreement" with the Government of Colombia.[22] However, the closure was subject to the following safeguards:

- *High level agreement*: The Agreement was countersigned by Colombian President Iván Duque.[23]
- *Stakeholder consultation*: The closure was decided on only after an open, wide-ranging stakeholder consultation.[24]

---

19 *Colombia: Preliminary Examination*, *supra* note 2.

20 Benchmarking Consultation, *supra* note 5, ¶ 36.

21 *Id.* ¶ 35.

22 Cooperation Agreement, *supra* note 4.

23 *Id.*

24 *Id.* at Preamble.

- *Long observation*: The ICC Prosecutors had observed the reality of Colombian justice in practice for years.[25]
- *Genuine commitment*: The ICC Prosecutor concluded that Colombia had demonstrated the ability and a willingness to pursue genuine justice.[26]
- *Relevant proceedings*: Without prejudice to the separation of powers, the Government committed to continue supporting relevant proceedings before ordinary justice, the Special Tribunal for Peace, and the Justice and Peace Law mechanism.[27]
- *Closure without prejudice*: The preliminary examination could be reopened if there is a significant change in circumstances.[28]
- *Indefinite duration*: There was no "sunset clause" in the Agreement.[29]
- *Structural stability*: The constitutional and legal status and structure for justice on which the ICC Prosecutor relies shall be preserved.[30]
- *Budgetary adequacy*: Colombia will continue to allocate a sufficient budget for justice.[31]
- *Information*: The Government will keep the ICC informed on a regular basis.[32]
- *Communication*: Lines of communication between the ICC and the Government will be maintained and strengthened.[33]
- *Annual visits and exchange:* ICC Prosecutors will visit Colombia and Colombian officials will visit The Hague.[34]
- *Access to records*: ICC Prosecutors will have access to relevant justice records.[35]
- *Mutual learning*: Both parties will take into account lessons learned and observations of best practices.[36]
- *Training*: The ICC will inform Colombian legal professionals of the latest developments and jurisprudence of the ICC.[37]

25 *Id.*
26 *Id.*
27 *Id.* art. 1.
28 *Id.* art. 6.
29 *Id.* art. 7.
30 *Id.* art. 1.
31 *Id.*
32 *Id.* art. 2.
33 *Id.* art. 6.
34 *Id.* art. 4.
35 *Id.* art. 2.
36 *Id.* art. 4.
37 *Id.* art. 5.

- *Punishments*: Punishments must be effective and proportional, and both retributive and restorative.[38]
- *Cooperation*: Among relevant state entities, cooperation must be maintained, particularly between the Attorney General and the Special Tribunal for Peace.[39]
- *Interference with Justice*: Such interference must be prevented.[40]
- *Safety and security*: Must be provided for judicial and prosecutorial personnel and participants in the proceedings.[41]
- *ICC prosecutor*: Will continue supporting justice in Colombia.[42]

The foregoing provisions provide a good template for the ICC to support national justice in prosecuting Rome Statute crimes generally. However, they would not be sufficient or appropriate in all cases. Unless the state involved, like Colombia at present in the ICC Prosecutor's estimation, has the "intent to bring the person concerned to justice,"[43] no accumulation of regular visits, informational exchanges and access to records will succeed in avoiding impunity. The safeguards listed above will be of practical value only when a state is "genuinely" willing to prosecute,[44] but not when it has a "purpose of shielding the person concerned from criminal responsibility."[45]

To ascertain a state's subjective "intent" is, of course, difficult at best. Hence the ICC Prosecutor is wise to look to the objective indicators enumerated above: structures, processes and outcomes, in order to decide whether to defer to national prosecutions.

2 Safeguards in Cases of Universal Jurisdiction

The safeguards agreed to between the ICC Prosecutor and Colombia were designed for cases of alleged war crimes and crimes against humanity committed by Colombians, against Colombians, in Colombia. But what if Colombia were to exercise jurisdiction over a foreign citizen for alleged war crimes

38 *Id.* art. 1.
39 *Id.*
40 *Id.*
41 *Id.*
42 *Id.* art 3.
43 Rome Statute, *supra* note 1, art. 17.2(c).
44 *Id.* art. 17.1(a).
45 *Id.* art. 17.2(a).

committed in foreign territory against foreign citizens, with no connection between the crime and Colombia, i.e., universal jurisdiction?

Imagine, for example, that Yevgeny Prigozhin, head of the Wagner Group fighters accused of atrocities in Ukraine,[46] were to take a flight to Russian ally Venezuela, only to have his plane encounter engine trouble and be diverted to land in neighboring Colombia.

Suppose Colombia invoked universal jurisdiction and took it upon itself to prosecute Prigozhin in Bogota rather than turn him over to The Hague. Would the ICC Prosecutor need to implement additional safeguards, beyond those currently in effect in Colombia, in order to acquiesce in an exercise of universal jurisdiction by Colombian courts?

The answer given two decades ago by three judges of the International Court of Justice is arguably "yes." In the case of an arrest warrant issued by Belgium for the former foreign minister of the Democratic Republic of the Congo, the judges considered the "question whether states are entitled to exercise jurisdiction over persons having no connection with the forum state when the accused is not present in the State's territory."[47]

They answered that a state could indeed exercise universal jurisdiction – provided that "certain safeguards are in place" which are "absolutely essential to prevent abuse" and to safeguard "stable relations between States."[48] Those safeguards are as follows:

- *Immunities*: The prosecution must respect the inviolability and immunities of the person concerned.[49]
- *National State*: A state contemplating bringing criminal charges based on universal jurisdiction must first offer to the national state of the prospective accused person the opportunity itself to act upon the charges concerned.[50]

---

46 *See, e.g.*, Louise Nordstrom, *Wagner Group's Bloody Year in Ukraine: From Murder Squad to Cannon Fodder*, FRANCE 24 (Feb. 22, 2023), https://www.france24.com/en/europe/20230222-wagner-group-s-bloody-year-in-ukraine-from-murder-squad-to-cannon-fodder (last visited October 4, 2023).

47 Arrest Warrant Case, *supra* note 9, at 63 ¶ 19 (The majority of the Court, holding that the former foreign minister was immune from prosecution in Belgium, did not reach the issues of universal jurisdiction.).

48 *Id.* ¶ 59.

49 *Id.*

50 *Id.*

- *Prosecutorial independence*: Further, such charges may only be laid by a prosecutor or juge d'instruction who acts in full independence, without links to or control by the government of that state.[51]
- *Special Circumstances*: Moreover, there must be "some special circumstances that do require the exercise of an international criminal jurisdiction" that have been brought to the attention of the prosecutor or juge d'instruction. "For example, persons related to the victims of the case will have requested the commencement of legal proceedings,"[52] and
- *Heinous crimes*: Universal criminal jurisdiction may be exercised "only over those crimes regarded as the most heinous by the international community."[53]

Granted, these safeguards apply to the exercise of universal jurisdiction where the alleged perpetrator is not present in the prosecuting state. However, that need not render them inapplicable to the case where he is present. His presence could simply be regarded as a "special circumstance" under the fourth safeguard.

Applying these five safeguards, then, to our hypothetical, Mr. Prigozhin has no official immunity from prosecution. He is a private businessman. Under the first safeguard, Colombia could prosecute him. In contrast, if the unfortunately diverted traveler were not Prigozhin, but Russian President Vladimir Putin, Colombia probably could not prosecute him because he enjoys official immunity while in office.[54]

In contrast, the ICC would not have to respect Putin's immunity.[55] It could prosecute him. Complementarity could thus play a role in prosecuting Prigozhin, but not Putin (as long as he remains in office). In the case of a private citizen, the ICC Prosecutor could allow Colombia to prosecute (assuming the other safeguards are met), whereas in the case of an official with immunity, the prosecution probably could be conducted only in The Hague (or, theoretically, in Russia).

Under the second safeguard, Colombia would be required to offer Russia the opportunity to prosecute Prigozhin. But would a Russian proposal to prosecute Prigozhin, an alleged crony of Putin, be credible? Unless a situation very different from current realities were to arise, making a Russian prosecution of Prigozhin credible, the ICC Prosecutor should insist that

51 *Id.*

52 *Id.*

53 *Id.* ¶ 60.

54 Arrest Warrant Case, *supra* note 9, at 3 ¶ 61.

55 Rome Statute, *supra* note 1, art. 27.2.

Colombia not send Progizhin to Moscow. Assuming the other safeguards were met, Prigozhin could be prosecuted in Colombia. Or if not, then in The Hague. Sending him back to Russia would in effect be to shield him from justice.

The third safeguard, prosecutorial independence from the government, should arguably apply regardless of whether Colombian prosecutes its own nationals or a foreigner like Prigozhin.[56]

The fourth safeguard, "special circumstances," should give the ICC Prosecutor pause in accepting a Colombian prosecution under universal jurisdiction. If the accused is present in Colombia, as in our Prigozhin hypothetical, his presence should be a special circumstance sufficient to justify Colombia in exercising jurisdiction.[57] But if Prigozhin is not in Colombia – suppose his plane managed to land safely in Venezuela, some other special circumstance would be required in order to justify a Colombian exercise of universal jurisdiction over him. Absent that, the ICC Prosecutor should not defer to Colombia to prosecute. Instead, the Prosecutor should demand that Venezuela, as a state party to the ICC, send Prigozhin to The Hague (unless Venezuela somehow makes a credible case that it would prosecute Prigozhin genuinely and fairly).

The fifth and final safeguard, a heinous offense, would probably allow the ICC Prosecutor the same options in a universal jurisdiction case as in a usual case. The ICC Prosecutor could defer to a Colombian prosecution if it is genuine and fair and comports with the other safeguards. If not, the Prosecutor could ask Colombia to send the suspect to The Hague. If Colombia were to refuse, the ICC Prosecutor could ask the ICC judges to issue an arrest warrant. Colombia, as a state party to the ICC, would then be legally obligated to honor the warrant.

The five safeguards proposed twenty years ago in *dicta* by the three judges of the ICJ are not binding international law. Nonetheless, they are entitled to respectful consideration. Their authors were not only ICJ judges, but also respected scholars of international law. Therefore, in evaluating complementarity in a case of universal jurisdiction, whether pure or hybrid, the ICC Prosecutor would be well-advised to consider, in addition to the safeguards he agreed with Colombia in 2021, at least four of the five additional safeguards suggested by the three ICJ judges. (The fifth, prosecutorial

56 *See, e.g.*, Casa Nina v. Peru, Preliminary Objections, Merits, Reparations and Costs, Judgment, Inter-Am. Ct. H.R. (ser. C) No. 419, ¶ 72 (Nov. 24, 2020).

57 *Cf.* Questions Relating to the Obligation to Prosecute or Extradite (Belg. v. Sen.), Judgment, 2012 I.C.J. 422, ¶ 94 (July 20).

independence from politics, should be applied regardless of whether a prosecution is against a state's own national or against foreign citizens.)

3 Conclusion

Navigating the legal, practical and policy issues of what safeguards the ICC Prosecutor should adopt in evaluating complementarity is neither simple nor scientific. Professional judgment is required. Whatever choice the Prosecutor makes in debatable cases may well be challenged in good faith by reasonable observers. Instead of deciding individual cases on a purely ad hoc basis, the Prosecutor would be well-served by general guidelines which channel (but do not dictate) results. Such guidelines should help preserve the legitimacy, reputation and effectiveness of the ICC.

Supplementing the ICC Prosecutor's 2013 *Policy Paper on Preliminary Examinations,*[58] the safeguards agreed to by the ICC Prosecutor in Colombia are the best that experience to date has produced. In cases of universal jurisdiction, they should be augmented by the safeguards suggested by the three ICJ judges in *Congo v. Belgium.*

There are few more important questions in international criminal law than the threshold issues of who prosecutes and why. Ideally the ICC should be more of a stimulus than a substitute for national prosecutions.[59] For this to become a defensible reality, the ICC should not simply observe national proceedings passively. Where plausible, as in Colombia, the ICC should attempt positive and energetic complementarity, always bearing in mind the "twin principles of partnership and vigilance."[60] Only where national justice is implausible or at least quite dubious – a debatable judgment call in many situations – is the ICC left with no alternative but to face the difficult challenge of attempting to fill the justice gap for "the most serious crimes of concern to the international community as a whole."[61]

---

58 Preliminary Examinations, *supra* note 7.

59 *See* Office of the Prosecutor, *supra* note 11 (The ICC Prosecutor agrees).

60 Benchmarking Consultation, *supra* note 5, ¶ 9.

61 Rome Statute, *supra* note 1, art. 1.

CHAPTER 38

Guiding Principles in ICC Engagement with Regional and National Courts: Burden Sharing and Comparative Benefit

Margaret M. deGuzman

Over the two decades since the International Criminal Court (ICC or Court) became operational, any illusions its founders had that it alone could "end impunity" for serious international crimes have been dispelled. Although the ICC has made impressive strides, particularly in its expression of global norms concerning such under-prosecuted crimes as conflict-related sexual violence,[1] the use of child soldiers,[2] and the destruction of cultural heritage,[3] its resources are vastly disproportionate to the crimes being committed. To make progress toward the goal of ending impunity therefore the ICC must operate as part of a network of accountability mechanisms, including not only national courts with traditional forms of jurisdiction,[4] but also those exercising universal jurisdiction, as well as regional courts with jurisdiction over international crimes. The effectiveness of this accountability network depends on thoughtful, principled cooperation among institutions.

This contribution proposes two principles to guide the ICC Office of the Prosecutor (OTP)'s engagement with regional courts and national courts

1 *See, e.g.*, Prosecutor v. Bosco Ntaganda, Doc. No. ICC-01/04-02/06, Judgment, 536 (Trial Chamber VI, Jul. 8, 2019) (convicting Ntaganda of both rape and sexual slavery as war crimes and crimes against humanity, including when committed intra-group).

2 *See, e.g.*, Prosecutor v. Thomas Lubanga Dyilo, Doc. No. ICC-01/04-01/06, Judgment Pursuant to Article 74 of the Statute, ¶ 820 (Trial Chamber I, Apr. 5, 2012) (holding that, with regard to children under 15, "to participate actively in hostilities" includes any activities or roles which put them at risk of becoming a target, and is not limited to direct participation in combat).

3 *See, e.g.*, Prosecutor v. Ahmad Al Faqi Al Mahdi, Doc. No. ICC-01/12-01/15-171, Judgment and Sentence, 49 (Trial Chamber VIII, Sept. 27, 2016), https://www.icc-cpi.int/court-record/icc-01/12-01/15-171 (convicting Al Mahdi of war crimes related to the destruction of mosques and mausoleums).

4 These include, in particular, the states where crimes are committed and where defendants are nationals.

 | DOI:10.1163/9789004686755_047

exercising universal jurisdiction.[5] The first is burden sharing. Although many of the Court's founders seem to have envisioned the institution as operating in a hierarchically inferior position relative to national courts with traditional forms of jurisdiction, in practice the Court has adopted a horizontal, burden sharing approach in regard to those courts. This principle should also guide the OTP's engagement with regional courts and national courts exercising universal jurisdiction.

Second, the ICC should implement a principle of comparative benefit in determining when and how to interact with regional courts and national courts exercising universal jurisdiction. It should perform an assessment of the relative benefits and risks of harm from prosecutions in all potential fora to determine which institution is best placed to advance the most important goals of relevant communities. In this context, relevant communities include global and regional communities as well as the national communities most directly affected by the crimes. In establishing priorities among the goals of these diverse communities, the OTP should be careful to avoid causing harm to the communities most directly affected by the crimes.

1 Burden Sharing

To determine how the OTP should engage with other accountability mechanisms, such as regional courts or national courts exercising universal jurisdiction, it is important to establish the ICC's relationship to those institutions. The ICC might be considered a hierarchically superior forum for adjudicating international crimes in the sense that adjudication by the ICC has greater value than adjudication by other institutions. On this account, the ICC should focus its resources on bringing its own cases, rather than on providing assistance or support to other institutions. However, this view of ICC authority is largely confined to the past.[6]

5 I have made similar arguments concerning OTP engagement with national courts exercising traditional forms of jurisdiction. *See, e.g.*, Margaret M. deGuzman, 'Legitimate Supra-National Adjudication in the New Era: The Requirement of Comparative Benefit' (2023) 55 *Case W. Rsrv. J. Int'l L.* 105; Margaret M. deGuzman, 'Complementarity at the African Court', in Charles Jalloh et al. (eds.), *The African Court of Justice and Human and Peoples' Rights* (Cambridge: Cambridge University Press, 2019).

6 For example, some early discussions of a potential international criminal court envisioned it as having exclusive jurisdiction over certain international crimes. *See, e.g.*, Doudou Thiam, Special Rapporteur, *Tenth Report on the Draft Code of Crimes Against the Peace*

Alternatively, the ICC might be considered hierarchically inferior to other institutions, as suggested by the oft-invoked trope that the ICC is a "court of last resort."[7] This was a frequent mantra at the Rome Conference where the ICC was established.[8] It helped motivate the Rome Statute's complementarity regime whereby the Court must deem "inadmissible" any case that is being genuinely investigated or prosecuted by a state with jurisdiction.[9] This vision of the ICC's mandate suggests that national courts – at least those with traditional forms of jurisdiction – are superior adjudicative fora compared to the ICC.

The idea that national courts with traditional forms of jurisdiction are superior fora derives from their greater proximity to the crimes, defendants, and affected communities. A similar argument can be made regarding regional courts, which can be considered one step removed from the most affected communities, whereas the ICC is two steps removed. According to such hierarchical thinking, the priority of national courts exercising universal jurisdiction would depend on their proximity to the most affected communities. For instance, national courts exercising universal jurisdiction in the same region as the most affected states might be given priority over ICC adjudication. This view would suggest that in addition to assisting national courts in the most affected states, the OTP should prioritize assistance to

---

and Security of Mankind, ¶ 36, U.N. Doc. A/CN.4/442 (Mar. 20, 1992) (proposing the draft provision: "All States Parties to this Statute shall recognize the *exclusive and compulsory* jurisdiction of the Court in respect of the [enumerated] crimes.") (emphasis added); International Law Commission, *Report of the International Law Commission on the Work of its Forty-Fourth Session*, U.N. Doc. A/47/10, ¶ 41 (1992) ("Some other members felt that the proposed court could have exclusive jurisdiction on certain international crimes and concurrent jurisdiction with national tribunals on other crimes.").

7 *See, e.g.*, *About the Court*, INTERNATIONAL CRIMINAL COURT, https://www.icc-cpi.int/about/the-court (last visited Jul. 8, 2023) ("As a court of last resort, [the ICC] seeks to complement, not replace, national Courts.").

8 *See* U.N. Diplomatic Conference of Plenipotentiaries on the Establishment of an International Criminal Court, *Summary Records of the Plenary Meetings and of the Meetings of the Committee of the Whole*, U.N. Doc. A/CONF.183/13 (Vol. II), at 68, 88, 116, 187 (Jul. 17, 1998) (reporting comments by Canada, Spain, Yemen, and Jordan, respectively, on the importance of the ICC being a "court of last resort").

9 International Criminal Court, Rome Statute of the International Criminal Court, art. 17(1), U.N. Doc. A/CONF.183/9 (July 17, 1998) [hereinafter Rome Statute]; *See* William A. Schabas, *The International Criminal Court: A Commentary on the Rome Statute*, 2d. ed. (Oxford: Oxford University Press, 2016), p. 452 (The Statute's drafters almost certainly intended "with jurisdiction" to refer to the traditional bases of jurisdiction, such as territoriality and active personality).

any regional adjudicative efforts as well as universal jurisdiction cases sufficiently proximate to the most affected communities.

The OTP should reject such hierarchical thinking about the ICC's relationships with other courts, however. Instead, it should adopt a horizonal, burden sharing approach that recognizes the distinct interests of various communities and seeks to maximize overall benefits, while avoiding harm, especially to the communities most directly affected by international crimes. As I have elaborated elsewhere, although the global community is a "thin" community, it has distinct values and goals that the ICC, and courts exercising universal jurisdiction, may legitimately pursue.[10] Regional courts, such as the proposed African Criminal Court,[11] represent regional communities with their own sets of values and goals.[12] Although much of international law is based on state consent, suggesting the superior value of national interests compared to regional and global interests, international criminal law is a cosmopolitan project that views individuals as the ultimate units of interest.[13] As such, the various communities to which individuals belong each have legitimate claims to the pursuit of their own goals.

The ICC has largely adopted a burden sharing approach to its complementarity with national courts exercising traditional forms of jurisdiction. The Court has found cases inadmissible only when a state with jurisdiction

---

10 Margaret M. deGuzman, *Shocking the Conscience of Humanity: Gravity and the Legitimacy of International Criminal Law* (Oxford: Oxford University Press, 2019), pp. 18–33.

11 African Union [AU], *Protocol on Amendments to the Protocol on the Statute of the African Court of Justice and Human Rights*, (adopted Jun. 27, 2014) [hereinafter "the Malabo Protocol"] (The Malabo Protocol would afford criminal jurisdiction to the African Court of Justice and Human Rights. The Protocol was adopted in 2014 but has not taken effect because it has not been ratified by the required number of states.).

12 *See* deGuzman, *supra* note 5, at 672–73.

13 *See, e.g.*, Padraig McAuliffe, 'From Watchdog to Workhorse: Explaining the Emergence of the ICC's Burden-sharing Policy as an Example of Creeping Cosmopolitanism' (2014) 13 *Chinese J. Int'l L.* 259, 269

(Many of those who develop, theorize and practice international law (and international criminal law in particular) are driven by a normative ideal that development of the law may progressively catalyze the establishment of a cosmopolitan community which would accord all individuals equal moral status, regardless of any national borders.);

Darryl Robinson, 'A Cosmopolitan Liberal Account of International Criminal Law' (2013) 26 *Leiden J. Int'l L.* 127, 138

(Cosmopolitanism resonates with the aspirations of ICL: a concern for human beings that extends beyond borders, a willingness to embrace alternative governance structures to supplement state structures, and an inclusiveness of the concerns of the international community as a whole.) (citations omitted).

is actively investigating or prosecuting the same person and substantially the same conduct as the case before the ICC.[14] A strong commitment to serving as a "court of last resort" would suggest an interpretation of complementarity that grants states significantly more deference in determining how, when, and whom to investigate and prosecute to avoid ICC action. The ICC's willingness to accept state party referrals of situations on their own territories (without requiring demonstrated inability to prosecute) is also suggestive of a burden sharing approach to complementarity. The OTP explicitly endorsed burden sharing in its Policy Paper on Case Selection and Prioritization, noting that when the requirements of complementarity are met as to a case, the Prosecutor may turn his attention to "other perpetrators that form part of the same or a different case theory, in line with a burden-sharing approach."[15]

A burden sharing approach to engagement with regional courts and national courts exercising universal jurisdiction suggests the OTP should view the efforts of those institutions as potentially equally valuable to its own. As such, no default priority in resource allocation should be given either to opening ICC cases or to supporting those of other institutions. In line with the well-accepted principle of positive complementarity, the OTP may engage with other institutions in a variety of ways, including cooperation through sharing evidence, intelligence and the like, as well as providing assistance, such as training and other forms of capacity building. In determining how to allocate resources among all potential accountability efforts, including its own, the OTP should be guided by the principle of comparative benefit.

2 Comparative Benefit

Comparative benefit analysis involves making predictions about the likely future effects of different institutional actions on disparate communities and comparing them to assess their relative value. Comparing predicted

14 Prosecutor v. William Samoei Ruto, Henry Kiprono Kosgey and Joshua Arap Sang, Case No. ICC-01/09-01/11 OA, Judgment on the Appeal of the Republic of Kenya Against the Decision of Pre-Trial Chamber II of 30 May 2011 Entitled 'Decision on the Application by the Government of Kenya Challenging the Admissibility of the Case Pursuant to Article 19(2)(b) of the Statute', ¶ 40 (Aug. 30, 2011).

15 Office of the Prosecutor, International Criminal Court, Policy Paper on Case Selection and Prioritisation 11 (2016), https://www.icc-cpi.int/sites/default/files/itemsDocuments/20160915_OTP-Policy_Case-Selection_Eng.pdf.

effects is both complicated and unstable in light of continually evolving social and political realities. Nonetheless, comparative benefit analysis is necessary to ensure that engagement efforts are both legitimate and efficient uses of scarce resources. This section sketches the contours of comparative benefit analysis in the context of engagement efforts and concludes with a call for greater dialogue about how it can best be performed.

The first step in comparative benefit analysis is to identify the likely net benefits of adjudication in each potential forum. This requires considering all potential benefits to each of the communities with an interest in a situation, as well as any potential harms that may result from adjudication. For instance, a case might provide opportunities for the pursuit of national goals of preventive punishment, regional goals of coordinated action, and global goals of norm expression. It is possible that prosecution by an institution outside the most affected state or states, whether at the ICC, a regional court, or a national court exercising universal jurisdiction, could fulfill all these goals simultaneously, albeit to different degrees. Often, however, the goals of one or more of these communities are in tension. In that case, priorities must be established, which may result in harm to some communities. For example, if a state adjudicating an international crime has different punishment norms than the state that suffered most directly from it, the former may impose punishment that undermines the goals of the latter. This could be considered a harm to the most affected national community, which may experience the punishment as an injustice. In such circumstances, it may be preferable for the ICC not to support the state seeking to exercise universal jurisdiction, especially if a more beneficial alternative is available.

In weighing potential benefits to different communities, special attention should be paid to the needs of the communities directly harmed by the crimes. Their interests are most strongly affected by adjudicative efforts, and decision-makers at the ICC and other institutions external to those communities should prioritize avoiding harm to them. This means that even if adjudication would provide benefits to the global community or a regional community, it should not be undertaken if there is a significant risk of harm to the most affected national communities. Such harm might arise, for instance, if the most affected communities prefer a non-criminal means of addressing serious crimes, such as a justice mechanism focused on reconciliation rather than punishment. Likewise, potential harm to affected communities might arise in situations where ongoing conflicts exist that might be exacerbated by prosecutorial efforts. If the OTP deems that the prosecutorial efforts of a regional court or national court exercising universal jurisdiction risk these or other harms to the most affected national communities, it should not provide support.

Where harm to affected communities is not suspected, the OTP should seek to determine the likely net benefits of an adjudicative effort and compare them to other options in deciding whether, and to what degree, to provide support. Generally, national courts exercising universal jurisdiction should be viewed as pursuing global justice goals akin to those pursued at the ICC.[16] The benefits of universal jurisdiction cases therefore largely relate to the prevention of international crimes through norm expression.[17] Such cases may also contribute to global crime prevention through individual and collective deterrence, although the likelihood of universal jurisdiction prosecutions remains low enough that any such effects are likely to be quite small.[18] Some universal jurisdiction cases may also contribute to crime prevention by incapacitating particularly dangerous actors.

Regional adjudicative efforts can also help to prevent international crimes and may provide this benefit more strongly at the regional level compared to other adjudicative fora. Regional courts can also express uniquely regional norms, and their greater proximity to interested communities can magnify their impacts in this regard. The proposed African Criminal Court, for instance, will have jurisdiction over crimes of regional import, such as unconstitutional change of government.[19] It will thus be in a unique position to promote such norms within the region.

To determine the net benefits of a given adjudicative effort, the OTP must take account of any harms it may cause. In addition to the kinds of harm to directly affected communities discussed above, adjudicative efforts can harm all relevant communities when they lack sufficient legitimacy. Legitimacy is a complex concept that cannot be unpacked fully here,[20] but some of its basic features are worth mentioning. First, legitimacy, defined in terms of an institution's "right to rule,"[21] has both normative aspects, related, for instance, to the fairness of an institution's procedures and out-

16 deGuzman, *supra* note 10, at 29.

17 *Id.* at 140.

18 *Id.* at 192.

19 Malabo Protocol, *supra* note 11, art. 28E.

20 For a discussion of various kinds of legitimacy *see* deGuzman, *supra* note 10, at 9–14.

21 Allen Buchanan and Robert O. Keohane, 'The Legitimacy of Global Governance Institutions' (2006) 20 *Ethics & Int'l Affs.* 405.

puts, and sociological components, referring to perceptions of the same.[22] In either respect, legitimacy should be treated as a (mostly) scalar, rather than binary, concept. Although an institution might be declared entirely illegitimate below a threshold, such as when it shows blatant disregard for human rights, generally it is more appropriate to evaluate institutional legitimacy by degrees.

In deciding whether, and to what extent, to cooperate with another institution, the OTP must evaluate the institution's legitimacy. If an institution fails to satisfy threshold legitimacy requirements it should receive no support from the OTP. Above the threshold, however, decisions about whether, and how much, to cooperate should depend on a combination of the strength of the institution's legitimacy and the benefits it is likely to provide. For instance, a regional court that is moderately legitimate, perhaps because it has significant resources challenges, but is expected to provide an important regional benefit by expressing regional norms, likely merits ICC support. In contrast, a national court exercising universal jurisdiction that has moderate legitimacy and is unlikely to contribute significantly either to global prevention or to the goals of most affected communities likely does not merit ICC support.

Once the ICC determines that the net benefits of a particular adjudicative effort may warrant its support, a cost-benefit analysis should be conducted. That is, the benefits of assisting another institution in its investigative and prosecutorial efforts should be weighed against the costs to the ICC of such assistance. The greater the benefits from non-ICC adjudication, the more assistance is warranted. However, if the ICC expects its own cases to provide greater benefits than those anticipated from the institution seeking support, it should direct its resources internally. In conducting this cost-benefit analysis, the OTP should bear in mind the potential multiplier effect of assistance to regional courts and national courts exercising universal jurisdiction. Cooperative efforts such as sharing evidence and providing training in one case are likely to have carry-on effects, enhancing the jurisdiction's ability to engage in future prosecutions of international crimes. Where this

22 *See, e.g.*, Daniel Bodansky, 'Legitimacy in International Law and International Relations', in Jeffrey L. Dunoff and Mark A. Pollack (eds.), *Interdisciplinary Perspectives on International Law and International Relations: The State of the Art* (Cambridge: Cambridge University Press, 2012), p. 327 ("Normative legitimacy depends on whether an institution *objectively* has a right to rule – whether its claim is in some sense true.... In contrast, [sociological] legitimacy concerns whether actors *subjectively* believe that an institution has a right to rule.") (emphasis in original).

multiplier effect is likely to be significant, such as when a national jurisdiction intends to pursue a significant number of universal jurisdiction cases, the OTP may determine that the benefits of engagement outweigh those of bringing additional cases before the ICC.

3 Conclusion

Although the ICC Statute does not explicitly task the Court with supporting and strengthening the accountability network, its preamble affirms the importance of ensuring the effective prosecution of "the most serious crimes of concern to the international community as a whole" "by taking measures at the national level and by enhancing international cooperation."[23] OTP engagement with regional courts and national courts exercising universal jurisdiction is an important way to promote these goals. Practitioners, scholars, and supporters of international criminal justice should devote greater attention to developing principles to guide such engagement, including further developing the principles of burden sharing and comparative benefit.

---

23 Rome Statute, *supra* note 9, at Preamble.

CHAPTER 39

Cooperation between the Office of the Prosecutor of the ICC and States Exercising Universal Jurisdiction

Ladislav Hamran

On 17 July 1998, at the end of a six-week diplomatic conference in Rome attended by over 160 States, an agreement was reached that would forever change the global legal landscape.[1] For the first time in the history of mankind, a permanent, treaty-based International Criminal Court (hereinafter "ICC" or "Court") was to be set up with the mandate to exercise jurisdiction over persons for the most serious crimes of international concern.

The founding treaty of the Court, the Rome Statute, defined a new international criminal justice mechanism that became known as the Rome Statute system. This system is composed of two independent building blocks: domestic proceedings in front of national courts and international proceedings carried out by the ICC. Their mutual relationship is governed by the principle of complementarity, as defined in Paragraph 10 of the Preamble, and Articles 1 and 17 of the Rome Statute.

The complementarity principle puts sovereign states at the forefront of the fight against impunity for the most serious international crimes committed during armed conflicts. It reminds the international community of the fact that the prime responsibility for bringing perpetrators of war crimes, crimes against humanity, and genocide to justice lies with national jurisdictions.[2] The role of the ICC is complementary and the Court may only exercise its jurisdiction if a state party is unwilling or unable to carry out national proceedings in a particular case.

As a rule, states prosecute crimes committed either on their territory, or committed by or against their own nationals. However, during armed conflicts, national authorities are not always in the position to meet the

1 The presented opinions are exclusively the author's and do not represent the official position of Eurojust or any other institution.

2 The mutual relationship between States and the International Tribunal for Former Yugoslavia and the International Criminal Tribunal for Rwanda was different. Both tribunals had primacy over national courts.

 | DOI:10.1163/9789004686755_048

obligation to investigate or prosecute suspects of core international crimes. In some cases, there is an unwillingness to conduct objective, impartial and independent investigations and prosecutions. Corrupt national proceedings either shield perpetrators from criminal responsibility or result in unjustified delays that are inconsistent with a genuine intent to ensure accountability. In other cases, states affected by an armed conflict are unable to effectively prosecute war criminals due to a substantial or total collapse of their national judicial system.

In principle, the absence of (effective) national proceedings could justify the exercise of jurisdiction by the ICC. However, Paragraph 6 of the Preamble of the Rome Statute calls on every state to exercise its criminal jurisdiction over those responsible for international crimes. They could do so based on the principle of universal jurisdiction, reflecting that:

> [C]ertain crimes are so harmful to international interests that States are entitled – and even obliged – to bring proceedings against perpetrators, regardless of the location of the crime and the nationality of the perpetrator or the victim.[3]

This gives states the possibility to investigate crimes committed thousands of miles away with no personal link to their own territory.

Many states have introduced the principle of universal jurisdiction into their national criminal codes.[4] However, the mere existence of domestic legislation does not automatically mean that states can also carry out effective investigations into core international crimes. In fact, only a relatively small number of states[5] have been applying universal jurisdiction in practice and the reasons for this are manifold. As in any criminal proceeding, the road towards justice must be paved by solid and admissible evidence.

3 Mary Robinson, 'Foreword', in Stephen Macedo (ed.), *The Princeton Principles of Universal Jurisdiction* (Princeton: Princeton University Program in Law and Public Affairs, 2001), p. 16.

4 Amnesty Int'l, *Universal Jurisdiction: A Preliminary Survey of Legislation Around the World – 2012 Update*, Index No. IOR 53/019/2012 (Oct. 9, 2012), https://www.amnesty.org/en/documents/ior53/019/2012/en/ (last visited October 10, 2023) (According to this 2012 article, 166 (approximately 86%) of the 193 UN Member States have defined one or more of four crimes under international law (war crimes, crimes against humanity, genocide and torture) as crimes in their national law and 147 (approximately 76.2%) out of 193 States have provided for universal jurisdiction over one or more of these crimes.).

5 For example, Argentina, Australia, Austria, Belgium, Canada, Denmark, Finland, France, Germany, Israel, Mexico, the Netherlands, Senegal, Spain, Sweden, Switzerland, the United Kingdom, and the United States.

Reconstructing and proving the circumstances under which a core international crime was committed can be like solving a 1000-piece puzzle without having the final image to guide you. It requires many hours of labor carried out by highly qualified personnel as well as robust political support.

Even with the abovementioned general conditions in place, the outcome remains uncertain. Police and judicial authorities have no access to the territory of the conflict, so they have to interview thousands of victims and witnesses who fled to various jurisdictions, and they need to validate, analyze and categorize unprecedented amounts of digital evidence located on cloud servers, social media networks and different electronic devices. At the same time, they face difficulties related to establishing the physical location of war criminals, cooperating with a wide range of stakeholders and working with different languages and dialects. Add to those more practical considerations concerning the available resources and conflicting national prosecutorial priorities, and no wonder that many states think twice before exercising universal jurisdiction in relation to core international crimes.

Despite these challenges, the number of universal jurisdiction investigations has been growing steadily over the years. According to the EU Network for investigation and prosecution of genocide, crimes against humanity and war crimes, the overall number of newly opened cases in EU Member States increased by 44 percent between 2016 and 2021.[6] More and more cases involving universal jurisdiction are also reported by Trial International, a Geneva-based NGO.[7] This encouraging development can be attributed to the long term and collective efforts to build up a critical mass of trained staff with the necessary knowledge and expertise. Moreover, improved legislation and institutional frameworks have started to bear fruit.

The recent presence of armed conflicts in Europe has sparked a debate about the need for a collective legal response to core international crimes. The war in Ukraine in particular, has taken the accountability efforts to a new level by bringing together states, international organizations, EU institutions and agencies, non-governmental organizations and civil society organizations. Only a few weeks after the start of the war, 21 states in Europe and beyond activated their national provisions on universal jurisdiction – in many cases after being dormant for years or even never used before. On 25 March 2022, Lithuania, Poland and Ukraine signed a Joint Investigation

6 *Key Factors for Successful Investigations and Prosecutions of Core International Crimes*, Eurojust, https://www.eurojust.europa.eu/publication/key-factors-successful-investigations-and-prosecutions-core-international-crimes (last visited October 8, 2023).

7 TRIAL Int'l, https://trialinternational.org (last visited October 12, 2023).

Team (hereinafter "JIT")[8] agreement with the aim to start documenting crimes committed during the invasion.[9]

One month later, the Office of the Prosecutor of the ICC (hereinafter "OTP-ICC") became a participant in this JIT. It was the first time that the OTP-ICC joined a JIT, thereby enhancing the possibilities for coordination between the ongoing national investigations and the independent investigation by the OTP-ICC. As such, it was an important milestone for the interpretation and practical implementation of the principle of complementarity, confirming that the exercise of universal jurisdiction by a state is not an obstacle for the OTP-ICC to act. At the time, ICC Prosecutor Karim A. A. Khan QC stated that:

> [T]he Ukraine situation, in particular, demands collective action so as to secure relevant evidence and ultimately ensure its effective use in criminal proceedings.[10]

The benefits of close cooperation between the OTP-ICC and states that are exercising universal jurisdiction for core international crimes are both manifold and mutual. Due to its limited capacity and resources, the OTP-ICC cannot possibly carry out all the tasks attributed to it in the Rome Statute. Sharing the workload with states could offer some relief and reduce the pressing need to increase national contributions to the ICC's annual budget. The OTP-ICC could further profit from the forensic and analytical capacity available at national level. This is increasingly essential in most investigations, for example when large amounts of digital evidence are involved.

8 A JIT is a formal legal agreement between the judicial authorities of two or more countries. JITs enable the easy exchange of information and evidence between prosecutors, judges and law enforcement officials, while allowing JIT members to be present during investigative measures on each other's territories.

9 This was the second JIT created for the investigation of core international crimes. The first was established in 2018 between Germany and France focusing on crimes committed in Syria. Thanks to the evidence collected by the JIT, the German Higher Regional Court in Koblenz convicted the former head of the investigations section in the Syrian General Intelligence Directorate for crimes against humanity. The evidence collected by the JIT compellingly proved that the suspect was guilty of killing 27 members of the opposition as a result of torture and inhumane treatment.

10 Statement, Karim A.A. Khan, Prosecutor, Int'l Crim. Ct., Office of the Prosecutor Joins National Authorities in Joint Investigation Team on International Crimes Committed in Ukraine (Apr. 25, 2022), https://www.icc-cpi.int/news/statement-icc-prosecutor-karim-aa-khan-qc-office-prosecutor-joins-national-authorities-joint (last visited October 6, 2023).

Closer cooperation with states may also lead to a better understanding of national prosecutorial strategies or priority crime areas, which in turn can contribute to a more efficient use of the ICC's resources.

States exercising their universal jurisdiction can equally benefit from regular interactions with the OTP-ICC. By providing information, evidence, advice or expertise, the OTP-ICC may significantly advance national investigations and help to overcome both evidentiary and legal hurdles. The OTP-ICC may supply a missing piece of information or evidence when national investigators cannot secure the cooperation from the state involved in the armed conflict. The OTP-ICC could also help national authorities to legally establish contextual elements, because confirming the link between a certain crime and an armed conflict is a prerequisite for obtaining a conviction. The OTP-ICC can even conduct an investigation on the territory of a state when authorized by the Pre-Trial Chamber and provided that the conditions specified in Article 57 paragraph 3(d) of the Rome Statute are met.

Having briefly described the benefits of increased interaction and cooperation between the OTP-ICC and states, I also see several obstacles that will have to be addressed. The first experience in forming a JIT between states and the OTP-ICC has revealed certain gaps in national legislations. Some states may only conclude JIT agreements with other states while lacking the legal basis to engage with the OTP-ICC in this context. States may also be reluctant to engage in joint investigations with the OTP-ICC due to disclosure obligations.

Another potential issue can be found in the somewhat old-fashioned provisions for international judicial cooperation in Part 9 of the Rome Statute. They are a reminder of the situation in the early 90s, when this cooperation was still mostly routed through diplomatic channels and central authorities. The Rome Statute has no provision for the spontaneous exchange of information between the OTP-ICC and state or non-state parties carrying out investigations based on universal jurisdiction.

Fortunately, the lack of such a provision is partially offset by the other possibilities offered by the Rome Statute concerning the cooperation between the OTP-ICC and national authorities. According to Article 54 paragraph 3(d) of the Rome Statute, the OTP-ICC may enter into arrangements or agreements that are necessary to facilitate the cooperation of a state party, intergovernmental organization or person. Similarly, Article 93 of the Rome Statue concerns requests for assistance from the Court to state parties (Paragraph 1) and vice versa (Paragraph 10). While both paragraphs contain a list of the types of assistance foreseen, they also both specify that this list is non-exhaustive. This opens the possibility for enhanced cooperation between the OTP-ICC and states, for example in the form of a JIT.

My plea for this enhanced cooperation seems to be in line with a trend witnessed in the context of the United Nations, where accountability efforts rely on national courts rather than the establishment of a new international court or a tribunal. The last three investigation mechanisms established by the United Nations – the United Nations Investigative Team to promote accountability for crimes committed by Da'esh/ISIL in Iraq (UNITAD),[11] the International, Impartial and Independent Mechanism (IIIM)[12] and the Independent Investigation Mechanism for Myanmar (IIMM)[13] – are all mandated to ensure the use of the evidence collected before national courts and therefore by default obliged to seek effective cooperation with different national jurisdictions.

In the same way, the ICC should invest in building the legal, institutional and technical architecture required for cooperation with all states exercising universal jurisdiction, regardless of their affiliation to the Rome Statute. In legal terms, formalizing this cooperation in an arrangement or agreement could ensure that the competent national authorities will systematically exchange information and evidence about core international crimes with the OTP-ICC. Institutionally, and insofar as not already established, it could be beneficial to introduce dedicated national units in charge of the cooperation with the OTP-ICC. Finally, the exchange of evidence and operational information should be done through modern and secure communication tools, replacing the traditional and cumbersome diplomatic channels.

Conclusion

In this article, I have attempted to demonstrate that the principles of universal jurisdiction and complementarity are by no means competitors. They should work together towards one and the same objective: closing the impunity gap for the most serious international crimes. Bringing a core international crime case to a national authority for the purpose of its investigation and prosecution is certainly not a failure of the ICC. In this respect I agree with Mr. Luis Moreno Ocampo, the first Prosecutor of the Court, who already in 2003 mentioned that:

11 S.C. Res. 2379 (Sep. 21, 2017).

12 G.A. Res. 71/248 (Dec. 16, 2016).

13 Human Rights Council Res. 39/2, U.N. Doc. A/HRC/RES/39/2 (October 3, 2018).

> [A]s a consequence of complementarity, the number of cases that reach the Court should not be a measure of its efficiency. On the contrary, the absence of trials before this Court, as consequence of the regular functioning of national institutions, would be a major success.

CHAPTER 40

Modern Guidelines for Universal Jurisdiction

Devika Hovell

Introduction

The "justice cascade" may have started as a trickle but is generating momentum.[1] The last few decades have witnessed the establishment of a steady stream of international criminal tribunals, including ad hocs, hybrids, specialist courts, and of course the permanent International Criminal Court. In more recent years, there has been a surge in the domestic prosecution of international crimes through the mechanism of universal jurisdiction. This bricolage of international criminal prosecutions is increasingly in need of systematization.

This is not a call for a hierarchy of courts, with the ICC at its apex. A common mistake, at least in the public mindset, is to see the ICC as the ultimate terminus for international criminals. As is well known by international criminal lawyers, the ICC was not created as a "last stop" but as a "last resort." As the first ICC Prosecutor declared at his swearing-in, "the absence of trials before [the ICC], as a consequence of the regular functioning of national institutions, would be a major success."[2] In his latest Annual Report, the current ICC Prosecutor Karim Khan explained the importance of transforming the role of the ICC from an "apex court" into a "hub" for cooperation and engagement.[3] While the ICC was established to generate a caseload of international criminal prosecutions, the goal was not simply to attract cases to the ICC but to deflect cases to other fora, encouraging burden-sharing of the prosecution load with domestic courts. The justice cascade must be mainstreamed through domestic legal systems if international criminal law is to have the capacity to fulfil its objectives.

1 Kathryn Sikkink, *The Justice Cascade: How Human Rights Prosecutions Are Changing World Politics* (2011).

2 Luis Moreno-Ocampo, *ICC Prosecutor, Ceremony for the Solemn Undertaking of the Chief Prosecutor of the International Criminal Court* (Jun. 16, 2003).

3 Office of the Prosecutor, Int'l Crim. Ct., *Annual Report* (Dec. 1, 2022), https://www.icc-cpi.int/sites/default/files/2022-12/2022-12-05-annual-report-of-the-office-of-the-prosecutor.pdf.

 | DOI:10.1163/9789004686755_049

Universal jurisdiction offers great potential for expanding the reach of international criminal law. Yet it also creates difficult and under-appreciated challenges for domestic courts. Universal jurisdiction involves the prosecution of extraordinary crimes through ordinary means. Yet much about international criminal law can be lost through recourse to the ordinary. The under-appreciated factor is that such trials share more in common with international criminal law than domestic criminal law. While the temptation is for domestic judges to proceed with "business as usual" in the conduct of universal jurisdiction trials, this can ignore certain incompatibilities between domestic and international criminal justice. The DNA of universal jurisdiction trials differs in important ways from other domestic criminal trials, connecting domestic courts to a different set of communities, interests, crimes, and cultures.

This essay proposes the development of a set of guidelines – an optimistic precursor to an eventual treaty – to guide the conduct of universal jurisdiction trials. The guidelines could be developed under the auspices of the ICC, building in an advisory role for the ICC in monitoring and guiding the conduct of universal jurisdiction prosecutions. A modest starting-point is provided in the Annex to this comment, outlining modern guidelines for the conduct of universal jurisdiction trials (hereinafter Modern Guidelines). The idea is to update our understanding of universal jurisdiction, explaining the contemporary contribution of universal jurisdiction, its distinctive nature, and the particular challenges generated by its trials. In particular, four distinct problems are identified that need to be addressed in its contemporary application: the public problem, the selectivity problem, the proof problem and the translation problem.

1 The Public Problem: Remoteness from Political Community

The first point to clarify is that universal jurisdiction trials are conducted on behalf of a different community than domestic criminal trials. Most lawyers have a clear understanding that domestic criminal trials are conducted on behalf of the domestic public. Therefore, in the United Kingdom, criminal matters are described as Rex v. X, capturing the conception of being answerable to a local sovereign; in the United States, cases are labelled as People v. X, capturing the idea of being liable to one's fellow citizenry; in France, criminal judgments are issued au nom du peuple français, while in China, criminal cases are in the name of the "People's Procuratorate" at various local levels.

The community addressed by universal jurisdiction trials is quite different. Hannah Arendt famously disparaged the "common illusion that the crime of murder and the crime of genocide are essentially the same," explaining that "[t]he point of the latter is that an altogether different order is broken and an altogether different community is violated."[4] The problem is that there is not yet a clear understanding of the political community on whose behalf universal jurisdiction prosecutions are undertaken. A number of alternatives present themselves, including the inter-state community, the international community, the affected victim community, and the domestic community of the prosecuting state.[5] The paradox is that, of these, the political community with the most remote interest in the trial is very often that of the prosecuting state.

This question is of more than academic relevance. Domestic criminal trials respond deliberately to the community on whose behalf they are conducted, drawing juries from within that community, prosecuted by representatives of that community, conducted in the language of that community, enforcing laws enacted for that community, publicized by media within that community, overseen by and accountable to that community. By contrast, universal jurisdiction produces deracinated trials, uprooted from their natural social, geographical, linguistic, and cultural environments. Domestic criminal courts are not accustomed to engaging with external communities, providing little scope for any ethic of responsibility toward external communities, participants, or interests.

It is important that domestic courts develop an understanding of the communities on whose behalf universal jurisdiction trials are conducted. The ICC can help frame an understanding of the polycentric interests engaged by universal jurisdiction trials. A proposed definition of universal jurisdiction is included in Modern Guideline 1.1, understanding universal jurisdiction as a license provided by the inter-state community to universalize the right of access to justice for victim communities so that the prosecuting state can prosecute certain heinous crimes of concern to the international community. Recognition of the communities implicated in universal jurisdiction trials provides the foundation for a trial that can better serve those on whose behalf it is conducted.

4 Hannah Arendt, *Eichmann in Jerusalem: A Report on the Banality of Evil* (1963).

5 Devika Hovell, *The Authority of Universal Jurisdiction*, 29 EUR. J. INT'L L. 427 (2018).

2 The Selectivity Problem: Remoteness of Interests

Where there is a disconnect between the legal communities of the prosecutor and the prosecuted, an impression can be created that a trial is simply political. The objectivity of the courtroom becomes questionable where it is a device through which one community imposes its laws upon another. The politics of universal jurisdiction are magnified by the fact that international criminal law can only ever be selectively enforced. One response to this is that prosecuting all persons responsible for international crimes is impossible. Yet problems arise where case selection is perceived as based on irrelevant or illegitimate interests.

It has become popular to describe universal jurisdiction in terms of an imperialist mission. A map of the nationalities of prosecutors and accused in universal jurisdiction prosecutions reveals a familiar though uncomfortable pattern. A survey of completed universal jurisdiction trials until 2020 shows that the seventy-five trials were conducted by eighteen prosecuting states, sixteen of which form part of the "Western European and Others" group in the United Nations.[6] Conversely, the accused in universal jurisdiction trials (if we exclude the five trials against accused former Nazis) are drawn from thirteen states, none of whom are from the "Western European and Others" group and all of whom are classified as developing economies. The survey seems to repeat a historical pattern, evoking the spectre of a "newfangled civilizing mission" with domestic criminal courts in the global north delivering the rule of law to the global south.

Another common anxiety about universal jurisdiction extends to a concern that foreign domestic prosecutions could be manipulated or deployed as an instrument of legal warfare against political adversaries. This problem was raised by Henry Kissinger, himself a target of attempted universal jurisdiction prosecutions, who described universal jurisdiction as a form of "judicial tyranny" which could "[turn] into a means to pursue political enemies rather than universal justice."[7]

The potential intellectual misstep in both the imperial and lawfare critiques is that they misconstrue the driving force behind universal jurisdiction prosecutions. While there may be significant rhetorical force in imagining universal jurisdiction oscillating ambivalently between imperialist interventions and aggressive show trials, these arguments are based more

6 Leslie Johns, Máximo Langer & Margaret E. Peters, *Migration and the Demand for Transnational Justice*, 116 AM. POL. SCI. REV. 1184, 1189-90 (2022).

7 Henry A. Kissinger, *The Pitfalls of Universal Jurisdiction*, FOREIGN AFF. (Jul. 1, 2001).

on reasonable suspicion than reasonable evidence. The reality is that states are not, and have never been, the main drivers of universal jurisdiction prosecutions. In practice, most if not all universal jurisdiction trials occur as a result of pressure from victims and victim-support groups. The problem is therefore not generally state overzealousness but state reluctance to prosecute. In practice, universal jurisdiction trials tend to be the result of a sensible wager on the part of the prosecuting state in each individual case, weighing diplomatic credit for participating in the prosecution of international crimes against the economic and diplomatic cost in international relations terms.[8]

These are important insights, not only because of their descriptive accuracy but also because of their normative implications. By defining with more particularity the legal interests rightly engaged by universal jurisdiction prosecutions, it becomes possible to situate decision-making about case selection within a potential legal framework. Recharacterizing universal jurisdiction as an individual right rather than a state right (Modern Guidelines 1.1 and 1.2) provides access to the human rights proportionality framework, enabling states to balance individual rights against their own legitimate aims and interests (Modern Guideline 2.8). It is necessary to develop a coherent set of criteria by which states can achieve proportionality between affected communities and other legitimate aims of the prosecuting state. As suggested in Modern Guideline 2.9, criteria to be weighed in the balance should include:

1. international consensus as to the seriousness of the crime;
2. desire by victims or victim organizations for access to justice;
3. danger that offenses would not otherwise be prosecuted;
4. location of the accused;
5. effective administration of justice given quantity and quality of available witnesses and evidence;
6. vulnerability and security of victims;
7. impact on standing, reputation and diplomatic relations of the prosecuting state; and
8. cost.

Though a long way off, it is possible to envisage a time when the ICC could act as a court of review in relation to decisions to accept or decline jurisdiction against these criteria (Modern Guideline 6.1).

8 Máximo Langer, *The Diplomacy of Universal Jurisdiction: The Political Branches and the Transnational Prosecution of International Crimes*, 105 AM. J. INT'L L. 1 (2011).

Of course, the risk of future abuse of the principle of universal jurisdiction should not be entirely disregarded. Universal jurisdiction should be exercised in good faith in accordance with a state's rights and obligations under international law (Modern Guideline 2.2), with respect for rules relating to immunity (Modern Guidelines 2.5–2.7) and double jeopardy (Modern Guideline 2.4). Recognition of universal jurisdiction as a mechanism to provide victims with a right of access to justice in circumstances where it is not otherwise available also supports recognition of a principle of complementarity as between the prosecuting state and the territorial state or state of nationality. Universal jurisdiction should only be exercised where the territorial state or state of nationality is genuinely unwilling or unable to do so (Modern Guideline 2.10). Greater understanding of the objectives of universal jurisdiction also guides the way to recognition of criteria for the resolution of potential conflicts of jurisdiction between states (elaborated in Modern Guideline 2.11).

3 The Proof Problem: Remoteness of Evidence

A further problem universal jurisdiction trials must address is the prosecuting state's remoteness from the evidence. Remoteness from the evidence can be measured not only in geographical but also in psychological and physical terms, complicating the collection of, recollection of, and connection to evidence. The geographical distance, impact of trauma, justifiable fear by witnesses of retribution, and complexity of chains of command can build serious fault lines between what happened and what can be proved in universal jurisdiction trials.

In geographical terms, almost all relevant evidence and witnesses in universal jurisdiction trials will be located in a foreign country to which investigators and prosecutors may be denied access. This creates obvious problems for the collection of evidence. In the absence of direct access to evidence, it becomes necessary for domestic investigators and prosecutors to rely on indirect means of obtaining access, often through the "first responders" to atrocity, namely non-governmental organizations (NGOs). The involvement of NGOs in evidence collection can create problems for domestic courts not accustomed to accommodating third party investigators. NGOs are also increasingly having to come to terms with adapting their information-gathering techniques and developing more rigorous methodologies where there is a possibility this information may be used as criminal evidence in a foreign court (Modern Guideline 5.2). The guidelines can provide access to guidance on these complex matters, linking to guidelines established by the ICC and Eurojust for NGOs to follow in documenting international crimes (Modern Guideline 5.3).[9]

In psychological terms, the trauma, fear, social chaos, and delay caused by mass criminality are far from ideal incubators of truth and memory. Given it is rare for senior political and military leaders to document their involvement in atrocity, the bulk of evidence in such trials tends to be in the form of witness testimony. Trauma and fear can subject evidence recollection to very human fallibilities and can interfere with the reliability and credibility of witnesses. The challenge for domestic courts is to develop procedures that will assist a judge or jury to disaggregate true from false memory in a way that is fair to the accused while not disproportionately impacting or impairing the rights of traumatized or vulnerable victims (Modern Guidelines 3.3–3.5). There is much scope for the ICC to provide guidance to domestic courts (and develop more detailed guidelines) on victim and witness protection and support, including victim witness familiarization and preparation, the impact of trauma on evidence, procedural and evidentiary rules that mitigate victim trauma, psychological counseling, and witness protection (Modern Guideline 3.12).

In physical terms, international criminal law's focus on higher-ranked individuals means universal jurisdiction trials must also factor in the accused's remoteness from physical acts of atrocity. In recognition of this, international criminal law has developed its own distinctive modes of liability, recognizing that the trial's focus is not the individual considered in abstraction but the individual as an element of the authority, institution, government, or even society the individual represents. Domestic criminal systems can face problems in circumstances where international criminal modes of liability are unfamiliar and where the idea of collective guilt is generally regarded as anathema to criminal justice. The ICC can play a role in encouraging greater adoption and guiding application of international criminal modes of liability in the prosecution of international crimes by domestic courts (Modern Guideline 3.7).

9 Eurojust & Int'l Crim. Ct. Off. of the Prosecutor, *Guidelines for Civil Society Organizations: Documenting International Crimes and Human Rights Violations for Accountability Purposes* (2022), available at https://www.icc-cpi.int/sites/default/files/2023-06/ICC-Eurojust-CSO-Guidelines-Eng.pdf.

4 The Translation Problem: Remoteness from Context

While the presence of foreign elements is not unique to universal jurisdiction trials, domestic courts are not always prepared for the linguistic and cultural disconnect between the domestic courtroom and foreign criminal context in universal jurisdiction trials, particularly in cases of trial by jury. The role of a jury is to build a bridge between the law and the community to which it is applied, with jurors typically engaged to bring their joint experience of life, and common sense, to judgment of the facts. The problem is that there is often little joint or common between a domestic jury's experience and the criminal context of foreign atrocity in universal jurisdiction trials. There is a strong argument for reconsidering the role of the jury in universal jurisdiction trials (Modern Guideline 3.1).

Of course, even in judge-led trials, the adjudication task is greatly hampered when the judge is not from the country in which the crime has occurred and has no knowledge of relevant factors such as language, geography, locations where the crime took place, distances, cultural idiosyncrasies, and relevant political or historical background. Judges sitting on universal jurisdiction trials should be encouraged to develop guided expertise on international criminal law, as well as on the historical, political, and cultural context in relation to which the alleged offense took place (Modern Guideline 3.2). Courts have demonstrated their capacity to build in adaptations where witnesses or defendants whose cultural attributes and communication style differ from those of courtroom personnel. For example, judges in Australia and Canada, working with indigenous populations, are required to participate in appropriate training and development programs, designed to explain contemporary Aboriginal society, customs, and traditions. The Dutch War Crimes Unit has employed an anthropologist as part of its team to enable a greater understanding of culturally contextual issues associated with universal jurisdiction trials. Germany is considering a move toward specialized war crimes chambers, with judges specially trained to deal with such cases.

The foreign language element also creates complications in universal jurisdiction trials. In linguistic terms, the nature of judicial proceedings is invariably altered when mediated through the mechanism of a foreign language interpreter. The domestic court must ensure it has access to adequately trained interpreters prior to the trial's commencement (Modern Guideline 3.8) and all court actors should inform themselves of, and be sensitive to, the challenges created by court interpretation (Modern Guideline 3.10). Helpful guidelines as to the numbers of interpreters, duration, and working conditions are available in the ICC's Registry Regulations, and could be elaborated in the guidelines.[10]

Finally, the problem of translation is not merely about how the courtroom understands foreign communities, but also how certain communities understand the foreign courtroom. International criminal law, like domestic criminal law, is ultimately a tool to achieve certain ends. These ends go beyond the individual accused, the individual victim, and the domestic community of the prosecuting state. The capacity for international criminal law to achieve its goals ultimately depends on the expressive function of individual trials as a venue for the reconciliation of the interests of the international community, the inter-state community, and victim communities. It is critical that domestic courts exercising universal jurisdiction establish effective lines of communication with affected communities, explaining and publicizing the trial and its outcomes among those communities (Modern Guidelines 4.1–4.3).

5 Conclusion

Remoteness is something of a leitmotif in universal jurisdiction trials. Universal jurisdiction trials are remote from the political communities on whose behalf they are undertaken, potentially compromised by external interests, physically distanced from the evidence to be considered, and lacking familiarity with the cultural context and language in which the crime occurred. These challenges can affect both the conduct of the trial and its impact. When a universal jurisdiction trial is poorly executed, the danger is that it has the capacity to serve as a corrosive rather than constructive agent, wasting the resources of domestic courts and failing to achieve the goals of international criminal law. This essay has sought to digest some of the lessons learned from universal jurisdiction trials to date and distil them into guidelines provided in the attached Annex. These guidelines include a role for the ICC in providing advice and guidance to domestic courts on case selection, conduct of, and outreach in universal jurisdiction trials. Given greater resources and state will, the ICC is professionally well equipped to act as a coordinating mechanism within the broader international criminal system, providing advice, assistance, and secondment of officials. It may even be possible to imagine that, one day, the ICC might act

10 Int'l Crim. Ct., *Regulations of the Registry* 27 (Aug. 1, 2018), available at https://www.icc-cpi.int/sites/default/files/Publications/Regulations-of-the-Registry.pdf.

as an avenue of judicial review to mediate the broad exercise of universal jurisdiction by states within an international criminal legal system.

Annex: Modern Guidelines for the Conduct of Universal Jurisdiction Trials

1 *Definition and Role*

1.1 Universal jurisdiction is a license by the inter-state community to universalize the right of access to justice for victim communities in relation to serious crimes of concern to the international community where this does not disproportionately affect the legitimate aims or interests of the prosecuting state.

1.2 Universal jurisdiction forms part of a state's contribution to the enforcement of international criminal law. It is not simply a state's right but in some cases is a duty owed by states under international law, either under international treaties or as a manifestation of its duty to provide individuals with access to justice.

2 *Scope and Limitations*

2.1 States may exercise universal jurisdiction:

(1) Where authorized to do so under a treaty; or

(2) In the case of other serious crimes of concern to the international community, where formally requested to do so by victims or a victim organization credibly and genuinely representing victims affected by the alleged crime.

2.2 States shall exercise universal jurisdiction in good faith and in accordance with their rights and obligations under international law.

2.3 Universal jurisdiction is not an absolute right or duty but may be balanced against the international obligations and other legitimate aims of prosecuting states. States may decline to exercise universal jurisdiction where international law prohibits them from doing so, where its exercise would disproportionately impact other legitimate aims or interests or where a state in a better position to prosecute is genuinely willing and able to do so.

a Ne Bis in Idem

2.4 No person who has been tried by another court for conduct shall be tried in universal jurisdiction proceedings with respect to the same conduct unless the proceedings in the other court were for the purpose of shielding the person concerned from criminal responsibility or otherwise were not conducted independently or impartially in accordance with international due process norms and were conducted in a manner inconsistent with an intent to bring the person concerned to justice.

b Immunity

2.5 In the exercise of universal jurisdiction, domestic courts must respect principles of international law on immunity.

2.6 Domestic courts shall respect the personal immunity of certain holders of high-ranking office in a state, such as the Head of State, Head of Government and Minister of Foreign Affairs, in civil and criminal matters. There is no exception to personal immunity in relation to international crimes. Individuals will lose personal immunity once they cease holding office or if their state of nationality waives immunity.

2.7 Functional immunity generally does not apply in relation to international crimes and does not prevent the exercise of universal jurisdiction.

c Disproportionate Interference With Legitimate Aims and Interests

2.8 Unless otherwise required to do so, states may elect not to exercise universal jurisdiction where it would not provide effective access to justice for victims or would disproportionately impact other legitimate aims or interests.

2.9 In determining whether to exercise universal jurisdiction in any particular case, the prosecuting state may assess whether providing a right of access to justice to victims would disproportionately impact other legitimate aims and interests. This decision should be based on an objective determination, reviewable by a court of law, having regard to: (1) international consensus as to the seriousness of the crime; (2) desire by victims or victim organizations for access to justice; (3) danger that offenses would not otherwise be prosecuted; (4) location of the accused; (5) effective administration of justice given quantity and quality of available witnesses and evidence; (6) vulnerability and security of victims; (6) impact on standing, reputation and diplomatic relations of the prosecuting state; and (7) cost.

d Complementarity and Conflict

2.10 A domestic court should only exercise universal jurisdiction where the state in whose territory the alleged crime was committed or state of nationality of the accused is unwilling or unable genuinely to do so.

2.11 In the event of conflict between states seeking jurisdiction, priority should be given to the court in the best position to judge the acts. This should be based on an objective determination, reviewable by a court of law, having regard to: (1) multilateral or bilateral treaty obligations; (2) request by affected victims or victim communities to prosecute; (3) the location of the accused; (4) the location of affected victims or victim community; (5) access to evidence; (6) linguistic and cultural connections between prosecuting state and accused, victims or location of crime; (7) fairness, independence and impartiality of the prosecuting court; (8) convenience to parties, witnesses and victims; and (9) interests of justice.

3 *Investigation and Trial Process and Procedure*

a Nature of Adjudicator

3.1 Where possible, universal jurisdiction trials should proceed before a judge or judges rather than a jury.

3.2 Judges should develop guided expertise on international criminal law, as well as on the history, political and cultural context in relation to which the alleged offense took place.

b Standard of Proof and Assessment of Evidence

3.3 An accused shall only be convicted in universal jurisdiction trials if the elements of the offense are proved beyond reasonable doubt.

3.4 Where insufficient direct evidence is available due to the circumstances of the crime, factual inferences may be drawn from circumstantial evidence. In such a case, the inference drawn from the circumstantial evidence must be the only reasonable one that could be drawn from the evidence presented.

3.5 In determining the reliability of witnesses, adjudicators should consider the situation of traumatized and vulnerable witnesses. They should develop evidentiary procedures for mitigating victim trauma and accommodate cogent and reasonable difficulties in providing a coherent, complete and logical account where this does not interfere with satisfaction of the standard of proof.

3.6 In assessing witness reliability in any particular case, judges may benefit from expert evidence on the impact of trauma on an individual's memory.

c Mode of Liability

3.7 Where possible, the liability of the accused in universal jurisdiction prosecutions should be determined according to international criminal modes of liability.

d Interpretation of Witness Evidence

3.8 In advance of the commencement of universal jurisdiction prosecutions, the availability of at least three properly trained and qualified court interpreters should be confirmed so as to provide the accused, witnesses and the court with access to interpretation.

3.9 Where possible, access to simultaneous interpretation should be provided to all actors in the courtroom, including the public gallery.

3.10 All court actors should conduct themselves in a manner sensitive to the challenges created by court interpretation.

e Rights and Protection of Accused, Victims and Witnesses

3.11 In exercising universal jurisdiction, a state and its judicial organs shall observe international due process norms during all stages of the investigation, trial, appeal, sentencing and enforcement, including but not limited to those relating to the rights of the accused and victims, fairness of the proceedings and the independence and impartiality of the judiciary.

3.12 States shall take all reasonable measures to guarantee the safety and physical and psychological wellbeing of victims, witnesses, experts and all other participants in universal jurisdiction proceedings, before, during and after the trial.

4 *Outreach*

4.1 States exercising universal jurisdiction shall develop effective lines of communication with affected communities and available outreach mechanisms through which to connect to these communities.

4.2 Where appropriate, prosecuting states should coordinate, cooperate and recognize the work of representative non-governmental organizations (NGOs). NGOs can provide valuable assistance in enabling and managing connections with victims and witnesses in preparation for, during and after universal jurisdiction prosecutions.

4.3 Courts should provide and publicize reasons for decisions in universal jurisdiction trials among affected communities and, where possible, explanation as to why reasoning may deviate from local norms or practices within the state or states most closely connected to the crime.

5 *Mutual Legal Assistance*

5.1 The competent state authorities shall assist one another in all proceedings initiated by virtue of the principle of universal jurisdiction, provided the prosecuting state acts in good faith.

5.2 NGOs can provide valuable assistance in identifying and locating victims and witnesses and mapping victimisation and alleged crimes. This information should be passed on to competent investigative authorities for future interviews.

5.3 Before taking witness accounts, NGOs are advised to consult the "Guidelines for Civil Society Organizations: Documenting International Crimes and Human Rights Violations for Accountability Purposes."[11]

6 *Settlement of Disputes*

6.1 Consistent with international law and the Charter of the United Nations, states should settle their disputes arising out of the exercise of universal jurisdiction by all available means of peaceful settlement of disputes. [Where all states to the dispute are parties to the Rome Statute, they may submit requests for resolution of disputes to the International Criminal Court.][12] All states may submit disputes to the International Court of Justice.

---

11 Guidelines, *supra* note 9.

12 Subject to the Assembly of States Parties to the International Criminal Court agreeing to provide this mechanism. This would require an amendment to the Rome Statute.

CHAPTER 41

The ICC Office of the Prosecutor and Support of Universal Jurisdiction Prosecutions before National Authorities

Máximo Langer

In the last forty years, there has been a remarkable expansion of efforts aimed at establishing criminal accountability for individuals involved in committing international crimes.[1] Prosecutions before national courts, ad hoc international criminal tribunals created by the United Nations Security Council (UNSC), hybrid criminal tribunals that have combined national and international elements in various ways, investigative mechanisms set to gather elements of proof to be used by various jurisdictions, proposals to create regional criminal tribunals, and the International Criminal Court have all collectively advanced the notion that those who commit international crimes should be held accountable for their actions.

Among these efforts, the International Criminal Court (ICC or the Court) is the only permanent international criminal court with jurisdiction over crimes against humanity, genocide, war crimes, and crimes of aggression. The ICC is the result of a treaty that was drafted with widespread participation from states and numerous nongovernmental organizations; it currently has 123 state parties. As such, the ICC and its Office of the Prosecutor (OTP) have played a unique role in holding those who commit these international crimes accountable since the Rome Statute came into effect on July 1, 2002.

Prior to, and concurrently with, the creation and work of the ICC, many states have made their laws extraterritorially applicable and granted universal jurisdiction to their courts over crimes against humanity, genocide, torture, and war crimes. Under universal jurisdiction, any state may prosecute certain crimes, even if the state in question lacked any territorial, national, or national-interest link with the alleged crime when the crime was

1 I would like to thank Francesca Allegra, Natalie Bryce, Annie Dulka, Macy Lerner, and Agustín Mogni for their assistance in updating my universal jurisdiction database in the last few years, and to The Promise Institute for Human Rights at UCLA School of Law for its support to make such updates, and to William Ayass for editing this essay.

 | DOI:10.1163/9789004686755_050

committed. The jurisdictional claim is rather based on the nature of the crime. Based on this principle, various states have launched prosecutions and held criminal trials before their national courts for the commission of international crimes within the territories of, involving, and against nationals of other states.

This essay argues that the ICC's Office of the Prosecutor should do more to support and engage with national authorities exercising universal jurisdiction for four reasons:

> First, both the ICC and universal jurisdiction prosecutions share the goal of holding accountable those who commit international crimes.
>
> Second, it is in the very nature of the ICC to collaborate with and support prosecutions and trials before national courts.
>
> Third, universal jurisdiction prosecutions before national courts have proven to possess the capacity to handle a greater number of cases than the ICC.
>
> Fourth, universal jurisdiction cases before national courts have supplemented the work of the ICC by concentrating on international crimes that fall outside the default jurisdiction of the Court.

Universal jurisdiction prosecutions also have the potential to supplement the ICC's work by addressing cases within the ICC's jurisdiction. However, universal jurisdiction prosecutions have not realized this potential. Thus, the OTP could do more to encourage and support universal jurisdiction prosecutions that fulfill this supplementary function.

1 The ICC as a System of Courts

From its very inception, the drafters of the ICC Statute conceived the ICC as a system of courts rather than one singular court. The Preamble of the ICC Statute affirms:

> [T]hat the most serious crimes of concern to the international community as a whole must not go unpunished and that their effective prosecution must be ensured by taking measures at the national level and by enhancing international cooperation.

The Preamble also recalls "that it is the duty of every state to exercise its criminal jurisdiction over those responsible for international crimes."

The complementarity principle, established in Article 17 of the ICC Statute, makes clear that a state with jurisdiction over a case should take priority over the ICC in investigating, prosecuting, and trying the case, unless the state in question is unwilling or unable to do so. The complementarity principle thus connects the OTP and the Court to the offices of the prosecutor and the courts of all its state parties, and even non-state parties, thereby making the ICC regime a system of courts. Part 9 of the Statute is also dedicated to international cooperation and judicial assistance between the ICC and national authorities and courts, setting the expectation that the ICC would collaborate with other offices of the prosecution and courts.

In this regard, the ICC regime has always been a system of "decentralized accountability." Within this system, national courts bear the primary responsibility for the prosecution and trial of international crimes, while the ICC plays a complementary role.

From the early years of the Court, the principle of complementarity was interpreted as establishing not only negative but also positive duties for the OTP and the Court. Article 17 sets negative duties by establishing that the Court should not admit a case that is being or was investigated, prosecuted, or tried by a state with jurisdiction over it. However, using the term "positive complementarity" or related notions, the first ICC Prosecutor,[2] state parties,[3] and commentators interpreted that the Court should also actively encourage and cooperate with national authorities to hold accountable those who committed international crimes.[4]

2 Luis Moreno Ocampo, *War and Justice in the 21st Century: A Case Study on the International Criminal Court and its Interaction with the War on Terror* (Oxford: Oxford University Press, 2022), pp. 86–7.

3 *See, e.g.*, International Criminal Court, Review Conference of the Rome Statute, *Stocktaking of International Criminal Justice Taking Stock of the Principle of Complementarity: Bridging the Impunity Gap*, RC/11, annex V(c).

4 *See, e.g.*, Mohamed M. El Zeidy, *The Principle of Complementarity in International Criminal Law: Origin, Development and Practice* (Boston: Martinus Nijhoff Publishers, 2008); Louis Arbour, 'Will the ICC Have an Impact on Universal Jurisdiction?' (2003) 1 *J. Int'l Crim. Just.* 585; William Burke-White, 'Proactive Complementarity: The International Criminal Court & National Courts in the Rome System of International Justice' (2008) 49 *Harv. Int'l L.J.* 53; Fausto Pocar and Magali Maystre, 'The Principle of Complementarity: A Means towards a More Pragmatic Enforcement of the Goal Pursued by Universal Jurisdiction', in Morten Bergsmo (ed.), *Complementarity and Universal Jurisdiction for Core International Crimes* (Oslo: Torkel Opsahl Academic EPublisher, 2010), p. 247; Carsten Stahn, 'Complementarity: A Tale of Two Notions' (2008) 19 *Crim. L. Rev.* 87.

The OTP implemented this positive complementarity principle in various ways. For instance, the announcement of preliminary examinations – a step prior to the launching of an investigation of a situation under the ICC Statute – and periodic reports about them were ways for the OTP to encourage national authorities to prosecute international crimes that had allegedly occurred within their territories or were committed by their nationals, under the "stick" that, otherwise, the OTP would prosecute these crimes.[5]

But this work has been mostly concentrated on encouraging prosecutions by the territorial or the active nationality state – i.e., by the state in whose territory international crimes were allegedly committed or by the state of nationality of the alleged participant in international crimes.

2 Universal Jurisdiction before National Courts and the ICC

The ICC's focus on encouraging prosecutions by the territorial or active nationality state is natural and sound. Everything else being equal, the territorial and active nationality state is the best venue to try international crimes for sovereignty, transitional justice, and logistical reasons. Despite all the changes of the last eight decades, we still live in an international order organized around sovereign states that, as such, have the primary responsibility of holding accountable those who commit serious crimes within their borders – and by extension, their nationals when they allegedly commit these crimes. It is also usually assumed that transitions from authoritarianism to democracy, and from armed conflict to peace, are more likely to reach domestic audiences and to be more successful if they are domestically driven. Logistically, evidence of the commission of international crimes is typically available in the place where the crimes occurred or where the perpetrators are located, and it is thus less costly to try alleged crimes where they took place.

However, states often do not hold those who commit international crimes within their borders or who are their nationals criminally accountable. State officials are typically involved in the commission of these crimes, and domestic criminal justice authorities may be in connivance with those officials or may not have sufficient power to hold them accountable. Those

5 Office of the Prosecutor, International Criminal Court, *Policy Paper on Preliminary Examinations* ¶ 100–3 (2013), https://www.icc-cpi.int/sites/default/files/iccdocs/otp/OTP-Policy_Paper_Preliminary_Examinations_2013-ENG.pdf (last visited August 29, 2023); Moreno Ocampo, *supra* note 2, at 312-313, 329, 540.

who commit international crimes also often migrate to other states for various reasons: because there is a regime change in the territorial state, they defect from the existing regime; they were not state officials in the first place; they were militarily defeated; or they leave looking for better life opportunities for themselves and their families. In addition, the territorial and active nationality state may not be able to hold these migrants accountable because the state does not know their whereabouts, does not have sufficient capacity or willingness to go after them, or the receiving states of the migrants may be unwilling to extradite or deport them to the territorial or active nationality state.

In situations where the territorial or active nationality state is unwilling or unable to hold those who commit international crimes accountable, universal jurisdiction prosecutions and trials before national courts and the ICC may then have a role to play. In this regard, it is important to note that universal jurisdiction cases before national authorities have held many more people criminally accountable than the ICC since the Court's Statute came into effect. According to my universal jurisdiction database, there have been eighty-seven universal jurisdiction trials for crimes against humanity, genocide, torture, or war crimes since the first case in the database against Adolf Eichmann in 1961 in Israel.[6] Seventy out of these eighty-seven universal

6 As I have explained in previous work, I use data that was originally published in Máximo Langer, 'The Diplomacy of Universal Jurisdiction: The Political Branches and the Transnational Prosecution of International Crimes' (2011) 105 *Am. J. Int'l L.* 1 [hereinafter The Diplomacy]; and subsequently updated and expanded in Máximo Langer and Mackenzie Eason, 'The Quiet Expansion of Universal Jurisdiction' (2019) 30 *Eur. J. Int'l L.* 779 [hereinafter The Quiet Expansion]; Leslie Johns, Máximo Langer and Margaret E. Peters, 'Migration and the Demand for Transnational Justice' (2022) 116–4 *Am. Pol. Sci. Rev.* 1184 [hereinafter Migration]; and further expanded to write this Comment. These universal jurisdiction data contain information on every known criminal complaint (or case considered by public authorities on their own motion) that involved the alleged commission of one or more of the four core international crimes – crimes against humanity, genocide, torture, and war crimes – by physical individuals; was filed or initiated between 1957 and 2020; and fully or partially relied on universal jurisdiction. That data thus does not include information on civil lawsuits. They also do not include criminal cases against corporations or other nonphysical entities. To create the original database, two research assistants independently found and coded cases using judicial decisions; LEXIS-NEXIS and Westlaw; law journals; books on universal jurisdiction and international criminal law; websites of the Center for Constitutional Rights, the Hague Justice Portal, Human Rights Watch, the International Center for Transitional Justice, the International Federation of Human Rights and TRAIL International; reports by Amnesty International, Human Rights Watch, and Redress; newspaper articles and other media documents; and the Google search engine. The last comprehensive update of the database was done in 2021. But since

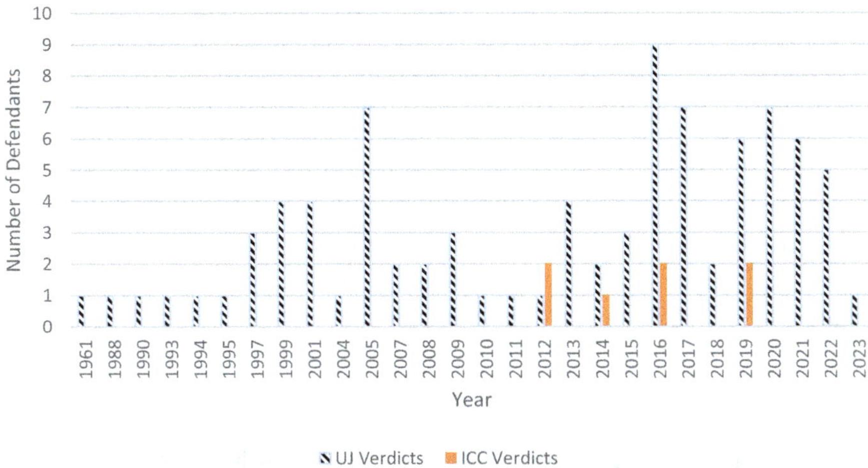

FIGURE 41.1 Universal jurisdiction and ICC verdicts for core international crimes
SOURCES: UNIVERSAL JURISDICTION DATABASE AND ICC WEBSITE

jurisdiction trials have taken place since the ICC Statute came into effect on July 1, 2002. In contrast, in the same period, the ICC has issued verdicts after trial against only six defendants.[7]

To be sure, universal jurisdiction and ICC trials are not always fully comparable because while the universal jurisdiction trials have often been held against low-level and middle-level defendants, ICC trials have typically been held against high-level defendants.[8] Trials against high-level defendants tend to be more complex than against low and middle-level defendants because the former are not always involved in the direct perpetration of international crimes and tend to be responsible for a larger number of crimes. However, the much larger quantity of universal jurisdiction verdicts than ICC verdicts highlights the important role that universal jurisdiction trials before domestic courts have played since the ICC Statute came into effect in

then, with the assistance of the people mentioned in the acknowledgements of this Comment, I have also done partial updates on individual variables, such as trials.

7 These include a conviction entered after a defendant admitted his guilt at the trial opening. I am not including here the ICC convictions for crimes against the administration of justice issued against five defendants because these are not core international crimes. I am not including here either two ICC trials against three defendants that did not end in a verdict because the trial chamber terminated the trial after the presentation of the case of the prosecution or after the defendant died.

8 *See* The Diplomacy, *supra* note 6 (Discussing which universal jurisdiction cases are likely to go to trial and why).

advancing the notion that people who commit international crimes should be held criminally accountable. They also show that universal jurisdiction states collectively have more capacity than the ICC to prosecute international crimes.

Given that the ICC – as the only permanent international criminal court within a broader system of courts – has a role to play in encouraging and cooperating with criminal accountability efforts by national authorities, the OTP and the Court ought to explore ways in which they could collaborate more closely with the authorities of universal jurisdiction states to foster and support these prosecutions.

3 Horizontal and Vertical Supplementarity with the ICC

To discuss ways in which the OTP and the Court could foster and support universal jurisdiction prosecutions, we can distinguish between two different ways in which universal jurisdiction prosecutions can supplement the ICC's work. In previous works, I have referred to these as horizontal supplementarity and vertical supplementarity.[9]

Universal jurisdiction prosecutions play a horizontal supplementarity role regarding the ICC when they prosecute defendants from situations that are not within the jurisdiction of the Court. Unless the UNSC refers a situation to the ICC, the Court only has jurisdiction over people who allegedly committed crimes against humanity, genocide, or war crimes on the territory of or who are nationals of an ICC state party or of a state that has otherwise accepted ICC jurisdiction.[10] When a situation is not within the ICC's jurisdiction, universal jurisdiction prosecutions before national courts may be used to supplement the ICC's work by holding criminally accountable those whom the Court does not have the authority to hold accountable.

Universal jurisdiction prosecutions play a vertical supplementarity role regarding the ICC when they prosecute defendants from situations under

9 See Máximo Langer, 'The Archipelago and the Wheel: The Universal Jurisdiction and the International Criminal Court Regimes', in Martha Minow, C. Cora True-Frost, and Alex Whiting (eds.), *The First Global Prosecutor: Promise and Constraints* (Ann Arbor: University of Michigan Press, 2015) 204, 223–224.

10 International Criminal Court, Rome Statute of the International Criminal Court, arts. 12, 13, U.N. Doc. A/CONF.183/9, (July 17, 1998); *see id.* at art. 15 *bis* (The ICC also has subject matter jurisdiction over the crime of aggression that has a different set of jurisdictional rules. But since most states have not claimed universal jurisdiction over the crime of aggression, this crime is beyond our analysis.).

preliminary examination or investigation by the ICC. As shown in FIGURE 41.1, the ICC has had the capacity to try only one to a handful of defendants in any given situation. Universal jurisdiction prosecutions can supplement the work of the ICC by prosecuting defendants from situations under preliminary examination or investigation by the Court that the OTP is not prosecuting. Thus, universal jurisdiction prosecutions may also be used to supplement the ICC's work by holding criminally accountable those whom the Court has the authority to try, but that the OTP does not prosecute due to logistical or public policy reasons.

Even if universal jurisdiction prosecutions have the potential to play both a horizontal and vertical supplementarity role vis-à-vis the ICC, these prosecutions have not fulfilled both roles to the same extent. Table 41.1 below shows that while universal jurisdiction cases and trials have served a horizontal supplementarity role in a substantial number of cases, they have played a vertical supplementarity role only in a few instances.

To further discuss this issue, Table 41.1 classifies universal jurisdiction complaints and universal jurisdiction trials into seven groups.[11] The first four groups involve international crimes committed before the ICC Statute came into effect.

The first group refers to international crimes committed before the 1990s – either before or during World War II by Nazis or during the Khmer Rouge in the 1970s. Some of the individuals who were alleged to have committed international crimes in these situations were prosecuted in the Nuremberg Trials and other post-World War II trials, as well as the Extraordinary Chambers in the Courts of Cambodia. In addition to these prosecutions, there were 374 universal jurisdiction complaints against these defendants – almost all of them against alleged Nazis – and 5 universal jurisdiction trials – all of them against alleged Nazis.

The second group involves former Yugoslavs for crimes that happened after 1991. The Office of the Prosecutor of the International Criminal Tribunal for the former Yugoslavia (ICTY) prosecuted 161 individuals in relation to this situation. In addition to these prosecutions before the ICTY, there

11 Under my universal jurisdiction database, "complaint" includes two types of situations: a) public authorities of the prosecuting state consider whether a certain person should be investigated for the commission of a criminal offense; or b) a private individual, NGO, another state, or other legal entities file a report before the authorities of the prosecuting state alleging that a person has committed a criminal offense. A "trial" refers to the adjudication stage at which a court or other adjudicating body decides whether the defendant is guilty or not guilty.

were also 257 universal jurisdiction complaints and eleven trials against this type of defendants before national authorities.

The third group involves Rwandans for international crimes that took place in Rwanda or committed by Rwandans in neighboring states in 1994. The Office of the Prosecutor of the International Criminal Tribunal for Rwanda (ICTR) prosecuted eighty-six of these defendants. In addition to these prosecutions before the ICTR, there have also been 142 universal jurisdiction complaints and twenty-five trials against them.

The fourth group refers to international crimes committed in Sierra Leone since November 30, 1996. The Special Court for Sierra Leone tried a few of these defendants. In addition to these trials before the Special Court, there have also been a handful of universal jurisdiction complaints and one universal jurisdiction trial regarding this situation.

The fifth group refers to international crimes committed in Syria since 2011. Unlike the previous four groups, these crimes were allegedly committed after the ICC Statute came into effect. However, since neither the UNSC has referred this situation to the ICC, nor has Syria ratified the ICC Statute or otherwise accepted the jurisdiction of the Court, these crimes have been beyond the ICC's reach. The United Nations General Assembly established the International, Impartial and Independent Mechanism to Assist in the Investigation and Prosecution of the Most Serious Crimes under International Law committed in the Syrian Arab Republic since March 2011. In addition to this effort, there have been a substantial number of universal jurisdiction complaints and trials that have played a horizontal supplementarity role with the ICC by holding individuals criminally accountable who were not under the jurisdiction of the Court.

The sixth group in Table 41.1 refers to alleged international crimes committed in situations under preliminary examination or investigation by the OTP. Table 41.1 shows that these universal jurisdiction complaints and trials have constituted only a small percentage of the total universal jurisdiction complaints and trials. This suggests that universal jurisdiction prosecutions have played a limited vertical supplementarity role with the ICC.

The final group involves universal jurisdiction cases from situations for which no international criminal tribunal or investigative mechanism was created, and that the OTP has not preliminarily examined or investigated. This group includes international crimes that took place before the ICC Statute came into effect – such as crimes committed in Latin America in the 1970s and the 1980s, as well as crimes that took place after the ICC Statute came into effect, such as crimes committed by members of the Islamic State in Iraq and other states – that have involved over 150 cases and eleven trials.

TABLE 41.1 Universal jurisdiction trials by type of situation

Type of situation	Percentage/total number of universal jurisdiction complaints out of all situations	Percentage/total number of universal jurisdiction trials out of all situations
Nazis/Khmer Rouge	16.94% (374 out of 2208)	5.75% (5 out of 87)
Former Yugoslavia	11.64% (257 out of 2208)	12.64% (11 out of 87)
Rwandans for 1994 Crimes	6.43% (142 out of 2208)	28.74% (25 out of 87)
Liberia/Sierra Leone	0.14% (3 out of 2208)	1.15% (1 out of 87)
Syria	23.96% (529 out of 2208)	22.99% (20 out of 87)
Situations under ICC preliminary examination or ICC investigation	1.40% (31 out of 2208)	3.44% (3 out of 87)
Other situations not involving international community's accountability effort	39.49% (872 out of 2208)	25.29% (22 out of 87)
Total	100% (2208 out of 2208 complaints)	100% (87 out of 87 trials)

SOURCE: UNIVERSAL JURISDICTION DATABASE

In these cases, universal jurisdiction prosecutions and trials have also played a horizontal supplementarity role with the ICC.

3.1 *What Could the OTP Do to Foster and Support Universal Jurisdiction Prosecutions before National Authorities?*

The previous section has shown that, while universal jurisdiction prosecutions have played a substantial horizontal supplementary role, they have played only a small vertical supplementarity role with ICC's work.

What could the OTP do to foster and support more of each type of universal jurisdiction prosecutions?

Regarding horizontal supplementary prosecutions, these are situations the OTP is neither examining nor investigating. Consequently, the OTP has neither elements of proof about, nor a direct institutional interest in these situations. However, these prosecutions still advance the goal of bringing criminal accountability for international crimes that the ICC has subject-matter jurisdiction over, and the OTP could take measures to foster these prosecutions. For instance, when conducting outreach to explain the OTP's work to audiences around the world, OTP staff could emphasize the personal jurisdiction gaps in the ICC regime and how universal jurisdiction cases can address some of these gaps.[12] Additionally, when the OTP responds to communications (i.e., the ICC equivalent of a crime report or complaint) by explaining that the ICC does not have jurisdiction over the alleged crime participants, the OTP could also remind those who filed the communication that there are other accountability mechanisms, such as universal jurisdiction prosecutions before national authorities that may have jurisdiction over these allegations.

As for vertical supplementarity prosecutions, these are situations the OTP has been examining and investigating. Consequently, the OTP has elements of proof about and a direct institutional interest in these situations. Considering that prosecuting only one or a handful of crime participants in a situation may not be sufficient to advance the goals of criminal punishment, among other ICC's goals, fostering and supporting universal jurisdiction prosecutions in these situations could be an important way for the OTP to advance these goals.

To identify ways to foster and support these vertical supplementarity prosecutions, it is helpful to first consider the experience of the ICTY and the ICTR, whose work was also vertically supplemented by universal jurisdiction complaints and trials. Table 41.1 above shows that there have been many more universal jurisdiction complaints and trials regarding the situations in the former Yugoslavia and Rwanda than there have been regarding all the situations under the OTP's preliminary examination and investigation combined.

There are multiple possible reasons why there have been more universal jurisdiction prosecutions against former Yugoslavs and Rwandans than against individuals who allegedly committed core international crimes in situations under OTP's preliminary examination or investigation. Given the

12 For a critical assessment of ICC outreach strategy, *see* Group of Independent Experts, International Criminal Court, *Review of the International Criminal Court and the Rome Statute System: Final Report*, ¶ 391, Res. 163–68 (Sep. 30, 2020), https://asp.icc-cpi.int/sites/asp/files/asp_docs/ASP19/IER-Final-Report-ENG.pdf (last visited August 31, 2023).

limited scope of this essay, I will only focus on two of them.[13] First, the situation in the former Yugoslavia generated significant public attention in Europe – where most universal jurisdiction states are – since it involved at the time the largest commission of international crimes in that continent since World War II. The situation in Rwanda also garnered considerable public attention in some European states, such as Belgium and France, because Belgian peacekeeping troops were killed during the genocide, and France had provided military and other forms of support to the Hutu regime in Rwanda.[14] Second, these two situations led to a large wave of migrants from the former Yugoslavia and Rwanda to European states, including crime participants, victims, witnesses, and a larger migrant community that contributed to the filing of complaints and the progression of these complaints toward trial.[15]

Except for the situation in Ukraine, none of the situations before the ICC have presented these two factors to the same extent. To be sure, the situation in Darfur generated a lot of international concern, but it neither involved Europeans nor led to large migration to European states. Additionally, crime participants did not have to migrate as they remained in power for a significant duration in that situation. The ongoing situation in Ukraine following the Russian invasion has garnered substantial public attention and concern in Europe due to serious allegations about the extensive commission of international crimes in this conflict. Moreover, it has led to a significant migration of Ukrainians to other European states. These two factors help explain why there have been multiple universal jurisdiction investigations opened in several states since 2022[16] – a development that Table 41.1 does not reflect, given that, as explained *supra* in note 6, the last

13 For deeper exploration on which factors drive universal jurisdiction cases, *see* The Diplomacy, *supra* note 6; Langer, *supra* note 9, at 223–28; The Quiet Expansion, *supra* note 6, at 790–99; Migration, *supra* note 6.

14 *See* Langer, *supra* note 9, at 225–26.

15 On migration as a factor that increases the likelihood of universal jurisdiction cases, *see* Langer, *supra* note 9, at 226–27; Frédéric Mégret, 'The 'Elephant in the Room' in Debates about Universal Jurisdiction' (2015) 6 *Transnat'l Legal Theory* 89; The Quiet Expansion, *supra* note 6, at 796–99; Migration, *supra* note 6.

16 For instance, in 2022, Germany initiated a structural investigation on war crimes committed in Ukraine in the context of the Russian invasion, and Sweden launched a universal jurisdiction preliminary investigation. *See* Statement, Federal Republic of Germany, The Scope and Application of the Principle of Universal Jurisdiction (Oct. 12, 2022), https://www.un.org/en/ga/sixth/77/pdfs/statements/universal_jurisdiction/12mtg_germany.pdf (last visited October 16, 2023); Ministry of Foreign Affairs, *How Sweden is Working to Hold Russia Accountable for Crimes in Ukraine*, GOV'T OFFICES OF

comprehensive update of my universal jurisdiction database was conducted in 2021, prior to the Russian invasion.[17]

But what could the OTP do to foster and support vertical supplementarity universal jurisdiction prosecutions in situations under OTP's examination and investigation that do not present these two factors? The OTP and the ICC cannot generate the type of public interest that the situations in the former Yugoslavia, Rwanda, and now Ukraine have generated by themselves, nor can they induce migration waves. However, there are still measures they could take to foster and support these types of prosecutions. Given the scope of this essay, I will mention only a few of them.

First, in recent years, the exercise of universal jurisdiction has been expanding geographically to states in the Global South.[18] When launching a preliminary examination or an investigation, the OTP could engage with public officials, NGOs, emigrée communities, and other actors from states outside of Europe – especially states from the same region as the state whose situation is under OTP's examination or investigation – as a means to foster potential universal jurisdiction cases in those states.

Second, one of the reasons that migration increases the likelihood of universal jurisdiction cases is that migrant communities may report crimes to police and prosecutors, mobilize public opinion in the receiving state, meet with public officials, and become parties in the criminal cases – a power available to complainants in many states around the world.[19] When launching preliminary examinations and investigations, the OTP could reach out to these emigrée communities and support their efforts to pursue universal jurisdiction cases.

Third, another way in which migration increases the likelihood of universal jurisdiction complaints is that migrants may also include perpetrators. The presence of perpetrators in the universal jurisdiction state increases the likelihood of a universal jurisdiction case because it may make the case salient, and it makes the case logistically easier and legally possible, since many states do not allow for trials in absentia.[20] In fact, several universal jurisdiction states have established protocols to identify potential

SWEDEN, https://www.government.se/articles/2023/03/how-sweden-is-working-to-hold-russia-accountable-for-crimes-in-ukraine/ (last visited August 29, 2023).

17 Since alleged Russian perpetrators have not migrated to European states, it remains to be seen how many of these complaints and investigations for alleged crimes committed in Ukraine are going to move towards trial.

18 *See* The Quiet Expansion, *supra* note 6, at 799–808.

19 Langer, *supra* note 9, at 226–27; Migration, *supra* note 6, at 1188-93.

20 Langer, *supra* note 9, at 226–27.

participants in international crimes among incoming migrants and asylum seekers.[21] Moreover, several states have formed specialized units comprising prosecutors, police officers, and/or judges to handle universal jurisdiction cases. National immigration authorities may refer potential cases they identify to these units. Consequently, when the OTP launches a preliminary examination or an investigation of a situation, the OTP could communicate with national authorities and encourage them to ascertain whether within their territory there are potential participants in international crimes related to the situation under OTP's preliminary examination or investigation.

Fourth, costs are another factor that affects the likelihood of universal jurisdiction complaints being filed and of universal jurisdiction trials being held.[22] Universal jurisdiction investigations, prosecutions, and trials can be costly, partly because it can be challenging to gather elements of proof for alleged crimes that occurred in the territory of another state and that may only be available in a foreign language. When the OTP launches the preliminary examination or investigation of a situation, it could offer universal jurisdiction states' national authorities information and elements of proof it has collected concerning the situation in general and regarding defendants it does not intend to prosecute.

4 Conclusion

This essay has argued that the OTP should foster and support universal jurisdiction prosecutions by national authorities to further the goals of the ICC. Universal jurisdiction cases and trials have been on the rise in recent years, yet they have primarily concentrated on situations that the OTP has not been investigating. This essay has explored the reasons behind this trend and has proposed ways in which the OTP could promote and support this kind of universal jurisdiction cases and trials.

---

21 *See* The Quiet Expansion, *supra* note 6, at 791–92, 796–99.

22 *Id.* at 792–796; Migration, *supra* note 6, at 1201.

CHAPTER 42

Partners in Accountability: The ICC and the Proposed Special Tribunal for Ukraine

Carrie McDougall

A special tribunal to prosecute crimes of aggression against Ukraine needs to be established in light of the lack of International Criminal Court (ICC) jurisdiction over these particular crimes of aggression, and the existence of significant impediments to any successful prosecution of these crimes domestically. Should the international community be able to agree on the proposed tribunal's establishment, the tribunal should be viewed as a natural partner in the ICC's fight against impunity, not a competitor. For this reason, the institutions should extend each other the greatest possible cooperation, limited only by conditions found in their respective legal frameworks, such as the need to take measures to ensure the protection of witnesses. Such mutual cooperation would be consistent with the Rome Statute, and should be governed by a cooperation agreement, complemented by any necessary arrangements covering matters that need to be kept confidential. The range of matters in respect of which cooperation would be beneficial is wide, but includes the sharing of information and evidence, and an agreement on the sequencing of the trials of persons indicted by both institutions.

The criminal justice response to the serious international crimes being perpetrated in Ukraine is extraordinary. It includes the referral of the situation in Ukraine to the International Criminal Court (ICC) by 43 states, eight years after Ukraine's initial ad hoc acceptance of the ICC's jurisdiction, but just days after the 24 February 2022 Russian invasion;[1] the provision of extensive international support for Ukraine's investigation and prosecution of serious international crimes;[2] and the opening of large-scale criminal

1 Statement, Karim A.A. Khan, ICC Prosecutor, On the Situation in Ukraine: Receipt of Referrals from 39 States Parties and the Opening of an Investigation (Mar. 2, 2022), https://www.icc-cpi.int/news/statement-icc-prosecutor-karim-aa-khan-qc-situation-ukraine-receipt-referrals-39-states (last visited September 29, 2023).

2 *See, e.g.*, Press Release, U.S. Dept. of State, Supporting Justice and Accountability in Ukraine: Fact Sheet (Feb. 18, 2023), https://www.state.gov/supporting-justice-and-accountability-in-ukraine/ (last visited October 1, 2023).

 | DOI:10.1163/9789004686755_051

investigations by a plethora of other states.[3] It is self-evident that this unprecedented accountability response will require extensive coordination and cooperation: a fact reflected in the establishment of multiple coordination mechanisms, including the Joint Investigation Team into alleged core international crimes committed in Ukraine (in which the ICC Office of the Prosecutor (OTP) is a participant),[4] the International Centre for the Prosecution of the Crime of Aggression against Ukraine (ICPA),[5] and the Atrocity Crimes Advisory Group.[6] Such coordination and cooperation must be extended to include the proposed special tribunal for the prosecution of crimes of aggression committed against Ukraine, should the political will for the establishment of such a tribunal be able to be generated.

1 The Rationale for the Establishment of a Special Tribunal

As I have outlined in detail elsewhere, there is little room to doubt that crimes of aggression have been committed against Ukraine by Russian (and potentially Belorussian) nationals.[7] While the ICC enjoys jurisdiction over any war crime, crime against humanity or crime of genocide committed on the territory of Ukraine, it lacks jurisdiction over these crimes of aggression. The provisions governing the ICC's aggression jurisdiction are complex, and their proper interpretation in various imagined scenarios is contested.[8] There is, however, no dispute over the fact that, in the absence of a Security

3 Investigations have been opened in more than 20 countries, including Lithuania, Poland, Estonia, Latvia, Slovakia and Romania.

4 *See Joint Investigation Team into Alleged Crimes Committed in Ukraine*, EUROJUST, https://www.eurojust.europa.eu/joint-investigation-team-alleged-crimes-committed-ukraine.

5 *See International Centre for the Prosecution of the Crime of Aggression against Ukraine*, EUROJUST, https://www.eurojust.europa.eu/international-centre-for-the-prosecution-of-the-crime-of-aggression-against-ukraine.

6 *See The European Union, the United States, and the United Kingdom Establish the Atrocity Crimes Advisory Group (ACA) for Ukraine*, U.S. DEPT. OF STATE (May 25, 2022), https://www.state.gov/creation-of-atrocity-crimes-advisory-group-for-ukraine/.

7 Carrie McDougall, 'The Imperative of Prosecuting Crimes of Aggression Committed against Ukraine' (2023) 28 *J. Conflict & Sec. L.* 203–30.

8 *See* Carrie McDougall, *The Crime of Aggression under the Rome Statute of the International Criminal Court*, 2d ed., (Cambridge: Cambridge University Press, 2021), pp. 258–352; Stefan Barriga and Niels Blokker, 'Conditions for the Exercise of Jurisdiction Based on State Referrals and Proprio Motu Investigations', in Claus Kreß and Stefan Barriga (eds.), *The Crime of Aggression: A Commentary* (Cambridge: Cambridge University Press, 2017), pp. 652–74.

Council referral, the ICC is unable to exercise jurisdiction over a crime of aggression involving a non-state party (such as Russia, or indeed Ukraine) as either aggressor or victim, as a result of the express exclusion from jurisdiction of non-state parties' nationals and their territory.[9] This was, in effect, the price paid to a small group of states led by the Permanent Five members of the Security Council for the adoption of the aggression amendments at the Rome Statute Review Conference in Kampala in 2010.

In the resolution under which those amendments were adopted, the States Parties decided to review the amendments seven years after the beginning of the ICC's jurisdiction over aggression, which will fall in 2025. In the wake of Russia's invasion of Ukraine, momentum is slowly building behind proposals to bring the jurisdictional provisions in line (or more in line) with the regime governing other crimes set out in Articles 12 and 13 of the Rome Statute.[10] This is clearly the most desirable end state, which would both help to reduce selectivity and underline the ICC's role as the permanent center-piece of the international criminal justice system. It must be acknowledged, however, that the crime of aggression has a controversial history because of its proximity to states' core national security interests, such that securing support for the proposed revision of the amendments is likely to be challenging. Add to this the fact that any amendments would have to be ratified by seven-eighths of states parties to enter into force,[11] and arguably could not have retrospective effect, and it becomes fairly obvious that this initiative is extremely unlikely to provide a path to the investigation and prosecution of crimes of aggression that have been committed against Ukraine.[12]

While a number of states have opened relevant criminal investigations, any domestic prosecution is likely to be beset by a range of challenges, including a possible lack of jurisdiction outside of the aggressor and victim

---

9 International Criminal Court, Rome Statute of the International Criminal Court, art. 15 *bis* (5), U.N. Doc. A/CONF.183/9, (July 17, 1998) [hereinafter Rome Statute].

10 *See, e.g.*, Ministerial Side-Event by Liechtenstein and Germany on the Occasion of the 25th Anniversary of the Rome Statute - The ICC and the Crime of Aggression: In Defense of the UN Charter, UNITED NATIONS (Jul. 17, 2018), https://media.un.org/en/asset/k1m/k1mdo8poz5.

11 Rome Statute, *supra* note 9, at art. 121(4).

12 *See* McDougall, *supra* note 7; Astrid Reisinger-Coracini, *Is Amending the Rome Statute the Panacea Against Perceived Selectivity and Impunity for the Crime of Aggression Committed Against Ukraine?*, JUST SEC. (Mar. 21, 2023), https://www.justsecurity.org/85593/is-amending-the-rome-statute-the-panacea-against-perceived-selectivity-and-impunity-for-the-crime-of-aggression-committed-against-ukraine/.

states; the applicability of immunities; an inability to secure the presence of the accused; the inevitable taint of victor's justice (or victim's revenge); and a lack of domestic expertise in the jus ad bellum.[13] In light of the ICC's lack of jurisdiction, and the unlikelihood of a successful domestic prosecution of those most responsible, Ukraine has called for the establishment of an special tribunal with jurisdiction over crimes of aggression committed against it,[14] and it has been widely recognized that this represents the only viable path to the prosecution of the crimes.[15]

At the time of writing, there is an ongoing debate among proponents as to the type of ad hoc tribunal that should be established. Ukraine has called for the establishment of an international tribunal;[16] states supportive of this model have, at least for now, coalesced around the proposal that such a tribunal be established by an agreement concluded between the United

13 For detailed explanations, *see* McDougall, *supra* note 7.

14 *See, e.g.*, Dmytro Kuleba, *A Criminal Tribunal for Aggression in Ukraine*, CHATHAM HOUSE, at 15:51 (Mar. 4, 2022), https://www.chathamhouse.org/events/all/research-event/criminal-tribunal-aggression-ukraine; Volodymyr Zelensky, *Speech by the President of Ukraine at the General Debate of the 77th Session of the UN General Assembly*, President of Ukraine (Sep. 22, 2022), https://www.president.gov.ua/en/news/vistup-prezidenta-ukrayini-na-zagalnih-debatah-77-yi-sesiyi-77905; Volodymyr Zelensky, *Speech to Representatives of the Public, Political and Expert Circles of the Kingdom of the Netherlands and International Institutions Based in The Hague*, President of Ukraine (May 4, 2023), https://www.president.gov.ua/en/news/vistup-volodimira-zelenskogo-pered-predstavnikami-gromadskos-82653.

15 *See, e.g.*, Philippe Sands, *Putin's Use of Military Force is a Crime of Aggression*, Financial Times (Feb. 28, 2022), https://www.ft.com/content/cbbdd146-4e36-42fb-95e1-50128506652c (last visited September 25, 2023); Jennifer Trahan, *UN General Assembly Should Recommend Creation of Crime of Aggression Tribunal for Ukraine: Nuremberg is not the Model*, JUST SEC. (Mar. 7, 2022), https://www.justsecurity.org/80545/u-n-general-assembly-should-recommend-creation-of-crime-of-aggression-tribunal-for-ukraine-nuremberg-is-not-the-model/ (last visited September 25, 2023); Oona Hathaway, *A Crime in Search of a Court: How to Hold Russia Accountable*, Foreign Affs. (May 19, 2022), https://www.foreignaffairs.com/articles/ukraine/2022-05-19/crime-search-court (last visited September 25, 2023); Tom Dannenbaum, 'A Special Tribunal for the Crime of Aggression?' (2022) 20 *J. Int'l Crim. Just.* 859–73; Anton Korynevych and Tymur Korotkyi, 'The Special Tribunal for the Crime of Aggression Against Ukraine: Realpolitik Versus the Inevitability of Punishment for the Crime of Aggression' (2022) 2 *Ukrainian J. Int'l L.* 33–42; Claus Kreß, Stephan Hobe & Angelika Nußberger, *The Ukraine War and the Crime of Aggression: How to Fill the Gaps in the International Legal System*, JUST SEC. (Jan. 23, 2023), https://www.justsecurity.org/84783/the-ukraine-war-and-the-crime-of-aggression-how-to-fill-the-gaps-in-the-international-legal-system/ (last visited September 26, 2023).

16 *See, e.g.*, Zelensky, *Speech to Representatives*, *supra* note 14.

Nations (U.N.) and Ukraine, negotiated by the U.N. Secretary-General at the request of the General Assembly (G.A.), and approved by the G.A. G7 states, on the other hand, have indicated that they are only prepared to support an "internationalized" tribunal (traditionally known as a hybrid), which would be embedded within Ukraine's national legal system, but have some international elements.[17] The resolution of this debate is immaterial to the need for cooperation, although it may have some impact on the shape of the instrument(s) that would govern such cooperation and their content, as outlined below.

2 The Proposed Tribunal and the ICC Would Be Natural Partners in the Fight against Impunity

ICC Prosecutor Karim Khan has made several comments that clearly signal his reservations in relation to the proposed establishment of a special tribunal. At the December 2022 meeting of the Assembly of States Parties, Khan stated that:

> Whilst we have seen a renewed focus on the crime of aggression in the light of the Ukraine Situation, it is my view that this is a very important moment to focus on the institutions we actually have, the institutions that you, civil society, and the Court have built together. When we recognize that there is a gap in that architecture, in my view, we should try to address it through the Rome Statute that was carefully negotiated and carefully built and which we are trying to fund to vindicate the rights of the survivors that I have mentioned. We don't want dilution, we want consolidation, and in this regard I stand ready and I am available at any time to explore how to strengthen this institution that you are collectively part of and that has been collectively built so that we can meet the needs of today but also the requirements of tomorrow.[18]

17 Press Release, *G7 Japan 2023 Foreign Ministers' Communiqué* (April 18, 2023), https://www.state.gov/g7-japan-2023-foreign-ministers-communique/ (last visited October 1, 2023) (The Communique was also issued in the name of the High Representative of the European Union.).

18 Karim A.A. Khan, Remarks at the Opening Plenary of the 21st Session of the Assembly of States Parties, (Dec. 5, 2022), https://asp.icc-cpi.int/sites/asp/files/2022-12/ASP21-STMT-PROS-ENG.pdf.

He has since suggested that the tribunal could be a distraction.[19] Asked directly if he supported the establishment of the proposed tribunal, Khan said:

> ...I think there needs to be a dose of realism. The ICC has been here for 20 years. It's been historically under-resourced. It has clear jurisdiction. And there are some perhaps unforeseen consequences or difficulties by creating other mechanisms. I think we should focus on mobilizing what is already here, what already exists. But we can become rather self-indulgent in creating things that we would like. I'd rather focus on what we have and put it into action effectively.[20]

One can perhaps understand why the Prosecutor is defensive of the ICC, given the institution has attracted unrelenting criticism in recent years. It is wrong to suggest, however, that the establishment of the proposed tribunal would come at the ICC's expense.

It is true that a key rationale for the establishment of a permanent international criminal court was to avoid the need to reinvent the wheel following mass atrocities by creating different ad hoc tribunals with narrow subject matter jurisdictions, which would simultaneously reduce selectivity, be more efficient, and lead to the consolidation of international criminal law's substantive rules. This naturally mitigates against the creation of new ad hoc tribunals. Clearly, however, there are many situations where the ICC currently lacks jurisdiction. In such cases, I share Khan's view that our first line of effort should always be to address that jurisdictional gap through a Security Council referral, the ratification of the Rome Statute, an ad hoc acceptance of the ICC's jurisdiction under Article 12(3), or the Rome Statute's amendment. However, as the Prosecutor will well know from his time leading the United Nations Investigative Team to Promote Accountability for Crimes Committed by Da'esh/ISIL, there are times when realpolitik makes such measures impossible. In these circumstances, the preeminence of the ICC as the only permanent international criminal justice institution is not a

19 Joe Barnes, *Nuremberg-Style Tribunal for Russian War Crimes Are Self-Indulgent*, The Telegraph (Jul. 15, 2022), https://www.telegraph.co.uk/world-news/2022/07/15/nuremberg-style-trials-russian-war-crimes-self-indulgen/ (last visited October 5, 2023).

20 Nick Schifrin, *International Criminal Court Prosecutor on the Pursuit of Justice for Russian War Crimes*, PBS NewsHour (Jun. 22, 2022), https://www.pbs.org/newshour/show/international-criminal-courts-top-prosecutor-discusses-justice-for-russian-war-crimes (last visited October 6, 2023).

compelling enough reason to deny justice by refusing to support the establishment of new accountability mechanisms. This is especially true in the current circumstances where the investigation and prosecution of crimes of aggression being committed against Ukraine is aimed at responding to one of the most egregious violations of the prohibition of the use of force witnessed in the post-Charter era, which could well have profound consequences for the international rules-based order and international peace and security long into the future.[21]

Proponents have deliberately called for the creation of a tribunal with a jurisdiction that is limited to the crime of aggression, and to the territory of Ukraine, precisely in order to avoid any existing jurisdictional conflict with the ICC, and to maximize the prospect of the ICC being positioned to exercise an expanded jurisdiction over crimes of aggression going forward through the amendment of the Rome Statute, so that future ad hoc tribunals are not needed. Thus, rather than setting up a competition with the ICC, this jurisdictional design ensures that the tribunal would complement the ICC's investigation into other Rome Statute crimes being committed on Ukrainian territory.

All evidence points to the provision of Ukrainian cooperation to the ICC,[22] and third states have pledged a hitherto unforeseen degree of support

---

21 For detailed arguments, *see* McDougall, *supra* note 7.

22 *See, e.g.*, Press Release, International Criminal Court, Ukraine and International Criminal Court Sign an Agreement on the Establishment of a Country Office (Mar. 23, 2023), https://www.icc-cpi.int/news/ukraine-and-international-criminal-court-sign-agreement-establishment-country-office (last visited October 5, 2023); Statement, Karim A.A. Khan, Prosecutor, Int'l Crim. Ct., ICC Prosecutor Karim A. A. Khan KC Concludes Fourth Visit to Ukraine: "Amidst this darkness, the Light of Justice is Emerging" (Mar. 7, 2023), https://www.icc-cpi.int/news/icc-prosecutor-karim-khan-kc-concludes-fourth-visit-ukraine-amidst-darkness-light-justice (last visited October 5, 2023). *See also* Про внесення змін до Кримінального процесуального кодексу України та інших законодавчих актів України щодо співробітництва з Міжнародним кримінальним судом, Document 2236-IX (adopted May 3, 2022) (Ukr.) (In May 2022, Ukraine added detailed sections to its Criminal Procedure Code (2013) to facilitate cooperation with the ICC.). *But see* Kai Ambos, *Ukrainian Prosecution of ICC Statute Crimes: Fair, Independent and Impartial?*, EJIL TALK! (June 10, 2022), https://www.ejiltalk.org/ukrainian-prosecution-of-icc-statute-crimes-fair-independent-and-impartial/ (last visited October 6, 2023) (As Kai Ambos has pointed out, the amendments are accompanied by an interpretive note, which problematically provides that:

> The effect of this section extends exclusively to cooperation with the International Criminal Court, with the aim of extending its jurisdiction to persons (citizens of Ukraine, foreign citizens and stateless persons) who, at the time of committing a crime falling under the jurisdiction of the International Criminal Court, were subordinated

for the ICC's investigation into the situation in Ukraine in the form of financial contributions, secondments, and offers to cooperate.[23] Indeed, the - extent of the support provided has drawn criticism based on how disproportionate it has been to the scarce support provided in relation to other situations currently being investigated by the Court.[24] Given the priority attached by states to the pursuit of accountability for serious international crimes being committed in Ukraine, there is no evidence to suggest that the establishment of an aggression-specific tribunal would divert resources or other forms of international cooperation away from the ICC.

Specifically in relation to funding, it is noted that much of the necessary evidence in relation to the state act elements of crimes of aggression that have been committed against Ukraine is readily available as a matter of public record, and that the tribunal will be able to collaborate with the existing ICPA in relation to the individual conduct elements, which will cap the new investigative resources needed. It has also been proposed that the tribunal utilize existing premises, and be established in a staged way (with, for example, judges only being appointed once it is necessary to convene different chambers). In other words, the cost of the tribunal will be minute compared to the incredible funds currently being spent to arm and otherwise support Ukraine. If G.A. support for the tribunal can be secured, there is also a reasonable prospect of it being funded through the U.N. regular budget. As such, while properly funding justice initiatives is, unfortunately, often a challenge, the tribunal would not represent a significant expenditure, and there is evidence that the political will exists in enough states to find the additional money needed to fund its activities.

---

and/or acted with the aim of carrying out armed aggression against Ukraine, and/or on the basis of decisions (orders, etc.) of officials, military command, or state authorities of the Russian Federation or another country that carried out aggression against Ukraine or contributed to it.).

23 *See, e.g.*, Press Statement, Karim A.A. Khan, ICC Prosecutor Karim A.A. Khan QC Announces Deployment of Forensics and Investigative Team to Ukraine, Welcomes Strong Cooperation with the Government of the Netherlands (May 17, 2022), https://www.icc-cpi.int/news/icc-prosecutor-karim-aa-khan-qc-announces-deployment-forensics-and-investigative-team-ukraine (last visited October 4, 2023); Sylvia Hui, *Millions in Extra Funding Pledged for ICC Work in Ukraine*, AP NEWS (Mar. 21, 2023), https://apnews.com/article/ukraine-uk-war-crimes-conference-icc-2facdba93e4dae9bb4d27027c6aadbe8 (last visited October 4, 2023).

24 *See, e.g.*, Maria Elena Vignoli, *Support Builds for ICC Ukraine Investigation: Governments Should Ensure Similar Support Across the Court's Mandate*, HUM. RTS. Watch (Mar. 20, 2023), https://www.hrw.org/news/2023/03/20/support-builds-icc-ukraine-investigation.

The principle of complementarity, which lies at the heart of the Rome Statute is, in essence, about the imperative of institutions working in harmony to end impunity. In the preamble of the Rome Statute, states affirmed "that the most serious crimes of concern to the international community as a whole must not go unpunished and that their effective prosecution must be ensured by taking measures at the national level and by enhancing international cooperation." From the outset, it has been universally recognized that the ICC cannot deliver justice alone. While the Court has focused on the importance of national efforts to investigate and prosecute Rome Statute crimes, there is no cogent reason to exclude international and regional accountability mechanisms from the role of partners in the fight against impunity. That this is not a radical idea is amply demonstrated by the fact that support for the proposed tribunal for crimes of aggression against Ukraine has won the support of states that rank among the ICC's most consistent political and diplomatic supporters,[25] as well as experts who are among the Court's greatest champions.

3 A Cooperation Agreement Would Be Needed

In the very first piece I published in support of the proposed tribunal in the early days of March 2022, I recommended that an agreement be concluded between the tribunal and the ICC "to emphasize their joint justice project and to deal with practical matters such as the sharing of evidence, and the sequencing of any trials of individuals wanted for prosecution by both institutions."[26] I remain of the view that such an instrument would be critical.

While also expressing the view that the conclusion of a cooperation agreement would be desirable, David Scheffer has stated that there is a plau-

25 For example, Albania, Belgium, Estonia, Guatemala, Latvia, Liechtenstein, Lithuania, Luxembourg, Marshall Islands, North Macedonia, Poland and Ukraine; *see also* Carrie McDougall, *Frequently Asked Questions: A Special Tribunal for the Crime of Aggression Against Ukraine* (unpublished manuscript) (on file with author).

26 Carrie McDougall, *Why Creating a Special Tribunal for Aggression against Ukraine is the Best Available Option: A Reply to Kevin Jon Heller and Other Critics*, Opinio Juris (Mar. 15, 2022), http://opiniojuris.org/2022/03/15/why-creating-a-special-tribunal-for-aggression-against-ukraine-is-the-best-available-option-a-reply-to-kevin-jon-heller-and-other-critics/ (last visited October 1, 2023).

sible argument that the ICC-UN Relationship Agreement[27] would apply to a UN-backed international tribunal.[28] Scheffer goes so far as to say that the application of the Relationship Agreement would work to the advantage of the ICC because it requires the UN to cooperate with the Court and to provide the Court with such information or documents as the Court may request pursuant to Article 87(6) of the Rome Statute,[29] but "[t]he reverse flow of evidence – from the ICC to the STCoA – would not be required unless negotiated between the two parties."[30]

Scheffer offers no arguments in support of his conclusion that the Agreement would apply, and I do not consider this contention to be correct. The entity bound by the Agreement is "the United Nations." In the context of provisions contemplating the conclusion of supplementary agreements or arrangements, the Relationship Agreement refers to "the United Nations or its programmes, funds and offices concerned".[31] The Office for Legal Affairs (OLA) authored *Best Practices Manual for United Nations – International Criminal Court Cooperation*[32] further explains that "[t]he Relationship Agreement provides a general framework for cooperation between all units and entities of the United Nations, including its offices, funds and programmes, on the one hand, and the International Criminal Court, including the Secretariat of the Assembly of States Parties, on the other."[33] OLA (which serves as the coordination point for ICC cooperation) has a consistent practice of interpreting these terms narrowly. An international tribunal established by an agreement concluded between the U.N. and Ukraine

27 Relationship Agreement Between the International Criminal Court and the United Nations, 2283 U.N.T.S. 196 (adopted October 4, 2004, entered into force October 4, 2004) [hereinafter Relationship Agreement].

28 David Scheffer, *Forging a Cooperative Relationship Between International Criminal Court and a Special Tribunal for Aggression against Ukraine*, JUST SEC. (Oct. 25, 2022), https://www.justsecurity.org/83757/forging-a-cooperative-relationship-between-intl-crim-court-and-a-special-tribunal-for-russian-aggression-against-ukraine/ (last visited October 1, 2023).

29 Rome Statute, *supra* note 9, at art. 15(1); *see also id.* at art. 18.

30 Scheffer, *supra* note 28.

31 Rome Statute, *supra* note 9, at art. 15(2), 18(4).

32 United Nations Office for Legal Affairs, *Best Practices Manual for United Nations – International Criminal Court Cooperation pursuant to The Relationship Agreement between the United Nations and the International Criminal Court (entry-into-force 4 October 2004) and General Assembly resolution 58/318* (2016), https://legal.un.org/ola/media/UN-ICC_Cooperation/Best%20Practice%20Guidance%20for%20UN-ICC%20cooperation%20-public.docx.pdf.

33 *Id.* at 4.

would be a separate international organization with international legal personality. An internationalized tribunal embedded in Ukraine's domestic legal system would also clearly fall outside of the Relationship Agreement. As such – and because the Relationship Agreement does not at any rate address the types of cooperation that would in fact be needed between two institutions with investigative, prosecutorial, and judicial capacities – at least one standalone cooperation instrument would need to be negotiated.

It is noted that the practice of the ICC OTP to date has been to rely principally on instruments of less than treaty status,[34] presumably because such instruments often cover investigative matters that are properly kept confidential. And it may indeed be that certain investigative and evidentiary matters would best be addressed in a confidential instrument concluded between the ICC and the proposed special tribunal. I would, however, maintain that certain key issues including the joint commitment to mutual cooperation, the ability to share information and documents in accordance with the institutions' respective legal frameworks, and the sequencing of trials and sentences, should properly be on the public record and addressed in a treaty. Thus, following the model of the UN-ICC Relationship Agreement, it would seem sensible to propose the conclusion of an overarching cooperation agreement, supplemented by any necessary agreements or arrangements.

4 The Proposed Tribunal and the ICC Have the Power to Conclude an Instrument Providing for Mutual Cooperation

While I am myself firmly of the view that the proposed special tribunal should be international, not internationalized, in nature,[35] the lack of agreement on this critical point means that, at present, there is some uncertainty as to whether the tribunal itself would have international legal personality

34 For example, the exchange of letters between the Prosecutor of the ICC and the Prosecutor of the Special Criminal Court of the Central African Republic. *See* Julian Elderfield, *The Rise and Rise of the Special Criminal Court (Part II)*, OPINIO JURIS (Apr. 7, 2021), https://opiniojuris.org/2021/04/07/the-rise-and-rise-of-the-special-criminal-court-part-ii/ (last visited October 5, 2023) (This would seemingly be an arrangement under Article 54(3)(d) of the Rome Statute).

35 *See* Carrie McDougall, 'Why Ukraine Needs an International – Not Internationalised – Tribunal to Prosecute the Crimes of Aggression Committed Against It' (forthcoming, 2023) *Polish Rev. Int'l & Eur. L.*

so as to enable it to conclude a cooperation agreement, or whether the agreement would need to be entered into with Ukraine (separate from existing arrangements in relation to the ICC's current investigation), perhaps supplemented by cooperation agreements with other partners, in addition to the aforementioned supplementary arrangements. In the event that sufficient political will can be generated to establish an international tribunal, the establishing agreement could require the conclusion of the contemplated cooperation agreement with the ICC, just as Article 2 of the Rome Statute required the ICC to be brought into a relationship with the U.N. through the conclusion of an agreement.

The legal capacity of the ICC to receive cooperation from, and to provide cooperation to, another international criminal tribunal is a little more complex.

The Rome Statute is primarily focused on cooperation provided by other entities to the Court. Under Article 86 of the Rome Statute, states parties have a general obligation to cooperate with the Court in the investigation and prosecution of crimes, which is elaborated upon in Part 9 of the Statute. Article 54(3)(d) of the Rome Statute empowers the Prosecutor to:

> [E]nter into such arrangements or agreements, not inconsistent with this Statute, as may be necessary to facilitate the cooperation of a State, intergovernmental organization or person.

Article 87(5) contemplates the voluntary conclusion of ad hoc arrangements and agreements with non-states parties, while Article 87(6) empowers the Court to ask any intergovernmental organization to provide information or documents and other forms of cooperation and assistance as may be agreed.[36]

One question that thus arises is whether the Court, or the OTP specifically, has the power to conclude cooperation instruments with international organizations that are not intergovernmental organizations. It could be that the drafters simply did not consider this scenario given cooperation with a new international criminal tribunal was not foreseen. In this context, it would be counterproductive to argue that the conclusion of such an agreement or arrangement is not permitted on the basis of a technicality. In my view it would be defensible to contend that the reference to "persons" in

36 I am grateful to Andrea Furger, Ph.D. Candidate, University of Melbourne, formerly of the ICC OTP, for discussing the OTP's past practice in relation to cooperation instruments with me, which informed much of my thinking in this section of this opinion.

Article 54(3)(d) should be interpreted as a reference to "legal persons," such that the list of entities with which at least the OTP is empowered to conclude agreements and arrangements is not limited to the entities that are explicitly enumerated.

The provision of ICC cooperation to other entities is exclusively governed by Article 93(10). Sub-paragraph (a) provides that:

> [T]he Court may, upon request, cooperate with and provide assistance to a state party conducting an investigation into or trial in respect of conduct which constitutes a crime within the jurisdiction of the Court or which constitutes a serious crime under the national law of the requesting State.

Under sub-paragraph (c), the Court is also empowered to grant requests for assistance in accordance with paragraph (10) from a non-state party. Two interpretive issues arise in this context: whether cooperation can be provided to entities other than states, and whether cooperation in relation to crimes of aggression falling outside the Court's personal jurisdiction is permitted.

Claus Kreß and Kimberly Prost in their commentary on Article 93 suggest that the absence of any reference to at least international organizations in the article is due simply to the fact that such organizations do no normally have the power to conduct criminal investigations and prosecutions, and they are of the view that the lack of an express reference does not prohibit cooperation with such organizations.[37] Such a purposive construction of the Statute is instinctively correct. A cogent legal argument in support of it can be based on Article 4(1) of the Rome Statute, which provides the Court with broad powers, specifically, "such legal capacity as may be necessary for the exercise of its functions and the fulfilment of its purposes." Arguably this provision is wide enough to empower the Court or any of its organs to conclude any instrument that would enhance its mandate to help "put an end impunity for the perpetrators of [serious crimes of concern to the international community as a whole] and thus to contribute to the prevention of such crimes,"[38] so long as the instrument is consistent with other relevant provisions of the Rome Statute. This would encompass the conclusion of an

37 Claus Kreß and Kimberly Prost, 'Article 93, Other Forms of Cooperation' in Otto Triffterer & Kai Ambos (eds.), *Rome Statute of the International Criminal Court: A Commentary*, 3d ed., (Oxford, United Kingdom: Hart, 2016), p. 2102.

38 Rome Statute, *supra* note 9, at Preamble.

instrument facilitating the provision of cooperation to another international criminal tribunal (and indeed, the receipt of cooperation from it as well).

A compelling answer to the second question has been offered by Frederica Gioia, who writes:

> Reverse cooperation is unquestionably admissible vis-a-vis conduct falling squarely within the jurisdictional reach of the Court ratione materiae, loci and temporis. Article 93(10) makes it equally admissible for conduct which would not fall within the jurisdiction of the Court ratione materiae. The interpreter is left alone in wondering whether reverse cooperation would be available for conduct characterized by factual circumstances which would be beyond the reach of the Court due to the absence of jurisdictional requirements other than the objective nature of the crime: namely, for the lack of the temporal, personal and/or territorial requirements. It is submitted that the statutory framework governing reverse cooperation, scant as it is, calls for an answer in the affirmative. It would indeed be contradictory to allow a state to request cooperation in respect of a conduct which could never come before the Court, since it does not amount to any of the crimes provided for in the Statute, on the one hand; and to prevent such a state from lodging a similar request for a conduct which might well come before the Court had it been committed by a national of a state party, or on the territory of a state party, or for which jurisdiction might be triggered by an ad hoc acceptance of the Court's jurisdiction by the relevant state, on the other hand.[39]

One could add that the crimes of aggression in question could, at least theoretically, come before the Court were the Security Council to refer the situation in Ukraine to the ICC pursuant to Article 15*ter*. While Article 93(10) is not directly applicable, its logic would presumably govern the provision of cooperation to another international criminal tribunal; in my view, and as reasoned by Gioia, the fact that the ICC currently lacks personal jurisdiction over these specific crimes is not a bar to cooperation.

The contention that mutual cooperation with the proposed special tribunal would be consistent with the Rome Statute is supported by existing ICC practice, such as the memorandum of understanding (MOU) governing

39 Frederica Gioia, 'Complementarity and "Reverse Cooperation"', in Carsten Stahn & Mohamed M. El Zeidy (eds.), *The International Criminal Court and Complementarity: From Theory to Practice* (Cambridge: Cambridge University Press, 2011), p. 822.

cooperation concluded between the ICC OTP and the International Commission on Missing Persons (ICMP) pursuant to Article 54(3)(d).[40] The ICMP is an international organization (not an intergovernmental organization),[41] thereby lending weight to the view that at least Article 54(3)(d) does not exhaustively list the entities from which cooperation can be sought.

The scope of cooperation covered by the MOU is set out in subparagraphs (2) and (3) of Article 1, which provide:

> 2. In accordance with the provisions of this Memorandum, the Parties shall, wherever possible, cooperate and assist each other in the discharge of their respective mandates, in conformity with the respective provisions of their respective legal frameworks.
>
> 3. Cooperation and assistance includes exchange of information, documents and records of mutual interest, including providing access to electronic and paper archives, as well as other databases maintained by either Party.

The MOU therefore clearly contemplates mutual cooperation, giving support to the view that the express references to states and non-states parties in Article 93(10) does not exclude the provision of cooperation to an international organization. This example thus suggests that any debate about the capacity of the ICC to conclude the recommended agreement, and any necessary supplementary arrangements, is an academic one only.

5 Key Provisions Needed in the Proposed Cooperation Agreement

The proposed agreement would need to cover a broad range of cooperation issues. These include the modalities for the making of cooperation requests, the conditions governing the sharing of information and evidence, the secure storage of information and evidence, conditions on the use of information and evidence, consultations with states surrendering persons to the ICC

40 Memorandum of Understanding Between the International Commission on Missing Persons and the Office of the Prosecutor of the International Criminal Court, Jul. 7, 2016, https://www.icc-cpi.int/sites/default/files/itemsDocuments/ICC_ICMP.pdf.

41 *See* Agreement on the Status and Functions of the International Commission on Missing Persons, arts. 1(1), 1(2), https://www.icmp.int/wp-content/uploads/2014/12/agreement-on-the-status-and-functions-of-icmp.pdf.

where transfer to the special tribunal is requested, access to persons in custody for the purpose of investigations, measures needed to ensure witness security, and the sequencing of any sentences handed down.

Perhaps of keenest interest will be the need to determine the sequencing of the trials of any persons indicted by both institutions – an issue that is of more than theoretical interest in light of the fact that President Putin is a prime suspect in relation to the crimes of aggression committed against Ukraine, and the ICC has already issued an arrest warrant against him for the war crimes of unlawful deportation, and the unlawful transfer of parts of the population of an occupied territory outside that territory. This issue will need to be governed by a cooperation agreement in order to avoid competition between the institutions given Article 17 of the Rome Statute does not contemplate the ICC's jurisdiction conflicting with another international criminal tribunal, meaning that there is no pre-existing legal framework to determine priority as between the institutions. Similarly, while ICC states parties owe clear legal obligations to ICC, including in relation to arrest and surrender,[42] the existence of these obligations does not answer the question of priority, as these obligations are only engaged in response to the issuing of an arrest warrant or other request for cooperation by the Court, and the ICC could agree to defer an issued but unexecuted warrant (or modify other types of cooperation requests in the unlikely event they created an impediment to cooperation with the special tribunal).

Assuming the special tribunal is established and functioning before the commencement of a relevant trial before the ICC, both institutions could command good arguments in favor of being given priority. On the one hand, the ICC's status as the only permanent international criminal court could be said to warrant primacy. At least as regards Putin, the ICC also issued an arrest warrant first. ICC supporters might also see the commencement of a proceeding against a government official, and one from a major power at that, as having the potential to materially boost the ICC's credibility in light of persistent criticisms that the Court has lacked the will or ability to pursue such cases effectively to date, such that the long-term well-being of the ICC would be well served by it being able to have first bite of the cherry, so to speak.

At the same time, there are countervailing considerations weighing in favor of proceedings before the special tribunal being given priority that, at

42 Rome Statute, *supra* note 9, at arts. 89, 92 (For completeness it is noted that Article 90 deals with competing requests from States, but requests from international criminal tribunals is not canvassed in this provision.).

least in my assessment, outweigh the arguments in favor of the ICC. First, while I am not in a position to speak on behalf of Ukraine, my impression, based on the import it has attached to the establishment of the special tribunal, is that it would prioritize an aggression prosecution. If Ukraine is characterized as a victim of at least the crime of aggression, its perspective should be a major consideration. Second, a conviction for one or more war crimes – or even a conviction for a suite of war crimes, crimes against humanity, and possibly even genocide – could not encompass the wrongs committed against all Ukrainian victims. As I have argued elsewhere,[43] Russia's aggression against Ukraine has opened the door to the commission of other crimes: it is the original and all-encompassing wrong. Its victims include not only Ukrainian civilians but also Ukrainian combatants, as well as members of the Russian armed forces who have reportedly been forced to fight a war on false premises. It is arguable that the indirect victims of Russia's aggression include all those who have been seriously impacted by the ongoing food and energy crises, and states whose interests have been threatened by the unprecedented attack on the international order. On this basis, I would argue that the interests of justice would best be served by the granting of priority to a prosecution before the special tribunal, which has the ability to deliver a measure of justice to literally all victims, and to reinforce the prohibition of the use of force, which is in the interests of all states.

6 Conclusion

It is imperative that the international community agree on the establishment of a tribunal for crimes of aggression committed against Ukraine. If this can be achieved, the ICC and the tribunal can and should provide each other with the greatest degree of cooperation possible under their respective legal frameworks. Rather than representing the fragmentation of the international criminal justice system, or a weakness on the ICC's part, this would demonstrate a mature recognition that the task of ending impunity is immense, and the existence of another credible institution that can respond to a gap in the Rome Statute and thereby help share the Sisyphean burden, is a very good thing indeed.

---

43 McDougall, *supra* note 7.

CHAPTER 43

The ICC and Regionalized Judicial Bodies in Africa

Bernard Ntahiraja

One of the most important principles of the Rome Statute is complementarity.[1] According to that principle, preventing and punishing atrocities is primarily the responsibility of states on whose territories they have been committed – or which might have jurisdiction on another accepted basis in international law. The International Criminal Court (ICC) intervenes when states fail to conduct investigations and prosecutions, or where they purport to do so but are unwilling or unable to genuinely carry out proceedings.[2] Luis Moreno Ocampo, the first ICC Prosecutor, was articulating complementarity when he stated that the Court's success was to be measured, not on the number of trials it would conduct but rather on the absence of trials if the latter was the result of the work of effective and functioning national systems.[3]

From its early years, the Office of the Prosecutor (OTP) has adopted what has been called a "positive approach" to complementarity.[4] This means that in addition to letting national authorities take the first initiatives for accountability, the OTP actively encourages them to do so and supports them as much as possible. For several reasons though, experience shows that national authorities do not often prosecute international crimes. For international criminal justice project to bear palpable fruits, it is therefore inevitable to look at the possibilities of involving other actors, i.e., regional and subregional organizations. One problem though is that the relationship between the ICC and any entity other than state parties and their judiciaries

1 International Criminal Court, Rome Statute of the International Criminal Court, Preamble ¶ 10, art. 1, U.N. Doc. A/CONF.183/9, (July 17, 1998) [hereinafter Rome Statute].

2 *Id.* at art. 17.

3 Office of the Prosecutor, International Criminal Court, Paper on Some Policy Issues Before the Office of the Prosecutor 4 (Sep. 2003), https://www.icc-cpi.int/sites/default/files/NR/rdonlyres/1FA7C4C6-DE5F-42B7-8B25-60AA962ED8B6/143594/030905_Policy_Paper.pdf (last visited October 7, 2023).

4 Chernor Jalloh, 'The Place of the African Criminal Court in the Prosecution of Serious Crimes in Africa', in Charles Chernor Jalloh and Ilias Bantekas (eds.), *The International Criminal Court and Africa* (Oxford: Oxford University Press, 2017) pp. 306–07.

 | DOI:10.1163/9789004686755_052

is still largely unregulated, the relationship with the Security Council of the United Nations being the exception.

This essay argues for the establishment of a sustainable cooperation mechanism between the International Criminal Court (ICC) and the African Union (AU) for the support of regionalized judicial bodies on the lines of the Extraordinary African Chambers (EAC) created within the Senegalese judicial system to try the former Chadian President, Hissène Habré. The essay first discusses why this is the preferable form of cooperation in today's African context, before discussing what the content of the potential agreement would be.

1 Why Regionalized Judicial Bodies?

In today's African context, as far as international criminal justice is concerned, national "regionalized" bodies are preferable first because the initially planned Criminal Section within the African Court on Human and Peoples' Rights is realistically not coming soon. It could also be argued that regionalized judicial bodies are (would be) closer to victims than proper regional courts or sections of regional courts on the Malabo-Protocol model. As part and parcel of national judiciaries, they would also have a more lasting impact and create foundations for a sustainable mechanism of international criminal law enforcement.

1.1 *Poor Prospects of the Planned Criminal Section within the African Court on Human and People's Rights versus the Promises of the EAC Formula*

In the African context, the first attempt to regionalize accountability for international crimes was made by adopting the "Protocol on the amendments to the Protocol on the Statute of the African Court of Justice and human rights," commonly referred to as the Malabo Protocol.[5] The Protocol was adopted on June 27th, 2014, by the twenty-third Ordinary Session of the Assembly of the African Union, held in Malabo, Equatorial Guinea. To enter into force, the Malabo Protocol needs to be ratified by fifteen states.[6] To

5 African Union [AU], *Protocol on Amendments to the Protocol on the Statute of the African Court of Justice and Human Rights*, (adopted Jun. 27, 2014) [hereinafter Malabo Protocol].

6 *Id.* at art. 11.

date, it has been signed by fifteen states but not even one state has ratified it.[7]

The absence of a single ratification of the Malabo Protocol, nine years after it was adopted, is not a sign of state enthusiasm for that instrument, to state the least. In the absence of a comprehensive study of the length of ratification processes in Africa, it is reasonable to rely on a comparison with other ratification processes, especially those of similar instruments, and from there have a perspective. In that regard, we can note that it took five years and three months for the African Charter on Human and Peoples' Rights, also known as the Banjul Charter, to enter into force. It is worth mentioning here that the entering into force of the Banjul Charter was much more demanding as it required ratification by a simple majority of member states of the then Organization of African Unity (OAU).[8] At that time, it meant twenty-six member states.[9] Another example is the ratification process of the Protocol on the establishment of the African Court on Human and Peoples' Rights, also known as the Ouagadougou Protocol. Almost as for the Charter itself, five years and seven months separated the adoption and the coming into force of that Protocol.[10] Fifteen instruments

---

7 *List of Countries Which Have Signed, Ratified/Acceded to the Protocol on the Statute of the African Court of Justice and Human Rights*, AFRICAN UNION, https://au.int/en/treaties/protocol-amendments-protocol-statute-african-court-justice-and-human-rights (click on "Status List") (last visited October 12, 2023).

8 Organization of African Unity [OAU], *African Charter on Human and Peoples' Rights*, art. 63 (adopted Jun. 1, 1981, entered into force Oct. 21, 1986) [hereinafter Banjul Charter].

9 *Afrique. 23e Sommet de l'O.U.A.*, ENCYCLOPÆDIA UNIVERSALIS, https://www.universalis.fr/evenement/27-29-juillet-1987-23e-sommet-de-l-o-u-a/ (last visited August 26, 2023) (In 1987, the OAU comprised fifty member states.) *See De l'OUA à l'Union africaine: histoire et institutions*, RFI, https://webdoc.rfi.fr/oua-union-africaine-histoire-institutions/chapitre-1.html (last visited Aug. 26, 2023) (Today's AU comprises fifty-five member states. The five members which joined/rejoined the OAU/AU after 1987 are the Republic of Namibia (1990), the Republic of Erythea (1993 ...), the Republic of South Africa (1994), the Republic of South Sudan (2011), and the Kingdom of Morocco (2017)).

10 For the ratification process and the status list of the Ouagadougou Protocol, *see* African Union, *List of Countries Which Have Signed, Ratified/Acceded to the Protocol to the African Charter on Human and Peoples' Rights on the Establishment of an African Court on Human and Peoples' Rights*, https://au.int/sites/default/files/treaties/36393-sl-PROTOCOL_TO_THE_AFRICAN_CHARTER_ON_HUMAN_AND_PEOPLESRIGHTS_ON_THE_ESTABLISHMENT_OF_AN_AFRICAN_COURT_ON_HUMAN_AND_PEOPLES_RIGHTS_0.pdf (last visited October 16, 2023).

of ratification were required.[11] There is therefore no exaggeration in suggesting that African States are not particularly interested in the Malabo project. Consequently, the African Court on Human and Peoples' Rights is not exercising criminal jurisdiction any time soon.

It should come as no surprise that African states are not enthusiastically ratifying the Malabo Protocol. From the time it was being discussed, some observers argued that the need to fight against impunity was not the main motivation behind the project. Chacha Murungu observed that the Malabo process was a reaction to the indictment and prosecution of African state officials either by the ICC or by the domestic courts of some European states, especially France, the United Kingdom, Spain, and Belgium.[12] The idea was, according to Murungu at least, to create a competitor to the Hague Court.[13] Others have seen in the Protocol an effort to score political points with the ICC rather than address the need for justice and accountability for crimes under international law.[14] Even voices generally sympathetic to the project recognized that the reaction against the ICC was a significant factor. One of them is Jalloh, who argued that AU's concerns in relation to the ICC led African leaders to start "fast-tracking"[15] their plans for the creation of a regional criminal court even if the said concerns were not the "impetus behind the proposal."[16] Indeed, when, in October 2013, the UN Security Council refused to consider Kenya's request to defer the ICC proceedings against its then President and Vice-President, the AU Assembly declared itself "deeply disappointed" and asked the Commission to "move with speed"[17] and conclude the process of extending the jurisdiction of the African regional criminal court.[18]

11 African Union [AU], Protocol to the African Charter on Human and Peoples' Rights on the Establishment an African Court on Human and Peoples' Rights, art. 34(3) (adopted Jun. 10, 1998, entered into force Jan. 25, 2004) [hereinafter Ouagadougou Protocol].

12 Chacha Bhoke Murungu, 'Towards a Criminal Chamber in the African Court of Justice and Human Rights' (2011) 9 *J. Int'l Crim. Just.* 1081.

13 *Id.*

14 *Id.*; *see also* Max Du Plessis, 'A New Regional International Criminal Court for Africa?' (2012) 2 *S. Afr. J. Crim. Just.* 286; Ademola Abass, 'The Proposed International Criminal Jurisdiction for the African Court: Some Problematical Aspects' (2013) 60 *Neth. Int'l L. Rev.* 37–42.

15 Jalloh, *supra* note 4, at 315.

16 *Id.*

17 African Union [AU], *Decision on the Progress Report of the Commission on the Implementation of the Decisions on the International Criminal Court*, Assembly/AU/Dec.493 (XXII), ¶ 13.

18 *Id.*

The political engagement of individual states also demonstrates the link between the Malabo project and ICC's activities in Africa. ICC situation countries were the most committed to the project. One example is Kenya whose then-President Uhuru Muigai Kenyatta and Vice President William Kipchirchir Samoei Arap Ruto were both indicted, as mentioned above.[19] While it has not ratified the protocol yet, Kenya is the single country to have made a financial pledge for the functioning of the would-be Court.[20] For obvious reasons, Kenya was also the most engaged country in the ICC's Assembly of States Parties pleading, among other reforms, for a rewording of the paragraph of the preamble on complementarity in the Rome Statute to include regional courts.[21]

Despite its vehement defense of immunity in favor of state officials, there is no reason to conclude that the AU is opposed to the international criminal justice project in its entirety. Even at the hottest moments of the AU-ICC tense relationship, the Organization kept reaffirming its "total rejection of impunity" in its resolutions.[22] Beyond rhetoric, a more meaningful example of that commitment is the Organization's support for the trial of the former Chadian President, Hissène Habré, by mandating the Republic of Senegal to try the suspect "on behalf of Africa."[23] It is for that purpose that the Extraordinary African Chambers (EAC) was created.[24]

The AU has manifested her willingness to use Habré's trial as a precedent and learn/build from it. In that regard, in July 2017, the AU Commission

19 Today, William Kipchirchir Samoei Arap Ruto is President of the Republic of Kenya.

20 Amnesty International, Malabo Protocol: Legal and Institutional Implications of the Merged and Expanded African Court 11 (2016), https://www.amnesty.org/en/wp-content/uploads/2021/05/AFR0130632016ENGLISH.pdf (last visited October 16, 2023).

21 *Submission by the Republic of Kenya on Amendments to Rome Statute of the International Criminal Court for Consideration by the Working Group on Amendments*, C.N.1026.2013.TREATIES-XVIII.10, ¶ 5 (Mar. 14, 2014), https://treaties.un.org/doc/publication/cn/2013/cn.1026.2013-eng.pdf (last visited October 16, 2023) (Here is the rewording suggested by Kenya to the Rome Statute's Preamble ¶ 10: "Emphasizing that the International Criminal Court established under this Statute shall be complementary to national and regional criminal jurisdictions.").

22 Among many documents, *see* African Union, Report of the Committee of Eminent African Jurists on the Case of Hissène Habré (Jul. 2006), https://thehagueinstituteforglobaljustice.org/files/legacy/justice/habre/ceja_repor0506.pdf (last visited October 16, 2023).

23 African Union [AU], *Decision on the Hissène Habré Case and the African Union*, Assembly/AU/Dec.127(VII) (2007).

24 *See* CHAMBRES AFRICAINES EXTRAORDINAIRES, http://www.chambresafricaines.org/ (last visited October 15, 2023) (For the AU-Senegal agreement to create the chambers, the Statute of the Chambers, and other relevant information on the EAC).

organized a seminar on "carrying forward the legacy of the Extraordinary African Chambers in the trial of Hissène Habré."[25] Its ambitious objectives were to engage African states in the progressive development of international criminal justice, build the capacity of the African judiciary, public prosecutors, civil society, and legal fraternities on international criminal justice; document and highlight EAC's contributions to international criminal justice; promote African support for international criminal justice; devise a framework for the exercise of international criminal justice in Africa; and promote accountability for the end of impunity for gross human rights violations.[26] It would therefore make sense to engage the AU on that basis.

1.2 *Decentralizing Accountability Even Further, and Better*

It is generally admitted that national prosecutions within territorial states are preferable in comparison with trials in international courts/tribunals. The United Nations' position on the question is also that tribunals are to be established as close to the concerned victims as possible to the extent that it is practicable.[27] In that regard, while a regional criminal court (based on the Malabo Protocol, for example) would unquestionably be further from victims than national courts, it would be significantly closer to them than an international court based in Europe. That reasoning can be pushed further to argue that national regionalized criminal courts are even better. This would still be the case even if they were to be established elsewhere than in the territorial state, provided that the deciding actors use some political common sense. In the African context, this would mean that the judicial institution would be created/chosen in the sub-region where the suspect comes from and where the victims live(d) (East, West, North, South, and Center of the continent, accordingly).

1.3 *Killing Two Birds with One Stone: Rendering Justice and Setting the Foundations of a Sustainable Enforcement Mechanism*

Regionalized solutions are not to be viewed as ends in themselves. Unlike regional permanent structures (Malabo Protocol – like chambers), they set

---

25 *A Seminar on Carrying Forward the Legacy of the Extraordinary African Chambers in the Trial of Hissène Habré*, AFRICAN UNION, https://au.int/en/newsevents/20170703/seminar-carrying-forward-legacy-extraordinary-african-chambers-trial-hiss%C3%A8ne (last visited October 14, 2023).

26 *Id.*

27 U.N. Secretary-General, *The Rule of Law and Transitional Justice in Conflict and Post-Conflict Societies*, ¶ 40, U.N. Doc. S/2004/616 (August 23, 2004).

the ground or reinforce national systems which are, by definition, the most sustainable. That is because they are integrated parts of national judiciaries.[28] An AU-ICC agreement to reinforce them would, by the same token, be contributing to the creation of a sustainable mechanism of international criminal law indirect enforcement.[29] This is of an even greater significance if the proceedings are to take place in a third country, basing its jurisdiction on universality, as was the case for Hissène Habré.

A legitimate question might be whether direct engagement with the country enforcing universal jurisdiction would not achieve the same or better result. It needs to be first highlighted that this essay is not advocating an AU-ICC cooperation mechanism as an alternative to ICC's direct engagement with states enforcing universal jurisdiction. On the contrary, the two approaches are complementary to each other if decentralized accountability is to be pursued. It is also worth mentioning that there are several obstacles to the enforcement of universal jurisdiction by individual states in the African context. One of them is the existence of a general framework for police/judicial cross-border assistance and cooperation. It comes as no surprise that, despite the existence of universal jurisdiction legislation in many countries across the continent, the first trial on that basis took place in a regionalized structure (the EAC), supported by the AU.[30]

2 What Can the ICC Do? What Forms of Cooperation with the African Union?

If a cooperation mechanism between the ICC and the AU is one day agreed upon, it is advisable that the agreement covers the judicial relationship between the ICC and the regionalized criminal courts to establish aspects of cooperation at a purely technical level.

28 In relation to the EAC, *see* Bernard Ntahiraja, 'Universal Jurisdiction and the Extraordinary African Chambers in the Senegalese Judicial System: Towards a Replicable Enforcement Model?' (2019) 24 *Afr. Y.B. Int'l L. Online*, 272–99 at 285–88.

29 *See* M. Bassiouni, 'Universal Jurisdiction for International Crimes: Historical Perspectives and Contemporary Practice' (2001) 24 *Va. J. Int'l L.* 81–161 at 82 (For enforcement of international criminal law, Bassiouni distinguishes between a "direct enforcement system" in the hands of international courts and an "indirect enforcement system" by national authorities).

30 *See* Amnesty International, Universal Jurisdiction: A Preliminary Survey of Legislation in the World (2011), https://www.amnesty.org/en/wp-content/uploads/2021/06/ior53 2004011en.pdf.

2.1 *Organizing the Judicial Relationship between the ICC and the Could-Be Regionalized Criminal Courts*

The complementarity regime of the Rome Statute does not textually contemplate a relationship between the ICC and a possible regional/sub-regional criminal court. This could create an overlap and raise a positive conflict of jurisdiction between the ICC and the African would-be regionalized judicial entity. In relation to the could-be Criminal Section in the African Court on Human and Peoples' Rights (based on the Malabo Protocol), Jalloh holds the view that while complementarity was initially conceptualized to regulate the relationships between the ICC and state parties to the Rome Statute, its regime is flexible enough to regulate the jurisdictional relationship between the ICC and regional criminal courts.[31] Jackson shares that view. He suggests that while Article 17 of the Rome Statute refers to states' jurisdictions, prosecutions by a regional criminal court should be seen as prosecutions by a state.[32] The argument is that regional criminal courts are to be seen as a lawful way for states to collectively exercise their primary responsibility to investigate and prosecute crimes within their jurisdiction.[33] Therefore, the regional court exercises jurisdiction by delegation.[34] The approach has been wrongly labelled as "hierarchical" in favor of the ICC.[35] Its critics argue that the model implies that the ICC would remain "at the apex of international criminal law enforcement."[36] They argue that the model envisages a situation in which a judgment by the regional court might be superseded by one of the ICC if the former's judgment is found "not to measure up to the standards of the ICC Statute and therefore to exemplify the inability or the unwillingness of the African Court to exercise jurisdiction in a particular case."[37] This is indeed the implication of considering the regional court as a national jurisdiction, but it does not make the

31 Jalloh, *supra* note 4, at 294.

32 Miles Jackson, 'Regional Complementarity: The Rome Statute and Public International Law' (2016) 14 *J. Int'l Crim. Just.* 1062.

33 *Id.* at 1067–68.

34 *Id.*

35 Balingene Kahombo, 'Towards Coordination of the Global System of International Criminal Justice with the Criminal Court of the African Union', in HJ van der Merwe and Gerhard Kemp (eds.), *International Criminal Justice in Africa* (Nairobi: Strathmore University Press, 2017), pp. 1–32.

36 *Id.* (citing Harmen van der Wilt, 'Complementary Jurisdiction (Article 46H)' in Gerhard Werle and Moritz Vormbaum (eds.), *The African Criminal Court: A Commentary on the Malabo Protocol* (Berlin: Springer, 2017), p. 191).

37 *Id.*

model "hierarchical." Complementarity does not give precedence to the ICC. On the contrary, it means that the Hague Court will always have to justify its intervention.

It is an open question whether the above solution would apply to regionalized judicial divisions created by an agreement between the AU and one of its member states. However, if that member state is also a state party to the Rome Statute, Jackson's approach is the only logical option, if conflicting obligations are to be avoided. An AU-ICC agreement could possibly extend the application of that solution even to situations where a regionalized court would be created in a non-state party to the Rome Statute.

The alternative to the AU-ICC agreement could be that the regionalized criminal court itself negotiates its relationships with the ICC as soon as it is established. In that case, the regionalized court would enter the negotiation with a pre-existing legal framework, i.e., its statute or constitutive instrument. There is no guarantee that that instrument would be compatible with the Rome Statute. If the hosting state is a party to the Rome Statute, it could run the risk of finding itself in conflicting obligations. In the African context, if the EAC is to create a precedent, i.e., if other regionalized courts/chambers are to be created in national judiciaries of African states, they are, more likely than not, to be created in states parties to the Rome Statute.[38] It is therefore safer to have the AU-ICC agreement in place at the time the instrument for the regionalized court is drafted. Such arrangements were not necessary for the EAC as no overlap with the ICC was to be envisaged, given the crystal-clear differences in their respective jurisdictions, ratione tempore.[39]

Even if the regionalized criminal court had to be created in a non-state party to the Rome Statute, an agreement between the ICC, on the one hand, and the AU or the hosting state, on the other, would be necessary. Its function would not be to prevent the hosting state from facing conflicting obligations but to organize a "division of labor" between the two judicial

38 It is reasonable to assume those states are more open to hosting sub-regional criminal courts than the states which are not parties to the Rome Statute. As of August 8th, 2023, 33 African states are parties to the Rome Statute.

39 *Statut des Chambres africaines extraordinaires au sein des juridictions sénégalaises pour la poursuite des crimes internationaux commis au Tchad durant la période du 7 juin 1982 au 1er décembre 1990*, art. 1 (Aug. 2012), *translated in Statute of the Extraordinary African Chambers*, HUM. RTS. WATCH (Sep. 2, 2013), https://www.hrw.org/news/2013/09/02/statute-extraordinary-african-chambers (While, roughly put, the ICC has jurisdiction for crimes committed after July 1st, 2002, the EAC were created to prosecute crimes committed in Chad between June 7, 1982 and December 1, 1990).

institutions and to prevent potential conflicts due to parallel proceedings or contradictory judgments.

Irrespective of the legal status of the hosting state of the regionalized court in relation to the ICC (party/not party to the Rome Statute), the Malabo Protocol's approach to complementarity should be avoided. Indeed, the Protocol does provide for complementarity, but only between the African Regional Court, on the one hand, and national courts, on the other, as well as courts of the regional economic communities.[40] Neither the ICC nor the Rome Statute are mentioned in the relevant provision.[41] The omission means that African leaders wanted to see the would-be African Criminal Court as an alternative, rather than a complement to the ICC, despite the fact many African states were already parties to the Rome Statute. This view is confirmed by AU's repetitive calls to its member states to not cooperate with the ICC.[42] If the African Regional Criminal Court (based on the Malabo Protocol) ever becomes operational, a conflict of jurisdiction with the ICC is more than likely, at least in relation to the four ICC crimes. Unlike the Malabo Protocol in relation to the ICC, the absence of reference to regional criminal courts by the Rome Statute is justified by the inexistence of such entities, functional or in sight, at the time the treaty was drafted.

2.2 *Technical Aspects of the Potential Cooperation Agreement*

For implementation of the complementarity principle, the ICC Office of The Prosecutor (OTP) can go beyond judicial relationships in the agreements it concludes. A recent example is the agreement concluded between the OTP and the government of Colombia on October 28th, 2021.[43] Among other aspects, the agreement includes commitments to exchange lessons learned and best practices between the OTP and Colombian institutions. It also mentions projects and programs aimed at Colombian legal professionals.[44] There is no apparent reason why a similar agreement would not be possible

40 Malabo Protocol, *supra* note 5, at art. 46H.

41 *Id.*

42 *See, e.g.*, African Union [AU], Decision on the International Criminal Court, Doc. EX. CL/1218(XXXVI), ¶ 3(i).

43 Cooperation Agreement Between the Office of the Prosecutor of the International Criminal Court and the Government of Colombia (2021), https://www.icc-cpi.int/sites/default/files/itemsDocuments/20211028-OTP-COL-Cooperation-Agreement-ENG.pdf.

44 *Id.* at Arts. 4, 5.

with a regional organization like the AU, especially given the number of member states which are also parties to the Rome Statute.[45]

There are nevertheless limits to what the ICC can do. Several times, the ICC Assembly of State Parties has reiterated that the Court is not a development agency.[46] It can therefore not engage in big and budget-consuming projects of capacity building. However, it is the view of this essay's author that this does not prevent short-time training sessions and judicial dialogue initiatives.

The exchange of experience during the drafting processes of the legal instruments of the could-be regionalized judicial divisions would be one of the most valuable aspects. This form of cooperation could have two benefits, at least. The first would be to help adopt a reasonably enforceable regime. Had the discussions/drafting of the Malabo Protocol involved lessons learned from the ICC, a more realistic instrument probably could have been drafted. The Malabo Protocol is indeed over-ambitious in several aspects. One example is the subject matter jurisdiction the instrument gives, or intends to give, to the African Court. The list of fourteen crimes is quite unprecedented in International Criminal Law.[47] If international criminal courts like the ICC struggle in carrying out their four-crimes mandate, it is almost a given that a judicial entity with significantly more limited resources would have enormous difficulties in carrying out a fourteen-crimes mandate, even within a limited geographical area.

The second benefit of that form of cooperation would be to help prevent ultra-regressive rules from being included in the constitutive instrument of the regionalized court. One example is the rules on immunities. Since the *Arrest Warrant* case and even before, it is largely admitted that personal immunities do not apply before international/internationalized courts.[48] Nevertheless, the Malabo Protocol included immunities for serving heads of

---

45 *The States Parties to the Rome Statute*, INT'L CRIM. CT., https://asp.icc-cpi.int/states-parties (As of today, there are 33 African states parties to the Rome Statute) (last visited August 8, 2023).

46 Assembly of States Parties, International Criminal Court, *Report of the Court on Complementarity*, Doc. No. ICC-ASP/10/23, pp. 5, 22 (Nov. 11, 2011), https://asp.icc-cpi.int/sites/asp/files/asp_docs/ASP10/ICC-ASP-10-23-ENG.pdf (last visited October 16, 2023).

47 Malabo Protocol, *supra* note 5, at art. 28A (The Criminal Chamber of the African Court would have jurisdiction over genocide, war crimes, crimes against humanity, aggression, unconstitutional change of government, piracy, terrorism, mercenarism, corruption, money laundering, trafficking in persons, trafficking in drugs, trafficking in hazardous wastes and illicit exploitation of natural resources.).

48 Case Concerning the Arrest Warrant of 11 April 2000 (Dem. Rep. Congo v. Belg.), Judgment, 2002 I.C.J. 3 (Feb 14, 2002), ¶ 61.

state and government as well as other "senior state officials."[49] The immunity rule of the Malabo Protocol has been one of the most criticized, both internally and externally. AU partners were vocal in their criticism of the rule. In the 2015 Judicial Dialogue, for example, the representative of the European Union announced that his organization would not support the project financially because of that rule – and the silence of the protocol on the relationship with the ICC.[50] It is less known that the immunity rule was also approved despite concerns raised within internal AU circles regarding its conformity with international law, domestic laws of member states, and jurisprudence.[51] There are therefore reasons to hope that AU-ICC engagements before and during the drafting processes would significantly reduce the probability of having such rules in the instruments to govern the regionalized criminal courts discussed in this essay.

The mechanisms to exchange information and evidence items on specific cases would properly be directly negotiated between the respective judicial bodies, i.e., the ICC and the regionalized criminal court. However, a commitment to put the necessary channels in place could be part of the AU-ICC agreement.

3 Conclusion

This essay has argued for the establishment of a cooperation mechanism between the International Criminal Court and the African Union aiming at supporting regionalized judicial divisions within national judiciaries as a mechanism to enforce international criminal law. The preference for regionalized chambers within national courts is in part justified by the poor prospects of the project to create a Criminal Section within the African Court on

49 Malabo Protocol, *supra* note 5, at art. 46A *bis*.

50 *EU Statement at the African Judicial Dialogue*, (Nov. 6, 2015), https://eeas.europa.eu/archives/delegations/african_union/documents/press_corner/eu-statement-judicial-dialogue-06-11-2015_en.pdf

(Regarding the matter of an expanded African Court, I can reconfirm that the EU is not in a position to support the Malabo Protocol creating the additional Criminal Chamber as it includes the provision of immunity for sitting Heads of State and Senior state officials and lacks complementarity with the ICC.).

51 This appeared, for instance, during discussions between delegations at the Ministerial Meeting. *See* African Union, *First Ministerial Meeting of the Specialized Technical Committee on Justice and Legal Affairs*, STC/Legal/Min/Rpt., ¶ 25, https://archives.au.int/bitstream/handle/123456789/9043/Assembly%20AU%208%20XXIII_E.pdf.

Human and Peoples' Rights. Those structures would also definitely bring justice closer to victims and could arguably increase the capacity of the national judiciaries for a more sustainable enforcement of international criminal law. The essay has also reflected on the major lines of a possible agreement between the International Criminal Court and the African Union for that purpose. If such an agreement is to be established, it will be preferable that it includes general principles on the judicial relationship between the ICC and the envisioned regionalized courts, as well as elements of a cooperation mechanism on purely technical aspects.

CHAPTER 44

Strengthening Cooperation between the ICC and National Authorities Exercising Universal Jurisdiction

Cedric M.J. Ryngaert

The International Criminal Court (ICC) is the most visible international criminal justice mechanism. However, it cannot possibly ensure accountability for international crimes on its own. Its jurisdiction and resources are limited, and its role is only complementary to that of states. States remain the primary purveyors of international criminal justice. This also includes states exercising universal jurisdiction (UJ), i.e., jurisdiction that is not based on a (territorial, national, or security) nexus with the prosecuting state, but is based on the gravity of the crime.[1] Over the years, UJ has been "quietly expanding,"[2] as a result of ICC implementation legislation, activism by non-governmental organizations, and the establishment of specialist law-enforcement units dedicated to the investigation and prosecution of international crimes[3].

As both the ICC and UJ states have jurisdiction over international crimes – and sometimes even exercise this jurisdiction over the same situation – the question arises how, and to what extent, the ICC should engage with national authorities exercising UJ. In this contribution, I argue that the ICC and UJ states may want to strengthen cooperation, including coordination of investigations and exchange of best practices. The ICC and UJ states that are members of the European Union (EU) have recently seized this

1 For an extensive discussion, *see* Luc Reydams, *Universal Jurisdiction International and Municipal Legal Perspectives* (Oxford: Oxford University Press, 2003).

2 *See also* Maximo Langer and Mackenzie Eason, 'The Quiet Expansion of Universal Jurisdiction' (2019) 30 *Eur. J. Int'l L.* 779.

3 *See* Council Decision 2003/335/JHA, of 8 May 2003 on the Investigation and Prosecution of Genocide, Crimes Against Humanity and War Crimes, 2003 O.J. (L 118) 4 (EU) ("Member States shall consider the need to set up or designate specialist units within the competent law enforcement authorities with particular responsibility for investigating and, as appropriate, prosecuting the crimes in question.").

 | DOI:10.1163/9789004686755_053

opportunity in the Ukraine situation: the ICC Office of the Prosecutor for the first time joined a Joint Investigation Team (JIT) established by Eurojust, the EU Agency for Criminal Justice Cooperation between EU Member States.[4] The ICC and UJ states may want to build on this experience for other situations as well, while nevertheless retaining their autonomy.

First, I briefly discuss the proper place for UJ in the international criminal justice project. Subsequently, I inquire how the ICC Prosecutor and UJ states could effectively team up in the investigation and prosecution of international crimes.

1 A Place for Universal Jurisdiction in the International Criminal Justice Project

UJ has a unique role to play for those international crimes committed on the territory (or by nationals) of states unwilling or unable to prosecute, and in respect of which the ICC does not have jurisdiction or no other international tribunal has been established. UJ is then the last resort for criminal accountability. A case in point is Syria. Syria is not a party to the ICC Rome Statute; the UN Security Council has not referred the situation in Syria to the ICC Prosecutor; nor is the establishment of an ad hoc tribunal envisaged. Faced with this apparent accountability deficit, some European states, egged on by non-governmental organizations, have started to exercise UJ over suspected Syrian war criminals. Germany has become "a poster child" for UJ, after German courts convicted Syrian intelligence officials for international crimes in 2021-22 (Al-Khatib or Koblenz trial).[5]

Also, where the ICC does have jurisdiction over a particular situation, there is a role for UJ, given that the ICC has limited budgetary resources and focuses on those perpetrators bearing the greatest responsibility. This is currently happening with respect to the situation in Ukraine, over which, apart from Ukraine itself, the ICC and UJ states exercise jurisdiction.[6]

4 Press Release, Eurojust, ICC Participates in Joint Investigation Team Supported by Eurojust on Alleged Core International Crimes in Ukraine (Apr. 25, 2022), https://www.eurojust.europa.eu/news/icc-participates-joint-investigation-team-supported-eurojust-alleged-core-international-crimes (last visited September 20, 2023).

5 Susann Aboueldahab and Fin-Jasper Langmack, 'Universal Jurisdiction Cases in Germany: A Closer Look at the Poster Child of International Criminal Justice' (2022) 31 *Minn. J. Int'l L.* 1.

6 Statement, Karim A.A. Khan, ICC Prosecutor, On the Situation in Ukraine: Receipt of Referrals from 39 States Parties and the Opening of an Investigation (Mar. 2, 2022), https://

Proper coordination between the ICC and UJ states will be called for in such a case.[7]

UJ prosecutions tend to focus on lower-level perpetrators as well as perpetrators who have fallen out of favor with their own government – which limits the potential for diplomatic fall-out.[8] UJ prosecutions are typically brought against presumed offenders who are already present on the territory of the prosecuting state, e.g., who have reached the territory by means of migratory streams from conflict zones.[9] Precisely because of this territorial presence, UJ states may consider the exercise of UJ to be in their interest, such as their interest to provide justice to and integrate victim communities (e.g., from Syria), which may in turn lead to societal stabilization.[10] Given states' tendency to couple the exercise of UJ with the pursuit

---

www.icc-cpi.int/news/statement-icc-prosecutor-karim-aa-khan-qc-situation-ukraine-receipt-referrals-39-states; Julia Crawford and Thierry Cruvellier, *Philip Grant: "Ukraine is Accelerating a Revival of Universal Jurisdiction"*, JUSTICE INFO (Nov. 29, 2022), https://www.justiceinfo.net/en/109532-philip-grant-ukraine-revival-universal-jurisdiction.html.

7 Mark Kersten, *Universal Jurisdiction in Ukraine: States Should Commit to Using Their Own Courts to Address Russian Atrocities*, JUSTICE IN CONFLICT (Oct. 17, 2022), https://justiceinconflict.org/2022/10/17/universal-jurisdiction-in-ukraine-states-should-commit-to-using-their-own-courts-to-address-russian-atrocities/ (recognizing that both states and the ICC have jurisdiction over the Ukraine situation, and submitting that UJ 'should be invoked [to] help fill gaps, spread the responsibility for accountability more evenly among states, and set new precedents for inter-state cooperation in international criminal law').

8 Maximo Langer, 'The Diplomacy of Universal Jurisdiction: The Political Branches and the Transnational Prosecution of International Crimes' (2011) 105 *Am. J. Int'l L.* 1.

9 Most states require the presence of the presumed offender before investigations can be initiated. The exercise of universal jurisdiction in absentia is a rare occurrence and controversial at that. *See* Tim Kluwen, 'Universal Jurisdiction in Absentia Before Domestic Courts Prosecuting International Crimes: A Suitable Weapon to Fight Impunity?' (2017) 8 *Goettingen J. Int'l L.* 7.

10 Frédéric Mégret, 'The 'Elephant in the Room' in Debates About Universal Jurisdiction: Diasporas, Duties of Hospitality, and the Constitution of the Political' (2015) 6 *Transnat'l Legal Theory* 89, 111

(The exercise of UJ is the manifestation and perhaps the act of constitution of a community composed of both native-born and immigrant, of those whose lives have been unperturbed by mass crime and those whose lives have been defined by it.);

Yuna Han, 'Should German Courts Prosecute Syrian International Crimes? Revisiting the "Dual Foundation" Thesis' (2022) 36 *Ethics & Int'l Affs.* 37, 56 ("Germany should administer UJ not only because it is acting on behalf of an amorphous international community but also because it allows the German state to enforce the rights of victims and recognize the status of refugees already within its territory as ontological subjects, giving them meaningful political agency in their new surroundings.").

of some form of national interest, UJ will remain a relatively exceptional phenomenon.[11]

2 UJ States and the ICC: Partners in International Criminal Justice

When states and the ICC exercise jurisdiction, they may mutually reinforce each other's work, especially when they investigate the same crime situation. Applying positive complementarity, the ICC Prosecutor already shares knowledge, expertise, and best practices with domestic law-enforcement agencies,[12] but more could perhaps be done with regard to UJ states.[13]

The Ukraine situation presents itself as a unique opportunity for the ICC and UJ states. Future cooperation, in respect of other situations, could build on what is currently unfolding. On 28 March 2022, Eurojust created a Joint Investigation Team (JIT) to support Member States exercising UJ to carry out investigations regarding crimes committed in Ukraine; this JIT was, for the first time ever, joined by the ICC Office of the Prosecutor on 25 April 2022.[14] On this occasion, ICC Prosecutor Karim Khan forcefully stated:

> [T]he participation of my Office in this JIT will not be a one-way street. We do not wish to only be the recipients of information and evidence. We also want to serve as an effective partner with respect to

11 Jeremy A. Rabkin and Craig S. Lerner, 'Criminal Justice Is Local: Why States Disregard Universal Jurisdiction for Human Rights Abuses' (2022) 55 *Vand. J. Transnat'l L.* 375, 431 (skeptically observing, in respect of UJ, that 'criminal justice remains stubbornly local in its aims and priorities').

12 Office of the Prosecutor, International Criminal Court, Policy Paper on Preliminary Examinations ¶ 2 (Nov. 2013) https://www.icc-cpi.int/sites/default/files/iccdocs/otp/OTP-Policy_Paper_Preliminary_Examinations_2013-ENG.pdf (last visited July 12, 2023); Emeric Rogier, *The Ethos of "Positive Complementarity"*, EJIL: TALK! (Dec. 11, 2018), https://www.ejiltalk.org/the-ethos-of-positive-complementarity/ (last visited November 7, 2023).

13 Valérie Paulet, The ICC & Universal Jurisdiction: Two Ways, One Fight, Coalition for the International Criminal Court (May 23, 2017), https://www.coalitionfortheicc.org/news/20170519/icc-universal-jurisdiction-two-ways-one-fight (last visited Sep. 25, 2023).

14 Press Release, Eurojust, ICC Participates in Joint Investigation Team Supported by Eurojust on Alleged Core International Crimes in Ukraine (Apr. 25, 2022), https://www.eurojust.europa.eu/news/icc-participates-joint-investigation-team-supported-eurojust-alleged-core-international-crimes (last visited Sep. 26, 2023).

> the conduct of domestic proceedings in relation to core international crimes, in line with the principle of complementarity. In that spirit, my Office will be seeking to identify all opportunities through which it can provide information and evidence to the concerned national authorities in support of their investigations and prosecutions.[15]

Eurojust's spokesman has clarified that: "the JIT countries and the ICC will exchange evidence necessary for the investigations and work in close cooperation."[16] In addition, investigators of selected EU Member States have been seconded to the ICC or worked with ICC teams on the situation in Ukraine.[17] Coordination will ensure that victims and witnesses are not retraumatized because of multiple interviews by the ICC and UJ states.[18]

This novel form of cooperation between the EU and European UJ states on the one hand, and the ICC on the other could finally make the ICC a "giant with arms," as the ICC Office of the Prosecutor may well be the main beneficiary of the evidentiary outcomes produced by the JIT.[19] Obviously, this does not mean that UJ states will be reduced to being subcontractors running errands for the ICC. The ICC will – and should – retain its autonomy and its own investigative capacity. UJ states, for their part, do not give up the power to initiate their own prosecutions. But they will benefit from information shared by the ICC (albeit on a discretionary basis), by other UJ

15 Press Statement, Karim A.A. Khan, ICC Prosecutor, Office of the Prosecutor Joins National Authorities in Joint Investigation Team on International Crimes Committed in Ukraine (Apr. 25, 2022), https://www.icc-cpi.int/news/statement-icc-prosecutor-karim-aa-khan-qc-office-prosecutor-joins-national-authorities-joint (last visited October 15, 2023).

16 Julia Crawford, *Ukraine, ICC and Eurojust: How Will That Work*, JUSTICEINFO.NET (May 5, 2022), https://www.justiceinfo.net/en/91763-ukraine-icc-eurojust-how-will-that-work.html.

17 David Bosco, *The ICC's Impact in Ukraine*, LAWFARE (Oct. 27, 2022), https://www.lawfaremedia.org/article/iccs-impact-ukraine.

18 Crawford, *supra* note 16; *see also* Brianne McGonigle, 'Using Strategic Litigation and Universal Jurisdiction to Advance Accountability for Serious International Crimes' (2022) 16 *Int'l J. Transnat'l Just.* 363, 372 (discussing the risk of retraumatization and interview fatigue).

19 Michele Caianiello, 'The Role of the EU in the Investigation of Serious International Crimes Committed in Ukraine. Towards a New Model of Cooperation?' (2022) 30 *Eur. J. Crime, Crim. L. & Crim. Just.* 219.

states (e.g., via the Eurojust Genocide Network),[20] and by UN mechanisms and teams (e.g., Syria, Myanmar, ISIL).[21]

Whether this model of cooperation between UJ states and the ICC could be replicated in other situations is not fully clear yet. Much will depend on the political willingness of UJ states and how cooperation on Ukraine will be assessed. The EU, in any event, appears to have the ambition to further strengthen cooperation across the board between EU member states exercising UJ and the ICC. Indeed, on 30 May 2022, the European Parliament and the Council amended the Eurojust Regulation, which explicitly provides henceforth that Eurojust will:

> [S]upport Member States' action in combating genocide, crimes against humanity, war crimes and related criminal offences, including by preserving, analyzing and storing evidence related to those crimes and related criminal offences and enabling the exchange of such evidence with, or otherwise making it directly available to, competent na-

20 Even regardless of the ICC's participation in the JIT on Ukraine, horizontal cooperation between (European) UJ states regarding Ukraine boosts the chances of UJ success. *Cf.* Kersten, *supra* note 7 ("those states can pool resources, intelligence, and evidence to make the exercise of universal jurisdiction more economical"). Note that the above-mentioned Al Khatib UJ trial in Germany resulted from a joint investigation team involving Germany and France, which holds the 'Caesar' files documenting the abuse of detainees in Syria. *See Syrian Official Sentenced to Life for Crimes Against Humanity with Support of Joint Investigation Team Assisted by Eurojust*, EUROJUST (Jan. 13, 2022), https://www.eurojust.europa.eu/news/syrian-official-convicted-crimes-against-humanity-with-support-joint-investigation-team (last visited October 11, 2023); *see generally* Beth van Schaack, *Imagining Justice for Syria* (Oxford: Oxford University Press, 2020), Chapter 7 (discussing mutual legal assistance regarding Syrian cases proceeding in domestic courts).

21 *E.g.*, International, Impartial, and Independent Mechanism to Assist in the Investigation and Prosecution of Persons Responsible for the Most Serious Crimes under International Law Committed in the Syrian Arab Republic since March 2011, https://iiim.un.org/ (last visited October 15, 2023); Independent Investigative Mechanism for Myanmar, https://iimm.un.org/ (last visited October 15, 2023); Investigative Team to Promote Accountability for Crimes Committed by Da'esh/ISIL, https://www.unitad.un.org/ (last visited October 15, 2023). *See* Catherine Marchi-Uchel, 'Klatsky Endowed Lecture in Human Rights' (2019) 51 *Case W. Rsrv. J. Int'l L.* 224-25 (These mechanisms conduct preparatory work "needed for accountability processes, regardless of what judicial avenues may emerge in the future"). Accordingly, they may 'feed' both the ICC and UJ states.

tional authorities and international judicial authorities, in particular the International Criminal Court.[22]

Accordingly, it is to be expected that European UJ states will more regularly make evidence available to the ICC. Such evidence-sharing will often result from structural UJ investigations (as for instance carried out by German authorities), which focus on an entire situation rather than on specific incidents or perpetrators.[23]

Cooperation between ICC and UJ states is most logical and practical where both parties investigate the same situation. Cooperation can also be envisaged, however, with respect to a situation that is investigated and prosecuted by only one party, e.g., where a UJ state has jurisdiction, but the ICC does not. In this case, cooperation will not concern the sharing of evidence, but may pertain more generally to an exchange of best practices on how to properly conduct an atrocity trial. For instance, the ICC could have advised German law-enforcement authorities on how to conduct the above-mentioned Al Khatib trial, which concerned atrocities committed in Syria over which the ICC does not have jurisdiction. Such cooperation could have prevented problems regarding access to translation and transcripts, outreach, truth-seeking, and witness protection which have cast a shadow over an otherwise exemplary trial.[24] Obviously, this type of ICC support will be dependent on a request by the UJ state, and on the availability of ICC resources.

Apart from cooperating on specific situations or cases, the ICC and UJ states may, more generally, exert mutual influence on each other through their respective contributions to the development of international criminal law and justice. Most obviously, in light of its international authority in the field of international criminal law (ICL), the ICC's application and interpretation of ICL will influence the practice of UJ states, especially states parties to the Rome Statute which have adopted ICC implementation legislation.

---

22 Regulation (EU) 2022/838 of the European Parliament and of the Council of 30 May 2022 amending Regulation (EU) 2018/1727 (new Article 4(1)(j)) (emphasis added).

23 Karolina Aksamitowska, Asser Institute for International and European Law, War Crimes Units: Legislative, Organisational and Technical Lessons 16 (Sep. 2021), https://www.asser.nl/media/795205/karolina-aksamitowska-war-crimes-units-legislative-organisational-and-technical-lessons-eng.pdf.

24 For a discussion of these problems, *see* Heidi Gilchrist, 'No Hiding from Justice: Universal Jurisdiction in Domestic Courts' (2022) 57 *Tex. Int'l L.J.* 215, 228-29; Aboueldahab, *supra* note 5.

But perhaps less obviously, in the reverse scenario, ICL practice of UJ states may impact, or at least provide inspiration for the ICC, in terms of, e.g., crime selection and procedural rights. Thus, it has been argued that UJ states may want to focus on sexual and gender-based violence, which has arguably not been satisfactorily addressed by the ICC.[25] It has also been submitted that UJ states may, at least on paper, provide more adequate protection than the ICC to victims, as strong victim protection legislation is already in place at the domestic level.[26] Such UJ best practices may ultimately migrate "upwards" to the ICC.

Regular consultations between UJ national prosecutors and the ICC Prosecutor through, e.g., the International Association of Prosecutors or Eurojust, may enhance mutual learning and prevent the normative fragmentation of ICL. They may even lead to the joint development of standards and guidelines for the prosecution of international crimes.[27] For instance, in September 2022, the ICC and Eurojust jointly presented guidelines for civil society on documenting international crimes.[28] Going forward, consultations could focus on those issues that are most salient from an ICL fragmentation perspective, e.g., modes of liability,[29] the prosecution of cor-

25 *Universal Jurisdiction Annual Review 2022*, TRIAL INT'L 10 (Mar 30, 2020), https://trialinternational.org/wp-content/uploads/2022/03/TRIAL_International_UJAR-2022.pdf; *But see* Joachim J. Savelsberg and Miray Philips, 'Epistemic Power of Universal Jurisdiction: Spreading Knowledge about Mass Atrocity Crimes' (2022) 31 *Minn. J. Int'l L.* 57, 94 (for a more positive assessment of the trial) ("The trial awakened, or re-awakened, public awareness of the massive violations of human rights committed by the regime of President Bashar al-Assad.").

26 McGonigle, *supra* note 18, at 371.

27 *Id.* at 378 (calling for the "adoption of special domestic international criminal procedural codes that would complement existing domestic criminal procedural codes").

28 Eurojust and The International Criminal Court Office of the Prosecutor, *Documenting International Crimes and Human Rights Violations for Criminal Accountability Purposes: Guidelines for Civil Society Organisations* (Sep. 2022), https://www.eurojust.europa.eu/sites/default/files/assets/eurojust-icc-csos-guidelines.pdf (last visited October 3, 2023).

29 The Rome Statute provides for modes of liability, such as complicity, but these are often already quite developed in domestic criminal law doctrine. For an inquiry, *see* Marina Aksenova, *Complicity in International Criminal Law* (Portland, Oregon: Hart Publishing, 2016). For a case application of domestic accessorial liability doctrines to international crimes prosecutions before domestic courts, *see* HR 30 juni 2009, NJ 2009, 481 n.k. (Openbaar Ministerie/Van Anraat) (Neth.) (Supreme Court judgment); GHSHE 21 april 2017, NJFS 2017, 153 (Openbaar Ministerie/Kouwenhoven) (Neth.) (Court of Appeals judgment).

porate actors,[30] or the prosecution of foreign terrorist fighters involved in atrocity crimes.[31]

3 Conclusion

The ICC and UJ national authorities are partners, not competitors. Both pursue the objective of accountability for international crimes. Accordingly, co-operation and coordination between the ICC Prosecutor and UJ national authorities is called for. It is heartening to witness the deep collaboration between the ICC Prosecutor and the Eurojust Joint Investigation Team on Ukraine, including the ICC Prosecutor's willingness to "seek to deepen ICC engagement with all actors in relation to the Ukraine situation," albeit in a manner consistent with his mandate as Prosecutor.[32] It is also encouraging to observe the joint adoption, by the ICC Prosecutor and Eurojust, of guidelines for civil society in documenting international crimes. It is hoped that such engagement is not a one-off, but could be repeated for other situations and topics, and also involve non-EU member states exercising UJ.

---

30 Pursuant to Article 25(1) of the Rome Statute, the ICC only has jurisdiction over natural persons. This provision extends to corporate officers, but not to corporations. The latter, however, may be held liable under domestic law, and some prosecutions are currently underway. *See, e.g.*, Sandra Cossart, Anna Kiefer, Cannelle Lavite, and Claire Tixeire, *Multinational Lafarge Facing Unprecedented Charges for International Crimes: Insights into the French Court Decisions*, OPINIO JURIS (Nov. 15, 2022), https://opiniojuris.org/2022/11/15/multinational-lafarge-facing-unprecedented-charges-for-international-crimes-insights-into-the-french-court-decisions/ (last visited October 12, 2023).

31 Genocide Network Secretariat, Eurojust, Cumulative Prosecution of Foreign Terrorist Fighters for Core International Crimes and Terrorism Related Offences (2020), https://www.eurojust.europa.eu/sites/default/files/Partners/Genocide/2020-05_Report-on-cumulative-prosecution-of-FTFs_EN.PDF.

32 Khan, *supra* note 15.

CHAPTER 45

The Promise and Perils of the ICC Prosecutor's Engagement with External Stakeholders

Leila Nadya Sadat

The Office of the Prosecutor (OTP) of the International Criminal Court is often requested or required to participate or collaborate with external stakeholders in achieving accountability for the commission of grave crimes under international law. Indeed, Prosecutor Khan's new Strategic Plan focuses extensively upon the engagement of the OTP with entities and persons outside the building, and five of the ten goals set forth in the Plan focus upon the Office's relationship with external stakeholders.[1] In addition to civil society and afflicted communities (strategic goal 4), the Prosecutor's Plan mentions national authorities (strategic goal 2), the global community (strategic goals 3 and 9), and an enhanced field presence in situation countries (strategic goal 7). The Strategic Plan envisages the OTP as a "hub for accountability efforts [...] working with situation and other countries, accountability mechanisms and other partners to ensure a coordinated and effective effort towards closing the impunity gap."[2] This effort to "reimagine" the Office is a nod to the reality that the ICC, as currently funded and conceived, will only be equipped to successfully handle a few cases in each situation, leaving, in most situation countries, a considerable impunity gap. That said, as a Court, and not a development agency, the Prosecutor's bold new vision faces obstacles in terms of funding, state opposition, and geopolitical realities and perceptions.

Due to space constraints, this contribution explores a few key issues. It will focus primarily upon the OTP's engagement with states in situation and in non-situation countries with respect to investigation and prosecution (but not enforcement of sentences), as well as its relationship with specialized international investigative mechanisms and tribunals. Section 1 addresses the promise and perils and benefits of cooperation with national

1 Office of the Prosecutor, International Criminal Court, Strategic Plan 2023-2025 (June 13, 2023), https://www.icc-cpi.int/news/office-prosecutor-strategic-plan-2023-2025 (last visited October 4, 2023) [hereinafter Strategic Plan].

2 *Id.* at ¶ 32.

 | DOI:10.1163/9789004686755_054

authorities. Section 2 addresses the promise and perils of cooperation with specialized international investigative mechanisms and tribunals. It is not possible in this short essay to address cooperation with regional authorities spanning the situation country, including, inter alia, Europol and Eurojust, although it will touch upon the role of the EU and the OTP as regards the proposals for a new tribunal on the crime of aggression for Ukraine.

I conclude that it will be important for the OTP not to take a "one-size fits all" approach in developing modalities for cooperation with national, regional, or other authorities or organizations in investigating and prosecuting international crimes. While keeping the OTP's door open for cooperation is important, and the Rome Statute contemplates this, there are challenges to implementing the hub system proposed by the Strategic Plan. Indeed, as regards situation countries, cooperation is likely to be more of an exception than a rule, even as regards ICC states parties.

A careful analysis of the ICC's activity to date suggests that direct cooperation with national authorities in self-referrals and proprio motu cases may often be politically fraught, and may sometimes be non-existent, although positive exceptions, such as the ongoing relationship between Bangladesh authorities and the ICC OTP can be found. Cooperation with national authorities in outside state referrals are more likely to be successful, but while some are enthusiastic in their welcome of the OTP, others are more reluctant partners. The Venezuela situation poses challenges to cooperation given the government's objection to the ICC investigation and credible allegations of attacks on victims and witnesses. Ukraine is a positive exception, representing a paradigmatic case of robust cooperation between the OTP and the situation country as well as other states and regional organizations. As for Security Council referrals, although the Council's Chapter VII powers have been invoked in those cases, cooperation has ranged from non-existent to challenging in the case of Sudan (with the exception of a short time after President Omar Al-Bashir's arrest, and prior to the current political unrest), and while much better, somewhat grudging in the case of Libya.

Interestingly, the OTP's most enthusiastic and willing partners will be found in non-situation countries that wish to assist the Court in a variety of ways or are conducting universal jurisdiction cases in their national systems. These partners may be intent upon working with the OTP to create a more effective global network of entities investigating and prosecuting international crimes. The ICC would indeed be a co-equal partner in this kind of cooperation, which is contemplated by Article 93(1) of the Rome Statute.

As regards international mechanisms, most will also be willing partners to the OTP, especially in situations such as Myanmar, which is already under the Court's jurisdiction and the subject of (limited) investigations. The proposed Special Tribunal for the Crime of Aggression (STA), however, if not managed carefully, could be a source of friction or disappointment, and states supporting its establishment should be careful not to compromise the ICC's independence, jurisdiction, or effectiveness, as well as be aware of the potential danger of a ne bis in idem challenge to action by the ICC if the STA moves forward in a case involving the same accused. Given that the ICC is already investigating the situation in Ukraine, it may be useful to wait and see how that investigation proceeds before establishing a new international court addressing the same situation, but different crimes.

Finally, in any cooperation efforts, the ICC Prosecutor must be mindful that independence and action "without fear or favor," must be the hallmark of the Office for the Court to retain its legitimacy. Staying squarely within its statutory mandate will help to insulate the Office from accusations of favoritism, double standards, and selectivity which so often drive discourse about the ICC in the public domain.[3]

1 OTP Cooperation with National Authorities

The ICC Prosecutor may need to engage with national authorities in situation countries, meaning countries in which the crimes are being committed (i.e., Ugandan authorities in the investigation of the LRA or Ukrainian authorities in the Ukraine situation) or with national authorities in non-situation countries, exercising their criminal jurisdiction extraterritorially (i.e., searching for LRA members wanted by the Court in African states outside of Uganda, interviewing Sudanese refugees in camps outside of Sudan, or assisting in the prosecution of cases involving universal jurisdiction). Some national authorities may be located in ICC states parties; others not (such as authorities in the United States).

1.1 *Cooperation with National Authorities of ICC States Parties*

The strongest legal framework for cooperation will inevitably be scenarios in which the Prosecutor is engaged with national authorities located in ICC states parties. Article 86 of the Rome Statute imposes a general obligation of cooperation upon ICC states parties, and Article 87(1)(a) allows the Court to make requests for cooperation to all states parties; Article 89(1) also imposes

3 Darryl Robinson, 'Inescapable Dyads: Why the International Criminal Court Cannot Win' (2015) 28 *Leiden J. Int'l L.* 323.

an obligation on states parties to comply, subject to the provisions of Part 9 of the Statute and national law, with a request for arrest and surrender of suspects. These formal obligations notwithstanding, engagement of the OTP with national authorities in both situation and non-situation countries presents both potential benefits and challenges.

1.1.1 In Situation Countries Involving Self-Referrals

With respect to national authorities in situation countries which have themselves reached out to the ICC for assistance in combatting the commission of Rome Statute crimes on their territories, it seems probable that national authorities would be eager to join with the Office in establishing "a forum or platform with relevant national authorities through which a community of practitioners can be developed for the sharing of information and expertise between the Office and national authorities."[4] After all, these are countries that have not only ratified the Statute, but they have also looked to the Court for help at a critical juncture. These countries currently include the Central African Republic, Côte d'Ivoire, Democratic Republic of the Congo, Mali, and Uganda.

At the same time, there is a risk involved in sharing evidence and supporting national systems if the government in-country is not dedicated to protecting and promoting human rights for all its citizens or is itself complicit in the commission of ICC crimes or human rights abuses. When ICC Prosecutor Luis Moreno Ocampo stood next to Ugandan President Yoweri Museveni and announced the opening of the situation involving the Lord's Resistance Army (LRA) in 2004, although his actions were viewed positively given the extensive crimes ongoing against civilians in Northern Uganda, some worried that the ICC had inappropriately cloaked allegations of serious crimes committed by Ugandan troops with a mantle of impunity.[5] With relative peace prevailing in Northern Uganda today, as well as the successful prosecution of Dominic Ongwen by the Court,[6] the decision to invite the Ugandan referral seems clearly to have been a positive development. Yet the nagging concern that the Ugandan government could be using the ICC

---

4 *Id.* at ¶ 35.

5 *ICC: Investigate all Sides in Uganda*, HUM. RTS. WATCH (Feb. 4, 2004), https://www.hrw.org/news/2004/02/04/icc-investigate-all-sides-uganda (last visited October 6, 2023).

6 Press Release, International Criminal Court, Ongwen Case: ICC Appeals Chamber Confirms the Conviction and Sentencing Decisions (Dec. 15, 2022), https://www.icc-cpi.int/news/ongwen-case-icc-appeals-chamber-confirms-conviction-and-sentencing-decisions (last visited October 14, 2023).

to defeat its opponents, and would never recognize that the Court's jurisdiction applied to its own activities, continues today, as human rights groups point to increasing numbers of unlawful killings, disappearances, arbitrary arrest, torture, and other abuses by Ugandan security forces.[7] As Kirsten Fisher has noted, the ICC needs to tread very carefully in self-referral cases to avoid reducing trust in the situation country, and ICC intervention has the capacity to reduce criminal activity in one area of the country while unfortunately permitting illiberal governments to increase their authority and attack their opponents.[8]

The Palestine situation is an interesting situation involving a declaration and self-referral;[9] although the OTP could endeavor to deepen its cooperation with the Palestinian Authority in the manner envisaged by the OTP Strategic Plan, it is difficult to imagine Israel doing so, and presumably some Israeli activity on the territory of the State of Palestine would be the subject of the ICC's investigation, in addition to any investigation involving allegations of wrongdoing by Palestinians. Although positive complementarity could play a constructive role in that situation as regards both Israeli authorities and the Palestinian Authority, as a non-state party, Israel would have no obligation to cooperate, and as a political matter, seems unlikely to do so.[10]

Thus, in carrying out some of the activities proposed by the Prosecutor in enhancing national prosecutorial efforts, the OTP will need to ensure that evidence and technology transfers are not misused or weaponized by

---

7 Press Release, Amnesty International, Uganda: Museveni's Latest Government Must Reverse Decline on Human Rights, May 12, 2021, https://www.amnesty.org/en/latest/press-release/2021/05/uganda-musevenis-latest-government-must-reverse-decline-on-human-rights/ (last visited October 14, 2023).

8 Kirsten J. Fisher, 'International Criminal 'Lawfare' and its Potential Effects on Post-Conflict Positive Peace' (2019) 19 *Int'l Crim. L. Rev.* 724.

9 Statement, Fatou Bensouda, ICC Prosecutor, Respecting an Investigation of the Situation in Palestine (Mar. 3, 2021), https://www.icc-cpi.int/news/statement-icc-prosecutor-fatou-bensouda-respecting-investigation-situation-palestine (last visited October 7, 2023).

10 Israel Ministry of Foreign Affairs, *The International Criminal Court's Lack of Jurisdiction Over the So-Called "Situation in Palestine"*, GOV.IL (Dec. 20, 2019), https://www.gov.il/en/departments/news/iccs-lack-of-jurisdiction-over-so-called-situation-in-palestine-20-dec-2019 (last visited October 10, 2023); Peter Beaumont, *ICC Opens investigation into war crimes in Palestinian territories,* THE GUARDIAN (Mar. 3, 2021), https://www.theguardian.com/law/2021/mar/03/icc-open-formal-investigation-war-crimes-palestine (Quoting Israeli prime minister Benjamin Netanyahu and foreign minister Gabi Ashkenazi protesting the ICC's decision to accept the referral as "undiluted antisemitism" and "morally and legally bankrupt").

national authorities against political opponents; that resources are not misallocated by the situation country; and that ICC personnel are not themselves placed in potentially compromising positions in assisting with national prosecutions. Accepting secondments from a situation country[11] opens the door to enhanced cooperation and knowledge transfer, but again, must be managed quite carefully to promote, rather than deter, the adoption of best practices in the national system.

1.1.2 In Other Situation Countries

Other situation countries in which the national authorities are ICC states parties fall into two categories: Proprio motu cases, and state referrals.

1.1.2.1 *Proprio Motu Referrals*

In these situations, the territorial state is unlikely to be cooperating with the ICC, and in fact, that is what has transpired thus far. In the Kenya situation, the OTP received some modicum of cooperation, but ultimately was faced with such an extensive lack of cooperation, and even interference, that it was impossible to move forward with trials of the accused.[12] Burundi and Philippines have withdrawn from the Statute, making the idea of direct engagement with national authorities seem even more remote. Likewise, in the Bangladesh/Myanmar situation, as in the Palestine situation discussed above, while Bangladeshi authorities could very well benefit from the kinds of cooperation envisaged by the Strategic Plan, Myanmar authorities are unlikely to cooperate with the OTP in any way, having responded to the Rohingya's allegations of deportation and other crimes as "meritless."[13] Prosecutor Khan has made two visits to Bangladesh both to meet with victims, and to

11 Strategic Plan, *supra* note 1, at para. 41.

12 For example, the ICC Prosecutor withdrew the charges in the case against Mr. Kenyatta, citing the non-cooperation of the Kenyan government with the proceedings in its application. *See* Statement, Fatou Bensouda, ICC Prosecutor, On the Status of the Government of Kenya's Cooperation with the Prosecution's Investigations in the Kenyatta case (Dec. 4, 2014), https://www.icc-cpi.int/news/statement-prosecutor-international-criminal-court-fatou-bensouda-status-government-kenyas. The case was subsequently terminated without prejudice. *See* Prosecutor v. Uhuru Muigai Kenyatta, Doc. No. ICC-01/09-02/11, Decision on the Withdrawal of Charges (Mar. 13, 2015).

13 *Myanmar to ICC: Rohingya Jurisdiction Request 'Should Be Dismissed'*, REUTERS (Aug. 9, 2018), https://www.reuters.com/article/us-myanmar-rohingya/myanmar-to-icc-rohingya-jurisdiction-request-should-be-dismissed-idUSKBN1KU1NG.

engage in deepening cooperation between the Office and the government of Bangladesh.[14]

1.1.2.2 *State Party Referrals*

As I have written elsewhere, these are the cases that were unexpected when the ICC was established in 1998.[15] The conventional wisdom, at that point, was that it would be the Security Council that would refer (if at all), and that no state would be willing to refer another state to the Court, given the fact that no inter-state complaints had been opened before any international human rights bodies at that time. That was the basis on which pressure was placed on the negotiators at Rome to provide for a proprio motu referral system.[16] As it turns out, both the Ukraine and the Venezuela situations have been referred by other ICC states parties – in the Ukraine situation, by 43 states with the active engagement and support of the government and the Prosecutor;[17] and in Venezuela I,[18] by six States in 2018 – Argentina, Canada, Colombia, Chile, Paraguay, and Peru. The Venezuelan government has tolerated the investigation by engaging with the OTP and not withdrawing from the Statute; however, Venezuelan civil society has reported repression and attacks, including murders and disappearances, with respect to individuals in country assisting with the ICC investigation.[19]

Unsurprisingly, the Venezuela situation has posed challenges to positive complementarity. In 2021, Prosecutor Khan opened a preliminary examination. On April 15, 2022, Venezuela asked the ICC to defer on the grounds

14 Press Release, International Criminal Court, ICC Prosecutor Karim A. A. Khan KC Concludes Second Visit to Bangladesh: "The Rohingya must not be forgotten. Together, we can deliver on their legitimate expectations of justice." (Jul. 10, 2023), https://www.icc-cpi.int/news/icc-prosecutor-karim-khan-kc-concludes-second-visit-bangladesh-rohingya-must-not-be-forgotten.

15 Leila Nadya Sadat, 'The International Criminal Court of the Future', in Carsten Stahn (ed.) *The International Criminal Court at 20: Reflections on the Past, Present and the Future* (forthcoming 2023), https://papers.ssrn.com/sol3/papers.cfm?abstract_id=4346095.

16 *Id.*

17 *Situation in Ukraine: ICC-01/22*, INT'L CRIM. CT., https://www.icc-cpi.int/situations/ukraine (investigation opened March 2, 2022) (last visited October 15, 2023).

18 Situation in the Bolivarian Republic of Venezuela I, Doc. No. ICC-02/18-1-AnxI, Notification: Referral from a Group of Six States Parties Pursuant to Article 14(1) of the Rome Statute Regarding the Situation in Venezuela (Sep. 27, 2018).

19 Presentation from Venezuelan Civil Society, ICC ASP, December 2023; Situation in the Bolivarian Republic of Venezuela I, Doc. No. ICC-02/18, Prosecution Request to Resume the Investigation Pursuant to Article 18(2), ¶ 19 (PTC I, Nov. 1, 2022).

that it was pursuing cases. However, in November 2022 Prosecutor Khan sought authorization to resume the ICC investigation on the grounds that the government of Venezuela had "not adequately demonstrated, in accordance with article 18(2), that it has investigated or is investigating its nationals or others within its jurisdiction" for ICC crimes.[20] Pre-trial Chamber I granted the request, finding that virtually all of the 1,875 submissions of views from the victims wanted the ICC investigation to continue,[21] and, based upon the information the prosecution had provided Venezuela under Article 18 in terms of the likely scope of the OTP investigation, concluded that "Venezuela appears to admit that it is not investigating the factual allegations underlying the contextual elements of crimes against humanity."[22] Moreover, the few prosecutions that had occurred were of low-level, rather than high-level individuals, and there had been insufficient investigation of sexual and gender-based crimes. For those reasons, the Chamber found that the ICC investigation could proceed, subject to future admissibility challenges that Venezuela might bring.

Venezuela represents a case of grudging cooperation with the Court; it is engaging with the process, but given that victims are complaining of retaliation, blacklisting, publishing of personal information, surveillance and monitoring, stripping of citizenship, extortion, expropriation, and the use of extreme violence by the authorities, including sexual and gender-based crimes,[23] it will be difficult for the OTP to engage with national authorities without potentially compromising its own investigation and the safety of victims and witnesses. As a recent Human Rights Watch essay noted, "[t]he ICC's interactions with national systems are complex, but this cooperation is crucial to maintain accountability."[24]

The most successful example of cooperation between the OTP, national, regional, and other authorities is the Ukraine situation. Indeed, the combination of the state's eagerness for the investigation, the fact that the crimes have been committed by a state outside the Rome Statute system, and the

20 Situation in the Bolivarian Republic of Venezuela, Case No. ICC-02/18, Prosecution Request to Resume the Investigation Pursuant to Article 18(2), ¶ 3 (PTC I, Nov. 1, 2022).

21 *Id.* at ¶ 18 (Only four potential victims demurred, citing concern for their safety).

22 *Id.* at ¶ 104.

23 Presentation from Venezuelan Civil Society, ICC ASP, December 2023; Situation in the Bolivarian Republic of Venezuela I, Case No. ICC-02/18, Prosecution Request to Resume the Investigation Pursuant to Article 18(2), ¶ 19 (PTC I, Nov. 1, 2022).

24 Tamara Taraciuk Broner, *In Venezuela, a Delicate Balance for the ICC*, HUM. RTS. WATCH (Dec. 8, 2022), https://www.hrw.org/news/2022/12/08/venezuela-delicate-balance-icc (last visited October 15, 2023).

fact that Ukraine is a member of the Council of Europe, has led not only to extensive support for Ukraine itself, but a deep and comprehensive engagement of Ukraine's national authorities, regional authorities (Eurojust and Europol), the creation of an Atrocity Crimes Advisory Group (ACA) established by the United States, the European Union, and the United Kingdom to help Ukrainian authorities investigate and prosecute war crimes,[25] and extensive cooperation between the ICC, Ukraine, and the ACA, among others.

While concerns have been voiced about too many resources being devoted to the Ukraine situation at the ICC, there have been many fewer concerns about the OTP "standing with Ukraine" regarding the crimes being committed on its territory by Russian forces and mercenaries, or concerns about unwittingly assisting the Ukrainian government in the repression of its own people by engaging in cooperation. Instead, Ukraine is a paradigmatically successful example of the kind of strategic and operational cooperation that the Prosecutor's 2023-2025 Strategic Plan envisages. It is, however, more likely to represent the exception than the rule.

1.2 *Cooperation with National Authorities in Non-States Parties*

1.2.1 In Situation Countries

Non-states parties have no formal obligation to cooperate with the ICC unless a Security Council resolution adopted under Chapter VII requires them to do so. Article 87(5) however, allows the Court to invite "any State not party to the Statute" to provide assistance on the basis of an ad hoc arrangement with that state. The situation in Ukraine, of course, involves such an arrangement; as discussed in Section 1.1 above, it is more analogous to a situation in which OTP is seeking to cooperate with a state party, given Ukraine's article 12(3) declarations, but, formally speaking, given that Ukraine is not a state party, an ad hoc arrangement is required.

The other two non-state party situation countries before the ICC currently are Sudan and Libya, both of which were referred by the Security Council to the ICC under Chapter VII of the U.N. Charter. While some cooperation has been evidenced by Sudanese authorities following the fall of former President Omar Al-Bashir's government, including a promise to hand over the former President to the ICC, prior to that time, non-cooperation was the rule of the day, as President Al-Bashir himself traveled to dozens of

25 *Ukraine Advisory Group* (ACA), U.S. DEPT. OF STATE, https://www.state.gov/ukraine-advisory-group-aca (last visited October 15, 2023).

countries (including to ICC states parties) despite the two ICC arrest warrants that had been issued against him.[26]

Libya has, since the beginning of the ICC referral by the Security Council, engaged more consistently with the OTP, and in his latest report to the Security Council, Prosecutor Khan noted that the Office had carried out "20 missions, collecting over 500 items of evidence, including video and audio material, forensic information and satellite imagery," as well as filed new arrest warrants.[27] The Libyan government has often asserted admissibility challenges and was successful in the Al Senussi case,[28] causing the ICC to stand down. That said, tensions have arisen between the government and the Court, particularly in the early days of the investigation during which time four members of the Court's staff were detained for several weeks during a visit to Libya.[29]

1.2.2 Outside of Specific ICC Situations (Universal Jurisdiction)

As the Prosecutor's Plan suggests, cooperation between the ICC and national authorities investigating ICC crimes may be highly effective. ICC situations will often generate significant refugee flows bringing both victims and perpetrators to third countries. Developing networks of cooperation to address those cases can be especially useful to the ICC and to national authorities. That said, the Court must employ firewalls to avoid compromising the security of its information. The Ukraine situation, which unites a situation country ready and willing to cooperate with both the ICC and outside jurisdictions, as well as regional and international criminal justice mechanisms, is a paradigmatic example of positive complementarity in action, and should be carefully studied as investigations and prosecutions progress so that best practices can be adopted, and lessons learned.

---

26 Alexa Koenig, Victor Peskin & Eric Stover, *Arrest Bashir: How the Sudanese Leader is Getting Away with Murder,* FOREIGN AFFS. (Jul. 13, 2016), https://www.foreignaffairs.com/articles/sudan/2016-07-13/arrest-bashir (last visited October 14, 2023).

27 Press Release, Security Council, 'Cause for Optimism' in Delivering Justice to Libyan People, International Criminal Court Prosecutor Tells Security Council, Citing Progress in Past Six Months, U.N. Press Release SC/15280 (May 11, 2023).

28 Prosecutor v. Gaddafi, ICC-01/11/-01/11 OA 6, Judgment on Appeal, (Jul. 24, 2014).

29 Press Release, International Criminal Court, Four ICC Staff Members Detained in Libya; Immediate Release Requested (Jun. 9, 2012), https://www.icc-cpi.int/news/four-icc-staff-members-detained-libya-immediate-release-requested (last visited October 3, 2023); Hadeel Al Shalchi, *Libya Frees Detained ICC Staff After Apology*, REUTERS (Jul. 2, 2012), https://www.reuters.com/article/uk-libya-icc/libya-frees-detained-icc-staff-after-apology-idUKBRE8610K120120702 (last visited October 4, 2023) (The ICC staff members were released by Libya in July 2012).

As regards atrocities occurring or that have occurred in countries not currently within the jurisdiction of the Court, such as Syria, the establishment of other international mechanisms to address those crimes means that the "hub" will be those entities as opposed to the ICC itself; at the same time, the ICC OTP will connect and coordinate with national authorities in appropriate circumstances. For those countries for which no international mechanisms are presently collecting information that could lead to investigations or prosecutions, the ICC OTP may have no formal role, but may nonetheless be aware of and open to cooperation as appropriate.

During the Kampala Review Conference for the Court, the idea of the ICC OTP engaging in assistance to other countries in developing their infrastructure relating to the investigation and prosecution of mass crimes was raised. It is clear that developing national capacity is critical to the success of the ICC's complementarity regime given that the ICC is a Court of last, not first, resort.[30] During the "stocktaking exercise" that occurred, general agreement was reached that it is states and civil society that would play the leading role in encouraging and assisting states in enacting national implementing legislation and investigating "serious international crimes committed on their territory or by their nationals."[31] This work would be facilitated by, but not conducted by, the ICC itself, so as not to deprive the Court – including the OTP – of resources that could otherwise be used to investigate and prosecute crimes. In the words of one delegate to the conference, the ICC should not function "as a development agency."[32]

2 Cooperation with Specialized International Investigative Mechanisms and Tribunals

The OTP could be asked, or could be required to engage, with a specialized international criminal tribunal or investigative mechanism, as permitted by Article 87(6), such as the proposed Special Tribunal for the Crime of Aggres-

30 Morten Bergsmo, Olympia Bekou and Annika Jones, 'Complementarity after Kampala: Capacity Building and the ICC's Legal Tools' (2010) 2 *Goettingen J. Int'l L.* 791.

31 *Id.* at 802.

32 Kampala Review Conference, Author's notes (on file with author); *see also* Hans Peter Kaul, 'Kampala June 2010 – A First Review of the ICC Review Conference' (2010) 2 *Goettingen J. Int'l L.* 649, 655 (the ICC is not an "organization which provides development aid").

sion (STA) that has been proposed to address the gap in the ICC's jurisdiction in that crime as regards the Ukraine situation, as well as the establishment of the European Union's International Centre for the Prosecution of the Crime of Aggression (ICPCA), which began work in The Hague in July 2023,[33] to collect data, interview witnesses, and build evidentiary files. The ICPCA is embedded in Eurojust which already maintains a Core International Crimes Evidence Database, is located in The Hague, and already cooperates with the ICC Prosecutor, meaning that it did not need to start "from scratch" in terms of organization and modalities.

Other situations, however, have required considerable time to staff up and become operational, including United Nations entities such as the International, Impartial and Independent Mechanism (IIIM for Syria), for example, created in 2016 by the U.N. General Assembly to assist in the "investigation and prosecution of persons responsible for the most serious crimes" committed in Syria since March 2011,[34] the United Nations Investigative Team to Promote Accountability for Crimes Committed by Da'esh/ ISIL (UNITAD) by the Security Council in 2017,[35] and the Independent Investigative Mechanism for Myanmar (IIM for Myanmar) established by the Human Rights Council in 2018.[36] These mechanisms themselves have needs for external cooperation with states and regional and international authorities; just as the ICC will wish to coordinate and work with them both informally and formally to exchange information.

As noted above, the Ukraine situation is a paradigmatic case of ICC cooperation with external stakeholders. The possible creation of a Special Tribunal for the Crime of Aggression (STA), however, is one situation in which there is a need for cooperation and there is also the specter of possible

33 *International Centre for the Prosecution of the Crime of Aggression against Ukraine*, EUROJUST, https://www.eurojust.europa.eu/international-centre-for-the-prosecution-of-the-crime-of-aggression-against-ukraine (last visited October 11, 2023).

34 G.A. Res. A/71/248 (Dec. 21, 2016) (adopted by a vote of 105 for, 15 against, 52 abstentions); See also INTERNATIONAL, IMPARTIAL AND INDEPENDENT MECHANISM TO ASSIST IN THE INVESTIGATION AND PROSECUTION OF PERSONS RESPONSIBLE FOR THE MOST SERIOUS CRIMES UNDER INTERNATIONAL LAW COMMITTED IN THE SYRIAN ARAB REPUBLIC SINCE MARCH 2011, https://iiim.un.org/ (last visited October 15, 2023).

35 S.C. Res. 2379 (September 21, 2017) (adopted unanimously); *See also* INVESTIGATIVE TEAM TO PROMOTE ACCOUNTABILITY FOR CRIMES COMMITTED BY DA'ESH/ISIL, https://www.unitad.un.org/ (last visited October 15, 2023).

36 Human Rights Council Res. 39/2, U.N. Doc. A/HRC/RES/39/2 (October 3, 2018); *See also* INDEPENDENT INVESTIGATIVE MECHANISM FOR MYANMAR, https://iimm.un.org/ (last visited October 2, 2023).

competition and conflict between the ICC and any future STA. This is because the STA would likely be investigating and prosecuting the same individuals targeted by the ICC, including President Vladmir Putin and members of his cabinet and high command. Former U.S. Ambassador for War Crimes, David Scheffer has suggested that it is more than possible – and even desirable – for the ICC and a future STA to exercise custody over the same individual and to try them for separate crimes.[37] Others, however, have expressed doubts that the ne bis in idem provision of the Rome Statute (Article 20), may not permit the ICC to move forward on atrocities committed during a war after someone has been convicted for launching the war itself, especially given the characterization of aggression (by some) as a continuing crime. Others have argued that the "conduct" bar is narrower and permits trial before both jurisdictions. Obviously, a careful agreement on cooperation would need to be negotiated; and evidence, witnesses, and victims would need to be protected as well as shared.

---

37 David Scheffer, *Forging a Cooperative Relationship Between International Criminal Court and a Special Tribunal for Aggression Against Ukraine,* JUST SEC. (Oct. 25, 2022), https://www.justsecurity.org/83757/forging-a-cooperative-relationship-between-intl-crim-court-and-a-special-tribunal-for-russian-aggression-against-ukraine/ (last visited October 1, 2023).

Index

www.ingramcontent.com/pod-product-compliance
Lightning Source LLC
LaVergne TN
LVHW012051011026
849162LV00017B/138